CRITICAL SURVEY
OF
SHORT FICTION

CRITICAL SURVEY

OF

SHORT FICTION

Second Revised Edition

Volume 3

James T. Farrell - W. W. Jacobs

Editor, Second Revised Edition
Charles E. May
California State University, Long Beach

Editor, First Edition
Frank N. Magill

SALEM PRESS, INC.
Pasadena, California   Hackensack, New Jersey

Managing Editor: Christina J. Moose
Research Supervisor: Jeffry Jensen
Acquisitions Editor: Mark Rehn
Photograph Editor: Philip Bader
Manuscript Editors: Lauren M. Mitchell
Melanie Watkins
Research Assistant: Jeff Stephens
Production Editor: Cynthia Beres
Layout: Ross Castellano

Library of Congress Cataloging-in-Publication Data

Critical survey of short fiction / editor, Charles E. May. — 2nd rev. ed.

    7 v. ; cm.

  First edition edited by Frank Northen Magill.

  Includes bibliographical references and index.

  ISBN 0-89356-006-5 (set : alk. paper) — ISBN 0-89356-007-3 (v. 1 : alk. paper) — ISBN 0-89356-008-1 (v. 2 : alk. paper) — ISBN 0-89356-009-X (v. 3 : alk. paper) — ISBN 0-89356-010-3 (v. 4 : alk. paper) — ISBN 0-89356-011-1 (v. 5 : alk. paper) — ISBN 0-89356-012-X (v. 6 : alk. paper) — ISBN 0-89356-013-8 (v. 7 : alk. paper)

  1. Short story. 2. Short story—History and criticism. 3. Short story—Bio-bibliography. I. May, Charles E. (Charles Edward) 1941 -   . II. Magill, Frank Northen, 1907-1997.

PN3321 .C7 2001
809.3′1—dc21

00-046384

Sixth Printing

CONTENTS

COMPLETE LIST OF AUTHORS

Volume I

Volume II

Volume III

Volume IV

Volume V

Volume VI

CRITICAL SURVEY

OF

SHORT FICTION

F

JAMES T. FARRELL

Born: Chicago, Illinois; February 27, 1904
Died: New York, New York; August 22, 1979

PRINCIPAL SHORT FICTION

Calico Shoes and Other Stories, 1934
Guillotine Party and Other Stories, 1935
Can All This Grandeur Perish? and Other Stories, 1937
Fellow Countrymen: Collected Stories, 1937
The Short Stories of James T. Farrell, 1937
$1,000 a Week and Other Stories, 1942
Fifteen Selected Stories, 1943
To Whom It May Concern and Other Stories, 1944
Twelve Great Stories, 1945
When Boyhood Dreams Come True, 1946
More Fellow Countrymen, 1946
More Stories, 1946
The Life Adventurous and Other Stories, 1947
A Hell of a Good Time, 1948
An American Dream Girl, 1950
French Girls Are Vicious and Other Stories, 1955
An Omnibus of Short Stories, 1956
A Dangerous Woman and Other Stories, 1957
Saturday Night and Other Stories, 1958
Side Street and Other Stories, 1961
Sound of a City, 1962
Childhood Is Not Forever, 1969
Judith and Other Stories, 1973
Olive and Mary Anne, 1977

OTHER LITERARY FORMS

In James T. Farrell's vast publications (more than sixty volumes) are included essays, critical writing, plays, novels, and social commentary. His novel, *Studs Lonigan: A Trilogy* (1935), was the basis for a film in 1960, then was adapted for television and presented, to critical acclaim, in 1979.

ACHIEVEMENT

Although he wrote more than two hundred short stories, many of them closely related to his acclaimed novels, James T. Farrell is seldom discussed as a short-story writer or represented in anthologies of fiction. He is, above all, a novelist, one who has incorporated many of his shorter works into his later novels, thereby subordinating them to the longer works. As a politically committed writer, he was also out of fashion in a country where writers with communist or socialist leanings were unpopular. Since many of his stories do concern the plight of political writers, they seem a bit dated to the contemporary reader unfamiliar with the Trotsky/Lenin wings of the Communist Party. In some respects, the short stories have suffered from their close ties to the novels, which themselves have declined in popularity beginning in the 1950's.

BIOGRAPHY

Born and reared on the south side of Chicago, James Thomas Farrell was educated at a series of parochial schools, attended the University of Chicago sporadically for three years during the 1920's, and attended New York University in 1941. The son and grandson of Irish teamsters, Farrell was also a teamster for a time and worked, variously, as a cigar-store clerk, a filling-station attendant, and a part-time newspaper reporter. He married Dorothy Patricia Butler in 1931, was divorced, married the actress Hortense Alden, whom he also divorced, and remarried Dorothy Butler Farrell in 1955, but they separated three years later. He had one child by his second wife. He received a John Simon Guggenheim Memorial Foundation Fellowship for creative writing in 1936, a Book-of-the-Month Club prize for *Studs Lonigan* in 1937, and a Newberry Library Fellowship in 1949.

He was a member of the National Institute of Arts and Letters and the Overseas Press Club. He died in 1979.

Analysis

James T. Farrell's stories, because of their often graphic language and action and because, perhaps, of their relatively uneven quality, are not often anthologized. His best work comes from the early collections such as *Calico Shoes, Guillotine Party*, and *$1,000 a Week*. When his stories remain within the realm of his Chicago youth, he is at his best—even later stories set in Chicago reflect the tough vibrance evident in the likes of "Willie Collins," "The Triumph of Willie Collins," and "Saturday Night."

Farrell's characters never seem fabricated. They strut and boast. They cringe at frightening things, and they suffer from the inexorable progress of time—perhaps the dominant theme in Farrell's work. Never conventionally literary, the real nature of Farrell's stories makes them compelling if not always tasteful and appealing. There is no varnish on Farrell's rough exterior. The reader is expected to accept the stories in their raw, immediate sense.

The individual is the unsteady center of Farrell's stories; a large number of his stories are almost vignettes of individuals as they function in daily life. It is this attention to the individual which sets Farrell's work apart. Farrell's universe does not admit of predestiny or fortune or, despite his rich Irish Catholic milieu, divine intervention; his individual succeeds or fails by virtue of his own efforts and abilities. The only force beyond the control of the individual is time, and, along with the freedom of the individual will, time rules Farrell's work. There is a consistent determination on the part of Farrell's characters to recapture the past, elude the present, or rush into the future. In each instance, despite their strivings, they inevitably fail. Farrell does not celebrate the failure, but he portrays it honestly, and failure sets the tone of his stories.

"When Boyhood Dreams Come True"

Both of Farrell's major themes are projected in "When Boyhood Dreams Come True." Tom Finnegan, a man trying to understand and recapture his past, fails in a dream world which is reminiscent of

James T. Farrell (Library of Congress)

the *Inferno* (c. 1320), *The Pilgrim's Progress* (1678), and the Catholic catechism, but Finnegan, on awakening, forgets the dream except for the one synthetic revelation that "almost explained the meaning of life." Finnegan is made aware that "the past was dead, gone. All his life had led up to this minute. Only this minute was real. The past was unreal. . . . It was gone." Finnegan fails to recapture the past and, at the end of the story, he is uncertain of his future, but the moment of reality, the now, is left for him to manipulate—to use or misuse as he is able. It is this juxtaposition of the impact of the past and of failure on which Farrell thrives.

Joe Eliot, in the story of the same name, struggles with the past in a similar fashion, but, unlike Finnegan, he is trapped—hamstrung by his failure and frustration. What Joe calls failures, however, are merely results of his inability to cope with things over which he has no control. When Joe refuses to ride home on the same car with this supervisor, he reflects "contempt," and the reader sees him as "uninterested," "bored," and passive to the point of giving his unfinished evening paper to his supervisor to get rid of him. Joe's reaction to his supervisor is typical of his relationship with humankind. His contempt for and passive reaction to other men are direct results of his frustration with past failure and himself.

In the second of five parts, Joe sinks into a reminiscence of his past which begins with bittersweet memories of the Seine in 1918 while he was in World War I and with remorseful recriminations against his wife, who died of peritonitis while he was in France. The reader learns that Joe has a Harvard University degree, was an All-American halfback, and felt that he "could have been something big." The reader also learns that he has had a break with his rich father (probably over Joe's marriage) and that he refuses a reconciliation despite overtures from his father. Farrell presents Joe as bitter and lonely but does not demand the reader's sympathy or pity. Joe deserves no pity in a situation he will not attempt to alter. The narrator declares of Joe: "He hadn't fitted into the world, and he didn't give a good goddamn."

After eating in a second-rate establishment, Joe walks through the Loop in Chicago. The narrator makes a point of coloring the scene with natural commentary about the soft night and the sunset, but Joe is unaffected by it all until, as he convinces himself he is a "failure," he suddenly notices "as if it were a discovery, a sky streaming with stars that were radiant on the surface of a deep blue." While the vision touches Joe, he belittles the experience and himself for standing on the corner gawking at the stars, "but he walked with the happy feeling that he just sucked a flashing moment from the weltering insignificance of human life." The revelation is only momentary, and the insignificance he attributes to human life brings him back to his "failure." He wanders to Lake Michigan musing over his lost promise, his dead wife and daughter, and the fact that "mistakes could not be rectified." He even berates death for being a "messy conclusion to a mess."

The moment of illumination, Farrell seems to tell the reader, is enough to remind Joe of something other than his self-imposed failure and frustration, but it is not enough to draw him out of himself—it cannot save him from himself. The sojourn beside

Lake Michigan nearly allows him to effect a reconciliation with himself. The mesmerizing nature of the waves calms his frustration but reminds him of the fruitless nature of people's efforts when compared to the effortless and inexorable presence of nature. Nature, Joe reminds the reader, will be here when Chicago crumbles, and the waves will go on when the city and humans are no more. The waves also remind Joe of his loss of faith and of his attempt to regain that faith with the Catholics; but he is revulsed by the Catholics' "eating their God" and admits the need for a "Presbyterian God." Joe cannot function socially or spiritually in human society, and nature only reminds him of his isolation and, thus, that he is a stranger. He is alone with himself. He is afraid to die. He "almost ached for the past. . . . He found himself wanting them [events of the past] all back." Despite the turmoil in his mind, Joe reaches "a womb of calm" before leaving the lake, but as he leaves, he watches a young couple making love on the beach. The moment of reconciliation is gone. His examination of himself has culminated in watching man procreating beside the forces of nature which calmed him. As he walks back into the city, his frustration returns.

Joe is frustrated by humankind, by nature, and by himself. He does not want to leave a restaurant because he is anonymous while in that group. He does not want to go home because he will be alone. He is fond of the night in the city because he does not have to cope with all the people who normally fill the empty offices, but he still feels surrounded by the city. The city at night and its "many little worlds and private universes were only reflected things." As a reflection, the city does not intrude on Joe's existence but is a sort of iron womb in which he can avoid the natural calm of the lake and turn back into the solace of his frustration. As a result, there is no final revelation, no change, no alteration in Joe. His failures are all that are real and his principal failure is the inability to cope with himself. He cannot regain the past and he cannot deal with his memories of that past. Farrell's world is full of such isolated, ostracized people. The past is an intrinsic part of their failures, and inordinate attention to or desire for the past enhances its impact. Farrell also makes it clear, however, that lack of concern for the past is just as fatal as preoccupation with it.

"THE FASTEST RUNNER ON SIXTY-FIRST STREET"

In "The Fastest Runner on Sixty-first Street," Morty Aiken is successful, but his preoccupation with the future blinds him to the importance of the present, and his failure to attend carefully to that present is a direct influence on the outcome of the story. The story of the boy who could outrun and outskate everyone in his neighborhood is a classic success story with a twist. The reader knows from the beginning that Morty is the All-American boy. He enjoys running and skating faster than anyone else—he does not revel in the victory, but in the performance itself. He is well liked and respected as a direct result of his abilities, and he is fascinated with his promise for the future. He views the present as little more than a way station to becoming the greatest runner in the world. At every turn the reader is reminded of Morty's self-assuredness and of his dreams: "Although he was outwardly modest, Morty had his dreams." Morty dreams of going to high school and prospering under high-school coaching. He dreams of college track meets and, ultimately, the Olympics. He also dreams of girls. He dreams that "girls would all like him, and the most beautiful girl in the world would marry him." He dreams of Edna, his ideal of the moment; when he runs, he dreams he is running for Edna. He dreams of ways to give Edna one of the medals he has won for speed. In all of his dreams, however, running is the all-important thing. Everything else in the world is simply an excuse to run and feel the exhilaration of speed and of his body accomplishing that speed.

Tony Rabuski is another accessory to Morty's speed. Tony, the "toughest" and "poorest" boy in school, is befriended by Morty, and Morty uses his speed to keep other boys from teasing Tony by chasing down Tony's tormentors and holding them until Tony can catch up and "exact his revenge." Morty's friendship changes Tony from a sullen outcast to a member of the "gang," but the change does not materially affect Morty. Morty uses Tony as another excuse to run—just as he uses his dreams of Edna and

his hopes for the future. In essence, there is no present for Morty, only the future.

It is only in the final sections of the story, after Morty is graduated from grammar school and begins summer vacation, that any sense of temporality enters his life. As Morty whiles away a summer "as good as any summer he could remember," he becomes embroiled in the racial problems of Chicago. Washington Park and Morty's neighborhood are being infiltrated by blacks, and there is a typical gang reaction to this move. One never sees Morty as a racist, only as the "catcher" for the gang. Morty runs ahead of the mob, tackles the "dark clouds" and holds them until the gang can catch up and beat them; it is precisely the scheme he and Tony had "doped out" earlier. The reader is never led to believe that Morty hates the blacks or has any interest in the situation at all except in the sense that it gives him another reason to run. As he runs after blacks, he dreams the same dreams of Edna, of glory, of running. He does not consider the blacks' fate or why he is catching them; he thinks only of running. It is this lack of concern for the real, present world that is Morty's undoing.

When Morty, in the finale of the story, runs ahead of a mob formed by Tony Rabuski, he is doing only what he does naturally—running. He chases two blacks who escape behind a funeral train (blatant foreshadowing) and then begins the final race to catch a lone black boy. With the mob howling behind him, Morty runs with the idea of catching the black and for the sheer joy of running. As he chases the black, however, the closer he comes to his quarry, the more he outdistances the mob. The closer he comes to his immediate goal, the further he runs ahead of his world, his present. The black runs into a predominantly black area; Morty, innocently, follows him; the black disappears; Morty is "caught and pinioned . . . his throat slashed," and the mob arrives to find no blacks in sight and to view the remains of the fastest runner on Sixty-first Street lying in a pool of his own blood.

Morty has never had time to live in the present. His dreams, his pleasure with his own body and his own future, and his lack of attention to the present which will become his past are fatal. If he had been attentive, he would have been more aware of the danger of entering the black neighborhood alone. He is trapped not by the past but by his ignorance of it, and the reader is warned against that ignorance by the image of his body.

Farrell was a fatalist, a determinist, a naturalist, and a realist, all in one turn. There is no success for Farrell, only endurance. His stories leave the reader with a very real sense of the character's failure and with a sense of the ongoing nature of that failure in the everyday world. Farrell's characters are hurt and they scream as a result of the pain, but no one is listening.

OTHER MAJOR WORKS

LONG FICTION: *Young Lonigan: A Boyhood in Chicago Streets*, 1932; *Gas-House McGinty*, 1933; *The Young Manhood of Studs Lonigan*, 1934; *Judgment Day*, 1935; *Studs Lonigan: A Trilogy*, 1935 (collective title for *Young Lonigan*, *The Young Manhood of Studs Lonigan*, and *Judgment Day*); *A World I Never Made*, 1936; *No Star Is Lost*, 1938; *Tommy Gallagher's Crusade*, 1939; *Father and Son*, 1940; *Ellen Rogers*, 1941; *My Days of Anger*, 1943; *Bernard Clare*, 1946; *The Road Between*, 1949; *This Man and This Woman*, 1951; *Yet Other Waters*, 1952; *The Face of Time*, 1953; *Boarding House Blues*, 1961; *The Silence of History*, 1963; *What Time Collects*, 1964; *When Time Was Born*, 1966; *Lonely for the Future*, 1966; *New Year's Eve/1929*, 1967; *A Brand New Life*, 1968; *Judith*, 1969; *Invisible Swords*, 1971; *The Dunne Family*, 1976; *The Death of Nora Ryan*, 1978.

PLAYS: *The Mowbray Family*, pb. 1946 (with Hortense Alden Farrell).

POETRY: *The Collected Poems of James T. Farrell*, 1965.

NONFICTION *A Note on Literary Criticism*, 1936; *The League of Frightened Philistines and Other Papers*, 1945; *The Fate of Writing in America*, 1946; *Literature and Morality*, 1947; *The Name Is Fogarty: Private Papers on Public Matters*, 1950; *Reflections at Fifty and Other Essays*, 1954; *My Baseball Diary*, 1957; *It Has Come to Pass*, 1958; *On Irish Themes*, 1982.

BIBLIOGRAPHY

Branch, Edgar M. *James T Farrell*. Minneapolis: University of Minnesota Press, 1963. Although his monograph is an overview of Farrell's life and work, Branch devotes considerable attention to Farrell's short stories, which he regards as closely linked to the novels. The stories are often preliminary experiments, deletions, or parts of abandoned projects, and they are consistent in tone and style with the larger works.

Fanning, Charles. "Death and Revery in James T. Farrell's O'Neill-O'Flaherty Novels." *In The Incarnate Imagination: Essays in Theology, the Arts, and Social Sciences, in Honor of Andrew Greeley: A Festschrift*, edited by Ingrid H. Shafer. Bowling Green, Ohio: Bowling Green State University Popular Press, 1988. Although Fanning is primarily concerned with Farrell's novels, he does identify themes that pervade all Farrell's fiction: the artist as an isolated being, the role of memory and dreaming in achieving the necessary isolation, and the relationship of the isolation to the experience of death.

Farrell, James T. *Selected Essays*. Edited by Lunor Wolf. New York: McGraw-Hill, 1967. This book, which contains an overview of Farrell's literary criticism, reprints many of Farrell's most significant essays, among them "On the Function of the Novel" and "The Writer and His Conscience." Also contains discussions of naturalism, Leo Tolstoy, and the American literary tradition.

Freedman, Samuel G. "Echoes of Lonigan, Fifty Years After." *The New York Times Book Review* 90 (March 17, 1985): 45. Argues that Farrell's *Studs Lonigan* trilogy still conveys the essence of Chicago life; states his portrayal of the Lonigans' bigotry still rings true; argues that the trilogy is valuable on aesthetic as well as sociological grounds and that Farrell deserves recognition as a prime influence on writers like Nelson Algren, Saul Bellow, Bette Howland, and David Mamet.

Fried, Lewis F. *Makers of the City*. Amherst: University of Massachusetts Press, 1990. Fried argues that Farrell portrays the city as a liberalizing and democratizing force. Fried does an excellent job of weaving together discussion of Farrell's life, career, and fiction. He also provides a helpful bibliographical essay on other studies of Farrell.

Pizer, Donald. "James T. Farrell and the 1930's." In *Literature at the Barricades: The American Writer in the 1930's*, edited by Ralph F. Bogardus and Fred Hobson. University: University of Alabama Press, 1982. Pizer argues convincingly that Farrell's literary roots are in the 1920's, that he owes as much to the Chicago school of philosophical pragmation as to naturalism, and that James Joyce and Sherwood Anderson also influenced Farrell's fiction. To demonstrate his theses, Pizer analyzes the *Studs Lonigan* trilogy.

Smith, Gene. "The Lonigan Curse." *American Heritage* 46 (April, 1995): 150-151. Claims that while the character of Studs Lonigan became Farrell's most popular creation, it was also his biggest personal albatross; notes that after killing Studs off, Farrell had trouble getting his work published and came to look back at his earlier work with loathing.

Wald, Alan M. *James T. Farrell: The Revolutionary Socialist Years*. New York: New York University Press, 1978. Wald's chapter "The Literary Record" demonstrates the intent of Leon Trotsky's influence on Farrell's fiction, and several short stories ("John Hitchcock," "The Dialectic," "The Renegade") receive extensive political readings. Wald identifies the real persons represented by Farrell's fictional characters and focuses on Farrell's treatment of the plight of the socialist writer. Contains an excellent bibliography with many political entries.

Clarence O. Johnson, updated by Thomas L. Erskine

WILLIAM FAULKNER

Born: New Albany, Mississippi; September 25, 1897
Died: Byhalia, near Oxford, Mississippi; July 6, 1962

PRINCIPAL SHORT FICTION
These Thirteen, 1931
Doctor Martino and Other Stories, 1934
Go Down, Moses, 1942
The Portable Faulkner, 1946, 1967
Knight's Gambit, 1949
Collected Short Stories of William Faulkner, 1950
Big Woods, 1955
Three Famous Short Novels, 1958
Uncollected Stories of William Faulkner, 1979

OTHER LITERARY FORMS
    William Faulkner published nearly twenty novels, two collections of poetry, and a novel-drama, as well as essays, newspaper articles, and illustrated stories. His early work has been collected and his University of Virginia lectures transcribed. As a screenwriter in Hollywood, he was listed in the credits of such films as *The Big Sleep* (1946), *To Have and Have Not* (1944), and *Land of the Pharaohs* (1955).

ACHIEVEMENTS
    William Faulkner is best known for his novels, particularly *The Sound and the Fury* (1929), *Absalom, Absalom!* (1936), and *As I Lay Dying* (1930), all of which have been translated widely. *A Fable* (1954) and *The Reivers* (1962) won Pulitzer Prizes, and *A Fable* and the *Collected Short Stories* won National Book Awards. Faulkner received the Nobel Prize in Literature for 1949.

    Film versions have been made of several of his works: *Sanctuary* (1961), *Intruder in the Dust* (1949), *The Sound and the Fury* (1959), *The Reivers* (1969), and *Pylon* (1957; or *Tarnished Angels*). Others (*Requiem for a Nun*, 1951, and "Barn Burning") have been filmed for television.

Such attention attests to the fact that Faulkner has been one of the most influential writers in the twentieth century—both in the United States, where his work suggested to an enormous generation of southern writers the valuable literary materials that could be derived from their own region, and in Europe, particularly in France. He has had a later, but also profound, effect on Latin American fiction, most noticeably in the work of Colombian writer Gabriel García Márquez, who seeks, as Faulkner did, to create a fictive history of a region and a people. Faulkner's work has also been well received in Japan, which he visited as a cultural ambassador in 1955.

BIOGRAPHY

William Faulkner spent most of his life in Mississippi, although as a young man he went briefly to

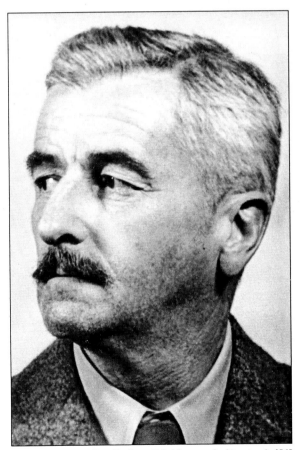

William Faulkner, Nobel Laureate for Literature in 1949
(©The Nobel Foundation)

Paris and lived for a time in New Orleans, where he knew Sherwood Anderson. He trained for the Royal Air Force in Canada during World War I, but the war was over before he saw action. He attended the University of Mississippi in Oxford for a year, where he published poems and reviews in a campus periodical; and after dropping out, he worked for a time in the university post office. He married Estelle Oldham, and they had a daughter, Jill. Except for periodic and often unhappy stays in Hollywood to work on screenplays—in order to support a large number of dependents—Faulkner lived and wrote in Oxford, where he had available to him in the town and surrounding countryside the prototypes for the characters that inhabit his major works. In the late 1950's, he accepted a position as a writer-in-residence at the University of Virginia and traveled to Japan on behalf of the Department of State. Although his literary reputation waned in the 1940's, when virtually all of his earlier works were out of print, Faulkner's stature as a writer grew after 1946, when *The Portable Faulkner* was published by Malcom Cowley and especially after 1950, when he accepted the Nobel Prize, when his collected stories were published, and when his novels began to be reprinted. Faulkner drove himself harder physically as he grew older, and he was troubled throughout his life with alcohol binges into which he would often fall after completing a book. These factors contributed to his death in 1962.

ANALYSIS

William Faulkner has been credited with having the imagination to see, before other serious writers saw, the tremendous potential for drama, pathos, and sophisticated humor in the history and people of the South. In using this material and, in the process, suggesting to others how it might be used, he has also been credited with sparking the Southern Renaissance of literary achievement that has produced much of the United States' best literature in the twentieth century.

In chronicling the tragedy of southern history, he delineated a vision tempered by his historical perspective that has freed the region from the popular conception of its character as possessing a universal gentility and a pervasive aristocracy, and he portrayed realistically a population often idealized and caricatured in songs, movies, and pulp fiction. In undercutting the false idealizations, Faulkner often distorted the stereotypes and rendered them somewhat grotesque in the interest of bringing them to three-dimensional life; and he attempted to show in the political and social presumptions of the South the portent of its inevitable destruction—first through war and then through an insidious new social order based on commercial pragmatism and shortsighted lust for progress. In this sense, the New South is shown to have much in common with mainstream America.

Faulkner's themes are often conveyed in an elaborate baroque style noted for its long, difficult sentences that challenge the reader to discern the speaker, the time, and even the subject of the narrative. Faulkner makes considerable use of stream-of-consciousness interior monologues, and his frequent meshings of time reinforce his conviction that the past and present are intricately interwoven in the human psyche.

"A ROSE FOR EMILY"

"A Rose for Emily," frequently anthologized and analyzed, is probably Faulkner's best-known story. Because of its elements of mystery, suspense, and the macabre, it has enjoyed a popular appeal. That Emily Grierson, an aging southern belle, murders the lover who spurned her and sleeps beside his decaying body for a number of years is only the most sensational aspect of the story. What is more interesting to the serious reader of Faulkner is the interplay between Emily Grierson and the two generations of townspeople who attempt to cope with her—one the old guard and the other a new generation with "modern ideas."

The opening paragraphs of the story inform the reader that when Miss Emily died, the whole town turned out for her funeral. She was a "fallen monument . . . a tradition, a duty and a care; a sort of hereditary obligation upon the town." The townspeople, who are by the time of Emily's death mostly of a generation younger than her own, have never been able to incorporate her into their community. For them, as well as for their fathers, she has stood as an embodiment of an older ideal of southern womanhood—

even though in her later years she has grown obese, bloated, and pale as dough. The older generation, under the mayoralty of Colonel Sartoris ("who fathered the edict that no Negro woman should appear on the streets without an apron"), has relieved Miss Emily of her taxes and has sent its children to take her china-painting classes "in the same spirit that they were sent to church on Sunday with a twenty-five-cent piece for the collection plate." The new generation, however, is not pleased with the accommodations its fathers made with Miss Emily; it tries to impose taxes upon her and it no longer sends its children to take her lessons. Miss Emily has been encouraged in her ways by the old guard, however; she refuses to pay the town's taxes, telling the representatives of the new generation to "see Colonel Sartoris," who has been dead for ten years. The town is unable to handle Emily; it labels her "insane" and likewise comes to see her as the ghost of a feminine ideal out of the past. She becomes a recluse, living alone in her house with her black servant; and in her claim to privilege and impunity, she stands as a reminder to the town of the values—and sins—of its fathers, which are visited upon the third generation.

It is tempting to think of Miss Emily as merely a decadent and perverse relic of the South's antebellum past; indeed, this is how the story has often been read. Such a neat interpretation, however, would seem to be defeated by the time element in the story. Emily lives in a house spiraled and cupolaed in the architectural style of the 1870's, on a once-elegant street that has been altered by industry and commercial development. Although the rickety town fathers of the Civil War era come to her funeral dressed in their dusty uniforms and even believe that she was of their own generation and that they had danced with her when she was a young woman, clearly Emily is not of that generation; she is of the postwar South. She has not lingered as a relic from a warped racist culture; she has instead been created by defeated members of that culture who have continued to yearn after a world they have lost, a world that might well have existed largely in their imaginations, but a concept so persistent that the newer generation, for all its modern ideas, is powerless to control it. The reader is told that the town had long thought of Emily and her dead father "as a tableau, Miss Emily a slender figure in white in the background, her father a spraddled silhouette in the foreground, his back to her and clutching a horsewhip, the two of them framed by the backflung front door." It is clear that the newer generation of the twentieth century has adopted certain popular ideas about the old South. This "tableau" could serve as the dust jacket for any number of romantic novels set in the plantation days.

Thus, the two generations are complicit in ignoring the real Emily and creating and maintaining the myth of Emily as an exemplum of southern womanhood from a lost age, just as the town aldermen— "three graybeards and one younger man, a member of the rising generation"—have conspired to cover up Emily's horrible crime. When the smell of the corpse of Emily's decaying lover, Homer Barron, had become so strong that it could no longer be ignored by the town, the aldermen had scattered lime around Emily's house secretly at night, although they knew she had recently purchased arsenic from the druggist and that Barron had disappeared; and when the smell went away, so did the town's concern about the matter. The old guard cannot bear, and does not wish, to accept the grim essence of the dream it has spun; the new generation, under the influence of the old, grudgingly accepts its burden of the past, but then wrenches it into a romantic shape that obscures the "fat woman in black" (overindulgent, moribund) that is Emily Grierson.

The story, then, is a comment on the postbellum South, which inherited the monstrous code of values, glossed over by fine words about honor and glory, that characterized the slave era; that postbellum South learns to ignore the unsavory elements of its past by ignoring Emily the recluse and murderess and by valorizing the romantic "tableau." This is, however, a complex matter. The new generation—a generation excluded from the nominal code of honor, valor, and decorum that the old Confederates believed to have sustained them and excluded from the benefits that were to be gained from the slave system of the "glorious" old South—sees the Griersons as "high and mighty," as holding themselves "a little too

high for what they really were." The new generation, pragmatic and small-minded, for the most part, has inherited a landscape sullied by cotton gins and garages. Miss Emily Grierson, as a privileged person and as a reminder of what the older generation forfeited in its defeat, is a goad in the minds of the uncharitable newer generation, which, when she does not marry, is "vindicated." When it hears the rumor that she has inherited nothing but the decaying house from her father, it is glad: "At last they could pity Miss Emily." Miss Emily out of sight, destitute, "insane," and deprived too of the lost legacy of the old South can be recreated as a fictional heroine in white, part of the backdrop against which the popularized hero, her father, stands with his horsewhip—a faceless silhouette, cruel and powerful, an "ancestor" who can be claimed by the dispossessed generation as its own.

The incestuous image of the father and daughter suggests the corrupt nature of the new South, which, along with the corrupt nature of the old South, is a favorite Faulknerian concern. Granted, the "tableau" on the face of it appears to be the cover of a romantic novel, and in that sense it seems to be merely a popular rendering of history; but it is the townspeople who arrange *father and daughter* in the lurid scene. It is the men of the new generation who black out the distinguishing features of Emily's dead father in their creation of the tableau, leaving a dark masculine space (more, one would guess, in the shape of foreman Homer Barron than of Mr. Grierson) into which they can dream themselves, as masters of a glorious age, as potent heroes for whom the wispy heroine wanes in the background. The newer generation has the "modern ideas" bred of the necessity of surviving in the defeated, industrialized South; but in its attitudes toward Emily Grierson, it reveals the extent to which the old decadent values of the fathers have been passed along.

The narrator of the story, one of the townspeople himself, has proved unreliable. While it is true that Emily seems to be "a tradition, a duty, a care, . . . an hereditary obligation," a relic of the past miraculously sprung into being in spite of the disparity between her time and the historical time with which she is associated, the narrator only inadvertently reveals the truth of the matter: that both generations of the town are guilty of the desires and misplaced values that not only allow Miss Emily the murderess to come into being but also lead them to cover her crime and enshrine her in a tableau into which they, in their basest longings, can insert themselves. There is an incestuousness to all of this, an unhealthy interbreeding of values that allows each generation to perform despicable acts in the process of maintaining its ideas of what it would like to be. It is true that Emily is a "fallen monument"; but what the narrator fails to spell out explicitly is that the monument has been erected not only by the historical grandeur of her family, but also by the dispossessed generations that interpret her to their own ends. The monument is toppled by death, not by an ethical evolution in the town. The narrator is redeemed to some extent by "his" pity for Emily and by the recognition that the town, by driving her into mad isolation, has treated her badly.

As for Emily herself, she would seem to represent the worst elements of her neighbors, carried to their extreme conclusions. As the antebellum masters of the slaves presumed an all-powerfulness that allowed them to believe that they could own people, so does Miss Emily presume. Alive, Homer Barron—the outsider, the Yankee, a curious vitality in the pallid town—is outside Miss Emily's control. Dead, however, she can own him, can dress his corpse like a groom, can sleep beside him perhaps every night at least until her hair turns gray. As the new generation can blind itself to unpleasant truths about its history and itself, so can Emily become lost in delusion: Her father, dead for three days, is proclaimed not dead and she refuses to bury him; Homer's corpse is a "groom" (and, perhaps in some further depraved vision, connected with the dead father). Emily represents not only the decadence of Colonel Sartoris's racist era but also the decadence of the "modern" generation's use of that era. Thus "A Rose for Emily," often dismissed as Faulkner's ghost story, proves to be a clear expression of a recurring motif in Faulkner's works: the complexity of the connections between the present and the past.

"The Bear"

These connections are explored in a less sensational manner in "The Bear." This story, which Faulkner also made the centerpiece of his novel *Go Down, Moses*, is another of the most anthologized, most studied pieces of Faulkner's short fiction. Composed of five sections (although often only four are printed in anthology versions, the long and complex fourth section being omitted), "The Bear" covers the history of Isaac (Ike) McCaslin, heir to the land and to the shame of his slave-owner grandfather, L. P. C. McCaslin, who committed incest with his illegitimate daughter, thereby driving her mother to suicide. After discovering this horrifying ghost in old plantation ledgers, Ike feels bound to repudiate the inheritance that has descended to him from his grandfather— even though the repudiation costs him his wife and any hope of progeny—in an attempt to expiate his inherited guilt and to gain a measure of freedom from the vicious materialism that brought the slavery system into being. Thus he allows his patrimony to pass to his cousin McCaslin Edmonds, who plays devil's advocate in Ike's attempt to understand the South and his own place in it, the tragedy of the blacks and of his own class, and the significance of what he possesses without inheriting: an instinctual knowledge of nature and an infallible sense of what is just.

"The Bear" may be seen as a hunting story, part of the *Big Woods* collection that includes "The Bear Hunt" and "Race at Morning." As a hunting story it is concerned with Ike's maturing, with his pilgrimage year after year to the hunting grounds where he and a group of adult hunters stalk the ancient bear, Old Ben, an enduring symbol of nature. Ike's guide and teacher is Sam Fathers, an aging Native American who still holds a sure instinct for the truths to be found in nature, and under whose tutelage Ike comes to form a system of values that later will lead him to renounce his inheritance. From Sam, Ike acquires a sense of nature's terms and of humanity's need to meet her on her own terms—of the necessity of according dignity to the force of nature and to all creatures through whom it courses. To meet the embodiment of that force in Old Ben, Ike must leave behind the instruments of civilization: the gun, the compass, the watch. Eventually Ike is able to track down Old Ben with regularity, but even when he encounters the bear and is armed, he refuses to shoot it.

It would seem that the proof of nature's endurance, represented in the bear, is of paramount concern to Ike. When Old Ben is finally killed and Sam Fathers dies, the ritual of the hunt is over for Ike. Yet two years later, he returns to the woods and sees in its organic and deathless elements, which have incorporated the remains of Old Ben and Sam Fathers, a proof of nature's dualistic power to absorb death and bring forth new life from it. This force is at the same time awesome and terrifying, and it must be revered and confronted if humanity is to live meaningfully. Even as Ike makes this last pilgrimage, however, a lumber company hacks away at the forest and a train cuts through the wilderness, underscoring the idea of the damage a materialistic civilization can do to even the most powerful aspects of nature. Faulkner shows an era of United States history passing—an era of abundance and of human appreciation of what nature requires from humanity in their mutual interest.

When "The Bear" is examined from the point of view of the intricate fourth section, it goes beyond being merely a hunting story to comment profoundly on the passing age and that which is replacing it. The scene shifts from the vast wilderness of nature to the intense confines of Ike McCaslin's consciousness, which struggles to find a way to atone for the sins of his ancestors and of his class. The entanglement of past and present here is more complex than it is in "A Rose for Emily," for Ike must face the knowledge that bloods mingled in the past—black and white, slave and owner—have flowed in grossly inequitable courses to the present, as reflected in the sufferings of his mixed-blood relatives. Therefore, he renounces his patrimony, he sets out to redress old wrongs with his black relatives, and he seeks to give full recognition to the brotherhood he shares with these relatives by recognizing the strengths they contribute to his family and to southern society—the virtues of "pity and tolerance and forbearance and fidelity and love of children."

In contrast to the self-serving generation of post-bellum townspeople in "A Rose for Emily," Ike—also of that era—is a man of conscience. This is not to suggest, however, that Ike is particularly "modern" in his ideas; rather he has modeled himself on older examples of integrity, not only Sam Fathers but also his father and his uncle, who had turned over their own inherited house to their slaves and built a humbler cabin for themselves. In Ike's own case, the personal sacrifices to integrity and conscience have been enormous—his wife's love; his hope of a son to carry on his mission; living alone and ultimately uncertain that his sacrifice will bear fruit beyond his limited scope to influence events. Nevertheless, Faulkner illustrates through his invention of Ike McCaslin the extent to which idealism can flourish, even when constantly challenged by the grimmest vestiges of past evils.

"BARN BURNING"

"Barn Burning" is an inversion of "The Bear" in that its protagonist, ten-year-old Sarty Snopes, is seeking the world that Ike McCaslin wishes to repudiate. Not of the landed class, but the son of a tenant farmer who is always on the move because arson is his means of creating justice, Sarty associates the landed gentry with a "peace and dignity" and a civilized justice that is the direct opposite of the "fear and terror, grief and despair" that characterizes his life with his father, Ab Snopes. Ab uses fire as a weapon against the ruling class that he sees as the shaper of his economic fate, and he exhorts Sarty to be true to the blood ties which Ab sees as the only protection for his kind against the forces of an exploitative aristocracy. Sarty, however, rejects the "old blood" that he has not chosen for what seems to him a higher concept of fairness, and he longs to be free of his family and the turmoil it generates in his life.

For Sarty, Major DeSpain is the antithesis of Ab. DeSpain owns the farm on which Ab has most recently contracted to work. To Sarty, DeSpain and his columned house, as big as a courthouse, represent not what Ab sees, the sweat of black and white people to produce someone else's wealth, but the peace and dignity for which Sarty yearns and a sys tem of justice that operates on principles of law rather than on personal revenge. Sarty's view is based on a naïve trust in civilization that blinds his inex perienced eyes to the inescapable connections between wealth and the mechanism of civilization.

Ab provokes a confrontation with DeSpain by deliberately tracking horse manure on an expensive rug. A series of moves and countermoves by Ab and DeSpain brings the pair to the point where, although DeSpain cannot begin to recover his loss from Ab, the local court nevertheless rules that Ab must take responsibility, within his means, for his act. This is enough to satisfy Ab yet again that the social system only works in behalf of the rich, and he sets out that night to redress this wrong by burning DeSpain's barn. Sarty cannot bear to allow this injustice, and so he is torn between real loyalty to his family and commitment to an ideal of justice. Specifically, he must decide whether to support his father's crime through silence or to betray the familial bond and warn DeSpain. Sarty chooses the ideal, warns DeSpain even as the barn begins to burn, and then flees the scene, unsure whether the shots he hears wound any of his family. Having made his choice, Sarty must set out alone to forge his own life.

"Barn Burning" offers a helpful picture of how Faulkner sees the economics of the postbellum South, where the poor whites remain the underclass rivals of black sharecroppers. Faulkner shows in other works how a new social order eventually evolved in which the descendants of Ab Snopes slip into the defeated, genteel society like silent bacteria and take over its commerce, coming finally to own the mansions that had previously belonged to the DeSpains and Compsons and Sartorises. Again and again Faulkner reiterates that it was the corrupt systems of slavery and of the plantation that ultimately ensured the fall of the Old South. Yet his view of Snopeses—violent, relentless, insidious men and inert, cowlike women, who by their numbers and crafty pragmatism will wrench the land and the wealth from the depleted gentility— is hardly positive.

In fact, "Barn Burning" is singular in that it is perhaps the only example of Faulkner's fiction in which the Snopeses are depicted sympathetically without first being made to appear ridiculous. As is often the case, Faulkner is extremely sensitive to the young boy caught in a painful rite of passage—as true for Sarty Snopes as it is for Ike McCaslin, Lucius Priest, Chick Mallison, and others not of the threatening Snopes clan. Moreover, "Barn Burning" makes an interesting case for Ab Snopes as the pitiable creation of the landed aristocracy, who seeks dignity and integrity for himself, although his only chance of achieving either would seem to lie in the democratic element of fire as the one defense available to all, regardless of social class. In this story, Ab is placed in the company of Wash Jones, Joe Christmas, and other members of the underclass that Faulkner views with sympathy and whose portrayals are in themselves indictments of the civilization that has forced them to desperate means.

While none of these examples quite suggests the very humorous ends to which Faulkner often turns his southern materials, it should be remembered that he was highly aware of the potential for comedy in all the situations described here and that even such delicate matters as the tensions between the races and the revolution in the social order are, in Faulkner's hands, as frequently the catalysts of tall tales and satire as they are of his most somber and lyrical prose. It is true that "A Rose for Emily" hints at a typically Faulknerian humor in that a whole town is turned on its end by the bizarre behavior of one of its citizens; but the grotesque nature of Miss Emily's secret smothers the promise of comedy in the story. Those seeking to experience Faulkner's comic voice are better served by reading such stories as "Shingles for the Lord," "Mule in the Yard," and "Spotted Horses."

In any case, whatever the mode Faulkner adopted in creating his Yoknapatawpha County and thereby recreating the South, he produced a stunning body of work, and in both matter and style, his works have had an equally stunning impact on modern letters.

OTHER MAJOR WORKS

LONG FICTION: *Soldiers' Pay*, 1926; *Mosquitoes*, 1927; *Sartoris*, 1929; *The Sound and the Fury*, 1929; *As I Lay Dying*, 1930; *Sanctuary*, 1931; *Light in August*, 1932; *Pylon*, 1935; *Absalom, Absalom!*, 1936;

The Unvanquished, 1938; *The Wild Palms*, 1939; *The Hamlet*, 1940; *Intruder in the Dust*, 1948; *Requiem for a Nun*, 1951; *A Fable*, 1954; *The Town*, 1957; *The Mansion*, 1959; *The Reivers*, 1962; *The Wishing Tree*, 1964 (fairy tale); *Flags in the Dust*, 1973 (original version of *Sartoris*); *Mayday*, 1976 (fable).

SCREENPLAYS: *Today We Live*, 1933; *To Have and Have Not*, 1945; *The Big Sleep*, 1946; *Faulkner's MGM Screenplays*, 1982.

POETRY: *The Marble Faun*, 1924; *A Green Bough*, 1933.

NONFICTION: *New Orleans Sketches*, 1958; *Faulkner in the University*, 1959; *Faulkner at West Point*, 1964; *Essays, Speeches and Public Letters*, 1965; *The Faulkner-Cowley File: Letters and Memories, 1944-1962*, 1966 (Malcolm Cowley, editor); *Lion in the Garden*, 1968; *Selected Letters*, 1977.

MISCELLANEOUS: *The Faulkner Reader*, 1954; *William Faulkner: Early Prose and Poetry*, 1962.

BIBLIOGRAPHY

Blotner, Joseph. *Faulkner: A Biography*. New York: Random House, 1964. This extensive but readable two-volume biography is the major source for details about Faulkner's life. It contains many photographs and a useful index.

Brooks, Cleanth. *William Faulkner: The Yoknapatawpha County*. New Haven, Conn.: Yale University Press, 1963. Brooks has written several excellent books on Faulkner, but this venerable classic of Faulkner criticism is one of the best introductions, treating Faulkner's characteristic themes, historical and social background, and offering detailed readings of the major novels and stories. His carefully prepared notes, appendices, and character index can be immensely helpful to beginning readers trying to make sense of mysterious events and complex family relations.

Broughton, Panthea. *William Faulkner: The Abstract and the Actual*. Baton Rouge: Louisiana State University Press, 1974. Of several fine critical studies that attempt to see Faulkner whole and understand his worldview, this is one of the best, especially for readers just beginning to know Faulkner. Broughton sees the tension between the ideal and the actual as central to understanding the internal and external conflicts about which Faulkner most often writes.

Carothers, James. *William Faulkner's Short Stories*. Ann Arbor, Mich.: UMI Research Press, 1985. This study gives special attention to interrelations among the short stories and between the stories and the novels. Carothers offers balanced and careful readings of the stories and a useful bibliography.

Ferguson, James. *Faulkner's Short Fiction*. Knoxville: University of Tennessee Press, 1991. An attempt to redress the critical neglect of Faulkner's short fiction. Discusses Faulkner's poetic and narrative impulses, his themes of loss of innocence, failure to love, loneliness, and isolation; comments on his manipulation of time and point of view and how his stories relate to his novels.

Ford, Marilyn Claire. "Narrative Legerdemain: Evoking Sarty's Future in 'Barn Burning.'" *The Mississippi Quarterly* 51 (Summer, 1998): 527-540. In this special issue on Faulkner, Ford argues that Faulkner experiments with the doubling of perspective in "Barn Burning" in which the omniscient narrator fuses with the protagonist to create a story with multiple narrative layers.

Hoffman, Frederick, and Olga W. Vickery, eds. *William Faulkner: Three Decades of Criticism*. New York: Harcourt, Brace, 1960. Though there are more recent collections of critical essays on Faulkner, this volume remains one of the most useful. It contains the important *The Paris Review* interview of 1956, the Nobel Prize address, and twenty-two essays, many of them seminal, on Faulkner's work and life.

Jones, Diane Brown. *A Reader's Guide to the Short Stories of William Faulkner*. New York: G. K. Hall, 1994. Discusses more than thirty of Faulkner's stories in terms of publishing history, circumstances of composition, sources/influence, and relationship to other Faulkner works; includes interpretations of the stories and summarizes and critiques previous criticism.

McHaney, Thomas. *William Faulkner: A Reference Guide*. Boston: G. K. Hall, 1976. Though somewhat difficult to use, this guide provides an admirably complete annotated listing of writing about Faulkner through 1973. Because Faulkner is a world-class author, a tremendous amount has been written since 1973. A good source of information about later writing is *American Literary Scholarship: An Annual.*

Minter, David. *William Faulkner: His Life and Work.* Baltimore: The Johns Hopkins University Press, 1980. Shorter and less detailed than Joseph Blotner's biography, this volume gives more attention to exploring connections between Faulkner's life and his works.

The Mississippi Quarterly 50 (Summer, 1997). A special issue on Faulkner, including articles that discuss displaced meaning, dispossessed sons, the wilderness and consciousness, and subjectivity in *Go Down, Moses.*

Singal, Daniel J. *William Faulkner: The Making of a Modernist.* Chapel Hill: The University of North Carolina Press, 1997. A study of the thought and art of Faulkner, charting the development of his ideas from their source in his reading to their embodiment in his writing. Depicts two Faulkners: the country gentleman and the intellectual man of letters.

Wagner-Martin, Linda. *New Essays on "Go Down, Moses."* Cambridge, England: Cambridge University Press, 1996. After an introduction that summarizes contemporary reception and critical analysis of *Go Down, Moses,* Wagner-Martin collects essays that approach the work from the perspective of race, environment, gender, and ideology.

Constance Pierce,
updated by Terry Heller

F. SCOTT FITZGERALD

Born: St. Paul, Minnesota; September 24, 1896
Died: Hollywood, California; December 21, 1940

PRINCIPAL SHORT FICTION

Flappers and Philosophers, 1920
Tales of the Jazz Age, 1922
All the Sad Young Men, 1926
Taps at Reveille, 1935
The Stories of F. Scott Fitzgerald, 1951
Afternoon of an Author: A Selection of Uncollected Stories and Essays, 1958
Babylon Revisited and Other Stories, 1960
The Pat Hobby Stories, 1962
The Apprentice Fiction of F. Scott Fitzgerald, 1907-1917, 1965,
    The Basil and Josephine Stories, 1973
Bits of Paradise, 1974
The Price Was High: The Last Uncollected Stories of F. Scott Fitzgerald, 1979

OTHER LITERARY FORMS

Four novels, four short-story collections, and a play make up the nine F. Scott Fitzgerald books published in his lifetime. They were issued in uniform editions by Scribner's with a British edition of each. His short stories were widely anthologized in the 1920's and 1930's in collections such as *The Best Short Stories of 1922, Cream of the Jug,* and *The Best Short Stories of 1931. The Vegetable: Or, From President to Postman* (1923) was produced at the Apollo Theatre in Atlantic City, and, while Fitzgerald was under contract to MGM, he collaborated on such screenplays as *Three Comrades, Infidelity, Madame Curie,* and *Gone with the Wind.* There have been numerous posthumous collections of his letters, essays, notebooks, stories, and novels; and since his death there have been various stage and screen adaptations of his work, including film versions of *The Great Gatsby* (1925) and *Tender Is the Night* (1934).

ACHIEVEMENTS

F. Scott Fitzgerald, considered "the poet laureate of the Jazz Age," is best remembered for his portrayal of the "flapper" of the 1920's, a young woman who demonstrated scorn for conventional dress and behavior. Fitzgerald's fiction focuses on young, wealthy, dissolute men and women of the 1920's. His stories written for popular magazines such as the *Saturday Evening Post* and, later, *Esquire* were very much in demand. Fitzgerald's literary reputation, however, is chiefly based on the artistry of stories such as "Babylon Revisited" and "The Rich Boy," as well as the novel *The Great Gatsby*. In this important novel, Fitzgerald uses rich imagery and symbolism to portray lives of the careless, restless rich during the 1920's and to depict Jay Gatsby as the personification of the American dream, the self-made man whose quest for riches is also a futile quest for the love of the shallow, spoiled Daisy.

F. Scott Fitzgerald (Library of Congress)

BIOGRAPHY

F. Scott Fitzgerald was educated at St. Paul Academy and at the Newman School in Hackensack, New Jersey. While attending Princeton University he wrote for the *Princeton Tiger* and *Nassau Literary Magazine*. He left Princeton without a degree, joined the army, and was stationed near Montgomery, Alabama, where he met Zelda Sayre. In 1920, they were married in New York City before moving to Westport, Connecticut. Their only child, Frances Scott Fitzgerald, was born in 1921. In the mid-1920's the Fitzgeralds traveled extensively between the United States and Europe, meeting Ernest Hemingway in Paris in 1925. The decade of the 1930's was a bleak one for the Fitzgeralds; Zelda had several emotional breakdowns and Scott sank into alcoholism. They lived variously in Montgomery and on the Turnbull estate outside Baltimore. Fitzgerald went to Hollywood for the second time in 1931. After that they lived for a time in Asheville, North Carolina, where Zelda was hospitalized and where Fitzgerald wrote the Crack-up essays for *Esquire*. In 1937, Fitzgerald met Sheila Graham while he was living in Hollywood and writing under contract to MGM. He began writing *The Last Tycoon* in 1939 and died, before it was completed, on December 21, 1940, at the age of forty-four.

ANALYSIS

F. Scott Fitzgerald was a professional writer who was also a literary artist. In practical terms this meant that he had to support himself by writing short stories for popular magazines in order to get sufficient income, according to him, to write decent books. Indeed, most of the money that Fitzgerald earned by writing before he went to Hollywood in 1937 was earned by selling stories to magazines. In his twenty-year career as a writer, he published 164 magazine stories; other stories were never published. All but eight of the stories that originally appeared in magazines became available in hardcover editions.

As one would expect of a body of 164 stories written in a twenty-year period mainly for popular consumption, the quality of the stories is uneven. At the bottom of this collection are at least a dozen stories, most of them written for *Esquire* during the last years of his life, which have few redeeming qualities; at the top of the list are at least a dozen stories which rank among the best of American short stories. One should not, however, be led to believe that these, as well as the hundred or more "potboilers" in the middle, do not serve a useful role in his development as an artist. Fitzgerald in the 1920's was considered the best writer of quality magazine fiction in America, and his stories brought the highest prices paid by slick magazines; the *Saturday Evening Post*, for example, paid him four thousand dollars per story even during the Depression. Dorothy Parker commented that Fitzgerald could write a bad story, but that he could not write badly. Thus each story, no matter how weak, has the recognizable Fitzgerald touch—that sparkling prose which Fitzgerald called "the something extra" that most popular short stories lacked. Fitzgerald also learned at the beginning of his career that he could use the popular magazines as a workshop for his novels, experimenting in them with themes and techniques which he would later incorporate into his novels. An understanding of a Fitzgerald story should take into account this workshop function of the story as well as its artistic merits.

Fitzgerald's career as a writer of magazine fiction breaks logically into three periods: 1919-1924, years during which he shopped around for markets and published stories in most of the important periodicals of the times; 1925-1933, the central period characterized by a close association with the *Saturday Evening Post*—a relationship which almost precluded his publication of stories in other magazines; and 1934-1940, a period beginning with the publication of his first *Esquire* story and continuing through a subsequent relationship with that magazine which lasted until his death. During the first of these periods, Fitzgerald published thirty-two stories in ten different commercial magazines, two novels (*This Side of Paradise*, 1920, and *The Beautiful and Damned*, 1922), two short-story collections (*Flappers and Philosophers* and *Tales of the Jazz Age*), and one book-length play (*The Vegetable*). In the second period, during which *The Great Gatsby* and a third short-story collection (*All the Sad Young Men*) appeared, he enjoyed the popular reputation he had built with readers of the *Saturday Evening Post* and published forty-seven of the fifty-eight stories which appeared during this nine-year period in that magazine; the remaining

eleven stories were scattered throughout five different magazines. In the final period, Fitzgerald lost the large *Saturday Evening Post* audience and gained the *Esquire* audience, which was smaller and quite different. Of the forty-four Fitzgerald stories to appear between 1934 and his death, twenty-eight appeared in *Esquire*. In addition to *Tender Is the Night*, which was completed and delivered before Fitzgerald's relationship with *Esquire* began, Fitzgerald published his final short-story collection (*Taps at Reveille*); he also drafted *The Last Tycoon* (1941) during the *Esquire* years. Twelve stories, nine of which have appeared in *Esquire*, have been published since his death.

An obvious conclusion may be drawn about Fitzgerald's professional career: He was at his best artistically in the years of his greatest popularity. During the composition of *The Great Gatsby*, Fitzgerald's commercial fiction was in such demand that large magazines such as the *Saturday Evening Post, Hearst's*, and *Metropolitan* competed for it. *Tender Is the Night* was written during the time when Fitzgerald's popularity with slick magazine readers was at its all-time high point; for example, in 1929 and 1930, important years in the composition of *Tender Is the Night*, he published fifteen stories in the *Saturday Evening Post*. In sharp contrast to the 1925-1933 stories, which are characteristically of an even, high quality, and many of which are closely related to two novels of this period, the stories of the *Esquire* years are, in general, undistinguished. In addition, with minor exceptions, the stories written in this final period have little relation to Fitzgerald's last "serious" work, *The Last Tycoon*. The *Esquire* years thus constitute a low point from both a popular and an artistic standpoint. They are years during which he lost the knack of pleasing the large American reading public and at the same time produced a comparatively small amount of good artwork.

In the first two years of Fitzgerald's storywriting, his sensitivity to audience tastes was naïve. "May Day" and "The Diamond as Big as the Ritz," not only the two best stories from these years but also two of the best stories in the Fitzgerald canon, were written for sale to mass-circulation magazines. Both, however, were too cynical about American values to be acceptable to a large, middle-American audience. By 1922 and the publication of "Winter Dreams" in *Metropolitan*, Fitzgerald had learned how to tailor his stories for slick magazine readers while at the same time using them to experiment with serious subjects and themes that he would later use in longer works.

"WINTER DREAMS"

Viewed in association with *The Great Gatsby*, "Winter Dreams" provides an excellent illustration of Fitzgerald's method of using his stories as a proving ground for his novels. In a letter to Maxwell Perkins, Fitzgerald describes "Winter Dreams" as a "sort of 1st draft of the Gatsby idea," and indeed, it contains sufficient similarities of theme and character to be called a miniature of *The Great Gatsby*. Parallels between Dexter Green and Jay Gatsby are striking: Both men have made a total commitment to a dream, and both of their dreams are hollow. Dexter falls in love with wealthy Judy Jones and devotes his life to making the money that will allow him to enter her social circle; his idealization of her is closely akin to Gatsby's feelings for Daisy Buchanan. Gatsby's idealized conception of Daisy is the motivating force that underlies his compulsion to become successful, just as Dexter's conception of Judy Jones drives him to amass a fortune by the time he is twenty-five. The theme of commitment to an idealized dream that is the core of "Winter Dreams" and *The Great Gatsby* and the similarities between the two men point up the close relationship between the story and the novel. Because "Winter Dreams" appeared three years before *The Great Gatsby*, its importance in the gestation of the novel cannot be overemphasized.

Important differences in Fitzgerald's methods of constructing short stories and novels emerge from these closely related works. Much of the effectiveness of *The Great Gatsby* lies in the mystery of Gatsby's background, while no such mystery surrounds the early life of Dexter Green. In "Winter Dreams," Dexter's disillusionment with Judy occurs suddenly; when he learns that she is no longer pretty, the "dream was gone. Something had taken it from him . . . the moonlit veranda, and gingham on the golf links and the dry sun and the gold color of her neck's soft down. . . . Why these things were no longer in the

world!" Because his enchantment could be shattered so quickly, Dexter's commitment to Judy is not of the magnitude of Gatsby's commitment to Daisy. Gatsby's disenchantment could only occur gradually. When he is finally able to see Daisy, "the colossal significance of the green light . . . vanished forever," but his "count of enchanted objects" had only diminished by one. Even toward the end of the novel, there is no way of knowing that Gatsby is completely disenchanted with Daisy. Nick says that "perhaps he no longer cared." The "perhaps" leaves open possibilities of interpretation that are closed at the end of "Winter Dreams." While Dexter can cry at the loss of a dream, Gatsby dies, leaving the reader to guess whether or not he still held on to any fragment of his dreams about Daisy. The expansiveness of the novel obviously allowed Fitzgerald to make Gatsby and his dream believable while he could maintain the mystery of Gatsby's past and the origins of his dream. Fitzgerald could not do this as well with Dexter in "Winter Dreams." The point is that in writing "Winter Dreams" Fitzgerald was giving shape to his ideas about Jay Gatsby, and, after creating the story, he could better see the advantages of maintaining the sense of mystery that made Gatsby a more memorable character than his counterpart in "Winter Dreams."

"THE RICH BOY"

Like "Winter Dreams," "The Rich Boy," published a year after *The Great Gatsby*, clearly illustrates the workshop function that the stories served. The story's rich boy, Anson Hunter, falls in love with the beautiful and rich Paula Legendre, but he always finds some reason for not marrying her, although he maintains that his love for her never stops. Anson, the bachelor, ironically becomes an unofficial counselor to couples with martial difficulties and, in his role as protector of the family name, puts an end to an affair that his aunt is having. Paula marries another man, divorces him, and, when Anson encounters her late in the story, he finds her happily remarried and pregnant. Paula, whose revered place has been jeopardized by her pregnancy, finally dies in childbirth, symbolically taking with her Anson's youth. He goes on a cruise, disillusioned that his only real love is gone. Yet he is still willing to flirt with any woman on the ship who will affirm the feeling of superiority about himself that he cherishes in his heart.

In "The Rich Boy," then, Fitzgerald uses many of the themes—among them, lost youth and disillusionment in marriage—that he had covered in previous stories; in addition, he uses devices such as the narrator-observer point of view that had been successful in *The Great Gatsby*, and he pulls from the novel subjects such as the idealization of a woman who finally loses her suitor's reverence. "The Rich Boy" also blends, along with the themes he had dealt with before, new topics that he would later distill and treat singly in another story, just as he first deals explicitly with the rich-are-different idea in "The Rich Boy" and later focuses his narrative specifically on that idea in "Six of One." Finally, particularly in the use of the theme of bad marriages in "The Rich Boy," there are foreshadowings of *Tender Is the Night* and the stories which cluster around it.

"BABYLON REVISITED"

The best of these *Tender Is the Night* cluster stories is "Babylon Revisited," which earned Fitzgerald his top *Saturday Evening Post* price of four thousand dollars and which is generally acclaimed as his finest story. "Babylon Revisited" represents a high point in Fitzgerald's career as a short-story writer: It is an artistically superior story which earned a high price from a commercial magazine. In the story's main character, Charlie Wales, Fitzgerald creates one whose future, in spite of his heroic struggle, is prescribed by his imprudent past, a past filled with heavy drinking and irresponsibility. He is destined to be haunted by reminders of his early life, embodied by Lorraine and Duncan, drinking friends from the past; to be judged for them by Marion, his dead wife's sister who, like Charlie's conscience personified, is disgusted by his past and demands punishment; and to be denied, for his penance, any right to fill the emptiness of his life with his daughter Honoria, who is in Marion's custody and who is the only really meaningful thing left. Fitzgerald fashions Charlie as a sensitive channel through which the reader can simultaneously view both Paris as it existed for expatriate wanderers before the Depression and the now-dimmed Paris to which Charlie returns.

The contrast is masterfully handled in that the course of Charlie's emotional life closely parallels the changing mood of the city—a movement from a kind of unreal euphoria to a mood of loss and melancholy. The contrast at once heightens the reader's sense of Charlie's loneliness in a ghost town of bad memories and foreshadows his empty-handed return to Prague, his present home. All of Charlie's present misery has resulted, in Fitzgerald's precise summary, from his "selling short" in the boom—an allusion to the loss of his dead wife Helen. Charlie, however, refuses to be driven back to alcohol, even in the face of being denied his daughter Honoria. Although he might easily have done so, Fitzgerald avoids drawing the reader into a sentimental trap of identification with Charlie's plight, the responsibility for and consequences of which must finally be borne only by Charlie. As he later did in Dick Diver's case in *Tender Is the Night*, Fitzgerald has shown in "Babylon Revisited" how one man works his way into an existence with *nada* at the core; how he manages to dissipate, "to make nothing out of something," and thus prescribe for himself a future without direction. It is also in the creation of this mood of Charlie's isolation that the artistic brilliance of the story, as well as its kinship to *Tender Is the Night*, lies.

The popular thrust of "Babylon Revisited" is a dual one in which Fitzgerald plays on what were likely to be ambivalent feelings of popular readers toward Charlie. On the one hand, he is pictured first as an expatriate about whose resolution to remain abroad American audiences may have been skeptical. On the other, Charlie appears to have reformed and obviously loves his daughter. Marion, by contrast, is depicted as a shrew, and the reader is left to choose, therefore, between the punishment of a life sentence of loneliness for a penitent wrongdoer and the granting of his complete freedom and forgiveness rendered against the better judgment of the unsympathetic Marion. Fitzgerald guarantees that the reader will become emotionally involved by centering the story around the highly emotional relationship between a father and his daughter. Because Charlie is, in fact, guilty, to let him go free would be to let wrongdoing go unpunished—the strictest kind of violation of the

Puritan ethic. To deprive Charlie of Honoria, however, would be to side with the unlikable Marion. Fitzgerald, then, resolves the conflict in the only satisfactory way—by proposing a compromise. Although Marion keeps Honoria for the moment, Charlie may be paroled, may come back and try again, at any time in the future.

The story, therefore, is successful on three major counts: It served as a workshop in which Fitzgerald shaped the mood of *Tender Is the Night*; it entertained with the struggle against unfair odds of a well-intentioned father for the affection of his daughter; and it succeeded on the mythic level, suggested in the title, as a story in which all ingredients conspire to lead to Charlie's exile—an isolation from the city that has fallen in the absence of a now-reformed sinner, carrying with it not only the bad but also the good which Charlie has come to salvage.

ESQUIRE STORIES

About four years after the publication of "Babylon Revisited," Fitzgerald had lost the knack of writing *Saturday Evening Post* stories, and he began writing shorter pieces, many of which are sketches rather than stories, for *Esquire*. *Esquire*, however, was not a suitable medium to serve a workshop function as the *Saturday Evening Post* had been. On the one hand, it did not pay enough to sustain Fitzgerald through the composition of a novel; even if it had, it is difficult to imagine how Fitzgerald would have experimented in the framework of short *Esquire* pieces with the complex relationships that he was concurrently developing in *The Last Tycoon*. Moreover, there is the question of the suitability of Fitzgerald's *The Last Tycoon* material, regardless of how he treated it, for *Esquire*: The Monroe Stahr-Kathleen relationship in *The Last Tycoon*, for example, and certainly also the Cecelia-Stahr relationship, would have been as out of place in *Esquire* as the *Esquire* story of a ten-year binge, "The Lost Decade," would have been in the *Saturday Evening Post*. In short, *Esquire* was ill-suited to Fitzgerald's need for a profitable workshop for *The Last Tycoon*, and it is difficult to read the *Esquire* pieces, particularly the Pat Hobby stories about a pathetic movie scriptwriter, without realizing that every hour Fitzgerald spent on them could have been better spent

completing *The Last Tycoon*. From a practical standpoint, it is fair to say that the small sums of income for which Fitzgerald worked in writing the *Esquire* stories may have interfered with the completion of his last novel, whereas the high prices Fitzgerald earned from the *Saturday Evening Post* between 1925 and 1933 provided the financial climate which made it possible for him to complete *Tender Is the Night*.

Indeed, if the *Esquire* stories in general and the Pat Hobby stories in particular, close as they were in terms of composition to *The Last Tycoon*, marked the distance Fitzgerald had come in resolving the professional writer-literary artist dichotomy with which he had been confronted for twenty years, any study of the function of the stories in Fitzgerald's overall career would end on a bleak note. Two stories, "Discard" and "Last Kiss," neither of which was published in Fitzgerald's lifetime, indicate, however, that he was attempting to re-create the climate of free exchange between his stories and novels characteristic especially of the composition period of *Tender Is the Night*. "Last Kiss" provides a good commentary on this attempt. When the story appeared in 1949, the editors remarked in a headnote that the story contained "the seed" that grew into *The Last Tycoon*. The claim is too extravagant for the story in that it implies the sort of relationship between the story and the novel that exists between "Winter Dreams" and *The Great Gatsby*, a relationship that simply does not exist in the case of "Last Kiss" and *The Last Tycoon*. There are, however, interesting parallels.

"LAST KISS"

Fitzgerald created in "Last Kiss" counterparts both to Monroe Stahr and Kathleen in the novel. Jim Leonard, a thirty-five-year-old film producer in "Last Kiss," is similar to Stahr in that he possesses the same kind of power: When the budding starlet, Pamela Knighton, meets Leonard, her agent's voice tells her: "This *is* somebody." In fact, on the Hollywood success ladder he is in Fitzgerald's words "on top," although like Stahr he does not flaunt this fact. Although Pamela is fundamentally different from Kathleen in her self-centered coldness, they also share a resemblance to "pink and silver frost" and an uncertainty about Americans. Kathleen is no aspiring actress, but her past life, like Pamela's, has an aura of mystery about it. Moreover, the present lives of both are complicated by binding entanglements: Pamela's to Chauncey Ward, and Kathleen's to the nameless man she finally marries. There are other parallels: The first important encounter between Leonard and Pamela, for example, closely resembles the ballroom scene during which Stahr becomes enchanted by Kathleen's beauty. In fact, the nature of Leonard's attraction to Pamela is similar to that of Stahr's to Kathleen; although there is no Minna Davis lurking in Leonard's past as there is in Stahr's, he is drawn to Pamela by the kind of romantic, mysterious force which had finally, apart from her resemblance to Minna, drawn Stahr to Kathleen. Moreover, both attachments end abruptly with the same sort of finality: Pamela dies leaving Jim with only film fragments to remember her by, and Kathleen leaves Stahr when she marries "the American."

That these parallels were the seeds of *The Last Tycoon* is doubtful. The important point, however, is that "Last Kiss" is a popular treatment of the primary material that Fitzgerald would work with in the novel: Jim's sentimental return to the drugstore where he had once seen Pamela and his nostalgic remembrance of their last kiss earmark the story for a popular audience which, no doubt, Fitzgerald hoped would help pay his bills during the composition of the novel. Fitzgerald was unable to sell the story, probably because none of the characters generates strong emotion. It is sufficiently clear from "Last Kiss," however, that Fitzgerald was regaining his sense of audience. In the process of demonstrating how well he understood Hollywood, the story also captured much of the glitter that is associated with it in the popular mind. In order to rebuild the kind of popular magazine workshop that he had had for *Tender Is the Night*, it remained for him to subordinate his understanding of Hollywood to the task of re-creating its surface. If he had continued in the direction of "Last Kiss," he would perhaps have done this and thus returned to the kind of climate which had in the past proven to be most favorable for his serious novel work—one in which he wrote handfuls of stories for popular magazines while the novel was taking shape. It is also possible that he might have used such stories to make *The Last Tycoon* something more than a great fragment.

Regarding the role of the stories in Fitzgerald's career, one can finally state that they functioned as providers of financial incentive, as proving grounds for his ideas, as workshops for his craft, and as dictators of his popular reputation. The problem for the serious student of Fitzgerald's works is whether he should examine the popular professional writer who produced some 164 stories for mass consumption or limit his examination of Fitzgerald to his acclaimed works of art, such as "Babylon Revisited," "The Rich Boy," *The Great Gatsby*, and *Tender Is the Night*. To do one to the exclusion of the other is to present not only a fragmented picture of Fitzgerald's literary output but also a distorted one. Just as the stories complement the novels, so do the novels make the stories more meaningful, and the financial and emotional climate from which they all came illuminates the nature of their interdependence.

OTHER MAJOR WORKS

LONG FICTION: *This Side of Paradise*, 1920; *The Beautiful and Damned*, 1922; *The Great Gatsby*, 1925; *Tender Is the Night*, 1934; *The Last Tycoon*, 1941.

PLAYS: *The Vegetable: Or, From President to Postman*, pb. 1923.

NONFICTION: *The Crack-Up*, 1945; *The Letters of F. Scott Fitzgerald*, 1963; *Letters to His Daughter*, 1965; *Thoughtbook of Francis Scott Fitzgerald*, 1965; *Dear Scott/Dear Max: The Fitzgerald-Perkins Correspondence*, 1971; *As Ever, Scott Fitzgerald*, 1972; *F. Scott Fitzgerald's Ledger*, 1972; *The Notebooks of F. Scott Fitzgerald*, 1978; *F. Scott Fitzgerald on Authorship*, 1996.

BIBLIOGRAPHY

Bloom, Harold, ed. *F. Scott Fitzgerald: The Great Gatsby*. New Haven, Conn.: Chelsea House, 1986. A short but important collection of critical essays. This book provides an introductory overview of Fitzgerald scholarship (five pages), as well as readings from a variety of perspectives on Fitzgerald's fiction.

Bruccoli, Matthew J. *Some Sort of Epic Grandeur.* New York: Harcourt Brace Jovanovich, 1981. In this outstanding biography, a major Fitzgerald scholar argues that Fitzgerald's divided spirit, not his lifestyle, distracted him from writing. Bruccoli believes that Fitzgerald both loved and hated the privileged class that was the subject of his fiction.

Conroy, Frank. "Great Scott." *Gentlemen's Quarterly* 66 (December, 1996): 240-245. A reconsideration of Fitzgerald on the centenary of his birth; Conroy argues that one of Fitzgerald's great strengths as a writer was his ability to make the metaphysical beauty of his female characters believable.

Eble, Kenneth. *F. Scott Fitzgerald.* Rev. ed. Boston: Twayne, 1977. A clearly written critical biography, this book traces Fitzgerald's development from youth through a "Final Assessment," which surveys scholarship on Fitzgerald's texts.

Gale, Robert L. *An F. Scott Fitzgerald Encyclopedia.* Westport, Conn.: Greenwood Press, 1998. Provides everything students should know about Fitzgerald's life and works. Indispensable.

Jefferson, Margo. "Still Timely, Yet a Writer of His Time." *The New York Times*, December 17, 1996, p. C17. A brief biography of Fitzgerald on the occasion of his centennial year; calls him one of those rare artists with a cultural radar system that is constantly picking up sensations, responses, and fresh thoughts.

Lee, A. Robert, ed. *Scott Fitzgerald: The Promises of Life.* New York: St. Martin's Press, 1989. An excellent collection of essays by Fitzgerald scholars, this book includes an introduction that surveys scholarship on the texts. Topics addressed include Fitzgerald's treatment of women, his notion of the decline of the West, his "ethics and ethnicity," and his use of "distortions" of the imagination.

Mangum, Bryant. *A Fortune Yet: Money in the Art of F. Scott Fitzgerald's Short Stories.* New York: Garland, 1991. Discusses all of Fitzgerald's stories, both those in collections and those uncollected, focusing on their relationship to his novels and their role as a proving ground for his ideas.

Meyers, Jeffrey. *Scott Fitzgerald: A Biography.* New York: HarperCollins, 1994. In this biography, which makes use of previously unknown materials about Fitzgerald's life, Meyers discusses how such writers as Edgar Allan Poe, Ernest Hemingway, and Joseph Conrad influenced Fitzgerald's fiction.

Miller, James E., Jr. *F. Scott Fitzgerald: His Art and His Technique.* New York: New York University Press, 1964. An expanded version of *The Fictional Technique of Scott Fitzgerald*, originally published in 1957, this book emphasizes Fitzgerald's technique, focusing on the impact of the "saturation vs. selection" debate between H. G. Wells and Henry James; it also adds critical commentary and interpretations of the later works.

Oxford, Edward. "F. Scott Fitzgerald." *American History* 31 (November/December, 1996): 44. A biographical sketch that notes that Fitzgerald was able to convey the energy and image of the 1920's, only to become an ironic witness to the death of that era. Discusses Fitzgerald's life with Zelda and his literary career.

Petry, Alice Hall. *Fitzgerald's Craft of Short Fiction.* Ann Arbor: UMI Research Press, 1989. A study of Fitzgerald's short stories in relationship to his novels, American society, and his personal life. Summarizes and critiques critical reception to his short-story collections and discusses his relationship with his editor Max Perkins; analyzes all the major stories and a number of minor ones.

Tate, Mary Jo. *F. Scott Fitzgerald A to Z: The Essential Reference to His Life and Work.* New York: Facts on File, 1998. A comprehensive study of the man and his oeuvre. Provides bibliographical references and an index.

Bryant Mangum, updated by Mary Ellen Pitts

GUSTAVE FLAUBERT

Born: Rouen, France; December 12, 1821
Died: Croisset, France; May 8, 1880

PRINCIPAL SHORT FICTION

Trois Contes, 1877 (*Three Tales*, 1903)
Novembre, 1885 (wr. c. 1840; *November*, 1932)

OTHER LITERARY FORMS

Gustave Flaubert is best known for his novels *Madame Bovary* (1857; English translation, 1886) and *L'Éducation sentimentale* (1869; *A Sentimental Education*, 1898), which offer a realistic view of life in his native Normandy and, in the latter somewhat autobiographical novel, in Paris. He also wrote narratives of his travels to the Pyrenees and Corsica in 1840 (1927), to Italy in 1845, and to Egypt and the Middle East in 1849-1851 (*Notes de voyage*, 1910). Much of the exotic material gleaned on these trips helped inspire *La Tentation de Saint Antoine* (1874; *The Temptation of Saint Anthony*, 1895) and *Salammbô* (1862; English translation, 1886), novels in which he fictionalized figures from history.

ACHIEVEMENTS

Gustave Flaubert's *Madame Bovary* may be regarded as the great French novel, but upon its publication, in 1857, it was attacked for its immorality, and a famous lawsuit attempted to suppress it. In a sense, Emma Bovary differs little from many heroines of earlier novels, who engaged in enough amorous adventures to attract avid readers but whose eventual punishment served to uphold a moral perspective sufficient to keep the books socially respectable. What is new in *Madame Bovary*, as in Flaubert's other realist work, lies in the author's style. His detailed documentation of the society in which Emma lived emphasized the hypocrisy endemic in that society. Careful control of physical description delineates the personalities of the various characters and creates a style that has strongly influenced subsequent writers.

Flaubert's realistic compositions form only one aspect of his literary production. His other works, closer to the romantic tradition of the historical novel, testify to his depth and versatility.

BIOGRAPHY

Gustave Flaubert was the second of three surviving children of a provincial doctor. Although it was Gustave's older brother, Achille, who would succeed their father in his medical practice, young Gustave accompanied his father even into the dissecting room, where he gained a knowledge of anatomy and a habit of close observation that would contribute to his future literary style. Unlike Emma's husband, the inept country doctor Charles Bovary, Achille-Cléophas Flaubert was a respected professional. Even after his father's death, Flaubert wrote to his mother from Egypt of his pleasure at meeting during his travels a man who knew and respected his father's reputation.

Flaubert began the study of law but discontinued in part because of his poor health. Epileptic, he had infrequent seizures, but despite his robust appearance, his friends and family sought to protect him from excess strain. Flaubert's only sustained professional activity was as an author. Although he lacked other employment, he felt no particular pressure to rush his works into publication. During the years 1835 to 1840, he composed a number of short pieces of prose, some fictitious and some personal memoirs, yet he published little. Most of these juvenilia were collected for publication only after his death.

During 1843-1845, Flaubert composed the first version of his autobiographical novel, *A Sentimental Education*, which would finally be published in a considerably revised version in 1869. The story that it tells of young Frédéric Moreau and his frustrated love for an older, married woman parallels Flaubert's own passion for the wife of Maurice Schlésinger, a financially successful bourgeois who provided a vehicle for the criticism of a materialistic society.

Flaubert's hesitation to publish increased in 1849 as the result of his reading of the manuscript of *The Temptation of Saint Anthony* to his friends Maxima Du Camp and Louis Bouilhet, who harshly criticized it. In October, 1849, Flaubert and Du Camp set out together on a trip to Egypt and the Mediterranean coast as far as Constantinople. During the early part of this journey, Flaubert suffered from considerable depression, which he related to the poor reception of his book and doubts about his literary future. These doubts seem ironic in retrospect, given that in the fall of 1851 he was to begin writing *Madame Bovary*.

Despite a lengthy relationship with Louise Colet, Flaubert never married. His numerous affairs may have been somewhat compromised after his tour of the Orient, however, in that he returned home suffering from syphilis. The publication of *Madame Bovary* in 1857 brought Flaubert both fame and notoriety because of the accusation of its immorality. During the remaining years of his life, Flaubert divided his time between his residence in Paris and his country house in Normandy. He also occasionally traveled to North Africa, the setting of his novel *Salammbô* published in 1862, and to Germany and England. In 1877, three years before his death, he

Gustave Flaubert (Library of Congress)

published what are now his best-known short stories, in *Three Tales*.

ANALYSIS

Gustave Flaubert's *Three Tales*, published during the year 1877, when he was fifty-six years old, reflects the variety of styles of his literary production as a whole. "Un Cœur simple" ("A Simple Heart") employs the Norman realism of *Madame Bovary*. "La Légende de Saint Julien l'hospitalier" ("The Legend of St. Julian, Hospitaler") reflects the preoccupation with exotic locales and the history of the early Christians evident in *The Temptation of Saint Anthony* and Flaubert's travel narratives. "Hérodias" retains this exotic context while focusing on a singular heroine from the past, as Flaubert had done in *Salammbô*.

These three texts, Flaubert's only short fiction to be widely read, provide the usual choices for modern readers seeking an introduction to his work. Flaubert wrote them in a spontaneous burst of activity between September, 1875, and February, 1877, as if he were capping his career with a demonstration piece of his various styles.

"A SIMPLE HEART"

"A Simple Heart," the life story of the good-hearted servant Félicité, draws its material from Flaubert's own life. In 1825, a servant, Julie, joined the Flaubert household and may have provided a model for the character of Félicité. Critics have further suggested comparisons between Félicité and the old woman Catherine Leroux, who, in the *Comices agricoles* scene of *Madame Bovary* (part 2, chapter 8), is awarded "for fifty-four years of service on the same farm, a silver medal—valued at twenty-five francs." Twenty-five francs may at that time have represented a fairly impressive sum but was nevertheless a mediocre value to place on fifty-four years of service. Flaubert, echoing his habit of undercutting both characters and social conventions with a final, damning detail, ends the official statement addressed to Catherine Leroux on this materialistic note.

In "A Simple Heart," as in *Madame Bovary*, the materialism of Norman society appears in the form of a continual preoccupation with money. Yet in both works, this harsh theme contrasts with a persistent romanticism linked to the vain hopes of the various characters. Cupidity in the form of jealousy appears in the very first sentence of "A Simple Heart": "For half a century, the bourgeois women of Pont-l'Évêque envied Madame Aubain because of her servant, Félicité." The motivations of characters throughout the story revolve around money, often to the disadvantage of trusting Félicité. Some figures appear prejudged, as society would have classified them economically, from their very first mention in the text. Thus, Madame Aubain's uncle, an impoverished aristocrat who visits early in the second section of the story, "always arrived at lunch time, with a horrid poodle whose paws spread dirt on all the furniture."

Even the characters dearest to Félicité do not hesitate to hurt her when money is involved. When Félicité befriends Nastasie Barette, who does exploit her by accepting numerous presents, Madame Aubain cuts off this opportunity for friendship by decreeing their prompt return from Trouville to Pont-l'Évêque. Even Félicité's beloved nephew, Victor, imposes on her generosity, although he does bring back to her gifts from his travels. His sudden departure on a voyage to the United States throws Félicité into despair, augmented by Madame Aubain's insensitive incomprehension of her suffering when she learns of Victor's death.

Throughout, characters are defined, usually in a negative manner, by the objects that surround them, objects that often appear in themselves hostile. The initial description of Madame Aubain's house in Pont-l'Évêque tells the reader that "it had interior differences of level that made people trip," and the family members appear through the presentation of their rooms, where the "two children's beds without mattresses" and the attic room of Félicité testify to the subordinate status of children and servants. Yet appearances can be deceiving, still with a bias toward the negative. Because of her harsh life and limited diet, Félicité "at the age of twenty-five appeared to be forty years old."

The considerable catalog of objects in these defining descriptions parallels Flaubert's technique in *Madame Bovary* and echoes much of the realistic style of Honoré de Balzac, whose death in 1850 had appeared to Flaubert as a great loss. Thus, the detailed menu of the lunch at the Liébard farm recalls the even more expansive description in Emma Bovary's view of the dinner at the château, and Virginie, after her death, survives in memory in her clothes—reminiscent of the wedding bouquet of Charles's previous wife that greets Emma upon her arrival at the house at Tostes—clothes that Madame Aubain could bring herself to inspect only when "moths flew out of the wardrobe."

The central documentation, however, must be that of Félicité's own room. Flaubert makes a significant decision to withhold this description until the very end of the story. The mention of Félicité's room in the opening pages tells the reader only that it was in the attic and had a view over the fields. There is no description of the interior. By the time it is revealed, the room contains the debris of Félicité's life and "had the appearance both of a chapel and a bazaar, as it contained so many religious objects and varied things." The separation of the religious objects here from the others underlines their dual role. Religion, as will be seen, held great importance for Félicité, but the objects that represent her devotion share with the others in her room echoes of deterioration and loss. Further, the distinction blurs between religious and secular: "On the dresser, covered with a cloth like an altar, was a box made of seashells that Victor had given her." She retains with religious veneration objects linked to her memories.

Negative emphasis within the realistic catalog again parallels *Madame Bovary*. The determining events of Félicité's unhappy memories grow from the same avaricious society that surrounded Emma. The one man she loved, Théodore, abandoned her to marry "a very rich old woman," an action analogous both to Charles Bovary's first, arranged marriage to Héloïse and to Paul's later marriage in "A Simple Heart" to the daughter of a man who could help his career. Victor's death, attributed to poor medical treatment of his case of yellow fever, recalls Charles Bovary's unfortunate failure in the operation on Justin, and the heirs who pillage Madame Aubain's house parallel the actions of Emma's creditors.

The most obvious negative emphases, however, result from a series of exclusions. The bad can be defined most easily by contrast with the good. Often, this ranking comes from the arbitrary expectations of society, expectations that Flaubert documented in his *Dictionnaire des idées reçues* (1910, 1913; *Dictionary of Accepted Ideas*, 1954). Thus, Charles Bovary bought for Emma "a second-hand vehicle that, once equipped with new lanterns and pierced leather mud flaps, almost resembled a tilbury," and at the beach at Trouville, Virginie "went swimming in a shirt, for lack of a bathing costume; and her maid dressed her in a customs-inspection cabin that served for the bathers." Things, not allowed to be as they naturally exist, are described as "almost" something more prestigious.

Those moments of high prestige in which the characters participate, however, disappear from the text. At Virginie's funeral, for example, readers see the preparation of the body for the burial but not the more uplifting religious ceremony. Flaubert states simply, "after mass, it took three quarters of an hour to get to the cemetery." Similarly, though romance dominates Emma Bovary's life, Flaubert never shows her at the moment of central significance when she is a bride in church. Again, he emphasizes distance to be traversed: "The town hall being at half a league from the farm, they went there on foot, and came back in the same manner, once the ceremony was over at the church." The last phrase, added almost as an afterthought, effectively deemphasizes what could have been the most positive moment of Emma's life. One may certainly argue that liturgy, with its set patterns, need not be described in detail to be understood. Still, as Alphonse Daudet so aptly demonstrated in "Les Trois Messes basses," the personal circumstances woven into each liturgy make it a unique event. This must hold especially true for both weddings and funerals.

Although the drama of liturgical moments disappears from Flaubert's texts, a current of romanticism persists throughout "A Simple Heart." Linked in part to the religious element in the story, this romanticism includes references both to traditional romantic themes and to other passages in which Flaubert appears to parody such themes. This again echoes *Madame Bovary* and Flaubert's dual feelings concerning romantic passion. Emma Bovary's emotional confusion clearly derives from the false ideas of love, which she had taken from sentimental novels. Immediately after her marriage, she "sought to know exactly what people meant in real life by the words *felicity, passion* and *intoxication* that had appeared so beautiful to her in books." Flaubert's use of the word *félicité* in this description of Emma's disappointment anticipates the irony in the choice of the word as the name for his heroine in "A Simple Heart." Félicité does occasionally achieve joy but only despite the numerous forces working against her happiness.

Religion provides the central solace of Félicité's life. At the beginning of the story, she rises at dawn to attend mass and falls asleep each night with her rosary in her hand. She derives a dual joy from attending catechism classes with Virginie. She admires the beauty of the stained-glass windows, much as Emma Bovary "rather than following the mass looked at the holy pictures framed in azure in her book," and thus Félicité gains a rudimentary religious education, such training "having been neglected in her youth." The repeated images in the church of the Holy Spirit in the form of a bird prepare for Félicité's vision at the end of the story.

Along with religion, a romantic joy in external nature touches Félicité. In a way that underlines her solitude, however, these fleeting moments of happiness come to Félicité only with the rare experience of love. Flaubert tells the reader very early that Félicité "had had, like anyone else, her tale of love," thus deemphasizing this formative experience. Still, during her interlude with Théodore, they were surrounded by the beauty of nature: "The wind was soft; the stars shone," but as Emma could not regain the luxury of the ball at the château, Félicité only rarely returns to the joys of nature. One other such interlude does occur when she accompanies the Aubain family to the countryside. This enjoyment coincides with the fulfillment that Félicité feels in taking care of Paul and Virginie when they are children, but even here there is a sense of deterioration from a better state of things past. The house they visit "was all that remained of a vacation house, now disappeared."

Consistent with the romantic pathetic fallacy identifying elements of nature with the emotional condition of the protagonist, nature remains pleasant in "A Simple Heart" while Félicité is relatively happy. Later, as she worries about Victor, who has gone to sea, she focuses on violent storms and finally learns that, "as in a memory of engravings in a geography book, he was eaten by savages, trapped in a forest by monkeys, or dying on a deserted beach." Like Emma, she takes her imaginings from an overly literal application of material from books.

As Flaubert cites these tales of savages and monkeys, modern elements of romantic travel literature, he draws on a rich source of contemporary allusion. Elsewhere, the names of Paul and Virginie he chooses for Madame Aubain's children recall the novel *Paul et Virginie* (1788), by Jacques-Henri Bernadin de Saint-Pierre, the exotic setting of which provided a model of preromantic nature description. Later, the appearance of the de Larsonnière family with their black servant and their parrot continued this current of exotic allusion.

Flaubert's critique of romanticism leads him to use a degree of exaggeration that approaches parody. When their uncle gives the children a geography book with engravings, "they represented different scenes of the world, cannibals with feathers on their heads, a monkey carrying off a young girl, bedouins in the desert, a whale being harpooned. . . ." These dramatic choices may have been typical of geography books of the time, but in Flaubert's description of Virginie after her death, the choices are entirely his own. He begins with a conventional tableau, where Virginie's pale face contrasted with a black crucifix echoes the contrast of light and darkness dear to the romantics. As Félicité remains "for two nights" near the body, however, the description, drawn from Flaubert's realistic medical observations, inclines toward the grotesque.

Grotesque exaggeration linked to the theme of death culminates in the story of Félicité's parrot. She had become so attached to the bird, the last voice audible to her as she became progressively deaf, that she had it stuffed after its death. Its place among the religious objects in her room reinforced an association: "In church she always contemplated the Holy Spirit and observed that he somewhat resembled the parrot." The bird, however, badly preserved, deteriorated. At the end, when Félicité's friend brought the parrot to her to kiss, "worms were devouring it."

Félicité does not see the deterioration of the parrot. Her eyes as well as her ears are failing. The brief fifth and final section of the story brings the reader at last to the perspective of Félicité herself, who, thanks to the very narrowness of her perceptions, achieves the happiness promised in her name. Earlier references have slighted Félicité's intelligence and alluded to her lack of education, but what she does not know may protect her. The fifth section opens with the line "The grass sent the odor of summer," appealing to one sense that Félicité retains and bringing back to her the sense of joy in nature. A religious procession is about to pass by the house, and readers see it through Félicité's imagination. The holy sacrament is displayed on an altar containing many objects representative of life in the local area, including the stuffed parrot, Loulou. This accumulation of mismatched objects, however, no longer conveys the lack of aesthetic sense that it might have represented earlier. It has become a "mound of bright colors" amid which "Loulou, hidden under some roses, showed only a blue forehead, like a piece of lapis." Properly selected and arranged, even the realistic debris of village life can present a form of beauty. At the end, Félicité is vindicated in that her "simple heart" had led her to make instinctive choices that protect what beauty there was in her world.

The complex style of "A Simple Heart" derives from the tension between its realistic and romantic elements. A similar contrast in "La Légende de Saint Julien l'Hospitalier" ("The Legend of St. Julian, Hospitaler"), however, produces a much simpler narrative, where quantities of relatively generic images replace the nuances of the objects in Félicité's surroundings.

"THE LEGEND OF ST. JULIAN, HOSPITALER"

"The Legend of St. Julian, Hospitaler" conveys the life of its protagonist from birth to death, neatly divided into three parts: the growing violence of the young man, who fears that he will fulfill a prophecy that he will kill his parents, a period of flight that ends with Julien unwittingly killing his parents when they come to seek him, and his final repentance and salvation.

The story, set in a vaguely described medieval Europe, contains numerous exotic elements that link it to Flaubert's *The Temptation of Saint Anthony*. While Antoine spends the greater part of his story doing penance and resisting temptations, however, Julien's violent years dominate a story with only a brief phase of penitence. The fairy-tale opening of "The Legend of St. Julian, Hospitaler"—"Julien's father and mother lived in a chateau, in the middle of a wood, on the slope of a hill"—contrasts with the more theatrical style with extensive dialogue that dominates *The Temptation of Saint Anthony*.

Exotic elements proliferate in "The Legend of St. Julian, Hospitaler" from the very first description, where the family's castle contains armaments of foreign origins, to the Asian merchants and pilgrims from the Holy Land who describe their journeys and to the diverse adversaries whom Julien faces during his extensive travels as a soldier. The analogy with the story of Oedipus, similarly destined to kill his father, adds a foreign element, but description in "The Legend of St. Julian, Hospitaler" lacks the details and contrasts of the Norman scene. When Julien kills animals while hunting and later finds himself surrounded by beasts intent on avenging his excessive savagery, the catalog of creatures retains the artistic sense of animals highlighted in a tapestry: "A marten slipped quickly between his legs, a panther bounded over his shoulder, a serpent wound around an ash tree." Except for the stag that speaks to Julien to warn him of his fate, the animals and other objects Julien encounters remain generic, devoid of descriptive detail.

Similarly, the pathetic fallacy linking landscape to emotion disappears in this text. When, in the second part, Julien marries and attempts to lead a settled life, the sky over his château "was always blue." Even in the emotional hunting scene that reawakens his savagery and leads to the death of his parents, readers see him surrounded by natural beauty: "The shadows of trees spread out across the moss. Sometimes the moon dappled the clearings."

Occasionally, description does serve, as elsewhere in Flaubert's work, to define the mood of characters. As Julien grows more ferocious in hunting, he returns home one night "covered with blood and dirt, with thorns in his hair and smelling like savage beasts." Flaubert, however, continues here, "He became like the beasts." The symbolism is more explicit and heavy-handed than in Flaubert's more realistic texts. A night lamp "in the form of a dove" symbolizes his parents' care for Julien but with a more simplistic suggestion than that in Félicité's vision of the Holy Spirit.

If the characters are not seen as motivated by the objects that surround them, a strong theme of fate provides an alternate controlling force. When Julien's thirst for blood is first aroused and he begins to kill birds with stones, "the wall being broken at that place, a piece of stone happened to be under his fingers. He turned his arm and the stone knocked down the bird." The stone, not Julien, is responsible, and later, when Julien attempts to repent, violent dreams come unbidden to renew his desire to kill.

Fate finds its voice in the prophecies governing Julien's life. At his birth, a beggar, "a Bohemian with plaited beard, silver rings on his arms, and blazing eyes," warns Julien's father of the violence to come, much as the beggar in *Madame Bovary* foreshadows Emma's death. At the end of the story, the leprous traveler whom Julien rescues flashes the same blazing eyes just before Julien is carried off to heaven. This salvation, ordained by Christ, responds to another kind of external—this time divine—manipulation.

"HÉRODIAS"

Just as Julien's story follows what has been preordained, "Hérodias" must not depart from the set sequence of events from the biblical story. This time, Flaubert narrates not the entire life of his protagonist but the events of a single day. During the first two parts of the story, a delegation arrives from Rome and, while searching Herod's cellars for treasures, finds the imprisoned John the Baptist, called here Iaokanann, who rails against Herod's incestuous marriage. The third part narrates the banquet where Salomé's dance earns Iaokanann's death.

Again, Flaubert uses a considerable amount of description, much of it derived from his own visit to the shores of the Dead Sea, but the view remains that of the camera, avoiding detailed analysis of the characters' emotions. Readers first see Herod on a terrace with a panoramic view of the surrounding country. The descriptive catalog of the terrain and Herod's embattled position parallel the situation at the beginning of *Salammbô*. Later, an enumeration of armaments in Herod's cellars recalls the similar listing in "The Legend of St. Julian, Hospitaler," but very little of this relates to character exposition. Only the menacing "hot wind with the odor of sulfer" that blows as Hérodias, Herod's wife, arrives hints at the personal confrontations to come. Even when, at the end of the first part, Herod's view of a beautiful young girl on another terrace foreshadows Hérodias's manipulation of him, the portrait of the girl herself has the impersonality of an Asian painting.

A principal animation of "Hérodias" comes from recurrent animal imagery. Iaokanann appears in prison, covered with animal skins, "in the depths of his lair." He screams that he will cry out "like a bear, like a wild ass" and forces Hérodias finally to "roar" like a lion. Contrasting with this animal imagery, however, Salomé's dance appears mechanical. In a parallel scene in *Salammbô*, the heroine dances with a python "placing the middle of its body around the back of her neck," but Salomé, instructed by her mother, remains externally controlled "like a flower shaken by a storm."

Inevitably Iaokanann is beheaded. The story ends as two Christians carry the head away toward Galilee: "Since it was very heavy, they took turns carrying it." This final realistic touch parallels the closing of "The Legend of St. Julian, Hospitaler," where Flaubert adds, "There is the story of Saint Julien l'Hospitalier approximately as one finds it on the church window in my country." Each story, exoticism notwithstanding, ends grounded by a realistic touch.

Flaubert's instinctive return to realism reflects the importance of the documentary style, founded on his detailed observation of Norman life, through which he orchestrated objects to reflect the psychological composition of his characters. A comparison of "A Simple Heart" with Flaubert's more exotic short stories reveals a shift in the latter toward a formal objectivity. Animals like those of a tapestry and the image of a girl portrayed as if in a painting distance themselves from the emotional content of the story.

Flaubert's realistic manner bridges this distance. In "A Simple Heart," as in *Madame Bovary*, he develops a complexity that relies on the careful selection of objects to define both the feelings of his characters and the societal forces that often conflict with them. This conflict, closely tied to the clash of romantic and realistic elements, provides the basic tension that gives life to Flaubert's work.

OTHER MAJOR WORKS

LONG FICTION: *Madame Bovary*, 1857 (English translation, 1886); *Salammbô*, 1862 (English translation, 1886); *L'Éducation sentimentale*, 1869 (*A Sentimental Education*, 1898); *La Tentation de Saint Antoine*, 1874 (*The Temptation of Saint Anthony*, 1895); *Bouvard et Pécuchet*, 1881 (*Bouvard and Pécuchet*, 1896); *La Première Éducation sentimentale*, 1963 (written 1843-1845; *The First Sentimental Education*, 1972).

PLAYS: *Le Candidat*, pr., pb. 1874 (*The Candidate*, 1904); *Le Château des cœurs*, pb. 1885 (wr. 1863, with Louis Bouilhet); *The Castle of Hearts*, 1904).

NONFICTION: *Par les champs et par les grèves*, 1885 (with Maxime Du Camp; *Over Strand and Field*, 1904); *Correspondance, 1830-1880*, 1887-1893; *Dictionnaire des idées reçues*, 1910, 1913 (*Dictionary of Accepted Ideas*, 1954); *Notes de voyage*, 1910.

MISCELLANEOUS: *The Complete Works*, 1904 (10 volumes); *Œuvres complètes*, 1910-1933 (22 volumes).

BIBLIOGRAPHY

Addison, Claire. *Where Flaubert Lies*. Cambridge, England: Cambridge University Press, 1996. A detailed study of Flaubert's life and art, focusing on the relationship between his personal life, historical context, and his fiction.

Bart, Benjamin F. *Flaubert*. Syracuse, N.Y.: Syracuse University Press, 1967. This chronologically arranged and detailed biography places Flaubert's works in the context of the events of his life. Chapter 24, devoted to the *Three Tales*, stresses psychological elements and events from Flaubert's life that contributed to the compositions as well as noting revisions that the stories underwent. Includes a note listing manuscript sources and an index.

Bloom, Harold, ed. *Gustave Flaubert*. New York: Chelsea House, 1989. This collection of fourteen essays with an introduction by Bloom covers multiple aspects of Flaubert's life and work. Jane Robertson writes on the structure of "Hérodias," noting the relative difficulty of the work. Shoshana Felman's essay on "The Legend of St. Julian, Hospitaler" stresses legendary and symbolic elements in the story. Contains a chronology of Flaubert's life, a bibliography, and an index.

Brombert, Victor. *The Novels of Flaubert: A Study of Themes and Techniques*. Princeton, N.J.: Princeton University Press, 1966. This work devotes a chapter to each of the *Three Tales*. Brombert's thematic approach emphasizes Flaubert's adaptation of the legend in "The Legend of St. Julian, Hospitaler," the tension between sentiment and irony in "A Simple Heart," and exotic descriptions, some derived from Flaubert's own trip to Egypt, in "Hérodias." Bibliography, index.

Cronk, Nicholas. "Reading *Un Cœur Simple:* The Pleasure of the Intertext." *Nineteenth-Century French Studies* 24 (Fall/Winter, 1995/1996): 154-161. Discusses the story's allusion to eighteenth century works from the Rousseauesque tradition of sentiment and the Voltairean tradition of satire. Claims that Flaubert appropriates a character of Bernardin de Saint-Pierre's as a model for Félicité.

Greenbaum, Andrea. "Flaubert's *Un Cœur Simple*." *The Explicator* (Summer, 1995): 208-211. Discusses the satire in Flaubert's story, particularly its mockery of religious devotion by means of the parrot, the story's satirical centerpiece.

Nadeau, Maurice. *The Greatness of Flaubert*. Translated by Barbara Bray. New York: Library Press, 1972. This biographical work devotes chapter 16 to the *Three Tales*, stressing how these works evolved from ideas that Flaubert had accumulated during his previous writing. Sources considered are largely biographical, and the chapter details the immediate context in which the three stories were written. Supplemented by a chronology and a bibliography.

Porter, Laurence M., ed. *Critical Essays on Gustave Flaubert*. Boston: G. K. Hall, 1986. This collection of sixteen essays includes work by a number of authorities in the field. Two studies treat the *Three Tales:* Raymonde Debray-Genette studies "Narrative Figures of Speech" in "A Simple Heart" in a structural analysis that still insists on the importance of illusion, and Benjamin F. Bart examines "Humanity and Animality" in "The Legend of St. Julian, Hospitaler." Bibliography, index.

Starkie, Enid. *Flaubert, the Master: A Critical and Biographical Study, 1856-1880*. New York: Atheneum, 1971. A biography considering Flaubert's life only after *Madame Bovary*, this study devotes chapter 12 to the short stories. Special attention is given to sources and to events in Flaubert's life, particularly close to the time of composition, that may have influenced the stories. With a bibliography and index.

Stipa, Ingrid. "Desire, Repetition, and the Imaginary in Flaubert's *Un Cœur Simple*." *Studies in Short Fiction* 31 (Fall, 1994): 617-626. Argues that although Flaubert maintains an ironic perspective in the story, a pattern of repetitions of imagery makes the transformation of the parrot into a sacred symbol acceptable to the reader, a tactic that protects the protagonist from being the victim of the irony.

Tarver, John Charles. *Gustave Flaubert as Seen in His Works and Correspondence*. 1895. Reprint. Port Washington, N.Y.: Kennikat Press, 1970. This relatively complete biography devotes only chapter 18 to the *Three Tales*. The bulk of the chapter summarizes the story of "The Legend of St. Julian, Hospitaler." Index.

Williams, Tony, and Mary Orr, eds. *New Approaches in Flaubert Studies*. Lewiston, N.Y.: E. Mellen Press, 1999. Part of the Studies in French Literature series, this is a contemporary study of Flaubert's works. Provides bibliographical references and an index.

Dorothy M. Betz

RICHARD FORD

Born: Jackson, Mississippi; February 16, 1944

PRINCIPAL SHORT FICTION

Rock Springs: Stories, 1987
Wildlife, 1990 (novella)
Women with Men: Three Stories, 1997

OTHER LITERARY FORMS

Richard Ford made his reputation as a novelist before turning to short fiction. His first novel, *A Piece of My Heart* (1976), marked him as a southern writer, since it was set primarily in Arkansas and on an uncharted island in the Mississippi River. *The Ultimate Good Luck* (1981) told the story of a Vietnam veteran, Harry Quinn, in Mexico, on a quest to get his girlfriend's brother out of jail. *The Sportswriter* (1986) is set in New Jersey and tells the story of a failed novelist trying to put his professional and personal life in order. *Independence Day* (1995) is a sequel to *The Sportswriter*. Ford's short-story collection *Rock Springs* and his novella *Wildlife* are set in Montana. In 1991, Ford's screenplay *Bright Angel*, also set in Montana and adapted from stories in the *Rock Springs* collection, was made into a film directed by Michael Fields and released by the Hemdale Film Corporation.

ACHIEVEMENTS

Richard Ford, a writer's writer, has been praised for his clean style and craft by other writers such as Raymond Carver, E. L. Doctorow, and Joyce Carol Oates, who described him as "a born story teller with an inimitable lyric voice." Walker Percy called *The Sportswriter*, which won the PEN/Faulkner Award for Fiction, a "stunning novel." Over the years, Ford earned several fellowships. From 1971 to 1974, he was a University of Michigan Fellow, and he went on to become a John Simon Guggenheim Memorial Foundation Fellow (1977-1978) and a National Endowment for the Arts Fellow (1979-1980). *A Piece of My Heart* was nominated for the Ernest Hemingway Award for the Best First Novel of the Year in 1976.

Independence Day won the Pulitzer Prize and the PEN/Faulkner Award in 1996, becoming the first novel ever to win both prizes. Ford won the Rea Award in 1995.

Such recognition, however, was slow in coming. According to Ford's friend and Michigan classmate Bruce Weber, the combined sales of Ford's first two novels amounted to fewer than twelve thousand copies. *The Sportswriter*, which sold sixty thousand copies, was the turning point in Ford's career and encouraged the publisher to put the first two novels back in print. The hard-cover edition of *Rock Springs* published by Atlantic Monthly Press sold twenty-five thousand copies, and the Vintage paperback edition was then scheduled for an initial run of fifty thousand copies.

BIOGRAPHY

Though he does not consider himself a southern writer, Richard Ford was born in the Deep South in Jackson, Mississippi, in 1944, and he grew up there. Like Sam Newel, one of the two principal characters of *A Piece of My Heart*, Ford's father was a traveling salesman whose territory might have coincided with that of Sam Newel's salesman father in the novel. In 1952, Ford's father suffered a heart attack, after which Richard lived with his grandparents, who ran a hotel in Little Rock, Arkansas. Ford grew into a relatively wild teenager, and, according to Bruce Weber, his mother "kept him from serious scrapes with the law." Ford's father died in 1960, and in 1962 Ford went to East Lansing to study literature at Michigan State University, where he met Kristina Hensley, whom he later married. For a year after graduation, Ford taught high school in Flint, Michigan, then enrolled for one semester as a law student at Washington University in St. Louis. Thereafter, he worked briefly in New York City as assistant editor for a trade magazine, *The American Druggist*.

He then seriously began pursuing his career as a writer, studying at the University of California at Irvine with Oakley Hall and E. L. Doctorow. He also

Richard Ford (James Hamilton)

lived in Chicago and Mexico, where his novel *The Ultimate Good Luck* is set. He taught at the University of Michigan, Princeton University, Goddard College, and Williams College. Ford told *People* magazine in 1990 that he had lived in twelve places in twenty-two years.

Ford has worked effectively to erase regional traces from his later writing in an effort to shed his identity as a southern writer. His first novel, *A Piece of My Heart*, is set mainly in Arkansas, after one of the two central characters crosses the South, coming east from California to get there. Most of the other characters are southern gothic types, and reading the novel one would suppose that it must have been written by a southerner. On the other hand, if one turns to a later Ford novel, such as *The Sportswriter*, set in New Jersey, one could easily believe that the novelist had spent all of his life in the New York-New Jersey area. Then, turning to his short-story collection *Rock Springs*, one might think that the writer had grown up in Montana. Interviewed in Salisbury, Maryland, in April of 1988, just after the publication of *Rock Springs*, Ford remarked that he did not want to be known as a southern writer, that his stories and char-

acters were universal and did not depend upon the peculiarities of any particular region.

Ford has lived in many places, urban and rural, but he settled in Montana to learn the locale that would be the setting for his *Rock Springs* story collection and for *Wildlife*. He and his wife continued to spend part of their time in a rented house in Highwood, Montana, about thirty miles east of Great Falls, and the rest of their time in New York, New Orleans, and other places remote from their Montana hideaway. As a writer, Ford has lived on fellowships as well as on the income generated from his writing and occasional lectures and readings. Although he has taught and lectured in the past, he clearly takes the vocation of writing most seriously.

ANALYSIS

Richard Ford's fiction probes the lives of ordinary people, fascinated and troubled by the unpredictability of life. In some cases, the stories reflect on some catastrophe experienced in adolescence or before, when a family crisis changed comfortable patterns of life.

"OPTIMISTS"

In the story "Optimists," in the *Rock Springs* collection, for example, the narrator recalls a traumatic event that occurred in Great Falls, Montana, when he was fifteen years old, in 1959, "the year my parents were divorced, the year when my father killed a man and went to prison for it." The family situation in this story resembles the one in the later novella *Wildlife*. In both cases, the father reacts badly and emotionally and ruins both his life and the marriage while the son watches, horrified and dumbfounded.

In fact, the wildlife metaphor of the later novella is explained in the story "Optimists," when the mother tells the boy Frank about a flock of migrating ducks that she saw resting on the Milk River once, when she was a girl, and winter was approaching. A friend of hers clapped her hands to startle the ducks into motion, but one stayed, its feet frozen to the ice. Her mother's friend explained, "It's wildlife. Some always get left behind." In other words, such things happen in life as a natural consequence. Nature will have its way, and disaster cannot be avoided.

In the story "Optimists," Frank's father, Roy Brinson, a railway worker, returns home early one night, shaken because he has witnessed a man's death in a railway accident. Returning home, he finds his wife playing cards and drinking with another couple, Penny and Boyd Mitchell. Boyd has had too much to drink and foolishly baits the disturbed father into an argument about unions. The father loses his temper and hits Boyd "square in the chest," a blow that kills the man. The police come, the father is taken away, and the boy's life is forever changed. "We'll all survive this," Frank's mother reassures him. "Be an optimist." Mere survival, however, is not the issue here. The father serves five months in prison for accidental homicide, but thereafter he loses his job, divorces his wife, turns to drinking, gambling, and embezzlement, and abandons his family. The son survives, but the optimistic title of the story is surely ironic.

"GREAT FALLS"

Fatherhood is a major theme in Ford's fiction, where men often go haywire, and many of his stories are built on father-and-son relationships and broken families, men trying to be good husbands and fathers, stumbling and failing in their attempts and perplexed by their failures. Jack Russell, the father of the story "Great Falls," takes his son Jackie duck hunting and attempts to give the boy advice. He remembers something Jackie's mother had once said to him: "Nobody dies of a broken heart," adding "that was the idea she had. I don't know why." The boy has fears: "I worry if you're going to die before I do," he tells his father, "or if Mother is. That worries me."

When Jackie and his father return home, they find a twenty-five-year-old stranger named Woody in the kitchen. The father goes berserk, ordering the mother to pack her bags, after which there is a standoff, with the father holding a loaded pistol just under Woody's chin, out in the yard by Woody's Pontiac, as the mother and son watch. "I did not think she thought my father would shoot Woody," the boy speculates, but he thinks his father did think so, "and was trying to find out how to." When asked in 1988 about his fictive strategy in this story and the dramatic possibilities, Ford explained:

When I wrote that story, I did something that I almost never do. I didn't know when I was writing the story if someone was going to get shot or not. But I got to the point in writing the story at which . . . I realized that if someone did get shot, that a whole lot of dramatic possibilities that went on beyond that would be foreclosed for me. And in part, at least, for that reason I didn't do it.

Ford also commented on the unpredictability that somehow infects his stories. "Well, when a man is standing in front of another man holding a gun to his chin and he hasn't shot him yet," Ford responded, "he either will shoot him, or he won't. And probably he doesn't know until he does or doesn't do it if he's going to."

"ROCK SPRINGS"

"Rock Springs," the title story of the collection, sets the tone of quiet desperation that dominates the book. Earl Middleton, the central character, is a fugitive and a thief who is trying to escape from Montana to Florida in a stolen Mercedes with his daughter Cheryl, and a divorced woman named Edna. When the Mercedes develops mechanical problems, they decide to leave it and steal another car when they get to Rock Springs, Wyoming. Three miles out of town, the car breaks down, and Earl calls a taxi. Their spirits are lifted momentarily when they see a gold mine on the outskirts of town; when they arrive at a Ramada Inn, however, Edna decides to go back to Montana, not because she does not love Earl but because she wants more permanence and security than he can offer. The story ends with Earl casing cars in the dead of night, wondering which one to steal and wondering

"what would you think a man was doing if you saw him in the middle of the night looking in the windows of cars in the parking lot of the Ramada Inn? . . . Would you think he was trying to get ready for a day when trouble would come down on him? . . . Would you think he was anybody like you?

When asked how he found such a perfect line to end that story, Ford responded,

"Sometimes you get lucky. You put yourself at the end of your story, and you know in fact it's the end of your story, and you get down to the last few gestures you've got left. You hope to put yourself in a state of mind where you could write a good sentence. That's . . . what I'm always trying to do—to write a good sentence.

Rock Springs offers the reader a multitude of good sentences.

"SWEETHEARTS"

Earl Middleton in the story "Rock Springs" is the fictive cousin of Robard Hewes in *A Piece of My Heart*, but with Earl and some of the other characters of the *Rock Springs* collection Ford pushes this prototype toward criminality while still putting the characters' humanity on display. In "Sweethearts," for example, Russ, the narrator, describes the day he and his live-in Arlene took her ex-husband Bobby to jail to serve time for passing bad checks and robbing a convenience store. "You have to face that empty moment," Bobby says to Russ. "How often have you done that?"

Bobby looks "like a man who knows half of something and who is supposed to know everything, who sees exactly what trouble he's in and is scared to death by it." Bobby is desperate and pulls a gun just as their car reaches the jail but finally decides not to use it to kill Arlene, for whatever crazed motive, though after Bobby surrenders, Russ and Arlene discover the gun was not loaded. As in "Great Falls," the story is not over until Russ and Arlene digest their own feelings and set the course for their own lives, though Russ understands "how you become a criminal in the world and lost it all," like Bobby, and like Earl in "Rock Springs." Again and again, Ford reveals a sense of closure that is distinctively effective and affecting.

WILDLIFE

Another character type that recurs frequently in *Rock Springs* and *Wildlife* is that of the disturbed child who senses that his life is being changed by forces beyond his control and would like to intervene to maintain the status quo but is not empowered to do so. All the character can do is to endure and survive in an unhappily changing world. Ford's adult characters are often faced with the same dilemma, but it is more pathetic when it visits children, such as the boy

in "Optimists," Jackie in "Great Falls," or Les in "Communist," who, on a goose hunt with his mother's friend Glen, has "a feeling that something important was about to happen to me, and that this would be a day I would always remember." As Les notes later, "too much awareness too early in life" can be a problem.

Human motivation is always the central puzzle in the fiction of Ford, a mystery that his characters do not pretend to understand. Ford probes the human heart, seeking to understand why it is often disconnected from the human mind. His characters can be painfully sympathetic and wholly decent and admirable as they drift into dilemmas that they cannot control. Fate is a blind mechanism that can cause love to atrophy or die as his characters struggle to control their lives. There is dignity in that struggle, and an ineffable melancholy that Ford seeks to convey.

In the novella *Wildlife*, teenager Joe Brinson sees his mother and father drifting apart and their marriage collapsing. He loves his parents and would do anything to save their marriage, but since his parents themselves do not understand what has gone wrong with their marriage after his father loses his job as a golf professional and his self-respect, how could a sixteen-year-old boy do anything to reverse the situation? The unemployed father goes out to fight forest fires for three days. Devastated, and perhaps fearing that he will never return home, the mother has a fling with an older man, perhaps because she merely seeks comfort and security, then leaves the family after the father returns home and discovers that she has been unfaithful. It is not at all clear that she understands her own motives. The son is made to understand that nothing in life is permanent or can be taken for granted. Happiness is a phantom that can be quickly dissipated. Grown-ups can be as unpredictable and as irrational as children. The only reality is the coldness of the oncoming winter and, potentially, of life.

Fears and self-doubts and frustrations flare up and spread as irrationally and as unpredictably as the forest fires that the father fights, which are finally brought under control not by the will of men but by the changing seasons and the passage of time. They will run their natural course. "This is a wild life, isn't it son?" the father asks after the mother announces her intention to leave him. The father's reaction to this news is also irrational and potentially dangerous to himself and others; at least in this fable, however, all ends well, after a fashion, though relationships cannot be fully restored after they are once broken, despite good intentions. Life is raw and fragile here, and art does not intrude to presume to make it better.

One critic has argued that transience is the major theme in Richard Ford's fiction, as well as in his transient lifestyle. In Montana, Ford seems to have found an appropriate setting for his stories about ordinary Americans—their hopes and aspirations, their failures, losses, and disappointments. In this respect, Ford seems to be telling the same story over and over, populating it differently, but always trying to get it right, demonstrating that life is fraught with frustration and the unexpected, and that the measure of a person's character is an ability to endure the worst and hope for the best.

Women with Men

This collection of three novellas develops one of Ford's favorite subjects, the position of the person who finds it difficult to look outside himself and into the life of someone who loves him. Ford has said that he likes the form of the long story and finds it congenial to this sort of subject. In the first of the stories, "The Womanizer," Martin Austin meets a French woman, Joséphine Belliard, during a business trip to Paris. He is excited and compelled by her apparent self-sufficiency and her resistance to his interest, even by her passivity when he kisses her. Back home, he instigates a quarrel with his wife and leaves to return to Paris and Joséphine. She is surprised but not very interested to hear from him.

When he arranges to meet her, he offers to stay with her six-year-old son Léo while she meets with her lawyer. Austin does not particularly like children, and he is unsure how he will entertain a small child whose language he does not speak. He finally decides to take the child to the nearby park, where Léo disappears. After some hours of searching by Austin and the police, the child is found. He is hysterical after having been attacked sexually. Coldly furious, Joséphine tells Austin that he is the same as dead. As

the story ends, Austin is meditating on the problem of being attached to another human being.

The second story, "Jealous," is set in Montana, where seventeen-year-old Donny is living with his father on a remote farm after his mother has left them to move to Seattle. On this snowy night, Donny's flamboyant aunt, Doris, is driving him to the station in Dutton so that he can visit his mother. While they wait in a bar for the train, they witness a shooting, one more unsettling event in a series for Donny, the last being his aunt's revelations about her bisexuality. The story leaves Donny feeling that his aunt is right in saying that he cannot trust the truth, a claim which leaves him strangely detached and calm.

Like "The Womanizer," "Occidentals" is set in Paris. Once again, the central character is a middle-aged novelist, Charley Matthews, divorced this time, who is visiting Paris with Helen Carmichael, a large blond woman for whom he feels a lukewarm affection. Helen is enthusiastic about the trip; she has always wanted to visit Paris. After several uncomfortable experiences, however, Charley's distaste for the French and the city erupt in bad temper, despite Helen's cheerfulness. When Helen dies unexpectedly, Charley meets the crisis with the same passive intelligence and vague optimism exhibited by Donny and Martin Austin at similar crises in their stories. Like many of Ford's characters, they ruminate on their futures in the tattered midst of their present lives.

Other major works

LONG FICTION: *A Piece of My Heart*, 1976; *The Ultimate Good Luck*, 1981; *The Sportswriter*, 1986; *Independence Day*, 1995.

SCREENPLAY: *Bright Angel*, 1991.

NONFICTION: *Good Raymond*, 1998.

Bibliography

Alcorn, Ellen. "Richard Ford: His Novels Are a Medicine Against Pain." *GQ* 60 (May, 1990): 224-225. A profile of the writer at age forty-six. Attempts to show how Ford found his inspiration for the novella *Wildlife* from his own difficult childhood. For Ford, storytelling is a kind of "medicine against pain."

Ballantyne, Sheila. "A Family Too Close to the Fire." Review of *Wildlife*, by Richard Ford. *The New York Times Book Review*, June 17, 1990, 3, 12. This review essay is perceptive in finding at the heart of *Wildlife* "a deep nostalgia for that moment when a person recognizes a true perfection in the way things once were, before the onset of ruin and great change." It describes the narrative structure of the story as resembling a memoir, though lacking "a memoir's breadth and scope."

Folks, Jeffrey J. "Richard Ford: Postmodern Cowboys." In *Southern Writers at Century's End*, edited by Jeffrey J. Folks and James A. Perkins. Lexington: The University Press of Kentucky, 1997. A discussion of *Rock Springs* as a postmodern Western whose characters are colonials and victims of a restrictive social environment. Argues that Ford's fiction is marginal literature in which all personal relationships are shadowed by political facts.

Ford, Richard. "First Things First." *Harper's Magazine* 276 (August, 1988): 72-77. Ford offers a first-person account of his life and career as a writer, from the early period when his stories were rejected, and how he dealt with such disappointments, to his eventual success and recognition. Along the way, Ford comments on the "business" of literary production and book publishing in the United States.

_____. "Interview." In *Speaking of the Short Story: Interviews with Contemporary Writers*, edited by Farhat Iftekharuddin, Mary Rohrberger, and Maurice Lee. Jackson: University Press of Mississippi, 1997. Ford discusses the process of writing such stories as "Rock Springs" and "Empire," talks about the difference between the short story and the novel, and responds to negative criticism of some of the characters in his short stories.

_____. "Interview with Richard Ford." Interview by Matthew Gilbert. *The Writer* 109 (December, 1996): 9-10. Ford discusses his views on the practice of writing, his love of moving around to different places, his rejection of the view that his books appeal more to men than women, and his approach to writing a novel.

Schroth, R. A. "America's Moral Landscape in the Fiction of Richard Ford." *The Christian Century* 106 (March 1, 1989): 227-230. Schroth believes that Ford's fiction reflects "America's search for integrity," a quest that certainly is central to *The Sportswriter*. The essay also covers *The Ultimate Good Luck* and *Rock Springs*.

Weber, Bruce. "Richard Ford's Uncommon Characters." *The New York Times Magazine*, April 10, 1988, 50-51, 59, 63-66. Weber, a friend and erstwhile classmate of the writer, offers a personalized biographical portrait and an analysis of Ford's fiction. He discusses Ford's penchant for telling "stories of Americans ennobled by hardship." A full context is given for the writer's interest in changing locales. This profile followed the publication of *Rock Springs*.

James Michael Welsh, updated by
Ann Davison Garbett

E. M. FORSTER

Born: London, England; January 1, 1879
Died: Coventry, England; June 7, 1970

PRINCIPAL SHORT FICTION

The Celestial Omnibus and Other Stories, 1911
The Eternal Moment and Other Stories, 1928
The Collected Tales of E. M. Forster, 1947
The Life to Come and Other Stories, 1972
Arctic Summer and Other Fiction, 1980

OTHER LITERARY FORMS

E. M. Forster wrote six novels, one of which (*Maurice*, 1971) was published posthumously because of its homosexual theme. He also wrote travel books, essays, reviews, criticism, biography, and some poetry. Together with Eric Crozier he wrote the libretto for the four-act opera *Billy Budd* (1951), adapted from Herman Melville's famous work.

ACHIEVEMENTS

As a novelist of rare distinction and one of the great literary figures of the twentieth century, E. M. Forster enjoyed international recognition and received many literary awards and honors. In 1921, as private secretary to the Maharajah of Dewas State Senior, he was awarded the Sir Tukojirao Gold Medal. The publication of *A Passage to India* (1924) brought him much acclaim, including the Femina Vie Heureuse Prize and the James Tait Black Memorial Prize in 1925. In 1927, he was elected Fellow of King's College, Cambridge, and he delivered Clark Lectures at Trinity College. In 1937, the Royal Society of Literature honored him with the Benson Medal. In 1945, he was made Honorary Fellow, King's College, Cambridge, where he remained until his death in 1970. In 1953, he was received by Queen Elizabeth II as a Companion of Honor. Between 1947 and 1958, several universities, including Cambridge, conferred on him the honorary degree of LL.D. In 1961, the Royal Society of Literature named him a Companion of Literature. He attained the greatest recognition when, on his ninetieth birthday, on January 1,

1969, he was appointed to the Order of Merit by Queen Elizabeth II.

BIOGRAPHY

Edward Morgan Forster was born in London on January 1, 1879. He was the great-grandson of Henry Thornton, a prominent member of the Evangelical Clapham Sect and a member of parliament. His father, an architect, died early, and he was brought up by his mother and his great-aunt, Marianne Thornton (whose biography he published in 1956). He received his early education at Tonbridge School, but he did not like the public school atmosphere. His bitter criticism of the English public school system appears in his portrayal of Sawston School in his first two novels, *Where Angels Fear to Tread* (1905) and *The Longest Journey* (1907). From Tonbridge, Forster went on to the University of Cambridge—thanks to the rich inheritance left by his aunt, Marianne Thornton, who died when he was eight—where he came under the influence of Goldworthy Lowes Dickinson (whose biography he wrote in 1934) and quickly began to blossom as a scholar, writer, and humanist.

After graduating from King's College, Cambridge, Forster traveled, with his mother, to Italy and Greece in 1901. His first short story, "Albergo Empedocle," was published in 1903. Between 1903 and 1910, he published four novels, nine short stories, and other nonfictional items. His travels to Greece and Italy led to his representation of life in those countries as being less repressive than life in England. During World War I, he served as a volunteer with the Red Cross in Alexandria, Egypt. His stay there resulted in *Alexandria: A History and a Guide* (1922) and *Pharos and Pharillon* (1923). His two visits to India, the first in 1912 in company of Goldworthy Lowes Dickinson and the second in 1921 as private secretary to the Maharajah of Dewas State Senior, provided him material for his masterpiece novel *A Passage to India* (1924) and *The Hill of Devi* (1953). With *A Passage to India*, Forster's reputation was established as a major English novelist of the twentieth century. He made a third visit to India in 1945 to attend a conference of Indian writers at Jaipur. He then wrote, "If Indians had not spoken English my own life would have been infinitely poorer." He visited the United States in 1947 to address the Symposium on Music Criticism at Harvard and again in 1949 to address the American Academy of Arts and Letters.

Though Forster stopped publishing fiction after 1924, he continued to produce significant nonfiction writing to the end. In a statement at the beginning of B. J. Kirkpatrick's *A Bibliography of E. M. Forster* (1965), Forster said: "The longer one lives the less one feels to have done, and I am both surprised and glad to discover from this bibliography that I have written so much." He died on June 7, 1970, at the age of ninety-one. Throughout his life he kept his faith in liberal humanism, in the sanctity of personal relationships, and, above all, in individualism. His charismatic personality and his personal warmth have led many people to believe that the man was greater than his books.

ANALYSIS

All of Forster's best-known and most anthologized stories appeared first in two collections, *The Celestial Omnibus* and *The Eternal Moment*. The words "celestial" and "eternal" are especially significant because a typical E. M. Forster story features a protagonist who is allowed a vision of a better life, sometimes momentarily only. Qualifications for experiencing this epiphany include a questioning mind, an active imagination, and a dissatisfaction with conventional attitudes. The transformation resulting from the experience comes about through some kind of magic that transports him through time—backward or forward—or through space—to Mt. Olympus or to heaven. Whether or not his life is permanently changed, the transformed character can never be the same again after a glimpse of the Elysian Fields, and he is henceforth suspect to contemporary mortals.

Forster termed his short stories "fantasies," and when the discerning reader can determine the point at which the real and the fantastic intersect, he will locate the epiphany, at the same time flexing his own

E. M. Forster (Archive Photos)

underused imaginative muscles. Perhaps "The Machine Stops," a science-fiction tale about a world managed by a computer-like Machine that warns men to "beware of first-hand ideas," was at the time of its writing (1909) the most fantastic of Forster's short fiction, but its portrayal of radio, television, and telephones with simultaneous vision seems to have been simply farsighted.

Forster frequently uses a narrator who is so insensitive that he ironically enhances the perception of the reader. In "Other Kingdom," for example, when Mr. Inskip finds it "right" to repeat Miss Beaumont's conversation about a "great dream" to his employer, the reader correctly places the tutor on the side of unimaginative human, rather than in the lineup of Dryads to which the young lady will repair. When the narrator of "The Story of a Panic" boasts that he "can tell a story without exaggerating" and then unfolds a tale about a boy who obviously is visited by Pan and who finally bounds away to join the goat-god, the reader knows that he must himself inform the gaps of information. When the same narrator attributes the death of the waiter Gennaro to the fact that "the miserable Italians have no stamina. Something had gone wrong inside him," the reader observes the disparity between the two statements and rightly concludes that Gennaro's death has a supernatural cause—that he had been subjected to the same "panic" as had Eustace, and that only the latter had passed the test.

In *Aspects of the Novel* (1927), Forster suggests that fiction will play a part in the ultimate success of civilization through promotion of human sympathy, reconciliation, and understanding. In each of the short stories the protagonist gets a finger-hold on the universal secret, but he sometimes loses his grip, usually through the action of someone too blind, materialistic, or enslaved by time to comprehend the significance of the moment.

If, as Forster himself declares, the emphasis of plot lies in causality, he allows the reader an important participation, because the causes of transformation are never explicit, and the more mundane characters are so little changed by the miraculous events taking place around them that they are not puzzled or even aware that they occur.

"THE ETERNAL MOMENT"

In "The Eternal Moment," the stiffly insensitive Colonel Leyland, Miss Raby's friend and traveling companion, is just such a character. While Miss Raby is determined to accept the responsibility for the commercialization of the mountain resort Vorta engendered by her novel, Colonel Leyland can understand her feelings no more readily than can Feo, the uneducated waiter who is the immediate object of Miss Raby's search. While Miss Raby ostensibly has returned to the village to see how it has been affected by tourism since she made it famous, she also is drawn to the spot because it was the scene of the one romantic, although brief, interlude of her life. For twenty years she has recalled a declaration of passionate love for her by a young Italian guide whose advances she had rejected. This memory has sustained her because of its reality and beauty. She finds the once rustic village overgrown with luxury hotels, in one of which Feo, her dream-lover, is the stout, greasy, middle-aged, hypocritical concierge. Miss Raby, whose instincts have warned her that the progress of civilization is not necessarily good, sees that "the passage of a large number of people" has cor-

rupted not only the village and its values, but also Feo. Observing that "pastoral virtues" and "family affection" have disappeared with the onslaught of touristry, she accosts the embarrassed peasant who had once offered her flowers. In a scene that is the quintessence of a human failure to communicate, Feo believes that she is attempting to ruin him, while she is actually appealing to him to help the old woman who owns the only hotel untouched by modernity. Colonel Leyland, who cannot bear the thought, much less the reality, of such intimate contact with a member of the lower class, gives up his idea of marrying Miss Raby. The rich novelist, whose entire life has been enriched by the "eternal moment" when she briefly and in imagination only had spanned class barriers, asks Feo if she can adopt one of his children. Rebuffed, she will live alone, able perhaps to blot out reality and relive the happiness that the memory of the "eternal moment" has brought her.

Another misunderstood protagonist is Eustace, the fourteen-year-old English boy considered a misfit by the group of tourists with whom he is seeing Italy. Listless and pampered, bad-tempered and repellent, Eustace dislikes walking, cannot swim, and appears most to enjoy lounging. Forced to go to a picnic, the boy carves from wood a whistle, which when blown evokes a "catspaw" of wind that frightens all of the other tourists into running. When they return to their picnic site in search of Eustace, they find him lying on his back, a green lizard darting from his cuff. For the first time on the trip the boy smiles and is polite. The footprints of goats are discerned nearby as Eustace races around "like a real boy." A dazed hare sits on his arm, and he kisses an old woman as he presents her with flowers. The adults, in trying to forget the encounter, are cruel to Eustace and to Gennaro, a young, natural, ignorant Italian fishing lad, who is a "stopgap" waiter at the inn, and who clearly understands the boy's experience. As Eustace and Gennaro attempt to flee to freedom from human responsibility, the waiter is killed, the victim of a society which in its lack of understanding had attempted to imprison Eustace, oblivious to his miraculous change, or at least to its significance. He has turned into an elfin sprite of the woods, to which he escapes forever, leaving behind him

Forster's customary complement of complacent, non-plussed tourists.

"OTHER KINGDOM"

No Pan, but a Dryad is Evelyn Beaumont of "Other Kingdom." Mr. Inskip, who narrates the tale, has been hired as a tutor of the classics by handsome, prosperous, and pompous Harcourt Worters. Inskip's charges are Worters's fiancé Miss Evelyn Beaumont and his ward Jack Ford. When Worters announces that he has purchased a nearby copse called "Other Kingdom" as a wedding gift for Evelyn, she dances her gleeful acceptance in imitation of a beech tree. On a celebratory picnic Evelyn asks Jack to stand in a position that will hide the house from her view. She is dismayed to learn that Worters plans to build a high fence around her copse and to add an asphalt path and a bridge. Evelyn values the fact that boys and girls have been coming for years from the village to carve their initials on the trees, and she notes that Worters finds blood on his hands when he attempts to repeat the romantic ritual. Upon hearing that Worters has obtained Other Kingdom by taking advantage of a widow, she realizes that he is a selfish person who views her as one of his possessions to be enjoyed. Broken in spirit, she apparently agrees to his plan of fencing in the copse, but she dances away "from society and life" to be united with other wood nymphs and likely with Ford, who knows intuitively that she is a free spirit that can never be possessed.

"THE ROAD FROM COLONUS"

While Eustace in "Story of a Panic" is a Pan-figure, Evelyn a Dryad, and Harcourt Worters a prototype of Midas, Mr. Lucas of "The Road from Colonus" is associated with Oedipus. The tale's title is reminiscent of Sophocles' play, and Ethel, Mr. Lucas's daughter, represents Antigone. As do Miss Raby, Eustace, and Evelyn Beaumont, Mr. Lucas enters into a special union with nature and mankind. Riding ahead of his daughter and her friends, he finds the "real Greece" when he spies a little inn surrounded by a grove of plane trees and a little stream that bubbles out of a great hollow tree. As he enters this natural shrine, he for the first time sees meaning to his existence, and he longs to stay in this peaceful spot. The other tourists, however, have schedules and

appointments to adhere to, and they forcibly carry Mr. Lucas away from the scene of his revelation. That night the plane tree crashes to kill all occupants of the inn, and Mr. Lucas spends his remaining days fussing about his neighbors and the noises of civilization, especially those made by the running water in the drains and reminiscent of the pleasant, musical gurgles of the little stream in Greece.

"THE CELESTIAL OMNIBUS"

More fortunate than Mr. Lucas is the boy who rides "The Celestial Omnibus" from an alley where an old, faded sign points the way "To Heaven." After the driver Sir Thomas Browne delivers the boy across a great gulf on a magnificent rainbow to the accompaniment of music, and back home to his nursery, the boy's parents refuse to believe his tale. Mr. Bons, a family friend, attempts to prove the boy is lying by offering to make a repeat journey with him. On this trip the driver is Dante. Even though Mr. Bons is finally convinced that the boy has actually met Achilles and Tom Jones, he wants to go home. When Mr. Bons crawls out of the omnibus shrieking, "I see London," he falls and is seen no more. His body is discovered "in a shockingly mutilated condition," and the newspaper reports that "foul play is suspected." The boy is crowned with fresh leaves as the dolphins awaken to celebrate with him the world of imagination. Mr. Bons, when accosted with this world, rejected it so violently that he suffered physical pain.

In all of these "fantasies," a gulf separates reality from illusion, and the latter is clearly to be preferred. If a person must inhabit the real world, one can bear its existence and even love its inhabitants if that person is one of the fortunate few receptive to a special kind of vision.

OTHER MAJOR WORKS

LONG FICTION: *Where Angels Fear to Tread*, 1905; *The Longest Journey*, 1907; *A Room with a View*, 1908; *Howard's End*, 1910; *A Passage to India*, 1924; *Maurice*, 1971 (wr. 1913).

PLAYS: *Billy Budd*, pb. 1951 (libretto, with Eric Crozier).

NONFICTION: *Alexandria: A History and a Guide*, 1922; *Pharos and Pharillon*, 1923; *Aspects of the*

Novel, 1927; *Goldsworthy Lowes Dickinson*, 1934; *Abinger Harvest—A Miscellany*, 1936; *Virginia Woolf*, 1942; *Development of English Prose Between 1918 and 1939*, 1945; *Two Cheers for Democracy*, 1951; *The Hill of Devi*, 1953; *Marianne Thornton: A Domestic Biography, 1797-1887*, 1956; *Commonplace Book*, 1978.

BIBLIOGRAPHY

Beauman, Nicola. *E. M. Forster: A Biography*. New York: Alfred A. Knopf, 1994. In this biography devoted primarily to the first forty-five years of Forster's life when he was developing as a fiction writer, Beauman discusses the origins of Forster's fictional themes in his family background and claims that his most successful years as a writer were also his unhappiest as a person due to his sexual repression and his conflicts over his homosexuality.

Caporaletti, Silvana. "Science as Nightmare: 'The Machine Stops' by E. M. Forster." *Utopian Studies* 8 (1997): 32-47. Discusses the dystopian theme in the story; claims the story denounces materialism and conformism imposed by rigid social conventions that repress diversity, spontaneity, and creativity.

_____. "The Thematization of Time in E. M. Forster's 'The Eternal Moment' and Joyce's 'The Dead.'" *Twentieth Century Literature* 43 (Winter, 1997): 406-419. Discusses how the two stories are influenced by Henri Bergson's dual concept of time as sequential and psychological. Argues that most of the characters in the stories reflect the contrast between these two modes of time.

Eldridge, C. C. *The Imperial Experience: From Carlyle to Forster*. New York: St. Martin's Press, 1996. Examines the political and social views of Forster and Thomas Carlyle, as well as imperialism in their literature.

Furbank, Philip N. *E. M. Forster: A Life*. New York: Harcourt Brace Jovanovich, 1978. In this authorized biography of E. M. Forster, Furbank successfully re-creates an authentic, intimate, and illuminating portrait of the man behind the writer and controversial public figure. The wealth of new material contained in this biography makes it an indispensable source on Forster's life, times, and work.

Gardner, Philip, ed. *E. M. Forster: The Critical Heritage*. New York: Routledge, 1997. Critical essays on Forster's works. Includes bibliographical references and an index.

Iago, Mary. *E. M. Forster: A Literary Life*. New York: St. Martin's Press, 1995. A succinct study of Forster's novels and work for the British Broadcasting Corporation. Helpful notes.

McDowell, Frederick P. W. *E. M. Forster*. Rev. ed. Boston: Twayne, 1982. A brilliant, well-balanced, and compendious overview of Forster's life, times, career, work, and achievement. This book contains a useful chronology, a select bibliography, and an index. It also offers a concise and perceptive analysis of Forster's short stories.

Seabury, Marcia Bundy. "Images of a Networked Society: E. M. Forster's 'The Machine Stops.'" *Studies in Short Fiction* 34 (Winter, 1997): 61-71. Discusses the story as a vision of the computer revolution. Examines interrelations between technology and religious thinking in the story; explores what happens to people when they spend much of their time connected to computer networks.

Stone, Wilfred. *The Cave and the Mountain: A Study of E. M. Forster*. Stanford, Calif.: Stanford University Press, 1966. A well-researched and scholarly book. Contains a vast amount of useful information about Forster's background, career, esthetics, and work. Includes a detailed and illuminating chapter on the short stories. Using psychological and Jungian approaches, Stone offers insightful and masterly critiques of Forster's fiction. Supplemented by notes and a comprehensive index.

Thomson, George H. *The Fiction of E. M. Forster*. Detroit: Wayne State University Press, 1967. Thomson presents a critical study of Forster's novels and short stories in terms of their symbolical and archetypal aspects. He argues that Forster's symbols "achieve archetypal significance and mythic wholeness" through "the power of ecstatic perception" in his work. Complemented by notes and a valuable appendix on the manuscripts of *A Passage to India*.

Trilling, Lionel. *E. M. Forster: A Study*. Norfolk, Conn.: New Directions, 1943. A pioneer study, instrumental in establishing Forster's reputation.

This book assesses Forster's artistic achievement in terms of his liberal humanism and moral realism.

Sue L. Kimball,
updated by Chaman L. Sahni

JOHN FOWLES

Born: Leigh-on-Sea, England; March 31, 1926

PRINCIPAL SHORT FICTION

The Ebony Tower, 1974 (novella, 3 short stories, and translation of a French medieval romance)

OTHER LITERARY FORMS

John Fowles is principally known for his long fiction, but, in addition to his collection of short stories, he has written a volume of poetry, *Poems* (1973); a philosophical work, *The Aristos: A Self-Portrait in Ideas* (1964); a historical work, *A Brief History of Lyme* (1981); and a number of essays accompanied by photographs, including *Shipwreck* (1974), *Islands* (1978), *The Tree* (1980), and *The Enigma of Stonehenge* (1980; with Barry Brukoff). *Wormholes: Essays and Occasional Writings*, a nonfiction work, was published in 1998.

ACHIEVEMENTS

John Fowles has achieved the enviable position of being both well regarded by critics and well received by readers. Three of his novels—*The Collector* (1963), *The Magus* (1965, 1977), and *The French Lieutenant's Woman* (1969)—were made into films. His first novel, *The Collector*, was an immediate critical and popular success. Readers of his long fiction can generally expect to find a good story with a passionate love interest, complex characters, and a healthy smattering of philosophy, all presented within the context of a plot.

Because Fowles rarely tells the same story in the same way, genre is a topic of discussion among his critics. His fiction reflects not only his interest in var-

ious genres but also his questioning of authorial voice, his examination of the decline of language, his fascination with moments out of time, and his interest in split viewpoint, a story within a story, and other forms of experimentation. Critics slice away multiple layers to get at the existential, historical, philosophical, and psychological levels of meaning therein. More than a dozen books have been published about him, and several journals have devoted special issues to him, including the *Journal of Modern Literature* (1981), *Modern Fiction Studies* (1985), and *Twentieth Century Literature* (1996).

BIOGRAPHY

John Fowles was born in Leigh-on-Sea, Essex, England, on March 31, 1926. During World War II, his family was evacuated to the remote village of Ippeplen, South Devon, and it was there that Fowles discovered the beauty of the countryside that later figured so prominently in his fiction. In these early years, he loved nature as a collector, patterning Frederick Clegg's butterfly-collecting obsession in his novel *The Collector* after his own. It was not until later that he learned to love nature for itself.

As a student at the exclusive Bedford School, Fowles studied German and French literature, eventually rising to the powerful position of head boy. At the Bedford School, he learned to love literature and power; only later did he learn to hate the latter. From Bedford, he went into military service, spending six months at the University of Edinburgh and completing training as a lieutenant in the merchant marine just as World War II was ending. Following the war, he continued his education in German and more par-

John Fowles (Camera Press Ltd./Archive Photos)

ticularly French literature at New College, the University of Oxford, where he graduated in 1950 with a B.A. with honors. His fiction owes many debts to his study of French literature, particularly his early interest in existentialism and his continuing interest in the Celtic romance, from which stems his express belief that all literature has its roots in the theme of the quest. His inclusion of his translation of Marie de France's Celtic lay in *The Ebony Tower* is a way of paying homage to this influence.

Following graduation, Fowles taught English at the University of Poitiers. A year later, he took a job teaching English on a Greek island, the grist for his first written (although not first published) novel, *The Magus*. It was also on this island that he met Elizabeth Whitton, whom he married three years later. Having taken up writing, he still continued to teach in and around London until the success of his first published novel, *The Collector*, allowed him to quit teaching to become a full-time writer. Two years later, *The Magus* was published, after twelve years of writing and revision. Still not happy with it despite its good reception, he revised and republished it in 1977.

In 1966, he and Elizabeth moved to Lyme Regis in Dorset, a small seaside town away from London, where they settled. Their first residence was a farm at the edge of the Undercliff, after which they moved to an eighteenth century house overlooking Lyme Bay. All figure prominently in *The French Lieutenant's Woman*, both the book and the film. *The Ebony Tower* was written as a break in the midst of his writing *Daniel Martin* (1977). In *The Ebony Tower*, Fowles experimented with the genre of short fiction. Three years later, *Daniel Martin* was published, marking the high point of his popular success.

While other novels followed and were variously received by the critics, their experimental nature has made them less accessible to the public. In his later works, Fowles became interested in philosophical pieces about nature, which have been published largely as photographic essays. After suffering a mild stroke in early 1988, he stopped publishing new fiction, although the nonfiction *Lyme Regis Camera* (1990) and *Wormholes: Essays and Occasional Writings* (1998) were published.

ANALYSIS

John Fowles's fiction has one main theme: the quest of protagonists for self-knowledge or wholeness. The collection of short stories in *The Ebony Tower* is no exception, as Fowles's working title for the volume, *Variations*, suggests. The working title was abandoned in favor of the title of the novella in the collection when first readers did not see the connections, but the connections are clearly there. In each of the stories of *The Ebony Tower*, the protagonist is faced with having to learn how to choose, having to learn how to quest in a world in which today's quester is cut off from the traditions and rituals of the past that gave questers of old a purpose and direction. Despair permeates the vision of contemporary life in these stories. All Fowles's characters are unable to communicate with others successfully. His translation and inclusion of Marie de France's quest tale is in homage to the connection that he recognizes between the ancient quest pattern and the pattern not only of his fiction but also of all Western fiction. The five stories of *The Ebony Tower*—elegant tales written for an elite audience—are variations on the Celtic romance, a form which Fowles regards as the origin of all fictional forms.

What separates the journey of the Fowlesian hero from the journey of the medieval hero is that much of it has become internalized. Whereas the quester of old fought actual battles with dragons, monsters, and mysterious knights, the modern quester has no such obvious obstacles. For today's quester, the battles are largely inward as the quester must struggle against ignorance and inertia. Thus, the modern journey can be seen in psychological terms with the results measured by the quester's ability to attain self-understanding. In the stories in *The Ebony Tower*, Fowles experiments not only with the genre of the short story but also with the darker aspects of the failed journey, a motif he developed earlier, in *The Collector*.

"THE EBONY TOWER"

The Ebony Tower includes the title story, followed by "A Personal Note," about his inclusion of "Eliduc" (c. 1150-1175), Marie de France's medieval romance, and the stories "Poor Koko," "The Enigma," and "The Cloud." The first and longest story, "The Ebony Tower," sets the stage in terms of theme and tone for those which follow. It is also intended as a modern mirror to the medieval romance which comes next.

David Williams, the protagonist of "The Ebony Tower," is the typical Fowlesian protagonist in his complacency about his unexamined life. When challenged, as all of Fowles's questers are, he finds that the surface veneer or mask which he wears so cleverly hides a lack of creativity that prevents him from being a great painter or a whole person. He has the opportunity, however, in the "mythic landscape" of Coetminais, to change. Coetminais is the French estate of Henry Breasley; its name means "wood of the monks." It becomes Williams's dark tower. His experiences there recall those of Childe Roland in Robert Browning's poem "Childe Roland to the Dark Tower Came." Williams recognizes the challenge and sees the path but does not take it. The knowledge he gains concerns the realization of his failure to break out of his safe world into a higher state of consciousness

and expression in his art. Williams is a divided man, one caught between two worlds and one who suffers from what poet T. S. Eliot calls "dissociation of sensibility." Like Eliot's J. Alfred Prufrock, Williams survives but does not succeed.

Breasley, the famous old rake whom the much-younger Williams wants to interview for a book to be called *The Art of Henry Breasley*, represents all that Williams is not. A traditionalist who continues to live life to the fullest, the seventy-seven-year-old Breasley challenges Williams to move beyond the safe abstraction of his art and life, which he calls "the ebony tower," and to reconnect with the lifeblood of his own being and art. Breasley's art is called "mysterious," "archetypal," and "Celtic"; Williams's is called "architectonic." Also, Breasley has been a lifelong profligate, who has two mistresses living with him presently. Williams has a wife and a daughter back in England and has never had an affair. Notably, the setting for Williams's adventure at Coetminais is "a garden of Eden," one in which the Eve character is a young girl named Diana—nicknamed by Breasley "the Mouse"—an aspiring artist who was formerly a talented student at the prestigious Royal College of Art where she had what she calls a disastrous affair. She tempts Williams, but to his own regret he does not fall.

Williams's problem is typical of many of Fowles's protagonists, especially Nicholas Urfe in *The Magus* and Charles Smithson in *The French Lieutenant's Woman*. Like Williams, they are caught up too much in the "head" side of life and the rational analysis of mystery, and they fail to understand the "heart" side, the intuitive response to mystery. Williams needs to express himself verbally, to compartmentalize all experience within the boundaries of language. Breasley's broken sentences and half-formed thoughts, though laden with meaning, contrast sharply with Williams's precise, fully formed sentences. When the drunken Breasley, a British expatriate, attacks Williams after dinner one evening for being "a gutless bloody word-twister," Williams responds coolly by saying, "Hatred and anger are not luxuries we can afford anymore." Williams does not want to offend Henry Breasley. The conflicting views of the two form the essence of the argument and the challenge. Will Williams live his life through carefully controlled language structures, which his abstract art also presents carefully, or will he abandon controls, as Breasley has done, to experience the intuitive life force, the feeling side? The story deals for the most part with issues of art but ends with Williams's deciding whether to bed "the Mouse."

It is through the feeling side that Williams responds so readily to the Mouse. His moment of temptation, his quest for true knowledge, comes in a garden walk at night among "ghostly apple trees." Rather than act in response to his feelings, Williams seeks the comfort of speech, trying to talk through his feelings. The Mouse retreats to her room and locks the door. The rest of the story presents Williams's analysis of the reasons for his problems at Coetminais.

The connections of "The Ebony Tower" to "Eliduc," the medieval tale that follows, are many. Williams has a challenge similar to that of Eliduc. Both have to choose between two women. For Williams these are his wife Beth, who could not come with him to Coetminais because their daughter was sick, and Diana, "the Mouse." Williams does not rise to the challenge. In "Eliduc" it is Eliduc's wife who does so at the end of that story. The weasel that Williams runs over on the road after leaving Coetminais dies and will not be revived, as happens in "Eliduc" when a weasel and a wife restore loved ones with a magical red flower. In "The Ebony Tower" only the head of the dead weasel survives intact, suggesting that the "head" side of Williams has survived too. When Williams meets Beth at Orly after his weekend at Coetminais, he tells her he has "survived."

"Eliduc"

In "Eliduc" a Breton knight is forced by evil rumors to be dismissed from court. He then bids adieu to his beloved wife Guildeluec and travels abroad to the port of Totnes in Devon. There he falls in love with the king's beautiful daughter, Guilliadun. Eventually, the two go to Brittany. On the way Guilliadun discovers that Eliduc is married, and she falls into a swoon, apparently dead. Eliduc takes her to a local chapel where his wife Guildeluec happens to find her

and heal her with a weasel's flower. Subsequently, Guildeluec enters a convent so that Eliduc and Guilliadun can marry and be happy. The story deals with the contradictions inherent in certain kinds of duty: duty to superiors, duty to loved ones, and duty to spouses.

"Poor Koko"

The remaining stories in Fowles's collection are connected to the title story through the theme of lost opportunities. In "Poor Koko" the sixty-six-year-old narrator is a writer who is robbed by a young burglar, who burns the writer's most valued possession, a manuscript for a book on the nineteenth century British author Thomas Love Peacock.

The story involves the writer's attempt to comprehend this seemingly meaningless deed. Like David Williams, he comes to an understanding of the experience, without the means or the will to take action. He struggles to make sense of the thief's act and also of the thief's final gesture: the raising of a cocked thumb. After dismissing several possibilities, the scholar finally concludes that the gesture is a signal similar to the one used by football players to connote courage. Only then does the writer realize that there was a match played out between himself and the young thief, in which the thief felt the need for bravery because he recognized that the writer had the upper hand. The scholar then continues his analysis of the situation by studying the thief's use of language. He hopes this will yield a clue to what has happened. He decides that the thief, with his impoverished language, is frustrated by his interest in a dead author and unwillingness to talk about it with someone younger. Fowles's deliberately obscure title for the story, as well as his use of an obscure quotation from a dead language for the story's ending, points up the writer's power to illuminate the meaning of language. Fowles notes that "Poor Koko" refers in Japanese to the correct filial relationship between father and son (one which the writer and the thief should have had) and that people need to build a bridge between the generations by passing on the magic of language, something that does not happen often in modern times. This failure could result in the loss of communication, a scenario conveyed by the Old Cornish expression which concludes the story: "Too long a tongue, too short a hand;/ But tongueless man has lost his land."

"THE ENIGMA"

In the next story, "The Enigma," a mystery of a different kind is presented. Fifty-seven-year-old John Marcus Fielding, a wealthy, happily married member of Parliament, disappears. Sergeant Michael Jennings is charged with investigating Fielding's disappearance. The answer to this mystery seems to be that the owner of Tetbury Hall in East Anglia has deliberately walked out on a life which appeared to offer everything but which must have left him feeling hollow and unfulfilled—another case of failed communication. Longing for a sense of mystery that his life lacks, Fielding creates his own. However, Fielding's final gesture seems a failure.

When he goes to the British Museum for what he hoped would be a rendezvous with his son's girlfriend, he finds out that she is not there, and he leaves his briefcase behind in the reading room of the museum. Since Fielding never reappears, the focus of the story shifts to the investigator and his investigation of the people close to Fielding, particularly Isobel Dodgson, the twenty-four-year-old girlfriend of Fielding's son Peter. Upon first meeting her, Sergeant Jennings feels her sense of vitality, which contrasts with everything else around him, which seems dead and controlled.

Now the unfolding mystery becomes about the developing relationship of these two. As is true with other protagonists in Fowles's work, the male needs a female to bring out the feeling side buried in him. Jennings relates to Isobel on a sensual as well as a feeling level. She discusses with Jennings the imaginative possibilities of the Fielding case. She treats the enigma as a literary text, perhaps because she works for a publisher and is trying to publish a novel. In a sense, she seduces Jennings with her speculations. While the reader does not see the full development of their story, its open ending allows one to conclude that Jennings, unlike any of the other characters in Fowles's collection of stories, has the potential to move a bit closer to self-knowledge, deciding to see Isobel again when he is off-duty.

"THE CLOUD"

The last story in *The Ebony Tower*, "The Cloud," is the most mysterious and open-ended. Fowles said that the tale is indebted to the fiction of Katherine Mansfield. Like Mansfield's fiction, "The Cloud" has an impressionistic style. It begins by painting a picture of a promising summer day for picnicking in the tranquil French countryside, but the eight English tourists of the tale have shallow conversations and are divided into sun and shadow, aspects which suggest a breakdown in communications. Again, as in "The Ebony Tower," Fowles associates the scene of the story with paradise. However, the world of this dreamy tale is actually a wasteland, one without renewal. It is a ruined paradise, in which the participants are strangers and a poisonous adder is present.

The main characters are Peter, Paul, and the sisters Annabel and Catherine. The latter is the focal point of the story. She is in deep depression over the loss of her husband. Although "The Cloud" contains some shifting points of view, Catherine narrates much of the story in a kind of stream of consciousness, seeming to have lost her connection to the world and to those around her. She cannot find anything to live for and feels that she will never love again. Her thoughts reflect her sense of being on an island where language does not provide a bridge. At the insistence of her niece, Catherine tells a story about a princess, using language to create a myth that she wants to enter, in much the same way that Isobel in "The Enigma" creates a story about the missing Mr. Fielding. Catherine's story ends with the princess waiting for the return of her prince, who has abandoned her but who may return soon. The connection to Catherine's own sense of having been abandoned by her deceased husband and of wanting to be reunited with him is clear.

Catherine's depression deepens following her meaningless sexual encounter with Peter, who, like the apostle for whom he is named, denies having seen her when he descends from a hill. As Catherine's companions emerge into a clearing, they see an ominous black cloud, one which Catherine also sees while still in the woods. She has entered the fairy tale that she has created. Presumably, she has committed suicide in a fit of black despair. With this implication, Fowles seems to suggest that romance in contemporary times is hopeless. Notably, the final image of the black cloud here follows from the first image of the ebony tower in the title story, uniting the theme of the collection under the darker aspects of failed journeys. Most of these stories show what can happen if a person is cut off from the mysteries of life. Although the general tone of the tales in *The Ebony Tower* is dark, the overall view of Fowles's longer fiction is more optimistic, or at least more open to the possibilities of life.

OTHER MAJOR WORKS

LONG FICTION: *The Collector*, 1963; *The Magus*, 1965, 1977; *The French Lieutenant's Woman*, 1969; *Daniel Martin*, 1977; *Mantissa*, 1982; *A Maggot*, 1985

POETRY: *Poems*, 1973

NONFICTION: *The Aristos: A Self-Portrait in Ideas*, 1964; *Shipwreck*, 1974; *Islands*, 1978; *The Tree*, 1980; *The Enigma of Stonehenge*, 1980 (with Barry Brukoff); *A Brief History of Lyme*, 1981; *Lyme Regis Camera*, 1990; *Wormholes: Essays and Occasional Writings*, 1998.

MISCELLANEOUS: *The Ebony Tower*, 1974 (novella, 3 short stories, and translation of a French medieval romance).

BIBLIOGRAPHY

Acheson, James. *John Fowles*. New York: St. Martin's Press, 1998. An excellent introduction to the life and works of Fowles.

Aubrey, James R., ed. *John Fowles and Nature: Fourteen Perspectives on Landscape*. Madison, N.J.: Fairleigh Dickenson University Press, 1999. Explores the use of nature in Fowles's fiction. Includes illustrations.

Barnum, Carol M. "The Quest Motif in John Fowles's *The Ebony Tower:* Theme and Variations." In *Critical Essays on John Fowles*, edited by Ellen Pifer. Boston: G. K. Hall, 1986. Provides a full treatment of the stories, including "Eliduc," using the quest theme as the basis of comparison with the longer fiction. Pifer's introduction provides a good overview of the entire fictional canon.

Bevis, Richard. "Actaeon's Sin: The 'Previous Iconography' of Fowles's 'The Ebony Tower.'" *Twentieth Century Literature* 42 (Spring, 1996): 114-123. In this special issue on Fowles, Bevis shows how the story's plot and characters are linked to the Greek mythological figures of Diana and Actaeon.

Butler, Lance St. John. "John Fowles and the Fiction of Freedom." In *The British and Irish Novel Since 1960*, edited by James Acheson. New York: St. Martin's Press, 1991. A discussion of Fowles's coming to terms with freedom in his fiction in an existential sense. Argues that Fowles's development as a writer followed the same course as that of existentialism. Discusses the centrality of freedom in Fowles's fiction.

Humma, John B. "John Fowles' *The Ebony Tower:* In the Celtic Mood." *Southern Humanities Review* 17, no. 1 (1983): 33-47. Treats the collection as a criticism of the modern age, with the characters representing the flawed modern view in that each enters the world of nature, representing the medieval or Celtic view, generally without much evidence of regeneration.

McDaniel, Ellen. "Fowles as Collector: The Failed Artists of *The Ebony Tower*." *Papers on Language and Literature* 21, no. 1 (1987): 70-83. Compares the characters in the stories to those of the novels in terms of their ability to evolve. Points out the failure of the characters in the stories to move beyond stasis. At the same time, McDaniel suggests that the plot of each story focuses on what little progress the characters do make, in thought if not in deed.

Martínez, María Jesús. "Astarte's Game: Variations in John Fowles 'The Enigma.'" *Twentieth Century Literature* 42 (Spring, 1996): 124-144. Discusses the story's intertextual relationship to the detective-story genre; shows how Fowles parodies the basic detective-story convention by presenting a mystery with all the available evidence and then refusing to solve it.

Modern Fiction Studies 31, no. 1 (Spring, 1985). This

special issue on Fowles presents the stories as an interconnected web based on a central theme. Argues that they should be read as a whole, with each enlarged by its interconnectedness to the others. Also of interest are the interview by Carol Barnum, which raises several points about the short stories, and the selected checklist of additional references by Ronald C. Dixon.

Salys, Rimgaila. "The Medieval Context of John Fowles's *The Ebony Tower.*" *Critique: Studies in Modern Fiction* 25, no. 1 (1983): 11-24. Sets up a fine comparison between "The Ebony Tower" and the themes of medieval romance in the light of the actions of the characters in the modern story. Describes the archetypal patterns of the quest motif in the story.

Carol M. Barnum,
updated by James Norman O'Neill

ANATOLE FRANCE
Jacques-Anatole-François Thibault

Born: Paris, France; April 16, 1844
Died: La Béchellerie, near Tours, France; October 12, 1924

PRINCIPAL SHORT FICTION

Nos Enfants, 1886
Balthasar, 1889 (English translation, 1909)
L'Étui de nacre, 1892 (*Tales from a Mother of Pearl Casket*, 1896)
Le Puits de Sainte-Claire, 1895 (*The Well of Saint Clare*, 1909)
Clio, 1900 (English translation, 1922)
Crainquebille, Putois, Riquet, et plusieurs autres récits profitables, 1904 (*Crainquebille, Putois, Riquet, and Other Profitable Tales*, 1915)
Les Contes de Jacques Tournebroche, 1908 (*The Merry Tales of Jacques Tournebroche*, 1910)
The Garden of Epicurus, 1908
Les Sept Femmes de la Barbe-Bleue et autres contes merveilleux, 1909 (*The Seven Wives of Bluebeard*, 1920)
The Wisdom of the Ages and Other Stories, 1925
Golden Tales, 1926

OTHER LITERARY FORMS

Anatole France was the kind of thoroughgoing professional man of letters who did almost every conceivable kind of writing in his time: in verse and in prose, works of the imagination and works of scholarship, journalism, polemical tracts, and autobiography. Fame of international proportions came late in his career—he had passed his fiftieth birthday by the time he was recognized as one of his country's great writers—and its basis was certainly his work in fiction, both novels and short stories. His first publication, however, was a work of literary criticism, and he achieved recognition as one of the best and most widely read critics and book reviewers in France during the 1880's and 1890's. He published two volumes of not-very-distinguished verse in the 1870's, and over a period of twenty-five years, he patiently compiled a controversial but well researched historical study of the life of Joan of Arc, published in 1908. His polemical writings, some of them the texts of speeches made at public meetings, were related to two major events of his lifetime—the Dreyfus affair and World War I; in the former, he was a leading pro-Dreyfus spokesman, and in the latter he defended a pacifist point of view. For a time he also wrote polemical articles for a socialist newspaper. He ventured only once into theatrical writing, with a comedy published in 1908, based on the medieval tale of the man who married a dumb wife. His autobiography is mildly fictionalized, although accurate in essentials, and runs to four volumes spread over a period of more than thirty years. For all the variety of his chosen forms, however, his most characteristic literary posture was that of the storyteller. Even his work as literary critic and historian emphasizes the anecdotal approach, and the Nobel Prize in Literature, which he won in 1921, certainly honored, above all else, the novelist and short-story writer.

ACHIEVEMENTS

Anatole France occupies an unusual place in cultural history; he is an author who achieved great fame but who had neither disciples nor documented influence upon subsequent generations. The suddenness of the collapse of his reputation after his death in 1924 was dramatic. Moreover, the revival of his literary fame over the past few decades, while genuine, has been limited.

Anatole France's writing is renowned for its combination of an inveterate skepticism with a celebrated style, a carefully crafted classical simplicity and subtle wit that is graceful yet elusive. Even without direct influence, Anatole France's career left its mark on French letters, particularly in the domain of the short

Anatole France (Library of Congress)

story. He was the most distinguished practitioner of the genre after Guy de Maupassant. The last decade of Anatole France's life brought many literary honors. He was elected a member of the French Academy in 1896 and was awarded the Nobel Prize in Literature in 1921.

BIOGRAPHY

Far more than for most writers, for Anatole France (born Jacques Anatole François Thibault) the world of the book was the central arena of his life. He was the son of a well-known Paris bookseller, and he grew up and was largely educated in the atmosphere created by the bookshop and its customers. His first employment was as researcher for reference works in preparation, and as editor in a publishing house. For some years he worked in the library of the French Senate, and much of the journalism he did while getting established as a writer took the form of book criticism. The subject matter of most of his novels and short stories either was derived from books or, not infrequently, was about writers and intellectuals. The immersion in the book world was so complete that his life apart from books had little substance, even in those years when he seemed actively involved in public events such as the Dreyfus affair. Most of the "events" of his eighty years were publications; nothing else in his life really mattered.

Perhaps the most interesting feature of his biography is that, although he never seems to have contemplated any vocation other than that of man of letters, it took him a very long time to become securely established as a writer. He was twenty-four years old when his first publication appeared; it was a critical study of the recently decreased poet, Alfred de Vigny. He was almost thirty when the traditional first volume of verse appeared, inaugurating his career as a writer; and he was nearly forty when he attracted his first critical attention with a novel—not a popular success by any means, but it did gain some recognition. It was not until 1890, when he was forty-six, that he published a book which won both critical acclaim and popular success, enabling him to resign his library position and his weekly journalistic commitments. Thereafter, he enjoyed the fruits of a growing fame, writing the masterpieces on which his reputation still rests and becoming drawn into certain public controversies because he was a celebrity. The public arena, however, never held his attention for long. He was uncomfortable as an orator or polemicist and preferred the solitude of his study, where he could give free rein to his skeptical mind. Thus, he spent his approximately thirty years of fame as an aging sage, occasionally in public view for some cause but mostly alone in his study, meditating and writing. When he died in 1924, he was given a public, national funeral—a final irony, for he had always been, fundamentally, a very private man, a dweller in the world of books.

ANALYSIS

Storytelling, which was the heart of Anatole France's literary career, was an art he mastered only after a very long apprenticeship. He began that apprenticeship in the traditional way, with a thinly disguised novel about his own youthful growing pains. It was the kind of personal novel of sensibility which had been the fashionable first composition for aspiring novelists since François René de Chateaubriand's *René* (1802), but he himself found the result so muddled and pointless that he put the manuscript away in a drawer in 1872 without offering it for publication. A decade later, he revised the manuscript extensively and published it as *Les Désirs de Jean Servien* (1882; *The Aspirations of Jean Servien*, 1912), but it went unnoticed, deservedly, by both critics and public. His sense of failure in 1872 kept him away from fiction for seven years thereafter. He tried again with two relatively long short stories which he published together as a small volume in 1879, but they attracted no attention, and their author understood that neither story had the coherence and focus necessary to hold a reader's interest. He persevered in fiction nevertheless and was rewarded when another small volume, this time containing two stories held together by a common central figure, came out in 1881 to considerable critical acclaim and respectable sales. *Le Crime de Sylvestre Bonnard* (1881; *The Crime of Sylvestre Bonnard*, 1890) was labeled a novel, although it was in reality two separate tales, and it gave Anatole

France his first taste of success in fiction, at the age of thirty-seven. He was encouraged to believe that fiction was his talent, and that the amusing and gentle irony that had succeeded in *The Crime of Sylvestre Bonnard* was his true creative vein. Yet he would spend the entire decade of the 1880's struggling still with the techniques of fiction writing, searching for the appropriate form for his talent as a storyteller.

After nearly a decade of experimentation and slow, painfully won progress, Anatole France published his first important collection of short stories in 1889, giving the entire volume the title of its best tale, *Balthasar*. What he had chiefly mastered by means of his experimentation was the art of concentration: choosing a central point or idea for each story and curbing his digressive tendencies so as to move the narrative unequivocally forward to its central point without confusing the reader with subplots and side issues. It was a difficult discipline for him to learn, since it went against his open curiosity, and, although he was not wholly successful in *Balthasar*, he had visibly come a long way in it, even since the modest success of *The Crime of Sylvestre Bonnard* eight years before.

"BALTHASAR"

The title story, for example, focuses on one of the three wise kings who, according to the Bible, followed a star to the birthplace of Jesus Christ in Bethlehem. The object of the story is to recount the circumstances which led Balthasar to decide to follow the wondrous star. The mocking imitation of biblical diction instructs the reader from the start to expect an ironic tale, undercutting the simple piety of the traditional Christmas legend. Balthasar is depicted as a naïve youth who receives a painful sentimental education at the hands of the cruelly capricious Queen of Sheba, Balkis, with whom he falls in love. It is the experience of being cast aside by Balkis when she is tired of him that turns Balthasar to the study of the stars, for consolation, and that places the journey to Bethlehem in an ironic light as the gesture of a despairing lover rather than a pilgrimage of pious devotion. The central idea of the story is thus clear, and kept in sharp focus for the reader by the carefully controlled narrative style which parodies and mocks its biblical model. It is only on the last page that the story falters: At the moment of choosing between Balkis and the star, Balthasar is described, with no hint of irony, as undergoing a spiritual transformation, and in a few rapid sentences the reader is told of Balthasar's meeting with the other two kings and his arrival in Bethlehem. The sudden change of tone is disconcerting, for it casts doubt on all that has preceded, as though the author had not quite been able to follow his own idea to its logical conclusion. Except for the ending, however, the story is well constructed, coherent, and skillful.

"M. PIGEONNEAU"

Another story in the same collection, "M. Pigeonneau," exhibits the same virtues and the same defect in the ending; It is a delightful tale of a solemn pedant led into a farcical adventure by a hypnotist. The particular audacity of this tale is that the narrator is the title character, who recounts his own ridiculous experiences in the solemn prose of the scholar, unaware that he is himself the butt of the joke. The premise of the story, however, that the pedant never realizes what he is revealing about himself, forces the author to leave the story unfinished, trailing off while M. Pigeonneau is still under the hypnotic spell. Until the disappointing conclusion, however, the story is an artfully sustained satire.

It was the following year, 1890, that saw publication of Anatole France's first genuine success, satisfactory in both content and form, and lauded both by the public and the critics. This was the remarkable novel *Thaïs* (1890; English translation, 1891), which told the story of the saint who would save the sinner only to fall into sin himself when he succeeded. The theme of ironic reversal gave the story a form which won immediate admiration and announced that Anatole France had, at last, mastered the art of fiction. Not by accident was the author's first draft of *Thaïs* cast in the form of a short story, for that was the literary form which he had been most insistently trying to solve for more than a decade. The success of *Thaïs* was almost immediately followed by his first true and acclaimed success in the short-story form, the collection suggestively titled *Tales from a Mother of Pearl Casket*. The most famous "jewel" in the box

was the story called "Le Procurateur de Judée" ("The Procurator of Judea"), still a model of short-story form, and one of the most widely anthologized short stories ever written.

"THE PROCURATOR OF JUDEA"

The principal narrative device in the story is to introduce the reader at the outset to Pontius Pilate in his old age, thus setting up the reader's natural expectation that the story will concern Jesus at some point. The reader receives, instead, a fascinating account of events in Judea as Pilate viewed them, in his office as Procurator, hence the representative of Rome, and the reader is drawn all the way to the end of the story before Jesus is even mentioned. The last line, in which Pilate reveals that he does not remember any Judean named Jesus of Nazareth, is no mere surprise or trick ending but the inevitable consequence of all that has gone before, and the sudden retrospective revelation of the story's import. The reader of the last line does not feel "taken in," but rather enlightened, recognizing that historical truth has been communicated from an unexpected angle of vision. The story thus resonates in the reader's mind long afterward, compelling ironic meditation about the paradoxes and complexities of the past and the probable distortions of official history. At the base of the story, in other words, is a profound idea about history, which has intricate ramifications; and the effect of the story is to make the reader think about those ramifications. Anatole France had, at last, found both a technique and a form which could yield the best he had to offer in the medium of the short story.

"THE JUGGLER OF OUR LADY"

The magisterial quality of "The Procurator of Judea" has tended to cast the other stories of the collection into limbo, for they suffer by comparison; but many of them are fine compositions in their own right and demonstrate how fully and consciously Anatole France had arrived at mastery of the genre by 1892. One might consider, as a typical example, the story "Le Jongleur de Notre-Dame" ("The Juggler of Our Lady"), which utilizes a medieval legend about a mountebank's gesture of piety, using the only skill he possessed to pay tribute to the Virgin Mary. In Anatole France's hands, however, the touching naïveté of the tale takes on a subtle suggestion of irony, simply by being addressed to a sophisticated modern audience. A tinge of parody of the narrative style of the Middle Ages haunts every line; although it is barely perceptible in any one sentence, the tinge of parody is so pervasive and cumulative in its effect that the reader is led to a detached and amused view of the tale, from which the sentimental religiosity has been drained.

"CRAINQUEBILLE"

After 1892, Anatole France regularly produced new collections of short stories intermingled with novels and other kinds of writing, thus displaying a faithfulness to the genre that attested to his sense of its importance and its value. Five collections of stories appeared after *Tales from a Mother of Pearl Casket*, each with at least one or two memorable stories, exploiting the hard-won mastery of the form which he had by then achieved. Probably the best of the collections is the one which appeared in 1904, containing several noteworthy masterpieces, among them the celebrated story of Crainquebille, the humble pushcart merchant who suffered a traumatic encounter with the law. Because "Crainquebille" recounts a case of a man unjustly convicted of breaking the law, and because it first appeared while the Dreyfus affair still raged, it has always been read as a specific satire of that event. Time, however, has provided a better perspective, and one can see that a subtler idea animates the story, namely, that the awesome machinery of the law can by itself make a mockery of justice. Crainquebille is not condemned (as was Dreyfus) by a conscious conspiracy designed to protect a traitor, but simply because the judge, preoccupied with the proper forms of judicial process, never really listened to Crainquebille's case, and Crainquebille never understood a word of what transpired in court. The man and the institution never established contact with each other, and judicial error became inevitable. The story is a masterpiece of social criticism, beautifully conceived, and executed with disciplined control and unfailingly sharp focus on the central idea.

"PUTOIS"

In the same collection appeared another delightful social satire called "Putois," in which Anatole France managed to invent an example of how a myth is created in a society. The story begins when a fictitious gardener is invented one day to give substance to a "white lie." The gardener soon becomes so useful socially that he is endowed with the name Putois and assigned certain attributes. Eventually the townspeople, accepting the invention, become convinced that they know him and have seen him. Soon a whole history of deeds and misdeeds accumulates around his name; Putois becomes a "presence" in the town, and even the inventor of the character forgets his origin and begins to think of him as a real person. The tale is in the author's best comic vein, a good illustration of the kind of gentle mockery which critics call "Francian" and which amuses while provoking serious thought.

The Francian short story is, more than anything else, a fiction of ideas, and it is that characteristic which sets his work apart from other short-story writers in the nineteenth century. Anatole France had little power of invention and not much interest in observation or in character. Books and ideas alone nourished his creative imagination, almost as though the external world did not exist for him. On that basis, he created a body of short fiction in which the pleasures were those of the mind and in which skepticism and irony were the presiding deities. At their best, his stories have the effect of opening up perceptions and lines of thought which reverberate in the reader's mind long after the last word has been read. At their worst, they can be trivial—when founded upon an idea of insufficient power, for example, or when based upon an inconsequential anecdote. In such a voluminous production, such embarrassments do occur, but of both the best and the worst, it can always be said that the style remains polished, classically pure, and a cause for rejoicing even when the content is less than compelling. Anatole France was one of the master storytellers of French literature and a master stylist as well.

OTHER MAJOR WORKS

LONG FICTION: *Le Crime de Sylvestre Bonnard*, 1881 (*The Crime of Sylvestre Bonnard*, 1890); *Les Désirs de Jean Servien*, 1882 (*The Aspirations of*

Jean Servien, 1912); *Thaïs*, 1890 (English translation, 1891); *La Rôtisserie de la Reine Pédauque*, 1893 (*At the Sign of the Reine Pédauque*, 1912); *Le Lys rouge*, 1894 (*The Red Lily*, 1898); *L'Orme du mail*, 1897 (*The Elm Tree on the Mall*, 1910); *Le Mannequin d'osier*, 1897 (*The Wicker Work Woman*, 1910); *L'Anneau d'améthyste*, 1899 (*The Amethyst Ring*, 1919); *Monsieur Bergeret à Paris*, 1901 (*Monsieur Bergeret in Paris*, 1922; *L'Histoire contemporaine*, 1897-1901, collective title for previous 4 novels; *Contemporary History*); *Histoire comique*, 1903 (*A Mummer's Tale*, 1921); *L'Île des pingouins*, 1908 (*Penguin Island*, 1914); *Les Dieux ont soif*, 1912 (*The Gods Are Athirst*, 1913); *La Révolte des anges*, 1914 (*The Revolt of the Angels*, 1914).

PLAYS: *Crainquebille*, pb. 1903 (English translation, 1915); *La Comédie de celui qui épousa une femme muette*, pb. 1903 (*The Man Who Married a Dumb Wife*, 1915).

NONFICTION: *Alfred de Vigny*, 1868; *La Vie littéraire*, 1888-1892 (5 volumes; *On Life and Letters*, 1911-1914); *Le Jardin d'Épicure*, 1894 (*The Garden of Epicurus*, 1908); *Vers les temps meilleurs*, 1906, 1949; *La Vie de Jeanne d'Arc*, 1908 (*The Life of Joan of Arc*, 1908); *Le Génie latin*, 1913 (*The Latin Genius*, 1924); *Sur la voie glorieuse*, 1915.

MISCELLANEOUS: *The Complete Works*, 1908-1928 (21 volumes); *Œuvres complètes*, 1925-1935 (25 volumes).

BIBLIOGRAPHY

Axelrad, Jacob, *Anatole France: A Life Without Illusions*. New York: Harper and Brothers, 1944. In this eminently readable biography, Axelrad focuses on Anatole France's impact as a social critic and partisan of justice. While the research is carefully undertaken and generally accurate, the point of view is overly sentimental, unabashedly admiring, and insufficiently critical and analytical.

Chevalier, Haakon M. *The Ironic Temper: Anatole France and His Time*. New York: Oxford University Press, 1932. Although dated, this book is insightful and engagingly written. Its purpose is to study a character, not to evaluate the artistic achievement of its subject. It sets an excellent analysis of Anatole France's ironic view of the world against a detailed portrait of the political climate in which he lived and wrote. Includes photos and a bibliography.

Hamilton, James F. "Terrorizing the 'Feminine' in Hugo, Dickens, and France." *Symposium* 48 (Fall, 1994): 204-215. Argues that these authors repress the feminine side in their depiction of the Terror by cold mechanical reasoning; argues the reign of such reason oppresses the feminine and creates a self-defeating force of violence.

Jefferson, Carter. *Anatole France: The Politics of Skepticism* New Brunswick, N.J.: Rutgers University Press, 1965. This work emphasizes the historical and political, as opposed to the literary, ideas of Anatole France and is especially informative with respect to the complex and shifting political positions he assumed in the last two decades of his life. The book's five chapters cover the conservative, anarchist, crusader, socialist, and "bolshevik" stages of Anatole France's thought. Contains a bibliography.

Sachs, Murray. *Anatole France: The Short Stories*. London: Edward Arnold, 1974. This brief but penetrating analysis focuses on Anatole France's career as a writer of short fiction. The primary aim of the study is to define and evaluate his distinctive contribution to the evolution of the short story as a literary form.

Stableford, Brian M. "Anatole France." In *Supernatural Fiction Writers: Fantasy and Horror, 1: Apuleius to May Sinclair*, edited by Everett Franklin Bleiler. New York: Scribner's, 1985. Brief introduction to France's treatment of the Christian myth and his fantastic fiction; discusses individual works.

Virtanen, Reino. *Anatole France*. New York: Twayne, 1968. Intended as a general introduction to the author's work, this insightful volume is accurate and sound in its evaluation of Anatole France's life and career. It is also of use to the general reader in its detailed analysis of Anatole France's most significant literary works.

Murray Sachs,
updated by Genevieve Slomski

BENJAMIN FRANKLIN

Born: Boston, Massachusetts; January 17, 1706
Died: Philadelphia, Pennsylvania; April 17, 1790

PRINCIPAL SHORT FICTION

"The Bagatelles," 1722-1784 (miscellaneous tales and sketches)
"Dogood Papers," 1722
"Busy-Body Papers," 1729
"Speech of Polly Baker," 1747
The Way to Wealth, 1758
"Extract from an Account of the Captivity of William Henry," 1768
"Letter from a Gentleman in Portugal," 1786

OTHER LITERARY FORMS

Benjamin Franklin excelled in a dazzling variety of literary forms. He initiated the United States' first successful periodical series, the "Dogood Papers"; he wrote and published *Poor Richard's Almanack*, an annual compilation of weather predictions, jokes, tales, proverbs, and miscellaneous materials; he published numerous scientific papers, such as the description of his famous kite experiment which identified lightning as a form of electricity; he wrote piercing satires such as the delightful "The Sale of the Hessians" and brilliant bagatelles such as "The Ephemera"; and the most important of his many political efforts may have been his editorial contributions to the Declaration of Independence and to the United States Constitution. At the end of his life, he produced one of the most popular, most widely praised, and most influential autobiographies in world literature.

ACHIEVEMENTS

Benjamin Franklin's monumental contributions to science, diplomacy, and politics have been in large measure conveyed through his clear and forceful prose, and the universal recognition accorded to these accomplishments takes into account his literary skills. Franklin was appointed Joint-Deputy Postmaster General of England in 1753; he was awarded the Copley Medal of the Royal Society of London in 1754 and was elected to membership in 1756. He was awarded an honorary degree of Doctor of Laws from the University of St. Andrews in 1759, and an honorary degree of Doctor of Civil Law from the University of Oxford in 1762. Franklin was also elected president of the American Philosophical Society (1769); chosen delegate to the Second Continental Congress (1775); elected Minister Plenipotentiary to France (1778); elected member of the Royal Academy of History of Madrid (1784); elected President of the Supreme Executive Council of Pennsylvania (1785); and elected delegate to the Federal Constitutional Convention (1787).

BIOGRAPHY

The fifteenth son of a Boston candlemaker, Benjamin Franklin began America's first genuinely classic success story when he ran away to Philadelphia at age seventeen and achieved both wealth and fame before the age of thirty. He retired from his printing business and lucrative almanac a wealthy man at age forty-two. Having already excelled as a writer, journalist, and businessman, in the following decades he distinguished himself in science, studying earthquakes, fossils, and the Gulf Stream, and developing experimental gardens in addition to his pioneering work in electricity. He also excelled in technology, inventing bifocals, the Franklin stove, and the lightning rod; in music, creating the glass harmonica for which Wolfgang Amadeus Mozart, Franz Joseph Haydn, and others wrote music; as a public servant, heading the Post Office and founding libraries, insurance organizations, and a charity hospital; as an educator, helping organize the University of Pennsylvania and the American Philosophical Society; and as a statesman, serving as America's first ambassador to France and helping draft the Constitution and the Declaration of Independence. He died the most beloved man in America and the most respected American in the world.

ANALYSIS

No American writer before Washington Irving produced more brilliant short fiction or approached the modern short story quite so closely, or quite so often, as Benjamin Franklin. The modern short story developed in America when Irving and others managed to blend the best of two quite distinct traditions: the essay-sketch tradition and the tale tradition. Scholars agree that Benjamin Franklin was the very first American to imitate the Addisonian periodical essay in America and that he had a genius for manipulating elements of the tale tradition: folklore, hoaxes, tall tales, and so on.

Franklin's first published prose, the first of his fourteen Addisonian Dogood papers, appeared on April 2, 1722, in the *New England Courant*. Taking the form of a letter to the paper, the sketch introduces the marvelously characterized persona Franklin adopted for the series, Mistress Silence Dogood; her fondness for gossip, mother wit, humane concern for others, eye for detail, sense of humor, earthiness, and well-deserved vanity make her one of the best-developed and most utterly charming characters of eighteenth century American literature. Apart from her rather more conventional moral system, Mistress Dogood in some respects recalls Daniel Defoe's Moll Flanders, another vital widow powerfully addicted to life.

"BUSY-BODY PAPERS"

Franklin further improved his writings skills in the Busy-Body essays which he penned some six years later, but the lightly sketched persona of this series cannot begin to approach Mistress Dogood's vitality. Some parts of the series, however—the eighth essay, for example—do tentatively approach the short story. Somewhat later, as seen on July 10, July 24, and September 12 of 1732, Franklin became interested enough in character for its own sake that he abandoned even the quite loose structure of the periodical essay and launched into independent character sketches. Each satirizes a distinct character type. "Anthony Afterwit" depicts a man who is tricked into marrying a woman without a dowry and nearly ruined by her extravagance, who finally reestablishes a rule of economy and common sense in the household when his wife absents

herself for a brief vacation. "Celia Single" in a charming scene and apt dialogue reports some of the aftermath in the Afterwit household and comments tellingly, with examples, on imprudence in the male of the species. The best of the three—and each is decidedly lively and entertaining—characterizes Alice Addertongue, a dedicated scandalmonger and one of Franklin's most brilliantly realized creations.

Mistress Addertongue opens her piece, a mock letter to the newspaper (*The Pennsylvania Gazette*, in which all three of these pieces appeared), commenting about recent newspaper essays on scandal and wittily employing an impeccable logic to demonstrate that only immoral "blockheads" complain of backbiting and gossip:

> They represent it as the worst of Crimes, and then roundly and charitably charge the whole Race of Womankind with it. Are they not then guilty of what they condemn, at the same time that they condemn it?

Let those who accuse Franklin of an incurable didacticism digest that moral and Mistress Addertongue's

Benjamin Franklin (Library of Congress)

introduction to the next section: "Let us leave then these Idiot Mock-Moralists, while I entertain you with some Account of my Life and Manners." A "young Girl of about thirty-five," she is unmarried and economically independent but still lives with her mother. Alice first prefers self-praise to scandal of others, but, on the one hand, she is censured and whipped for such display of ill manners and, on the other, finds herself much more likely to please an audience by attacking third parties rather than by praising herself. Franklin here as elsewhere economizes, describing the vice, exploring scandalmongers' motives, and vividly characterizing his protagonist at one stroke.

In illustration of the latter principle, Alice recalls an incident wherein she vanquishes her mother's antipathy to the vice. During a tea party in the parlor, her mother brutally bores her company with a drizzling litany of praise of their various neighbors; Alice decamps to the kitchen where she contrarily entertains the girls with "a ridiculous Story of Mr.——'s Intrigue with his Maid, and his Wife's Behaviour upon the Discovery." By and by the mother finds herself destitute of company and in turn adjourns to the kitchen, a convert to Alice's cause.

Mistress Addertongue next describes how she has succeeded in making herself "the Center of all the *Scandal* in the Province." One principle involves sound business practices: Whenever someone tells her one foul story she punctually repays it with two. Another principle dictates that if she has never heard of scandal attached to any given individual's name, she first imputes the lack not to virtue but to "defective Intelligence." Next, if she hears scandal of a woman, she praises her before other women for beauty, wit, virtue, or good management; if her prey is a man, she praises him "before his Competitors in Love, Business, or Esteem on Account of any particular Qualification." The latter technique proves superfluous in the case of politicians. Another principle of Alice's success involves keeping strict accounts (she is trained as a bookkeeper) of those from whom she has received or to whom she has retailed scandalous tales. Alice also generously declares that after profound reflection she determines few people allow more than a fifth of their scandalous

behavior to be known; therefore she feels herself justified in improving her stories by inventing sundry details and by modest exaggeration: "I think I keep within Bounds if in relating it I only make it *three times* worse than it is."

In her conclusion, Alice laments that for several days a severe cold and a terrible toothache have prevented her from talking and thus from balancing her accounts; she begs the editor to assist her by printing the material she encloses, an "Account of *4 Knavish Tricks, 2 crakt Maidenheads, 5 Cuckoldoms, 3 drubbed Wives*, and *4 Henpecked Husbands.*" She promises to send more should the toothache continue. In an editorial note the publisher one-ups poor Alice, however, desiring to be excused from printing "the Articles of News she has sent me; such Things being in Reality *No News at all.*"

"ALICE ADDERTONGUE"

If didactic, "Alice Addertongue" represents the most enlightened form of didacticism. Franklin does instruct the reader at length in the nature, conduct, and personnel involved in scandal, as if any of this were really necessary. He also underlines the transparent rationalization involved; more charmingly he identifies the true motive for scandal as a perverted impulse of self-praise—prevented from elevating oneself, one denigrates others—as Alice so convincingly demonstrates in her tactics for learning of scandal. Toward the end, in a marvelous twist, she implicitly generalizes her topic by relating scandal in one form to the basis of contemporary political campaigning and of journalism. Who among Franklin's readers could have been innocent of practicing or enjoying scandalmongering in one form or the other? The final mark of genius involves the enormous charm with which Franklin endows Alice. She is vital, magnetic, dynamic, self-assured, and absolutely amoral—rather possessing the attributes of scandal itself. The reader should not like Alice but cannot help it—much the same situation in which one finds oneself regarding scandal. Could Franklin possibly have analyzed scandal more tellingly?

"SPEECH OF POLLY BAKER"

Franklin produced a marvelous array of delightful short fictions. The "Speech of Polly Baker" takes the form of a mock oration in which Miss Baker argues on the basis of industry, economy, and nature to defend herself against the calumny associated with her having brought five bastard children into the world; the introduction indicates she represented herself well enough that one of her judges married her the next day and subsequently had fifteen children by her.

"THE EPHEMERA"

"The Ephemera," a bagatelle, gently satirizes human ambition, learning, politics, and art—human life in sum—through the device of recounting the narrator's eavesdropping on a May fly. Franklin's famous letter to Madame Helvétius, another bagatelle, attempts to seduce her by means of a dream in which Franklin learns of "new connections" permitted in the afterlife; in fact, he learns that in this afterlife Mrs. Franklin and Monsieur Helvétius have formed precisely the sort of liaison Franklin devoutly hopes to establish with Madame Helvétius in the here and now.

Franklin's two most impressive works of fiction came from his pen after his sixtieth year. They are genuine tales, not periodical essays such as his "Dogood Papers" and "Busy-Body Papers" or short sketches such as his "Speech of Polly Baker." Their content, moreover, has nothing in common with the satirical character delineations of his newspaper sketches or with the homely wisdom of Poor Richard but is exotic and fanciful. The earliest of these pieces, published during Franklin's middle age, concerns the mythology of Native Americans, and the latter piece, written a few years before his death, concerns everyday life in China.

"EXTRACT FROM AN ACCOUNT OF THE CAPTIVITY OF WILLIAM HENRY

In 1768, Franklin published in two issues of the *London Chronicle* a pretended "Extract from an Account of the Captivity of William Henry in 1755, and of His Residence Among the Senneka Indians Six Years and Seven Months Till He Made His Escape from Them, Printed at Boston, 1766." Like the "Speech of Polly Baker," the piece is a journalistic hoax. There was no William Henry taken captive by the Indians and no account of such an experience published in Boston. The narrative is based instead on Franklin's personal experience with Native Americans in Pennsylvania and a string of treaties between the colony and the local tribes that he published on his own press. Franklin's main literary source was an anonymous deistical essay that used Native Americans as a vehicle for describing and extolling the religion of nature. Franklin's protagonist details long conversations with the tribal chieftain and younger braves, analyzes Native Americans principles of rhetoric, and repeats one of the creation myths of the tribe. In this myth, nine warriors while out hunting see a beautiful woman descend from the clouds. Realizing that she is the daughter of the Great Spirit, they go to welcome her and give her food. She thanks them and tells them to return after twelve moons. They do so and discover various new agricultural products where the parts of her body had touched the ground. Franklin introduced this myth in his "Remarks Concerning the Savages of North America" in 1784.

"A LETTER FROM CHINA"

Franklin's narrative concerning China has the same plot structure of an ordinary Englishman forced by circumstances to live in close contact with an alien culture, but it belongs to the literary genre of imaginary voyages. Given the title "A Letter from China," when it appeared in Jared Sparks's edition of Franklin's works in 1839, it should more properly be treated under Franklin's original title in the *Columbia Magazine*, where it was published in 1786 as "Letter from a Gentleman in Portugal to His Friend in Paris, Containing the Account of an English Sailor Who Deserted in China from Capt. Cooke's Ship." This is also the title on Franklin's manuscript copy in the American Philosophical Society Library. The work, with resemblances to both Jonathan Swift's *Gulliver's Travels* (1726, 1727) and the second part of Daniel Defoe's *Robinson Crusoe* (1719) is pure imaginative fiction with no utilitarian purpose. It was partially inspired, however, by Captain James Cook's voyages, which also furnished local color. The sailor, whose adventures are recounted, was seized by pirates, rescued by the authorities, and sent to work on a farm in the interior of China, where he became a quasi member of the family with whom he lived. In a style suitable to a literate sailor, who has many characteristics in common with Franklin himself, the narrator introduces in a fictional setting the most popular topics in contemporary Western writing about China.

OTHER MAJOR WORKS

NONFICTION: *A Dissertation on Liberty and Necessity, Pleasure and Pain*, 1725; *A Modest Enquiry into the Nature and Necessity of a Paper Currency*, 1729; *Plain Truth: Or, Serious Considerations on the Present State of the City of Philadelphia and Province of Pennsylvania*, 1747; *Proposals Relating to the Education of Youth in Pensilvania*, 1749; *Experiments and Observations on Electricity*, 1751, 1754; *The Interest of Great Britain Considered, with Regard to Her Colonies*, 1760; *On the Slave Trade*, 1790; *Mémoires de la vie privée ecrits par lui-même*, 1791 (*Life of Doctor Benjamin Franklin*, 1793; *Memoirs of the Life*, 1818; best known as *Autobiography*).

BIBLIOGRAPHY

Aldridge, A. Owen. *Benjamin Franklin and Nature's God*. Durham, N.C.: Duke University Press, 1967. This study of Franklin's theology treats his religious beliefs in relation to both his practice and his literary works, including "Speech of Polly Baker," "Extract from an Account of the Captivity of William Henry," and "Letter from a Gentleman in Portugal." Intended for the serious student, it is particularly relevant to Franklin's views on metaphysics and personal conduct.

Anderson, Douglas. *The Radical Enlightenments of Benjamin Franklin*. Baltimore: Johns Hopkins University Press, 1997. A study that focuses on the literary and intellectual career of Franklin in his early years; provides a close reading of a number of Franklin texts.

Campbell, James. *Recovering Benjamin Franklin: An Exploration of a Life of Science and Service*. Chicago: Open Court, 1999. A thoughtful look at Franklin's life.

Durham, Jennifer L. *Benjamin Franklin: A Biographical Companion*. Santa Barbara, Calif.: ABC-CLIO, 1997. A good, contemporary biography of Franklin.

Franklin, Benjamin. *Benjamin Franklin's Autobiography*. Edited by J. A. Leo Lemay and P. M. Zall. New York: W. W. Norton. 1986. This critical edition presents the authoritative text of Franklin's *Memoirs of the Life*, superseding those in all multivolume editions of Franklin's writings. Particularly useful are thirty pages of biographical notes concerning the contemporary and historical figures mentioned in the autobiography. Other valuable sections contain relevant extracts from Franklin's letters and selected commentaries by outstanding critics from Franklin's times to the mid-1980's.

_____. *Benjamin Franklin's Writings*. Edited by J. A. Leo Lemay. New York: Library of America, 1987. This outstanding anthology—by far the best in print—contains not only the quintessence of Franklin's literary production but also valuable annotations and a thorough index.

Granger, Bruce I. *Benjamin Franklin: An American Man of Letters*. Ithaca, N.Y.: Cornell University Press, 1964. In order to prove that Franklin is an important man of letters, Granger subjects his periodical essays, almanacs, letters, bagatelles, and autobiography to close stylistic analysis, developing the "persona" of his sketches and the tropes of his essays and conversely dissecting "such rhetorical figures as analogy, repetition, proverb and pun." This stylistic analysis is successful as far as it goes, but it fails to consider the intensely human message of Franklin's best writing.

Locker, Roy N., ed. *Meet Dr. Franklin*. Philadelphia: Franklin Institute, 1981. Sixteen prominent historians contribute to this compilation of essays analyzing various aspects of Franklin's career, including the literary. Intended for the nonspecialist, the essays cover the essentials of Franklin's life and thought.

Van Doren, Carl. *Benjamin Franklin*. New York: Viking, 1938. This biography, although old, is the most readily obtainable, most comprehensive, and most adapted to the general reader. Extensive quotations from Franklin's works provide a "speaking voice" for both the historical figure and the human personality. The text is long but brings the whole of Franklin's life into a single narrative.

Wood, Gordon S. "Not So Poor Richard." *The New York Review of Books* 43 (June 6, 1996): 47-51. Claims that Franklin is the hardest of all the Founding Fathers to understand; provides a biographical sketch, noting particularly the apparent

contradiction between his image as a rustic, industrious, prototypical American and his image as an urbane and aristocratic European.

Walter Evans,
updated by A. Owen Aldridge

MARY E. WILKINS FREEMAN

Born: Randolph, Massachusetts; October 31, 1852
Died: Metuchen, New Jersey; March 13, 1930

PRINCIPAL SHORT FICTION

A Humble Romance and Other Stories, 1887
A New England Nun and Other Stories, 1891
A Pot of Gold and Other Stories, 1892
Young Lucretia and Other Stories, 1892
Silence and Other Stories, 1898
The People of Our Neighborhood, 1898
The Love of Parson Lord, and Other Stories, 1900
Understudies, 1901
Six Trees, 1903
The Wind in the Rose-Bush and Other Stories of the Supernatural, 1903
The Givers, 1904
The Fair Lavinia and Others, 1907
The Winning Lady and Others, 1909
The Copy-Cat and Other Stories, 1914
Edgewater People, 1918
Best Stories, 1927

OTHER LITERARY FORMS

While Mary E. Wilkins Freeman's current reputation rests almost exclusively on her numerous collections of short stories for adults, her thirty-nine published works also include poems and stories for children, novels, and a play, *Giles Corey, Yeoman* (1893), a historical tragedy which, in part, dramatizes her ancestors' involvement in the Salem witch trials of 1692. Some forty stories, together with a handful

of articles, magazine verse, and other fugitive pieces, remain uncollected.

ACHIEVEMENTS

In August, 1890, *Critic* magazine conducted a public opinion poll to establish "Twenty writers whom our readers deem truest representative of what is best in cultivated American womanhood." Mary E. Freeman was included among the twenty, along with Harriet Beecher Stowe, Sarah Orne Jewett, and Rose Terry Cooke. Seven years later the same periodical conducted another poll to determine the twelve best American short stories. The winning list included Freeman's "The Revolt of 'Mother,'" and the second best list included "A Humble Romance." In still another display of public favor, the New York *Herald*'s 1908 "Anglo-American Competition" awarded Freeman five thousand dollars for *The Shoulders of Atlas* (1908). Perhaps the two most significant recognitions of her literary accomplishments were awarded in 1926: Freeman became one of the first four women to be elected to the National Institute of Arts and Letters, and she won the William Dean Howells Gold Medal for Fiction awarded by the American Academy of Letters.

BIOGRAPHY

Reared in an orthodox Congregationalist family, Mary Ella (later altered to Eleanor) Wilkins spent her early life in Randolph, Massachusetts. She moved with her parents to Brattleboro, Vermont, in 1867;

following her graduation from high school, she took courses at Mt. Holyoke Female Seminary and Glenwood Seminary (West Brattleboro) during 1870-1871. After an unsuccessful attempt at teaching school in 1873, she began writing poetry and short stories; her first significant work appeared in *Harper's Bazaar* and *Harper's New Monthly* in the early 1880's. Her first two collections of stories for adults, *A Humble Romance and Other Stories* and *A New England Nun and Other Stories*, generally considered her finest work, established her reputation as a professional writer. Upon her marriage to Dr. Charles Freeman in 1902, she moved to his home in Metuchen, New Jersey, where she resided for the remainder of her life. Personal tragedy marked her later years: She began suffering from deafness in 1909, and she was legally separated from her husband in 1922 as a result of his incurable and destructive alcoholism. Notable among her later works are two novels, *The Shoulders of Atlas*, which won the New York *Herald's* transatlantic novel-writing contest, and *The Whole Family: A Novel by Twelve Authors* (1908), written collaboratively with William Dean Howells, Henry James, and others.

ANALYSIS

Invariably set in the rural areas of Massachusetts or Vermont, Mary E. Wilkins Freeman's most engaging stories focus on troubled characters who encounter situations that jeopardize their quest for happiness and personal fulfillment. In prose as angular and unornamented as the characters she portrays and with masterful detachment from them, Freeman typically develops a story around the main character's response to a personal crisis. Depending on the degree of resoluteness that they possess and the seriousness of the circumstances that they face, her characters react in several ways: Some openly rebel, exerting their will with great courage and determination; others passively accept their lot, preferring to continue what may be a meaningless existence; still others act self-destructively, revealing a masochistic tendency toward self-punishment. Although she wrote about men, her most fascinating characters are women, especially older ones, and in her best work, *A Humble*

Mary E. Wilkins Freeman (Library of Congress)

Romance and Other Stories and *A New England Nun and Other Stories*, from which the following stories are taken, Freeman's heroines are depicted with extraordinary sensitivity and insight. The major theme running through all her fiction is the struggle of every human being to preserve his or her dignity and self-respect when confronted with difficult decisions.

"THE REVOLT OF 'MOTHER'"

As its title indicates, "The Revolt of 'Mother'" has as its protagonist a character who boldly asserts herself. Freeman's most widely anthologized story, it humorously dramatizes the clash of wills between Sarah Penn, a dutiful, God-fearing wife, and her stubborn husband, Adoniram. One spring on the very spot where he had promised to build their new house when they got married forty years earlier, Adoniram begins erecting a new barn for their small New England farm. Having patiently and quietly endured the cramped and outdated quarters of their old house for all these years and wanting her daughter, Nanny, to be married in the new house in the fall, Sarah confronts her husband, accusing him of "lodgin'" his "dumb beasts" better than his "own flesh an' blood." Adoniram refuses to honor his long-standing promise. In fact, he obstinately refuses even to discuss the matter, continually replying with Yankee terseness, "I ain't got nothin' to say." Tearfully reconciling herself to the situation, Sarah chooses not to force the issue, content at present to continue her role as an obedient wife.

When the barn is completed in late July, Adoniram plans to transfer his livestock from the old barn on a Wednesday. On the day before, however, learning of an opportunity to buy "a good horse" in neighboring Vermont, he decides to defer the move until his return on Saturday. Convinced that his absence is an act of "providence," Sarah and Nanny pack the family's belongings and carry them into the spacious new barn. Within a few hours, with a little imagination and ingenuity, Sarah begins to transform the barn into the house of her dreams.

News of her rebellious activities soon spreads, and by Friday she is the main subject of village gossip. The minister, hoping to persuade her to undo the deed before Adoniram returns, tries to reason with her, but his efforts are in vain. When he returns the following day, Adoniram enters the house shed first, only to discover that one of his cows has taken up residence there. In a state of disbelief he then enters the new barn and is flabbergasted when he discovers what has happened during his absence. Assuring him that she "ain't crazy," Sarah releases her pent-up emotions, justifies her actions, and, to his amazement, orders him to complete the conversion. After being served his favorite supper, which he eats silently, Adoniram retreats to the front step and cries. Later comforted by Sarah, he obediently promises to finish converting the barn and humbly confesses to her, "I hadn't no idee you was so set on't as all this comes to."

Like other characters who are constitutionally unable to endure the role that they have been forced to play by family or society—for example, Candace Whitcomb in "A Village Singer"—Sarah Penn ultimately resorts to open rebellion as a means of expressing dissatisfaction. Their self-respect threatened, Freeman's psychologically healthy characters refuse to accept the intolerable situation that causes their unhappiness. Most of her protagonists, however, are not as successful in dealing with crises, for their twisted and lonely lives are so devoid of purpose and meaning that they do not even realize that they are partially or wholly responsible for their plight. The tragic vision set forth in these stories is far more typical of her fiction than the comic mood seen in "The Revolt of 'Mother.'" In this regard "A New England Nun" and "A Poetess," two of her most critically acclaimed stories, are more representative in tone, incident, and artistry.

"A New England Nun"

In the title story of *A New England Nun and Other Stories*, an illuminating study of self-imposed spinsterhood, Freeman analyzes the crippling emotional paralysis that prevents the heroine, Louisa Ellis, from marrying her fiancé of fifteen years, Joe Dagget. For the first fourteen years of their engagement, Joe had worked in Australia "to make his fortune." Faithful to each other but seldom exchanging letters, Joe and Louisa assume that nothing has happened during their separation that would stop the wedding from taking place as scheduled upon his return. Much, however, has happened to Louisa, and her first reaction to Joe's return is "consternation." His biweekly visits with her are marked by stiff formality, banal conversation, and emotional uneasiness. He is puzzled by her lack of passion; her cool behavior toward him makes him uncomfortable. During one of their awkward meetings for example, Joe unintentionally tracks in some dust, nervously fidgets with her carefully arranged books, and accidentally knocks over her sewing basket, all of which irritates her.

With remarkable insight, Freeman traces the development of Louisa's emotional paralysis and neurotic meticulousness. Following the deaths of her mother and brother while Joe was in Australia, which "left her all alone in the world," Louisa had steadily drifted into the private world of her house and garden. Rather than seeking out the company and friendship of other people, Louisa has retreated into her self-imposed convent and over the years has found comfort and pleasure in growing lettuce "to perfection," keeping her bureau drawers "orderly," cleaning her windowpanes, and "polishing her china carefully." Her sewing apparatus has become "a very part of her personality," and sewing itself one of her great obsessions. Hopelessly inured to her soul-killing routines, Louisa wants nothing to disturb her placid, well-ordered life, including Joe Dagget.

Freeman skillfully employs three important symbols to represent the futility of her life and the potential unhappiness that Joe would face being married to her. One of Louisa's favorite pastimes is distilling aromatic essences from her roses and mint. The numerous vials of essences that she has collected over the years serve no purpose whatsoever and are clearly a tangible measure of the meaninglessness of her life. Marriage would destroy this self-indulgent hobby, for in being responsible to someone else "there would be no time for her to distil for the mere pleasure of it." What would happen to Joe if he married her is symbolized in part by her caged canary, which always flutters "wildly" when he visits as if to warn him of his fate. The most important symbol of bondage, however, is the chain on which for fourteen years she has kept her supposedly vicious dog, Caesar. "A veritable hermit of a dog" and kept "a close prisoner," Caesar has been "shut out from the society of his kind and all innocent canine joys." Joe, knowing that Caesar is not really mean and subconsciously reflecting on what might happen to himself, continually tells Louisa that he will one day set the dog free. For Louisa, too, the chain has symbolic significance: Joe's promise to set the dog free represents a threat to the continuance of her secure, reclusive existence.

Joe does not fully understand the changes that Louisa has undergone and politely continues to tolerate her icy attitude toward him. Louisa, feeling obligated to marry the man who has sacrificed so much of his life for her, is unwilling either to alter her life or to tell him frankly that she prefers monasticism to marriage. Impassive, she does nothing. Having received no passionate responses from Louisa, Joe finds himself becoming attracted to Lily Dyer, a beautiful, warmhearted woman who is helping his sick mother. Lily grows fond of Joe, but neither of the two lets the relationship become serious since both feel that the fifteen-year-old engagement should be sacredly honored. One evening about a week before the wedding, Louisa, who knows nothing about Joe and Lily, takes a walk and inadvertently overhears

them talking. Lily is about to leave town to prevent further complications; with mixed emotions Joe agrees with her decision. Realizing that Joe and Lily love each other and sensing an opportunity to get out of the marriage gracefully, Louisa frees Joe the next night. Without mentioning Lily, Louisa finally admits that "she had lived so long in one way that she shrank from making a change." While Louisa does confess to her inadequacies and while her decision is in part a noble one, it is also self-serving for it allows her to avoid any long-term responsibility to another human being. To achieve this desire, Louisa condemns herself to a life of seclusion.

Freeman's profound understanding of the atrophy of the human will is revealed in a number of stories, most notably "A Symphony in Lavender," "A Lover of Flowers," "A Village Lear," "A Kitchen Colonel," and "Sister Liddy." As in "A New England Nun," Freeman carefully avoids passing judgment on the paralyzed characters in these stories, but she leaves little doubt that total passivity is one of the worst of human failings. The unwillingness to take command of one's life, Freeman demonstrates in these stories, eventually leads to the fatally mistaken assumption that one cannot and should not alter one's pattern of living, even if that life has lost purpose and meaning.

"A POETESS"

If some of Freeman's protagonists aggressively assert themselves or passively accept the status quo, others react in ways that show a tendency toward self-punishment. Such is the case with Betsey Dole in "A Poetess," which traces the invidious effects of gossip on a person who ends up lashing herself rather than the author of her humiliation, the village minister. Fifty-years-old, unmarried, and consumptive, Betsey has acquired a modest reputation in the town as a writer of poetry, which is every bit as saccharine as the sugar cubes that she feeds her canary. Like Louisa Ellis, Betsey has created a world the source of whose meaning is not other people. Betsey lives only for her poetry. Poor, she has never made any money from her writing. Her only income for the past twenty years has been the interest generated from her deceased father's modest savings account. Impractical as well as poor, she prefers growing flowers rather than the vegetables that she needs for her very nourishment. Her life is characterized by eccentricity.

One summer morning she is visited by Mrs. Caxton, who is dressed in mourning because of the recent death of her young boy, Willie. Wanting her son to be commemorated in verse, she asks Betsey to write a fitting obituary poem. After they weep together for several minutes, Mrs. Caxton informs Betsey that she is going to have copies printed for friends and relatives. Betsey, promising to do "the best" she can, tells her that the poem will be written in the afternoon.

Raptly working through lunch and even experiencing visions of little Willie as a human and as angel, Betsey looks "like the very genius of gentle, old-fashioned, sentimental poetry." She lies awake all that night mentally revising her sixteen-verse poem; and on the next day she delivers the final copy of the maudlin tribute to a very appreciative and tearful Mrs. Caxton. Having been promised a printed copy, Betsey feels "as if her poem had been approved and accepted by one of the great magazines."

Too poor even to have it framed, she pins the printed copy on her living-room wall and subtly calls attention to it when visitors come. Only two weeks later, however, "the downfall of her innocent pride came." The key word is "innocent," for Betsey has naïvely assumed that everyone in the village appreciates her poetry. She is informed by Mrs. Caxton that Reverend Lang, who has some literary taste and who has had some of his poetry published in magazines, has called her poem "poor." Worse, he is reported to have said that Betsey has never written anything that could rightly be regarded as poetry. Stunned, she says nothing. After Mrs. Caxton leaves, Betsey begins talking as if there were a listener in the room:

> I'd like to know if you think it's fair. Had I ought to have been born with the wantin' to write poetry if I couldn't write it—had I? Had I ought to have been let to write all my life, an' not know before there wa'n't any use in it?

Her listener is God, and her bitter questioning reveals the extent to which she is overly dependent on her poetry for any meaning in her life. Thoroughly hu-

miliated, she proceeds to burn all of her poems: "Other women might have burned their lovers' letters in agony of heart. Betsey had never had any lover, but she was burning all the love-letters that had passed between her and life." Unable to forget the poems, she puts the ashes in her blue china sugar bowl. Burning the poems symbolizes not only her disillusionment with God but also the destruction of her reason for existing. The almost perverse pleasure that she takes in burning the poems and then keeping the ashes as a painful reminder of them suggests the unhealthiness of her will.

Having destroyed the only activity that has ever meant anything to her, she steadily loses her desire to live. By fall she is bedridden and on the verge of death. Shortly before dying, she requests that Reverend Lang visit her. The minister, assuming that Betsey wants to clear her conscience before dying, is unaware that her real purpose is to embarrass him, to make him feel guilty. She asks that he bury the ashes of the poems with her, gets him to admit that he has some literary pretensions, and says that none of her poetry was ever "good." Bewildered by the nature of her death-bed conversation, he remains oblivious to her real intention. Her final request is that he write an obituary poem for her. As Betsey had told Mrs. Caxton, the minister promises to do "the best" he can. Even after this pointed reference, he is completely unaware of the connection between Betsey's behavior and the comments he had made about her poetry several months before. Ironically, Betsey dies falsely believing that Reverend Lang will live with a guilty conscience. Rather than passively living with her limitations as Louisa Ellis chooses to do or boldly asserting her dignity as Sarah Penn ultimately decides, Betsey Dole follows a self-destructive path.

Thoroughly familiar with the conscience and the will, Freeman created a wide range of literary portraits that are remarkable for their psychological verisimilitude. While most other regional writers represented in their fiction little more than the surface of New England life, Freeman consistently tried to bare the very mind and soul of her compatriots. With the possible exception of Sarah Orne Jewett, none of her contemporaries was as successful in delineating the character of New Englanders. At her best, particularly in *A Humble Romance and Other Stories* and *A New England Nun and Other Stories*, her fiction transcends "local color." Although her characters and settings are clearly regional, the underlying subject of her stories—the human condition—is universal. Freeman is not overtly didactic, but the reader may readily infer from her stories that happiness and self-fulfillment are the result of the often difficult struggle to secure and maintain dignity and self-respect. Her fiction is a forceful reminder that while some people succeed, many others fail.

OTHER MAJOR WORKS

LONG FICTION: *Jane Field*, 1892; *Pembroke*, 1894; *Madelon*, 1896; *Jerome, a Poor Man*, 1897; *The Jamesons*, 1899; *The Heart's Highway: A Romance of Virginia*, 1990; *The Portion of Labor*, 1901; *The Debtor*, 1905; *"Doc" Gordon*, 1906; *By the Light of the Soul*, 1907; *The Shoulders of Atlas*, 1908; *The Whole Family: A Novel by Twelve Authors*, 1908; *The Butterfly House*, 1912; *The Yates Pride: A Romance*, 1912; *An Alabaster Box*, 1917 (with Florence Morse Kingsley).

PLAY: *Giles Corey, Yeoman*, pb. 1892.

NONFICTION: *The Infant Sphinx: Collected Letters of Mary E. Wilkins Freeman*, 1985.

CHILDREN'S LITERATURE: *Goody Two-Shoes*, 1883 (with Clara Doty Bates); *The Cow with the Golden Horns and Other Stories*, 1886; *The Adventures of Ann: Stories of Colonial Times*, 1886; *Once Upon a Time and Other Child Verses*, 1897.

BIBLIOGRAPHY

Daniel, Janice. "Redefining Place: *Femmes Coverts* in the Stories of Mary Wilkins Freeman." *Studies in Short Fiction* 33 (Winter, 1996): 69-76. Discusses the many images in Freeman's stories that suggest covering or containing women. Argues that the women in the stories reject restrictive places imposed from the outside, choose their own places, and enclose themselves in choices that are conducive to their own affirmation of self.

Feinberg, Lorne. "Mary E. Wilkins Freeman's 'Soft Diurnal Commotion': Women's Work and Strategies of Containment." *The New England Quarterly* 62, no. 4 (1989): 483-504. "How is women's work to be valued in the marketplace" is the question Feinberg struggles with as she looks at Freeman's short stories dealing with the conception of "women's sphere" and the economics of women's work. To help answer this question, Feinberg discusses Catherine Beecher and Charlotte Perkins Gilman's ideas on the ways value was assigned to women's work. Stories mentioned are: "A New England Nun," "An Honest Soul," "A Humble Romance," "A Church Mouse," and "The Revolt of 'Mother.'"

Freeman, Mary E. Wilkins. *The Infant Sphinx: Collected Letters of Mary E. Wilkins Freeman*, edited by Brent L. Kendrick. Metuchen, N.J.: Scarecrow Press, 1985. Kendrick suggests that although the author's letters were written for practical literary reasons and are a bit mundane, they are a valuable source for autobiographical information. Kendrick warns that it may be difficult to recognize and appreciate the autobiographical details tucked away that reflect her external and internal life, but he insists that they do exist for the patient reader.

Mann, Susan Garland. "Gardening as 'Women's Culture' in Mary E. Wilkins Freeman's Short Fiction." *The New England Quarterly* 71 (March, 1998): 33-53. Claims that gardening in Freeman's stories indicates women's culture imposed by a hierarchical society. Argues that Freeman subverted woman's sphere by focusing on domestic areas where they received personal gratification.

Marchalonis, Shirley, ed. *Critical Essays on Mary Wilkins Freeman*. Boston: G. K. Hall, 1991. A collection of essays ranging from early reviews to a number of essays influential in starting a revival of interest in Freeman's stories. Includes an essay that surveys a hundred years of criticism on Freeman's work, as well as five essays written especially for this collection.

Reichardt, Mary R. "'Friend of My Heart': Women as Friends and Rivals in the Short Stories of Mary Wilkins Freeman." *American Literary Realism*,

1870-1910 22, no. 2 (1990): 54-68. Reichardt contends that evidence is lacking in Freeman's canon for upholding current feminist ideas of nineteenth century matriarchal worlds and strong women's friendships. Instead, Reichardt's article shows a variegated pattern in Freeman's work of domineering or proud women rejected or humbled, while meeker and more dependent women quietly triumph.

_____. *Mary Wilkins Freeman: A Study of the Short Fiction*. New York: Twayne, 1997. An excellent examination of Freeman's short stories. Includes bibliographical references and an index.

_____. "Mary Wilkins Freeman: One Hundred Years of Criticism." *Legacy* 4, no. 2 (1987): 31-44. Reichardt offers an extensive, although not complete, critical and historical context for Freeman and her work. Reveals specific areas of attention given to Freeman over time that serve as a "barometer of our cultural attitudes toward gender in the 100 years that have elapsed since Freeman embarked on her literary career in 1887."

_____. *A Web of Relationship: Women in the Short Fiction of Mary Wilkins Freeman*. Jackson: University Press of Mississippi, 1992. Argues that Freeman's best stories focus on women who struggle against forces that control them, such as marriage, family, and poverty. The book focuses on four types of conflicted relationships in Freeman's stories: women and parents, women and husbands, women and friends, and women alone.

Toth, Susan Allan. "'The Rarest and Most Peculiar Grape': Versions of the New England Woman in Nineteenth-Century Local Color Literature." In *Regionalism and the Female Imagination: A Collection of Essays*, edited by Emily Toth. New York: Human Sciences Press, 1985. Freeman's use of marriage, or lack thereof, in her short stories is the focus of Toth's article. She maintains that one of Freeman's specialties is the portrait of neurotic single women who eschew marriage and find other sources of emotional fulfillment. Curtailing the theme of marriage, Toth briefly mentions the protectiveness, strength, and sentimentality Freeman develops in her characters who are mothers.

Westbrook, Perry D. *Mary Wilkins Freeman*. Rev. ed. Boston: Twayne, 1988. With an informative look at Freeman's pre-1900 work written for adults, Westbrook provides background on the socioeconomic and religious situation of backcountry New England. Westbrook also offers information on the reception of Freeman's work as it was published.

*Larry A. Carlson,
updated by Karin A. Silet*

BRUCE JAY FRIEDMAN

Born: New York, New York; April 26, 1930

PRINCIPAL SHORT FICTION

Far from the City of Class and Other Stories, 1963
Black Angels, 1966
Let's Hear It for a Beautiful Guy, and Other Works of Short Fiction, 1984
The Collected Short Fiction of Bruce Jay Friedman, 1995

OTHER LITERARY FORMS

Bruce Jay Friedman has written several novels, the most commercially and critically successful of which have been *Stern* (1962, 1988) and *A Mother's Kisses* (1964). Among his later novels are *The Current Climate* (1989) and *A Father's Kisses* (1996). His other works include essays in popular periodicals; two major plays, both produced in New York; screenplays; a parody of contemporary self-help manuals; book reviews; and journalistic pieces. In

1995, he published a sequel to *The Lonely Guy's Book of Life* (1978), entitled *The Slightly Older Guy*. His play *Have You Spoken to Any Jews Lately?* was produced at the American Jewish Theater in New York in 1995.

ACHIEVEMENTS

Bruce Jay Friedman is an American short-story writer, novelist, playwright, scriptwriter, journalist, and editor who has a talent for examining the ironic and often comic aspects of contemporary Jewish life. He named, and has often been linked to, the black humor tradition arising out of the 1960's. In this literary movement, writers emphasize the absurdities of existence through irreverent or grotesque humor. Friedman's central characters are usually middle-class Jews who are alienated from their roots and from mainstream society. They are shallow creatures lost in a fragmented, absurd America, searching for acceptance and strength. Friedman's work has often been compared to that of Saul Bellow, Philip Roth, and Bernard Malamud. He is less intellectual than the aforementioned—more visceral in his approach. Friedman has achieved critical success in different genres, including the short story, the novel, and drama. Although best known as a novelist, he has also devoted time to adapting material for the screen. Friedman won the prestigious Obie Award for his play *Scuba Duba: A Tense Comedy* (1968). His *The Collected Short Fiction of Bruce Jay Friedman* was published in 1996 to excellent reviews.

BIOGRAPHY

Bruce Jay Friedman was born in New York City in 1930. He attended the University of Missouri in Columbia, which awarded him a degree in journalism in 1951. After graduation, he joined the Air Force and served as correspondent for the in-house journal *Air Training*. He was discharged in 1953, the same year in which he published his first short story in *The New Yorker*. In 1954, he married the actress and model Ginger Howard, and they had three children. In 1977 Friedman and his wife were divorced. From 1954 until 1966, Friedman worked as an executive for the Magazine Management Company in New York. By

Bruce Jay Friedman in 1970 (AP/Wide World Photos)

1966 he had established himself as an independent writer, having published two novels, two collections of short stories, a play, and the influential anthology *Black Humor* (which he edited). In 1974, he became visiting professor of literature at York College, City University, in New York, a position he held for two years. He continued to produce fiction, and he also began to devote his attention to dramatic and cinematic forms. In the early 1990's, Friedman said he fired his agent because he was too good at getting him work as a screenwriter, which left him too little time for writing stories, novels, and theater plays. He said he hated screenwriting, although he won an Oscar nomination for his screenplay for *Splash*. In 1984, his nonfiction book *The Lonely Guy's Book of Life* was made into the film *The Lonely Guy*, starring Steve Martin.

ANALYSIS

Bruce Jay Friedman condemns his succession of fictional schlemiels, losers, "lonely" and fall guys to a violent, morbid, and paranoic world; his terrain is a stark, post-Thurberesque hell haunted by the enfeebled ghosts of Franz Kafka and Søren Kierkegaard (the first "Modern Day Lonely Guy," according to Friedman). The author claims that he has merely attempted to mirror the surreal montage of the first page of *The New York Times*. In such a world, anonymous victims that no one could imagine happy trudge their daily Sisyphean hills. Those sensitive or foolish enough to wonder, why me? deserve whatever additional anxieties hyperconsciousness assures.

Indeed, the only Friedman characters to escape the avenging furies of their own souls are those who cannot or do not think at all, and those who thrive as caricatures of themselves (such as the notorious "Jewish mothers" cluttering the novels and short stories). Such characters possess little genuine self, and, for Friedman, self and suffering form the two halves of a terrible equation. One should not assume something Christlike in this sacrificial formula, however; Brooklyn and New York City are not exactly Golgotha. Hence, lacking this saving archetypal dimension, Friedman's characters bear their insipid *papier-mâché* crosses in a cultural and spiritual vacuum. No bands of scraggly disciples witness their travail or await their return, and their passage thus proves all the more torturous. (It takes Stern, in the novel of that title, more than one year to "get even" with a man who has insulted his wife. Meanwhile, Stern develops ulcers and has a nervous breakdown.)

The element of "sick" humor in Friedman's fiction is probably what prompted critics of the 1960's to describe it and similar work by writers such as Vladimir Nabokov, Joseph Heller, James Purdy, Thomas Pynchon, and Terry Southern as "black humor." Friedman himself popularized the term when he edited the anthology of short fiction, *Black Humor*, in 1965. Critic Max Schulz seems to have identified black humor correctly as a phenomenon of its time. Perhaps this is because, as Friedman recognized in an influential introduction to his anthology, the phrase fails to convey the essence as well as the comic seriousness of fiction which, for whatever reasons, finds itself so classified. Then again, there is the wider generic question of comedy in general to consider.

Friedman claims in his introduction that black humor has always been and always will be written—"as long as there are disguises to be peeled back. . . ."

Black humor, he suggests, asks "final questions"; it announces to the world—"be preposterous, but also make damned sure you explain yourself." One does wonder, given these qualifications, how black humor differs from the traditional satiric humor of, say, a Jonathan Swift or a Petronius. Critics and theorists, nevertheless, have taken pains to distinguish the two forms. Charles Harris, for one, emphatically denies any satiric function in black humor; so does Robert Scholes, and so, somewhat contradictorily, does Friedman. Black humor apparently shrugs off any hope of personal redemption or social reform; its sole purpose is the exposure of absurdity. In this sense, black humor can be regarded as a kind of vaudevillian naturalism devoid of the scientific and deterministic restraints peculiar to classical naturalism. The only solace it promises is relief through laughter for its own sake. The world, Friedman proclaims, is a tense, brutal affair, and you might as well laugh at what little of it you can; if nothing else, discharge muscular tension.

There is, however, more to Friedman's fiction than pure gag or memorable one-liners or even a peculiar and rather perverse comic vision. This extra dimension develops most definitively in the novels, but one can also catch glimpses of it in the short stories that make up the author's first two collections. Beyond the subsuming survival motive of Friedman's neurotic anti-heroes, certain old-fashioned virtues and values do emerge as possible alternatives to meaninglessness. Courage, for example, would eliminate many otherwise humiliating compromises; love, forever elusive in Friedman's work, might cushion every fell blow; and compassion would neutralize hatred, bad vibrations, and egotistical self-dotage, but courage, love, and compassion—defenses, all, against what Friedman describes as the "new Jack Rubyesque chord of absurdity [that] has been struck in our land"—lie buried deeply beneath the Sisyphean hill. Friedman's characters remember them fondly, as they would childhood baubles. Eternally lost, their very absence makes them the most conspicuous themes in Friedman's fiction. Evil and accident result, then, as consequences of the *lack* of goodness and order. Without knowing it, perhaps, the Jewish

Friedman delineates an Augustinian world. (Judaism does have its Augustinian equivalents in certain gnostic scriptures.)

Against courage, love, and compassion Friedman assembles an entire arsenal of badness: germs, disease, physical deformity, violence, humiliation, embarrassment, despair, free-floating anxiety, nervous breakdowns, failure, divorce, infidelity, loneliness, isolation, everyday banalities, and—encompassing them all—the fear of death. In practically every story the central character recognizes but fails to overcome some major obstacle, and minor obstacles also abound.

CASTRATING MOTHER STORIES

In a group of stories involving "castrating" mothers (almost certainly leftover material from the novel, *A Mother's Kisses*), the protagonists cannot escape their mothers' omnivorous presence. In "The Trip," for example, a young man's mother accompanies her son to the Midwest to make sure he gets off to a good start in college. The mother, like all Friedman mothers, is loud, crude, brash, and offensive and thrives on the fantasy that strangers will mistake her for her son's lover. The student desperately wants his mother to act like ordinary mothers, for her power not so much inhibits his style as renders him styleless: "I was marked as a fellow with a mother," he groans. In a related story, "The Good Time," a young soldier's mother visits her furloughing son in Philadelphia to, as she puts it, show him "a good time." She succeeds only in embarrassing and oppressing the anguished son. In still another story, "The Enemy," the men of a typical Jewish family appear weak and impotent when pitted against the voracious, saw-toothed females of the clan.

UNMANAGEABLE WOMEN STORIES

In general, Friedman's world is full of unmanageable women. The wives of his characters, while inhabiting a different domain entirely, prove no better than their mothers. While the mothers, however perversely, do in a sense remain faithful to their weak sons, the wives constantly drift away from their husbands, emotionally, physically, and legally. Friedman wives, insubstantial intellectually and often emotionally vapid, refuse to remain homebodies, mothers, and kitchen drudges. Their rebellion, if it can be called that, involves nothing so abstract and ideological as the lure of independence or feminist ideals; rather, it takes the form of vague dissatisfaction, diffuse ennui, and an ultimate rejection of the shortcomings of men in general. The husbands, equally fed up and bored with their wives, react in two ways; either they attempt to make amends and sincerely desire to patch up a shattered marriage, or they abandon their wives for the prospect of nervous one-night stands and ubiquitous nubile flesh in a sexually revolutionized world for which they are little prepared.

Castrating mothers, unsatisfactory wives, problematic girlfriends, and sexual objects—these are the women who populate Friedman's fiction. Their purpose, which they serve by *existing*, is to expose men where they are most vulnerable, as heroes and/or lovers. Perhaps Friedman spares women no mercy precisely because they undermine all of the splendid myths men have created about themselves. In "The Punch," a recently married public relations man named Harris describes his marriage as a "series of tense situations." The mere presence of his sexy young wife erodes Harris's confidence and masculinity, and he responds by resorting to violence as "the need to hit someone . . . gathered up like an abscess." Harris feels the only way he can impress his wife is to slug another human being. Yet the fear unsettles him: He knew that "no matter how smoothly things were running, always, at a party . . . there would arise some confrontation in which he would be brought to the edge of violence and then, in some way or other, fail to throw a punch." Finally, to his wife's immense delight, Harris manages to punch a stranger on the street. Once he proves his manhood—that is, after the fact—Harris realizes that what he really wanted to do was punch the infuriating creature who had so disrupted his life. Thus, violence precipitates more violence.

NEUROTIC MEN STORIES

Missing the comforts of domestic, conjugal, and romantic fulfillment, Friedman's male characters develop numerous real and psychosomatic ailments. Stefano, in "Black Angels," describes his life as a "sea of despair"; the patient in "The Investor" observes his fever rise and fall with the fluctuations of

Plimpton Rocket Fuel stock; Gorsline, in "The Death Table," draws a roulette card that promises him early demise via heart attack; Mr. Kessler, in "When You're Excused You're Excused," claims that bad health excuses him from family and social obligations; Merz, in "A Foot in the Door," arranges a Faustian pact by accepting an ulcer and asthma in order to get the woman he wants; and the lead character in "Mr. Prinzo's Break-through" spends his last cent on psychoanalysis. (The paragon of hypochondriacs in Friedman's fiction is Stern in *Stern*.) Freudian critics, particularly those who follow Leslie Fiedler's perceptive analyses, might interpret this widespread hypochondria, as well as the general disrespect for women in Friedman's work, as a sign of latent homosexuality. Homosexuality does not, latent or otherwise, seem to preoccupy Friedman, however, except occasionally, when he adds it to the ever-growing list of deleterious options threatening contemporary man. It is altogether safer, and more accurate, to assume that the neuroses of Friedman's characters are metaphysical rather than psychological in nature.

Not surprisingly, perhaps their very Jewishness remains the sole, frayed connection Friedman's comic wretches can make with their culture, their tradition, their heritage, and their brethren. Thematically, Jewishness offers these characters what Faulkner might have called an "eternal verity." For Friedman, however, one is Jewish practically by default. In *The Dick* (1970), the protagonist changes his name from Sussman to LePeters in order to enter mainstream America, and in one of Friedman's best stories, "When You're Excused You're Excused," Mr. Kessler seems more interested in avoiding Jewish holiday rituals than he does in restoring his health at Vic Tanny's gym, where he decides to work out on the eve of Yom Kippur. Throughout the story, Mr. Kessler tries to convince himself that he has been excused from Jewishness for a while. He gets together with a group of unsavory characters and indulges himself shamelessly. In the end, however, Mr. Kessler punches a man in the nose for never having heard of the Jewish baseball hero, "Phumblin' Phil" Weintraub. That was too much for any Jew on Yom Kippur. "I may have been excused," Mr. Kessler mutters, "but I wasn't that excused."

HARRY TOWNS STORIES

Harry Towns is a sort of black-humor Everyman—a bit of a loser, a bit of a creep, somewhat pathetic, somewhat despicable. In "The Partners," Harry is in Las Vegas with his young son in an effort to spend more time with him in preparation for a divorce. This idealistic notion is "black humorously" spoiled by the fact that Harry has venereal crabs and has trouble getting away from the boy long enough to satisfy his gambling habit and his sexual desires. Although the boy is hurt by a falling barbell in a gym to which Harry takes him, that does not deter Harry from leaving him in the hotel room while he goes to gamble and visit a hooker. When the boy has him paged, Harry is at first angry, but then he feels guilty when the boy, who wants to be with his father regardless of the setting, says he loves Las Vegas more than any place in the world. The only way Harry can show his fatherly love is to give the underage boy a handful of coins with which to play the slot machines and then to stand by him to ward off the casino guard, saying he will kill anyone who dares to come within ten feet of the two of them.

The "lady" in the Harry Towns story "Lady" is cocaine, and Harry is a drug user who also uses cocaine to get women. When Harry's mother dies, her death becomes the opportunity for his meeting a new dealer who gets him some of the best cocaine he has ever had; he has no scruples about exploiting the mother's funeral for the sake of his habit. However, similar to the ending of the previous story about the father-son bonding around the slot machines in Las Vegas, Friedman creates an ironic version of Harry's saving grace at the end of this story. In the only moral gesture toward his mother's memory that Harry is capable of, he vows to finish the cocaine before dawn of the day of the funeral so he can start off the day clear. He vows that no matter what someone might offer him on the day of the funeral, even cocaine used for brain surgery, he will turn it down. In an ironic and unknowing reference to himself, Harry swears that anyone who sticks so much as a grain of cocaine up his nose on the day of the funeral had to "be some new and as yet undiscovered breed of sonofab—. The lowest."

"Pitched Out" is a kind of black-humor coda to Harry's not-so-noble adventures. At age fifty-seven, he is a writer sunk so low that he is unsuccessfully trying to pitch a show about a dog to network executives. While in Los Angeles, he meets a friend for dinner and laments that he is getting old and is coming up empty in Hollywood. Both men bemoan their lost youth which they still try to maintain by hustling women in the bar. As they watch beautiful young girls come out of a night spot, Harry knows that any one of them could have slipped past the fence he had built around himself when he met the woman he now lives with. Typically, Harry knew "there were still some adventures up ahead."

Friedman's work, in general, exaggerates and exposes the neurotic condition of Jews in America; but as the alienated Jew comes to represent contemporary Everyman, so Friedman's stories transcend their Jewishness and read like absurd vignettes of any postindustrial civilization. It would not take much to convert such vignettes into minor tragedies—a laugh less here, a bit more pathos there—and this is exactly why Friedman's humor seems so right for this Age of Anxiety. Saving graces and verities are there, but no one seems to know what to do with them.

OTHER MAJOR WORKS

LONG FICTION: *Stern*, 1962, 1988; *A Mother's Kisses*, 1964; *The Dick*, 1970; *About Harry Towns*, 1974; *Tokyo Woes*, 1985; *The Current Climate*, 1989; *A Father's Kisses*, 1996.

PLAYS: *Scuba Duba: A Tense Comedy*, pr. 1967; *Steambath: A Play*, pr. 1971; *Have You Spoken to Any Jews Lately?*, pr. 1995.

SCREENPLAYS: *The Owl and the Pussycat*, 1971 (based on the play by William Manhof); *Stir Crazy*, 1980; *Doctor Detroit*, 1983 (with Carl Gottlieb and Robert Boris; based on a story by Friedman); *Splash*, 1984 (with Lowell Ganz and Babaloo Mandel).

NONFICTION: *The Lonely Guy's Book of Life*, 1978; *The Slightly Older Guy*, 1995; *Even the Rhinos Were Nymphos: Best Nonfiction*, 2000.

EDITED TEXT: *Black Humor*, 1965.

BIBLIOGRAPHY

Gefen, Pearl Sheffy. "Bear of a Man." *The Jerusalem Post*, December 5, 1996, p. 4. A biographical sketch, combined with an interview of Friedman. Friedman talks about the ups and downs of his career, his encounters with Hollywood screenwriters, his relationship to his family, and his reaction to reviewers.

Nolan, Tom. "Master of His Universe." Review of *The Collected Short Fiction of Bruce Jay Friedman*, by Bruce Jay Friedman. *The Los Angeles Times Book Review*, March 3, 1996, p. 4. Nolan discusses Friedman's flair for bizarre comedy, his talent for fantasy, and his focus on the recurring character Harry Towns in several of his stories.

Schulz, Max. *Black Humor Fiction of the Sixties: A Pluralistic Definition of Man and His World*. Athens: Ohio University Press, 1973. Schulz has made a career of examining black humor writers in general, Friedman in particular. He develops the concept of the emergence of black humor in the 1960's, defines it, and examines its leading exponents. In a separate chapter on Friedman, his novel *Stern* is compared and contrasted to Charles Wright's *The Wig* (1966).

_____. *Bruce Jay Friedman*. New York: Twayne, 1974. Schulz has emerged as Friedman's leading essayist and critical admirer. He places Friedman directly into the mainstream of black humor (Friedman actually coined the term), considering him its leading exponent. The author carefully examines Friedman's wide range of tastes with separate chapters on the various genres. The author predicts a bright future for him. A good introduction to Friedman's work. Supplemented by a chronology and a select bibliography.

_____. *Radical Sophistication: Studies in Contemporary Jewish-American Novelists*. Athens: Ohio University Press, 1969. Limiting his study to only a handful of Jewish writers, such as Isaac Bashevis Singer, Bernard Malamud, Saul Bellow, Normal Mailer, and Leslie Fiedler, Schulz includes a separate chapter on Friedman and compares his handling of the theme of love in *Stern* to Edward Lewis Wallant's *The Pawnbroker* (1961). The chapter is a reprint of a 1968 article in *Critique: Studies in Modern Fiction.*

Seed, David. "Bruce Jay Friedman's Fiction: Black Humor and After." *Thalia: Studies in Literary Humor* 10 (Spring/Summer, 1988): 14-22. A good, brief look at Friedman's major work and his importance as a writer. Seed points out that Friedman has been sadly overlooked by his critics except for Schulz and that his work deserves greater attention. He believes Friedman is at his best when he turns everyday notions completely upside down through his characters and their bizarre adventures.

Taylor, John. "The Funny Guy's Book of Life." *New York* 22 (October 9, 1989): 46-50. A biographical sketch that comments on Friedman's success in

the 1960's, his slide from fame, his scriptwriting, and his efforts to make a comeback with fiction in the 1980's.

Trachtenberg, Stanley. "The Humiliated Hero: Bruce Jay Friedman's *Stern.*" *Critique: Studies in Modern Fiction* 7 (Spring/Summer, 1965): 91-93. Trachtenberg briefly examines Friedman's *Stern*, the novel about a Jew named Stern looking for someone to torment him, finding his nemesis in an anti-Semitic neighbor. The author praises the book and considers it significant. He notes that Friedman can vividly bring out the laughter behind the grotesque horror.

Louis Gallo,
updated by Terry Theodore

BRIAN FRIEL

Born: Killyclogher, near Omagh, Northern Ireland; January 9, 1929

PRINCIPAL SHORT FICTION

The Saucer of Larks, 1962
The Gold in the Sea, 1966
The Saucer of Larks: Stories of Ireland, 1969
Selected Stories, 1979 (reprinted as *The Diviner*, 1982)

OTHER LITERARY FORMS

Although Brian Friel began his literary career writing short stories, he has achieved critical acclaim and popular success with his plays, the most famous of which are *Philadelphia, Here I Come!* (pr. 1964), *Translations* (pr. 1980), and *Dancing at Lughnasa* (pr., pb. 1990).

ACHIEVEMENTS

Brian Friel is a member of the Irish Academy of Letters and Aosdana, the national treasury of Irish letters. He received an honorary doctorate from the

National University of Ireland in 1982. In 1986, he accepted a seat in the Irish senate, the lower house of the Irish parliament. *Aristocrats* (pr. 1979) won him a 1989 New York Drama Critics Circle Award for best foreign play, and *Dancing at Lughnasa* won him an Olivier Award in 1991. His play *The Loves of Cass McGuire* was produced on television in Dublin.

BIOGRAPHY

According to his birth certificate, Bernard Patrick Friel was born in Killyclogher, near Omagh, Northern Ireland, on January 9, 1929. However, according to the parish register, his name at baptism was Brian Patrick O'Friel, the substitution of the more Anglo version of his name perhaps owing to the Protestant bureaucracy's habit of discouraging Gaelic names at the time of his birth. He was educated at Long Tower School and Saint Columb's College in Derry, after which he earned a B.A. degree at St. Patrick's College in Ireland's national seminary at Maynooth in Kildare. After training to be a teacher at St. Joseph's Teacher Training Center in Belfast, he began a ten-year career as an educator in Derry. He married Anne Morrison in 1954 and began publishing short stories in the early 1950's; within a few years he had secured a contract with *The New Yorker*.

After having a number of stories published and two radio plays broadcast, Friel retired from teaching in 1960 to write full-time. He spent several months in 1963 at the Guthrie Theater in Minneapolis, Minnesota, learning stagecraft; the following year his first major play, *Philadelphia, Here I Come!*, made a highly successful debut at the Dublin Theatre Festival, followed by another successful run on Broadway in 1966. His best-known play, *Translations*, was produced in 1980 by the Field Day Theatre Company, established by Friel and actor Stephen Rea. He is one of Ireland's best-known and most respected living playwrights. Friel, who settled in a rural area of County Donegal, is a member of the Irish senate.

ANALYSIS

The author of thirty-one stories in two collections, *The Saucer of Larks* and *The Gold in the Sea*, eighteen of which were selected and republished in *The Saucer of Larks: Stories of Ireland*, Brian Friel once made a distinction between the relationship between the storyteller he began as and the playwright he became. Whereas the playwright must always be concerned with using stealth to evoke a fresh response from the complacent theater audience, the storyteller mimics a personal conversation implicitly prefaced with, "Come here till I whisper in your ear."

However, there is perhaps more similarity between Friel's stories and his plays than there are differences. First of all, his stories are conventionally organized, built on the substructure of a relatively straightforward thematic idea that can be illustrated by moving simple characters about on a limited stage. Friel has been compared to Anton Chekhov and Ivan Turgenev, and whereas there is a surface similarity, he lacks the character complexity found in Chekhov and Turgenev.

Friel has been criticized by some critics for writing stories that, while often situated on the politically charged boundary between the Republic of Ireland and Northern Ireland, belie the existence of that

boundary and the bloody history that stains it. The conflicts that beset his characters are not political but personal, and the past that Friel evokes is romantic rather than rebellious. Although such slighting of political rhetoric by Friel in favor of universal longings and romantic illusion may irritate social critics who want fiction to carry political freight, Friel's short fiction is firmly within the Irish folk tradition.

"AMONG THE RUINS"

A typical Friel story, "Among the Ruins" is structured conventionally around the main character's discovery about the irretrievable nature of the past. Margo, Joe's wife, arranges, for the children's sake, to take a family day-trip to Donegal, where Joe was born and raised. Although at first he resists the idea, saying he is not sentimental and that he does not see the point in the trip, on the way he becomes excited, not because he wants to show his children where he played as a boy, but because he wants to recapture some lost magic.

However, when he tries to explain to his wife the significance of the imaginative games he once played in a secret bower with his sister, he realizes that the past is an illusion, a mirage that allows an escape from the present. When he finds his son playing his own imaginative game in the woods, he understands that the past belongs not to him, but to his son, in a long line of generations, all finding some meaning in the magic of irretrievably lost childhood. Thematically, the story suggests that the past has meaning not as something that once happened, but as something that continues to happen, repeating itself over and over again.

"THE DIVINER"

The Irish stereotypes of the alcoholic husband and the shamed and embarrassed wife form the basis of "The Diviner." The twist that Friel plays on the story is that Nelly Devenny, the shamed wife, is freed from her alcoholic husband in the first paragraph of the story and, after a suitable period of mourning, decides to marry again, this time to a respectable retired man from western Ireland. The story actually begins when, three months after Nelly marries the man, he is drowned in a lake. After divers fail to find the body, a diviner is brought in, who, like a priest, can smell out the truth. The truth, which Friel saves until the end of the story, is revealed when the body is brought to the surface and two whisky bottles are found in the pocket. Nelly's wailing, which ends the story, is not so much for the dead husband as for the respectability she almost gained but which now is lost.

"FOUNDRY HOUSE"

"Foundry House" is Friel's best-known and most widely respected story, primarily because it features a cast of well-balanced characters in a dramatic scene that presages Friel's later triumphs in stage drama. The story is also appealing to many readers because the dramatic oppositions derive from Irish history and reflect a clearly defined class distinction that once was known as the "Big House" system, in which English Protestants lived in large manor homes with Irish Catholic peasants who were dependant on them. However, because Friel is not really interested in these political or religious distinctions, he makes both Joe Brennan, the working class descendant of the peasant class, and the Hogan family, who still live in the big house, Irish Catholic.

Friel symbolizes the difference between the dying, old way and the competent, new, industrial way by making the Hogans aging and sterile and Joe a radio and television repairman. When Joe is called to the house to show the family how to play a tape recording from one of the daughters, a nun in Africa, he is asked to stay and listen, but the father, now infirm, snaps at him, calling him "boy" as in the old days. However, when Joe returns home and is queried by his curious wife about the big house, he can only say, as he dresses his baby for bed, that they are a great, grand family.

"THE SAUCER OF LARKS"

The magic of the natural world and its momentary superiority over the public world of rules and protocol dominates "The Saucer of Larks." The protagonist is a police sergeant in Donegal during World War II, who escorts two German officials to disinter the body of a young German pilot who has crashed in the area. The landscape has a significant effect on the sergeant, making him feel that he would not mind being buried out here, for with so much life around, one does not have a chance to be really dead. When they reach the grave site, they hear hundreds of larks singing, which inspires the sergeant further in his lyrical response to nature. Arguing that after being buried in one of the big cemeteries in Dublin, one is finished complaining about how man destroys beautiful areas such as the place known as "the saucer of larks," he tries to convince the Germans to leave the young pilot where he is; but the Germans, in stereotypical fashion, can think only of orders and duty. At the end of the story, when the sergeant is back at the station, he wonders what came over him, puzzling that he has never done anything like that before and blaming it on the heat and his age.

"MY FATHER AND THE SERGEANT"

The title of this Friel story sufficiently signifies its meaning, for the father and the Sergeant are one and the same; the story is told by a young man whose father, a teacher at the school in Donegal, where he is a student, is secretly nicknamed "the Sergeant" by his students; thus he is both a kind, silent man troubled by ambition and a stern, hard-driving, humorless task-master. The story is not dependent so much on theme or complexity of character as it is on a reminiscent tone of gentle, sad memory.

When passed over for a better post, the father decides he will show his superiors what a good teacher he is by preparing four of his students for the regional scholarship exams. However, when he is stricken by pleurisy and a substitute is called in, the young man becomes so popular with his charges that the father's position is made even more precarious. The story comes to a climax when the substitute is accused of kissing one of the young girls, the protagonist's girlfriend, and is sent packing by the priest. When the father returns and some of the boys tease the young girl, saying that she will be wrestling on the couch with the Sergeant next, the protagonist reacts violently, crying, "He's my father." However, rather than tell his father what the boys have said, the protagonist says only that he hit one of the boys because he called him "the Sergeant."

OTHER MAJOR WORKS

PLAYS: *A Doubtful Paradise (The Francophile)*, pr. 1959; *The Enemy Within*, pr. 1962; *The Blind*

Mice, pr. 1963; *Philadelphia, Here I Come!*, pr. 1964; *The Loves of Cass Maguire*, pr. 1966; *Lovers*, pr. 1967; *Crystal and Fox*, pr. 1968; *The Mundy Scheme*, pr. 1969; *The Gentle Island*, pr. 1971; *The Freedom of the City*, pr. 1973; *Volunteers*, pr. 1975; *Living Quarters*, pr. 1977; *Aristocrats*, pr. 1979; *Faith Healer*, pr. 1979; *American Welcome*, pr. 1980; *Translations*, pr. 1980; *Three Sisters*, pr., pb. 1981 (adaptation of Anton Chekhov's play); *The Communication Cord*, pr. 1982; *Selected Plays of Brian Friel*, pb. 1984; *Fathers and Sons*, pr., pb. 1987; *Making History*, pr. 1988; *Dancing at Lughnasa*, pr., pb. 1990; *The London Vertigo*, pb. 1990; *A Month in the Country: After Turgenev*, pb. 1992; *Wonderful Tennessee*, pr., pb. 1993; *Molly Sweeney*, pr. 1994; *Give Me Your Answer, Do!*, pr. 1999.

RADIO PLAYS: *A Sort of Freedom*, 1958; *To This Hard House*, 1958.

BIBLIOGRAPHY

Bonaccorso, Richard. "Back to 'Foundry House': Brian Friel and the Short Story." *The Canadian Journal of Irish Studies* 17 (December, 1991): 72-77. Claims the story can be read as a satire of two bankrupt worlds or as an elegy of a lost past; argues that part of the problem with the story is Friel's reticence and use of the dramatic mode without commentary.

_____. "Personal Devices: Two Representative Stories by Brian Friel." *Colby Quarterly* 32 (June, 1996): 93-99. Discusses the comic-elegiac tone and the transactions between character and community in "The Flowers of Kiltymore" and "The Saucer of Larks." Argues that in Friel's stories technique is embodied in the creation of characters whose hearts are free.

Cronin, John. "'Donging the Tower'—The Past Did Have Meaning: The Short Stories of Brian Friel." In *The Achievement of Brian Friel*, edited by Alan J. Peacock. Gerrards Cross: Colin Smythe, 1993.

1-13. Discusses how Friel's stories anticipate themes and techniques used more effectively in his plays. Argues that the stories are largely derivative of other Irish writers but contain hints of what is to come.

Dantanus, Ulf. *Brian Friel: The Growth of an Irish Dramatist*. Göteborg, Sweden: ACTA Universitatis Gothoburgensis, 1985. Although most of this study focuses on the plays, a long chapter on the short stories explores the physical and political landscape of Friel's fiction, including his focus on community, imagination, poverty, the past, and family. Includes a detailed discussion of "Foundry House."

Maxwell, D. E. S. *Brian Friel*. Lewisburg: Bucknell University Press, 1973. A chapter on the short stories provides a general introduction to Friel's basic themes, with discussions of several major stories. Argues that although Friel's stories are not political, they feature recurring motifs of flight, exile, and shifting allegiances.

O'Brien, George. *Brian Friel*. New York: Twayne, 1990. The first chapter of this general introduction to Friel's works provides an overview of his short stories. Argues that his stories speak for a culture, not a political entity; thus, Friel does not deal with the ideological division between the Republic of Ireland and Northern Ireland. Discusses the themes in a number of Friel's stories.

Pine, Richard. *Brian Friel and Ireland's Drama*. London: Routledge, 1990. In his chapter on the short stories, Pine argues that Friel's main themes are illusion, expectation, and dignity; claims that Friel's basic technique is to draw the reader into the characters' illusions, disillusions, and attempts at dignity and thus involve the reader in the resolution of such crises as loss of faith, disintegration of the family, and failure of memory.

Charles E. May

CARLOS FUENTES

Born: Panama City, Panama; November 11, 1928

PRINCIPAL SHORT FICTION

Los días enmascarados, 1954
Aura, 1962 (novella; English translation, 1965)
Cantar de ciegos, 1964
Zona sagrada, 1967 (novella; *Holy Place*, 1972)
Cumpleaños, 1969 (novella)
Poemas de amor: Cuentos del alma, 1971
Chac Mool y otros cuentos, 1973
Agua quemada, 1980 (*Burnt Water*, 1980)
Constancia y otras novelas para vírgenes, 1989
　　(*Constancia and Other Stories for Virgins*, 1990)
Días enmascarados, 1990 (includes *Los días
　　enmascarados* and *Cantar de ciegos*)
El naranjo: O, Los círculos del tiempo, 1993 (*The
　　Orange Tree*, 1994)
*La frontera de cristal: Una novela en nueve
　　cuentos*, 1995 (*The Crystal Frontier: A Novel in
　　Nine Stories*, 1997)

OTHER LITERARY FORMS

Known primarily as a novelist, Carlos Fuentes has also written three plays and has collaborated on several screenplays. His numerous nonfiction works include political tracts, essays on Mexican life, and literary criticism. He has also been a frequent contributor to periodicals in the United States, Mexico, and France.

ACHIEVEMENTS

Carlos Fuentes is regarded by many as Mexico's foremost contemporary novelist. Perhaps the most valuable contribution of Fuentes's writing is that it introduced innovative language and experimental narrative techniques into mainstream Latin American fiction. His concern for affirming a viable Mexican identity is revealed in his allegorical and thematic use of his country's history and legends, from the myths of the Aztecs to the Mexican Revolution.

Aside from receiving honorary degrees from numerous colleges and universities, such as Columbia College, Harvard University, and Washington University, Fuentes has won many literary awards. These include the Rómulo Gallegos prize (Venezuela) in 1977 for *Terra nostra* (1975; English translation, 1976), the Alfonso Reyes Prize (Mexico) in 1979 for the body of his work, the National Award for Literature (Mexico) in 1984 for *Orquídeas a la luz de la luna* (pb. 1982; *Orchids in the Moonlight*, 1982), the Miguel de Cervantes Prize from the Spanish Ministry of Culture in 1987, and the Rubén Darío Order of Cultural Independence (Nicaragua), and the literary prize of Italo-Latino Americano Institute, both in 1988.

Fuentes received the Capita Maria Medal (1991), the Chilean Order of Merit (1992), the French Legion of Honor (1992), and the Menendez Pelayo International Award from the University of Santander (1992). He was named honorary citizen of Santiago de Chile, Buenos Aires, and Veracruz (1993) and received the Principe de Asturias Prize (1994). He was a candidate for the Neustadt International Prize for Literature (1996) and received honorary degrees from Bard College, Cambridge University, Columbia College, Chicago State University, Dartmouth College, Essex University, Georgetown University, Harvard University, and Washington University.

BIOGRAPHY

Carlos Fuentes was born into a Mexican family that he later characterized as typically petit bourgeois. Son of Rafael Fuentes, a career diplomat, and Berta Macias Rivas, Carlos traveled frequently and attended the best schools in several of the major capitals of the Americas. He learned English at the age of four while living in Washington, D.C. After he was graduated from high school in Mexico City, he studied law at the National University and the Institut des Hautes Études Internationales in Geneva, Switzerland. Fuentes also lived in Santiago, Chile, and Buenos Aires, Argentina.

From 1950 to 1952, Fuentes was a member of the Mexican delegation to the International Labor Organization in Geneva. Upon his return to Mexico, he became assistant head of the press section of the Ministry of Foreign Affairs in 1954. While he was head of the department of cultural relations at the Ministry of Foreign Affairs (1957-1959), he also founded and edited *Revista mexicana de literatura* (Mexican review of literature). He later edited or coedited the leftist journals *El espectador, Siempre*, and *Política*.

In 1954, Fuentes published his first book, a collection of short stories, entitled *Los días enmascarados* (the masked days). About this time, Fuentes devoted himself to writing full-time—novels, book reviews, political essays, screenplays (for Luis Buñuel, among others), and plays.

La muerte de Artemio Cruz (1962; *The Death of Artemio Cruz*, 1964), a novel which treats the Mexican Revolution and its betrayal in modern Mexican society through the memories of Cruz, as he lies dying, is generally regarded as Fuentes's most successful work and has been translated into fifteen languages. For the next several years, Fuentes lived primarily in Paris. He moved back to Mexico in 1969 and joined with his literary colleague Octavio Paz, among others, in an attempt to challenge the monopoly of Mexico's official political party (the Partido Revolucionario Institucional) and to advocate more responsive democratic governmental structures. From 1975 to 1977, Fuentes served as Mexico's ambassador to France. In 1989, he became president of the Modern Humanities Research Association. Fuentes also became a member of the Mexican National Commission of Human Rights.

ANALYSIS

Fundamentally a realist, Carlos Fuentes's search for the quintessence of Mexican reality often led him to its mythological roots. Yet, for him, Mexico's Aztec, Christian, and revolutionary past is not merely a literary theme but a powerful force to be dealt with when representing contemporary society. The foremost concern of his fiction is the Mexican Revolution and its eventual betrayal, a subject that has earned for him both the hostility of the Mexican establishment and the admiration of new generations looking to him for ideological leadership. The form of this literary

search for Mexico's past has been termed "Magical Realism." Fuentes states that he has "always attempted to perceive behind the spectral appearance of things a more tangible, more solid reality than the obvious everyday reality."

Fuentes began his literary career with a collection of six short stories, *Los días enmascarados*, published in 1954. In this work, the author denounces customs and primitive modes of life that he views as burdensome to modern Mexican life. The stories are fantastical. Like *Aura*, Fuentes's 1962 magical novella about the desire for eternal youth, the stories contain eruptions of the fantastic into everyday life and can be included in the category of Magical Realism.

"CHAC MOOL"

"Chac Mool," the first story in *Los días enmascarados* (and also in a later collection, *Burnt Water*), records the "takeover" of the protagonist, Filiberto, by a statue of the ancient rain god—the Chac Mool—that he had bought at a flea market. The Chac Mool reemerges into the twentieth century, but with this rebirth come old age and presumably death. This story illustrates well the major themes and styles of

Carlos Fuentes

Fuentes's fiction, since it combines the author's penchant for fantasy and joins two periods of time—or, more precisely, it demonstrates how the past continues to be a vital element of the present. The story describes the residual impact of the primitive gods on the subconscious mind of a man who was born of Mexican heritage and who must eventually come to terms with that heritage.

CANTAR DE CIEGOS

The seven stories contained in the volume *Cantar de ciegos*, published in 1964, portray various psychological or social deviations; they are not magical but are often bizarre. In the ten years between the two collections, the development of the writer and artist is significant. Although Fuentes has denied any close connection between these stories and the scriptwriting that he was doing at the time, several of the stories appear to be conceived in cinematic terms. The attitude common to these stories is that modern society is decadent and that the few "decent" individuals encountered are eventually destroyed by this decadence.

The first story, "Las dos Elenas" ("The Two Elenas"), is a subtle study in amorality. It is a triple character sketch constructed around a young wife, the first Elena, her husband, Victor, and her mother, the second Elena. The wife, a very modern young woman, attempts to persuade her husband of the theoretical acceptability of a *ménage á trois* as a way of life. The irony is that the husband is already carrying on an affair with his mother-in-law, the second Elena. The true decadent element is that the wife is naïvely honest in her approach to the problem of marital boredom, while her husband and her mother play the game of adultery furtively, in the age-old dishonest and traditional way. The author seems to imply that so-called modern morality may actually be an innocent sort of naïveté when compared with the old dishonesty. Fuentes's incongruous realism produces a chillingly controlled effect.

"Vieja moralidad" ("The Old Morality"), often considered the most accomplished story of the collection, again echoes the theme of loss and innocence, as it recounts the disruption of an eccentric but happy household by traditionally moral but inwardly corrupt meddlers. The provincial atmosphere, with its moral and sexual hypocrisy, links this story to the novel *Las buenas conciencias* (1959; *The Good Conscience*, 1961). In this story, the presentation is much more straightforward than in "The Two Elenas," and amorality is again seen to be more honest than the "old morality" of the title, although now the old morality is not so much presented as decadent but rather as a form of psychological ignorance. The characters are tortured into perversion and incestuous outlet because of an unreasonable adherence to the old, hypocritical ethics of Mexican Catholicism.

AURA, HOLY PLACE, *and* CUMPLEAÑOS

Aura, Holy Place, and *Cumpleaños* (birthday) are three novellas comprising a trilogy. In the novella *Aura*, Fuentes displays less concern with social criticism than in previous works and makes greater use of bizarre images and fantastic developments. The novella's use of witchcraft and archaic rituals and its defiance of chronological time all contribute to making it one of Fuentes's most fascinating works. Clearly, it is structured around two sets of doubles, Consuelo de Llorente as Aura and Felipe Montero as the long-dead General Llorente. Through her satanic rituals, Consuelo creates a double, an alternative personality, identical to herself when younger, which she controls and through which she has sexual intercourse with Montero. In a more obscure fashion, however, Montero is also a re-creation of the general. In some way, Montero is identical to Llorente, as Aura is to Consuelo.

This amazing identity cannot be attributed to some sort of ritual practice of Consuelo, as is the case with Aura. Although she conducts an erotic ritual that seems to be akin to a black mass, it is never indicated that Felipe has been altered physically. Possibly he is a reincarnation of the general.

The fragmentation of time is one of Fuentes's favorite themes, and something close to reincarnation or at least continuing consciousness across time is a major thread in *Cumpleaños*. There is no real indication, however, of this concept in *Aura*. One critic suggested that *Aura* may be a subjective experience, either a dream or something close to it. Another maintains that the story is narrated by an unreliable narrator as madman. Thus, the doubling in the story is not only a structural device but also a thematic one. *Aura* may be read as the record of one man's delusion.

Holy Place is, in one sense, a series of scenes from a descent into madness, a graphic voyage into hell. There are a number of resemblances to *Aura*. Aside from the doubling technique, particularly significant is the mythic structure, here carried to an extreme degree of complexity, embodying both pre-Hispanic and Greek mythological constructions. Also significant is the characteristic flight from chronological time. In addition, the protean structure of the novel reflects the attempts of the characters to re-create and thus perpetuate themselves through constant change. They seek to defy the corrupting course of chronological time that will lead them inevitably toward decay and death.

One of the chief resemblances to *Aura* is the unreliable narrator, trapped in a destructive Oedipal conflict. His beloved apartment, his sacred place, is something out of a *fin-de-siècle* dream. The protagonist, Mito, is obsessed by incestuous desires, potentially homosexual; he is a sadist as well. Finally, he is reduced to total dissociation as he adopts the role of a dog, completing the sadomasochistic compulsion that animates him. To accept the version of reality offered by Mito is to ignore the fact that he is incapable of anything resembling objective narration. His tale is hopelessly suspect. His vision is of a disturbed world created by his own psyche.

Of the three novellas, *Cumpleaños* is the densest and most difficult. Like *Aura*, the atmosphere is magical, but the narrative does not build toward a climax in the same way. It is rather more fragmented and experimental. A birthday marks the passage of time: The stark one-word title accentuates the work's abstract focus on time without a mitigating social context. The conspicuous absence of "happy," most frequently modifying "birthday," suggests the inexorable rather than the joyful nature of birthdays and reflects the longing for eternal life that appears in the novel. *Cumpleaños* is a total fiction that abandons rational, chronological, or causal progression in favor of a dreamlike multiplication and conflation of times, places, and figures. Contradictions and paradoxes are

often recounted with the dreamer's mixture of acceptance and puzzlement.

Within the narration, which seems to have no clear beginning or end, times are reversed: George the dreamer/narrator sees himself as an old man—and perhaps also as a boy. The labyrinthine house is simultaneously itself, the city of London, and a Jamesean house of fiction. The whole narration, dreamlike as it is, finds itself confirmed, recorded, in the mind of Siger de Brabant, a polemical thirteenth century philosopher. In this novella, Fuentes has constructed narrative analogues for Siger's theses, and, like those theses, whose notions of multiple times and souls were heretical, Fuentes's text with its plurality of times and voices constitutes a kind of narrative heresy.

THE CRYSTAL FRONTIER

Subtitled *A Novel in Nine Stories*, Fuentes's next book is a collection of related stories that focus somewhat nebulously on Don Leonardo Barroso, a sort of Mexican millionaire "Godfather," who symbolizes what Fuentes has called the "scar" of the Mexican/American border. Although the book falls short of the politically complex novel of ideas that Fuentes perhaps intended it to be, it does explore a variety of controversial issues—drug traffic, immigration restrictions, and government corruption—that plague the transparent but inflexible frontier between the two countries.

"A Capital Girl," which many reviewers recognize as the strongest story in the collection, focuses on Don Barroso's ruthlessness in getting what he wants, even to the extent of grooming his beautiful young goddaughter to be the wife of his bookish son so that Barroso himself can have her as a lover. Other stories deal with more political issues, such as factory workers on the border, the importing of cheap labor into the United States, and blacklisted union organizers. In some of these "issue" stories, Fuentes's effort to create a political novel that criticizes both Mexican and American officials, who ignore the real lives of ordinary people, often leads him to didactic excesses, stick-figure stereotypes, and stilted dialogue.

Two stories have been singled out for praise by critics. "Pain" is about a young medical student, Juan

Zamora, for whom Barroso has provided a scholarship to Cornell. While there, Juan, whose homosexuality makes him feel doubly alienated, pretends to be rich for his American hosts, who have no idea of the poverty in Mexico. The title story, "Crystal Frontier," focuses on Lisandro Chavez, a young man from Mexico City who is brought to New York to work as a janitor. To manifest the "crystal frontier" between Mexico and America, Fuentes creates a delicate scene in which Chavez, while washing windows at a Manhattan skyscraper, sees Audrey, an advertising executive, catching up on work alone. After communicating through the window by pantomime, they put their lips to the glass: "Both closed their eyes. She didn't open hers for several minutes. When she did, he was no longer there."

The final "chapter" in the collection is Fuentes's lyrical attempt to pull the various strands of the stories together by presenting a poetic summary of Mexican history, situating himself within the story in the persona of Jose Francisco, a writer stopped by Mexican and American guards for taking literature across the border. The resultant image is a central metaphor for Fuentes's efforts to create a cultural meeting point between two nations:

> The manuscripts began to fly, lifted by the night breeze like paper doves able to fly for themselves. They . . . went flying from the bridge into the gringo sky, from the bridge to the Mexican sky . . . and Jose Francisco gave a victory shout that forever broke the crystal of the frontier.

OTHER MAJOR WORKS

LONG FICTION: *Las región más transparente*, 1958 (*Where the Air Is Clear*, 1960); *Las buenas conciencias*, 1959 (*The Good Conscience*, 1961); *La muerte de Artemio Cruz*, 1962 (*The Death of Artemio Cruz*, 1964); *Cambio de piel*, 1967 (*A Change of Skin*, 1968); *Terra nostra*, 1975 (English translation, 1976); *La cabeza de hidra*, 1978 (*The Hydra Head*, 1978); *Una familia lejana*, 1980 (*Distant Relations*, 1982); *Gringo viejo*, 1985 (*The Old Gringo*, 1985); *Cristóbal nonato*, 1987 (*Christopher Unborn*, 1989); *La Campaña*, 1990 (*The Campaign*, 1991; first volume of trilogy *El tiempo romántico*); *Diana: O, La*

Cazadora Solitaria, 1994 (*Diana, the Goddess Who Hunts Alone*, 1995); *Los años con Laura Díaz*, 1999 (*The Years with Laura Díaz*, 2000).

PLAYS: *Todos los gatos son pardos*, pb. 1970; *El tuerto es rey*, pb. 1970; *Orquídeas a la luz de la luna*, pb. 1982 (*Orchids in the Moonlight*, 1982); *Ceremonias del alba*, rev. ed. pb. 1991.

SCREENPLAYS: *El acoso*, 1958 (an adaptation of Alejo Carpentier's *El acoso*, with Luis Buñuel); *Children of Sanchez*, 1961 (an adaptation of Oscar Lewis's *Children of Sanchez*, with Abby Mann); *Pedro Páramo*, 1966; *Tiempo de morir*, 1966; *Los caifanes*, 1967.

NONFICTION: *The Argument of Latin America: Words for North Americans*, 1963; *Paris: La revolución de mayo*, 1968; *La nueva novela hispanoamericana*, 1969; *El mundo de José Luis Cuevas*, 1969; *Casa con dos puertas*, 1970; *Tiempo mexicano*, 1971; *Cervantes: O, La crítica de la lectura*, 1976 (*Don Quixote: Or, The Critique of Reading*, 1976); *Myself with Others: Selected Essays*, 1988; *Valiente mundo nuevo: Épica, utopía y mito en la novela*, 1990; *El espejo enterrado*, 1992 (*The Buried Mirror: Reflections on Spain and the New World*, 1992); *Geografia de la novela*, 1993; *Tres discursos para dos aldeas*, 1993; *Nuevo tiempo mexicano*, 1994.

BIBLIOGRAPHY

Brody, Robert, and Charles Rossman, eds. *Carlos Fuentes: A Critical View*. Austin: University of Texas Press, 1982. This well-written collection of essays takes various critical approaches to Fuentes's major works of prose, drama, and literary criticism. The work also includes bibliographical references and a chronology.

Brushwood, John S. *Mexico in Its Novel*. Austin: University of Texas Press, 1966. This book takes account of a nation's search for identity through an examination of its fiction. The section devoted to Fuentes discusses the author's major works (published before 1966). Brushwood underscores Fuentes's belief that Mexico has accepted realities that prevent the realization of its potential. Contains a chronological list of Mexican novels and a select bibliography.

Duran, Gloria. *The Archetypes of Carlos Fuentes: From Witch to Androgyne*. Hamden, Conn.: Archon Books, 1980. The first work in English to deal exclusively with the body of Fuentes's novels that have been translated into English. Duran maintains that an examination of the place of witchcraft and occultism is critical to an understanding of Fuentes's work as a whole. Contains biographical data, an appendix, and a bibliography.

Fainaru, Steve. "Poisoned Pen." *The Boston Globe*, November 4, 1997, p. E1. A detailed account of the bitter feud between Fuentes and Octavio Paz; discusses the origin of the feud in the 1980's over an attack on Fuentes that Paz allowed to be published in a journal he helped establish.

Faris, Wendy B. *Carlos Fuentes*. New York: Frederick Ungar, 1983. Faris's book offers both biographical information and an insightful critical assessment of Fuentes's early novels, short fiction, and plays. Complemented by a useful bibliography, a chronology, and an index.

Guzmán, Daniel de. *Carlos Fuentes*. New York: Twayne, 1972. The author provides a brief but insightful view on the historical context (specifically, the Mexican Revolution) of Fuentes's fiction. Guzman's book also includes a select bibliography, an appraisal of the author's works, a historical and sociocultural background, and a chronology of Fuentes's works.

Helmuth, Chalene. *The Postmodern Fuentes*. Lewisburg, Penn.: Bucknell University Press, 1997. Studies the postmodern features in Fuentes's novelistic production, particularly since 1975. According to Helmuth, the postmodern novels hold a nonmimetic view of the textual representation of reality, which becomes evident when considering the continual reminders of the artificial nature of the written word that Fuentes scattered in his later narratives.

Ibsen, Kristine. *Author, Text, and Reader in the Novels of Carlos Fuentes*. New York: Peter Lang, 1993. A reader-oriented analysis of four major novels: *A Change of Skin*, *Terra Nostra*, *Distant Relations*, and *Christopher Unborn*.

O'Connor, Anne-Marie. "The Sum of Unequal Parts." *Los Angeles Times*, October 24, 1997. An extended discussion, based on an interview with Fuentes, of his treatment of the border between Mexico and the United States in his *The Crystal Frontier*. Fuentes talks of Latin American writers and intellectuals, criticizes the news media for ignoring the plight of the poor, and comments on his efforts to reflect the changes that have taken place in Mexican society.

Van Delden, Maarten. *Carlos Fuentes, México and Modernity*. Nashville, Tenn.: Vanderbilt University Press, 1998. Analyzes the ongoing tension in Fuentes's works between nationalism and cosmopolitanism, which stands in a complex relationship to the problem of Latin American modernization.

Weiss, Jason. "At the Frontier." Review of *The Crystal Frontier*, by Carlos Fuentes. *The Boston Globe*, November 16, 1997, p. L1. A review of Fuentes's collection, praising especially "Rio Grande, Rio Bravo"; criticizes the frequent didactic message in many of the stories.

Williams, Raymond Leslie. *The Writings of Carlos Fuentes*. Austin: University of Texas Press, 1996. Considering *Terra Nostra* a keystone in Fuentes's narrative production, the author maintains that the early novels contained all major themes and topics later developed by the writer and, by the same token, that the later novels are reworkings and expansions of many of the motifs found in Fuentes's masterpiece.

Genevieve Slomski,
updated by Charles E. May

G

ERNEST J. GAINES

Born: Oscar, Louisiana; January 15, 1933

PRINCIPAL SHORT FICTION
Bloodline, 1968
A Long Day in November, 1971

OTHER LITERARY FORMS

Aside from his short fiction, Ernest J. Gaines published several novels, including *Of Love and Dust* (1967), *The Autobiography of Miss Jane Pittman* (1971), *In My Father's House* (1978), *A Gathering of Old Men* (1983), and *A Lesson Before Dying* (1993).

ACHIEVEMENTS

Ernest J. Gaines won the Joseph Henry Jackson Award of the San Francisco Foundation in 1959 for the short story "Comeback." He received a Rockefeller Foundation grant (1970), a John Simon Guggenheim Memorial Foundation Fellowship (1971), and a John D. and Catherine T. MacArthur Foundation Fellowship (1993). The Commonwealth Club of California honored him with the fiction gold medal in 1972, for *The Autobiography of Miss Jane Pittman*, and in 1984, for *A Gathering of Old Men* (1983). Gaines also won the American Academy of Arts and Letters literary award in 1987 and the National Book Critics Circle Award in 1993, for *A Lesson Before Dying*, which was nominated for a Pulitzer Prize. A few of Gaines's novels, including *The Autobiography of Miss Jane Pittman*, *A Gathering of Old Men*, and *A Lesson Before Dying*, were turned into made-for-television movies, and "The Sky Is Gray," a short story, was dramatized for the Public Broadcasting Service short-story series.

BIOGRAPHY

As a boy, Ernest James Gaines lived in rural Louisiana, where he often worked in the fields. At the age of fifteen he moved to Vallejo, California, to live with his mother and stepfather. In 1955, after his release from the Army, he entered San Francisco State College, from which he graduated in 1957. In 1958 two of his stories helped him win a Wallace Stegner Creative Writing Fellowship for graduate study at Stanford University. After 1966, when he received a grant from the National Endowment for the Arts, Gaines garnered many awards and honors, especially in the wake of the 1974 television version of *The Autobiography of Miss Jane Pittman*. He also enjoyed a successful career as lecturer and teacher, working at Stanford, California's Whittier College, and the University of Southwestern Louisiana in Lafayette. He married for the first time at age sixty.

ANALYSIS

Strongly influenced by the folkways of rural Louisiana, Ernest J. Gaines's narratives all reflect a cultural heritage enriched by a strong oral tradition. Although his fiction's main focus is on the African American community, the author's work also reflects the cultural diversity of his native parish, Pointe Coupee, by Creoles, Cajuns, and Anglo-American entrepreneurs, overseers, and law officials. Among Gaines's acknowledged literary mentors are the nineteenth century Russian masters, for their treatment of peasantry; Ernest Hemingway, for his understatement and "grace under pressure" theme; and William Faulkner, for his mastery of locale and the oral narrative.

BLOODLINE

Gaines, although popular, is a very serious and methodical writer. He works very hard to fashion a distinct voice richly imbued with its unique traditions. He also spins compelling stories, which are collected in the single volume *Bloodline*, first published in 1968. *Bloodline* contains five long stories, all of which deal with a place and a people Gaines expresses so fully and so vividly that they are recognized as his own exclusive fictional property: the southern black communities living on a stretch of low-lying cotton and sugarcane country between the Atchafalaya and Mississippi Rivers, west and northwest of Baton Rouge. Setting is a central force in Gaines's work, and his fiction often focuses on this distinctive Louisiana region.

All the stories in *Bloodline* take place in and around the fictional town of Bayonne, a small country town not too far from the actual city of Baton Rouge. The lives of Gaines's men and women are shaped by fields, dirt roads, plantation quarters, and the natural elements of dust, heat, and rain. Whatever the differences among his characters—he has a rich diversity of race and culture to work with—the Cajun sharecroppers, the black tenants, and the white plantation owners all consider the soil and the crops part of their daily weather. Bayonne and the surrounding countryside provide local and cultural unity for the stories in *Bloodline*.

Ernest J. Gaines (©Jerry Bauer)

Equally important to the unity of *Bloodline* is the way the stories are presented. All of them are written in the form of oral narratives told by the characters in their own words. The first four stories are told by individual African Americans who participate in or are deeply affected by the stories they tell. The tellers range in age from the six-year-old boy of "A Long Day in November" to a seventy-year-old man in the title story. The final story, "Just Like a Tree," is told by a group of relatives and friends, each in turn, as they attend the leave-taking ceremonies surrounding Aunt Fe, an old black woman who has been invited North to escape white reprisals against the Civil Rights movement. In all these stories the sound of individual voices rings out clearly and convincingly. Gaines has a keen, sure ear for his native speech patterns and recognizes the power of language in a predominantly oral culture to assert, affirm, and keep hold of personal and collective values. His stories deliberately call attention to the special virtues of the spoken word as a rich storehouse capable of keeping alive an otherwise impoverished community.

There is, however, a deeper unifying force to the stories than a common setting, race, and dependence on the spoken word. It consists of the movement of the stories through individual lives toward a sort of communal consciousness. There is a hint of this movement in the successive voices of the five stories. The first two are accounts of two young boys, the third of a young man in jail, the fourth of an old man of seventy, and the fifth of a household of friends, relatives, and one stranger. *Bloodline* begins with the private experience of a little boy and ends with a public event that affects the entire community.

The impression of development is strengthened by the recurrence in each story of one of Gaines's major themes, the impact of personal and communal codes of honor colliding with various forms of hostility, especially, in the last four stories, the discrimination, injustice, and violence the African American faced in the segregated South. This is not to imply that polemics or ideologies ever prevail over character in Gaines's stories. What interests him first and foremost is black experience, and some of his best writing centers on the lives and relationships of southern blacks within their own community, with sometimes little direct reference at all to the world of the whites around them. Inasmuch as discrimination and the crimes of segregation were an inescapable fact of southern black experience, the world Gaines describes is always—overtly or not—conditioned by the tensions of racial claims. In *Bloodline*, the questions raised by such claims become progressively more insistent, and the stories themselves roughly follow the chronology of the changing mood among blacks in modern times. Specific dates are not mentioned, but the stories obviously stretch back to the 1940's rural South of "A Long Day in November" up to the 1960's Civil Rights movement in Louisiana alluded to in the last story, "Just Like a Tree."

"A Long Day in November"

In the first story, "A Long Day in November," there are no direct references to racial struggles. It is a long tale told in the voice of a six-year-old boy, Sonny, whose world is suddenly shattered by the separation of his parents. His mother, Amy, leaves her husband, Eddie, because she feels he has become overenthusiastic about his car to the point of neglecting his family. She takes Sonny to her mother's house, and the remainder of the story charts Eddie's unsuccessful attempts to bring his wife home. Finally, on the advice of the local Voodoo woman, Madame Toussaint, Eddie burns his car publicly, and Sonny and Amy return home. For the entire story, Sonny does not act; he observes and suffers. He sees the world in terms of basic feelings—warmth, cold, hope, fear—and desires simply that his disrupted world be restored. The story ends where it began, with Sonny in bed, snug and safe under the blankets, only this time the night is not disturbed by his mother's calls or crying. Instead, Sonny is rocked to sleep by the sound of the springs in his parents' bed.

Gaines is a master at re-creating the words and sensations of children, and one of his main concerns in "A Long Day in November" is to contrast Sonny's simple, innocent needs of love and security with the complex world of adult conflicts. Neither his parents nor his grandmother seems to offer him what he needs most. His mother has become hard and bitter, and his father, more gentle, shows a weak streak and

tends to use Sonny to win back his wife. The grandmother's irritability may be comic for the reader, but for Sonny she is the most hateful person in his life, rough spoken, harsh, and complaining. She is the one person Sonny would most like to be free of: "Lord knows I get tired of Gran'mon fussing all the time." The main character in the story, however, is Sonny's mother. She may be harsh and bitter, but she has forged for herself a code of personal behavior that finally brings her family into a new relationship. She forces the change at a great cost, especially in regards to her son.

One important feature of "A Long Day in November" is the presence of a well-defined community—the schoolteacher, the preacher, the schoolchildren, the Voodoo woman, Eddie's friends, and Amy's relatives—where conflict and separation may occur, but whose shared assumptions are not questioned. Increasingly, as the stories progress, not only individual codes but also communal values are brought under pressure.

"The Sky Is Gray"

The second story in *Bloodline*, "The Sky Is Gray," is also narrated by a small boy. One of the most successful stories in the volume, it consists of thirteen episodes spanning the day James, eight years old, goes with his mother to a dentist in Bayonne. Like Sonny in "A Long Day in November," James suffers more than he acts, but already, even at eight years old, he is beginning to adopt the code of stoic pride his mother is constantly encouraging. His world is even bleaker than Sonny's. His father has been called into the Army, and his mother is left with three children and great poverty. Throughout the story, her hard words and harsh judgments must be measured against the fact that she has been placed in a situation in which mere survival is not always certain. She feels compelled to teach her oldest son how to take care of his family and to survive with dignity as a man.

While waiting in the dentist's office, James watches a young, educated African American argue with an older man who looks to James like a preacher. The young black has no faith in religion but reacts in such an extreme, self-confident way that he challenges their religious beliefs. Still, when he is hit by the "preacher," a man who maintains that no questions at all should be asked about God or traditional beliefs, it is the young man who wins the admiration of James: "When I grow up I want be just like him. I want clothes like that and I want keep a book with me, too."

The point seems to be that given the extent of black suffering, most reactions tend to assume extreme, absolute forms that destroy man's full nature. The preacher is at once too submissive and too aggressive; the young man asserts his right to disbelieve but is unable to make sense out of his contradictory certitudes; and James's mother so overemphasizes stoic resistance that, in a later episode, she is incapable of compromising her rigid pride even when it means a meal for her son. Fortunately, the white lady who offers the meal knows exactly how to circumvent such pride so that natural help is not construed as demeaning charity. Such generosity has been too rare in the past, however, even among her fellow blacks, and the mother's attitude remains unchanged. At first, the story as a whole seems to reveal a world where gentleness and love and flexibility have no place: "The sleet's coming down heavy, heavy now, and I turn up my coat collar to keep my neck warm. My mama tells me to turn it right back down. 'You not a bum,' she says. 'You a man.'" James nevertheless knows that his mother loves her children and that they love her.

"Three Men"

The third story, "Three Men," may have been placed at the center of the collection as a sort of hub toward which the first two stories approach and around which the whole book swings to return to the traditional rural society of the final stories, still rural and traditional, but now in the new context of the Civil Rights movement. Certainly it is the only story in which the central character undergoes anything resembling a change of heart or self-discovery.

Again, like the other stories, "Three Men" centers on a personal code of honor, this time specifically related to racial domination. A nineteen-year-old youth, Proctor Lewis, turns himself in to the law in Bayonne after stabbing another man in a fight over a girl. The

story takes place in jail where his cellmates, an old convict, Munford, and a homosexual, Hattie, argue with each other and talk to Proctor. Munford, full of hate for a society based on racial stereotypes, hates himself for allowing his life to gratify the expectations of those same stereotypes. Recalling the way his own past has swung back and forth between fights and jail, he poses the dilemma of the story: whether Proctor should choose to get out of jail by accepting the bond he initially hopes the white plantation owner will pay, or whether he should stay in jail, suffer the certain beating of the guards, and eventually go to the state penitentiary. Munford claims that the latter choice is the only way for Proctor to keep his manhood, something both Munford and Hattie have surrendered.

As the story ends, Proctor has almost made up his mind to refuse the bond and to abide by the code Munford has described. Although he is finally not sure if he can stand by his decision, a shift of attitude has been made, and the right questions have been clearly articulated. "Three Men" looks back to the seemingly fatalistic rounds of poverty, frustration, and rigid codes of the first two stories and anticipates the last two stories, in which individual acts of self-affirmation seem to offer something more than mere stoic resistance.

"Bloodline"

The last two stories are best treated together, since they both return to the rural world of the plantation suddenly introduced to the rising violence of black activism. "Bloodline," the title story of the collection, raises the old southern problem of mixed blood, but in a new context, the "postsegregation" South. The story is told by a seventy-year-old African American, Felix, who works for the plantation's present owner, Walter Laurent. Copper, the half-white illegitimate son of Laurent's dead brother, has returned to the plantation seeking what he considers his birthright, the land on which his "father" raped his mother. He calls himself the General and refuses to go through the back door of the plantation house to meet his uncle. Finally, after Copper has thwarted all attempts by Laurent to force him through the back door, Laurent relents and goes to meet him. Their meeting symbolizes the old order making way for the new. Laurent does not change his mind about the old rules; he simply stops applying them for a time. Copper represents the transformation that will eventually change the caste system of white over black and rewrite the rules Laurent is constantly talking about: "I didn't write the rules, and I won't try to change them."

The old men, Walter and Felix, are clearly part of the old order, but Gaines is careful to show how they both, especially Felix, manage to retain their individual dignity even though bound to the established tradition. There is a give and take between "master" and "servant" common to men who speak the same language, know the same people, and who have lived near each other all their lives. From this perspective, Copper comes back to his birthplace as an outsider, isolated from the rest of the blacks, whom he considers childlike lackeys. He embodies the same sort of absoluteness and aloofness represented earlier by the young man in the dentist's office in "The Sky Is Gray," but he also embodies the necessary wave of change that will eventually sweep through the plantation, a change whose consequences are already being felt in the final story, "Just Like a Tree."

"JUST LIKE A TREE"

"Just Like a Tree" revolves around Aunt Fe, an old black woman who is being taken North to escape the violence that has begun on the plantation. A young man, Emmanuel, has begun working for change, and in retaliation a tenant house has been bombed and a woman and her two children killed. More than any other story in the collection, "Just Like a Tree" affirms the force of the community. The only outsider, an African American from the North, is clearly alien to the shared assumptions and beliefs of the others. He speaks a different "language"; he sets himself apart by his loud manners, his condescension, and his lack of feeling. The other people gathered in the house, even the white lady who has walked to the house to say good-bye, form a whole, united by shared speech and shared feelings. The ceremony itself of farewell, and the narrative mode of the story— told in turn by several of the visitors—affirm the strong communal bonds of rural black society. Unlike the young man in "The Sky Is Gray" or the General in "Bloodline," Emmanuel belongs to the community

even as he acts to change the old ways. He is a type of activist represented best in Gaines's work by Jimmy in *The Autobiography of Miss Jane Pittman.*

Aunt Fe's longtime presence in the community, her having touched, in some loving way, every member of the community, and her impending removal to the North provide clues to the tree symbolism of the story's title: Like a great, old, shade tree she has protected and sheltered other living creatures, and her departure will leave a spiritual hole in the life of the community, like the hole that the removal, roots and all, of a large tree will leave in a meadow. Aunt Clo predicts that Aunt Fe will die when she is "transplanted" to the North. The personal diaspora being forced upon Aunt Fe also represents the mass diasporas suffered by African Americans through the centuries.

The story and the book end with Aunt Fe's death. She has refused to be moved, and once again the strong vital roots of individual pride show their strength. The difference is that Aunt Fe's pride affirms its strength within the community, not in aloof isolation from it. In terms of *Bloodline* as a whole, "Just Like a Tree" offers the conclusion that change must involve sacrifice, but that change must take place. The farewell ceremony and Aunt Fe's death also offer the reminder that the traditional community had values that the new order can deny only at its own peril and loss.

The stories of *Bloodline* illustrate two other major themes in Gaines's writing. First, there is the presence and influence of strong female figures such as Octavia, Aunt Fe, and Amy, who are, in various ways, early prototypes of such heroines as Miss Jane Pittman in Gaines's later fiction. Manhood becomes a significant achievement for several male characters in *Bloodline*—James, Eddie, and Proctor—who anticipate even larger treatment of the male-maturation theme in Gaines's novels from *The Autobiography of Miss Jane Pittman* through *A Lesson Before Dying,* one of his most powerful works.

OTHER MAJOR WORKS

LONG FICTION: *Catherine Carmier,* 1964; *Of Love and Dust,* 1967; *The Autobiography of Miss Jane*

Pittman, 1971; *In My Father's House*, 1978; *A Gathering of Old Men*, 1983; *A Lesson Before Dying*, 1993.

MISCELLANEOUS: *Porch Talk with Ernest Gaines*, 1990.

BIBLIOGRAPHY

Babb, Valerie Melissa. *Ernest Gaines*. Boston: Twayne, 1991. A solid introduction to the author and his works. Includes a bibliography and an index.

Burke, William. "*Bloodline:* A Man's Black South." *College Language Association Journal* 19 (1976): 545-558. This study centers on the design of the five stories in *Bloodline* and argues that they are a coherent record of changing race relations prompted by the African American male's recovery of his masculinity.

Gaines, Ernest J., Marcia G. Gaudet, and Carl Wooton. *Porch Talk with Ernest Gaines: Conversations on the Writer's Craft*. Baton Rouge: Louisiana State University Press, 1990. A transcription of an intimate interview conducted by colleagues of Gaines, this work offers an insightful look at how the author has transmuted his Louisiana heritage, familial experiences, literary influences, and strong folk tradition into fiction with a distinct voice.

Jones, Suzanne W. "New Narratives of Southern Manhood: Race, Masculinity, and Closure in Ernest Gaines's Fiction." *Critical Survey* 9 (1997): 15-42. Discusses Gaines's deconstruction of stereotypes and presentation of new models of black and white southern manhood. Asserts that Gaines suggests that in order to reconstruct the South, black and white men must reject the traditional Western model of manhood that links masculinity and violence.

Lowe, John, ed. *Conversations with Ernest Gaines*. Jackson: University Press of Mississippi, 1995. A selection of interviews in which Gaines speaks about his life, his themes, and his works. Includes and index and chronology of his life.

Magnier, Bernard. "Ernest J. Gaines." *The UNESCO Courier* 48 (April, 1995): 5-7. In this interview, Gaines discusses his childhood and family background, the books that most influenced him, his feelings about Africa, and other topics.

Papa, Lee. "'His Feet on Your Neck': The New Religion in the Works of Ernest J. Gaines." *African American Review* 27 (Summer, 1993): 187-193. Claims that Gaines is concerned with characters who must make a personal test of religion, not accept it as imposed by institutional Christianity.

Peterson, V. R. "Ernest Gaines: Writing About the Past." *Essence* 24 (August, 1993): 52. A brief biographical sketch that discusses Gaines's background, his typical themes, and the development of his writing career.

Shelton, Frank W. "Ambiguous Manhood in Ernest J. Gaines' *Bloodline*." *College Language Association Journal* 19 (1975): 200-209. Shelton notes that although the African American males in Gaines's stories strive for manhood and dignity, they are only partially successful in their quests.

Simpson, Anne K. *A Gathering of Gaines: The Man and the Writer*. Lafayette: Center for Louisiana Studies at the University of Southwestern Louisiana, 1991. Simpson's study, well documented with excerpts from Gaines's personal papers, offers a biographical sketch, an examination of his stylistic influences and characteristics, and a critical overview of his fiction. It includes an unannotated but thorough bibliography.

Ben Forkner,
updated by John W. Fiero and Philip A. Tapley

MARY GAITSKILL

Born: Lexington, Kentucky; November 11, 1954

PRINCIPAL SHORT FICTION
Bad Behavior, 1988
Because They Wanted To, 1997

OTHER LITERARY FORMS

Mary Gaitskill published her first novel, *Two Girls, Fat and Thin*, in 1991. She has published articles, especially on feminist issues, in major magazines, most notably her essay, "On Not Being a Victim: Sex, Rape, and the Trouble with Following Rules," in *Harper's Magazine* (1994).

ACHIEVEMENTS

In 1981 Mary Gaitskill received the Jule and Avery Hopwood Award from the University of Michigan for "The Woman Who Knew Judo and Other Stories." Her story "The Nice Restaurant" was anthologized in *Nothing But You: Love Stories from "The New Yorker."* Gaitskill was nominated for the 1998 PEN/Faulkner Award for Fiction.

BIOGRAPHY

Mary Gaitskill was born in Lexington, Kentucky, on November 11, 1954. Her mother, Dorothy Jane Gaitskill (née Mayer), was a social worker and homemaker; her father, Lawrence Russell, was a teacher. She grew up in Livonia and Northville, suburbs of Detroit, Michigan, in a home environment that she once described in an interview as "a whole huge mess." At age sixteen Gaitskill ran away from home and became, among other things, a stripper. She lived in Toronto for a few years and later returned to Michigan to attended the University of Michigan as a journalism student. After she received her B.A. in 1981 and won her first adult award for her fiction, she moved to New York and worked on her first collection of short stories, *Bad Behavior*, until it was published in 1988. In 1991 she published *Two Girls, Fat and Thin*, her first novel. Gaitskill has spent time in mental institutions and for a while bounced back and

forth between her New York home and her much quieter home in Marin County, California, before settling in San Francisco. In 1997 she published her second collection of short stories, *Because They Wanted To*.

ANALYSIS

In his 1997 review of *Because They Wanted To*, Craig Seligman compared Mary Gaitskill's writings favorably with those of Flannery O'Connor. The driving forces behind most of Mary Gaitskill's characters are the need for self-understanding and the need to connect with other people, both of which are irrevocably linked as each character fights for identity. Most of the characters in Gaitskill's first collection of stories, *Bad Behavior*, share one huge problem: Each of them tries desperately to cling to the wrong person. Sometimes this seeming mistake leads a character closer to self-discovery, but, as often as not, it leads to that simplest of literary ironies where the reader can clearly see what the character cannot. The motivation of the characters in Gaitskill's second collection, *Because They Wanted To*, is essentially escape from a past they feel defines them in a way they cannot fully accept. Both collections are filled with what might be called "weird" sex (prostitution, sadomasochism, rapes, gang bangs, date rapes, fetishes, role playing) often in very graphic detail, but the stories are less about sex than they are about the opportunity for connection, escape from isolation, and feelings of alienation. Even when the opportunities are missed—as they usually are—the characters and the story are enriched by revelations. The major difference in the two collections of stories is maturity. As should be expected, the more recent stories show a more stylistically even hand. The message most consistently delivered in both books is that separation and isolation are often necessary, even desirable.

"DAISY'S VALENTINE"

"Daisy's Valentine" showcases three characters, none of whom has any hope of ever being in a normal, enduring relationship. Joey, a delusional, epileptic speed freak, lives with Diane, a paranoid, epileptic speed freak living on government checks. When Diane learns that Joey has slept with a character named Daisy, she attacks him, rips out his earring, and throws him out of their apartment. Joey thinks he is falling in love with Daisy, a poster child for the insanely insecure, who works with him at a bookstore. Daisy lives with an abusive man, the only kind of man she thinks she can love. Joey spends much of his time daydreaming about rescuing Daisy from muggers, terrorists, and natural disasters. The heart of this story is in the disparities between how each character interprets his or her own motivations, how each of the other characters views them, and the impressions their actions and reactions leave on the reader. One major accomplishment of this story is that Gaitskill makes the reader care about people who are otherwise very hard to care about.

"SOMETHING NICE"

"Something Nice" is one of the few Gaitskill stories in which the leading male character is not a clear-cut villain. This is a story filled with ironies, the greatest of which is that readers see some of this man's better qualities through an affair he has with a prostitute while his wife is out of town. After his first visit with the prostitute, he becomes so enamored of her that he comes back every night, except for one he takes off so she will not get bored with him. She is different from any prostitute he has ever seen. He offers her five hundred dollars to take a night off from the escort service and spend it with him alone—a night on the town with dinner and a movie that he has arranged for the night before his wife returns. The prostitute stands him up, and when he calls the escort service to set up an appointment, he is told that she no longer works for them. Almost a year later, he sees her in a restaurant with a young man and learns by eavesdropping on them that her job in a museum may be in jeopardy and that she may have to "survive on free-lance work."

"TINY, SMILING DADDY"

Stew, the father in "Tiny, Smiling Daddy," and his daughter Kitty suffer from a malady common to many of Gaitskill's characters: the need to understand each other in the face of facts and circumstances that make communication with each other all but impossible. Both are products of their generations and victims of the chasm that separates them, but the larger part of the blame for their inability to reach each other rests on Stew. He cannot understand that her changes in behavior, her rebelliousness, and her frequent need for time alone are part of her growing up. The most visible problem is that he cannot accept that his daughter is a lesbian. At the beginning of the story, he is awakened from a dreamy afternoon nap and sent into a panic by a phone call from a friend informing him that the latest issue of the magazine *Self* contains an article "that Kitty wrote about fathers and daughters talking to each other." While waiting for his wife to come home with their only car so he can go get a copy of the magazine, he broods over confrontations that he and Kitty had as she was growing up and recalls with great pain the miserable ways his father treated him as a child, but he never seems to make the connection.

"BECAUSE THEY WANTED TO"

"Because They Wanted To" is the story of a girl's maturation that fails to happen because there has been no mature, nurturing person in her life. Elise is a sixteen-year-old runaway, trying to escape a home made unbearable by an incestuous relationship with her brother. She lies about her age so she can hitch a ride across the Canadian border with a couple of horsemen who curse her and chase her off when they find out how young she is. In Vancouver, she panhandles for food money and shares housing with Mark, another runaway. She answers an ad for a baby-sitting job, and the woman who placed the ad, Robin, asks if she will watch her kids while she looks for a job, promising to pay her out of her first paycheck. Desperate for money, Elise agrees to take the job and to wait for her pay. Robin promises to be back home by six. Elise is a wreck long before six, and as it gets later and later, she loses patience and finally tells a man who lives downstairs that she has to leave. As she walks by the house the next morning, she sees that the window she left open is still open, a metaphor for her past and possible future.

"THE GIRL ON THE PLANE"

As in many of her stories, one of the main themes

in Gaitskill's "The Girl on the Plane" is the seeming impossibility of objectively defining "consensual sex." On a flight to Cincinnati, a man sits next to a woman who, after a bit of scrutiny, reminds him of a girl who had a crush on him in college. The girl on the plane reveals to him, in the spirit of Alcoholics Anonymous, that she has had problems with alcoholism, and he confesses to her that once the college girl with the crush became drunk at a party and willingly had sex with most of the men at the party, including him. This game of "true confessions" continues until he says to her, "If you want to talk about mistakes . . . I raped somebody. Somebody I liked." Instantly, her entire demeanor changes. She wrestles her hand away from his and says, "Don't touch me again." In spite of all his attempts to explain that it was not really rape—"it was complicated"—she throws up an impenetrable wall. When the plane lands he tries to follow her and explain, but she butts her way past him and never looks back.

OTHER MAJOR WORKS

LONG FICTION: *Two Girls, Fat and Thin*, 1991.

BIBLIOGRAPHY

Contemporary Literary Criticism 69: 198-209. Contains a comprehensive collection of reviews of the stories in *Bad Behavior* from Michiko Kakutani, Barry Walters, George Garrett, Carol Anshaw, and many more. Especially interesting is Regina Weinreich's explanation of how Gaitskill, inspired in her youth by *Playboy* cartoons, aspired to become a prostitute and how that experience later leaked into her fiction.

Gaitskill, Mary. "On Not Being a Victim: Sex, Rape, and the Trouble with Following Rules." *Harper's Magazine* (March, 1994): 35-44. Gaitskill gives straightforward accounts of times when she has been raped and explanations of other experiences in her life that have led to examinations and explorations of definitions of "rape," "date rape," "consensual sex," and similar terms that play major parts in several of her stories, including "The Blanket," "The Girl on the Plane," and "The Nice Restaurant." She provides in-depth analysis of how she evolved from a very "politically correct" feminist to an individual thinker and writer more concerned with personal responsibility and trying to understand what things really motivate her characters and the characters of other writers.

Graff, E. J. "Mixed Emotions." *Women's Review of Books* 14 (May, 1997): 8-9. Review of several stories from *Because They Wanted To*, critical comments on *Bad Behavior*, and comparisons of the works of Gaitskill with work by Amy Bloom. Both authors use sex as a dramatic tool in their writing. Both write fiction that has been categorized as "postqueer."

Edmund August

MAVIS GALLANT

Born: Montreal, Canada; August 11, 1922

PRINCIPAL SHORT FICTION

The Other Paris, 1956

My Heart Is Broken: Eight Stories and a Short Novel, 1964 (pb. in England as *An Unmarried Man's Summer*, 1965)

The Pegnitz Junction: A Novella and Five Short Stories, 1973

The End of the World and Other Stories, 1974

From the Fifteenth District: A Novella and Eight Short Stories, 1979

Home Truths: Selected Canadian Stories, 1981

Overhead in a Balloon, 1985

In Transit, 1988

Across the Bridge, 1993

The Moslem Wife and Other Stories, 1994

The Collected Stories of Mavis Gallant, 1996

OTHER LITERARY FORMS

A journalist and essayist as well as a writer of fiction, Mavis Gallant has chronicled various social and historical events, such as the case of Gabrielle Russier, a young high school teacher in Marseille, who was driven to suicide by persecution for having become romantically involved with one of her students. *Paris Notebooks: Essays and Reviews* (1986) is a collection of essays in which Gallant offers observations relating to her many years spent in France, scrutinizing French culture and life in general. Her accounts of the student revolt of 1968 are particularly riveting.

In addition, Gallant wrote *The War Brides* (1978), a collection of biographical articles, and the play *What Is to Be Done?* (pr. 1982), a drama about two young women who idealize communism. Her essays, articles, and reviews have appeared regularly in *The New Yorker*, *The New York Times Book Review*, *The New Republic*, *The New York Review of Books*, and *The Times Literary Supplement*.

ACHIEVEMENTS

Mavis Gallant's stature as a writer of short fiction is unsurpassed. The elegant simplicity of her pieces is an unchanging trait of her work and was in fact recognized in her first published piece, "Madeleine's Birthday," for which *The New Yorker* paid six hundred dollars in 1951. In 1981, Gallant was awarded Canada's Governor-General's Literary Award for fiction for *Home Truths*. Other awards include the Canadian Fiction Prize (1978), Officer of the Order of Canada (1981), and honorary doctorates from the University of Saint Anne, Nova Scotia (1984), York University (1984), the University of Western Canada (1990), Queen's University (1992), University of Montreal (1995), and Birnap's University (1995). She has also received the Canada-Australia Literary Prize (1985) and the Canadian Council Molson Prize for the Arts (1997).

BIOGRAPHY

Born in Montreal in 1922, Mavis Gallant (née Mavis de Trafford Young), an only child, was placed in a Catholic convent school at the age of four. She attended seventeen schools: Catholic schools in Montreal, Protestant ones in Ontario, as well as various boarding schools in the United States. After the death of her father, Gallant lived with her legal guardians in New York, a psychiatrist and his wife. At the age of eighteen, Gallant returned to Montreal. After a short time working for the National Film Board of Canada in Ottawa during the winter of 1943-1944, Gallant accepted a position as reporter with the *Montreal Standard*, which she left in 1950. In 1951, Gallant began contributing short-fiction stories to *The New Yorker*. In the early 1950's, she moved to Europe, living in London, Rome, and Madrid, before settling in Paris in the early 1960's. It was through her travels and experiences in France, Italy, Austria, and Spain that she observed the fabric of diverse societies. During the initial years of her life in Europe, Gallant lived precariously from her writings, ultimately becoming an accomplished author, depicting loners, expatriates,

Mavis Gallant (©Miriam Berkley)

and crumbling social structures. Gallant settled in Paris, working on a history of the renowned Dreyfus affair in addition to her work in fiction. Gallant settled in Paris, occasionally traveling to Canada, the United States, and England.

ANALYSIS

The often somber tone of Mavis Gallant's work is strengthened by the combination of acute lucidness and understated stylistic richness. Gallant is a remarkable observer. She succeeds in creating worlds that are both familiar and foreign, appealing yet uninviting. Her mastery in the restrained use of language and in her incomparable narrative powers make her undeniably one of the world's greatest fiction writers.

"THE OTHER PARIS"

The title story of Mavis Gallant's first collection strikes the pitch to which the others that follow it are tuned. Most of these stories are about young Americans in Europe just entering into marriage, uncertain about what they should feel, unsure of their roles, and unable to find appropriate models around them for the behavior that they think is expected of them. The young protagonists in the stories grope through their

ambivalences, looking for guidance in others who seem more sure of themselves, or clutching written words from some absent sibling—advice recorded in a letter, or written down by themselves about appropriate responses to their present situation. In the other stories in which a parent is present, the other parent, usually ill or divorced, is absent, and the rules of conduct become equally tenuous because of that absence. The European stories are set in the early 1950's, when the devastations of World War II are still being felt. Refugee figures haunt the fringes.

"The Other Paris" refers to the romantic illusions generated by films about that city which Carol feels she is missing. She is about to be married to Howard Mitchell, with whom she works in an American government agency, and with whom she is not yet in love. She keeps remembering her college lectures on the subject to reassure herself. Common interests and similar economic and religious backgrounds were what mattered. "The illusion of love was a blight imposed by the film industry, and almost entirely responsible for the high rate of divorce." Carol waits expectantly for the appropriate emotions to follow the mutuality of their backgrounds: Their fathers are both attorneys, Protestants, and from the same social class. In Carol's mind, the discovery of that mysterious "other Paris" is linked with the discovery of love. She believes the Parisians know a secret, "and if she spoke to the right person or opened the right door or turned down an unexpected street, the city would reveal itself and she would fall in love." She tries all the typical tourist things, such as listening to carols at the Place Vendôme, but everything has been commercialized. Newsreel cameras and broadcast equipment spoil the atmosphere she seeks. Plastic mistletoe with "cheap tinsel" is tied to the street lamps.

Odile, Howard's secretary, invites her to a private concert. Excitedly Carol thinks that she has finally gained entrance into the aristocratic secrets that are hidden from foreigners. Instead of the elegant drawing room she had anticipated, it is an "ordinary, shabby theatre" on an obscure street, nearly empty except for a few of the violinist's relatives. Odile is thin, dark, seldom smiles, and often sounds sarcastic because of her poor English. She is involved with Felix, pale, ill, hungry, and without papers, who sells things on the black market. He is twenty-one, she is more than thirty years old, and Carol finds the gap in their ages distasteful. They have no common interests, no mitigating mutual circumstances; yet, one night in Felix's dark, cluttered room, she discovers that they love each other. The thought makes her ill. In that dusty slum, with revulsion, she discovers that, at last, she has "opened the right door, turned down the right street, glimpsed the vision." On this paradox, that the sordid reality reveals the romantic illusion, the story closes with a time shift to the future in which Carol is telling how she met and married Howard in Paris and making it "sound romantic and interesting," believing it as it had never been at all.

"AUTUMN DAY"

"Autumn Day" is another initiation story of a nineteen-year-old who follows her Army husband to Salzburg. She has a list of instructions: "Go for walks. Meet Army wives. Avoid people on farm." She attributes her unhappiness, her failure to feel like a wife, to the fact that they have no home. They are boarding in a farmhouse from which she takes dutiful long walks under the lowering Salzburg skies, gray with impending snow. An American singer practices a new setting of the poem "Herbsttag" ("Autumn Day"), whose most haunting line, which the narrator feels had something to do with her, is "who does not yet have a home, will never have one." She feels that the poet had understood her; it was exactly the life she was leading, going for lonely walks. She slides a note under the singer's door, asking if they might meet. After a complicated day in which she has had to listen to two sets of confessions, Laura's and Mrs. de Kende's, she returns to the farmhouse to find the singer had invited her to lunch and had returned to America. Walt, her bewildered husband, finds her crying. He tries, timidly, to console her by insisting that they "will be all right" when they get their own apartment. She wonders if her present mood is indeed temporary or whether their entire marriage will be like this.

Your girlfriend doesn't vanish overnight. I know, now, what a lot of wavering goes on, how you step forward

and back again. The frontier is invisible; sometimes you're over without knowing it. I do know that some change began then, at that moment, and I felt an almost unbearable nostalgia for the figure I was leaving behind.

It is in depicting these border states of consciousness that Gallant excels. Her portraits of girls who are trying to become women without having internalized a strong role model to emulate are moving because the portrayal of their inner sense of being lost is augmented by the setting; it is externalized into the girls' awareness of being foreigners alone in a strange country. The psychic territory has been projected outward into an alien land. Both Carol and Cissy have heard music which they feel contains some secret knowledge that can help them understand their feeling of having been somehow left out, excluded from a love they would like to feel. Both accommodate themselves to lives that are less than the songs promised they might be. "Autumn Day" closes with Cissy's ritually repeating the magic formula, like an incantation, like a figure in a fairy tale casting a spell over her own anxiety, "We'll be all right, we'll be all right, we'll be all right."

"POOR FRANZI"

"Poor Franzi" is also set in Salzburg and in the same wavering space. The young American Elizabeth is engaged to the grandson Franzi of Baroness Ebendorf, an Austrian aristocrat, who dies in the course of the story. Because Franzi refuses to go to the funeral, Elizabeth feels obligated to attend. A party of American tourists serves as choric voices. They insinuate that the young Austrian has become engaged to the American girl simply to escape from the country. They gossip about his failure to visit the old woman in her last illness, his refusal to pay for the funeral, and his having burned her will. Her landlady, "out of helplessness and decency," had arranged for the last rites, which she could ill afford, a peasant paying homage to a noble line.

Elizabeth's nearsightedness is a physical correlative of her failure to see her fiancé's faults, which are obvious to everyone else. "Blind as a bat!" the other Americans mutter as she walks straight past them.

She gazes at the edge of the horizon, but her myopia prevents her from distinguishing whether she is seeing clouds or mountains. She sees Franzi in this same suffused haze. Instead of the cynicism and selfishness his behavior so clearly outlines, there is a fuzzy aura blurred by her feeling of having to be protective of his great grief. Poor thing, he is all alone now; he must never suffer again. The soft shapes, "shifting and elusive," which better eyes than hers saw as the jutting rocks of the Salzburg mountains, become an emblem of her emotional condition. The story closes on this ambiguous haze: "What will happen to me if I marry him? she wondered; and what would become of Franzi if she were to leave him?"

THE COLLECTED STORIES OF MAVIS GALLANT

This anthology contains fifty-two stories that appeared in *The New Yorker* magazine. Gallant has divided her anthology into nine sections: thirty-five stories, with settings chronologically arranged between 1930-1990; five autobiographical stories with Linnet Muir, a young Canadian girl, as the main character; four about the Canadian Carette Sisters; four focused on Edouard, a Frenchman and his two "wives"; and four featuring Henri Grippes, a French "hack" writer and charlatan.

In the introduction, Gallant says she gets her ideas for stories through imaginary flashes. She compares it to looking at a snapshot. Then she begins by developing a unique character with a name, age, nationality, profession, voice and accent, family history, destination, personality quirks, secrets, ambitions, and attitudes toward love, money, religion. Next, she writes scenes between her characters with dialogue and develops a plot that is "entire but unreadable." She says that revision takes her a long time; it is a "slow transformation from image to story."

The stories are written in a powerful and fluent style with precise details. Many have settings during and after World War II in Canada, France, and Germany, when people's lives are in a state of flux. Gallant's settings and characters are reproduced like filmed images, complete with background noise and dialogue. However, her extraordinary ability to get inside her characters' minds provides ironic contrast between external events and their fragmented thoughts and confused emotions. Typically, her main characters are rootless young women trapped by the past in an existential world, lonely, isolated, and uncertain of the direction their lives should take. Secondary characters often include neglected, love-starved children, surrounded by insensitive adults.

"THE MOSLEM WIFE"

The title of this story does not refer to a North African setting or to the Islamic religion. It refers to the role of Moslem women, who traditionally submit to the domination of fathers and husbands. These women have great responsibility for the management of their homes and the well-being of their families. Most have limited contact with the outside world.

Gallant compares the Moslem wife's lifestyle to that of Netta Asher, an inexperienced young English girl, whose family ties and cultural roots have been severed by death and circumstance. Netta's dying father provides for her future by signing a one-hundred-year lease on his resort hotel in southern France and marrying her to Jack, a philandering cousin. Thus, locked into her role as owner/manager of the hotel, Netta leads a confined life, while Jack enjoys much freedom. On the eve of Adolf Hitler's European conquest, Jack goes on holiday to England and does not return until World War II is over. Meanwhile, Netta takes care of Jack's temperamental mother and survives deprivation and the presence of Italian and German soldiers billeted at the hotel. Miserable and lonely, Netta longs to escape her "prison." However, when Jack, the perpetual adolescent, returns, Netta, still dependent on his masculine charm, remains locked into her role as "The Moslem Wife."

"ACROSS THE BRIDGE"

"Across the Bridge" is a lighthearted initiation story, set in Paris in the 1950's. It gives insight into postwar French families and their attempt to reestablish social classes and tradition. American teenagers, who enjoy considerable freedom to select their own love interests without parental involvement, will consider this story old-fashioned and foreign. However, ethnicity, religious background, and economic and social status are realistic factors that continue to influence a person's selection of a mate.

After much negotiation, teenaged Sylvie Castelli's

parents arrange her marriage to Arnaud Pons, a quiet, unromantic young man. The Italian/French Castellis have a modest fortune, but the Pons family has an old and respected name. On a bridge en route to having wedding invitations printed, Sylvie confesses to her mother that she is in love with Bruno, a boy she met at the park. Her doting parents allow her to break her engagement to Arnaud, and Mr. Castelli contacts Bruno's wealthy parents, who deny their son's interest in Sylvie and humiliate the Castellis. Eventually, Sylvie "crosses the bridge" from romantic, adolescent dreams to realistic maturity and on her own, without parental involvement, selects Arnaud as her fiancé. The question of whether pragmatic considerations offset romantic ideals and physical attraction remains unanswered as Sylvie and Arnaud begin their new relationship.

"THE DOCTOR," "IN YOUTH IS PLEASURE," AND "BETWEEN ZERO AND ONE"

The Linnet Muir stories are fictionalized, coming-of-age memoirs based on Gallant's own experiences as a member of a dysfunctional family. Biographical data confirms much, but not all, of the content of the stories. During her childhood, Gallant, like Linnet, observed her parents' unhappy marriage. In "The Doctor" a precocious Linnet recalls the sterile and bewildering relationship between her parents, Charlotte and Angus Muir, and their eccentric friends, Mrs. Erskine and Dr. Chauchard, Linnet's pediatrician, who is treating her for a lung disease from which she recovers.

After Gallant's father's untimely death, her mother placed her in a series of boarding schools and left her care and education to strangers. In her late teens, Gallant, like Linnet, attempted a reconciliation with her mother that failed. "In Youth Is Pleasure," an ironic title because of somber events in the story, eighteen-year-old Linnet asserts her independence, breaks off an unhappy relationship with her mother, and returns to Montreal from New York. There, she discovers family secrets: that her father suffered from tuberculosis of the bone and committed suicide and that her mother ran off with a lover.

Gallant became a successful journalist in Canada, an experience she considered boring, but one that sharpened her writing skills and techniques of obser-

vation. After selling her first short story, she left Canada and moved to France, where she hoped to establish new roots and become a successful writer. Similarly, in the story "Between Zero and One," Linnet works at a boring government job surrounded by men who are either too old or disabled to serve in the army during World War II. At first they resent Linnet, but later accept her. When Mrs. Ireland, an outspoken feminist, arrives, dynamics in the office change. After looking at a graph of statistics, Linnet becomes more assertive. She discovers that what occurs during a person's life-graph "Between Zero and One" determines the future.

OTHER MAJOR WORKS

LONG FICTION: *Green Water, Green Sky*, 1959; *Its Image on the Mirror*, 1964; *A Fairly Good Time*, 1970.

PLAY: *What Is to Be Done*, pr. 1982.

NONFICTION: *The Affair of Gabrielle Russier*, 1971; *The War Brides*, 1978; *Paris Notebooks: Essays and Reviews*, 1986.

BIBLIOGRAPHY

Besner, Neil. *The Light of Imagination: Mavis Gallant's Fiction*. Vancouver: University of British Columbia Press, 1988. An extremely thorough analysis of Gallant's fiction from *The Other Paris* to *Overhead in a Balloon*. Includes a biographical review as well as a useful critical bibliography.

Dobozy, Tamas. "'Designed Anarchy' in Mavis Gallant's *The Moslem Wife and Other Stories*." *Canadian Literature*, no. 158 (Autumn, 1998): 65-88. Discusses an anarchic aesthetic in the collection in which the stories challenge the impulse to create a master narrative and instead allow a variety of competing narratives that prevent a unified vision.

Hatch, Ronald. "Mavis Gallant." In *Canadian Writers Since 1960: First Series*. Vol. 53 in *Dictionary of Literary Biography*, edited by W. H. New. Detroit: Gale Research, 1986. A thorough general introduction to Gallant's fiction up to, and including, *Home Truths*. Supplemented by a bibliography of interviews and studies.

Jewison, Don. "Speaking of Mirrors: Imagery and Narration in Two Novellas by Mavis Gallant." *Studies in Canadian Literature* 10, nos. 1, 2 (1985): 94-109. A study of *Green Water, Green Sky* and *Its Image on the Mirror*. Focuses on the importance of mirrors from the perspective of imagery as well as of narration.

Keefer, Janice Kulyk. *Reading Mavis Gallant*. Toronto: Oxford University Press, 1989. A comprehensive study of Gallant's fiction and journalism. Discusses the prison of childhood and the world inhabited by women, in addition to Gallant's conception of memory.

Merler, Grazia. *Mavis Gallant: Narrative Patterns and Devices*. Ottawa: Tecumseh Press, 1978. This critical study of Gallant's narrative technique includes a bibliography and an index.

Schaub, Danielle. *Mavis Gallant*. New York: Twayne, 1998. A book-length discussion of Gallant's fiction focusing on the relationship between thematic tensions and narrative devices. Argues that Gallant's irony, stylistic devices, atmosphere, and structure create a tension that reflects the disconnectedness of her characters. Features chapters on Gallant's major short-story collections from *The Other Paris* to *Across the Bridge*.

Schenk, Leslie. "Celebrating Mavis Gallant." *World Literature Today* 72 (Winter, 1998): 18-26. In this interview, Gallant discusses the short story as a genre, the extent to which her stories are biographical or autobiographical, and her relationship to contemporary France. She also discusses some of her stories, including "Across the Bridge."

Simmons, Diane. "Remittance Men: Exile and Identity in the Short Stories of Mavis Gallant." In *Canadian Women: Writing Fiction*, edited by Mickey Pearlman. Jackson: University Press of Mississippi, 1993. Discusses characters in a number of Gallant's short stories who, suffering some early loss, are adrift and, by choosing to live abroad, are acting out their inner sense of exile.

Smythe, Karen E. *Figuring Grief: Gallant, Munro, and the Poetics of Elegy*. Montreal: McGill-Queen's University Press, 1992. Discusses Gallant's use of elegiac romance conventions and modes of mourning in her stories, as well as her critique of historiography and the ethical implications of writing about the past.

_____. "The Silent Cry: Empathy and Elegy in Mavis Gallant's Novels." *Studies in Canadian Literature* 15, no. 2 (1990): 116-135. A study discussing the ways in which the reader is forced to become involved in the emotional and empathetic elements present in *Green Water, Green Sky; Its Image on the Mirror*; and *A Fairly Good Time*.

Ruth Rosenberg, updated by Kenneth W. Meadwell and Martha E. Rhynes

JOHN GALSWORTHY

Born: Kingston Hill, England; August 14, 1867
Died: London, England; January 31, 1933

PRINCIPAL SHORT FICTION

From the Four Winds, 1897 (as John
    Sinjohn)
A Man of Devon, 1901 (as John Sinjohn)
A Commentary, 1908
A Motley, 1910
The Inn of Tranquility, 1912
Five Tales, 1918
Tatterdemalion, 1920
Captures, 1923
*Caravan: The Assembled Tales of John
    Galsworthy*, 1925
Two Forsyte Interludes, 1927
On Forsyte 'Change, 1930
Soames and the Flag, 1930
Forsytes, Pendyces, and Others, 1935

OTHER LITERARY FORMS

Short fiction was a minor vein for John Galsworthy, although he published many collections and is known for several fine stories. His contemporaries acclaimed his plays, whereas posterity knows him chiefly as the novelist who chronicled the family fortunes of the Forsytes in *The Forsyte Saga* (1922) and *A Modern Comedy* (1929).

ACHIEVEMENTS

John Galsworthy refused a knighthood in 1917, but he did accept England's highest literary honor, the Order of Merit. In 1921, Galsworthy became the first president of the International Association of Poets, Playwrights, Editors, Essayists, and Novelists (PEN). During his travels, he was awarded honorary degrees by seven leading universities in England, Scotland, and the United States. Shortly before his death, he became the fourth British writer to win the Nobel Prize in Literature. More important to Galsworthy than honors and prizes were the social reforms—in the penal system, the status of women,

labor conditions, and the treatment of animals—that his essays and stories helped effectuate.

BIOGRAPHY

Born into a rich middle-class family, John Galsworthy followed the usual path of privileged youth. He was graduated from Harrow and Oxford, was called to the Bar, and traveled widely in Canada and Australia. Back in England, he put himself beyond the pale by becoming lover and all-but-husband to his cousin's wife Ada in 1895. Excluded from polite society until 1905, when they were able to marry, the Galsworthys set what was to be the pattern of their life together: Utterly devoted to each other, they traveled abroad or perched at some English location, John writing and ministering to his delicate wife, Ada assisting "her writer." Ada was the model for her husband's most memorable fictional creation, Irene, in *The Forsyte Saga*. In 1906, the success of a novel (*The Man of Property*) and the production of a play (*The Silver Box*) won Galsworthy the esteem of his compatriots, and from then on he was a public figure, a respected writer, and social reformer. Having been found unfit for active duty in World War I, Galsworthy served as a masseur for the wounded, wrote patriotic pieces, and gave at least half his income to the war effort. His crusading optimism was a casualty of the European conflict; in the 1920's he turned to writing the nostalgic novels that gained him his greatest popularity. Galsworthy died in January, 1933.

ANALYSIS

John Galsworthy's works have undergone critical and popular reappraisals since his death. During the last years of his career, he ranked higher in esteem than D. H. Lawrence, E. M. Forster, or even Joseph Conrad. Yet within five years of his death, his reputation suffered dramatic reversal. As the Western world plunged more deeply into the Great Depression, the public lost interest in the values, manners, pastimes, and possessions of the privileged class Galsworthy so expertly delineated. In the decades that followed, the fiction was respectfully remembered more as social history than as living literature, while Galsworthy's plays were relegated to community and university theater production. Only *The Forsyte Saga* retained a sustained readership, even receiving Hollywood attention from time to time. Critics generally concluded that while Galsworthy's writing had forcefully protested social injustices of his time, it had failed to attain either the universality or the vital uniqueness that would permit it to survive the passing of the world it mirrored.

A twenty-six-hour serialization of "The Forsyte Chronicles" by the British Broadcasting Corporation (BBC) decisively undermined this judgment. Faithful to the original material, the television series, which first aired in England on January 7, 1967, became a resounding international success, eventually appearing in more than forty countries and many languages, including Russian. Millions of people, to whom the Forsytes seemed as real as neighbors, demanded new editions and translations of Galsworthy's novels and stories. Suddenly the books were better known than they had been even during the author's lifetime, as paperback editions proliferated. The short fiction, too, was being more frequently anthologized than ever before.

"THE APPLE TREE"

"The Apple Tree," one of Galsworthy's finest tales, reveals both the strengths and the weaknesses of his art. The germ of Galsworthy's story is the West Country tradition associated with "Jay's Grave," a crossroads on Dartmoor where is buried a young girl said to have killed herself out of disappointed love. The tale's title and its epigraph, "The Apple-tree, the singing, and the gold," relate Galsworthy's modern treatment of destructive love to Euripides' *Hippolytus* (428 B.C.E.), but the differences in the two works are perhaps more striking than the similarities. The Greek tragedy centers on psychological truths in its portrayal of Hippolytus and Phaedra, the respective embodiments of amorous deficiency and excess; Galsworthy's story makes a social point. His young lovers, Frank Ashurst and Megan David, contrast in various ways—they are male and female, Anglo-Saxon and Celt, scion of civilization and child of na-

John Galsworthy, Nobel Laureate for Literature in 1932
(©The Nobel Foundation)

ture, gentleman and common girl. All these differences are aspects of what for Galsworthy is the one great polarity: exploiter and exploited.

The story opens on a splendid spring day, the twenty-fifth anniversary of Frank and Stella Ashurst, who in honor of the occasion have driven out into the Devon countryside not far from where they first met. They stop by a grave at a crossroad on the moor. Stella brings out her colors to paint, but a vague discontent rises in Frank, who regrets his inability to seize and hold the ecstatic beauty of the spring day. Suddenly he knows that he has been here before. His mind takes him back twenty-six years to when, a young man of independent means with Oxford just behind him and the world before him, he had curtailed a walking tour at a nearby farm. There he had met Megan David, a country girl with the loveliness of a wild flower. The season and his youth, the beauty of the countryside, and the maiden combined to capture his susceptible fancy; she was dazzled by the attentions of a lordly aesthete from the Great World.

After a midnight tryst in the apple orchard, they fell deeply in love. Charmed almost as much by her innocence as by the prospect of his own chivalry, Frank proposed that they elope together, to live, love, and perhaps finally marry in London. Megan acquiesced, and he departed for the nearby resort town of Torquay to procure money for the trip and a traveling wardrobe for his rustic beauty.

At Torquay, Frank encountered an old Rugby classmate, Halliday, and his sisters, Stella, Sabina, and Freda. In their company he enjoyed the ordinary holiday pleasures of the leisure class, exploring and sea bathing, taking tea, and making music. Soon the moonlit idyll in the orchard came to seem merely an interlude of vernal madness. In the company of the amiable Hallidays, particularly Stella, Ashurst's conscience and class consciousness revived: He saw his intended elopement for what it would be, not romance but seduction: "It would only be a wild love-time, a troubled, remorseful, difficult time—and then—well, he would get tired, just because she gave him everything, was so simple, and so trustful, so dewy. And dew—wears off!" Resolving to do the decent thing, Frank never went back to claim and compromise the waiting Megan, and a year later he married Stella.

Although the young Ashurst may have rationalized his actions as unselfishness, now as a man twenty-six years older, he learns the lesson of the *Hippolytus*—that Love claims her victims despite human magnanimity. The grave on the moor, he discovers from an old laborer, is Megan's. Unable to endure the loss of her love, she had drowned herself in the stream by the apple tree where they had met: "Spring, with its rush of passion, its flowers and song—the spring in his heart and Megan's! Was it just Love seeking a victim!" Ironically, this man who half thinks himself too intense for the bread-and-butter love of married life must recognize that his own escape is due less to the strength of his "civilised" virtue than to the weakness of his "civilised" passion.

ON FORSYTE 'CHANGE

Galsworthy wrote about his Forsytes, those pillars of Empire whose instincts for possession and property amounted to a kind of genius, in his short fiction as well as in *The Forsyte Saga* and *A Modern Comedy*. The family first appears in the short piece "The Salvation of a Forsyte," in which old Swithin, on his death bed, relives the one impulsively romantic interlude in his eminently practical bachelor's life; and it furnishes the material for Galsworthy's last completed book, *On Forsyte 'Change*, a collection of tales ranging from Aunt Ann's recollection of her father, "Superior Dosset" Forsyte, under the reign of George IV, to "Soames and the Flag," in which Galsworthy shows how his epitome of middle-class sense and honor reacted to World War I and the Armistice. Perhaps the most charming and substantial of the short Forsyte pieces is "The Indian Summer of a Forsyte," a tale that brought the family back to life for their creator, just as the madeleine in lime-flower tea revived all Combray for Marcel Proust, and spurred Galsworthy on to write his sequels to the hitherto freestanding *The Man of Property*. This Forsyte interlude centers on old Jolyon, the most sympathetic of the brothers and a man patterned on Galsworthy's own father. Like "The Apple Tree," "The Indian Summer of a Forsyte" reveals Galsworthy's love of the English countryside and his skill in portraying the aesthetic sensibility.

"THE INDIAN SUMMER OF A FORSYTE"

As the story opens, old Jolyon, his family abroad, is spending the summer alone except for his granddaughter Holly at Robin Hill, the country house he bought from his nephew Soames when the wife of that "man of property" fled from their marriage. Although his body is not in the best of health, Jolyon's fine spirit has mellowed with his eighty-four years. The orthodoxy of his class has fallen away, "leaving him reverent before three things alone—beauty, upright conduct, and the sense of property; and the greatest of these was now beauty." Jolyon's quiet pleasures—the summer countryside, music, his cigars—are enhanced when beauty in woman's form enters his life. Walking on his grounds, Jolyon encounters Irene, Soames's runaway wife, who has come to commune with her memories of her dead lover, the architect who had designed Robin Hill. The old man and the young woman appreciate each other's fineness, and a friendship emerges. So intensely, in fact, does Jolyon come to care for his niece by marriage that he decides to pay her a Forsyte's supreme compliment: He will leave her a bequest. Although the old man's spirit is rekindled by this radiant and mysterious woman's presence in his life, his frail body is weakened by his excited anticipation of her visits and his journeys to London to treat her to dinner and the Opera. In letting this spiritual romance enter his contemplative life, old Jolyon finally and utterly transcends his Forsyte practicality:

> For it is written that a Forsyte shall not love beauty more than reason; nor his own way more than his own health. And something beat within him in these days that with each throb fretted at the thinning shell. His sagacity knew this, but it knew too that he could not stop that beating, nor would if he could. And yet, if you had told him he was living on his capital, he would have stared you down.

Live on his capital old Jolyon does, however, until finally one drowsy and perfect summer day, he exhausts it. Expecting a visit from Irene, Jolyon dies quietly as he watches for beauty to cross his sunlit lawn: "Summer—summer—summer—the soundless footsteps in the grass!"

As susceptible to beauty as old Jolyon, Galsworthy could never quite bring himself to pay the high price of devotion, which in his case would have involved embracing artistic self-centeredness. Galsworthy was always too scrupulous in fulfilling his other obligations—giving Ada the personal attention and social success she needed, campaigning for decent treatment of his various "lame ducks," churning out prose for the war effort—to fully cultivate his art as he would have liked. His judgment surpassed his performance; and despite the world's acclaim, he felt a failure. Thus, his story "Spindleberries," which presents the plight of an artist who, like Andrea Del Sarto, aims low and succeeds completely, is a window on Galsworthy's own dissatisfied soul.

The story is a simple series of encounters between two painters, the celebrated Scudamore, "whose studies of Nature had been hung on the line for so many years that he had forgotten the days when, not yet in the Scudamore manner, they depended from the sky," and his cousin, the eccentric Alicia. As the story opens, Alicia enters with a spray of dull pink spindleberries. "Charming! I'd like to use them!" Scudamore exclaims. Repelled by his pragmatism, she hurries contemptuously away. Alicia's disapproval, and perhaps his own supressed agreement with her feeling, set Scudamore's mind on a journey reliving other such encounters that proceed from spring to winter, from the cousins' youth to late middle age. In each meeting, Scudamore endorses expedience: He is a Forsyte with a paint brush. Alicia, a female Don Quixote, perversely flings away every opportunity in her absolute devotion to beauty. She refuses Scudamore's love; destroys her wondrous study of night—a creation Scudamore recognizes as far better than anything he or she has done before or ever will do—because any attempt to capture a summer night seems "blasphemy"; rejects a legacy that would mean comfort and security; and gazes at the stars in bitter weather until pneumonia prostrates her.

Scudamore pities the impractical Alicia: "A life spoiled! By what, if not by love of beauty? But who would ever have thought that the intangible could wreck a woman, deprive her of love, marriage, motherhood, of fame, of wealth, of health? And yet—by George—it had!" All the same, part of him whispers, perhaps her sacrifice has been worthwhile. Alicia has remained true to the pursuit from which worldly compromises have distracted him. She has refused to sell her vision and has not seen the world's loveliness fade to the stuff of a transaction. "Who could say that she had missed the prize of life?" With a wistful sigh that must have been Galsworthy's as well, Scudamore turns from this idealism so uncomfortable to contemplate. "And he set to work to paint in his celebrated manner—spindleberries."

OTHER MAJOR WORKS

LONG FICTION: *Jocelyn*, 1898 (as John Sinjohn); *Villa Rubein*, 1900 (as John Sinjohn); *The Island Pharisees*, 1904; *The Man of Property*, 1906; *The Country House*, 1907; *Fraternity*, 1909; *The Patrician*, 1911; *The Dark Flower*, 1913; *The Freelands*, 1915; *Beyond*, 1917; *The Burning Spear*, 1919, 1923;

Saint's Progress, 1919; *In Chancery*, 1920; *To Let*, 1921; *The Forsyte Saga*, 1922 (includes *The Man of Property*, "*Indian Summer of a Forsyte*," "*Awakening*," *In Chancery*, and *To Let*); *The White Monkey*, 1924; *The Silver Spoon*, 1926; *Swan Song*, 1928; *A Modern Comedy*, 1929 (includes *The White Monkey*, *The Silver Spoon*, *Two Forsyte Interludes*, and *Swan Song*); *Maid in Waiting*, 1931; *Flowering Wilderness*, 1932; *Over the River*, 1933; *End of the Chapter*, 1934 (includes *Maid in Waiting*, *Flowering Wilderness*, and *Over the River*).

PLAYS: *The Silver Box*, pr. 1906; *Joy*, pr. 1907; *Strife*, pr., pb. 1909; *Justice*, pr., pb. 1910; *The Little Dream*, pr., pb. 1911; *The Eldest Son*, pr., pb. 1912; *The Pigeon*, pr., pb. 1912; *The Fugitive*, pr., pb. 1913; *The Mob*, pr., pb. 1915; *A Bit o'Love*, pr., pb. 1915; *The Little Man*, pr., pb. 1915; *The Foundations*, pr. 1917; *Defeat*, pr. 1920; *The Skin Game*, pr., pb. 1920; *A Family Man*, pr. 1921; *The First and the Last*, pr., pb. 1921; *Hall-marked*, pb. 1921; *Punch and Go*, pb. 1921; *The Sun*, pb. 1921; *Loyalties*, pr., pb. 1922; *Windows*, pr., pb. 1922; *The Forest*, pr., pb. 1924; *Old English*, pr., pb. 1924; *The Show*, pr., pb. 1925; *Escape*, pr., pb. 1926; *Exiled*, pr., pb. 1929; *The Roof*, pr., pb. 1929.

POETRY: *The Collected Poems of John Galsworthy*, 1934 (Ada Galsworthy, editor).

NONFICTION: *The Little Man*, 1916; *A Sheaf*, 1916; *Another Sheaf*, 1919; *Castles in Spain*, 1927; *Candelabra: Selected Essays and Addresses*, 1932; *Letters from John Galsworthy, 1900-1932*, 1934 (Edward Garnett, editor).

MISCELLANEOUS: *The Works of John Galsworthy*, 1922-1936 (30 volumes).

BIBLIOGRAPHY

Dupre, Catherine. *John Galsworthy: A Biography*. New York: Coward, McCann & Geoghegan, 1976. A well-researched and thoughtful biography that is less impressive in its critical evaluations of the writings. Judgments of merit and influence are not substantiated by current developments.

Frechet, Alec. *John Galsworthy: A Reassessment*. Totowa, N.J.: Barnes & Noble Books, 1982. A sound, balanced assessment of Galsworthy's career. Provides a good analysis of the stylistic qualities of the literary artist.

Holloway, David. *John Galsworthy*. London: Morgan-Grampian, 1969. A concise but accurate and perceptive survey of the life and career of Galsworthy. Especially good in identifying ways that Galsworthy's life is directly used in the fiction.

Marrot, H. V. *The Life and Letters of John Galsworthy*. New York: Charles Scribner's Sons, 1936. Both the strengths and weaknesses of an authorized biography are evident in this work commissioned by Galsworthy's widow. A personal friend of the author, Marrot had access to information unavailable to others. Yet Galsworthy is idealized in order to present an official portrait sanctioned by his family.

Mottram, R. H. *For Some We Loved: An Intimate Portrait of Ada and John Galsworthy*. London: Hutchinson University Library, 1956. Though an uncritical, adoring portrait of Galsworthy, written by a disciple, this study is valuable for its glimpses of the author's home life and his interactions with other persons of letters of his period. Highly readable. Admittedly "an intimate portrait of Ada and John Galsworthy."

_____. *John Galsworthy*. London: Longmans, Green, 1956. A concise introduction of forty pages, including notes and bibliography. Although basic facts are efficiently presented, Mottram's work is uncritical.

Rønning, Anne Holden. *Hidden and Visible Suffrage: Emancipation and the Edwardian Woman in Galsworthy, Wells, and Forster*. New York: Peter Lang, 1995. See chapter 1, "The Social Context of Edwardian Literature," chapter 4, "Marriage in Galsworthy, Wells, and Forster," and chapter 6, "Galsworthy's View on Suffragism." Includes notes and bibliography.

Ru, Yi-ling. *The Family Novel: Toward a Generic Definition*. New York: Peter Lang, 1992. Examines Galsworthy's *The Forsyte Saga* as an example of the family novel. Other authors, including Roger Martin du Gard and Chin Pa, are examined as well.

Smit, J. Henry. *The Short Stories of John Galsworthy*. New York: Haskell House, 1966. An idiosyncratic little book, but with a number of brief comments on Galsworthy's stories.

Sternlicht, Sanford. *John Galsworthy*. New York: Twayne, 1987. A well-written, complete, yet concise survey of Galsworthy's life and achievement. The best single introduction to the subject.

Weiss, Rudolf. "John Galsworthy's *Strife:* Striving for Balance or the Audience as Jury." *Theatre Research International* 20 (Spring, 1995): 7-18. Discusses Galsworthy's play from four different perspectives: theater history, textual history, dramatic analysis, and critical reception.

Peter W. Graham,
updated by Allene Phy-Olsen

GABRIEL GARCÍA MÁRQUEZ

Born: Aracataca, Colombia; March 6, 1928

PRINCIPAL SHORT FICTION

La hojarasca, 1955 (novella; translated as *Leaf Storm* in *Leaf Storm and Other Stories*, 1972)

El coronel no tiene quien le escriba, 1961 (novella; translated in *No One Writes to the Colonel and Other Stories*, 1968)

Los funerales de la Mamá Grande, 1962 (*Big Mama's Funeral*, stories included in *No One Writes to the Colonel and Other Stories*, 1968)

Isabel viendo llover en Macondo, 1967 (*Monologue of Isabel Watching It Rain in Macondo*, 1972)

No One Writes to the Colonel and Other Stories, 1968

Relato de un náufrago: Que estuvo diez días a la deriva en una balsa sin comer ni beber, que fue proclamado héroe de la patria, besado por las reinas de la belleza y hecho rico por la publicidad, y luego aborrecido por el gobierno y olvidado para siempre, 1970 (*The Story of a Shipwrecked Sailor: Who Drifted on a Liferaft for Ten Days Without Food or Water, Was Proclaimed a National Hero, Kissed by Beauty Queens, Made Rich Through Publicity, and Then Spurned by the Government and Forgotten for All Time*, 1986)

La increíble y triste historia de la Cándida Eréndira y de su abuela desalmada, 1972 (*Innocent Eréndira and Other Stories*, 1978)

Leaf Storm and Other Stories, 1972

El negro que hizo esperar a los ángeles, 1972

Ojos de perro azul, 1972

Todos los cuentos de Gabriel García Márquez, 1975 (*Collected Stories*, 1984)

Crónica de una muerte anunciada, 1981 (novella; *Chronicle of a Death Foretold*, 1982)

Doce cuentos peregrinos, 1992 (*Strange Pilgrims: Twelve Stories*, 1993)

OTHER LITERARY FORMS

Besides his short fiction, including short stories and novellas, Gabriel García Márquez's fictional work includes full-length novels, such as his masterpiece and best-known novel, *Cien años de soledad* (1967; *One Hundred Years of Solitude*, 1970), *El general en su laberinto* (1989; *The General in His Labyrinth*, 1990), and *Del amor y otros demonios* (1994; *Of Love and Other Demons*, 1995). In addition, during his long career as a journalist, he has written numerous articles, essays, and reports on a variety of topics, particularly relating to Latin American life and politics. His nonfiction works include *La aventura de Miguel Littín' clandestino en Chile* (1986; *Clandestine in Chile: The Adventures of Miguel Littín*, 1987), *Por un país al alcance de los niños* (1996; *For the Sake of a Country Within Reach of the Children*, 1998), and *Noticia de un secuestro* (1996; *News of a Kidnapping*, 1997), an account of the nefarious activities of drug lord Pablo Escobar in 1990.

ACHIEVEMENTS

In 1967, Gabriel García Márquez's highly acclaimed novel *One Hundred Years of Solitude* appeared and was immediately recognized by critics as a masterpiece of fiction. As a work of high literary quality, this novel was unusual in that it also enjoyed tremendous popular success both in Latin America and in translation throughout the world. This work made García Márquez a major figure—perhaps *the* major figure—of contemporary Latin American literature.

García Márquez's work has been praised for bringing literary fiction back into contact with real life in all of its richness. His combination of realism and fantasy known as Magical Realism *(realismo mágico)* sets the stage for a full spectrum of Latin American characters. His stories focus on basic human concerns, and characters or incidents from one work are often integrated into others, if only with a passing reference.

García Márquez won the Colombian Association of Writers and Artists Award in 1954, for the story "Un dia despues del sabado." The novel *One Hundred Years of Solitude* garnered the French Prix de Meilleur Livre Étranger, the Italian Chianciano Award, and the Venezuelan Rómulo Gallego Prize. Awarding him the Nobel Prize in Literature in 1982, the Nobel committee compared the breadth and quality of his work to that of such great writers as William Faulkner and Honoré de Balzac. In 1988 García Márquez won the *Los Angeles Times* Book Award, for *El amor en los tiempos del cólera* (1985; *Love in the Time of Cholera*, 1988).

BIOGRAPHY

Gabriel García Márquez was born in Aracataca, a town near the Atlantic coast of Colombia, on March 6, 1928. His parents, Luisa Santiaga and Gabriel Eligio Márquez, sent him to live with his mater-

Gabriel Garcia Márquez (©The Nobel Foundation)

nal grandparents for the first eight years of his life. He attended school in Barranquilla and Zipaquirá and went on to law studies at the Universidad Nacional in Bogotá.

His first short story was published in 1947 in the Bogotá newspaper *El Espectador*. The literary editor praised the work, and in the next five years several more short fictions were also published. When his studies were interrupted by political violence in 1948, García Márquez transferred to the Universidad de Cartagena, but he never received his degree. Instead, he began his career as a journalist, writing for *El Universal*. He soon had a daily column and became friends with the writers and artists of the "Barranquilla group." In 1950, he moved to Barranquilla and in 1954 to Bogotá, continuing his work as a journalist. During this time, he also published *Leaf Storm and Other Stories* and received a prize from the Association of Artists and Writers of Bogotá.

In 1955, he was sent to Geneva, Switzerland, as a European correspondent. When *El Espectador* was closed down in January, 1956, García Márquez spent a period of poverty in Paris, working on *La mala hora* (1962; *In Evil Hour*, 1979) and writing some freelance articles. In the summer of 1957, he traveled through eastern Europe before moving to Caracas, Venezuela, as a journalist. With the prospect of a steady job, he married Mercedes Barcha in March, 1958.

Interested since his university days in leftist causes, García Márquez worked for the Cuban news agency Prensa Latina in Bogotá after Fidel Castro came to power in 1959, then in Havana, Cuba, and later New York. After leaving the agency, he moved to Mexico City, where he worked as a journalist and screenwriter with Carlos Fuentes during the period 1961-1967. In 1962, *In Evil Hour* was published and won the Esso Literary Prize in Colombia. That same year, a collection of stories, *Los funerales de la Mamá Grande*, also appeared. Then, in a spurt of creative energy, García Márquez spent eighteen months of continuous work to produce his best-selling novel *One Hundred Years of Solitude*, which won book prizes in Italy and France in 1969. In order to be able to write in peace after the tremendous success of this book, he moved to Barcelona, Spain, where he met Peruvian author Mario Vargas Llosa. In 1972, he won both the Rómulo Gallego Prize in Venezuela and the Neustadt International Prize for Literature. The money from both prizes was donated to political causes.

García Márquez left Barcelona in 1975 and returned to Mexico. That same year, *El otoño del patriarca* (1975; *The Autumn of the Patriarch*, 1975), about the life of a Latin American dictator, was published, and in 1981, his *Chronicle of a Death Foretold* appeared. His news magazine, *Alternativa*, founded in 1974 in Bogotá to present opposing political views, folded in 1980, but García Márquez continued his activism by writing a weekly column for Hispanic newspapers and magazines. His Nobel Prize speech in 1982 made a strong statement about conditions in Latin America yet sounded the note of hope in the face of oppression.

García Márquez continued his literary production after receiving the Nobel Prize, publishing, among other works, *El general en su laberinto* in 1989 (*The General in His Labyrinth*, 1990), based on the life of South American revolutionary leader Simón Bolívar. He also continued his political work, appearing at conferences with, variously, Colombian, Venezuelan, Mexican, and U.S. presidents on such issues as civil war and drug trafficking. In 1999 he fell ill in Bogotá, in one of his seven houses, and was diagnosed with cancer.

ANALYSIS

Gabriel García Márquez's fiction is characterized by a thread of common themes, events, and characters that seem to link his work together into one multifaceted portrayal of the experiences of Latin American life. From the influences of his early childhood, when he learned from his grandmother how to tell the most fantastic stories in a matter-of-fact tone, to his later observations of the oppression and cruelties of politics, García Márquez captures the everyday life of the amazing people of coastal Colombia, with its Caribbean flavor, as well as the occasional resident of the highlands of Bogotá. He has an eye for the details of daily life mixed with humor and an attitude of acceptance and wonder. His characters experience the magic and joy of life and face the suffering of solitude and isolation but always with an innate dignity. García Márquez's vision touches real life with its local attitudes and values, and in the process it also reveals a criticism of politics, the church, and U.S. imperialism, as they contribute to the Latin American experience.

García Márquez's body of work portrays a complete reality breaking out of conventional bounds. Characters from one story regularly show up or are mentioned in another, while his complex mix of fantasy and reality reveals a consummate storyteller capable of bringing to his work the magic of his non-European world. His impact as a writer lies in the fact that although his work describes the Latin American experience of life, it also goes beyond to reveal a universal human experience.

OJOS DE PERRO AZUL

García Márquez's earliest stories have a bizarre, almost surreal, tone, reminiscent of Franz Kafka. Collected in *Ojos de perro azul*, these stories represent an experimental phase of García Márquez's development as a writer. They exemplify his new, or strange, realism, extending the reality of life into and beyond the experience of death. "La tercera resignación" ("The Third Resignation"), for example, deals with the thoughts and fears of a young man in his coffin. "Nabo, el negro que hizo esperar a los ángeles" ("Nabo, the Black Man Who Made the Angels Wait") tells of a man who is locked in a stable because he goes insane after being kicked in the head by a horse.

In "Isabel viendo llover en Macondo" ("Monologue of Isabel Watching It Rain in Macondo"), published the same year as his first novella, *Leaf Storm*, García Márquez captures the atmosphere of a tropical storm through the eyes of his protagonist. Here, the world of Macondo, used in *Leaf Storm* as well and made world-famous in *One Hundred Years of Solitude*, is presented amid the suffocating oppressiveness of tropical weather. Here as later, nature itself is often a palpable force in the fiction of García Márquez—often exaggerated and overwhelming in order to reflect the reality of Latin American geography and the natural forces within it. The repetition underscores the monotony of the continuing deluge, and the theme of solitude is reflected in the imagery as well as in the personal relationship of Isabel and Martin: "The sky was a gray, jellyish substance that flapped its wings a hand away from our heads."

NO ONE WRITES TO THE COLONEL

After demonstrating his ability to capture the tropical atmosphere, García Márquez shows himself capable of capturing a portrait in words with his well-structured novella *No One Writes to the Colonel*. The central character is a dignified man with a deep sense of honor who has been promised a military pension. Every Friday, he goes to the post office to wait for mail that never comes, and then he claims that he really was not expecting anything anyway. He is a patient man, resigned to eternal waiting and hope when there is no reason to expect that hope to be fulfilled. "For nearly sixty years—since the end of the last civil war—the colonel had done nothing else but wait. October was one of the few things which arrived." His

other hope is his rooster, which belonged to his son, who was executed for handing out subversive literature, but since he is too poor to feed the rooster, some townspeople work out an arrangement to provide food until after the big fight. The political background is introduced subtly as the story opens with the funeral of the first person to die of natural causes in this town for a long time. Violence, censorship, and political repression are a given, as is the pervasive poverty. The colonel continues passing out the literature in his son's place and waiting for his pension. His dignity sustains him in the face of starvation.

The dialogues between the colonel and his practical wife of many years are woven through the novella and reach a climax at the very end of the story. She presses him to sell the rooster, asking plaintively and persistently what they will eat:

> It had taken the colonel seventy-five years—the seventy-five years of his life, minute by minute—to reach this moment. He felt pure, explicit, invincible at the moment when he replied:
> "S—!"

LOS FUNERALES DE LA MAMÁ GRANDE

The image of dignity is developed again in the first story of *Los funerales de la Mamá Grande*, entitled "La siesta del martes" ("Tuesday Siesta") and also set in Macondo. Said to be García Márquez's favorite, it tells of a woman and her young daughter who arrive by train in the stifling heat at siesta time. The woman asks the priest to be allowed to visit her son in the cemetery. The young man was shot for being a thief, but she proudly claims him as her own with quiet self-control: "I told him never to steal anything that anyone needed to eat, and he minded me."

The title story, "Los funerales de la Mamá Grande" ("Big Mama's Funeral"), still set in Macondo, breaks the tone of the other stories into a technique of hyperbole, which García Márquez later used in *One Hundred Years of Solitude* to good effect. The opening sentence sets the tone:

> This is, for all the world's unbelievers, the true account of Big Mama, absolute sovereign of the King-

dom of Macondo, who lived for ninety-two years, and died in the odor of sanctity one Tuesday last September, and whose funeral was attended by the Pope.

The panorama and parody of the story mention Mama's power and property in high-sounding phrases, many from journalism. The pageantry is grandiose to the point of the absurd for this powerful individual, a prototype of the patriarch who appears in García Márquez's later work. She is a legend and local "saint," who seemed to the local people to be immortal; her death comes as a complete surprise. The story criticizes the manipulation of power but also skillfully satirizes the organized display or public show that eulogizes the holders of power with pomp and empty words. The story ends when the garbage men come and sweep up on the next day.

INNOCENT ERÉNDIRA AND OTHER STORIES

Fantastic elements characterize the collection entitled *Innocent Eréndira and Other Stories*. Two of the stories, "Un señor muy viejo con unas alas enormes" ("A Very Old Man with Enormous Wings") and "El ahogado más hermoso del mundo" ("The Handsomest Drowned Man in the World"), have adult figures who are like toys with which children, and other adults, can play. With the second story, García Márquez also tries a technique of shifting narrators and point of view to be used later in the novel *The Autumn of the Patriarch*.

A political satire is the basis for another story, "Muerte constante más allá del amor" ("Death Constant Beyond Love"). The situation that forms the basis for the satire is also incorporated into the longer "Innocent Eréndira." Geographically, in this collection García Márquez has moved inland to the barren landscape on the edge of the Guajiro desert. Here, he sets a type of folktale with an exploited granddaughter, a green-blooded monster of a grandmother, and a rescuing hero named Ulises. Combining myth, allegory, and references from other works, García Márquez weaves a story in which "the wind of her misfortune" determines the life of the extraordinarily passive Eréndira. Treated as a slave and a prostitute by her grandmother, Eréndira persuades Ulises to kill the evil woman—who turns out to be amazingly hard

to kill. Throughout the story, García Márquez demonstrates the ability to report the most monstrous things in a matter-of-fact tone. Some critics have pointed out that the exaggeration that seems inherent in many of his tales may have its roots in the extraordinary events and stories that are commonplace in his Latin American world.

CHRONICLE OF A DEATH FORETOLD

In *Chronicle of a Death Foretold*, García Márquez blends his experience in journalism with his mastery of technique to tell a story based on an actual event that took place in 1955 in Sucre, where he lived at the time. Using records and witness testimony, he unfolds his story on the lines of a detective story. The incident is based on the revenge taken by Angela Vicario's brothers on their friend Santiago Nasar, who supposedly took Angela's virginity (although some doubt is cast on this allegation). The story is pieced together as the townspeople offer their memories of what happened, along with excuses for not having warned the victim. Tension builds as the reader knows the final outcome but not how or why it will occur. The use of dreams (ironically, Nasar's mother is an interpreter of dreams), the feeling of fatalism, and submission to the code of honor, all of which form a part of this society's attitudes, play a central role in the novella, as do García Márquez's use of vision and foreshadowing. Although the basis for the story is a journalistic report of a murder, the actual writing captures the themes of love and death as well as the complex interplay of human emotions and motives in a balanced and poetic account, which reveals García Márquez's skill as a writer.

STRANGE PILGRIMS

Strange Pilgrims picks up the Magical Realism of the earlier short stories, orchestrating twelve works written between 1976 and 1982 so that seven stories, having to do with the death-force of life, are followed by five stories which evoke the vitality of death. The opening story portrays a septuagenarian ex-president whose imminent death proves to be illusory; the seventh story portrays a septuagenarian woman, to whom the approach of death proves to be illusory. In both stories, dying is detailed as a form of intensified living. The second and sixth stories deal with the supernatural, one through a corpse that does not putrefy and the other through a haunted bedroom, and both include Italian settings. The third and fifth stories carry fairy-tale variations: a sleeping beauty who, unkissed, awakes of her own volition, and a lady in distress who, imprisoned in a madhouse, transcends her incarceration. In the fourth story, the umbilicus of the seven, a woman, whose life consists of dreaming, awakens from her dreams only through death. The concluding five stories present, first, two stories of murder—between which is a story of suicide—and two stories dealing with strange fatalities. In one, the wave function of light drowns persons without diving gear; in the other, an apparently negligible rose-thorn prick on a young bride's ring fingertip inexorably causes her death.

OTHER MAJOR WORKS

LONG FICTION: *La mala hora*, 1962, revised 1966 (*In Evil Hour*, 1979); *Cien años de soledad*, 1967 (*One Hundred Years of Solitude*, 1970); *El otoño del patriarca*, 1975 (*The Autumn of the Patriarch*, 1975); *El amor en los tiempos del cólera*, 1985 (*Love in the Time of Cholera*, 1988); *El general en su laberinto*, 1989 (*The General in His Labyrinth*, 1990); *Collected Novellas*, 1990; *Del amor y otros demonios*, 1994 (*Of Love and Other Demons*, 1995).

NONFICTION: *La novela en América Latina: Diálogo*, 1968 (with Mario Vargas Llosa); *Cuando era feliz e indocumentado*, 1973; *Chile, el golpe y los gringos*, 1974; *Crónicas y reportajes*, 1976; *Operación Carlota*, 1977; *Periodismo militante*, 1978; *De viaje por los países socialistas*, 1978; *Obra periodística*, 1981-1983 (4 volumes, includes *Textos costeños*, 1981; *Entre cachacos I*, 1982; *Entre cachacos II*, 1982; and *De Europa y América, 1955-1960*, 1983); *El olor de la guayaba: Conversaciones con Plinio Apuleyo Mendoza*, 1982 (*The Fragrance of the Guava: Plinio Apuleyo Mendoza in Conversation with Gabriel García Márquez*, 1983; also known as *The Smell of Guava*, 1984); *La aventura de Miguel Littín, clandestino en Chile*, 1986 (*Clandestine in Chile: The Adventures of Miguel Littín*, 1987); *Notas de prensa 1980-1984*, 1991; *Por un país al alcance de los niños*, 1996 (*For the Sake of a Country Within*

Reach of the Children, 1998); *Noticia de un secuestro*, 1996 (*News of a Kidnapping*, 1997).

BIBLIOGRAPHY

Bell-Villada, Gene H. *García Márquez: The Man and His Work*. Chapel Hill: University of North Carolina Press, 1990. This well-written book traces the forces that have shaped the life and work of García Márquez and analyzes his short fiction as well as his novels. Includes an index and a fine selected bibliography of sources in English and Spanish, as well as a listing of works by García Márquez and of available English translations.

Bloom, Harold, ed. *Gabriel García Márquez*. New York: Chelsea House, 1989. Essays by eighteen critics, with an introduction by Bloom, on the fiction of García Márquez. Includes two studies of *Chronicle of a Death Foretold*, estimates of the influences of Kafka and Faulkner, analyses of narrative stylistics, and inquiries into the author's types of realism.

Byk, John. "From Fact to Fiction: Gabriel García Márquez and the Short Story." *Mid-American Review* 6 (1986): 111-116. Discusses the development of García Márquez's short fiction from his early imitations of Kafka to his more successful experiments with Magical Realism.

Gerlach, John. "The Logic of Wings: García Márquez, Todorov, and the Endless Resources of Fantasy." In *Bridges to Fantasy*, edited by George E. Slusser, Eric S. Rabkin, and Robert Scholes. Carbondale: Southern Illinois University Press, 1982. Argues that the point of view of "A Very Old Man with Enormous Wings" makes readers sympathize with the old man by establishing his superiority over the villagers.

Hart, Stephen M. *Gabriel García Márquez: "Crónica de una Muerte Anunciada."* London: Grant & Cutler, 1994. A thorough critical guide to *Chronicle of a Death Foretold*.

McMurray, George R., ed. *Critical Essays on Gabriel García Márquez*. Boston: G. K. Hall, 1987. A collection of book reviews, articles, and essays covering the full range of García Márquez's fictional work. Very useful for an introduction to specific novels and collections of short stories. Also includes an introductory overview by the editor and an index.

McNerney, Kathleen. *Understanding Gabriel García Márquez*. Columbia: University of South Carolina Press, 1989. An overview addressed to students and nonacademic readers. After an introduction on Colombia and a brief biography, the five core chapters explain his works in depth. Chapters 1 through 3 discuss three novels, chapter 4 focuses on his short novels and stories, and chapter 5 reviews the role of journalism in his work. Includes a select, annotated bibliography of critical works and an index.

McQuirk, Bernard, and Richard Cardwell, eds. *Gabriel García Márquez: New Readings*. Cambridge, England: Cambridge University Press, 1987. A collection of twelve essays in English by different authors reflecting a variety of critical approaches and covering García Márquez's major novels as well as a selection of his early fiction: *No One Writes to the Colonel, Innocent Eréndira*, and *Chronicle of a Death Foretold*. Also includes

a translation of García Márquez's Nobel address and a select bibliography.

Minta, Stephen. *García Márquez: Writer of Colombia*. New York: Harper & Row, 1987. After a useful first chapter on Colombia, the book traces García Márquez's life and work. Minta focuses his discussion on the political context of the *violencia* in *No One Writes to the Colonel* and *In Evil Hour*. Includes two chapters on Macondo as García Márquez's fictional setting and another chapter with individual discussions of *The Autumn of the Patriarch, Chronicle of a Death Foretold*, and *Love in the Time of Cholera*. Includes a select bibliography by chapter and an index.

Oberhelman, Harley D. *Gabriel Gárcia Márquez: A Study of the Short Fiction*. Boston: Twayne, 1991. Argues that García Márquez's short fiction is almost as important as his novels. Suggests that his stories have the same narrative pattern as his novels. Includes five interviews with García Márquez and essays by four critics.

Susan L. Piepke,
updated by Roy Arthur Swanson

JOHN GARDNER

Born: Batavia, New York; July 21, 1933
Died: Susquehanna, Pennsylvania; September 14, 1982

PRINCIPAL SHORT FICTION

The King's Indian: Stories and Tales, 1974
The Art of Living and Other Stories, 1981

OTHER LITERARY FORMS

Extraordinary variety and productivity marked John Gardner's literary career: He published two collections of short fiction, numerous novels, three books of tales and one of verse for young readers, an "epic," a book of poems, opera librettos, a radio play, and reviews. Since he was an academic as well as an imaginative writer, Gardner also published scholarly

books and articles—most, however, directed chiefly at nonspecialists, with the aim of making the literature more accessible (his translations of medieval poetry, for example, or his biography of Geoffrey Chaucer). His interest in contemporary fiction and in teaching fiction writing resulted in his most controversial book, *On Moral Fiction* (1978), and in two related books of advice and encouragement for young writers, *On Becoming a Novelist* (1983) and *The Art of Fiction* (1984).

ACHIEVEMENTS

The publication of his third novel, *Grendel* (1971), a postmodern retelling of *Beowulf* (c. 1000) from the monster's point of view, brought John Gardner critical acclaim and a measure of commercial success. His next three novels—*The Sunlight Dialogues* (1972), *Nickel Mountain* (1973), and *October Light* (1976)—all became best-sellers, and the last one won the 1977 National Book Critics Circle Award for fiction. Gardner's other awards and honors include Woodrow Wilson, Danforth, and John Simon Guggenheim Memorial Foundation fellowships (1955, 1970-1973, and 1973-1974, respectively), election to the American Academy of Arts and Letters, the Armstrong Prize for his radio play *The Temptation Game* (1977), and a Lamport Foundation award for his essay "Moral Fiction." The book from which that essay was drawn, *On Moral Fiction*, became the focus of a national literary debate over the nature and purpose of contemporary fiction.

BIOGRAPHY

John Champlin Gardner, Jr., was born on July 21, 1933, in the farming community of Batavia in western New York, the setting of a number of his stories and novels. His literary interest can be traced back to his mother, an English teacher, and to his father, a farmer, lay preacher, and opera lover. "Bud" (Welsh for poet) began writing stories when he was eight, but it was the death of his brother Gilbert on April 4, 1945, in a farm accident for which Gardner held himself responsible, that appears to have influenced him most deeply. Gilbert's death and the part that Gardner believed he played in it are the subject of one of his finest stories, "Redemption," and serve as the subtext of nearly all of his fiction.

During his high school years, Gardner studied the French horn at the Eastman School of Music in nearby Rochester. He later attended DePauw University for two years (majoring in chemistry) before marrying Joan Patterson, a cousin, on June 6, 1953, and transferring to Washington University in St. Louis, where he began writing *Nickel Mountain*. He did his graduate work at the University of Iowa, dividing his time between the Writers' Workshop and medieval studies, submitting a collection of stories for his M.A. thesis and a novel, "The Old Men," for his Ph.D. dissertation. From Iowa, Gardner went on to hold faculty appointments at a succession of colleges and universities, including Oberlin College, San

Francisco State University, Southern Illinois University (his longest, 1965 to 1976), Bennington College, Williams College, George Mason University, and finally the State University of New York at Binghamton, where he directed the writing program.

The early years of Gardner's literary career were marked by obscurity; the next ones, from 1971 to 1976, by critical and commercial success; the last by notoriety; and all by unflagging, almost demonic, and at times certainly self-defeating energy. The heated debate at the National Book Critics Circle over the relative merits of *October Light* and Renata Adler's *Speedboat* (1976), the book that it narrowly defeated for that year's fiction prize, set the stage for the difficult times that soon followed: the breakup of his first marriage, a charge of plagiarism, a bout with cancer, trouble with the Internal Revenue Service, and the publication of *On Moral Fiction* and the sudden downturn in Gardner's critical reputation—all grist for the mill of his last and most autobiographical

John Gardner (©Joel Gardner)

novel, *Mickelsson's Ghosts* (1982). Gardner died in a motorcycle accident on September 14, 1982, a few months after his amicable divorce from the poet L. M. (Liz) Rosenberg and a few days before he was to marry Susan Thornton.

ANALYSIS

Although he published only two short-fiction collections during his brief but nevertheless prolific career, John Gardner took a serious and historically informed interest in short fiction's various forms. In addition to the nineteen stories, tales, and novellas collected in *The King's Indian* and *The Art of Living and Other Stories*, Gardner published five uncollected stories (the earliest in 1952 while still an undergraduate, the latest posthumously in 1984); a textbook, edited with Lennis Dunlap, significantly titled *The Forms of Fiction* (1962); three books of stories for children (1975-1977); a novella aimed at adolescent readers; one novel, *Grendel*, which initially appeared in abbreviated version (edited as a short story by *Esquire's* Gordon Lish, not Gardner); and another novel, *Nickel Mountain*, originally conceived as a set of interrelated stories. *The King's Indian* and *The Art of Living and Other Stories* do not, therefore, adequately represent the extent of Gardner's interest in the short story and its allied forms. They do, however, evidence the consistency of Gardner's aesthetic vision and, more important, his remarkable technical virtuosity, ranging from the fantastic and parodic at one extreme to the realistic and didactic at the other. Neither *The King's Indian* nor *The Art of Living and Other Stories* merely collects previously published works; rather, they are carefully and cleverly constructed. *The King's Indian* explores and celebrates the art of narrative, whereas *The Art of Living and Other Stories* pursues the moral fiction idea, which, by the late 1970's, had become the author's chief obsession.

THE KING'S INDIAN

The King's Indian offers an oblique and exuberant commentary on contemporary writing, which Gardner believed was unnecessarily pessimistic and/or overly concerned with its own verbal texture. *The King's Indian* is divided into four parts, the first enti-

tled "The Midnight Reader." Against the progressive darkness of the first four stories of the first part, Gardner posits both the hopeful vision of the fifth story and—less overtly but also perhaps more effectively—the wildly playful voices of all five narrators, metafictional and moral-fictional versions of Samuel Taylor Coleridge's Ancient Mariner.

"PASTORAL CARE"

In "Pastoral Care," the voice belongs to a John Updike-type minister beset by doubts about his congregation, his world, and himself. Unable to raise the social consciousness of his congregation in Carbondale, Illinois, the Reverend Eugene Pick, standing on a footstool that he keeps hidden behind the pulpit, does reach a tall, bearded stranger who acts on Pick's advice, though in a way that the minister never intended: The stranger bombs the local police station and, as Pick later learns, a church (perhaps his own). Implicated, the minister flees, only, like Jonah, to learn that there is no escape from either the stranger or responsibility (pastoral care). When a girl high on drugs falls from the train, Pick, full of misgivings, attempts to comfort her boyfriend, another bearded stranger. Although he believes that "all systems fail," Pick also believes (adapting William Shakespeare) that "flexibility is all." "I force myself to continue," he says at the story's end. "I have no choice."

"THE RAVAGES OF SPRING"

Another person who apparently does not have a choice is the anonymous country doctor, identified only by the alias William Thorp, in the story "The Ravages of Spring," also set in Carbondale, sometime in the nineteenth century. The tornado, which sets the story in motion, is formidable but no match for the vortex of intertextual forces from which Gardner spins the story's befuddled, unprepossessing narrator and his playfully self-conscious narrative—bits and pieces from Edgar Allan Poe, Herman Melville, and Franz Kafka being the most prominent. Against the awed doctor's appreciation of "the beauty and grandeur of Nature in her rage," Gardner posits the geneticist Dr. Hunter (a cloned copy of the original doctor, dead some thirty years), and against cloning (the reproduction of exact copies), Gardner posits his own parodic method, part put-down, part homage. The tornado topples the Poesque House of Hunter; the doctor disappears, replaced by three infant copies whom the narrator, a bachelor, leaves in the care of an old woman who, believing them mad (and perhaps thinking she has the doctor's consent), subjects them to the "mandrake cure" from which the doctor is only able to save two. The good doctor is puzzled by events but accepting of them, including the fictively real children, the presumed offspring of a Dr. Hunter who may be little more than a character in a dream, the result of a storm-induced bump on the narrator's head.

"THE TEMPTATION OF ST. IVO"

Affirmation in the face of uncertainty is a major theme in all Gardner's fiction and more particularly in the three remaining stories of "The Midnight Reader." In "The Temptation of St. Ivo," the narrator, Brother Ivo, is a copyist who possesses a firm belief in order and a genius for decorating sacred manuscripts. Ivo manages to balance the imperatives of his fantastic art and the rules of his religious order (as well as his faith in those rules) successfully until Brother Nicholas arrives on the scene. "Your rules are absurd," Nicholas whispers, "The order of the world is an accident." Claiming to have found where the phoenix—the symbol of the resurrection and, not incidentally, the most artful of Ivo's many artful creations—lives, Nicholas in effect forces Ivo to choose between obeying the rules governing monastic life and acting on his faith in order to save not the phoenix, a myth, mere art, but whatever the phoenix may represent (perhaps a child whom Nicholas intends to kill, or even Nicholas's soul). Ivo chooses action over obedience, complex faith over simple order. He leaves the monastery at night and enters the dark Dantean wood where he soon loses his way: "The rules, techniques of a lifetime devoted to allegory, have ruined me." According to the usual Christian plot, Ivo must lose himself before he can be saved, but in Gardner's story, Ivo's salvation proves at best ambiguous—as ambiguous as the advice given by the knight errant whom he meets: "Nothing means anything."

"THE WARDEN"

The next story, "The Warden," does to the exis-

tentialist preoccupation with Nothing what much of postmodern fiction does: puts it to comic use, as in the joke line from Thomas Pynchon's *V.* (1963), "Nothing was coming; nothing was already here." The story draws heavily on Poe and Kafka, adds a dash of Samuel Beckett, and ends with the opening lines of Jean-Paul Sartre's *L'Être et le néant* (1943; *Being and Nothingness*, 1956). "The Warden" also leaves its narrator, Vortrab (perhaps a variant of the German *Vortrag*, meaning "performance"), in a far worse, and also more humorous, predicament than the soon-to-be-sainted Ivo, cut off from the guards and prisoners whom he nominally (but without any real authority) commands, from the warden who may be dead, and from his own family (especially his father, a painter). Josef Mallin, the villain of the piece, is a composite of the anarchist figures of the previous three stories, "a nihilist, destroyer of churches, murderer of medical doctors," who, until his execution, opposed all ideas on the grounds that they led people to believe in the possibility of a better world (according to Mallin, an illusion). Not much has changed by the story's end. Vortrab is still waiting for the warden to open his door ("The Parable of the Law" from Kafka's *The Trial*, 1937) and even says to the guard Heller what the warden previously said to Vortrab: "You and I are the only hope."

"JOHN NAPPER SAILING THROUGH THE UNIVERSE"

Vortrab's situation is not so much existentially tragicomic as it is comically parodic. The fifth of "The Midnight Reader's" five stories strikes a slightly different note and depends less on virtuoso technique than on willed affirmation. Gardner drops the literary masks (Poe, Melville, Kafka, and others) to speak, which is to say to narrate, in his own voice, the voice of "John Gardner," a fictive character and therefore, autobiographical appearances aside, another mask. Adrift in the same southern Illinois as the Reverend Pick and the country doctor, John and Joan Gardner take off for Europe in search of the jovial John Napper (a character based on the actual artist who illustrated Gardner's 1972 novel *The Sunlight Dialogues*). Arriving in Paris, they find that the Nappers are in London, but disappointment gives way to dismay when the house sitter shows them some paintings from an early period, the work of an artist the Gardners cannot recognize: "dark, furious, intellectual, full of scorn and something suicidal. Mostly black, with struggles of light, losing." Simply put, Napper was what Gardner the narrator/character now is. Gardner soon learns that what saved Napper was his discovery that the cheerful "nonsense" of his later paintings "lighted his sad wife's eyes." In the eyes of his own young daughter, in the painting that Lucy has "commissioned" for seven dark English pennies, Gardner sees the beginning of the very conflict that Napper's art—indeed any art—must depict and, even if only temporarily, offset: "In the pretty flowers, the pretty face, my daughter's eyes were calculating." It is an image that leaves Lucy poised between innocence and experience, between the taking of selfish advantage and paying the price, as Napper has, of selfless, although self-conscious, affirmation.

"TALES OF QUEEN LOUISA"

The three "Tales of Queen Louisa," which make up the book's second part, take the form of fairy tales and so can afford to be less ambiguously affirmative. In drawing on the fairy-tale form here and in his books for young readers, Gardner was contributing to what was fast becoming a postmodern practice: the retelling and defamiliarizing of simple narrative structures—myths and epics as well as fairy tales—by John Barth (*Chimera*, 1972), Donald Barthelme (*Snow White*, 1967, "The Glass Mountain"), Robert Coover (*Pricksongs and Descants*, 1969), Angela Carter (*The Bloody Chamber and Other Stories*, 1979), and others, including Gardner (*Grendel*). Dotted with allusions to contemporary affairs (for example, the war in Vietnam, the kidnapping of Patty Hearst), the three stories recycle traditional plots and character types for decidedly metafictional (but also moral-fictional) purposes. In the only kingdom where imagination rules (the mad Queen's imagination), art wins, righting all wrongs, transforming pregnant chambermaids into long-lost princesses.

"THE KING'S INDIAN"

In "The King's Indian," the Queen's metamorphosing imagination and the transcendent truth that it makes real by royal decree are outdone by the nar-

rative gamesmanship of John Gardner and Jonathan Upchurch. "The King's Indian" is a strange and exuberant work in the American tall-tale tradition, having characters, plots, and themes borrowed from Poe, Nathaniel Hawthorne, Melville, Jack London, Coleridge, Shakespeare, Percy Bysshe Shelley, Homer, and Frank L. Baum, among others, and told in a parodically and self-consciously metafictional manner through a relay of narrators. There is the tale's ostensible narrator, the walleyed Upchurch, who tells his tale in the manner of Coleridge's Ancient Mariner to a "guest" whose responses to Upchurch's alternately mesmerizing and infuriatingly "overblown" tale are duly noted. Then there is the barely perceptible narrator who apparently contrives Jonathan's "crafty fabulation" in a prison cell to pass the time before his execution and thus to keep his mind from the existential abyss into which Jonathan nearly tumbles. Finally, near the tale's end, John Gardner makes a "guest" appearance to announce that "The King's Indian" is not "a cynical trick, one more joke on exhausted art" but instead a monument, a collage, a celebration of all literature and life. It is, however, a claim about which even "John Gardner" has his doubts, doubts that the reader—recalling the conundrum of the Cretan barber who claims that all Cretans are liars—must necessarily share.

The relay of narrators mirrors the story's infinite regress of tales within tales, all stacked like a nest of Chinese boxes. Following the plot of Poe's *The Narrative of Arthur Gordon Pym* (1838), Upchurch finds himself aboard the whaler *New Jerusalem*, whose Captain Dirge turns out to be a ventriloquist's dummy crafted by the pseudonymous Swami Havananda (disguised as the mate Wilkins) and manipulated by master mesmerist and archtrickster Dr. Luther Flint (disguised as the blind seer Jeremiah). Like Harry Houdini, born Ehrich Weiss, Flint and his assistant play and prey upon the credulity of others yet nevertheless long for some one, stable, absolute truth in the world of illusion, which their theatrical artistry mimics and extends. Tricksters by "maniacal compulsion," they, like so many characters in Gardner's fiction (Grendel and the Sunlight Man in particular), long for a state that is unattainable and may not even exist (outside art and religion). Failing in their quest, they end up feeling betrayed. Upchurch learns that a wise man settles for less, "for Ithaca," which in his case translates to the cry "On to Illinois the Changeable," accompanied not by Dirge's beautiful daughter Augusta but by Flint's battered Miranda (Augusta unmasked). The reader faces a similar choice in judging a story that, on the one hand, offers the literary equivalent of "the magnificence of God and of all his Creation" and, on the other, suggests "mere pyrotechnic pointlessness."

THE ART OF LIVING AND OTHER STORIES

That is not a choice that a reader of *The Art of Living and Other Stories* must face. None of the ten stories is stylistically pyrotechnic; all are, if anything, too pointed. Except for "Trumpeter" (another "Queen Louisa" story, told from a dog's point of view), "The Library Horror" (a sophomoric response to William H. Gass's position on the autonomy and self-reflexiveness of all art), and "Vlemk the Box-Painter" (an overlong fairy tale that proves less imaginative and more didactic than *In the Suicide Mountains*, 1977, the novella that Gardner wrote around the same time for adolescent readers), the stories take a more of less realistic rather than (as in *The King's Indian*) self-consciously parodic approach. Realism, however, had always been an essential part of Gardner's immensely varied repertoire of narrative tricks: in *The Resurrection* (1966), *The Sunlight Dialogues, Nickel Mountain, October Light*, and *Mickelsson's Ghosts*, but not in *The Wreckage of Agathon* (1970), *Grendel*, or *Freddy's Book* (1980). "The Joy of the Just" was originally part of *Nickel Mountain* before Gardner decided to turn his collection of interrelated stories into a "pastoral novel," and "Stillness" was drawn from a novel (posthumously published) that Gardner wrote as a form of marriage therapy (the marriage failed but the novel, even though never revised for publication, is remarkable).

"REDEMPTION"

"Redemption" was also written as "bibliotherapy" and became the means by which Gardner began to come to terms with the guilt that he felt over the accidental death of his younger brother Gilbert in 1945.

The story is deeply autobiographical and, from its opening sentences, quietly devastating:

> One day in April—a clear, blue day, when there were crocuses in bloom—Jack Hawthorne ran over and killed his brother David. Even at the last moment he could have prevented his brother's death by slamming on the tractor's brakes, easily in reach for all the shortness of his legs; but he was unable to think, or, rather, thought unclearly, and so watched it happen, as he would again and again watch it happen in his mind, with nearly undiminished intensity and clarity, all his life.

After a long period of self-hatred, rage, and withdrawal (from others, especially his family, and into music), Jack will be redeemed—not, however, by his own playing but by that of his teacher, a master musician whose own sufferings during the Russian Revolution match Jack's. Realizing that he will never play as well as Yegudkin, Jack returns home, finding in the human herd that he, like Friedrich Wilhelm Nietzsche, had formerly scorned, a sense of belonging to something larger, more important, and more forgiving than himself. "Redemption" succeeds so well because it creates, but does not attempt to resolve, the tension between the greatness of what Gardner liked to call "true art"—its visionary power—and the failure of artists and indeed individuals to make their lives art's equal.

"COME ON BACK"

In "Come on Back," the immense gap between the visionary and the quotidian leads one character to take his life but leads the survivors to join in song and thus overcome their individual grief. In the title story, a small-town cook, Arnold Deller, overcomes the loss of a son in Vietnam by preparing a dish that his son had praised in a letter and that, despite their misgivings, members of a local motorcycle gang share with him in a bizarre but nevertheless religious communion. As the cook explains, "'Love by policy, not just instinct.' That's the Art of Living." Rewarding and quietly effective as "Redemption," "Stillness," "Come on Back," and the title story are, the collection as a whole lacks the disruptive energies that characterize *The King's Indian* and that make its affirmations aesthetically as well as morally interesting.

OTHER MAJOR WORKS

LONG FICTION: *The Resurrection*, 1966; *The Wreckage of Agathon*, 1970; *Grendel*, 1971; *The Sunlight Dialogues*, 1972; *Nickel Mountain: A Pastoral Novel*, 1973; *October Light*, 1976; *In the Suicide Mountains: A Pastoral Novel*, 1977; *Freddy's Book*, 1980; *Mickelsson's Ghosts*, 1982; "Stillness" and "Shadows," 1986 (with Nicholas Delbanco).

PLAYS: *The Temptation Game*, pr. 1977 (radio play); *Death and the Maiden*, pb. 1979; *Frankenstein*, pb. 1979 (libretto); *Rumpelstiltskin*, pb. 1979 (libretto); *William Wilson*, pb. 1979 (libretto).

POETRY: *Jason and Medeia*, 1973; *Poems*, 1978.

NONFICTION: *The Construction of the Wakefield Cycle*, 1974; *The Construction of Christian Poetry in Old English*, 1975; *The Poetry of Chaucer*, 1977; *The Life and Times of Chaucer*, 1977; *On Moral Fiction*, 1978; *On Becoming a Novelist*, 1983; *The Art of Fiction: Notes on Craft for Young Writers*, 1984.

CHILDREN'S LITERATURE: *Dragon, Dragon and Other Tales*, 1975; *Gudgekin the Thistle Girl and Other Tales*, 1976; *A Child's Bestiary*, 1977; *The King of the Hummingbirds and Other Tales*, 1977.

TRANSLATION: *Gilgamesh*, 1984 (with John Maier).

EDITED TEXTS: *The Forms of Fiction*, 1962 (edited with Lennis Dunlap); *The Complete Works of the Gawain-Poet*, 1965; *Papers on the Art and Age of Geoffrey Chaucer*, 1967 (edited with Nicholas Joost); *The Alliterative "Morte d'Arthure," "The Owl and the Nightingale," and Five Other Middle English Poems*, 1971.

BIBLIOGRAPHY

Chavkin, Allan, ed. *Conversations with John Gardner*. Jackson: University Press of Mississippi, 1990. Although the nineteen interviews collected here represent only a fraction of the number that the loquacious Gardner gave, they are among the most important and are nicely complemented by Chavkin's analysis of the larger Gardner in his introduction.

Cowart, David. *Arches and Light: The Fiction of John Gardner*. Carbondale: Southern Illinois University Press, 1983. Like so many Gardner critics, Cowart is too willing to take Gardner at his (moral fiction) word. Cowart is, however, an intelligent and astute reader. He devotes separate chapters to *The King's Indian*, the children's stories, and *The Art of Living and Other Stories*.

Fenlon, Katherine Feeney. "John Gardner's 'The Ravages of Spring' as Re-creation of 'The Fall of the House of Usher.'" *Studies in Short Fiction* 31 (Summer, 1994): 481-487. Shows how Gardner re-creates Poe's story and Americanizes its details, providing a comprehensive interpretation of "The Fall of the House of Usher." Argues that Gardner's story, which compares dreaming to artistic creation, interprets what happens in Poe's story as the construction of the art work.

Henderson, Jeff. *John Gardner: A Study of the Short Fiction*. Boston: Twayne, 1990. Henderson provides a detailed and comprehensive analysis of *The King's Indian, The Art of Living and Other Stories*, the tales for children, and Gardner's last published story, "Julius Caesar and the Werewolf." Henderson includes previously unpublished Gardner materials and excerpts from previously published studies.

_____, ed. *Thor's Hammer: Essays on John Gardner*. Conway: University of Central Arkansas Press, 1985. Of the fifteen original essays collected here, two will be of special interest to students of the short fiction: John Howell's excellent and groundbreaking essay on "Redemption" and Robert A. Morace's overview of Gardner's critical reception.

McWilliams, Dean. *John Gardner*. Boston: Twayne, 1990. McWilliams includes little biographical material and does not try to be at all comprehensive, yet he has an interesting and certainly original thesis: that Gardner's fiction may be more fruitfully approached via Mikhail Bakhtin's theory of dialogism than via *On Moral Fiction*. Unfortunately, the chapters (on the novels and *Jason and Medeia*) tend to be rather introductory in approach and only rarely dialogical in focus.

Morace, Robert A. *John Gardner: An Annotated Secondary Bibliography*. New York: Garland, 1984. Morace lists and annotates in detail all known speeches and interviews with Gardner and reviews and criticism of his work.

Morace, Robert A., and Kathryn Van Spanckeren, eds. *John Gardner: Critical Perspectives*. Carbondale: Southern Illinois University Press, 1982. This first book devoted to criticism of Gardner's work includes a discussion of "Vlemk the Box-Painter" (in Morace's introduction), separate essays on *The King's Indian* and the children's stories, and Gardner's afterword.

Morris, Gregory L. *A World of Order and Light: The Fiction of John Gardner*. Athens: University of Georgia Press, 1984. In his chapters on *The King's Indian* and *The Art of Living and Other Stories*, Morris, like David Cowart, stays within the framework that Gardner himself established; unlike Cowart, however, Morris contends that moral art is a process by which order is discovered, not (as Cowart believes) made.

Yardley, Jonathan. "The Moral of the Story." *The Washington Post*, April 17, 1994, p. X3. A review of Gardner's *On Writers and Writing*, a collection of his reviews and literary essays. Discusses Gardner's controversial insistence on fiction that was moral and affirmative and his distaste for fiction that celebrated technique for its own sake or for the sake of the author's personal amusement.

Robert A. Morace

HAMLIN GARLAND

Born: West Salem, Wisconsin; September 14, 1860

Died: Hollywood, California; March 4, 1940

PRINCIPAL SHORT FICTION

Main-Travelled Roads: Six Mississippi Valley Stories, 1891

Prairie Folks, 1893

Wayside Courtships, 1897

Other Main-Travelled Roads, 1910

They of the High Trails, 1916

The Book of the American Indian, 1923

OTHER LITERARY FORMS

Hamlin Garland's more than fifty published works include nearly every literary type—novels, biography, autobiography, essays, dramas, and poems. His best and most memorable novels are *Rose of Dutcher's Coolly* (1895), similar in plot to the later Theodore Dreiser novel, *Sister Carrie* (1900), and *Boy Life on the Prairie* (1899), chronicling the social history of Garland's boyhood. One book of essays, *Crumbling Idols* (1894), presents his theory of realism ("veritism"). His autobiographical quartet, *A Son of the Middle Border* (1917), *A Daughter of the Middle Border* (1921), *Trail-Makers of the Middle Border* (1926), and *Back-Trailers from the Middle Border* (1928), recounts the story of his family. *A Daughter of the Middle Border* won the Pulitzer Prize for 1922. These books contain episodes that are treated in greater detail in some of his short stories.

ACHIEVEMENTS

Hamlin Garland's work stands at an important transition point from Romanticism to realism, playing a role in ushering in the new literary trend. His best works are important for their depiction of a segment of society seldom delineated by other writers and for the relationship they show between literature and its socioeconomic environment. He used American themes—rather than Americanized European themes—and commonplace characters and incidents that turned the American writer away from his colonial complex, even away from the New England tradition of letters. His realism emancipated the American Midwest and West and the American farmer particularly from the romanticized conception that kept their story from being told before. Like Walt Whitman, Garland wanted writers to tell about life as they knew it and witnessed it. His realism foreshadowed the work of young writers such as Stephen Crane, E. W. Howe, and Harold Frederic. His naturalistic inclination, apparent in his belief that environment is crucial in shaping men's lives, preceded the naturalistic writing of Crane, Frank Norris, and Dreiser. Aside from their value as literature, Garland's best stories are a comprehensive record of an otherwise relatively unreported era of American social history. Much read in his prime, he enjoyed considerable popularity even while antagonizing, with his merciless word pictures, the very people about whom he wrote. Garland was awarded honorary degrees from the University of Wisconsin, the University of Southern California, Northwestern University, and Beloit College. In 1918, he was elected to the board of directors of the American Academy of Arts and Letters. He won the Pulitzer Prize for Biography and Autobiography in 1922.

Hamlin Garland (Library of Congress)

BIOGRAPHY

Of Scotch-Irish descent, Hannibal Hamlin Garland moved with his family from Wisconsin, where he was born in West Salem on September 14, 1860, to an Iowa farm while still a child. Years spent on the farm made him seek escape through a career in oratory. To this end, he attended Cedar Valley Seminary from which he was graduated in 1881. He held a land claim in North Dakota for a year, but mortgaged it for the chance to go East and enroll in Boston University. He succeeded in getting to Boston but was unable to attend the university; however, he embarked on a self-directed program of reading in the holdings of the Boston Public Library. While in Boston, he began writing, his first attempts being lectures, then stories and books. It was around this time also that he joined the Anti-Poverty Society and became an active reformer. He read Henry George and embraced the Single Tax theory as a solution to some of the many contemporary social problems.

Donald Pizer, along with many scholars, divides Garland's career into three general phases: a period of political and social reform activity that coincides with his most memorable fiction set in the Middle West (1884-1895); a period of popular romance-writing in which his settings shifted from the Midwest to the Rocky Mountains (1896-1916); and a period of increasing political and social conservatism, during which he wrote his major autobiographical works (1917-1940). In 1899, Garland married Zulime Taft, and they became parents of daughters born in 1904 and 1907. His list of acquaintances and friends grew to include such literary figures as William Dean Howells, Eugene Field, Joseph Kirkland, Edward Eggleston, Frank Norris, Stephen Crane, George Bernard Shaw, and Rudyard Kipling.

He lived the last years of his life in Hollywood, where he could be near his married daughter. In these later years, he turned more seriously to a lifelong fascination with the occult, producing two books on the subject. He died of cerebral hemorrhage in Hollywood on March 4, 1940.

ANALYSIS

Hamlin Garland's most enduring short stories are

those dealing with the Middle Border (the prairie lands of Iowa, Wisconsin, Minnesota, Nebraska, and the Dakotas). Collected for the most part in four books, they touch on nearly every subject of everyday life, from birth through youth, adulthood, courtship, and marriage, to death. They deal with the unromantic life of harassed generations on the farms and in the small towns of the prairie. Garland's belief that an author must write of "what is" with an eye toward "what is to be" causes him alternately to describe, prophesy, suggest, and demand. Although often subtle in his approach, he is sometimes, when championing the cause of the farmer, more the reformer than the artist. Social protest is the single most recurrent theme in his work. "A Stopover at Tyre" and "Before the Low Green Door" show with some skill the unrelenting drudgery of the farmer's life.

"UNDER THE LION'S PAW"

"Under the Lion's Paw," Garland's most anthologized story, is his most powerful statement of protest. In it, one man, Tim Haskins, like thousands of struggling farmers, is exploited by another man, representative of scores of other land speculators. Haskins, through months of arduous labor, pushing his own and his wife's energies to their limits, has managed to make the dilapidated farm he is renting a productive place of which he can be proud. He has begun to feel confident that he can buy the farm and make a success of it. The owner, however, has taken note of the many physical improvements Haskins has made and recognizes its increased value. Thus, when Haskins talks to the owner about buying the place, he is astonished to learn that the purchase price has doubled and the rent has been increased. Haskins is "under the lion's paw," caught in untenable circumstances that will hurt him no matter what he does. If he gives up the farm, as his angry indignation dictates, he will lose all the money and time he has invested in the farm's improvements. If he buys, he will be under a heavy mortgage that could be foreclosed at any time. If he continues to rent at the higher fee, all his work will almost literally be for the owner's benefit, not for himself and his family. The personally satisfying alternative of simply striking the man dead is wildly considered by Haskins momentarily until the thought

of the repercussions to his family brings him to his senses, and he agrees to buy on the owner's terms. The situation in itself is cruel. Garland clearly shows that it is even worse when one realizes that the exploitation of Haskins is only one of thousands of similar cases.

"LUCRETIA BURNS"

"Lucretia Burns," another social protest story, is longer and has more action and a more complex major character than the similar "Before the Low Green Door." Although some of its impact is diminished by its tiresome discussions on reform and by its weak denouement, Garland has created in Lucretia an unforgettable character who makes the story praiseworthy. Lucretia is a strong personality who had "never been handsome, even in her days of early childhood, and now she was middle-aged, distorted with work and childbearing, and looking faded and worn." Her face is "a pitifully worn, almost tragic face—long, thin, sallow, hollow-eyed. The mouth had long since lost the power to shape itself into a kiss. . . ." She has reached a point of desperation that calls for some kind of action: confrontation (with her husband), capitulation, or a mental breakdown. She chooses to renounce her soul-killing existence and operate on a level of bare subsistence, with no more struggling to "get ahead" or do what is expected. When the spirit of rebellion overcomes her, she simply gives in to her chronic weariness and refuses to do more than feed her children and the husband for whom she no longer cares.

For a successful conclusion to this powerful indictment against the farm wife's hopeless life, Garland had several choices. Unfortunately, he chose the ineffectual ending in which a dainty, young, idealistic schoolteacher persuades Lucretia to give life another try. The reader, having seen Lucretia's determination to stop the drudgery in her life forever, is dissatisfied, knowing it would have taken a great deal more than a sympathetic stranger to convince Lucretia that her life was worth enduring.

"A SOCIABLE AT DUDLEYS"

This kind of lapse is not Garland's only flaw. Occasionally, he leads on his readers, telling them what they should think about a character. In "A Sociable at Dudleys," for example, he describes the county bully:

"No lizard revelled in the mud more hideously than he. . . . His tongue dropped poison." Garland apparently abhorred the "vileness of the bully's whole life and thought." Moreover, in most of the stories, one can tell the heroes from the villains by the Aryan features and Scottish names of the former and the dark, alien looks of the latter. His heroes are further categorized into two prevailing physical types: Either they are tall, imposing, strong, even powerful and handsome (Tim Haskins is an older, more worn version of this type) or they are stocky, sturdy, ambitious, cheerful, and optimistic counterparts of the young Hamlin Garland as he described himself in *A Son of the Middle Border*. Will Hannan of "A Branch Road" falls into this category.

"A BRANCH ROAD"

"A Branch Road" develops another favorite theme of Garland—a romantic one in which boy meets girl; misunderstanding separates them; and then adversity reunites them. Although this plot is well-worn today, in the late 1800's and early 1900's, the reading public still liked it, and Garland occasionally catered to the larger reading public. "A Branch Road" is long enough for the author to develop character, setting, and plot in a more leisurely, less personal manner than in some of his other stories on the same theme, such as "A Day of Grace," "A Sociable at Dudleys," and "William Bacon's Man." In "A Branch Road," young Will Hannan and Agnes Dingman have fallen in love. Will is ecstatic when he goes to the Dingman farm to help with the threshing, secure in his belief that she cares as much for him as he for her.

Once at the farm, however, listening to the other men, both young and older, making casual, joking comments about Agnes's prettiness and her attraction to most of the young swains in the county, Will becomes apprehensive that they will notice her obvious preference for him and make light of his deep private feelings. To prevent this, he repays her smiling attentions to him with curt words and an aloof manner. Agnes is hurt and confused by this, not understanding his masculine pride and sensitivity to ridicule. She responds by keeping up a light-hearted demeanor by smiling and talking to the other men, who are delighted, a response that makes Will rage inwardly.

The day is a disaster for Will, but because he is to take Agnes to the fair in a few days, he is confident that he will be able then to set things right.

On the morning of the day of the fair, however, the hopeful lover sets out early, but promptly loses a wheel from his buggy, requiring several hours of delay for repair. By the time he gets to Agnes's house, she has gone to the fair with Will's rival, Ed Kinney. Will is so enraged by this turn of events that he cannot think. Dominated by his pride and jealous passion, blaming her and considering no alternatives, he leaves the county, heading West, without a word of farewell or explanation to Agnes.

Seven years later he returns to find Agnes married to Ed Kinney, mother of a baby, daughter-in-law to two pestering old people, and distressingly old before her time. Will manages to speak privately to her and learns how he and she had misunderstood each other's actions on that day long ago. He finds she had indeed loved him. He accepts that it is his fault her life is now so unhappy, that she is so abused and worn. In defiance of custom and morality, he persuades her to leave her husband and go away with him. They flee, taking her baby with them.

In outline, this is the familiar melodrama of the villain triumphing over the fair maiden while the hero is away; then, just in time, the hero returns to rescue the heroine from the villain's clutches. Actually, however, Garland avoids melodrama and even refrains from haranguing against farm drudgery. He avoids the weak denouement and chooses instead a rather radical solution to the problem: The abduction of a wife and baby by another man was a daring ending to an American 1890's plot. Yet Garland makes the justice of the action acceptable.

Will Hannan, a very sensitive young man living among people who seem coarse and crude, is propelled through the story by strong, understandable emotions: love, pride, anger, fear of humiliation, remorse, pity, and guilt. Love causes the anger that creates the confusion in his relationship with Agnes. Pride and fear of humiliation drive him away from her. Remorse pursues him all the time he is away and is largely responsible for his return. Pity and guilt make him steal Agnes away from the life to which he feels he has condemned her. Many of Garland's other stories do not have the emotional motivation of characters that "A Branch Road" has (in all fairness, most are not as long); nor are Garland's characters generally as complex. He seems less concerned with probing a personality's reaction to a situation than with describing the consequences of an act.

The theme of the return of the native to his Middle Border home is used in several stories, among them "Up the Coolly," "Mrs. Ripley's Trip," and "Among the Corn Rows."

"THE RETURN OF A PRIVATE"

Less pessimistic and tragic and more sentimental than these is "The Return of a Private," an elaboration of Garland's father's return from the Civil War as told in the first chapter of *A Son of the Middle Border*. The story describes the sadness which old war comrades feel as they go their separate ways home. It describes the stirring emotions which the returning soldier feels as he nears his home and sees familiar landmarks; when he first catches sight of the homestead; when he sees his nearly disbelieving wife and the children who hardly remember him. They are tender scenes, but Garland the artist cannot contain Garland the reformer, who reminds the reader of the futility facing the soldier, handicapped physically from war-connected fever and ague and handicapped financially by the heavy mortgage on his farm. The soldier's homecoming is shown as one tiny, bright moment in what has been and will continue to be an endless cycle of dullness and hardship. Garland obviously empathizes with the character and shows the homecoming as a sweet, loving time, but, as with so many of his stories, "The Return of a Private" is overcast with gloom.

Garland's stories show the ugly and the beautiful, the tragic with the humorous, the just with the unjust. He tries always to show the true, reporting the speech and dress of the people accurately, describing their homes and their work honestly. Truth, however, is not all that he seeks; he wants significance as well. To this end, his stories show the effects of farm drudgery on the men and women, of the ignorant practices of evangelists, of the thwarted ambitions of the youth because of circumstances beyond their control. Garland does not always suppress his reformer's instincts, and so in some stories he offers solutions. In his best stories, however, he simply shows the injustice and moves the reader, by his skillful handling of details, to wish to take action. Although his stories are often bitter and depressing, there is a hopefulness and optimism in Garland that compels him to bring them to a comparatively happy ending. In his best stories, he does for the Middle Border what Mary E. Wilkins Freeman does for New England, brings the common people into rich relation with the reader and shows movingly the plights of the less fortunate among them, especially women.

OTHER MAJOR WORKS

LONG FICTION: *A Member of the Third House*, 1892; *Jason Edwards: An Average Man*, 1892; *A Little Norsk*, 1892; *A Spoil of Office*, 1892; *Rose of Dutcher's Coolly*, 1895; *The Spirit of Sweetwater*, 1898 (reissued as *Witch's Gold*, 1906); *Boy Life on the Prairie*, 1899; *The Eagle's Heart*, 1900; *Her Mountain Lover*, 1901; *The Captain of the Gray-Horse Troop*, 1902; *Hesper*, 1903; *The Light of the Star*, 1904; *The Tyranny of the Dark*, 1905; *The Long Trail*, 1907; *Money Magic*, 1907 (reissued as *Mart Haney's Mate*, 1922); *The Moccasin Ranch*, 1909; *Cavanagh, Forest Ranger*, 1910; *Victor Ollnee's Discipline*, 1911; *The Forester's Daughter*, 1914.

PLAYS: *Under the Wheel: A Modern Play in Six Scenes*, pb. 1890.

POETRY: *Prairie Songs*, 1893.

NONFICTION: *Crumbling Idols: Twelve Essays on Art*, 1894; *Ulysses S. Grant: His Life and Character*, 1898; *Out-of-Door Americans*, 1901; *A Son of the Middle Border*, 1917; *A Daughter of the Middle Border*, 1921; *Trail-Makers of the Middle Border*, 1926; *The Westward March of American Settlement*, 1927; *Back-Trailers from the Middle Border*, 1928; *Roadside Meetings*, 1930; *Companions on the Trail: A Literary Chronicle*, 1931; *My Friendly Contemporaries: A Literary Log*, 1932; *Afternoon Neighbors*, 1934; *Joys of the Trail*, 1935; *Forty Years of Psychic Research: A Plain Narrative of Fact*, 1936.

BIBLIOGRAPHY

Garland, Hamlin. *Selected Letters of Hamlin Garland*. Edited by Keith Newlin and Joseph B. McCullough. Lincoln: University of Nebraska Press, 1998. The volume's introduction serves as a good entry into Hamlin's biography.

Joseph, Philip. "Landed and Literary: Hamlin Garland, Sarah Orne Jewett, and the Production of Regional Literatures." *Studies in American Fiction* 26 (Autumn, 1998): 147-170. Compares some of Garland's early stories with the stories in Jewett's *Country of the Pointed Firs* to examine ideological conflict within literary regionalism. Argues that while Garland's support for social reform leads him to challenge some of the conventions of late nineteenth century realism, Jewett does not see class differences as a hindrance to U.S. destiny.

Kaye, Frances. "Hamlin Garland's Feminism." In *Women and Western Literature*, edited by Helen Winter Stauffer and Susan Rosowski. Troy, N.Y.: Whitston, 1982. Kaye discusses Garland's deliberate feminism, identifying him as the only male author of note at the end of the nineteenth century who spoke in favor of women's rights, suffrage, and equality in marriage.

McCullough, Joseph. *Hamlin Garland*. Boston: Twayne, 1978. This study follows Garland through his literary career, dividing it into phases, with major attention to the first phase of his reform activities and the midwestern stories. A primary bibliography and a select, annotated secondary bibliography are included.

Martin, Quentin E. "Hamlin Garland's 'The Return of a Private' and 'Under the Lion's Paw' and the Monopoly of Money in Post-Civil War America." *American Literary Realism* 29 (Fall, 1996): 62-77. Discusses how Garland made money and power the central features in his two stories; discusses the connection between the stories and the financial system of Gilded Age America in the 1890's.

Nagel, James, ed. *Critical Essays on Hamlin Garland*. Boston: G. K. Hall, 1982. Nagel's introduction surveys the critical responses to Garland's work. This volume is especially rich in reviews of Garland's books, and it also includes twenty-six biographical and critical essays.

Newlin, Keith. "Melodramatist of the Middle Border: Hamlin Garland's Early Work Reconsidered." *Studies in American Fiction* 21 (Autumn, 1993): 153-169. Discusses Garland's development of a dramatic method to express the privation of the Middle Border; argues that he was torn between his admiration for the universal truths of melodrama and his realization that melodrama was limited in its realistic presentation of life.

Newlin, Keith, ed. *Hamlin Garland: A Bibliography, with a Checklist of Unpublished Letters*. Troy, N.Y.: Whitston Publishing, 1998. Basically a primary bibliography, with one section listing articles that addressed Garland extensively. The introduction surveys the availability of primary and secondary sources. Newlin includes a chronology and title index.

Pizer, Donald. *Hamlin Garland's Early Work and Career*. Berkeley: University of California Press, 1960. Pizer treats in careful detail Garland's intellectual and artistic development during the first phase of his literary and reformist career, from 1884 to 1895. He discusses Garland's development of his creed, his literary output, and reform activities in society, theater, politics, and the arts. Pizer includes a detailed bibliography of Garland's publications during these years.

Silet, Charles. *Henry Blake Fuller and Hamlin Garland: A Reference Guide*. Boston: G. K. Hall, 1977. This volume contains a comprehensive annotated guide to writing about Garland through 1975. For information about scholarly writing on Garland after 1975, see *American Literary Scholarship: An Annual*.

Silet, Charles, Robert Welch, and Richard Boudreau, eds. *The Critical Reception of Hamlin Garland, 1891-1978*. Troy, N.Y.: Whitston, 1985. This illustrated volume contains thirty-three essays that illustrate the development of Garland's literary reputation from 1891 to 1978. The introduction emphasizes the difficulty critics have had trying to determine the quality of Garland's art.

Taylor, Walter. *The Economic Novel in America*. Chapel Hill: University of North Carolina Press,

1942. Taylor examines Garland's work in the context of fiction that reflects economic issues and trends. In Garland's literary career he sees a reflection of the fall of pre-Civil War agrarian democracy with the halting of the advance of the frontier and the decline of populism.

Jane L. Ball,
updated by Terry Heller

GEORGE GARRETT

Born: Orlando, Florida; June 11, 1929

PRINCIPAL SHORT FICTION

King of the Mountain, 1958
In the Briar Patch, 1961
Cold Ground Was My Bed Last Night, 1964
A Wreath for Garibaldi and Other Stories, 1969
The Magic Striptease, 1973
An Evening Performance: New and Selected Stories, 1985
The Old Army Game: A Novel and Stories, 1994
Bad Man Blues: A Portable George Garrett, 1998

OTHER LITERARY FORMS

Although early in his career George Garrett was best known as a poet, he later gained recognition as an important contemporary novelist as well. He has written several plays and screenplays, and his *The Young Lovers* (1964) has become a cult favorite. Garrett has received particular acclaim for his historical novels, *Death of the Fox* (1971) and *The Succession* (1983), both set in Elizabethan England. Garrett has also written a biography and critical studies and has written, edited, and contributed to many books and journals on film, writing, and literary criticism. In 1998, *Days of Our Lives Lie in Fragments: New and Old Poems, 1957-1997*, a collection of his poems, was published.

ACHIEVEMENTS

George Garrett has been awarded fellowships from the National Endowment for the Arts and the John Simon Guggenheim Memorial Foundation, the Rome Prize of the American Academy of Arts and Letters, and a Ford Foundation grant, among many other honors. Through his teaching, editing, and writing, Garrett influenced contemporary American letters directly and significantly. Garrett received the T. S. Eliot Award for creative writing from the Ingersoll Foundation (1989), the PEN/Malamud Award for short fiction (1991), and the Hollins College Medal (1992). In 1994, he was awarded an honorary doctorate from the University of the South.

BIOGRAPHY

George Palmer Garrett, Jr., was born on June 11, 1929, in Orlando, Florida, one of three children and the only son of George Palmer and Rosalie Toomer Garrett. He was graduated from Sewanee Military Academy in 1946 and prepped at the Hill School in 1946-1947 before entering Princeton University. He was graduated from there in 1952 magna cum laude and a member of Phi Beta Kappa. He earned his M.A. in English from Princeton University in 1956 with a thesis on the poetry of William Faulkner, a work of scholarship which is still read by scholars who want to know the early Faulkner. Garrett enlisted in the U.S. Army Reserves in 1950 and was soon called to two years of active duty in Yugoslavia and Austria, before finishing his M.A. Garrett completed all work for the doctorate except for the dissertation; Princeton accepted his novels *Death of the Fox* and *The Succession* as fulfilling the dissertation requirement and awarded him the Ph.D. in 1985. Active in teaching young writers, Garrett held teaching positions at a number of universities, including the University of South Carolina, Columbia University, Princeton University, and the University of Virginia. In 1984, he became the Hoyns Professor of English at the University of Virginia at Charlottesville. In 1952, he married

George Garrett (©Miriam Berkley)

Susan Parrish Jackson; the marriage produced three children.

ANALYSIS

George Garrett's work spans many genres. Considered both a poet and fiction writer of considerable importance, Garrett produced a body of work that is varied, substantial, and highly regarded. In his two historical novels, *Death of the Fox* and *The Succession*, Garrett is considered to have elevated the level of a popular literary form to that of serious art. In his poetry and his fiction, Garrett's topics alternately range from classical to popular cultures, thus revealing and providing a unique perspective, which at once embraces the ancient and the modern.

"COLD GROUND WAS MY BED LAST NIGHT"

One of Garrett's persistent themes has been that of man's experience as prisoner. In "Cold Ground Was My Bed Last Night," all the characters are prisoners, no matter what side of the bars they live on, or whether, like the Goat Man, they live in the shifting netherworld between imprisonment *de facto* and imprisonment *de jure*. The story opens as deputy Larry Berlin, coming back to the county seat after patrol-ling all night, is almost hit by a car coming around a curve too quickly. Enraged, he turns around and chases it, overtakes it, and slides to a halt across its front, forcing the driver to stop. The driver gets out, pulls out a gun, and the deputy kills him with one shot. Then he discovers that there is someone else inside.

Meanwhile, the sheriff, Jack Riddle, is waiting for Berlin and his prisoner at the sheriff's office and half-seriously threatening the Goat Man, a habitué of the jail, with ninety days if he is caught drunk and disorderly again. He saves a little face, mostly for the sake of the Goat Man, by saying he does not want the goats to starve. The Goat Man, or the Balloon Man, is a leitmotif in Garrett's work, surfacing in places as disparate as the last scene of *The Young Lovers*, and the long story about Quirk. Here, he represents Nature, mindless, oblivious to law or regulation, and incorrigible, something that can imprison one if one believes that Nature will yield to rationalities. The sheriff is unusual; he carries no gun and is not without some compassion. Like most of Garrett's best characters, he is a man of the religious mode. In the office, there is a magazine open to the picture of a naked woman. She is the banal and two-dimensional embodiment of that goddess whom Riddle serves—respectability. The pinup is joined in the close, hot, dirty office by a fly, another objective correlative, this time of life itself, oblivious, buzzing, annoying life. Moreover, the fly seems to be the presiding genius of the place, its totem animal.

Ike Toombs, the other man in the car, is brought in. The sheriff envies him because he represents the open road; he is a shabby modern version of the wayfaring life, but he is a wayfarer nevertheless, and he even sings a verse of the traditional song which gives its name to this story. The sheriff sees in him almost a kindred spirit: Both men are chivalric figures, knight and troubadour.

This illusion, however, soon begins to break down. The prisoner tries to wheedle his release from the sheriff, who has established some kind of tacit understanding with the prisoner. Next, officers from the state police call and report that a service station has been held up and a teenage boy was shot the night before by a man driving the car in which Toombs was riding. His friend of the moment has decided Toombs's fate for him, and Toombs has had no hand in it; for now the disappointed sheriff is thrown back on his resources, which are meager once his confidence in himself and his faith in freedom are shaken. The sheriff angrily rejects the wayfarer even though he knows the jury will no doubt convict on circumstantial evidence. He refuses him his old cheap guitar, an act that brings tears to the eyes of the prisoner, and he throws the magazine away. One man has been killed, another sentenced, and another has died a spiritual death.

"A WREATH FOR GARIBALDI"

In another story, "A Wreath for Garibaldi," an American in Rome who "works" at the American Academy, a man who never names himself or is named, is at a party at which an Englishwoman he admires wants to recruit a volunteer to lay a wreath under the huge bronze statue of Giuseppe Garibaldi. There is an awkward silence. Political tension is very strong in Rome that year, old fascists and new radicals are looking very portentous, and a huge scandal has occurred because of an "orgy" at a big party. The government is obsessed with the idea that because Garibaldi Day is April 30 and the next day May Day, the international holiday that in Europe is New Year, Easter, and Christmas all rolled into one for the Second and Third and Fourth Internationals, any wreath honoring Garibaldi is probably a communist provocation.

The American volunteers to lay the wreath at Garibaldi's statue on the condition that he do it alone, no press, just a simple gesture; but he has to go through the ambassador to get permission. He is also asked to leave "a little bunch of flowers" at the bust of anti-fascist poet Lauro di Bosis. In the course of his official dealings with the government, he finds that the bureaucrats do not know who di Bosis is. It is all too evident that everyone knows who Garibaldi is.He is supposed to lay the wreath the next day, but he decides not to go through with it; it was not going to measure up to what the English lady had wanted done. He goes to where the statue of Garibaldi is. Garibaldi looks imperial. The equestrian

statue of his wife, Anna, baby in arms, firing behind her, horse at full gallop, looks silly. He goes across to the bust of di Bosis—"Pale, passionate, yes glorious, and altogether of another time. . . ." He thinks of those who died rushing the village in France in a stupid, pointless frontal attack, of those killed in police stations all over the civilized world, and his feelings change toward di Bosis: "It was a forlorn, foolish adolescent gesture. But it was a kind of beginning." He looks at the bust with "the feelings usually attributed to young girls standing at the grave of Keats."

"THE MAGIC STRIPTEASE"

The theme of mutability and the problem of the artist's acceptance are the two themes of Garrett's long short story, "The Magic Striptease," in the collection of the same name; the odd paradigms of grace and election have been set aside for the critics in this fable, which also has considerable stature as a moral fable. The story is about one Jacob Quirk, "Proteus of Impersonators," as he is briefly known, and the story is told through entries in Quirk's secret journal, through an omniscient narrator, and through trial transcripts. Through his racy, slangy, topical, simpleminded, vulgar, skeptical, weary, and thoroughly American diction, Garrett achieves some of his finest effects and creates a much-needed tension between the burdens of this long fiction and the expectations of his audience. The story follows Quirk through rapid, unremitting change, which happens, as does most change, as a result of inner and spiritual developments which inevitably bring about outer and tangible transformations.

In the State Orphan's Home, no one will adopt Quirk because, as the director says, no one wants a smart-aleck kid. Once grown, he becomes a nightclub performer specializing in impressions. At first, he impersonates famous persons, but this bores him, so he turns to people he has seen on the street, but finds this approach unsuccessful. Quirk, therefore, tells his agent that he does not want to be funny any more, that he wants to be an artist. His agent explains that performing is a business, art is for kids, and Quirk decides to leave him. He intends at first (as he says in his journal) to go where no poet or novelist has ever trod, despite the fact that he will be living characters that are fictional—in other words, that have no life once he leaves them. Moreover, he intends to use his talent coolly and logically.

Quirk's first impersonation is that of the neighborhood postman, whose duties he takes on. It is a sad and sobering experience for him. He discovers that a young man in the neighborhood is a drunkard. A woman upstairs offers herself for an eight-cent postage-due stamp; although her closets are overflowing with good clothes, she sleeps on an old ripped-up mattress, the only furniture in her apartment. Quirk's short tour of duty as a postman gives him "an intoxicated, dizzying sense of his own freedom" because he finds out that most people are totally incurious.

After more impersonations, all of them wildly successful, Quirk changes himself into a beautiful young man and through mere looks prompts a beautiful woman, obviously the mistress of an old, rich, powerful man, to slip him a note suggesting an assignation at the intermission of the opera where they have just met for the first time. They leave, passing a legless beggar. "Beautiful people are a law unto themselves," she says, and Quirk decides to teach her a badly needed object lesson in humility—or at least this is how he explains it to himself; the reader will be wiser. So, after they have made love and the girl is asleep, Quirk changes into the legless beggar, wakes her up, and crab-scuttles out of the room. He has miscalculated, however—her mind is ruined by the experience. For the first time in his life, he has intentionally hurt another human being. Quirk decides to atone. He too becomes maimed, ugly, despised; now he mimes those who are prisoners of fate or their ugly bodies, just as he is a prisoner of his special talent, unique in all the world. Quirk learns that the types and varieties of suffering "exceeded all the possibilities and subtleties of pleasure."

Quirk decides to go forth and tell humanity what he has learned. Unfortunately, when he decides to do so through his impersonation of Jesus Christ, he is arrested and sent to an insane asylum. Now, with Quirk as artist and man, citizen and student of the human condition, at the end of his rope, Garrett expands the allegorical content of his story and has Quirk decide that insanity and suicide are the only options left to a man of sense, feeling, and breeding in this world. The drill of the insane asylum, however, once settled into, unfortunately leaves plenty of time to think, and once more Quirk ponders his art. After all his experiences, Quirk now realizes in a momentous revelation that all along he has been ignoring whole new realms that could be conquered by his art: the animal kingdom, even in the form of a stray dog. Even more extreme, he can become, because of his great artistry, inanimate—even a fire hydrant, which is below the dog, which is below the crazy, which is below the religious teacher, below the untouchable, and so on back up the spiral. His journal ends: "Just look for me where you find me."

BAD MAN BLUES

In the foreword to this collection of stories, essays, sketches, and anecdotes, Richard Bausch insists that there is no writer in America with a more versatile and "restless" talent than George Garrett. Indeed, this miscellany is eloquent testimony to Bausch's accolade. The most significant part of the book is the section of eight stories, the two most important of which are "A Letter That Will Never Be Written" and "Genius Baby." The former is set in 1626 and features characters from Garrett's well-known Elizabeth trilogy: *Death of the Fox, The Succession,* and *Entered from the Sun.* In a short space, Garrett tackles religious obsession, political turmoil, and the creative vitality of Tudor England in an economical précis of the world of his trilogy treatment of the same material.

"Genius Baby" the most engaging story in the collection, is a comic rendering of a writer by a writer who refuses to take himself too seriously. Assuming the form of notes written on a yellow legal pad in a hospital lounge, the narrator tells about his decision to become a writer when, discovering that his wife was turned on by reading pornography and unable to find any of a literary quality, he began writing the stuff himself. However, the central focus of his account is his troubles with his gifted son Genius Baby, whom he cannot tolerate. The conflict between the two comes to a comic head when the child will not let his father in his room to watch Captain Kangaroo on Saturday morning, whereupon the narrator chops down the door with an axe and then destroys the television set and the rest of the furniture. The story ends when Genius Baby gets his revenge by putting alum in a glass of punch the father drinks, drying him up to absolute silence.

The title story of the collection, "Bad Man Blues," is a racial romp told with risky good humor by an African American man about the "last lynching" in Quincy County, Florida. The story is a classic tall tale, albeit about one of the most horrendous and stereotypical forms of racial persecution to take place in the South before the age of civil rights—the lynching of a black man accused of the rape-murder of a white woman. When the accused man, Buster Ford, the "baddest man to come out of Quincy County," is thrown to the lynch mob by the sheriff, he tricks them into chasing another black man and gets away; the ironic result is that the white folks in the town are so embarrassed at being outwitted by Buster that there has not been a lynching in Quincy County since.

In his essay, "Going to See the Elephant: Why We Write Stories," Garrett says the only advice he can give to aspiring young writers is that they are summoned to an "ancient and honorable enterprise" as old as the caves, where our ancestors painted animals on the wall to illustrate stories. For Garrett, people become storytellers because there is no choice; writers are like small boys "whistling in the dark, in a graveyard" to assure the dead that they are fearless.

OTHER MAJOR WORKS

LONG FICTION: *The Finished Man*, 1959; *Which Ones Are the Enemy?*, 1961; *Do, Lord, Remember Me*, 1965; *Death of the Fox*, 1971; *The Succession*, 1983; *Poison Pen*, 1986; *Entered from the Sun*, 1990; *The King of Babylon Shall Not Come Against You*, 1996.

PLAYS: *Sir Slob and the Princess: A Play for Children*, pb. 1962; *Garden Spot, U.S.A.*, pr. 1962; *Enchanted Ground*, pb. 1981.

SCREENPLAYS: *The Young Lovers*, 1964; *The Playground*, 1965; *Frankenstein Meets the Space Monster*, 1966 (with R. H. W. Dillard and John Rodenbeck).

POETRY: *The Reverend Ghost*, 1957; *The Sleeping Gypsy and Other Poems*, 1958; *Abraham's Knife and Other Poems*, 1961; *For a Bitter Season: New and Selected Poems*, 1967; *Welcome to the Medicine Show: Postcards, Flashcards, Snapshots*, 1978; *Luck's Shining Child*, 1981; *The Collected Poems of George Garrett*, 1984; *Days of Our Lives Lie in Fragments: New and Old Poems, 1957-1997*, 1998.

NONFICTION: *James Jones*, 1984; *Understanding Mary Lee Settle*, 1988; *My Silk Purse and Yours: The Publishing Scene and American Literary Art*, 1992; *The Sorrows of Fat City: A Selection of Literary Essays and Reviews*, 1992.

EDITED TEXTS: *New Writing from Virginia*, 1963; *The Girl in the Black Raincoat*, 1966; *Man and the Movies*, 1967 (with W. R. Robinson); *New Writing in South Carolina*, 1971 (with William Peden); *The Sounder Few: Essays from "The Hollins Critic,"* 1971 (with R. H. W. Dillard and John Moore); *Film Scripts One, Two, Three, and Four*, 1971-1972 (with O. B. Hardison, Jr., and Jane Gelfman); *Craft So Hard to Learn*, 1972 (with John Graham); *The Writer's Voice*, 1973 (with John Graham); *Intro 5*, 1974 (with Walton Beacham); *The Botteghe Oscure Reader*, 1974 (with Katherine Garrison Biddle); *Intro 6: Life As We Know It*, 1974; *Intro 7: All of Us and None of You*, 1975; *Intro 8: The Liar's Craft*, 1977; *Intro 9: Close to Home*, 1979 (with Michael Mewshaw); *That's What I Like (About the South), and Other New Southern Stories for the Nineties*, 1993 (with Paul Ruffin).

BIBLIOGRAPHY

Dillard, R. H. W. *Understanding George Garrett*. Columbia: University of South Carolina Press, 1988. The first major critical work on Garrett. Contains individual chapters on *The Finished Man, Which Ones Are the Enemy?, Do, Lord, Remember Me*, the two historical novels, *Poison Pen*, as well as a chapter on the poems and short stories. Supplemented by a helpful bibliography.

Garrett, George. "Going to See the Elephant: Why We Write Stories." In *Bad Man Blues: A Portable George Garrett*. Dallas, Tex.: Southern Methodist University Press, 1998. Talks about growing up in a large family of storytellers; discusses the deeper motivation of storytelling; suggests the duty of storytelling is like that of Pygmies hunting an elephant and then telling the story of the hunt.

George Palmer Garrett: A Bibliography and Index of His Published Works and Criticism of Them. Potsdam, N.Y.: Frederick W. Crumb Memorial Library, 1968. An annotated bibliography of works by and about George Garrett.

Horvath, Brooke, and Irving Malin, eds. *George Garrett: The Elizabethan Trilogy.* Huntsville, Tex.: Texas Review Press, 1998. A critical study of a number of historical figures as they relate to Garrett's work, including Sir Walter Raleigh and Christopher Marlowe. Includes a bibliography and index.

Meriwether, James B. "George Palmer Garrett, Jr." *Princeton University Library Chronicle* 25, no. 1 (1963): 26-39. An introductory article on Garrett's work, acknowledging his excellence in poetry at the time when he was turning his attention more to fiction. Southern and family themes are noted. Complemented by a checklist of Garrett's writings.

Mill Mountain Review 1, no. 4 (Summer, 1971). This special issue on Garrett includes critical essays and personal comments by Fred Chappell, Gordon Lish, and others.

Robinson, W. R. "Imagining the Individual: George Garrett's *Death of the Fox.*" *Hollins Critic* 8 (1971): 1-12. An exploration of the mixture of fact and creation that is inherent in fiction and the historical novel in particular, with extensive quotations from Garrett on the subject. Robinson argues that Garrett's work is a serious creation and surpasses conventional historical fiction.

Sheets, Anna J., ed. *Short Story Criticism: Excerpts from Criticism of the Works of Short Fiction Writers.* Vol. 30. Detroit, Mich.: Gale Research, 1999. Includes excerpts from Garrett, Shmuel Yosef Agnon, Gina Berriault, Theodore Dreiser, Conrad Ferdinand Meyer, Emilia Pardo Bazán, and Leo Tolstoy.

Slavitt, David R. "History—Fate and Freedom: A Look at George Garrett's New Novel." *The Southern Review* 7 (1971): 276-294. In this lengthy first review of *Death of the Fox,* Slavitt examines the novel in relation to Garrett's earlier works and considers the creative process.

Spears, Monroe K. "George Garrett and the Historical Novel." *The Virginia Quarterly Review* 61, no. 2 (Spring, 1985): 262-276. Spears considers how closely *The Succession* and *Death of the Fox* correspond to the traditional definition of the historical novel.

Wier, Allen. "Skin and Bones: George Garrett's Living Spirits." In *Bad Man Blues: A Portable George Garrett.* Dallas, Tex.: Southern Methodist University Press, 1998. Discusses Garrett's interest in the relationship between fact and fiction and the relationship between the present and the past. Comments on Garrett's experimentation with ways of telling stories.

John Carr, updated by Lou Thompson
and Charles E. May

WILLIAM H. GASS

Born: Fargo, North Dakota; July 30, 1924

PRINCIPAL SHORT FICTION

In the Heart of the Heart of the Country and Other Stories, 1968
The First Winter of My Married Life, 1979
The Cartesian Sonata and Other Novellas, 1998

OTHER LITERARY FORMS

Besides his collections of short fiction, William H. Gass has published the novels *Omensetter's Luck* (1966), *Willie Masters' Lonesome Wife* (1968), and *The Tunnel* (1995). He has also written several collections of essays, some of the most provocative literary theory of post-World War II literature, and the studies *Finding a Form* (1996) and *Reading Rilke: Reflections on the Problems of Translation* (1999).

ACHIEVEMENTS

William H. Gass is one of a handful of contemporary American writers who can justifiably be described as pioneers—that is, writers who eschew the well-trod ways of the mass of their fellow writers and chart new directions for literature. The fact that he has been as frequently assailed—most famously by the novelist John Gardner—as praised for his innovations is perhaps the best proof that Gass has indeed made his mark on the literary world. Along with John Barth, Donald Barthelme, and a few other innovators, Gass has shown the reader the artifice behind the art of fiction. At the same time, he has created memorable characters involved in gripping conflicts. Rather than an experimenter or old-fashioned storyteller, though, Gass may best be seen as an impeccable stylist. It is this interest in the relation among the sounds of words that most clearly unifies his short fiction, novellas, novels, and essays. Among his awards and honors are a Rockefeller Foundation Fellowship (1965), the Hovde Prize for Good Teaching (1967), a John Simon Guggenheim Memorial Foundation Fellowship (1969), and the National Institute for Arts and Letters prize for literature (1975). He has also re-

ceived the National Medal of Merit for fiction (1979), the National Book Critics Circle Award for criticism (1986) for *Habitations of the Word: Essays* (1985), the PEN/Faulkner Award for Fiction and the American Book Award (1996) for *The Tunnel* (1995), National Book Critics Circle Award for criticism award (1997) for *Finding a Form* (1996), and the Lifetime Achievement Award from the Lannan Foundation (1997). He has also received honorary doctorates from Kenyon College, George Washington University, and Purdue University.

BIOGRAPHY

William Howard Gass attended Kenyon College in Gambier, Ohio, for one year and Ohio Wesleyan University in Delaware, Ohio, for a brief period of study. During World War II, he served in the U.S. Navy and was stationed in China and Japan. After the war he returned to Kenyon College and was graduated in 1947 with a B.A. degree in philosophy. He earned his Ph.D. from Cornell University in 1954. Gass has taught philosophy at a number of colleges, including the College of Wooster in Ohio (1950-1955), Purdue University in Lafayette, Indiana (1955-1969), and Washington University in St. Louis, where he began teaching in 1969 and where he held the title of David May Distinguished University Professor in the Humanities. In 1990, Gass became the first director of the International Writers' Center at Washington University. Gass married Mary Patricia O'Kelly in 1952; they had two children. In 1969, he married Mary Alice Henderson; they became the parents of twin daughters.

ANALYSIS

William H. Gass joins a number of contemporary writers—including John Barth and Alain Robbe-Grillet, among others—who have made a significant contribution to the development of short fiction while publishing a relatively small number of stories. Aside from a few uncollected stories published in journals (and most of these are sections of longer works in progress), Gass's initial contribution to short fiction rests on one slender collection, *In the Heart of the Heart of the Country and Other Stories*, containing only five selections. Yet these five are enough to show that Gass is a master of the form, at once innovative and adept at manipulating characterization, plot, and tone, the conventions of the short story.

Calling Gass a master of the conventions of fiction is perhaps ironic, since the bulk of his own criticism seems to lead to the conclusion that one's perceptions of those conventions are generally skewed at best and are often completely wrongheaded. Yet Gass's theories represent less a prescription for writing than a description of what good writing has always involved. Gass emphasizes merely what he feels to be the obvious: that writing is an activity of word choice and placement. Plot, then, is not a sequence of actions but a sequence of words; a character is not a fictive "mirror" of a human being but a set of images, no more. Not surprisingly, Gass's primary concern is style; indeed, he prefers to call himself a "stylist" rather than a novelist or short-story writer. In the novella *The Cartesian Sonata*, he refers to his method of writing as "pencil carving," a habit of repeated light tracings that eventually burn into paper or wood grain. It is this layering of words that constitutes Gass's style.

How does this affect the reader's understanding of Gass's short stories? At the very least, one should be aware that Gass's fictions depend upon a developing pattern of imagery and that this pattern of imagery does not become more important than characterization or plot but that characterization and plot are no more than patterns of imagery themselves. Thus, one should see each of Gass's works as a developing metaphor, bound by its own rules, not the rules of the world.

This emphasis on imagery as metaphor indicates that the aesthetic foundation of Gass's work is poetic as well as fictive. As much as any prose writer in American literature, perhaps as much as any *writer* since Wallace Stevens, Gass is concerned with the sound of words and their rhythms. His prose is strikingly rhythmical and alliterative; in fact, in "In the Heart of the Heart of the Country" and *The Cartesian Sonata*, Gass quite deliberately employs prose rhyme. It is impossible, however, to read Gass's stories and be satisfied merely by an examination of his syntax, since the reader is constantly drawn into the characters' lives, their actions and motivations. The readers cannot help comparing the characters' worlds with their own, and Gass nowhere enjoins them from doing so; he simply reminds readers not to weigh down characters and plot with any more "reality" than inheres in the words that compose them.

An overview of Gass's stories reveals that the figures in his carpet of words are structural and thematic, as well as syntactical. Each story, for example, is told from a limited first-person point of view. Characters in effect create the world in which they live through the images in which, consciously or unconsciously, they perceive their world. Thus, the way the worlds appear is less a comment on the worlds than on the narrators. In essence, the fictive worlds are twice removed from "actual" reality: once by virtue of being Gass's creations, twice by virtue of being the narrators' creations.

William H. Gass (©Miriam Berkley)

"ORDER OF INSECTS"

This may perhaps be no more than an overly elaborate way of describing what happens with any limited perspective, yet Gass's fiction causes the reader more problems—intriguing problems—because his narrators are so unreliable. The narrator of "Order of Insects," for example, is a wife and mother who has moved into a new home, only to find it invaded by insects. She quickly becomes obsessed with the bugs; at first horrified, she comes to see their dead bodies as "wonderfully shaped." Her obsession is not shared by other members of the family, however; indeed, the reader is not certain that anyone else is aware of the bugs or that the insects even exist. Rather, her obsession is the chief manifestation of her unhappiness, her horror at her roles of woman, wife, and mother. She is never so interested in the insects alive as dead; she comes to see the lifeless husks as the true souls of the insects. To the wife and mother, what is eternal, what lasts, is not warmth and love but the dry, physical residue of life.

This reading of "Order of Insects" is not simply conjecture. The woman herself admits to being "ill": She is as aware as the reader that her obsession reflects an abnormal psychological stance toward life in general. Similarly, the narrator of "Icicles" is painfully aware that he is "not right" and that his obsession with icicles—he sees them as both beautiful and horrifying—is but an extreme symptom of his withdrawal from life. The motif of the withdrawal from life is found in all five stories. In "Mrs. Mean" and in "In the Heart of the Heart of the Country," the narrators have already retreated, psychologically and physically, to the position of passive observers of life; in "Icicles" and "Order of Insects," the narrators are in the process of withdrawal; the end of "The Pederson Kid" finds the narrator rejoicing in a "glorious" act of bravery as he sits curled in a cocoon of psychosis.

"THE PEDERSON KID"

"The Pederson Kid" is overtly Gass's most traditional story. It possesses an identifiable setting, rich, rounded characters, and action which marches toward a violent climax. Indeed, in the mind of one critic, the story recalls nothing so much as the Upper Michigan stories of Ernest Hemingway. The comparison is understandable, given the story's bleak landscape, mother/father/son conflict, and violent conclusion; yet a better comparison would be with William Faulkner's *As I Lay Dying* (1930), with its tenuous world built on the shifting perspectives of unreliable narrators.

A closer reading of "The Pederson Kid" reveals that, rather than being "traditional," the story is a perfect example of what Gass's theories amount to in practice. Describing the action, for example, *should* be easy enough. Apparently, one bleak winter morning Big Hans, a hired hand on a North Dakota farm, discovers the Pederson Kid, a boy from a neighboring farm, collapsed in the snow. In a delirium, the boy tells of a stranger in yellow gloves who forced his parents into a cellar while the boy escaped and ran miles through a blizzard for help. Jorge—the narrator, a boy a little older than the Pederson Kid—Jorge's father, and Big Hans start off on a wagon for the Pederson place. After some difficulties they get there and hide in the barn, but all three fear moving across the open space to the house. Finally, Jorge strikes off across the yard. When his father follows, a shot rings out, and his father falls dead. Jorge hides in the house, awaiting death, but the stranger never appears. At the end, Jorge sits in the Pederson house—convinced that the stranger has killed Big Hans and his mother, too, by now—but is "burning up . . . with joy" at the thought of his act of bravery.

Some critics contend that this straightforward plot summary is indeed an accurate rendering of what "actually" happened in the story. Others maintain that in all probability the stranger never existed and that "actually" Jorge shot his own father. In Gass's terms, however, nothing "actually" happens; the story is a series of words creating images that in turn make up a developing metaphor, a virtual world obeying its own rules and having no meaning beyond the words that compose it.

All the reader can know with any certainty is that Jorge loathes and fears his father, although at one time their relationship was at least a little more amicable; he loathes Big Hans, although once they, too, were much closer; he initially loathes the Pederson Kid, although at the end he comes to identify with him. At the end, in his own mind his act of "bravery" has apparently freed him from his father's yoke; but this act was largely without volition, and he has been freed less from his father than from any connection with the living world. The reader leaves him thankful for the snow and the "burning up . . . with joy": fire and ice, the twin images of Hell. No one interpretation of "The Pederson Kid" is any more demonstrably valid than another, and this contributes to, rather than detracts from, the work's power and endless fascination.

"Mrs. Mean"

A work of less intensity but open to even broader interpretation, perhaps, is "Mrs. Mean." Mrs. Mean is the name given by the narrator to a neighbor: the vulgar, shrill mother of a brood of children. The story is filled with mythic and religious allusions (as are most of Gass's stories), which have led certain critics to rather strained interpretations; once again, however, the allusions are the unreliable narrator's, and what really happens in his fictive world may be far different from his interpretation of it.

The story is composed almost entirely of the narrator's observations as he and his wife spy on Mrs. Mean from their house across the street. He sees a woman loud, vulgar, violent, and sadistic to her children; indeed, in the narrator's mind she assumes a malevolence of almost mythic proportions. Any parent reading the story, however, might see Mrs. Mean as simply a mother harried to distraction by a pack of children who seem to have very little fear of the "monster" that the narrator perceives. The narrator deems it "unnaturally sacrificial" when the children run *into* their house, not *away* from their house when chased by their mother. What is unnatural, however, is the narrator's inability to understand a simple domestic situation and his obsession with observing life instead of participating in it. At the end, he has withdrawn into his room, locked away even from his wife, but desperate to join the world of Mrs. Mean—which is, after all, simply the world of the living.

Another observer of, rather than participant in, life is the narrator of the title story.

"In the Heart of the Heart of the Country"

One of the most frequently anthologized stories of contemporary literature, "In the Heart of the Heart of the Country" is strikingly innovative; it achieves what all great writers strive for: the perfect wedding of form and content. The story concerns a poet, the narrator, who has "retired" to a small Indiana town after a failed love affair. He is in the heart of the country geographically, and in the heart of that heart since he is still in the heart's domain: the country of love.

The story is divided into sections ranging from a few sentences to a few pages in length, and each section is entitled with a descriptive phrase such as "Politics," "Vital Data," "Education," and so forth. In a sense, the story is an anatomy of a rural community, but, as in the other stories, what the narrator describes reveals more about him than about the objects of his descriptions. For example, although the sections may initially appear to be randomly arranged (there is a subtle movement from winter through spring, summer, fall, and back to winter at the story's end), certain recurring elements bind them together to form a psychological and spiritual portrait of the narrator. As much as he may try to make his descriptions flat and objective, for example, as much as he may try to refine himself out of his own story, the narrator can never escape his memories of love. He as much as admits that his interest in politics, for example, simply fills a vacuum left by lost love.

Even when his memories of love do not intrude directly into certain sections, his despair colors whatever he touches. For example, the persons to whom he returns again and again in his descriptions are the old, the feeble, the lonely: projections of himself. On the rarer occasions when he describes persons who are younger and more vital, he cannot empathize: They are faceless, dangerous. It is a measure of his fall when he thinks of his lost love in terms of "youth and child" but now is obsessed with the lonely and the dying.

The story is fragmented, then, because the narrator's psyche is fragmented; he is out of harmony with his own life. The "organic" qualities of the story, however, go beyond that. The narrator is a poet, and as a result "In the Heart of the Heart of the Country" is a "poetic" fiction. The sentences are rhythmical and alliterative; he even deliberately employs prose rhyme. The descriptions are imagistic, frequently recalling T. E. Hulme, Ezra Pound, Richard Aldington, and Robert Lowell more than any prose masters. Indeed, the first "Politics" section as a poem would rival some of the finest efforts of the contemporary period.

THE CARTESIAN SONATA

Gass's *The Cartesian Sonata* is a further examination of narrative fragmentation. The three-part narrative begins with the Sterne-like promise that "this is the story of Ella Bend Hess," a clairvoyant woman who is subjected to various abuses which she knows about in advance. What follows the opening line, though, are mutterings of the narrator and tergiversations of truth in connected digressive fragments, these all yielding a composite picture of Ella rather than a traditional story about her. The reader moves linearly through the asynchronous images of Ella getting her shoes from a traveling salesman, the salesman's uncle's story of a man shot in the foot, a description of the museum that displays the boot, Peg Crandall's nude portrait session and the artist's lust, the narrator's writing habit and interest in graffiti, an explanation of Ella's talent as due to ultrasensitivity ("She was almost totally attention and antennae"), and visits to other seers including Professor Logrus and Madame Betz. The concluding section is a circular stream-of-consciousness rendering of Ella's husband's thoughts. He reviews his abuse of Ella and the possibility of her death, and the section is peppered with vertical ellipsis and self-deprecation. The effect of these disjunctive elements is that of montage, of the reader's whole understanding of the subject as greater than the sum of the parts.

Hyperbole is hard to avoid when evaluating the work of Gass. He is an enormously talented writer and critic—so talented as to be initially daunting, perhaps, to some readers. That is unfortunate, for enjoyment of his stories never relies on knowledge of his theories or subtle grasp of his technical expertise, although these can add to the pleasure. "The Pederson Kid" and "In the Heart of the Heart of the Country," in particular, are destined to become hallmarks of contemporary short fiction.

OTHER MAJOR WORKS

LONG FICTION: *Omensetter's Luck*, 1966; *Willie Masters' Lonesome Wife*, 1968; *The Tunnel*, 1995.

NONFICTION: *Fiction and the Figures of Life*, 1970; *On Being Blue: A Philosophical Inquiry*, 1976; *The World Within the Word: Essays*, 1978; *Habitations of the Word: Essays*, 1985; *Finding a Form*, 1996; *Reading Rilke: Reflections on the Problems of Translation*, 1999.

BIBLIOGRAPHY
Busch, Frederick. "But This Is What It Is Like to Live in Hell: Gass's *In the Heart of the Heart of the Country*." *Modern Fiction Studies* 20 (Autumn, 1974): 328-336. This essay provides one of the earliest, and still one of the best, analyses of theme and style in one of Gass's most important short stories.

Gardner, James. "Transgressive Fiction." *National Review* 48 (June 17, 1996): 54-56. Agues that whereas fiction used to delight as well as edify, now it has split into different forms of fiction, with writers like Stephen King and Jackie Collins being read for entertainment value, while Thomas Pynchon and William Gass intentionally suppress the element of pleasure.

Gass, William. "An Interview with William Gass." Interview by Lorna H. Dormke. *Mississippi Review* 10, no. 3 (1987): 53-67. One of the most recent and most extensive interviews with Gass.

Hadella, Charlotte Byrd. "The Winter Wasteland of William Gass's *In the Heart of the Heart of the Country*." *Critique: Studies in Modern Fiction* 30 (Fall, 1988): 49-58. Hadella explores the wasteland theme and imagery in Gass's story and compares them with T. S. Eliot's use of the same themes in his great poem.

Holloway, Watson L. *William Gass*. Boston, Mass.: Twayne Publishers, 1990. A good critical study of Gass's fiction. Includes a bibliography and an index.

Kaufmann, Michael. *Textual Bodies: Modernism, Postmodernism, and Print.* Lewisburg, Pa.: Bucknell University Press, 1994. A thorough study of works by Gass, William Faulkner, Gertrude Stein, and James Joyce. Includes a bibliography and an index.

_____. "The Textual Body: William Gass's *Willie Masters' Lonesome Wife.*" *Critique* 35 (Fall, 1993): 27-42. Argues that the voice of the work is not the voice of the protagonist, Willie Masters' wife, but the voice of the text itself. Discusses Gass's experiments with typography and the physical form of the text.

Kellman, Steven G., and Irving Malin, eds. *Into "The Tunnel": Readings of Gass's Novel.* Newark: University of Delaware Press, 1998. Considers the psychological element in Gass's novel; includes a discussion of historians and college teachers in literature, a bibliography, and an index.

McCaffery, Larry. "A William Gass Bibliography." *Critique: Studies in Modern Fiction* 18, no. 1 (1976): 59-66. A useful bibliography of Gass scholarship.

Saltzman, Arthur. *The Fiction of William Gass: The Consolation of Language.* Carbondale: Southern Illinois University Press, 1986. Saltzman's book includes seven chapters on various aspects of Gass's fiction. Saltzman claims that Gass's short-fiction collection can best be read as a "series of variations on the theme of the pleasures and pitfalls of aesthetic isolation." The last chapter contains an interesting interview with Gass.

Stone, Robert. "The Reason for Stories: Toward a Moral Fiction." *Harper's* 276 (June, 1988): 71-76. Discusses Gass's argument about the estrangement of art and moral goodness in his essay "Goodness Knows Nothing of Beauty." Claims that Gass does not practice the ideas expressed in his essay, which are at odds with the imperatives of writing. Contends that in order to be independent of morality, fiction would have to be composed of something other than language, for the laws of language and art impose choices that are unavoidably moral.

Dennis Vannatta,
updated by Scott Vander Ploeg

DAVID GATES

Born: Middletown, Connecticut; January 8, 1947

PRINCIPAL SHORT FICTION
The Wonders of the Invisible World: Stories, 1999

OTHER LITERARY FORMS
David Gates is the author of the novels *Jernigan* (1991) and *Preston Falls* (1998).

ACHIEVEMENTS
David Gates was a finalist for the Pulitzer Prize for *Jernigan* and for the National Book Critics Circle Award for *Preston Falls*. His stories have been anthologized in *The Best American Short Stories* and *Prize Stories: The O. Henry Awards*.

BIOGRAPHY
David Gates was born in a small Connecticut town and received a B.A. from the University of Connecticut. While in graduate school at that university Gates met and married Ann Beattie, and together they took teaching positions at the University of Virginia and Harvard University, eventually returning to Connecticut when Beattie began to establish herself as a fiction writer. Gates's lack of career success, in tandem with Beattie's fast-growing literary reputation, led to marital tensions and, in 1972, to divorce.

In addition to his teaching jobs, Gates has worked as a wholesale food distributor, a cab driver, a phone operator for Western Union, a stock clerk, and a square dance musician. In 1979 Gates took a job in the correspondence department of *Newsweek* magazine, from which he rose to the position of senior writer in the arts section. During this period Gates also began to write fiction. His first novel, *Jernigan*, received high critical praise.

Gates's second marriage also ended in divorce. He married a third time, and he, his wife, and his stepdaughter divide their time between two homes: one in Granville, in upstate New York, and the other in Manhattan.

ANALYSIS

David Gates's first collection of stories, *The Wonders of the Invisible World*, is regarded as continuing the high caliber of work found in his earlier novels. Here, too, Gates has created an original narrative voice, whose rhythms, intonations, and cultural references seem to capture the tenor of contemporary American life perfectly. In addition to skillfully suggesting the American vernacular, Gates is able to shape the rhythms of the American voice into a highly strung, jazzy stream-of-consciousness both humorous and serious.

Although in his early novels Gates has taken as his protagonists culturally sophisticated but emotionally tormented middle-aged men with a history of difficult or broken marriages, this type of man is the center of consciousness in only a handful of his short stories. Other stories feature the perspectives of contemporary gay men or elderly men from a previous generation. Half of the stories feature female protagonists who are treated with a similar mix of irony and compassion, whether they be bitter, man-hating alcoholics, middle-aged, conflicted feminists, or isolated, desperate housewives. No matter what the age, gender, or sexual preference of Gates's characters, they are all struggling with either their own dark side or the dark sides of those close to them. This may involve alcohol or drug abuse, or relationship problems, such as infidelity, exploitation, abandonment, or divorce.

A clue to the general theme of the stories in *The Wonders of the Invisible World* can be gleaned from the title, which refers to the early American theologian Cotton Mather's description of demonic spirits.

For Gates, these demonic forces live within the individual, so that it is largely unconscious or rationalized evil motives and impulses that lead his men and women into loveless, lonely lives and to the subversion of their own best selves.

THE WONDERS OF THE INVISIBLE WORLD

The ten stories in this collection are told from the perspective of a variety of characters, young and old, male and female, straight and gay. However, the plots turn on the universal themes of disintegrating families, broken relationships, and unraveling lives. In the title story, "The Wonders of the Invisible World," the protagonist is divorced and losing touch with his grown daughter. He is having an affair with a woman whose possible pregnancy puts a serious strain on their relationship. The protagonist's hip, jazzy narrative voice, which threatens to disintegrate into incoherence, reflects the ragged quality of his life and his approach to it, which has gradually lapsed into a kind of moral inattention. When he loses his clarinet and alienates his girlfriend in the same evening, the reader sees that he is careless with regard to both his creative life and his love life. Acutely aware of his own fecklessness, he may not be aware, however, of the degree to which his losses may be the product of his own neurotic intentions.

A similar type of character appears in the story "A Wronged Husband." Here, the narrator and his wife weave a tissue of lies around their marriage, especially with regard to their infidelities. The lying and adultery, along with drugs and alcohol, are essentially escapist strategies meant to preserve the status quo. The lies and evasions, however, have in reality undermined and destroyed the marriage, an outcome the wife suggests may have been her husband's true intention.

Two other stories have a narrator who is male and homosexual. In each case the man must cope with the presence of a chaotic, self-destructive person in his life. "Star Baby" is told from the perspective of Billy, a gay man and the brother of a drug-addicted, self-destructive woman, Cassie, who has abandoned her seven-year-old son Deke to his care. During the course of looking after Deke, Billy's flippancy and defensive patterns give way to deeper feelings of genuine love. He is stunned by the realization that he will always be the only consistent, caregiving adult in the child's life. Another story, "The Intruder," also features a gay protagonist, a decent older man, whose devotion to a younger, selfish, unfaithful lover has placed his emotional life and his health in danger.

Gates uses a female narrative perspective in four of the stories in this collection. In "The Bad Thing," a pregnant woman feels trapped in her marriage in an isolated house in upstate New York and attempts to rationalize her secret drinking as an emancipatory gesture. In "Beating" the perspective is that of Dinah, a childless day-care worker married to an aging radical. Although a self-described feminist, Dinah is nevertheless responsible for all domestic chores and secretly and compulsively watches the film version of the romantic fairy tale "Beauty and the Beast." Her husband Tobias, who is obsessed with police beatings, is no longer the political idealist she married but has instead become a bitter and paranoid crank. Another unhappy wife can be found in "The Crazy Thought." Here the lonely and childless Faye feels stranded in Vermont and increasingly estranged from her insensitive husband Paul. Daydreaming of an old boyfriend and disturbed by her husband's purchase of a shotgun, she begins to wish for Paul's accidental death.

An unhappily married woman in the story "Saturn" tries various ways to relieve her sense of suffocation, including a clandestine love affair and self-improvement schemes, but like the planet Saturn, which is also the brand name of her automobile, which stops cold in a minor traffic accident, she evinces a paralyzing reluctance to change things.

Older men take over the narrative perspective of two other stories. Len, the elderly narrator of "Vigil," is left to hold things together after his daughter Bonnie is hospitalized when her car is struck by a drunken driver. Len, whose alcoholic wife Sylvia ran off to Phoenix with her marginally more successful boss years ago, has long been left in charge of Bonnie, a task he assumed with characteristic stoic competence. When Sylvia returns to see her hospitalized daughter, she frightens her grandson with violent, man-hating fantasies that significantly lessen the value of the domestic skills she also provides for the family. A turning point is reached when Bonnie's husband finally brings out into the open the fact that Bonnie's automobile accident occurred after a tryst with a secret lover. When, for good measure, he also accuses his mother-in-law of sexual promiscuity, Len can no longer deny the realities that are shattering his family.

An elderly man is also the narrator of the final story, "The Mail Lady," a tour de force reminiscent of the work of Gates's literary hero, the Irish author Samuel Beckett. The story is told from the perspective of an elderly stroke victim named Lewis Coley, whose damaged, sometimes nonsensical thought processes and speech become in Gates's hand a skillful stream-of-consciousness narrative that is both comic and tragic. Lew, once a scientist, heavy drinker, and authoritarian father, who prided himself on the strict discipline meted out to his daughter Wylie, has in his later years undergone a religious conversion that has made him something of a fanatic on the subject. Due to his stroke, he has also become completely dependent on his wife Alice. The female postal worker of the title comes to Lew's rescue after he shuts himself up in his car, which is slowly filling with carbon monoxide. Lew, who had been hoping to die a peaceful, spiritual death in his automobile, sees the Mail Lady as less his salvation than an agent of destiny returning him to a bleak, greatly diminished, and hellish life.

OTHER MAJOR WORKS

LONG FICTION: *Jernigan*, 1991; *Preston Falls*, 1998.

BIBLIOGRAPHY

Gates, David. "David Gates: Voices for Vices." Interview by Michael Coffey. *Publishers Weekly*, May 10, 1999, 42-43. Gates discusses his background, his vocation as a writer, and his two novels as well as his short-story collection. Much useful material, especially with regard to the influence of Gates's literary hero Samuel Beckett.

Grossinger, Harvey. "David Gates: Life's Hazards, People's Alienation," *Houston Chronicle*, July 18,

1999, p. 23. Interprets stories in *The Wonders of the Invisible World* from an existential perspective, praising them as well-crafted, gritty stories of contemporary malaise, alienation, and spiritual exhaustion. Also analyzes Gates's characters, concluding they are isolated and loveless, have lives marked by regret, and are unable to sustain serious relationships. Lengthy, insightful analyses of "Vigil" and "The Mail Lady."

Hynes, James. "More Hideous Men." Review of *The Wonders of the Invisible World*, by David Gates. *Washington Post*, July 8, 1999, p. X05. Concentrates on Gates's male characters, particularly in terms of their negative attributes. Describes Gates as continuing to mine the territory he staked out in his novels, with heroes who behave badly but are also self-aware and bitterly witty.

Kakutani, Michiko. "Thinking Too Much About Sour Relationships." Review of *The Wonders of the Invisible World*, by David Gates. *The New York Times*, July 6, 1999, p. E-6. Kakutani is critical of the collection's narcissistic, self-absorbed protagonists, finding them too similar to the heroes of Gates's novels. Also faults Gates for overreliance on what she describes as "terminal irony."

Marzorati, Gerald. "Hip, Free, and Middle Aged." Review of *The Wonders of the Invisible World*, by David Gates. *The New York Times Book Review*, July 18, 1999, 11. Praises the collection for its mordant humor and its bleak but sharp-witted vision of contemporary people and situations.

Ulin, David L. "Adrift in the Sea of Adulthood." Review of *The Wonders of the Invisible World*, by David Gates. *San Francisco Chronicle*, August 8, 1999, p. 3. This perceptive review notes that the collection's "low grade existential anguish" is similar to the emotional territory of the novels. Concludes that Gates's protagonists are "adrift in the amorphous sea of adulthood" and are unable to live up to their best possibilities. Especially praises Gates's ability to write endings that pull his stories together in surprising ways and concludes that Gates has developed into a writer to be reckoned with.

Wolfe, Linda. "A Talent for Misery." Review of *The Wonders of the Invisible World*, by David Gates. *Boston Globe*, June 27, 1999, p. D1. Insightful review praises Gates for his ironic approach, his ability to depict depression and bleakness, and his talent for suggesting the cadences and idioms of contemporary American speech. Especially useful comments on the way in which Gates's characters are driven by a hidden dark side. Explores the ways these inner forces of darkness drive Gates's characters to drink, drugs, and isolated, loveless narcissism.

Margaret Boe Birns

THÉOPHILE GAUTIER

Born: Tarbes, France; August 30, 1811
Died: Paris, France; October 23, 1872

PRINCIPAL SHORT FICTION

Les Jeunes-France: Romans goguenards, 1833
"Omphale," 1835 (English translation, 1902)
"La Morte amoureuse," 1836 (The Beautiful Vampire, 1926)
Fortunio, 1838 (novella; English translation, 1915)
"Une Nuit de Cléopâtre," 1838 ("One of Cleopatra's Nights," 1888)
"Le Roi Candaule," 1844 ("King Candaules," 1893)
Nouvelles, 1845
Un Trio de romans, 1852
Avatar, 1857 (English translation, 1900)
Jettatura, 1857 (English translation, 1888)
Romans et contes, 1863
Spirite: Nouvelle fantastique, 1866 (novella; Spirite, 1877)

OTHER LITERARY FORMS

Théophile Gautier made significant contributions in several different fields. His importance as a literary critic was established by his 1844 book *Les Grotesques* (*The Grotesques*, 1900). He also wrote several works of long fiction, including *Mademoiselle de Maupin* (1835-1836; *Mademoiselle de Maupin: A Romance of Love and Passion*, 1887), *Le Roman de la momie* (1856; *Romance of the Mummy*, 1863), and *Le Capitaine Fracasse* (1863; *Captain Fracasse*, 1880).

ACHIEVEMENTS

Théophile Gautier's interests extended well beyond France. In his poems, short stories, and novels, he made judicious use of aspects of Spanish and North African cultures and thus enriched the French literary landscape. He composed in 1841 the libretto for the ballet *Giselle: Ou, Les Wilis* (*Giselle: Or, The Wilis*, 1970), which has become part of the canon of classical ballet. He wrote the first truly successfully fantastic short stories in French by combining elements of realism and the marvelous. He received the French Legion of Honor in 1858.

BIOGRAPHY

Théophile Gautier was born on August 30, 1811, in the southern French city of Tarbes, where his father Pierre was a civil servant. In 1814, Pierre, his wife Antoinette, and their son Théophile moved to Paris, where Théophile lived until his death on October 23, 1872. Gautier had two sisters: Émilie, born in 1817, and Zoé, born three years later. He attended school in Paris and then studied painting in 1829. That same year he met writer Victor Hugo, who persuaded Gautier to become a writer.

During the 1830's, Gautier earned his living as a journalist. He also began his literary career by writing in several different genres, including fiction, poetry, plays, ballet librettos, and art criticism. He never married, but he did have three children out of wedlock. A mistress named Eugénie Fort gave birth to his only son, Théophile, in 1836. For many years he lived with his mistress Ernesta Grasi. Together they had two daughters: Judith, born in 1845, and Estelle, born two years later. Unlike many French writers of the nineteenth century, Gautier earned his living solely from his writings. He developed the argument that art existed only for art's sake. He stressed that the value of a literary work should be determined solely by aesthetic criteria. He was very interested in foreign cultures. He undertook extensive trips to Algeria, Spain, Italy, Egypt, Greece, Constantinople, and Russia and then published books on these trips. He died from heart problems in Paris on October 23, 1872.

ANALYSIS

Théophile Gautier's short fiction can be divided into two general categories: fantastic stories and stories dealing with Egypt and the Middle East. Thanks to the work of Jean-François Champollion, who deciphered the Rosetta Stone, ancient Egyptian culture became very popular and this explains Gautier's choice of ancient Egypt as the locale for his short stories "Une Nuit de Cléopâtre" ("One of Cleopatra's Nights") and "Le Roi Candaule" ("King Candaules").

Gautier's other major contribution to short fiction was his creative use of fantastic elements. The term "fantastic literature" may have two different meanings. It may refer to seemingly incomprehensible occurrences for which a logical explanation is given at the end of a short story. The term may also refer to occurrences for which no logical explanation exists or is given by the writer.

"OMPHALE"

"Omphale" is a first-person narrative told by a man who lived during his adolescence in a dilapidated house in Paris. The narrator clearly remembers that a rococo tapestry in his bedroom depicted Hercules and his lover Omphale. One night, possibly during a dream, the narrator sees Omphale leave her tapestry to talk with him. She explains to him that she was the Marquise of T***, who had married one of the narrator's ancestors. The ancestor had an artist depict his wife as Omphale and him as Hercules in the tapestry. The second night the marquise returns, goes to the narrator's bed, and begins to seduce the adolescent, who is afraid that the deceased marquis will be jealous. The attention and caresses from Omphale bring the seventeen-year-old much pleasure. Gautier never makes it clear whether this is a sexual fantasy or a supernatural appearance by a dead woman. After the death of his uncle, the tapestry is sold and the aged narrator expresses the tongue-in-cheek regret that he is now too old for attractive women to leave tapestries and caress him in bed.

"THE BEAUTIFUL VAMPIRE"

As in "Omphale," the mystery in Gautier's 1836 short story "La Morte amoureuse" ("The Beautiful Vampire") is never resolved. Neither Gautier nor his first-person narrator Fr. Romuald try to explain whether Fr. Romuald's obsession with Clarimonde is caused by delusions or whether Clarimonde is a female demon who tried to take over Fr. Romuald's mind. As this first-person narrative begins, the sixty-six-year old Fr. Romuald is telling a friend about a series of very disturbing events of forty years earlier, which he still does not understand. As a young semi-

Théophile Gautier (Archive Photos)

narian, his sole desire was to become a priest and serve God. During his ordination ceremony, however, he inadvertently looked away from the altar and toward the worshipers. He saw a beautiful and mysterious woman. This was a life-changing experience for him. His friend Fr. Sérapion is very perceptive, and he begins to realize what has happened. He warns him that Clarimonde is a devil whose goal is to lead him into a life of sin and to cause him to lose his immortal soul. One day Fr. Romuald is asked to go the house of a dying woman so that she can receive the sacrament of extreme unction. When he arrives, it is too late, but he sees that the dead woman is none other than Clarimonde. Fr. Sérapion tries to exorcize the demon from his friend's mind by digging up the grave of the long-deceased Clarimonde, forcing Fr. Romuald to view her earthly remains. Like the narrator in "Omphale," Fr. Romuald does not know what to think. He cannot decide whether Clarimonde is a female devil or whether he is suffering severe delusions. Once again, Gautier never answers this question. These two short stories are classic works of fantastic literature because the reader never knows whether the explanation for these strange occurrences is real or supernatural.

"ONE OF CLEOPATRA'S NIGHTS"

Gautier's 1838 short story "One of Cleopatra's Nights" also deals with obsessive love. Gautier describes Cleopatra as bored with her existence. She does enjoy throwing elaborate feasts and boating down the Nile River in her elegant ships, but she senses the need for new adventures to alleviate her boredom. Because of her reputation for great beauty, Cleopatra inspires passion even in men whom she has never met. Such a man is a commoner named Meiamoun. He risks his life to swim toward her boat. Gautier describes Cleopatra as capricious and cruel. She wants men to pay attention to her, but if any uninvited man dares to approach her, he is put to death. When Meiamoun is brought into her presence, she decides to toy with him. She spares his life temporarily and offers to throw an exquisite party in his honor. She mentions in passing, however, the he will exchange his life for one night of pleasure. Meiamoun does not believe that Cleopatra is serious, but it soon becomes clear to Gautier's readers that her intention is to poison him the next morning. Gautier describes in great style the details of the orgy organized by Cleopatra for Meiamoun. He stresses repeatedly that the French language is not sufficient to express the luxuriousness of this feast. The narrator disparagingly compares the feast to an orgy, in which grotesque and thus culturally strange dances are performed by Cleopatra's slaves. Through his narrator, Gautier distances himself from ancient Egyptian culture and portrays Cleopatra as a lascivious and rather sadistic person, who enjoys seeing Meiamoun enjoy ephemeral pleasures before she poisons him. When Marc Anthony enters and asks her why there is a dead man on the floor, she calmly answers that it is nothing more than an experiment designed to test the effectiveness of a newly created poison, which she planned to use on herself if Caesar Augustus tried to limit her freedom. There are several levels of irony in the ending of this short story. Cleopatra seems to the reader an extremely unsympathetic character, who

takes pleasure in misleading Meiamoun, but her reference to her suicide reminds us that she did, in fact, take her own life, albeit not with poison.

"KING CANDAULES"

Like "One of Cleopatra's Nights," Gautier's 1844's short story "King Candaules" also deals with an oriental theme. King Candaules married an exquisitely beautiful woman named Nyssia who refused to reveal anything other than her eyes in the presence of any man other than her husband. Nyssia explains very calmly to her husband that it is a tradition in her country for married women to be exceedingly modest. She is totally faithful to her marriage vows, and she hopes that her new husband will respect her wishes. King Candaules, however, views his wife as a sexual object, whose physical beauty he wants other men to admire as well. His desire is to discuss his wife's physical beauty with another man. He orders a servant named Gyges to hide behind a wall in their bedroom, and Candaules cuts a small hole in the wall so that Gyges can observe the disrobing of Nyssia. The description of this scene is highly voyeuristic, and Gautier suggests that Gyges becomes sexually aroused as he views Nyssia's naked body. Nyssia spots the small opening in the wall, and she feels defiled. She keeps quiet and plans her revenge. The very next day she calls Gyges into her apartment and gives him a choice. Either she will have Gyges killed, or he will kill Candaules. Gyges decides to save his own life, and he kills Candaules. Thanks to the efforts of Nyssia, the palace guards are persuaded to turn their allegiance to Gyges, who becomes the new king. "King Candaules" is a rather violent short story, but it does depict a powerful and resourceful woman who refuses to allow men to treat her as a sexual object.

OTHER MAJOR WORKS

LONG FICTION: *Mademoiselle de Maupin*, 1835-1836 (2 volumes; *Mademoiselle de Maupin: A Romance of Love and Passion*, 1887); *Le Roman de la momie*, 1856 (*Romance of the Mummy*, 1863); *Le Capitaine Fracasse*, 1863 (*Captain Fracasse*, 1880).

PLAYS: *Une Larme de diable*, pb. 1839; *Giselle: Ou, Les Wilis*, pr. 1841 (ballet scenario; *Giselle: Or, The Wilis*, 1970); *La Péri*, pr. 1843 (ballet scenario);

Le Tricorne enchanté, pr. 1845; *La Fausse Conversion*, pr. 1846; *Pierrot posthume*, pr. 1847; *Pâquerette*, pr. 1851 (ballet scenario); *Gemma*, pr. 1854 (ballet scenario); *Théâtre de poche*, pb. 1855; *Sacountala*, pr. 1858 (ballet scenario); *Yanko le bandit*, pr. 1858 (ballet scenario).

POETRY: *Poésies*, 1830 (English translation); *Albertus: Ou, L'Âme et le péché*, 1833 (enlarged edition of *Poésies*; *Albertus: Soul and Sin*, 1909); *La Comédie de la mort*, 1838 (*The Drama of Death*, 1909); *España*, 1845; *Poésies complètes*, 1845; *Émaux et camées*, 1852, 1872 (*Enamels and Cameos*, 1900); *Dernières Poésies* (1852).

NONFICTION: *Voyage en Espagne*, 1843 (*Wanderings in Spain*, 1853); *Les Grotesques*, 1844 (2 volumes; *The Grotesques*, 1900); *Salon de 1847*, 1847; *Caprices et zigzags*, 1852; *Italia*, 1852 (*Travels in Italy*, 1900); *Constantinople*, 1852 (*Constantinople of To-Day*, 1854); *Les Beaux-Arts en Europe, 1855*, 1855-1856 (2 volumes); *L'Art moderne*, 1856; *Honoré de Balzac: Sa Vie et ses œuvres*, 1858; *Histoire de l'art dramatique en France depuis vingt-cinq ans*, 1858-1859 (6 volumes); *Abécédaire du Salon de 1861*, 1861; *Trésors d'art de la Russie ancienne et moderne*, 1861; *Loin de Paris*, 1865; *Quand on voyage*, 1865; *Voyage en Russie*, 1867 (*A Winter in Russia*, 1874); *Ménagerie intime*, 1869 (*My Household of Pets*, 1882); *Tableaux de siège*, 1871 (*Paris Besieged*, 1900); *Portraits contemporains*, 1874 (*Portraits of the Day*, 1900); *Portraits et souvenirs littéraires*, 1875; *L'Orient*, 1877; *Fusains et eaux-fortes*, 1880; *Tableaux à la plume*, 1880; *Les Vacances du lundi*, 1881; *Guide de l'amateur au Musée du Louvre*, 1882 (*The Louvre*, 1900); *Souvenirs de théâtre, d'art, et de critique*, 1883; *Victor Hugo*, 1902; *La Musique*, 1911; *Critique artistique et littéraire*, 1929; *Les Maîtres du théâtre français de Rotrou à Dumas fils*, 1929; *Souvenirs romantiques*, 1929.

MISCELLANEOUS: *The Works of Théophile Gautier, 1900-1903* (24 volumes).

BIBLIOGRAPHY

Bowman, Frank. *French Romanticism*. Baltimore, Md.: The Johns Hopkins University Press, 1990. A thoughtful study which explores the importance of religion, eroticism, and psychological instability in numerous French works of short and long fiction written during the first half of the nineteenth century. Bowman's remarks are very relevant to Gautier's short stories.

Gordon, Rae Beth. *Ornament, Fantasy, and Desire in Nineteenth-Century French Literature*. Princeton, N.J.: Princeton University Press, 1992. A solid analysis which examines the representation of obsessive behavior and sexual fantasies in fiction by Gautier and other nineteenth century French writers.

Grant, Richard B. *Théophile Gautier*. Boston: Twayne, 1975. Albeit somewhat dated, this book still remains one of the best introductions in English to the writings of Théophile Gautier. It includes an annotated bio-bibliography of primary works in French, English translations, and critical studies in both French and English.

Marino, Virginia M. "The Devil's Discourse: The Meeting of Allegory and the Fantastic." *Journal of the Fantastic in the Arts* 31 (1997): 331-346. An insightful analysis of several short stories in which Gautier leaves it to the reader's imagination whether there is a real or a supernatural explanation for strange occurrences.

Smith, Albert B. *Théophile Gautier and the Fantastic*. University, Miss.: Romance Monographs, 1977. A book-length study on the various types of seemingly inexplicable occurrences depicted in works of both short and long fiction written by Gautier. Includes a clear discussion of what the notion of the fantastic meant to Gautier.

Smith, Nigel E. "Gautier, Freud, and the Fantastic: Psychoanalysis avant la Lettre." In *Functions of the Fantastic*, edited by Joe Sanders. Westport, Conn.: Greenwood Press, 1995. A Freudian analysis of obsessive behavior and sexual fantasies in several short stories by Gautier.

Edmund J. Campion

TIM GAUTREAUX

Born: Morgan City, Louisiana; 1947

PRINCIPAL SHORT FICTION

Same Place, Same Things, 1996
Welding with Children, 1999

OTHER LITERARY FORMS

Tim Gautreaux's Louisiana novel, *The Next Step in the Dance*, was published in 1998.

ACHIEVEMENTS

Tim Gautreaux's story "Same Place, Same Things" was chosen for *The Best American Short Stories 1992*, "Little Frogs in a Ditch" appeared in *The Best American Short Stories 1997*, "Welding with Children" appeared in that annual collection in 1998, and "The Piano Tuner" in 1999. Gautreaux has been the recipient of a National Endowment for the Arts Fellowship and the National Magazine Award for Fiction. In 1996, he was appointed the John and Renee Grisham Visiting Southern Writer-in-Residence at the University of Mississippi.

BIOGRAPHY

Tim Gautreaux was born in 1947 and grew up in Morgan City, Louisiana. His father was a tugboat captain and his grandfather was an engineer on a steamboat. He received his undergraduate degree from Nicholls State University. Although he originally intended to be a business major, he says that when someone stole his accounting books, he changed to English. He received his Ph.D. from the University of South Carolina. He has taught creative writing at Southeastern Louisiana University in Hammond, Louisiana, since 1972.

ANALYSIS

Tim Gautreaux is but the latest in a long line of fine short-story writers from Louisiana which includes Ellen Gilchrist, Robert Olen Butler, Shirley Ann Grau, and Moira Crone. His milieu is the rural farm country of southern Louisiana, populated with characters who live in small towns such as Tiger Island, Gumwood, and Pine Oil. Although his people are often down on their luck financially, mostly their moral values are sound, even when they are sorely tried. Gautreaux has said he considers himself a Catholic writer in the tradition of Walker Percy, saying that "if a story does not deal with a moral question, I don't think it's much of a story."

Gautreaux writes of Cajun country, about working-class men and women who come smack up against a challenge to their humaneness, and usually manage to meet it with courage and grace. Comparing him to Flannery O'Connor, critics have praised his stories as being morally complex in their depiction of human frailty and deceptively simple in their pellucid lyrical style.

"SAME PLACE, SAME THINGS"

The title story of Tim Gautreaux's first collection, an anthology favorite, is about Harry Lintel, a forty-four-year-old traveling pump repairman from Missouri who has "followed the droughts" to Louisiana to find work. After finding a dead man who has been electrocuted while trying to fix his pump, Harry is then pursued by the dead man's wife, who says she has spent her life seeing the "same place, same things." Since Harry is the only person she ever met who can go where he wants to go, and since because of poverty she has never been more than a hundred miles from her home, she urges him to take her with him.

However, although Harry is tempted because of the woman's good looks and seductive promise to be good to him, he is bothered by the woman's easy dismissal of her husband and the fact that two previous husbands have died. His revelation comes when he opens the electric fuse box at the woman's house and finds a switch wire cut into the circuit and running into the house. Then he knows that the woman switched on the current while her husband worked on the pump and murdered him. Although Harry is shaken "like a man who had just missed being in a terrible accident," he does not report the crime, happy to leave the town and the woman behind.

The climax of the story comes when he stops at a café and finds her hidden under the tarp in his truck bed. Although she begs him to take her with him, he says significantly, "Where you want to go, I can't take you." The woman hits Harry over the head with a heavy wrench, snarling, "I've never met a man I could put up with for long. I'm glad I got shut of all of mine." She then drives away in his truck. When he regains consciousness, Harry knows that whereas she was a woman who would never get where she wanted to go, he was always clear where he was going.

The story is an understated treatment of a man who almost makes a terrible mistake, but who finds meaning in his work. His basic contentment with the "same things" regardless of where he finds himself is contrasted with the discontent of the woman who will never find meaning regardless of the place she occupies.

"LITTLE FROGS IN A DITCH"

In his contributor's notes to this story in *The Best American Short Stories 1997*, Gautreaux says he got the central idea from a radio call-in show which asked listeners to tell about the "meanest trick" they had ever played on someone. One man called in and bragged how he had caught a bunch of common roof pigeons and sold them as untrained homing pigeons complete with instructions. Gautreaux says he wondered what kind of person would do such a thing and what it would be like to have such a person in his family.

The central character who plays the "mean trick" in Gautreaux's story is Lenny Fontenot, who is out of work and lives with his grandfather, his parents having left him to travel around the country in a Winnebago motor home. The story centers on one man, Mr. Lejeune, who buys a pigeon from Lenny for his crippled little nephew, who is staying with him. The moral conscience of the story is the grandfather, who puts Lenny out until he goes to a priest and makes a confession of what he has done. The title of the story comes from the grandfather's warning Lenny that if he closes his eyes before he goes to confession his sins will make a noise. "They'll cry out like little frogs in a ditch at sundown."

The final revelation of the story occurs when the pigeon sold to Mr. Lejeune returns to the grandfather's house and he takes it to the new owner to make it appear it has truly "returned home." He discovers that Lejeune knew the pigeon was a fake and that he bought it for his nephew purposely to provide him with a lesson about disappointment. Although the boy has never had a father and his mother is addicted to crack cocaine, he lives in a fairy-tale world in which he thinks his mother will return. Lejeune says he has to toughen up, that maybe if he learns to deal with the little things, it will teach him to deal with the big thing. The story parallels these two men, both of whom are responsible for wards who are crippled in different ways. It ends with the grandfather not being sure about whether what he and Lejeune are doing is the "right thing."

"WELDING WITH CHILDREN"

This is one of Gautreaux's most admired stories, for it combines comic characterization and dialogue with a poignant and deeply felt human realization. The central character is a grandfather whose four unmarried daughters leave their children—who have names such as "Nu-Nu," "Moonbean," and "Tammy-nette"—with him. He lives in the small central Louisiana town of Gumwood and has an old greasy car engine hanging from a K-Mart chain in his yard. When he takes the kids to the Pak-a-Sak store in his old Chevy Caprice to get Icees, he feels shame when he overhears some men saying, "Here comes Bruton and his bastardmobile."

The highlight of the story is a comic dialogue between Bruton and the grandchildren about their profane language and lack of religious training. The comedy increases when he reads them the Genesis story of creation, which they compare to the movie *Conan the Barbarian* because it has swords and snakes in it. When Bruton insists the Bible is not a movie, Tammynette says, "I think I seen it down at Blockbuster."

After entertaining fantasies of moving up north with the kids and starting over again, Bruton decides to stay and do better by them than he did by his daughters. He turns off the electricity to the television set, begins reading to them, takes them to church, and cleans up his property so it does not look like white trash live there. The story ends with him planning to put a tire swing up on the tree where the old motor once hung.

The story works because of the humanity of the grandfather, who feels badly that he has let things slide with his daughters. Forced into uncomfortably seeing himself as white trash, he makes a last ditch effort to salvage something of his family; if it is too late for his children, he thinks, then maybe it is not too late for his grandchildren.

"THE PIANO TUNER"

This story is similar to "Same Place, Same Things" in that it involves a common Gautreaux technique of focusing on service people. Gautreaux has said that he likes to write about such people who "visit our homes and get just a little entangled in our lives." In this story, Claude, a piano tuner, who, his wife says, "invented reality by saying it," gets entangled in the life of a down-and-out and depressed woman whom he helps get a job playing the piano in the bar at the Lafayette Motel.

As he frequently does in his stories, Gautreaux adroitly mixes comedy with poignant humanism here. In the most hilarious scene, the woman, who has bought a new piano, tries to get her old one out of the house with a tractor the size of a locomotive. In the process, the tractor gets away from her, not only pulling out the piano but also pulling the whole house down, igniting a gas fire that destroys what is left of the house.

However, Gautreaux's characters have staying power above all else. The story ends a year later when Claude goes to hear the woman play and she tells a story about how Scott Joplin died crazy from syphilis on April Fool's Day, 1917. She then delivers the defining line of the story, which also describes the characteristic tone of many of Gautreaux's stories: "That's kind of funny and sad at the same time, isn't it?"

OTHER MAJOR WORKS

LONG FICTION: *The Next Step in the Dance*, 1998.

BIBLIOGRAPHY

Blouin, Keith. "People Who Live There Know That Hope Springs Eternal Deep in Louisiana Territory." *The Tampa Tribune*, October 17, 1999, p. 4. Compares Gautreaux to Flannery O'Connor in his ability to portray faithfully "good country people." Discusses his familiarity with the people of Louisiana and his celebration of human strengths and weaknesses and "our everlasting capacity for hope."

Grossinger, Harvey. "A Trip Through Cajun Country." Review of *Welding with Children*, by Tim Gautreaux. *Houston Chronicle*, December 19, 1999, p. 14. Says Gautreaux is at the top of the list of gifted short-story writers writing in America. Discusses what he calls the "brilliant" title story and describes "The Piano Tuner" as a "masterpiece of delicate shading and method."

Jacobs, Hal. "Poignant Messages Emerge in *Welding with Children*." *The Atlanta Journal and Constitution*, November 28, 1999, p. 13K. Says Gautreaux's stories have all the same ingredients as Garrison Keillor's popular stories: humor, warmth, irony, suspense, and uplifting endings.

Larson, Susan. "Swamp Boogie" and "The Writer Next Door." *The Times-Picayune*, May 15, 1998, p. D6, E1. In these two articles, Larson talks about the Louisiana elements in Gautreaux's writing; says he is a sensualist who can render with equal detail the clank of machinery and the smell of boiled crabs. Provides some biographical background and describes Gautreaux's Acadian home in the woods outside Hammond, Louisiana.

Gautreaux, Tim. *Novel Approach: Tim Gautreaux Takes "The Next Step."* Interview by Christina Masciere. *New Orleans Magazine* 32 (March, 1998): 31. Gautreaux repudiates the notion that he is a "southern" writer, allying himself more closely with the frontier humorists. He also acknowledges the role that his Catholic Louisiana milieu has had on his life and work.

Paddock, Polly. "*Same Place* Mines Louisiana for Extraordinary Folk Tales." Review of *Same Place, Same Things*, by Tim Gautreaux. *The Arizona Republic*, September 29, 1996, p. E10. Says that although he writes about the Cajun country he knows so well, the stories in this collection transcend locale and plumb the "deepest reaches of the human heart."

Stroup, Sheila. "He's Got the Write Stuff." *The Times-Picayune*, January 26, 1993, p. B1. In this interview story, Gautreaux says he learned to like to tell stories from reading *The Catholic Messenger* out loud when he was in elementary school. Gautreaux discusses the origins of some of his stories, including how his fascination with obsolete machinery gave rise to the title story of his first collection *Same Place, Same Things*.

Wanner, Irene. "An Imaginative Teller of Tales." Review of *Welding with Children*, by Tim Gautreaux. *The Seattle Times*, October 10, 1999, p. M8. Notes that Gautreaux's "adventurous imagination and perfect pitch for the right phrase" make his stories so special. Singles out for particular praise the title story for its "heartbreaking voice" and "The Piano Tuner" for its "generosity of details."

Charles E. May

ELLEN GILCHRIST

Born: Vicksburg, Mississippi; February 20, 1935

PRINCIPAL SHORT FICTION

In the Land of Dreamy Dreams, 1981
Victory over Japan, 1984
Drunk with Love, 1986
Light Can Be Both Wave and Particle, 1989
I Cannot Get You Close Enough, 1990 (novellas)
The Age of Miracles, 1995
Rhoda: A Life in Stories, 1995
The Courts of Love, 1996
Flights of Angels: Stories, 1998
The Cabel and Other Stories, 2000

OTHER LITERARY FORMS

Ellen Gilchrist has found her most comfortable literary form to be the short story, although her first published work was a collection of poems, *The Land Surveyor's Daughter* (1979). She published the novels *Anabasis: A Journey to the Interior* (1994) and *Sarah Conley* (1997). She has also written magazine articles and a television play, *The Season of Dreams* (1968), based on some of writer Eudora Welty's short stories. *Falling Through Space: The Journals of Ellen Gilchrist* (1987) is a collection of essays drawn from her journals and presented on National Public Radio.

ACHIEVEMENTS

Ellen Gilchrist's fiction uses a rich tangle of family relationships and realistic settings, often southern settings. Because of that, Gilchrist has sometimes been considered a regional writer, sometimes a women's writer, though most reviewers believe that she rises above the limitations those labels imply. Although her subjects are often the messy lives of the wealthy and talented, she creates lively pictures of other types too, male as well as female. Her portraits of children are especially vivid, and although she often writes about the South, she has also used settings from California to Maine. *The Season of Dreams* won the National Scriptwriting Award from the National Educational Television Network in 1968. Gilchrist won Pushcart Prizes for "Rich" (1979-1980) and "Summer: An Elegy" (1983). In 1984, she won the American Book Award for *Victory over Japan*, and in 1985, she won the J. William Fulbright Award for literature. The Mississippi Academy of Arts and Sciences honored her in 1985, 1990, and 1991.

BIOGRAPHY

Ellen Gilchrist was born into a family of plantation owners in Mississippi and remained in the South almost all of her life, except for several of her adolescent years during World War II. During that time, her father, an engineer for the Army Corps of Engineers, moved the family through several small towns in the Midwest. When she was fourteen, Gilchrist began her career in journalism by writing a column for a local newspaper in Franklin, Kentucky. At nineteen, she dropped out of school and ran away to North Carolina to marry an engineering student. Together they had three children. Divorced in 1966, Gilchrist entered Millsaps College, where she studied creative writing under Eudora Welty. During the next years, Gilchrist continued to write, and she was married and divorced three more times, once to her first husband. It was toward the end of that period that she took real steps toward a career as a professional writer. The first of those steps was a position as editor for the New Orleans newspaper *Vieux Carré Courier*.

Gilchrist reported that by the late 1970's she was tired of the social world of New Orleans, where she had lived during her marriages. At about the time she began working at the *Vieux Carré Courier* she sent some of her poems to Jim Whitehead, poet and novelist in the writing program at the University of Arkansas, Fayetteville. He urged her to join his writing class, and she did so. Gilchrist said that the instant she saw Fayetteville, Arkansas, she felt that she had arrived where she belonged. She liked its unpretentious social world, where people from the university and community met as equals. In 1981, the University of Arkansas Press published Gilchrist's first short-story collection, *In the Land of Dreamy Dreams*. Its sales were remarkable, about ten thousand copies in the Southwest alone—good sales by any standard but especially for a book brought out with no budget for elaborate advertising and promotion. The word-of-mouth praise that *In the Land of Dreamy Dreams* received brought it to the attention of Little, Brown, the company that published Gilchrist's next two books and that reissued *In the Land of Dreamy Dreams* in 1985.

Gilchrist's novel *The Annunciation* (1983) received a rather cool critical reception, but critical attention to her later work, particularly her short fiction, was more evenly positive. In the mid-1980's, her growing reputation made her an interesting choice for a weekly series of "journal entry" essays on National Public Radio's *Morning Edition* (some of these were later collected in *Falling Through Space*). Many of these essays originated in Fayetteville, Arkansas, and dealt with local characters and places (much as *The Annunciation* itself did). At the same time, they communicated Gilchrist's delight in human relationships and in the demands of her craft, as well as the world around her. Gilchrist continued to write fiction as well as to give public readings and lectures, remaining in her beloved Fayetteville.

ANALYSIS

Any reader of Ellen Gilchrist's fiction quickly comes to recognize some of her people, places, and preoccupations. She writes about women, very often about wealthy southern women who are coming to terms with their own boredom and self-indulgence. Sometimes she writes about creative women, writers and poets and scholars whose impulses lead them into tight situations from which only drastic actions can rescue them. In fact, desperate circumstances—pregnancy, even murder—mark the central action of many Gilchrist stories. Gilchrist also peoples her fiction with children, particularly adolescent girls whose growing self-awareness and sexuality often draw them into the sort of circumstances their creator most enjoys exploring.

Gilchrist frequently revisits favorite characters at several ages in their lives, so that reading successive stories about them becomes a bit like reading a short novel. In fact, Gilchrist frequently interweaves motifs, linking stories within as well as across collections. In her work, characters appear and reappear from one collection to the next, sometimes with new names, sometimes with slightly different families or backgrounds, but always with recognizable characteristics that take on greater depth as the reader sees them from multiple angles. Gilchrist treats settings the same way, using real geographic detail about places such as New Orleans, California, or Charlotte, North Carolina, to create the canvas on which she works, linking the various frames of that canvas through repetition.

"RICH"

In "Rich," an early story from *In the Land of Dreamy Dreams*, Tom and Letty Wilson are wealthy New Orleans socialites. Their lives have brought them everything they have ever wanted, including each other. Tom is a banker who likes to quote Andrew Carnegie: "Money is what you keep score with," he says. Letty has loved him since she saw him performing drunken fraternity stunts while they were both students at Tulane University. On one occasion, he stole a Bunny bread truck and drove through the Irish Channel district, a poor area of the city, throwing bread to the housewives. The one thing missing from Tom and Letty's lives is a child, and even that gap is filled when they adopt a baby girl named Helen. After the adoption, Letty has no trouble conceiving, and in short order, the Wilsons have four additional children. Of their children, only Helen is imperfect; she is plagued with learning disabilities and attention disorders; she must take drugs in order to be able to concentrate.

The Wilsons are also rich in maids, and the maids find Helen hateful to care for, especially because she can turn from loving to vicious in moments, shouting "nigger, nigger, nigger" at the maid who has crossed her will. In one such confrontation, Helen runs from the angry servant, crashes into the bassinet holding the smallest Wilson baby, and sends it rolling off the porch to crash on the sidewalk, killing the infant. The death ruins Tom. He begins to drink too much and makes bad banking decisions. The thought haunts him that people will think Helen is his illegitimate child. His life is crumbling to nothing. At last, driven beyond what he can tolerate, Tom takes Helen with him out to his duck camp. He takes along his prize Labrador puppy, a rifle, and a revolver, and after amusing Helen as tenderly as he can manage, he shoots first the puppy, then Helen, and then himself. Many things about this story are typical of Gilchrist's work, especially the violent ending and the detailed use of New Orleans for the setting. The reader, however, should also notice the realistic picture of Helen, whose psychic deformities are displayed without melodrama. What is less typical is the shifting point of view in the story; in later work, Gilchrist tends to use limited viewpoints or to write in first person.

"THE FAMOUS POLL AT JODY'S BAR"

"The Famous Poll at Jody's Bar" offers a good example of Gilchrist's fondness for returning to characters. In the story, nineteen-year-old Nora Jane Whittington, whom Gilchrist describes as "a self-taught anarchist," is trying to decide how to get the money to go to her boyfriend, Sandy, in San Jose. She and Sandy had lived together for fourteen months after she had finished high school. Sandy had taught Nora Jane many things, including an appreciation for jazz and an ability to plan holdups. Now she uses that ability, along with her skill in disguise, to hold up Jody's Bar, where the regulars include a judge and Jody himself who, ironically, keeps himself armed against the holdups he constantly expects. The poll of the title is being taken to let the bar's customers decide whether Prescott Hamilton IV should go on with his plans to be married. As she cleans out the till, Nora Jane adds her ballot to the jar; then, disguising herself as a nun, she leaves, headed for Sandy.

VICTORY OVER JAPAN

When the reader sees Nora Jane next, she is in California in "Jade Buddhas, Red Bridges, Fruits of Love," from Gilchrist's 1984 collection *Victory over Japan*. The story concerns Nora Jane's efforts to reconnect with Sandy, and it reveals how instead she takes up with Freddy Harwood. As often happens in Gilchrist's stories, biology plays a dramatic role in Nora Jane's destiny, and she becomes pregnant, perhaps by Freddy. In "The Double Happiness Bun" in the same collection, the reader begins to suspect that her baby is really twins. At the end of "The Double Happiness Bun," Nora Jane is caught on the Bay Bridge during an earthquake; she is entertaining the children of a stranger who is even more desperate than she. In the volume that follows, *Drunk with Love*, the reader actually experiences part of the story from the point of view of the twin fetuses. Although, like many Gilchrist women, Nora Jane seems trapped by her own sexuality and reproduction, it is a mistake to see her as a victim. Like Gilchrist's most vivid characters, she is also daring and resourceful. Her holdup demonstrates this, as does her courageous decision to help the stranger and her children in the earthquake disaster.

"Music," in *Victory over Japan*, is the story that most amplifies the character of Rhoda, a woman who appears in several stories over several collections. When readers piece together her background, they know that Rhoda's father is a self-made man; his fortune has come from geology, and he has moved his wife and daughter around the country—heartlessly moved them, his wife says—where his work has taken him. Rhoda appeared as a child in several stories in *In the Land of Dreamy Dreams*, sometimes with her own name, sometimes with another. In "Music," the reader sees a sulky, willful fourteen-year-old Rhoda who embodies many of the qualities of Gilchrist's older heroines. In addition to being unbearably self-centered, she is also intelligent and romantic; those are the parts of her character that prevent her from being a bore.

In this story, she has become the means by which her parents express their ongoing conflict. Furious at being dragged from Indiana to Kentucky by her father while the boy she is sure she loves, Bob Rosen, undergoes surgery for cancer far away in St. Louis, Rhoda does everything she can to make herself obnoxious to her parents. Along with her frequent assertions of her atheism, her constant smoking becomes her lever to rebellion. Both her parents detest the habit, but her weak mother cannot stop her. At last, her father takes her to see the strip mines in rural Kentucky. He has some limited success in preventing Rhoda from smoking during the trip, but he cannot stop her from seducing a boy she meets in a pool hall, and at last, in the midst of a union dispute, he must send her home in a chartered plane.

The last paragraphs of the story are set thirty years later, when Rhoda reads a letter from her father. In it, he tells her that he and her mother are ashamed of the book she has dedicated to them and that he wants their names removed from it. Rhoda, not surprisingly, has the last word. When she writes back, she tells him to take his name off the checks he sends to television preachers, and she reasserts her old arguments about evolution. Readers familiar with Gilchrist's women will recognize in Rhoda the spiritual sister of Amanda McCamey of *The Annunciation* and of Anna Hand in many of the later stories.

Victory over Japan also contains an important group of stories, which begin to introduce the complicated family that appears in much of Gilchrist's later work. One of the characters who does most to unify these tales is Traceleen, the black woman who has long worked as maid for Crystal and Manny Weiss and as nurse to the family's daughter Crystal Anne. Like many Gilchrist characters, Traceleen seems to have roots in William Faulkner's vision of the South; she is loyal, intelligent, devoted to the white family she works for but clear-eyed about its many faults. It is through her eyes that readers see Crystal's disintegrating marriage in "Miss Crystal's Maid Name Traceleen, She's Talking, She's Telling Everything She Knows" (that marital conflict forms the theme of several stories in which Traceleen appears). It is Traceleen who sees that Crystal's tragedy is her loveless marriage. "They're rich people, all the ones I'm talking about. Not that it does them much good that I can see," Traceleen says with her characteristic candor. The stories in the "Crystal" section describe Crystal's brother Phelan Manning, her lover Alan, and her son King by her first marriage. Gilchrist continues to explore these relationships increasingly in *Light Can Be Both Wave and Particle*, her novel *The Anna Papers*, and her three novellas in *I Cannot Get You Close Enough*.

DRUNK WITH LOVE

Gilchrist's 1986 collection, *Drunk with Love*, contains the Nora Jane story, which is concluded from the point of view of her unborn fetuses. As the fetuses speak, they look forward to their appearance on earth, which they know only by reputation. This collection also includes three Rhoda stories: "Nineteen Forty-one," which portrays Rhoda around the age of nine; "The Expansion of the Universe," which details Rhoda's romance with Bob Rosen, before his illness, and which concludes with Rhoda's family moving to Kentucky (a move that temporarily unites Rhoda and her mother against her father); and "Adoration," in which readers see nineteen-year-old Rhoda in her hasty new marriage, as she and her husband use her pregnancies as a means of denying their empty relationship.

Drunk with Love concludes with two important

stories. "Traceleen at Dawn" is the story of how Crystal quit drinking. Once again, Traceleen is a friendly but not entirely neutral narrator as she relates Crystal's efforts to quit. When Crystal falls off the wagon, she goes on an epic binge, which ends when she deliberately sets fire to her house. That is how she quits drinking at last. The story called "Anna, Part I" introduces Anna Hand on "the day she decided to give up being a fool and go back to being a writer." The story traces Anna's love affair with a married man; as the affair ends, readers see her opening a box of typing paper, determined to turn her experience into art. Anna's story is continued and in a sense concluded in Gilchrist's 1988 novel, *The Anna Papers*. In the course of the novel, Anna discovers her niece Olivia, who is her brother Daniel's child from his failed first marriage to a Cherokee woman whom he met in California in the 1960's. Although Olivia is poor and Anna has always had money, once Olivia is brought into the family, she proves to be Anna's spiritual daughter in terms of talent, intelligence, and nerve. At the end of the novel, Anna commits suicide rather than face treatment for a cancer she knows will be fatal. These details become important in *I Cannot Get You Close Enough*.

LIGHT CAN BE BOTH WAVE AND PARTICLE

Light Can Be Both Wave and Particle in many ways distills characters and themes from the earlier collections. "The Tree Fort" and "The Time Capsule" return to picture Rhoda as a child in wartime, trying to come to terms with her family's constant moving and her first intimations of what death means. Another Rhoda story, "Some Blue Hills at Sundown," confirms that Bob Rosen did indeed die of cancer. "The Starlight Express" documents the birth of Nora Jane's twins. They are delivered by Freddy Harwood at his eccentric house far out in the forest. Nora Jane is saved from bleeding to death only by the fortuitous arrival of the medical services helicopter, for in Gilchrist's work, birth is rarely a simple matter.

The title story of the collection involves the meeting of Lin Tan Sing, a third-year medical student from San Francisco, and Margaret McElvoy, from Fayetteville, Arkansas. They meet on a bridge over-

looking Puget Sound, fall in love, and eventually decide to have him meet Margaret's family, in Fayetteville. In Gilchrist's stories, the abrasions that arise from conflicting classes and cultures are often fatal to love. Part of the difficulties of Crystal's marriage, for example, rise from the fact that her husband is a Jew. Olivia, when she reenters the Hand family, is always conscious of her status as a Native American. In the case of Lin Tan and Margaret, however, things go well. Margaret's family is equal to the occasion; the story closes as her father prepares to play chess with his future son-in-law.

The volume closes with a long story, "Mexico," in which the reader sees Rhoda again, now divorced and spending time in Mexico with some of the same wealthy and self-indulgent people who have had roles in other Gilchrist stories; in fact, Crystal's brother, Phelan Manning, is here, and the reader also learns that Rhoda knew Anna before she killed herself. At the end of the story, Rhoda has broken her foot, and the resulting confinement leads her to try to make sense of her family and its relationships. As the story concludes, she has written a conciliatory letter to her brother Dudley, with whom her past relationship has been painful. (It is notable that the name Dudley is given to many of Gilchrist's least likable men.)

I CANNOT GET YOU CLOSE ENOUGH

Much of the Anna series is concluded in *I Cannot Get You Close Enough*. The first part is a posthumous manuscript from Anna, explaining her attempts to deal with her brother Daniel's treacherous former wife. The second details the early life in Oklahoma of Anna's niece, Olivia, and her joining the Hands in Charlotte, North Carolina. The last part takes place after Anna's death, when all the family females (including Traceleen and Crystal Anne and Olivia) spend the summer in Maine.

FLIGHTS OF ANGELS

This collection returns some of Gilchrist's liveliest characters—Rhoda, Traceleen, and Crystal—and continues their story, while also introducing new voices into the Gilchrist cast. "Miss Crystal Confronts the Past" is told through the frank voice of Traceleen, who describes herself as "old enough to know better" in reference to her trip with Crystal to Charlotte, North Carolina, to save Crystal's grandmother (a powerful force in her own right) and her estate from the manipulations of Phelan. Phelan may be unscrupulous, but he knows how to entertain the bored old woman; it is only after her death that the true nature of Phelan's Medicare scam comes to light.

In "A Sordid Tale: Or, Traceleen Continues Talking," Traceleen reveals what Crystal went through to try to keep her recently widowed friend Canada Marks from falling under Phelan's spell. Crystal knows that Phelan is mainly interested in her friend's money. The story also introduces Traceleen's feisty niece Andria, a television anchorwoman who has told her aunt, "Don't go writing any more of those crazy stories and casting yourself in the role of maid." Traceleen's charm is that while she may call Crystal "Miss Crystal," she is never blind to the truth—good or bad—about her employer.

As the collection's title from Horatio's farewell to the dying Hamlet suggests, many of these stories deal with death or loss. In "Mississippi," Larkin is on death row for the murder of a white supremacist who killed Larkin's African American friend Someral during a demonstration for integration. Larkin is a typical Gilchrist woman: self-willed, independent, and led by a strong sense of justice. In "A Tree to Be Desired," Juliet takes strength from her dying grandfather to confront her loveless marriage and to begin a love affair with the young black male nurse who tended him.

"The Triumph of Reason" introduces a new Gilchrist narrator, brilliant and outspoken seventeen-year-old Aurora Harris, who relates the story of her romance with a French boy (and justifies her subsequent abortion) in this story. In "Have a *Wonderful* Nice Walk" she chronicles the French boy's difficult visit to the United States, her discovery of her next love, and her comic relationship with her younger sister. The stories demonstrate Gilchrist's skill in creating credible voices of bright adolescents, making them funny and likable without downplaying their awful self-centeredness. "Down at the Dollhouse," one of the last stories in the collection, returns to the theme of death as it recounts how a spunky old lady spends the last hours of her life at a beauty salon, attending to the needs of her equally elderly friends. As always, the dominant concern is the weight of the past on present human relationships, one of Gilchrist's most persistent themes.

OTHER MAJOR WORKS

LONG FICTION: *The Annunciation*, 1983; *The Anna Papers*, 1988; *Net of Jewels*, 1992; *Starcarbon: A Meditation on Love, a Novel*, 1994; *Anabasis: A Journey to the Interior*, 1994; *Sarah Conley*, 1997.

TELEPLAY: *The Season of Dreams*, 1968.

POETRY: *The Land Surveyor's Daughter*, 1979; *Riding out the Tropical Depression: Selected Poems*, 1986.

NONFICTION: *Falling Through Space: The Journals of Ellen Gilchrist*, 1987.

BIBLIOGRAPHY

Allen, Kimberly G. Review of *I Cannot Get You Close Enough*, by Ellen Gilchrist. *Library Journal* 115 (September 15, 1990): 98-99. Praises the work's complex structure, which Allen describes as confusing but effective. Useful in its examination of the novellas' overlapping chronology.

Bauer, Margaret Donovan. *The Fiction of Ellen Gilchrist*. Gainesville: University Press of Florida, 1999. An excellent book-length study of Gilchrist's works and prevalent themes. Includes bibliographical references and an index.

Gilchrist, Ellen. Interview by Wendy Smith. *Publishers Weekly* 239 (March 2, 1992): 46-47. The interviewer claims that in her novels, Gilchrist creates an extended family that could no longer be comfortably handled in the short-story form. Discusses characters such as Rhoda Manning, Anna Hand, and others who reappear in Gilchrist's fiction.

Hoffman, Roy. Review of *Light Can Be Both Wave and Particle*, by Ellen Gilchrist. *The New York Times Book Review*, October 22, 1989, 13. Analyzes the work as a conclusion to *The Annunciation*; gives particular attention to "Mexico" and to the title story. The themes of the meeting of East and West in that story seem to suggest new directions that Hoffman believes Gilchrist's fiction is about to take.

McCay, Mary A. *Ellen Gilchrist*. New York: Twayne, 1997. Examines Gilchrist's life and her works, with a chapter on the short stories. Includes bibliographical references and an index.

Seabrook, John. Review of *Victory over Japan*, by Ellen Gilchrist. *The Christian Science Monitor*, December 7, 1984, p. 38. This balanced review offers a brief analysis of the stories' major characteristics, praising Gilchrist's prose style and dialogue but faulting the weakness of her character analysis. Seabrook likes her humor but finds the behavior of her characters baffling.

Shapiro, Harriet. "Southerner Ellen Gilchrist Is the Book World's Belle." *People Weekly* 23 (February 11, 1985): 75. A brief biographical sketch written when Gilchrist won the American Book Award for her collection *Victory over Japan*;

notes that her stories focus on independent "southern belles."

Thompson, Jeanie, and Anita Miller Garner. "The Miracle of Realism: The Bid for Self-Knowledge in the Fiction of Ellen Gilchrist." In *Women Writers of the Contemporary South*, edited by Peggy Whitman Prenshaw. Jackson: University Press of Mississippi, 1984. A useful close analysis of Gilchrist's early work. The authors see her treatment of women as essentially traditional, despite her interest in unconventional central characters. The essay gives most attention to *The Annunciation*, but it also discusses "Rich," "The President of the Louisiana Live Oak Society," and "Revenge." The authors look particularly at Gilchrist's fondness for central characters who are simultaneously charming and awful.

Ann Davison Garbett

PENELOPE GILLIATT

Born: London, England; March 25, 1932
Died: London, England; May 9, 1993

PRINCIPAL SHORT FICTION

What's It Like Out?, 1968 (pb. in United States as *Come Back If It Doesn't Get Better*, 1969)
Nobody's Business, 1972
Splendid Lives, 1977
Quotations from Other Lives, 1982
They Sleep Without Dreaming, 1985
Twenty-two Stories, 1986
Lingo, 1990

OTHER LITERARY FORMS

In addition to several collections of short stories, Penelope Gilliatt has published novels, collections of essays (including film reviews, profiles, interviews, and conversations), an award-winning screenplay, an opera libretto, and a study of comedy, which is an analysis of the comedic styles of famous comedians.

ACHIEVEMENTS

The "jet set," that chic world of international sophisticates, has found in Penelope Gilliatt one of its compelling literary representatives. Her talents as a purveyor of elitist wit and liberal sensibility have been prominently recognized, sometimes skeptically and even negatively, but, most generally, with acclaim and high praise. Scrupulous readers of her work, such as Anne Tyler and Anthony Burgess, appreciate her profound modernity, whereas the less astute see primarily, or exclusively, slickness and glibness. Her cinematic writing style was effectively conducive to her script for the John Schlesinger film *Sunday Bloody Sunday*, the 1971 film which received prizes as the best screenplay of the year from the National Society of Film Critics and the New York Film Critics, to be followed in 1972 by a prize from the Writers Guild of Britain and a nomination for an Academy Award. In 1972, Gilliatt also received an Award in Literature from the American Academy of

Arts and Letters and an election to the Royal Society of Literature.

BIOGRAPHY

Like Arabella Ridley—her brilliant and efficacious heroine in "They Sleep Without Dreaming," who "had written her Ph.D., in advance to save time, and then got her B.A."—Penelope Ann Douglass Conner, the daughter of Cyril and Mary Douglass Conner, exhibited her precocity by passing her University of Oxford entrance examinations before she was old enough to be admitted. That was in 1947, when she was fifteen. Her father, who was a lawyer, and her mother had reared their two daughters in Northumberland until 1942, during which year her parents' marriage had broken up and Penelope had elected, at age ten, to live with her father in wartime London. At Queens College, she gained proficiency in music, literary studies, and foreign languages. In 1948, still not old enough for Oxford, she made the first of her many swings across the Atlantic to study for one academic year at Bennington College in Vermont.

In London, during the early 1950's, Penelope Conner directed her writing talents toward magazine journalism and rose to the feature-editorship of *Vogue*. She trained her eye for cinema and theater by contributing reviews to *Vogue* and other magazines, including the *New Statesman*. At the beginning of the next decade, she became the film critic for London's *The Observer*. From 1961 to 1966, she gained prominence in this capacity, giving the last of these years over to theater criticism. Her reputation won her an invitation to serve as guest film critic for *The New Yorker*. Her success culminated in her sharing this post with Pauline Kael, each serving annually for half a year. In 1954, Penelope had married and subsequently divorced Roger William Gilliatt, who became a professor of clinical neurology at the University of London. Her second marriage, to the playwright John Osborne in 1963, ended in divorce after five years; Gilliatt's daughter, Nolan Kate, was born of this marriage.

During her marriage to Osborne, Gilliatt began her career as a novelist. She published *One by One* in 1965 and *A State of Change* in 1967. These were followed by *The Cutting Edge* (1978), *Mortal Matters* (1983), and *A Woman of Singular Occupation* (1988). The novels are generally praised in the context of Gilliatt's high intelligence and elegance of expression, qualities that marked her concurrent profiles and critical articles on film and theater for periodicals, including *The New Yorker*, but they are found somewhat wanting in continuity and characterization. A critic for *The Observer* said of the 1988 novel that "it's all talk" and is "a frustrating novel," and a reviewer for *The Times Literary Supplement* spoke of "characters who are lightly introduced and forgotten very soon." She ended her affiliation with *The New Yorker* in 1979.

Talk and minimal characterization are better suited to the short story, at which Gilliatt came to excel and from which her ear for conversation and her zoomlike pictorial eye brought her, by way of her incisive film reviews for *The New Yorker* (in which most of her short stories originally appeared), to the creation of her screenplay for Schlesinger's *Sunday Bloody Sunday* (adapted from *One by One*) in 1971. This achievement fulfilled, in large part, the promise of her childhood precocity, and the awards in recognition of the screenplay and subsequently for her

Penelope Gilliatt in the 1970's (Archive Photos)

writing in general ensured her identification as a significant twentieth century literary artist. As a dedicated socialist, Gilliatt sustained membership in the British Labour Party and studied conscientiously the cultures of Slavic countries, especially Russia, Poland, and Czechoslovakia. Gilliatt continued her association with *The New Yorker*, primarily as a fiction writer, and in the 1980's, she adapted several works from her fiction as plays and films. Remaining unmarried, she maintained her residence in London, until her death in 1993 after a protracted illness.

ANALYSIS

Penelope Gilliatt's short fiction illustrates the twentieth century phenomenon of the de-centered narrative. Breaching the Aristotelian holism of *mythos* (plot) comprising beginning, middle, and end, de-centered fiction disregards plot and eliminates one or two of the narrative stages. De-centering is not exclusively a matter of removing the middle and either leaving only beginning and end or presenting only the removed middle as the narrative. Rather, de-centering eschews the triad that is defined by a middle.

Other of Gilliatt's favored themes include Slavic culture, gourmet cooking and dining, appreciation of music (especially opera and modern music), language study (English, Greek, Latin, and modern foreign languages), dentistry, and the superiority of human brainwork to computerized authority. Her short fiction is also incident with eccentric affairs of affection, notably May-December romances and grandparent-grandchild attachments.

Discernible in each of her collections of short stories, moreover, is a thematic or imagistic continuity. The exception is *Twenty-two Stories*, which merely culls representative selections from the five preceding collections. The skull motif informs *What's It Like Out?*, with the word "skull" appearing in seven of the nine stories. In the two exceptions, "The Tactics of Hunger" and "Come Back If It Doesn't Get Better," a preoccupation with death substantiates the motif of the skull.

WHAT'S IT LIKE OUT?

In Gilliatt's first collection of short stories, for example, "Fred and Arthur" is a dyad consisting, first,

of Arthur teamed as a comic entertainer with Fred and, second, of Arthur living without Fred after his partner marries and then dies. With Fred, Arthur is fat and jocund; without him, Arthur becomes thin and serious. The triad, consisting of Arthur, Fred, and Fred's wife, destroys the duo of Fred and Arthur.

Aristotelian or classical logic, then, is rooted in triadism—for example, the syllogism. De-centering disestablishes classical logic. "Living on the Box" spotlights a vestigially classicist writer attempting to imbue his nature poetry with spatial logic and moral order. He attributes the staleness of his existence not to his own unawareness of creative disorder but to the world, to which he cannot adjust, and to his wife, whom he neglects. His wife sees through his inauthenticity and, after their inevitable separation, remains available to him in his unacknowledged dependence on her. The story, lacking any specific beginning or end, amounts to a juxtaposition of the limitations of logic with the inherence of chaos.

"The Redhead" holds up to view another person, a six-foot-tall woman upset by the "romanticism of the period," who opts for logic and finds it hellish but yields in time to the attraction of Newtonian mathematics. The narrative, which changelessly details the redhead's changelessness, doubly confutes logic. Harriet, the redhead, is said to be fifteen in 1912, which would make 1897 her birth date; later, she is said to have her fortieth birthday in 1943, which would set her birth date at 1903. Further, the second paragraph of the story relates the unchanged color of her hair "to the end of her life," and the penultimate paragraph of the story begins, "She is still alive." The story saw three editions without revision, making it clear that its plotlessness is abetted by contradictions that identify the narrative as an instrument of opposition to logic.

"What's It Like Out?," the last and titular story of the first collection, introduces a theme that becomes prominent in Gilliatt's short fiction: old age, or the final period of life, as the most efficacious period. The once-conventional notion of the triadic life—youth, maturity, age—was de-centered by the twentieth century's obsession with youth; Gilliatt elects an obsession with advanced age. Her octogenarian Milly and

Franklin Wilberforce, for all their age-related physical impairments, prove to be psychologically and intellectually superior to a young newspaper interviewer named Ben. Milly evinces her existentialist authenticity by her thought, twice expressed, that she will never become accustomed to the ravaging of old age and that she has not *any obligation to get used to it.* Fifteen of the sixty stories published through 1990 develop this theme, including the especially compelling "Cliff-Dwellers," a story in a one-act play format in which the octogenarian Emma and Henry sustain the full psychological experience of youth without a trace of self-deception.

NOBODY'S BUSINESS

Nobody's Business is primarily a collective variation on the theme of anticomputerism and, secondarily, a dyad consisting, first, of five stories in imitative evocation of literary works and, second, of four stories echoing such twentieth century trends as Freudianism, socialism, and astrology. The sequence begins with "FRANK" (Family Robot Adapted to the Needs of Kinship), a satire on cybernetics, which extends the cautionary observations about the mechanistic displacement of humankind in Karel Čapek's *R.U.R.* (1920; English translation, 1923) and concludes with the titular story, a celebration of the aged at the expense of the obnoxious young. "An Antique Love Story" places British Adam-and-Eve figures Amy and Ed in a seedily Edenic New York, where a Polish-Jewish child is educated by computerized telephone (Touch-Tone-Tuition), while a Mrs. Green, who insists that she is God, knits human organs; Amy plans a trip to Czechoslovakia, the homeland, incidentally, of Čapek. "Staying in Bed," inclusive of a theatrical seminar called "Computers—Whither?," is a suggestive version of Ivan Goncharov's *Oblomov* (1859; English translation, 1915); in Gilliatt's story a cellist refuses to get out of bed and assigns his own psychoanalysis to his pianist friend and former accompanist. "Property," in the form of a one-act play, is, with computer-controlled individuals, a variation on Jean-Paul Sartre's *Huis clos* (1944; *In Camera*, 1946; better known as *No Exit*, 1947). "Foreigners" employs the name Flitch (evocative of T. S. Eliot's "flitch of bacon") and a reflection of India to rehearse

the aura of *The Waste Land* (1922). The collection swings from technological science to social science with its concluding quartet, two stories picking up the Freudianism implicit in "Staying in Bed": one story glancing at the Communist Party as expressing "a sort of chivalrous exasperation at things as they would always be," and one, punctuated by astrological readings, being a de-centered account of a woman who, having given up computer programming, dabbles in astrology.

SPLENDID LIVES

Splendid Lives opens with its titular story about a racehorse-owning nonagenarian bishop and his octogenarian sister. The nine stories in the collection generally support an undercurrent of trades versus professions versus landed gentry and make a swipe, at once curiously both broad and subtle, at the British class system. The fifth story in the group, "Catering," works out an ingeniously cubistic double perspective on temporal movements: Time-forward moves through the week-long preparations for a wedding reception, and time-backward is retrospective of two generations of involvements in extramarital sex.

QUOTATIONS FROM OTHER LIVES

Although none of the twelve stories in *Quotations from Other Lives* carries the title of the collection, the title is apt because all the stories intone the existentialist Other, sometimes as subject, with "quotations" denoting words, and sometimes as object, with "quotations" connoting the value of persons as commodities. The opening selections concentrate on the proper name. In "Break," a Czechoslovakian of Scottish ancestry identifies himself with Nazi-harassed Jews by changing his name from Alastair to Eli. Near-Scottish provenance (Cumberland) in "Stephanie, Stephen, Steph, Steve" underlies the story of Stephen, a shipbuilder, who finds his identity in his namesake wife and daughter. Both "Teeth" and "When Are You Going Back?" subtextually quote or cite Sigmund Freud. In the latter, a young American woman experiences "otherness" as social displacement in English society. In "Teeth" a male dentist and a female sculptor find their love disapproved both by her family and by his reluctance to impinge in any way on her artistic independence. Subjective examples of eccentric affairs of affection follow in "As Is," in which a nineteen-year-old woman pursues intimacy with a sixty-four-year-old professor, and "Fakt," in which a Polish exile visits Warsaw and is received as a famous Polish exile with the same name; each exile appears in the company of his wife and a mistress who is sanctioned by the wife. The Polish corridor figures in both stories, analogically in "As Is" and literally in "Fakt." Wordplay marks the next pair of tales, taking the form of mottos and truisms in "Timely Is the Hand That Winds the Clock" and that of semanticism in "In Trust," which is composed as a three-act play. The concluding quartet of stories revolves around the vitality and special insights of the aged, one of whom, a ninety-three-year-old grandmother, is exemplary in her ability to see the Other as subject instead of object or commodity.

THEY SLEEP WITHOUT DREAMING

They Sleep Without Dreaming includes two stories on the superiority of the aged: the already mentioned "Cliff-Dwellers" and another, "Addio," in which a seventy-one-year-old opera soprano, who for fifty years of her career has played the boy Cherubino in *The Marriage of Figaro*, joins in song a brilliant young woman finalist at an audition, abbreviating thereby the qualitative distance between youth and age. The initial story, "The Hinge," is embossed in its lack of plot by the strength of the woman Kakia, an octogenarian survivor of Auschwitz upon whom many depend for help and advice. The titular story elaborates a theme introduced in "Twice Lucky," from the concluding quartet in *Quotations from Other Lives*, namely, the "aboriginal saying that a man who loses his dreaming is dead." Three stories—"The Nuisance," "Broderie Anglaise," and "Purse"—illustrate the means by which a woman, reduced to her own resources, achieves dignity. Particularly compelling is "Broderie Anglaise," in which "dainty," a word commonly evocative of femininity, subtextually sustains the irony of its derivation from Latin *dignitas* (dignity).

They Sleep Without Dreaming maintains imagistic or thematic continuity in repetitive or contrapuntal overlap. The first three stories have a café or restaurant setting. Stories three and four include, each, a prominent character named Joanna. Stories four and five involve music, stories five and six employees giving notice, six and seven taxation and characters named Peter, and seven and eight characters named Emma. In both story eight and story nine there is a duologue, in nine and ten the making of a carbon copy, and in ten and eleven the act of taking dictation. The dyadic quality manifest in this overlapping is also a part of Gilliatt's transnarrational technique. A few of the very many examples are as follows. Stories six ("Broderie Anglaise") and seven ("Suspense Item") of *They Sleep Without Dreaming* intensify thematic counterpoint by each including the phrase "Needlessly messy anarchy" in different contexts. In stories four ("Addio") and five ("They Sleep Without Dreaming"), there is variant use of the name Cherubino. The technique is a signature device in Gilliatt's short fiction. "Known for Her Frankness," in the first collection, quotes the German proverb, "A hungry belly has no ears"; in "Timely Is the Hand That Winds the Clock," from the fourth collection, the proverb reappears as a motto, "A hungry belly hath no ears." In "Foreigner" (from *Nobody's Business*), there is a passage, "I'll leap into my life, he thought, if it splits my face to bits"; this appears in "On Each Other's Time" (from *They Sleep Without Dreaming*) as "I must leap into my life if it cuts me to splinters." A Latin pun, *lucus a non lucendo* (something like "*park* is not derived from *Sparking*"), fits different contexts in "Autumn of a Dormouse" (from *Splendid Lives*) and the titular story of *They Sleep Without Dreaming*. The recurrences are not exclusively dyadic: A number of phrases and passages appear more than twice, but twice is the standard. Against any charge of careless or inadvertent repetition one need only note Gilliatt's impeccable command of language and her deliberateness in juxtaposing stories with recurrences, such as "Keep the mind busy and the body seated" ("Fleeced" in *Splendid Lives*) and "Keep the brain occupied and the physique seated" ("Phone-in," immediately following "Fleeced"), only thirteen pages away.

LINGO

Lingo, Gilliatt's 1990 collection of ten stories, restates concerns of the stories in her earlier collections. For example, "The Corridors of Mr. Cyril" expresses the same concern found in "Break" over the unpleasant fact that the word "monosyllable" has five syllables instead of one. Observations about linguistic peculiarities constitute the theme of the collection, to which titles such as "Lingo," "Hic Haec Hoc," and "Ex Libris" contribute thematic effect. Wordplay such as "Never trouble trouble till trouble troubles you" in "Hic Haec Hoc" is repeated from "Timely Is the Hand That Winds the Clock." The titular story tests the psycholinguistic difference between referring to one's self as "I" and as "one." "Fat Chance" includes the word "Etymolo-whatnots"; and "Lingo" follows, in interior repetition, with "Onomato-thing." In "Hurricane Ethelred," a plotless story about an oddly matched couple (an oboist named Nina, who is heir to a 150-year-old turtle, and a computer expert named Maximilian), a stormy night elicits semantically different qualifications: Maximilian calls the night "heavily metaphorical" and an elderly neighbor calls it "actual."

One of the most haunting of Gilliatt's images amounts to a comment on the moribundity of organized religion. In "The Redhead," the titular character's hair is likened to the "wisps" of orange hair on the skulls in the crypt of St Bride's Church. The same image is used in "Stephanie, Stephen, Steph, Steve"

> When the baby Stephanie was born, she had two tufts of bright red hair. They were the color that hair has turned on some of the skeletons in the crypt of St. Bride's.

The image is clarified as the Redhead's "wisps" of belief in an afterlife desert her irrevocably and as Stephanie dies shortly after she herself bears a daughter.

One critic calls Penelope Gilliatt's de-centered short stories "snippets"; another calls them "sketches"; another insists that they are not slices of life so much as "elegant slivers." Each of the labels is apt. The stories flash upon the retina of a reader's thought with a cinematic impact that is almost subliminal. "As for plot," writes Rosemary Dinnage, who provides the phrase "elegant slivers," "it's too coarse a concept altogether."

OTHER MAJOR WORKS

LONG FICTION: *One by One*, 1965; *A State of Change*, 1967; *The Cutting Edge*, 1978; *Mortal Matters*, 1983; *A Woman of Singular Occupation*, 1988.

PLAYS: *Property*, pr. 1980; *But When All's Said and Done*, pr. 1981.

SCREENPLAY: *Sunday Bloody Sunday*, 1971.

NONFICTION: *Unholy Fools: Wits, Comics, Disturbers of the Peace*, 1973; *Jean Renoir: Essays, Conversations, Reviews*, 1975; *Jacques Tati*, 1976; *Three-Quarter Face: Reports and Reflections*, 1980; *To Wit: Skin and Bones of Comedy*, 1990 (pb. in England as *To Wit: In Celebration of Comedy*, 1990).

BIBLIOGRAPHY

Broyard, Anatole. Review of *Splendid Lives*. *The New York Times Book Review*, January 29, 1978, 12. Mixing mild blame with high praise, Broyard touches upon a key characteristic of Gilliatt's short stories, namely, their breaking off, their "discontinuing in the middle of things."

Casson, Hugh, and Lord Snowdon. "True to Her Words." *The Guardian*, May 12, 1993, p. 11. Personal recollections of Gilliatt, just after her death, by two well-known men who knew her. Casson notes Gilliatt's passion for words, while Lord Snowdon remembers her inquisitiveness and her humor.

Dinnage, Rosemary. "Stylish Sketches." Review of *Quotations from Other Lives*, by Penelope Gilliatt. *The New York Times Book Review*, April 11, 1982, 6. Emphasizes Gilliatt's style, suggesting that its "clipped brilliance" may not wear well, and discusses Gilliatt's loving preoccupation with verbal oddities. Note is taken of the satisfaction to be derived from reading between Gilliatt's clever lines, but the writer considers that the lines themselves should be more substantial.

Glendinning, Victoria. "Watch Your Language." Review of *To Wit* and *Lingo*, by Penelope Gilliatt. *The Times*, February 17, 1990. This review by a well-known British writer maintains that Gilliatt's picture of an England that never was is funny, but not funny enough in her stories. Asserts they are stories of displacements, collisions, and rearrangements, but that the idioms in them seem anachronisms.

Jefferson, Margo. "Miniature Eccentrics." *Newsweek* (February 13, 1978): 90. A review of *Splendid Lives* that praises Gilliatt's whimsical and worldly tone but criticizes her for sacrificing character to atmosphere and detail. Claims the best story in the collection is "A Lovely Bit of Wood," but that Gilliatt's typical weakness can best be seen in "The Bishop of Hurlingham."

Kael, Pauline. "A Movie Classic Is Not Nothing." In *Deeper into Movies*. Boston: Little, Brown, 1973. In this review of the film *Sunday Bloody Sunday*, written for the October 2, 1971, issue of *The New Yorker*, Kael says much in clarification of Gilliatt's artistic motives. One statement about the film particularly encapsulates Gilliatt's literary direction: "A curious sort of plea on behalf of human frailty . . . that asks for sympathy for the nonheroes of life who make the best deal they can."

Kaveney, Roz. "Speaking for the Shabby-Genteel." Review of *They Sleep Without Dreaming*, by Penelope Gilliatt. *The Times Literary Supplement* (November 29, 1985): 1353. Kaveney observes Gilliatt's presentations of lives developing in sudden "cuts and shifts" over many years and notes that Gilliatt's characters "jump suddenly and radically in their speech as well." She is not entirely supportive of Gilliatt's defiance of strict logic or her "narrative tricks."

Kinkead, Gwen. Review of *Nobody's Business*, by Penelope Gilliatt. *The Harvard Advocate* (Winter, 1973). Kinkead nonjudgmentally summarizes the effect of Gilliatt's short fiction on readers and makes a statement that can be applied to all Gilliatt's short fiction: "We are spectators to involvements formed in invisible pasts, to conversations already three-quarters finished, situations interrupted, of endings not yet complete, and are expected with confidence to comprehend the ellipses."

Mars-Jones, Adam. "Far from the Truth About England: *To Wit* and *Lingo*." *The Independent* (February 18, 1990): 20. A review of a book of nonfiction and a collection of short stories by a well-known British short-story writer. Criticizes Gilliatt for situating the stories in a "second-hand England" of inadequately funny social comedies.

Roy Arthur Swanson

CHARLOTTE PERKINS GILMAN

Born: Hartford, Connecticut; July 3, 1860
Died: Pasadena, California; August 17, 1935

PRINCIPAL SHORT FICTION

"The Yellow Wallpaper," 1892
Charlotte Perkins Gilman Reader, 1981 (Ann J. Lane, editor)
The Yellow Wallpaper and Other Writings, 1989 (Lynne Sharon Schwartz, editor)
Herland and Selected Stories, 1992 (Barbara H. Solomon, editor; also published as *Herland, The Yellow Wall-Paper, and Selected Writings*, 1999, Denise D. Knight, editor)

"The Yellow Wall-Paper" and Selected Stories of Charlotte Perkins Gilman, 1994 (Denise D. Knight, editor)
The Yellow Wallpaper, and Other Stories, 1995 (Robert Shulman, editor)

OTHER LITERARY FORMS

Charlotte Perkins Gilman published a volume of poems, *In This Our World* (1893). Her nonfiction social criticism, notably *Women and Economics* (1898), was the basis of her contemporary reputation and her lecture career. Gilman also wrote utopian novels, including her famous *Herland* (1915). Her final work

Charlotte Perkins Gilman (Library of Congress)

was an autobiography, *The Living of Charlotte Perkins Gilman* (1935).

ACHIEVEMENTS

Charlotte Perkins Gilman was posthumously inducted into the National Women's Hall of Fame in Seneca Falls, New York, in 1994. During her life, she was a delegate to a number of international conventions, including the International Socialist and Labor Congress in London in 1896 and the International Women's Suffrage Congress in Budapest, Hungary, in 1913.

BIOGRAPHY

Charlotte Anna Perkins Gilman was born in Hartford, Connecticut, on July 3, 1860. Her father was Frederick Beecher Perkins, and her mother was Mary Fitch Westcott. The Beechers, including her early role model, Harriet Beecher Stowe, influenced her social convictions. Gilman married Charles Walter Stetson, a young artist, in 1884. Within the year, their daughter Katharine was born. Thereafter, Gilman suf-

fered bouts of depression stemming from her desire to work as artist, writer, and advocate of women's rights and the conflict between this desire and her more traditional role as wife and mother.

In 1886, Gilman had a breakdown and was treated for hysteria by neurologist S. Weir Mitchell, who prescribed total rest and abstinence from work. Despite the treatment, Gilman grew worse and feared for her sanity. She decided to take matters into her own hands, separated from Stetson, and moved to California, where she began to publish and lecture on the economic and domestic dependence of women.

During the 1890's, Gilman published the short story "The Yellow Wallpaper," based on her breakdown and rest treatment. During that time, she also published her first book of poetry, *In This Our World*, and a major volume of social criticism, *Women and Economics*. In 1900, Gilman married George Houghton Gilman. She continued to publish social criticism and fiction throughout the next decades. From 1909 to 1916, she single-handedly wrote and published the monthly magazine *The Forerunner*. Her husband died in 1934. Gilman, diagnosed with incurable breast cancer, took her own life on August 17, 1935.

ANALYSIS

Charlotte Perkins Gilman used her fiction to dramatize her vision of history, sociology, and ethics. Over the course of her career, she published close to two hundred pieces of fiction, mainly short stories, in periodicals or in her own *Forerunner* magazine.

Most of Gilman's stories belong to two categories: realistic stories that deal with the unhappy situations of the everyday world and utopian stories set totally in the world of the imagination.

In her fiction, Gilman suggests changes that might be made in preparation for the future world and asserts the need to break away from the traditions that limit human potential. While she is often identified with the feminist movement, her emphasis is on a utopian society in which men and women would be equal, a society she portrays in the novel *Herland*. Her stories are meant to be uplifting examples of her social philosophy. Because many of these stories have an ideal ending, rather than a probable one, many critics find them didactic or formulaic. They are not well regarded for their literary qualities.

Gilman did not have literary pretensions; she wrote quickly and without much revision. She did, however, aspire to write with "clearness and vivacity," so that her work would "be apprehended with ease and pleasure." Her style is direct; her message is clear.

"THE YELLOW WALLPAPER"

Of all Gilman's fiction, "The Yellow Wallpaper" stands out as a brilliant psychological study, apart from the rest of her work in its emotional intensity and introspection. It is considered by critics the only genuinely literary piece she wrote, in the literary tradition of the nineteenth century American short story, sustaining a single effect: here, madness, loneliness, and desperation with a psychological intensity best suited to short fiction.

The story is told in the first person by a young wife and mother. The narrator's physician-husband has ordered a rest cure for her nerves. The reference is clearly autobiographical; Gilman's stated intent is to indict the methods of Dr. S. Weir Mitchell, who ordered a similar cure of complete rest and absence of intellectual stimulation for Gilman to cure her depression and breakdown following her own marriage and motherhood. According to Gilman, this medical advice brought her nearer to the brink of "utter mental ruin." This story is unique in Gilman's canon in not resolving happily. The narrator, according to the traditional view of wife as dependent child, believes that her husband-doctor knows best and sinks into horrifying insanity. In her own life, Gilman was able to break out and save herself by moving away from her husband and resuming her work.

John, the well-meaning husband-doctor of the story, rents a large house isolated in the country to provide his ailing wife with perfect rest. Gradually she becomes confined to the nursery at the top of the house, forbidden to write to relieve her anxiety. As her condition worsens, the woman becomes obsessed with the yellow wallpaper in the nursery. She becomes convinced that the wallpaper menaces her, then that it holds a woman trapped behind bars. The poor young woman attempts to escape her confinement and the wallpaper by gnawing at the bed, which

is nailed down, and peeling off the wallpaper with her fingernails. Finally, she escapes into total madness, creeping round and round the room on her hands and knees.

"The Yellow Wallpaper" is a small literary gem, the most widely read and admired of Gilman's short fiction. It is the story of a woman's mental breakdown, narrated in a naïve, first-person voice with superb psychological and dramatic precision. The story is consciously autobiographical, achieving a genuine power, directness, and authenticity. From the time of its publication, the story was read and admired as a tale of horror and madness in the tradition of Edgar Allan Poe. Since the 1970's, it has most often been given a feminist reading as a symbolic tale of a woman trying to break free from her cage. Feminist critics view the story as a rare piece of literature by a nineteenth century woman who directly confronts the sexual politics of the male-female, husband-wife relationship.

"MAKING A CHANGE"

Julia is a young wife and mother on the verge of collapse. She is exhausted and hypersensitive from being kept awake at night by her screaming child. She believes it is her duty to care for her child and the home while her husband, preoccupied with earning money, has no understanding of her state of mind. Desperately, Julia tries to kill herself. Fortunately, her mother-in-law arrives in time to stop her, and the two women work out a plan of escape. Secretly, Julia pursues her career as a musician, while the widowed mother-in-law sets up a day care center. Both women find their problems are solved; both pursue meaningful work.

Julia's husband is angry when he discovers the arrangement, but finally realizes that all of them are happier and better off economically. "Making a Change" is an example of one of Gilman's stories suggesting social change as an alternative to frustrating, meaningless lives for women. The "baby-garden" of the story is a stable environment for children which allows mothers to seek work for which they are better suited and older women to find creative possibilities for their lives after husbands and children are gone. Julia's desperation, realistic and autobiographical for Gilman, is happily resolved through the intervention of a wise older woman.

"WHEN I WAS A WITCH"

First published in *The Forerunner* in 1910, "When I Was a Witch" is one of Gilman's utopian fantasies. The narrator is a modern woman who goes to work in an office in New York City while her sister keeps house. On Halloween, she acquires the magical power to have her wishes come true. Over the course of several days, she doles out punishments to fit the crimes of those who embody her pet peeves: abusers of animals; sellers of bad milk, eggs, and meat; the cruel; the pompous; those who take excessive profits at the expense of the poor.

Once she realizes what is happening, the narrator sets about reforming the city according to Gilman's imagination. Newspapers stop printing lies, the world becomes kinder and more truthful. In the end though, when she dares to wish for satisfaction and meaningful work for women, her magic fails her. Gilman's style in this story is light, humorous, entertaining and mischievous. It is pure fantasy, until the narrator is stopped short at the end, perhaps indicating that Gilman was aware that reform for women would not be so easily accomplished.

"MR. PEEBLES' HEART"

"Mr. Peebles' Heart" is another realistic situation mingled with utopian elements and a happy ending. In this story, the protagonist is an older man, illustrating Gilman's humanistic concern for older people and productive lives for all, men and women alike. Mr. Peebles is a slave of duty. All his life he has labored at work he dislikes in order to support his mother, his silly clinging wife, and his daughters. His sister-in-law, a "new woman" and a doctor, encourages him to travel around Europe for two years, wisely convinced this will improve the lives of all involved. In Gilman's view, conventional domestic arrangements trap men as well as women.

Mr. Peebles returns, healthier and happier. The change does his wife good, too, as she has learned to depend on herself and use her mind. As in "Making a Change," Gilman's formula is a happy ending coming about through the wise intervention of an intelligent person who can envision a better social order.

OTHER MAJOR WORKS

LONG FICTION: *What Diantha Did*, 1910; *The Crux*, 1911; *Moving the Mountain*, 1911; *Herland*, 1915 (serial), 1979 (book); *With Her in Our Land*, 1916; *Benigna Machiavelli*, 1994.

POETRY: *In This Our World*, 1893; *Suffrage Songs and Verses*, 1911; *The Later Poetry of Charlotte Perkins Gilman*, 1996.

NONFICTION: *Women and Economics*, 1898; *Concerning Children*, 1900; *The Home: Its Work and Influence*, 1903; *Human Work*, 1904; *Women and Social Service*, 1907; *The Man-Made World*, 1911; *His Religion and Hers*, 1923; *The Living of Charlotte Perkins Gilman*, 1935; *A Journey from Within: The Love Letters of Charlotte Perkins Gilman, 1897-1900*, 1995.

BIBLIOGRAPHY

Golden, Catherine. *The Captive Imagination: A Casebook on "The Yellow Wallpaper."* New York: The Feminist Press, 1992. Devoted entirely to "The Yellow Wallpaper." The "Backgrounds" section of the volume includes essays on nineteenth century attitudes and treatment of women's psychiatric complaints. The collection of criticism of Gilman's most-discussed story is extensive, including Elaine Hedges' 1973 feminist afterword to "The Yellow Wallpaper."

Hill, Mary A. *Charlotte Perkins Gilman: The Making of a Radical Feminist, 1860-1896*. Philadelphia: Temple University Press, 1980. Primarily a biographical exploration of the roots of Gilman's social theories, the insights of this work are based on a reading of Gilman's private journals and letters. Includes comments on the autobiographical short fiction, particularly "The Yellow Wallpaper."

Karpinski, Joanne B., ed. *Critical Essays on Charlotte Perkins Gilman*. Boston: G. K. Hall, 1991. This collection includes the Shelley Fishkin essay "Making a Change: Strategies of Subversion in Gilman's Journalism and Short Fiction."

Knight, Denise D., ed. *Charlotte Perkins Gilman: A Study of the Short Fiction*. New York: Twayne Publishers, 1997. A most useful volume of critical analysis of the short fiction. Part 1 discusses

Gilman's short fiction, its influences, "The Yellow Wallpaper," and other stories. Part 2 provides Gilman's reflections on writing, from primary sources, and Part 3 is a collection of criticism of several of Gilman's short stories. The editor makes a point of going beyond "The Yellow Wallpaper" so that readers may expand their appreciation of Gilman's range as a writer of short fiction.

Lane, Ann J. "The Fictional World of Charlotte Perkins Gilman." In *The Charlotte Perkins Gilman Reader*. New York: Pantheon, 1980. Lucid, concise analysis of Gilman's fiction as a whole.

_____. *To Herland and Beyond: The Life and Work of Charlotte Perkins Gilman*. New York: Pantheon, 1990. Primarily a biography. Recognizing the connection between Gilman's life and work, Lane devotes a solid pair of chapters to an analysis of the work. Detailed synopsis of *Women and Economics* as the foundation of Gilman's thought. Discussion of the short fiction is brief, but analytic and informative.

Scharnhorst, Gary. *Charlotte Perkins Gilman*. Boston, Twayne, 1985. Scharnhorst, an authority on Charlotte Perkins Gilman who has also compiled an extensive bibliography, has written a literary biography, a study of her imaginative work as a whole, relating her poetry and fiction to her pioneering nonfiction. The theme of this monograph is that Gilman's entire canon shares a unified didactic purpose.

Susan Butterworth

ELLEN GLASGOW

Born: Richmond, Virginia; April 22, 1873
Died: Richmond, Virginia; November 21, 1945

PRINCIPAL SHORT FICTION

The Shadowy Third and Other Stories, 1923
The Collected Stories of Ellen Glasgow, 1963

OTHER LITERARY FORMS

Ellen Glasgow's twenty-three published books include novels, short stories, poetry, criticism, and an autobiography. She is best known for her novels, particularly *Barren Ground* (1925), *The Romantic Comedians* (1926), *The Sheltered Life* (1932), and *In This Our Life*, which was awarded a Pulitzer Prize in 1941.

ACHIEVEMENTS

Ellen Glasgow spent her lifetime dedicated to the craft of writing, despite the cultural and literary prejudices of her time and place, which deplored the idea of an independent female author. She was at her finest writing fiction about women; many of her female characters' lives were distinctly unconventional for their time. Her exploration of women's lives, male-female relationships, and particularly the destructive effect of romantic notions of chivalry, innocence, and gender roles on the individual and society made her a best-seller during her lifetime but earned her limited critical recognition. She was awarded the Howells Medal by the American Academy of Arts and Letters in 1940, the *Saturday Review* Award for Distinguished Service to American Literature in 1941, and the Pulitzer Prize in 1942, three years before her death.

BIOGRAPHY

Ellen Anderson Gholson Glasgow's father was a strict Scotch Presbyterian; her mother was a member of an established Tidewater family. Glasgow was too nervous to attend school, so she was educated at home. In late adolescence, her attention was directed to the work of writers such as Charles Darwin and Friedrich Nietzsche, and she read extensively in philosophy, political economy, and literature. She began to go deaf at the age of sixteen, and throughout her life she felt handicapped in social situations. In 1918, after a quarrel with her fiancé, Glasgow attempted suicide. She was engaged twice, but she never married. Although she always regarded Richmond, Virginia, as her home, Glasgow traveled widely. She received honorary doctorates from the University of North Carolina (1937), the University of Richmond (1938), Duke University (1938), and the College of William and Mary (1939). She was elected to the National Institute of Arts and Letters in 1932, and to the American Academy of Arts and Letters in 1938. Glascow died in Richmond, Virginia, on November 21, 1945.

ANALYSIS

Ellen Glasgow's most frequently quoted observation is that "What the South most needs is blood and irony." She revolted against the affectedness, Romanticism, and excessive picturesqueness of much nineteenth and early twentieth century southern literature, and set out to produce a more realistic kind of fiction. She emphasized the wastage of life and of human energy which results from prejudice, illusion, impracticality, and a hostile environment; several of her most effective characters portray the frustration which comes from such wastage. Glasgow glorified strength, fortitude, energy, and a sense of duty. In fact, her characters are usually defined in terms of strength or weakness, rather than along the more conventional lines of good and evil.

Although Glasgow did introduce an element of realism into southern literature, she failed to accomplish her objectives fully. She remained a rather genteel southern lady whose attempt to depict the truth of the human situation was hampered by the limited range of her own experiences—she was shocked and horrified at the subject matter described by later southern realists, notably William Faulkner. Further, Glasgow seldom used a personal narrator, preferring an omniscient viewpoint. She often abused the technique, however, by inserting didactic or moralizing editorial observations into her fiction. As a result, much of her work tends to be talky and lacks the immediacy and impact of some other realistic fiction. Glasgow never entirely lost a sense of Romanticism or even sentimentality, and although those qualities

Ellen Glasgow (Library of Congress)

do appear, she did not associate them with her own writing.

Although Glasgow did not handle realistic materials as convincingly as some other writers have done, she did contribute to the growth of realism by introducing into southern literature a number of topics which had previously been glossed over. Some of these were suggested by her reading; some stemmed from her rebellion against her father's inflexible religion; and some were the product of her frustration with the weakness and ineffectuality of the southern aristocracy, of which she was a member through her mother's family. These comparatively new themes included determinism, social selection, the influence of heredity and environment, positive and negative energy, sexuality, feminism, industrialism, and criticism of the southern class system.

Most of Glasgow's twelve short stories, eleven of which were written before 1925, are adequate but not exceptional. She tended toward a rather diffuse style of writing and found it difficult to confine herself to the limitations of the short-story form. Although Glasgow never deliberately produced inferior work, she evidently wrote at least five of the short stories primarily for the sake of the high fees which magazines would pay for short fiction. Glasgow's short stories tend to focus on moral themes, particularly those which relate to male-female relationships, and these moral themes are not by any means confined to the issue of sexual morality. Glasgow was extremely concerned about the social and personal injustices which occurred because the "double standard" allowed men to behave differently than women.

"THE DIFFERENCE"

Glasgow's best-known story, "The Difference," is a scathing contrast between male and female attitudes toward love and marriage. The protagonist of the story, Margaret Fleming, is horrified when she discovers that her husband has been seeing another woman. Margaret learns about the affair from the mistress, Rose Morrison, who has written to Margaret asking her to give up her husband so that he might find happiness with Rose. Margaret goes to visit Rose, who is living in a villa belonging to George Fleming. Rose assures Margaret that she and George are very much in love, and that she understands George and can offer him far more excitement and satisfaction than Margaret can. Margaret, whose pale, grave beauty is beginning to fade, feels that George must have been attracted by the self-confident good looks of the red-haired Rose. She also wonders whether Rose's uninhibited sexuality is more alluring than her own well-bred reserve. She concludes that George must truly love Rose if he is willing to sacrifice his wife, and she resolves to give him his freedom, even if it costs her own happiness.

Margaret approaches George with the intention of telling him that, although she herself might have been capable of romance and adventure if he had only called forth those qualities in her, she is willing to step out of his life so that he can fulfill the burning love he feels for Rose. This love, she feels, is the only justification for his behavior and the only reason she will forgive him. When Margaret informs George that she has seen Rose, however, and that Rose has asked her to give up George, he stands with his mouth open in amazement. He tells Margaret that he has no intention of leaving her for Rose, and that he thinks of Rose as he thinks of golf—". . . just a sort of—well,

sort of—recreation." He then considers the subject closed and becomes restless for his supper. He cannot, in any case, see that Rose has anything whatever to do with Margaret. Remembering Rose's passion, and knowing the depth of her own responses, Margaret feels disillusioned and empty. She recognizes the truth of a remark which a friend had made earlier in the day: "Women love with their imagination and men with their senses." To a woman, love is "a thing in itself, a kind of abstract power like religion"; but to a man, "it is simply the way he feels."

"The Difference" illustrates both Glasgow's feminism and her lingering Romanticism. She does not simply conclude that what men call love is frequently sensual and/or unthinking; she concludes that that view of love is wrong. She speaks of love in terms of "imagination" almost in the sense that Samuel Taylor Coleridge uses the term. Yet Glasgow does succeed in introducing into her story an unconventional but realistic assessment of the moral questions involved in the double standard. George is wrong, not because he slept with another woman, but because he has treated both that woman and his wife as objects for his own convenience. Unlike her Victorian predecessors, Glasgow is not concerned with the religious aspects of extramarital affairs; or with Margaret's and George's mutual duties as husband and wife, as laid down by civil and ecclesiastical authorities. She dismisses the effect of infidelity and possible divorce on the family structure. It is not George's sexuality that Glasgow condemns, it is his selfishness. Glasgow underlines her point by setting up an unusual relationship in which the wife feels rage on the mistress's behalf because of "the bond of woman's immemorial disillusionment."

"ROMANCE AND SALLY BYRD"

This idea of female solidarity in the face of male selfishness is repeated in a later story, "Romance and Sally Byrd." Unlike "The Difference," this story is told from the point of view of the "other woman"; but the effect is the same. In the story, Sally Byrd Littlepage lives with her elderly grandparents and two aging aunts. Her Aunt Louisa is afflicted with neuralgia, and her Aunt Matilda is afflicted with religion. Sally Byrd, at nineteen, finds her dull existence enlivened by an admirer, Stanley Kenton, who has asked her to elope with him. Sally Byrd assumes that he means marriage, but he explains that he is already married, insisting that if she really loves him she will leave with him anyway. Sally Byrd refuses, not because of any strong moral indignation but because of the conviction that, like responding to thirst by getting drunk, this is something which one simply does not do. Having renounced her would-be lover, Sally Byrd feels a sense of romantic melancholy which she rather enjoys.

Some time after Stanley's departure, Sally Byrd Learns that he has been in an accident. His companion is dead, and he himself is badly hurt and will probably be permanently blind. Sally Byrd decides that it is her obligation to go to New York City and nurse him, since he and his wife are estranged and he has no one to care for him. She travels to New York and locates Stanley's luxurious apartment. There she is greeted by a large, firm woman with graying hair and an air of serenity. Sally Byrd explains why she has come. The woman turns out to be Stanley's wife, who gently lets Sally Byrd know that she is one of many women whom Stanley has admired. His latest mistress was the companion who was killed in Stanley's car accident. Mrs. Kenton explains that whenever Stanley needs support, he always returns to her, as he has done in the present instance. She herself is composed and impersonal because, as she explains, once the heart is broken it does not hurt any more. "You can't imagine the relief it is," she tells Sally Byrd, "to have your heart break at last." Sally stumbles out, sure that she is hurt for life, and resolved never to allow anything like this to happen again. On the train going home, however, she meets a personable young man who lives in the same town as she does; as she walks home from the station, she finds herself feeling happier at the thought of meeting him again.

"Romance and Sally Byrd" adds another dimension to the picture of male-female relationships drawn in "The Difference." In "The Difference," neither of the women has the advantage of knowing George's true nature until his wife discovers it in the final scene of the story. As a result, the issue of a woman's knowingly permitting herself to be used as a convenience by a man does not arise. In "Romance and Sally Byrd," however, Mrs. Kenton returns to Stanley whenever he wants her. In fact, she sits darning his silk socks as she talks with Sally Byrd. Her knowledge brings her only the negative satisfaction of a broken heart which no longer hurts. She makes no attempt to shape a life of her own. At the other end of the spectrum of experience, Sally Byrd quickly springs back from her disillusionment and begins daydreaming about another man. Despite her own adventure and the example of Mrs. Kenton, she still thinks of marriage as she had done earlier in the story: "as a passive and permanent condition of bliss."

Although Glasgow reserved most of her experimentation for her novels, she did incorporate into a few of her short stories a technique which she used nowhere else. Realist though she believed herself to be, Glasgow greatly admired the work of Edgar Allan Poe, and she produced a few ghost short stories which are indebted to him. The best of these are two stories which center around the image of an old house imbued with an aura or atmosphere which influences or reflects the actions of those who live there.

"DARE'S GIFT"

The earlier of these, "Dare's Gift," centers around an old Virginia mansion which had been built by a traitor, Sir Roderick Dare. A Washington lawyer takes a lease on the house as a desirable country residence for his wife, who is recovering from a nervous breakdown. At first her health seems to improve, but then her behavior becomes increasingly nervous and erratic. The lawyer, who is involved in a particularly important and delicate case, tells his wife about some evidence the disclosure of which would greatly injure his client. The evidence is disclosed, and the lawyer realizes that only his wife could have betrayed him. It turns out that this is the most recent of several similar cases which have occurred in Sir Roderick's house. The present owner, who lives in California, left the house because his trusted secretary had betrayed him there, and when the last Dares were living in the house, at the time of the Civil War, Miss Lucy Dare betrayed her fiancé to the soldiers who were seeking him.

"Dare's Gift" combines the occult image of a controlling atmosphere with the more realistic problem of personal loyalty versus loyalty to an ethic or to a cause. This theme is developed most fully in the case of Miss Lucy Dare, who had to decide between the Virginia code of personal loyalty and the duty she felt to the Confederate cause. The same theme is repeated when the lawyer's wife prevents his client from escaping the consequences of his dishonesty. The issue, however, does not seem to arise in the story of Sir Roderick, who built the house and presumably started the curse, nor in the case of the present owner's secretary. Here, as in her other ghost stories, Glasgow has some difficulty in balancing purely occult manifestations with the psychological elements which writers like Poe and Henry James express so well in their ghost stories.

"JORDAN'S END"

By far the best of Glasgow's ghost stories is "Jordan's End," which, like "Dare's Gift," is influenced by Poe's tale "The Fall of the House of Usher." Like the title "Dare's Gift," which is both the name of the house and an ironic allusion to the inheritance it carries, the title "Jordan's End" has a double meaning. It is the name of the crumbling southern mansion which is the main setting of the story, and it is also a reference to the decaying state of the Jordan family.

The opening of "Jordan's End" is very similar to the opening of Glasgow's important novel *Barren Ground*, which appeared two years after "Jordan's End" was published. A doctor, riding in a buggy, approaches a crossroads leading to an ancient southern farm. On the way he gives a ride to an old man, who tells him part of the history of Jordan's End. The present head of the family, Alan Jordan, lives there with his wife and son. The house is also inhabited by three eccentric elderly women: Alan Jordan's grandmother and two aunts. The men in the Jordan family have long been showing symptoms of insanity, and the marked oddity of the three old ladies suggests that the problem is spreading to the women.

When he arrives at Jordan's End, the doctor discovers that the once gracious house is crumbling, and that the lawns and gardens are unkempt. He meets Mrs. Alan Jordan, who tells him that her husband has

begun to show signs of the madness which has already claimed his father, grandfather, and uncles. Her chief fear is that her husband's great physical strength may condemn him to the kind of prolonged existence in a madhouse which his grandfather is presently suffering. The doctor leaves an opiate, and waits for the verdict of a nerve specialist who has promised to visit Jordan's End the next day.

Catching the nerve specialist as he boards a train to return home, the doctor learns that Alan Jordan is incurable. His insanity is the result of a long history of intermarriages within the Jordan family. The specialist has suggested to Mrs. Jordan that she place her husband in an institution. The next morning, however, the doctor is again summoned to Jordan's End, where he finds Alan Jordan dead, and the bottle of sleeping pills empty. His wife, composed and detached, suggests that she has fulfilled a promise she had made to her husband when he first learned of the possibility that he would go mad. The doctor does not inquire further, feeling that Mrs. Jordan's detachment and solitude remove her from any human touch.

"Jordan's End" anticipates the techniques, themes, and characterizations of Glasgow's major novels. For example, the issues of heredity, environment, and euthanasia which appear briefly in this story form the basis of several of her lengthier works. Similarly, her Hardyesque use of setting to reflect character is much more sophisticated here than in "Dare's Gift"; the decaying house, the twilight, the overcast skies, and the ragged vegetation function in "Jordan's End" as external manifestations of internal decay. The fall of the Jordans suggests the recurrent Glasgow theme of the decadence of the South in both blood and environment, and the strong figure of Mrs. Jordan, animated—despite the horrors she has endured—by a sense of duty and compassion, anticipates such major Glasgow heroines as Dorinda Oakley.

OTHER MAJOR WORKS

LONG FICTION: *The Descendant*, 1897; *Phases of an Inferior Planet*, 1898; *The Voice of the People*, 1900; *The Battle-Ground*, 1902; *The Deliverance*, 1904; *The Wheel of Life*, 1906; *The Ancient Law*, 1908; *The Romance of a Plain Man*, 1909; *The

Miller of Old Church, 1911; *Virginia*, 1913; *Life and Gabriella*, 1916; *The Builders*, 1919; *One Man in His Time*, 1922; *Barren Ground*, 1925; *The Romantic Comedians*, 1926; *They Stooped to Folly*, 1929; *The Sheltered Life*, 1932; *Vein of Iron*, 1935; *In This Our Life*, 1941.

POETRY: *The Freeman and Other Poems*, 1902.

NONFICTION: *A Certain Measure: An Interpretation of Prose Fiction*, 1943; *The Woman Within*, 1954; *Letters of Ellen Glasgow*, 1958.

BIBLIOGRAPHY

Glasgow, Ellen. *The Woman Within*. New York: Harcourt, Brace, 1954. Glasgow's autobiography is one of the best sources for the philosophy behind her fiction. This volume is more of a literary autobiography than a personal one, indicating shifts of perceptions, understanding, and attitude. It was published posthumously.

Godbold, E. Stanly, Jr. *Ellen Glasgow and the Woman Within*. Baton Rouge: Louisiana State University Press, 1972. A literary biography, interesting mainly as an example of prefeminist interpretation of Glasgow's work.

Goodman, Susan. *Ellen Glasgow*. Baltimore: The Johns Hopkins University Press, 1998. A biography that focuses on showing Glasgow's significance as a southern author at the turn of the century; discusses the gap between her reception by her contemporaries and her later reception.

McDowell, Frederick P. W. *Ellen Glasgow and the Ironic Art of Fiction*. Madison: University of Wisconsin Press, 1960. Interesting in-depth analysis of Glasgow's oeuvre mostly in terms of style, irony, and wit. Extensive bibliography.

Matthews, Pamela R. *Ellen Glasgow and a Woman's Traditions*. Charlottesville: University Press of Virginia, 1994. Discusses Glasgow's feminism and her place as a twentieth century southern female author. Includes bibliographical references and an index.

The Mississippi Quarterly 49 (Spring, 1996). A special issue on Glasgow with essays on her short stories which discuss her focus on struggling underprivileged farmers, her modernity, the effect of Henry Watkins Anderson on her work, and her use of clothing imagery.

Rouse, Blair. *Ellen Glasgow*. New York: Twayne, 1962. Presents facts, analyses, and interpretations of Glasgow's life, the nature and purposes of her writing, the scope of her work, and her attainment as an artist in fiction; the author is a southerner who was one of the first contemporary critics to appreciate Glasgow. Annotated bibliography.

_____. Introduction to *Letters of Ellen Glasgow*. Compiled and edited by Blair Rouse. New York: Harcourt, Brace, 1958. The introduction to this volume sketches Ellen Glasgow's achievement in relation to her letters and other autobiographical writings. Rouse also provides commentary on the letters.

Scura, Dorothy M., ed. *Ellen Glasgow: New Perspectives*. Knoxville: University of Tennessee Press, 1995. Detailed essays on Glasgow's major novels and themes, two essays on her autobiographies, and two essays on her poetry and short stories. Includes a helpful overview in the introduction and a bibliography.

Wagner, Linda W. *Ellen Glasgow: Beyond Convention*. Austin: University of Texas Press, 1982. An excellent, in-depth analysis of all Glasgow's work, placing it in the context of her time and place, as well as in relation to later work by American authors.

Joan DelFattore, updated by
Mary LeDonne Cassidy

GAIL GODWIN

Born: Birmingham, Alabama; June 18, 1937

PRINCIPAL SHORT FICTION
Dream Children, 1976
Mr. Bedford and the Muses, 1983

OTHER LITERARY FORMS

Gail Godwin has written ten novels, including *The Odd Woman* (1974), *A Mother and Two Daughters* (1982), *The Good Husband* (1994), and *Evensong* (1999). She edited, with Shannon Ravenel, *The Best American Short Stories* of 1985. She has also written several opera librettos, including *Remembering Felix* (pb. 1987), for composer Robert Starer.

ACHIEVEMENTS

Gail Godwin received a National Endowment for the Arts grant in 1974-1975, a John Simon Guggenheim Memorial Fellowship in 1975-1976, and the award in literature from the American Academy of Arts and Letters in 1981. *The Odd Woman* received a National Book Award nomination; *Violet Clay* and *A Mother and Two Daughters* received American Book Award nominations; and *A Southern Family* received the Thomas Wolfe Memorial Award. In 1988, Godwin received the Janet Heidinger Kafka Prize, presented by the University of Rochester.

BIOGRAPHY

Gail Kathleen Godwin was born in Birmingham, Alabama, on June 18, 1937. She attended Peace Junior College in Raleigh, North Carolina, before matriculating at the University of North Carolina at Chapel Hill, where she received a B.A. in journalism. For two years she was employed as a reporter for the *Miami Herald*, during which time she married Douglas Kennedy, a photographer. The marriage ended in divorce less than a year later. After leaving the *Herald*, Godwin worked and traveled in Europe for six years, settling in London, where she worked in the U.S. Travel Service at the American Embassy in London. She married Ian Marshall, a British physician; they

were divorced the following year. Godwin returned to the United States and entered the graduate writing program at the University of Iowa in 1967. She received her M.A. degree in 1968 and her Ph.D. in English in 1971, after which she devoted herself full time to writing, although she also accepted teaching positions at Vassar College in 1977 and Columbia University in 1978 and 1981.

ANALYSIS

Gail Godwin's two volumes of short stories have received little critical attention in spite of the fact that they anticipate many of the themes Godwin explores in her novels. One such overarching theme, for example, is the relationship between men and women, especially in marriage. Many stories in *Dream Children*, as in Godwin's early novels *The Perfectionist* and *Glass People*, explore the nature of women's subordination to men and the various strategies the women adopt to subvert it. There is a prevailing note of dissatisfaction, quest, rebellion, escape, and revenge, often frustrated revenge.

Unlike the realism of Godwin's early novels, however, *Dream Children* contains experiments with form (especially in "Notes for a Story") and explores elements of fantasy and the supernatural, including the nonrational dream world and how that impinges on everyday reality. In the title story, for example, a woman whose child was stillborn has a series of strange nocturnal "spirit" meetings with a child who, as a newborn, was briefly and mistakenly presented to her as her own baby. Sometimes the fantasy elements take on a dark coloring, but these are balanced by stories ("An Intermediate Stop," "The Woman Who Kept Her Poet") that hint cryptically and obliquely at mystical, spiritual moments of realization.

There is a shift in Godwin's second collection, *Mr. Bedford and the Muses*. Almost all the protagonists are writers, people whose lives center on the workings of the creative mind, and these stories tend to reflect a more optimistic perspective. The characters find greater possibilities for personal freedom and wholeness, even given the strange twists and turns that life takes—for example, a father whose young wife leaves him for his own son still finds a moment of perfection in his music; a young novelist falls in love with a woman more than twenty years his senior because he cannot help but see her as young. More fully developed and satisfying than many of the somewhat sketchy stories in *Dream Children*, this collection shows Godwin's mastery of the form.

"NOBODY'S HOME"

"Nobody's Home" expresses a highly critical view of marriage that was typical of feminist writers of the 1970's. The story explores the frustration of a lonely, middle-aged, middle-class woman trapped in a tedious marriage and her plan to escape. Mrs. Wakeley decides to leave her husband without explanation and rent an apartment directly opposite their house. It is as if she is an actress in a play she has come to loathe, and she wishes to remove herself from it and then observe the play run into chaos without her. This is the sublimated desire for revenge of a timid, weak-willed woman; Mrs. Wakeley's courage falters at the practical details. How will she open a bank account or get a Social Security card under her new alias of Clara Jones? How will she find a job knowing nothing about the world of work? She concludes she is not fully a person in her own right.

When her husband returns home in the evening, she finds herself diminished even further by his mere presence, although she cannot explain why. The narrator emphasizes the distance between husband and wife that lies behind the polite surfaces. The marriage continues in name only, and the reader is led to the conclusion that Mrs. Wakeley, although continuing to fantasize about her escape, will never muster the means to effect it: She has sacrificed her independence and individual identity (her first name is never mentioned) to her marriage.

"FALSE LIGHTS"

One of several stories in *Dream Children* about second wives or mistresses, "False Lights" is written in the form of an exchange of letters between Violet, the young wife of novelist Karl Bandema, and Annette, Karl's former wife, who is in her fifties. The two opening letters are brief and formal, but then Violet writes to the older woman at length. She reveals herself to be an idealistic, meditative, imaginative woman, given to philosophical speculation, and much in love with her husband, despite the fact that he seems to be a self-centered egotist.

Violet wants to befriend Annette and confides that the category of "wife" seems an ephemeral thing, almost meaningless in an infinite world of perpetual change. She speculates on what marriage will be like in the year 2075. Maybe it will be different, more pure, less petty, "all of us sailing through change as effortlessly as gulls through air." She also wonders whether marriage will even exist a hundred years from now.

As the title of the story may hint, Violet's flights of fancy do not strike a responsive chord within the older woman, who replies formally, rejecting Violet's notion that they could ever be friends. Perhaps Godwin is suggesting that although alternative attitudes to marriage may in theory be possible, for the present, marriages are likely to remain stuck in the familiar groove—temporary, unstable alliances that quickly become unsatisfactory for at least one partner.

Gail Godwin (©Jerry Bauer)

"THE LEGACY OF THE MOTES"

In this mystical story about awakening, an American student in London is finishing his Ph.D. dissertation on conceits in metaphysical poetry. Elliott is always in a hurry, impatient with the relaxed pace of living that the English prefer. He develops a problem with his eyes, seeing a pair of wings flying sideways across his line of vision. A librarian friend, Van Buren, hints that he may have been working too hard, a suggestion that Elliott dismisses. Although an eye specialist explains that the *muscae volitantes* (flying flies) pose no threat to his vision, Elliott becomes obsessively worried about them.

After Elliott has a breakdown in the British Museum, the narrative jumps ahead ten years, and the reader learns that Elliott abandoned his studies after making a deal with the *muscae:* If they let him go on seeing, he would not enter a library. Instead, the man who had scoffed at the English and their fondness for parks now finds pleasure in exploring the world, experiencing it at first hand, not through books. He is eventually persuaded by Van Buren to read George Herbert's poem "Easter-Wings." Typographically, this poem about human loss and divine redemption is shaped like a pair of wings. Elliott, weeping, realizes the significance of the real-life images of the *muscae* that were the cause of his own rebirth. Although Godwin does not make this explicit, the implication is that before, Elliott, for all his learning, knew nothing. Now he knows how to experience life fully; the *muscae*, far from being a curse, were divine promptings, nudging him to see things anew.

"AMANUENSIS"

The protagonist of "Amanuensis" is a writer, and the story explores the conditions under which her creativity waxes and wanes. Constance Le Fevre is an ambitious, successful novelist who has lost her inspiration. One day Jesse, a college student, arrives at her house offering to be Constance's amanuensis; Jesse wants to do the household chores so that Constance can concentrate on her work. This arrangement works well for a time. Constance gets used to Jesse's presence in the house, allows Jesse to nurse her through an illness, and becomes fond of her. Constance's creativity, however, does not return. The turning point comes appropriately one spring morning, when Constance, inspired by the sounds of Jesse going about her household tasks, for one brief moment realizes "how nice *just being* is," without the self-imposed pressure of ambition or the need to create.

Jesse departs without a trace that very day, and later Constance discovers that she was tricked—a disgruntled former lover planted Jesse in her house so that he could gather material for a novel of his own. What is really important is that Constance somehow finds herself liberated from her need for achievement and the habit of imposing on the world her concepts of events and their patterns. She sells her house and travels, determined to take no notes, simply to let life come and bring her what it will, without interference on her part. The strategy works; her creativity is restored, and she thinks of Jesse as her "angel of release."

OTHER MAJOR WORKS

LONG FICTION: *The Perfectionists*, 1970; *Glass People*, 1972; *The Odd Woman*, 1974; *Violet Clay*, 1978; *A Mother and Two Daughters*, 1982; *The Finishing School*, 1985; *A Southern Family*, 1987; *Father Melancholy's Daughter*, 1991; *The Good Husband*, 1994; *Evensong*, 1999.

PLAYS: *The Last Lover*, pr. 1975; *Journals of a Songmaker*, pr. 1976; *Apollonia*, pr. 1979; *Remembering Felix*, pb. 1987 (libretto).

EDITED TEXT: *The Best American Short Stories*, 1985 (with Shannon Ravenel).

BIBLIOGRAPHY

Crain, Jane Larkin. "Dream Children." *The New York Times Book Review* (February 22, 1976). In this review, Crain argues that the atmosphere of the stories is largely dark and defines Godwin as a "chronicler of life on the edge," depicting states of alienation, isolation, and madness. As in Godwin's novels, the principal concern in the stories is the nature of womanhood.

Gies, Judith. "Obligation, Fascination, and Intrigue." *The New York Times Book Review* (September 8, 1983): 14, 37. A critical review of *Mr. Bedford and the Muses*, which faults the stories for being too neatly resolved at the end and regrets the "chatty and oddly schoolmarmish" tone of the book. Regards "A Cultural Exchange" as the most successful story.

Halisky, Linda H. "Redeeming the Irrational: The Inexplicable Heroines of 'A Sorrowful Woman' and 'To Room Nineteen.'" *Studies in Short Fiction* (Winter, 1990): 45-54. Examines the parallels between Godwin's story in *Dream Children* and Doris Lessing's "To Room Nineteen." Argues that because these stories possess similar plots, Lessing's story is an analogue to Godwin's and can help to explain the behavior of Godwin's heroine.

Hill, Jane. *Gail Godwin*. New York: Twayne, 1992. The best study of Godwin for the general reader. Hill concentrates on the novels, while commenting that the stories deserve a study of their own. Hill approaches Godwin's work through plot and character, and although she acknowledges the regional and gender-related aspects of Godwin's work as a southern woman writer, she points out

that Godwin's novels also connect with the larger tradition of novels in America and Europe.

Westerlund, Kerstin. *Escaping the Castle of Patriarchy: Patterns of Development in the Novels of Gail Godwin*. Stockholm, Sweden: University of Uppsala, 1990. Discusses the short stories only briefly, noting that they frequently echo the main themes of Godwin's novels. Analyzes the novels up to *A Southern Family* in terms of female development, which is linked to Godwin's treatment of male-female relationships. Includes a chapter on Godwin and American feminism.

Xie, Lihong. *The Evolving Self in the Novels of Gail Godwin*. Baton Rouge: Louisiana State University Press, 1995. Argues that instead of accepting the postmodern deconstruction of the self, Godwin has constructed a concept of the self as evolving, finding itself not in essence but in process. The book explores the nature of this "self-in-the-becoming."

Bryan Aubrey

JOHANN WOLFGANG VON GOETHE

Born: Frankfurt am Main, Germany; August 28, 1749
Died: Weimar, Germany; March 22, 1832

PRINCIPAL SHORT FICTION

Die Leiden des jungen Werthers, 1774 (*The Sorrows of Young Werther*, 1779)
Unterhaltungen deutscher Ausgewanderten, 1795 (*Conversations of German Emigrants*, 1854)
Novelle, 1826 (*Novel*, 1837)

OTHER LITERARY FORMS

Johann Wolfgang von Goethe's genius extended beyond the short story to embrace all the major genres: the novel, drama, and lyric poetry, as well as nonfiction. Much of his work is autobiographical yet

goes well beyond the personal in its focus on the individual's place in society and the struggle of the artist to express his humanity in the face of opposing forces, both external and internal. His novels *Wilhelm Meisters Lehrjahre* (1795-1796; *Wilhelm Meister's Apprenticeship*, 1825), *Die Wahlverwandtschaften* (1809; *Elective Affinities*, 1849), and *Wilhelm Meisters Wanderjahre: Oder, Die Entsagenden* (1821, 1829; *Wilhelm Meister's Travels*, 1827) are the prototypcial *Bildungsromane*; his diverse lyrics and ballads are among the best in Western literature; and his nonfiction works—even extending to scientific treatises—chronicle some of the most important socio-literary thought of his day, especially his correspondence with Friedrich Schiller. Perhaps his crowning achievement, the Faust plays summarize the artistic and philosophical preoccupations not only of Goethe's Romantic age but also, in many senses, of the twentieth century as well.

ACHIEVEMENTS

Before World War II, Johann Wolfgang von Goethe was read by virtually the entire German populace. Even in the English world, where he has been neglected, largely because of the difficulty in translating the nuances of so sensitive an artisan, it has been commonplace to assign him a position in the literary pantheon of Homer, Dante, and William Shakespeare. Moreover, Goethe has had paramount influence on German literature, influencing writers such as Friedrich Hölderlin, Hermann Hesse, Thomas Mann, and Franz Kafka. In the English world, his influence is seen on Thomas Carlyle, Charles Dickens, Samuel Butler, and James Joyce; in the French world, on Romain Rolland and André Gide. Nothing escaped his observation; everything he wrote bears the stamp of monumental genius, whether one speaks of his short stories, novels, poems, or plays. Among modern readers, Goethe has been undergoing reappraisal, if not decline, particularly among younger Germans. This opposition, perhaps more social and political than aesthetic, is especially true for Marxists, who have historically resisted writing of nonpolitical orientation. In a day when human survival is at stake, Goethe can seem distant to the contemporary generation. Often his idiom is not so much difficult as it is ethereal; his message, in its optimism, more Victorian than modern. He consorted with aristocrats, despised the French Revolution, admired Napoleon. At times, he is viewed as moralistic, if not arrogant. On the other hand, he has often suffered from excess admiration. Ultimately his value may rest with the profundity of his psychological insights, his sense of the human quest with its pain, his mastery of lyric form. His work needs to be judged for itself, independent of biases. Certainly he has much to offer, given the Renaissance scope of his interests and achievements. His collected works comprise 143 volumes; his writings on science, fourteen volumes alone. If *Faust* were his only work, it would be sufficient to assure him a high place in literary annals with its affirmation

Johann Wolfgang von Goethe (Library of Congress)

of the human spirit and its confidence that humanity can transcend its errors.

BIOGRAPHY

Johann Wolfgang von Goethe was born into an upper-middle-class family in Frankfurt am Main, Germany, on August 28, 1749. Given a largely private education that included a rigorous study of ancient and modern languages, he came into contact with the theater at a very early age. At the age of sixteen, he studied law at Leipzig but was interrupted by a debilitating illness that nearly took his life. Two years later, he went on to the University of Strasbourg, where he completed his studies. While there, he met Johann Gottfried Herder, who introduced him to Homer, Shakespeare, Ossian, and folk literature. Herder also converted Goethe to the tenets of a new artistic credo which would become known as Romanticism. All these elements loom large in Goethe's work.

On his return to Frankfurt, Goethe engaged in law and writing. In 1773, he achieved immediate renown among his compatriots with the play *Götz von Berlichingen mit der eisernen Hand* (*Götz von*

Berlichingen with the Iron Hand, 1799). A year later, his reputation took on international stature with *The Sorrows of Young Werther*, his most noted work with the exception of *Faust*. In 1775, Goethe attracted the attention of the young Duke of Saxe-Weimar, who invited him to the capital city, Weimar. Except for a two-year interval when Goethe visited Italy, he would remain at Weimar all of his life. It was at Weimar that Goethe fell in love with the married Charlotte von Stein, a woman of high refinement and intellectual capability. Realizing that the ten-year affair was a romance without a future, Goethe departed for Italy in 1786, where he remained for nearly two years. The Italian sojourn affected him greatly and marks his embrace of classicism and his retreat from Herder's influence. Classicist norms are evident in his plays *Egmont* (1788; English translation, 1837), *Iphigenie auf Tauris* (1779, revised 1787; *Iphigenia in Tauris*, 1793), and *Torquato Tasso* (1790; English translation, 1827).

Several years after his return to Weimar, Goethe entered into the principal friendship of his life, with fellow artist Friedrich Schiller; each served as critic and motivator to the other until Schiller's death in 1805. On one occasion, Goethe confessed to Schiller that he owed him a second youth. Keenly intelligent, perhaps overly punctilious, Goethe seems to have intimidated many of his contemporaries. Hence, his last years were largely lonely ones. Nevertheless, during these years he produced some of his greatest works, among them *Faust*, a labor of love for nearly sixty years and, by common assent, some of the world's most sublime lyric verse. Literature, however, was not his only forte, for he was accomplished in fields as wide-ranging as botany and optics, mineralogy and anatomy. He died in 1832, already a legend in his lifetime.

ANALYSIS

Johann Wolfgang von Goethe did not invent the novella, or short fiction, genre in German literature, though he is rightfully given credit as its first master. Before Goethe, no German writer had given serious thought to composing a crafted fictional work. Initially, Goethe borrowed his materials. It is in his ad-

aptations, however, that these sources became transformed. In short fiction, Goethe's method usually followed the example of Giovanni Boccaccio, with his frame method of telling a series of stories within a social context. This appealed to Goethe's sense of formal integrity, or effecting of unity. Even in his novels, Goethe often interpolates short stories into his narratives, where they function largely to amplify the central theme.

It can be said that in Goethe's short fiction no two stories are ever quite alike, some of them being parabolic; others, psychological or sociological; a few, fables; still others, allegories. At times, Goethe is highly symbolic; at others, not so at all. His stories are often dilemma-centered and, consequently, demanding of resolution. If any overarching similarity exists in these stories, it may rest in the theme of love. In one story or another, love in one of its guises is surely present, whether of man for man, of man and woman for each other, or of human love for nature's world.

THE SORROWS OF YOUNG WERTHER

The Sorrows of Young Werther represents Goethe's entry into the realm of short fiction, here in the form of the novella. The plot is essentially uneventful; the protagonist, Werther, is engaged in writing after-the-fact letters to his friend Wilhelm, describing the waning fortunes of his enamoredness for the engaged, and later married, Lotte, daughter of a town official. Werther, realizing that his passion is an impossible one, seeks egress through diplomatic service elsewhere. Things do not go well even with a move, however, and he finds himself snubbed for his middle-class origins. He returns to his town, only to find that Lotte has married Albert. Distraught, Werther contemplates suicide. On a final visit to Lotte during Albert's absence, they read together from Macpherson's *Ossian*, and, overcome with the plight of the poem's anguished lovers, Werther kisses Lotte, who becomes alarmed and refuses to see him again. Werther leaves. Lotte's intimation of impending tragedy is confirmed later that evening when Werther takes his life.

Goethe was only twenty-four when he wrote this work, which would find its way into every European salon. Like nearly everything he wrote, the story has autobiographical roots; Goethe and Werther share even the same birthday. Goethe had been in love with Charlotte Buff, the fiancé of another man, named Kestner. Like Werther, Goethe left the community to escape his passion. He had also contemplated suicide, and he made that part of the story upon learning of the suicide of an acquaintance, an attaché named Karl Wilhelm Jerusalem. Jerusalem had fallen in love with a married woman and had undergone social snubbing.

Despite their parallel experiences, however, it is important to distinguish Goethe from his protagonist. Goethe intends a psychological portraiture of a mind in distress, moving inexorably toward self-destruction. Goethe, who in many ways possessed the "two souls" of rationality and intuition, is admonishing readers to avoid excesses of passion, which can render beautiful feelings into ugliness when no limits are imposed. Although there is much in this novella that is characteristic of the lyrical Goethe—the rhapsodizing of spring, for example—Goethe's emphasis is clear: Feelings have potential for producing good, but because the line between good and evil is not always a clear one, danger abounds. *The Sorrows of Young Werther* begins as a story of love; it ends as a story of death.

Historically, the importance of this early work lies in its departure from eighteenth century norms of rationality, with their proscriptions of objective criteria, particularly as to language. *The Sorrows of Young Werther* is powerfully told through imagery, not abstraction. While there were other epistolary novels in the century, this work gave readers an unparalleled look at an individual character, thus anticipating the modern novel, with its interior, or psychological, rendering.

Though he was very young at the time that he wrote *The Sorrows of Young Werther*, Goethe also shows himself in command of form: The novella divides into two parts having an ironic relationship. The first part deals with Werther's arrival up to his departure from the town and anticipates the tragedy of the second part. Both parts involve escape, one by going away, the other by self-inflicted gunshot. Neither escape proves to be a proper resolution. The tell-

ing irony of this novella is that Werther wants his suicide to represent the ultimate altruism of self-sacrifice. On the contrary, it represents the ultimate egotism. A sterile act, it changes nothing. Genuine love sacrifices by yielding, not by abrogating. Readers may be sorry for Werther, but they cannot absolve him.

Each part is also orchestrated in terms of the seasons. In the first part, it is spring and summer; in the second, autumn and winter. The seasons reflect the cycles of maturation and decline, birth and death. Hence they amplify the course of the novella's action.

"THE FAIRY TALE"

"Das Märchen" ("The Fairy Tale") reflects Goethe's fondness for the German folklore tradition. This tale, or *Erzählung*, originally appeared in *Conversations of German Emigrants*, comprising stories that Goethe wrote as imaginative pieces requiring the suspension of disbelief for their enjoyment. In this type of story, anything can happen and usually does. If the reader will be patient with the story, theme always emerges, for the archetypal elements are never lacking.

In "The Fairy Tale," a river divides two realms. A ferryman transports passengers from the east bank to the west bank. A giant's shadow returns visitors to the east bank. Those traveling westward visit Lily, whose realm suggests death. A Serpent, in this tale a heroic creature, sacrifices itself to make a bridge for the wayfarers from the east bank, or the realm of life. The story is replete with polarities, not only between East and West but also between light and darkness, the living and the dead, vegetables and minerals. Paradoxes extend to characters. The same Lily whose touch can kill can also restore life. The Man-with-the-Lamp, who comes from the East, appears to represent truth, which is that superlative goals can be reached only through collective effort, or self-abnegation. The Lily, however beautiful, cannot function meaningfully until the Prince (another character) dies willingly in her embrace, or as an act of love. Without love, life is sterility; existence, death. With the Serpent's act of self-sacrifice, a bridge is built. Separation ceases between the realms. Pilgrims move freely.

The journey is life. Life (the East) and Death (the West) are reconciled in the context of existence lived in love (the bridge). Meanings abound in a story as symbolic as this: Each is necessary to the other (the sociological); love is the one true regenerative power (the moral); Nature is paradoxically both destroyer and procreator (the mythic).

NOVELLE

Along with "The Fairy Tale," *Novelle* is the most renowned of Goethe's short fictions. Here, a princess takes an excursion into the countryside to see the ruins of a family castle destined to be restored. She is accompanied by the squire, Honorio, while her husband is away on a hunt. Proceeding initially through the town marketplace, they notice a caged tiger and lion surrounded by attention-getting placards focused on their ferocity, though the animals appear docile enough to the casual observer. As the day unfolds, a fire breaks out in the town, and the Princess turns back, only to encounter the tiger, who has escaped (along with the lion) in the aftermath of the fire. The tiger, which follows her, is killed by Honorio. At this point, a woman and her flute-playing son appear, protesting the killing of the "tamed" tiger. (She and her husband own the tiger and lion.) Soon, the Prince and his party, attracted by the fire, meet the Princess and spy the dead tiger. Just then, the woman's husband appears and begs the Prince to spare the life of the lion, who is nearby. The Prince agrees to this if it can be done safely. Playing his flute and singing his song, the child meets the escaped lion and woos him to his lap, before removing a thorn from one of its paws. The story ends with the child continuing his song with its admonition to employ love and melody to tame the wild.

This story, simple in format, is complex when it comes to interpretation. Like much of what Goethe wrote in his last years, the story is highly symbolic. It is certain that the story, on one level, involves the mutual animosity of humans and nature. Ironically, however, it is human beings who prove to be the aggressors, hence the appropriateness of the story's opening with the hunting expedition. In this connection, the motif of appearance and reality functions pervasively. That the tiger and lion prove docile and

the humans aggressive suggests that humans have not yet come to terms with their own repressed animality. In short, the story may be seen to have sociological implications: societies and nations preying upon each other. Through the child's song, Goethe hints at the source of man's healing of the internal "thorn": the transforming power of love, which can render antagonist into friend. Goethe is on the side of the peasantry in this tale, and herein lies an ecological theme as well. The owners of the tiger and lion succeed over nature, not through the power of a gun, but through the dynamic of empathy. Their simple, harmonious lives provide a model for humans' proper relation to the natural world.

OTHER MAJOR WORKS

LONG FICTION: *Wilhelm Meisters Lehrjahre*, 1795-1796 (4 volumes; *Wilhelm Meister's Apprenticeship*, 1825); *Die Wahlverwandtschaften*, 1809 (*Elective Affinities*, 1849); *Wilhelm Meisters Wanderjahre: Oder, Die Entsagenden*, 1821, 1829 (2 volumes; *Wilhelm Meister's Travels*, 1827).

PLAYS: *Die Laune des Verliebten*, wr. 1767, pr. 1779 (*The Wayward Lover*, 1879); *Die Mitschuldigen*, first version wr. 1768, pr. 1780, second version wr. 1769, pr. 1777 (*The Fellow-Culprits*, 1879); *Götz von Berlichingen mit der eisernen Hand*, pb. 1773 (*Götz von Berlichingen with the Iron Hand*, 1799); *Götter, Helden, und Wieland*, pb. 1774; *Clavigo*, pr., pb. 1774 (English translation, 1798, 1897); *Erwin und Elmire*, pr., pb. 1775 (libretto; music by Duchess Anna Amalia of Saxe-Weimar); *Stella*, first version pr., pb. 1776, second version pr. 1806 (English translation, 1798); *Claudine von Villa Bella*, first version pb. 1776, pr. 1779, second version pb. 1788 (libretto; *Die Geschwister*, pr. 1776; *Iphigenie auf Tauris*, first version pr. 1779, second version pb. 1787 (*Iphigenia in Tauris*, 1793); *Jery und Bätely*, pr. 1780 (libretto); *Die Fischerinn*, pr., pb. 1782 (libretto; music by Corona Schröter; *The Fisherwoman*, 1899); *Scherz, List, und Rache*, pr. 1784 (libretto); *Der Triumph der Empfindsamkeit*, pb. 1787; *Egmont*, pb. 1788 (English translation, 1837); *Torquato Tasso*, pb. 1790 (English translation, 1827); *Faust: Ein Fragment*, pb. 1790 (*Faust: A Fragment*, 1980); *Der Gross-Cophta*, pr., pb. 1792; *Der Bürgergeneral,* pr., pb. 1793; *Was wir bringen,* pr., pb. 1802; *Die natürliche Tochter,* pr. 1803 (*The Natural Daughter,* 1885); *Faust: Eine Tragödie,* pb. 1808 (*The Tragedy of Faust,* 1823); *Pandora,* pb. 1808; *Die Wette,* wr. 1812, pb. 1837; *Des Epimenides Erwachen,* pb. 1814; *Faust: Eine Tragödie, zweiter Teil,* pb. 1833 (*The Tragedy of Faust, Part Two,* 1838).

POETRY: *Neue Lieder,* 1770 (*New Poems,* 1853); *Sesenheimer Liederbuch,* 1775-1789, 1854 (*Sesenheim Songs,* 1853); *Römische Elegien,* 1793 (*Roman Elegies,* 1876); *Reinecke Fuchs,* 1794 (*Reynard the Fox,* 1855); *Epigramme: Venedig 1790,* 1796 (*Venetian Epigrams,* 1853); *Xenien,* 1796 (with Friedrich Schiller; *Epigrams,* 1853); *Hermann und Dorothea,* 1797 (*Herman and Dorothea,* 1801); *Balladen,* 1798 (with Schiller; *Ballads,* 1853); *Neueste Gedichte,* 1800 (*Newest Poems,* 1853); *Gedichte,* 1812, 1815 (2 volumes; *The Poems of Goethe,* 1853); *Sonette,* 1819 (*Sonnets,* 1853); *Westöstlicher Divan,* 1819 (*West-Eastern Divan,* 1877).

NONFICTION: *Von deutscher Baukunst,* 1773 (*On German Architecture,* 1921); *Versuch die Metamorphose der Pflanzen zu erklären,* 1790 (*Essays on the Metamorphosis of Plants,* 1863); *Beyträge zur Optik,* 1791, 1792 (2 volumes); *Winckelmann und sein Jahrhundert,* 1805; *Zur Farbenlehre,* 1810 (*Theory of Colors,* 1840); *Aus meinem Leben: Dichtung und Wahrheit,* 1811-1814 (six volumes; *The Autobiography of Goethe,* 1824; better known as *Poetry and Truth from My Own Life*); *Italienische Reise,* 1816, 1817 (two volumes; *Travels in Italy,* 1883); *Zur Naturwissenschaft überhaupt, besonders zur Morphologe,* 1817, 1824 (two volumes); *Campagne in Frankreich, 1792,* 1822 (*Campaign in France in the Year 1792,* 1849); *Die Belagerung von Mainz, 1793,* 1822 (*The Siege of Mainz in the year 1793,* 1849); *Essays on Art,* 1845; *Goethe's Literary Essays,* 1921; *Goethe on Art,* 1980.

MISCELLANEOUS: *Works,* 1848-1890 (fourteen volumes); *Goethes Werke,* 1887-1919 (133 volumes).

BIBLIOGRAPHY

Atkins, Stuart. *Essays on Goethe.* Columbia, S.C.: Camden House, 1995. Essays on the apprentice novelist and other topics, by the preeminent Goethe scholar.

Boyle, Nicholas. *Goethe: The Poet and the Age, Volume I: The Poetry of Desire (1749-1790).* Oxford, England: Clarendon Press, 1991. A monumental scholarly biography. See the index of Goethe's works.

Brodey, Inger Sigrun. "Masculinity, Sensibility, and the 'Man of Feeling': The Gendered Ethics of Goethe's *Werther.*" *Papers on Language and Literature* 35 (Spring, 1999): 115-140. Argues that Goethe's man of feeling renounces traditional masculine roles and instead exists on the edge of illness, madness, impotence, and silence.

Lange, Victor, ed. *Goethe: A Collection of Critical Essays.* Englewood Cliffs, N.J.: Prentice-Hall, 1968. The essays collected in this informative volume emphasize Goethe's extraordinary poetic range as well as the pervasive consequences of scientific and social concerns in his life and work. The wide-ranging critical debate over the author's classical synthesis of private and collective responsibility is well represented. Includes a chronology of significant dates and a select bibliography.

Lukacs, Georg. *Goethe and His Age.* New York: Grosset & Dunlap, 1968. While the essays in this volume originated in the 1930's, a knowledge of those cultural, ideological, and literary struggles that classical German literature and philosophy generated is useful in forming any modern literary assessment of Goethe's work. Lukacs, a renowned Marxist critic, views Goethe's work as a bridge between the great realism of the eighteenth and nineteenth centuries.

Pratt, Vernon. "Goethe's Archetype and the Romantic Concept of the Self." *Studies in History and Philosophy of Science* 27 (September, 1996): 351-365. Compares Goethe's concept of archetype with the romantic concept of self as a core plus the expression of the core; contends that Goethe's archetype is a kind of agent at the heart of a thing, striving for self-expression.

Reed, T. J. *The Classical Centre: Goethe and Weimar, 1775-1832.* New York: Barnes & Noble

Books, 1980. This book asserts that Goethe's work came as a fulfillment of a need felt by a culture that lacked the essentials of a literary tradition. Narrowing his discussion to the author's years in Weimar, Reed's analysis emphasizes Goethe as the center of German literature and the primary creator of German classicism.

Remak, Henry H. H. *Structural Elements of the German Novella from Goethe to Thomas Mann.* New York: Peter Lang, 1996. Tests the three constituents of Goethe's famous definition of the novella against his own novellas. Discusses Goethe's seminal role in the development of the novella as the supreme literary achievement of Germany in the nineteenth century.

Wagner, Irmgard. *Goethe.* New York: Twayne, 1999.

An excellent, updated introduction to the author and his works. Includes bibliographical references and an index.

Weisinger, Kenneth D. *The Classical Facade: A Nonclassical Reading of Goethe's Classicism.* University Park: Pennsylvania State University Press, 1988. The works covered by this interesting volume all come from the middle period of Goethe's life. In his analysis, Weisinger searches for a kinship between *Faust* and Goethe's classic works. The author asserts that all these classic works share a nonclassic common theme: the disunity of the modern world.

*Ralph R. Joly, updated by
Genevieve Slomski*

NIKOLAI GOGOL

Born: Sorochintsy, Ukraine, Russian Empire (now Ukraine); March 31, 1809
Died: Moscow, Russia; March 4, 1852

PRINCIPAL SHORT FICTION

Vechera na khutore bliz Dikanki, 1831 (vol. 1), 1832 (vol. 2; *Evenings on a Farm Near Dikanka*, 1926)
Mirgorod, 1835 (English translation, 1928)
Arabeski, 1835 (includes stories and essays; *Arabesques*, 1982)

OTHER LITERARY FORMS

Nikolai Gogol established his reputation on his remarkable short stories, but he is often better known in the West for his play *Revizor* (pr., pb. 1836; *The Inspector General*, 1890) and for the first part of his novel *Myortvye dushi* (1842; *Dead Souls*, 1887). Still the subject of much debate and criticism, his *Vybrannye mesta iz perepiski s druzyami* (1847; *Selected Passages from Correspondence with Friends*, 1969) represents a range from literary criticism to tendentious and presumptuous evaluation of Russia as seen from abroad.

ACHIEVEMENTS

In Russian literature of both the nineteenth and the twentieth centuries, it is impossible to overstate the importance of Nikolai Gogol as an innovator in style and subject matter. He created a great and enduring art form composed of the manners of petty officials, small landowners, and the fantastic and all-too-real people who inhabit the three worlds that he describes: the Ukraine, St. Petersburg, and the Russian heartland.

Outside Russia, his influence can be detected most noticeably in Franz Kafka's *Die Verwandlung* (1915; *The Metamorphosis*, 1936), which centers on a conceit not unlike Nikolai Gogol's hapless titular councillor in Gogol's "Nos" ("The Nose"). Inside Russia, Fyodor Dostoevski is reputed to have begun the saying that "we all came from under Gogol's 'Overcoat,'" meaning that Gogol's stories originated the themes, social and spiritual anguish, and other literary preoccupations of the rest of Russian literature.

Nikolai Gogol (Library of Congress)

BIOGRAPHY

Nikolai Vasilyevich Gogol was born in the Ukraine on March 31, 1809, to a Ukrainian land-owner, Vasily Afanasievich Gogol-Yanovsky, and his young wife, Mariya Ivanovna. Vasily Afanasievich wrote plays in Ukrainian and sponsored artistic evenings at his home. Nikolai would write almost nothing in Ukrainian throughout his life. On his father's estate, Nikolai would absorb the manner and, significantly, the pace of provincial life, which would flavor his works from his early stories through *Dead Souls*.

At school and later in the *Gymnasium*, Nikolai remained something of a loner. He participated in activities, especially in drama performances, where he is said to have excelled. His classmates called him "the mysterious dwarf," though, for his predilection to aloofness and his unassuming stature.

Gogol's first work, *Hans Kuechelgarten* (1829), which he published at his own expense, was received so poorly that he bought all the unsold copies, burned them, and never wrote in verse again. He fled the country (in what was to become a characteristic retreat) and took refuge in Germany for several weeks. When he returned, he occupied a minor post in the civil service in St. Petersburg and began writing the stories that would begin to appear in 1831 and subsequently make him famous. His first collection of stories, *Evenings on a Farm Near Dikanka*, met with great critical and popular acclaim and set the stage for the series of successes that his later stories were to have.

In 1836, however, his play *The Inspector General* premiered, was produced most outlandishly in Gogol's mind, and created a minor scandal. Although this initial reaction was reversed and, through the intercession of the czar himself, the play was to continue its run, Gogol was nevertheless mortified at the antagonism that he had aroused in the spectators. He again left the country, only this time—with the exception of two rather short trips back to Russia—forever.

His last and most enduring works, "Shinel" ("The Overcoat") and *Dead Souls*, were thus written abroad. The irony of the profound resonance that his writing enjoyed at home was not lost on him. He began to doubt his ability to convey the "truth" to the Russians from such a distance and began to search for artistic inspiration. His self-doubt gave birth to his last literary production, *Selected Passages from Correspondence with Friends*. This product of his doubt was met with indignation and even anger in Russia. Vissarion Belinsky wrote his famous letter excoriating Gogol for his "fantastic book" and for writing from his "beautiful distance." Had Gogol forgotten the misery of Russia, its serfdom and servility, its "tartar" censorship, its totalitarian clout? Belinsky believed that the public was justified in its censure of this work; the public has the right to expect more from literature.

Gogol spent the last six years of his life fighting depression and artistic barrenness, trying to reach the "truth" in the second part of *Dead Souls*. Unfortunately, he failed to finish this work and, shortly before his death, burned what he had written. Physically ill, spiritually empty, emotionally depleted, he died in pain in Moscow on March 4, 1852.

ANALYSIS

Nikolai Gogol combines the consummate stylist with the innocent spectator, flourishes and flounces with pure human emotion, naturalism with delicate sensitivity. He bridges the period between Romanticism and realism in Russian literature. He captures the "real" against the background of the imagined and, in the estimation of at least one critic, the surreal. Frequently, the supernatural or some confounding coincidence plays a major role in his works. His heroes of the "little man" variety imprinted the most profound impression on his readers and critics alike. These petty clerks, all socially dysfunctional in some major respect, nevertheless explore the great depth of the human soul and exhibit certain personality traits characteristic of the greatest heroes in literature.

Gogol focuses his major creative occupation on the manners of his characters; his creative energy is nowhere more apparent than in the "mannerizing" in which he describes and characterizes. His genius does not dwell in philosophical dialogues, allegory, or involved internal monologue as do the realist novels of the latter half of the century. Nor does he engender his heroes with abandon and ennui, as do his near contemporaries Alexander Pushkin and Mikhail Lermontov. The depth of his psychological portraiture and the sweep of his romantic apostrophes, however, remain powerful and fascinating. In his plays, speech is swept aside from its characteristic place in the foreground; the dramatic foreground is given over to the manner or mannerisms of the characters. The actions literally speak louder than words. The social satire, deeply embedded in the manners of the characters, unfolds without special machinations and with few unnatural speech acts, such as asides. It is a tribute to Gogol's skill that his characters do not necessarily become superficial or unidimensional as a result but are imbued with certain attributes that display a wide range of human passion, particularly human dignity and the cognizance of the injustices created in social stratification.

One of Gogol's favored narrative devices can be called the chatty narrator. This narrator, seemingly prolix and sometimes random, will supply the reader with most of the information that will ever be re-

vealed about a character. In a typical passage, the reader will encounter a character who might say something utterly commonplace such as: "I won't have coffee today, Praskovia Osipovna, instead I will take some hot bread with onions." The character says little that can be used to describe himself. The reader's attention, however, is then directed to the information supplied by the narrator: "Actually, Ivan Yakovlevich would have liked to take both, but he knew it was utterly impossible to ask for two things at the same time since Praskovia Osipovna greatly disliked such whims." Thus Ivan Yakovlevich is described by his manners—he speaks to his wife in a formal tone that relates very little information to the reader—but the narrator, in his chatty, nosy fashion reveals much about this individual and describes Ivan's wife, his subordinate position at home, and his struggle for dignity within this relationship at the same time. Thus, from a seeming excess of information, the reader becomes familiar with a character who might otherwise remain nondescript.

Gogol's narratives abound in descriptions, and these tend to be humorous. Many times, humor is created by the device of metonymy, whereby a part stands for the whole. Thus, women become "slender waists" and seem so light that one fears that they will float away, and men are mustaches of various colors, according to their rank. Another humorous effect might be created by the chatty narrator's remark about some individual in a very unfavorable light. This information that he, for some reason, knows in regard to the character informs the reader's opinion of that character and often lends either a humorous or a pathetic tone to his or her person. Also humorous is the effect created through realized metaphors, another favorite technique of Gogol. Thus, instead of "he ate like a pig," the person is actually transformed into a pig with all the attributes of a perfect pig, at least temporarily. In general, Gogol's works abound with descriptions packed with colors, similes, and wayward characterizations by his narrator or actors.

Gogol's works fall roughly into three categories, which in turn correspond approximately to three different periods in his creative life. The first period is represented solely by short stories that exhibit lush local color from the Ukraine and Gogol's own mixing of devils and simple folk. Seven of the eight stories from the collection *Evenings on a Farm Near Dikanka*, which appeared in 1831 (with the second part following in 1832), belong in this category, as well as the stories in *Mirgorod*, first published in 1835.

The second major period of Gogol's literary life features works either centered on a locus in the imperial center of Russia, St. Petersburg itself, or surrounding the bureaucrats and petty officials ubiquitous in the provinces of the empire. This period stretches roughly from 1835 to 1842 and includes the short stories "Nevsky Prospekti" ("Nevsky Prospect"), "Zapiski sumasshedshego" ("Diary of a Madman"), "The Overcoat," "The Nose," the play *The Inspector General*, and the novel *Dead Souls*. The short story "Portret" ("The Portrait"), although definitely a product of this period, is singular for its strong echoes of the devil tales in the early period.

The last period can claim only one published work, *Selected Passages from Correspondence with Friends*, and is typically interpreted as a reversal in Gogol's creative development. If the analyst, however, can keep in mind Gogol's rather fanatic attachment to his artistic life as a devotional to God, then perhaps this otherwise unexplainable curve in his creative evolution might seem more understandable.

The two volumes of *Evenings on a Farm Near Dikanka* contain eight stories. However atypical they were to become in terms of setting and subject matter, these tales of the Ukraine, with various elements of the supernatural adding terror, exhibit many of the qualities found in the mature writer of the second period. They are magical and engaging, heroic and base, simply enjoyable to read and quite poignant.

"A MAY NIGHT"

An excellent example of these tales is "Mayskaya Noch: Ili, utoplennitsa" ("A May Night: Or, The Drowned Maiden"). The plot is a simple love story in which the lovers are not allowed to wed because of the objection of the man's father. The seeming simplicity, however, is overwhelmed by acts of Satan, witches, and *rusalki*. (In folk belief, *rusalki* are female suicides who endlessly inhabit the watery depths of ponds, tempting men and often causing their deaths.) When the antics of Ukrainian cossack youths do not by themselves bring the matter to resolution, the *rusalka* puts a letter into the young man's hand, which secures for him his marriage.

The characters are depicted in ways highly reminiscent of the oral folktales. Levko, the hero, sings to his beloved to come out of her house. He speaks of his "brighteyed beauty," her "little white hands," and her "fair little face." All these figures of speech are fixed epithets common in folklore. He promises to protect her from detection—"I will cover you with my jacket, wrap my sash around you, or hide you in my arms—and no one will see us,"—forfending the possible intrusion three ways. Likewise, he promises to protect her from any cold—"I'll press you warmer to my heart, I'll warm you with my kisses, I'll put my cap over your little white feet"—that is, a threefold protection. The reinforcement of images in threes is also quite common in folklore. Thus, clearly, Gogol is invoking folklore in his artistic works. Nevertheless, there are hints of the mature Gogol in the landscape descriptions. Even the intervention of the supernatural to produce, in this case, the successful outcome of the story belongs to the second period as well as to the first.

"IVAN FYODOROVICH SHPONKA AND HIS AUNT"

One story, in retrospect, however, stands out clearly from the others. "Ivan Fyodorovich Shpon'ka i ego tetushka" ("Ivan Fyodorovich Shponka and His Aunt") certainly presages the later works that will come to be regarded as Gogol's most characteristic. Set in the Ukraine, the story begins with an elaborate frame involving the following: The original storyteller of the tale wrote the story entirely and gave it to the narrator (for reasons that are not explained), but the narrator's wife later used the paper to wrap her pies, so the end of the story was unfortunately lost. The reader is assured, however, that should he or she so desire, he or she may contact the original storyteller, who still lives in that village and who will certainly oblige in sharing the ending.

There are many details in this frame alone that are very typical of the mature Gogol. First, the narrator does not take responsibility for the story—that is, that it is left unfinished; the abrupt end is presented as something over which he has no control. Second, the woman is the undoing of the man, although, in this case, the undoing is caused by her stupidity (she is illiterate) and not by an inherent evil. Moreover, the narrator could have rectified the situation himself, but, seemingly, he was fated to forget to ask the storyteller for another copy of the ending. Most of all, the story in the frame abounds with chatty, seemingly irrelevant details that serve to characterize the narrator, his wife, and the storyteller but that, ultimately, motivate the plot and occasion the sometimes precipitous changes in the course of the narrative.

The motifs described above reappear in forms both changed and unchanged throughout Gogol's work. A woman will appear in many guises in three of the four stories in *Mirgorod*. In "Taras Bulba," a long story with the color and force of an epic, a Polish beauty causes the son, Andrei, to defect to the enemy. Later, the traitor will be murdered by his father's own hands, described in the father's own words as a "vile dog."

"VIY"

In another story from this collection, "Viy," a young student, Khoma Brut, meets an old woman on his way home on vacation. When he stays for the night in her barn, she comes after him with outstretched arms. Khoma tries to avoid her three different ways, but she persists and, to his amazement, he loses the use of his arms and legs. The old woman turns out to be a witch who wickedly torments and then rides on the back of the young philosopher. Remembering some exorcisms, however, he renders her harmless and, in fact, exchanges places with her, now riding on her back. Khoma makes an incredible trek in this fashion until she falls in a faint. Now, watching her prone form, he is amazed to find not a witch or an old woman but a fair young maiden. Khoma races off, making it all the way to Kiev, but is called back to watch over her corpse for three nights, which was the last request of the dying maiden. During the third night, he is overcome by the supernatural devil, Viy, who emanates from the dead woman and thus brings his own doom.

"THE TALE OF HOW IVAN IVANOVICH QUARRELED WITH IVAN NIKIFOROVICH"

Another story from this collection, "Povest o tom, kak possorilsya Ivan Ivanovich s Ivanom Nikiforovichem" ("The Tale of How Ivan Ivanovich Quarreled with Ivan Nikiforovich"), also revolves around the same motif of the evil woman, although almost imperceptibly. Here, it is a "stupid" woman who sets out the gun while cleaning the house, which causes Ivan Ivanovich to envy this possession of his neighbor Ivan Nikiforovich. This seemingly insignificant act is the very act that causes an ensuing argument and that in turn builds into a lasting enmity between the former friends and then lasts in the courts for a decade. In Russia, this story is often invoked when people quarrel over imagined improprieties or insignificant trifles.

"NEVSKY PROSPECT"

In *Arabesques*, the two most famous stories, "Nevsky Prospect" and "Diary of a Madman," similarly feature the demonic power of women over men. "Nevsky Prospect" indeed centers on this "demonic" nature of women. Two tales are told, one of the "sensitive young man," the artist Piskarev, and the other of a rather older, down-to-earth lieutenant named Pirogov. The artist, perhaps fooled by the falling darkness, is stunned by the dazzling beauty of a woman walking by on Nevsky Prospect, a main avenue in St. Petersburg. At the same moment, Pirogov notices and blindly takes off after a blonde woman, "convinced that no beauty could resist him." Piskarev, almost overwhelmed at his own audacity, meekly follows his beauty to her "home," only to find out that she is, indeed, a prostitute. This development soon becomes the undoing of the poor artist as he falls into daytime and nighttime dreaming in a vain attempt to rescue his former exalted vision and save her image from the reality of her vile lifestyle. He takes to opium and, finally emboldened, decides on the desperate act of proposing marriage to her. When she rebuffs him, he goes mad and takes his own life. Pirogov, on the other hand, for all of his self-confidence and experience, fares only slightly better after following his blonde beauty home—to her husband. He blindly but cunningly continues his pursuit of her, only to end up being humiliated and physically abused. Indignant, he sets out to put his case before the court, but, somehow, after eating a little and spending some time rather pleasantly, he becomes diverted and seemingly forgets the whole thing. The narrator then closes the story with the admonition not to trust Nevsky Prospect, since nothing is as it seems, especially not the ladies.

"DIARY OF A MADMAN"

"Diary of a Madman" appears to be the personal journal of Popryshchin, whose name sounds very much like "pimple." The story is written as a series of entries with the chronology becoming entirely skewed at the end in accordance with the degree of dementia within the protagonist. The appearance of Popryshchin, the poor government clerk, marks the introduction of a new incarnation of the meek Shponkin type who will populate many of Gogol's works thereafter and enter the world of Russian literature as a prototype for many writers, notably Dostoevski. Popryshchin, a rather older, undistinguished man, adores the director's daughter but recognizes that pursuing her is useless. Moreover, he sees that his infatuation for her will be his doom: "Dear God, I'm a goner, completely lost!" Virtually at the same moment that he admits his futile position, his attention is drawn to the thin voice of Madgie, the young lady's dog, who is speaking to Fido. This rather fantastic conversation is centered on the letter that poor Fido seemingly never received from Madgie. Popryshchin's delusions continue to build up, with him even reading the canine correspondence. It is actually through Madgie's letters that Popryshchin learns of the young lady's love for, and engagement to, a handsome young chamberlain. Moreover, Popryshchin finds the young man's description unflattering. The sentence, "Sophie always laughs at him," becomes the crowning blow to his sanity. Shortly thereafter he goes mad, imagining himself to be the King of Spain. He is committed to Spain, more accurately, to a mental hospital, where he is constantly tormented. The pathos of the "little man" is palpable, conveyed through the evocation of a beautiful image—a troika coming to fly to him and rescue him—juxtaposed to the hateful attendants dousing him repeatedly with cold water.

"THE OVERCOAT"

Another "little man" follows closely in Popryshchin's footsteps. In "The Overcoat," Akaky Akakievich, whose humorous name is a reminder of fecal matter (kaka), represents such a meek and orderly person that he can perform only one duty: copying papers. This duty he discharges perfectly and with great pleasure, sometimes so much so that he occasionally brings the document home and, in his spare time, copies it again. Akaky Akakievich lives in St. Petersburg, victim of almost unimaginable poverty with barely enough means to keep himself alive. It was, indeed, a terrible day when he could no longer convince his tailor to have his overcoat remade; he would have to buy a new one. The physical privations that were necessitated by this desperate position are reminiscent of saintly asceticism. However, Akaky begins to sublimate his anguish and dreams of the great overcoat as though of a wife. With the mention of the word "wife," the reader who is accustomed to Gogol might immediately suspect the potential danger of this coat, since women in Gogol's fiction are almost always the undoing of a man. True to form, after withstanding all the hardships, enduring all the misgivings and new sensations, Akaky wears the new coat only once before he is mugged and the coat stolen from him. Dazed and exposed in the cold of St. Petersburg, he musters the courage to petition a "Person of Consequence" who dismisses him pompously. Akaky then falls into a fever from which he will not emerge alive. The tale, however, takes on a fantastic ending. Akaky comes back from the dead, intimidates and robs the Person of Consequence of his overcoat, and then, apparently satisfied, leaves the scene forever.

The supernatural revenge makes "The Overcoat" quite singular in Gogol's work. The fantastic element, however, appears again in another story of the same period, "The Nose." A barber, Ivan Yakovlevich, takes a roll for breakfast and finds, much to his alarm, a human nose in it, and he recognizes the nose as that of the Collegiate Assessor Kovalyov. Ivan Yakovlevich tries to rid himself of the nose. Meanwhile, its erstwhile owner wakes up to find a completely smooth area where his nose and incipient pimple had been the previous evening. He sets out on foot with the empty spot concealed by a handkerchief, only to witness his own former nose walking about freely, moreover in the uniform of a civil councillor—that is, a higher-ranking individual than Kovalyov himself. He accosts the nose very deferentially, but the nose claims to be an independent individual and not part of Kovalyov at all. In desperation, he sets out for the police department but, thinking better of it, decides to place an advertisement in the local newspaper. There, the clerk, thinking about it, decides against publishing such an advertisement to avoid potential scandals for the paper. Luckily for Kovalyov, the nose is returned to him by a police officer, but to his horror, it will not stick to his face. Then, as absurdly as the story began, it ends. Kovalyov wakes up with the nose back in its former place, goes to Ivan Yakovlevich and has a shave (the barber now not touching the olfactory organ), and it is as though nothing happened.

Many of Gogol's characters have penetrated into everyday Russian speech. If someone works hard at a brainless job, he is called an "Akaky Akakievich," for example, an attestation how well the writer created a type of Russian "little man" who, however uncreative, still captures the hearts and alliances of readers. There is something real about these absurd, impossible characters, something in their unidimensionality that transcends their locus and becomes universal. Gogol, while embroidering in highly ornate circumlocution, directly touches the wellspring of humanity in even the lowliest, most unattractive character. In his descriptions, there are simultaneously resonances of slapstick humor and the depths of human misery and social injustice.

Gogol left quite an imprint on the course of Russian literature. Very few subsequent writers will produce anything that does not at all reverberate the Gogolian legacy. Even in the twentieth century, writers incorporate his artistic ideas or emulate his style to a degree.

OTHER MAJOR WORKS

LONG FICTION: *Taras Bulba*, 1842 (revision of his 1835 short story; English translation, 1886); *Myor-* *tvye dushi*, part 1, 1842; part 2, 1855 (*Dead Souls*, 1887).

PLAYS: *Vladimir tretey stepeni*, wr. 1832, pb. 1842; *Zhenit'ba*, wr. 1835, pr., pb. 1842 (*Marriage: A Quite Incredible Incident*, 1926); *Revizor*, pr., pb. 1836 (*The Inspector General*, 1890); *Utro delovogo cheloveka*, pb. 1836 (revision of *Vladimir tretey stepeni*; *An Official's Morning*, 1926); *Lakeyskaya*, pb. 1842 (revision of *Vladimir tretey stepeni*; *The Servants' Hall*, 1926); *Tyazhba*, pb. 1842 (revision of *Vladimir tretey stepeni*; *The Lawsuit*, 1926); *Otryvok*, pb. 1842 (revision of *Vladimir tretey stepeni*; *A Fragment*, 1926); *Igroki*, pb. 1842 (*The Gamblers*, 1926); *The Government Inspector and Other Plays*, pb. 1926.

POETRY: *Hanz Kuechelgarten*, 1829.

NONFICTION: *Vybrannye mesta iz perepiski s druzyami*, 1847 (*Selected Passages from Correspondence with Friends*, 1969); *Letters of Nikolai Gogol*, 1967.

MISCELLANEOUS: *The Collected Works*, 1922-1927 (six volumes); *Polnoe sobranie sochinenii*, 1940-1952 (fourteen volumes); *The Collected Tales and Plays of Nikolai Gogol*, 1964.

BIBLIOGRAPHY

Erlich, Victor. *Gogol*. New Haven, Conn.: Yale University Press, 1969. For nonspecialists, this book may be the most accessible and evenhanded. Erlich concentrates on Gogol's oeuvre without shortchanging the generally disavowed *Selected Passages from Correspondence with Friends*. He deals with much of the "myth" of Gogol and supplies interesting background to the making of Gogol's works.

Fanger, Donald L. *The Creation of Nikolai Gogol*. Cambridge, Mass.: The Belknap Press of Harvard University Press, 1979. Fanger presses deeply into the background material and includes in his purview works both published and unpublished, in his effort to reveal the genius of Gogol's creative power. This book is worthwhile in many respects, particularly for the wealth of details about Gogol's life and milieu. Includes twenty-eight pages of notes and an index.

Gippius, V. V. *Gogol.* Translated by Robert Maguire. Ann Arbor, Mich.: Ardis, 1981. Originally written in 1924, this famous monograph supplies not only the view of a fellow countryman but also a vast, informed, and intellectual analysis of both the literary tradition in which Gogol wrote and his innovation and contribution to that tradition. Vastly interesting and easily accessible. Contains notes and a detailed list of Gogol's works.

Hart, Pierre R. "Narrative Oscillation in Gogol's 'Nevsky Prospect.'" *Studies in Short Fiction* 31 (Fall, 1994): 639-645. Argues that the story is a commentary on the author's development of strategies to deal with reality; discusses the urban scene in the story, suggesting that the city forces the protagonist into a final defensive position.

Maguire, Robert A. *Exploring Gogol.* Stanford, Calif.: Stanford University Press, 1994. The most comprehensive study in English of Gogol's entire writing career. Incorporates a chronology, detailed notes, and an extensive bibliography.

Maguire, Robert A., ed. *Gogol from the Twentieth Century: Eleven Essays.* Princeton, N.J.: Princeton University Press, 1974. This collection of essays, with a lengthy introduction by the editor and translator, represents some of the most famous and influential opinions on Gogol in the twentieth century. Some of the most problematic aspects of Gogol's stylistics, thematics, and other compositional elements are addressed and well elucidated. Bibliography, index.

Rancour-Laferriere, David. *Out from Under Gogol's "Overcoat": A Psychoanalytic Study.* Ann Arbor, Mich.: Ardis, 1982. This specialized study proves very exciting to the reader of Gogol. Much of the discussion focuses on the particular usage of words by Gogol. Even students with no command of Russian will find the explication understandable since the examples are clear and self-defining. Much of the discussion comprises very modern literary-analytical technique and may prove of good use to the reader. Contains a bibliography that includes many background works.

Robey, Judith. "Modelling the Reading Act: Gogol's Mute Scene and Its Intertexts." *Slavic Review* 56 (Summer, 1997): 233-250. Discusses scenes in which viewers look at paintings in Gogol's fiction and essays; argues these moments correspond to a metanarrative in Gogol's works in which reading is depicted as a process that can lead to redemption and salvation.

Setchkarev, Vsevolod. *Gogol: His Life and Works.* Translated by Robert Kramer. New York: New York University Press, 1965. Still often recommended in undergraduate courses, Setchkarev's monograph concentrates on both the biography and the works, seen individually and as an artistic system. Very straightforward and easily readable, this work might be perhaps the best place for the student to begin.

Tosi, Alessandra. "Andrei Kropotov's 'Istoriia o Smurom Kaftane': A Thematic Source for Gogol's 'Shinel'?" *The Slavonic and East European Review* 76 (October, 1998): 601-613. Compares Gogol's "The Overcoat" with Kropotov's earlier story; in both stories a trivial garment takes on significance for the main characters and ultimately causes their ruin. Discusses the similarity in the twists in the plots; suggests that Kropotov's story may have been source for Gogol's.

Troyat, Henri. *Divided Soul.* Translated by Nancy Amphoux. Garden City, N.Y.: Doubleday, 1973. This study provides perhaps the most information on Gogol's life and demonstrates masterfully how Gogol's life and work are inextricably intertwined. Troyat does not neglect the important role that "God's will" played in Gogol's life, the thread that lends the greatest cohesion to the diverse developments in his creative journey. The volume contains some interesting illustrations, a bibliography, notes, and an index.

Christine Tomei

HERBERT GOLD

Born: Cleveland, Ohio; March 9, 1924

PRINCIPAL SHORT FICTION

Love and Like, 1960
The Magic Will: Stories and Essays of a Decade,
  1971
Stories of Misbegotten Love, 1985
Lovers and Cohorts: Twenty-seven Stories, 1986

OTHER LITERARY FORMS

Herbert Gold's memoirs, *Blind, Blind Date: Memoir* (1980), *Travels in San Francisco* (1990), *Best Nightmare on Earth: A Life in Haiti* (1991), and *Bohemia: Where Art, Angst, Love, and Strong Coffee Meet* (1993), are collections of personal reflections on his life and travels. Gold has also authored nearly two dozen novels, edited collections of short stories, and written the children's book *The Young Prince and the Magic Cone* (1973).

ACHIEVEMENTS

Herbert Gold was a Fulbright fellow at the Sorbonne, University of Paris, in 1950, a *Hudson Review* fellow in 1956, and a John Simon Guggenheim Memorial Foundation fellow in 1957. In 1954 he received an Inter-American Cultural Relations grant to Haiti. He has also received an Ohioana Book Award, a National Institute of Arts and Letters grant, a Longview Foundation Award, and a Ford Foundation theater fellowship. He received the California Literature Medal in 1968 for *Fathers: A Novel in the Form of a Memoir* (1967), the Commonwealth Club Award for best novel in 1982 for *Family: A Novel in the Form of a Memoir* (1981), and the Sherwood Anderson Prize for fiction in 1989. His short stories have appeared in numerous publications, including *The New York Times Book Review*, *Harper's Bazaar*, *Atlantic*, *Esquire*, *Playboy*, *Partisan Review*, and *Prize Stories: The O. Henry Awards*.

BIOGRAPHY

Herbert Gold was born in Cleveland, Ohio, in 1924. After working for U.S. Army Intelligence from 1943 to 1946, he received his B.A. and M.A. from Columbia University, in 1946 and 1948, respectively. He was married to Edith Durbin from 1948 to 1956 and to Melissa Dilworth from 1968 to 1975; both marriages ended in divorce. Gold has a number of children: Ann and Judith from his first marriage, and Nina, Ari, and Ethan from his second marriage.

Gold's first published story appeared in *Harper's Bazaar* while he was still in college, and he was firmly established as a full-time writer by the time he was in his thirties. In 1960, Gold left the Midwest permanently; he moved to San Francisco, settling in a small apartment on Russian Hill above North Beach, which continued to be his permanent residence during his extensive travels. Most of his later fiction is set in San Francisco, while his essays reflect his travels, especially in Haiti. Gold has taught at several universities, including the University of California at Berkeley, Stanford University, and Harvard University.

ANALYSIS

Herbert Gold's short fiction depicts realistic themes and settings—most often dealing with male-female relationships or the broader theme of families. He has a keen eye for contemporary manners and mores, and his fiction and essays often investigate how people deal with life, their environment, and one another. Much of Gold's short fiction features middle-aged men, divorced or unhappily married, who have passionate but brief relationships with younger women. In these stories, the men typically are presented as innocent victims of manipulative women. Other stories illuminate the broader network of family relationships, and his treatment of the elderly can be particularly sensitive.

In most of his stories, the situations and personalities are very close to his own life story. Gold has said he writes "semi-automatically" so as to get in touch with his dreams, fantasies, and recollections, especially in his fiction; when he writes less intuitively, he produces essays, which are outlined in advance. Gold's dialogue is frequently wry and witty; his style is often conversational, and he avoids overt symbolism, as he prefers to let the story create its symbols in the reader's mind. Often the story's end is not definitive but leaves the next step in the character's evolution to the reader's imagination.

In some stories, Gold objectifies one or more characters by not naming them—in fact, in his novel *He/She* (1980), the names of the main characters, a divorcing couple, are never mentioned. From 1986 to 1999, Gold's output comprised three collections of nonfiction and three novels.

"THE HEART OF THE ARTICHOKE"

Perhaps Gold's best-known work of short fiction, "The Heart of the Artichoke" (1951) describes the conflicts between twelve-year-old Daniel and his father, whom he deeply loves and admires. His parents insist Daniel work in the family grocery store, a job about which he feels embarrassed. He feels that he has been branded a lower-class immigrant, not only in his own eyes but also, and more devastatingly, in the eyes of Pattie, the wealthy girl on whom he has a crush. His father, who came to America to start a new life against his own father's wishes, does not see that Daniel now faces a similar conflict with his father.

When a class field trip is scheduled for one of the busiest days of the year at the store, Daniel sneaks out of work to join his friends. When Pattie shares her lunch with him and lets him walk her home, Daniel is thrilled and confesses he likes her. Her dismissive response that he is just a grocery boy devastates him. The story concludes with an intensely emotional and physical conflict between Daniel and his father.

In "The Heart of the Artichoke," food is a family symbol of love, security, and abundance, and the father relishes procuring and selling excellent food as much as eating it. Gold uses food analogies, particularly those of the artichoke, to illustrate both the conflicts inherent in the adolescent's struggle to make his or her own way and the problems between immigrant parents and their children.

LOVERS AND COHORTS

Gold's 1986 collection of twenty-seven essays

Herbert Gold (©Miriam Berkley)

and short stories includes a number of stories already collected in *Love and Like* and *The Magic Will: Stories and Essays of a Decade*, along with later works, several of which were previously unpublished. A number of the selections are set in Haiti; several other stories involve men, often married, often teachers at a college, who become involved with younger women, often students, then find that they are the ones being used by the vibrant, young women. The men feel betrayed, ignoring the hypocrisy inherent in the fact that they are betraying their own wives and children. The feelings of their wives are barely discussed in most of the stories.

Many of the short stories seem to flow toward a predictable ending, until the last paragraph, when a quick remark truncates the story with a different twist than might be expected. Because Gold's essays often incorporate stylistic elements more often associated with fiction and his fiction often draws heavily on his personal life, the reader may not always be sure which selections are fictional and which are not. For example, one of the most amusing stories in *Blind, Blind Date* is a wry look at dating in San Francisco that is so outlandish, it almost has to be true, but it reads like a humorous piece of fiction.

"LOVE AND LIKE"

First published in *The Hudson Review* in 1958, this story is somewhat unusual in Gold's fiction in its in-depth examination of the feelings of the children of a failed marriage. Newly divorced Dan Shaper has moved to New York from Cleveland because he feels unable to live in close proximity to his former wife. The story unfolds when Shaper makes his first visit back to Cleveland to see his young daughters, Paula and Cynthia, and his girlfriend, Sally. While married, his wife was determined to have a son, and she became focused on determining the ideal timing, diet, and techniques for conceiving a boy. The marriage collapsed when she learned that while she had turned their lovemaking into a clinical pursuit of a son, he had sought refuge in an affair with a student. Although all the other characters in the story are named, the wife's name is never mentioned: When speaking to her, Shaper always calls her "kid," an appellation she detests; to others, he refers to her as "my wife," although Sally constantly points out that the woman is his former wife.

Shaper insists he likes Sally and claims to like his wife, but he says he loves only his children. When he tries to convince six-year-old Paula that although he and their mother merely like each other, this does not change his love for his daughters, Paula cuts through her father's hypocrisy and word games. As he leaves, Paula challenges him, shouting, "Oh, how I'm sick of those words love and like!" At the end of his visit, the former wife becomes angry that Shaper says he cannot afford tuition at a private school for their older daughter and screams that whereas he never satisfied her sexually, her new boyfriend does. The story ends with Shaper standing in front of Sally's doorway, toying with the idea of suicide but concerned about its effect on his children.

"COHORTS"

In "Cohorts," Gold switches his focus from the problems that man have with women to a touching tale of two brothers spending the day with their aged father. The narrator, who is never named, has flown from California to Cleveland to visit his parents and brother.

The strength of this brief story is in the economical way in which Gold paints a picture of the defeated father Sam, who is waiting to die, and the son's feeling of helplessness in the face of his father's decline. "My father is tired of growing old. . . . He helped me to grow up. Why can't I help him now?" the narrator cries. Sam is often confused, his hearing and sight are fading, his energy is low, and he is embarrassed to admit he now loses control of his bowels and bladder. In one breath, Sam tells his visiting son to go out and have fun but not to leave him.

When the mother, also nameless, goes to a meeting, the visiting son and his brother decide to ignore their mother's wish that they feed their father at home and instead take him to the deli where they often went as a family years earlier. At the deli, waitresses and customers come up to the three men, calling Sam by name, reminding him of their names. Although he has turned off his hearing aid, he cheerfully greets the other customers. After they leave the deli, the brothers ask who all the people were, but Sam laughs as if it were a joke and admits he has no idea.

OTHER MAJOR WORKS

LONG FICTION: *Birth of a Hero*, 1951; *The Prospect Before Us*, 1954 (reprinted as *Room Clerk*, 1955); *The Man Who Was Not with It*, 1956 (published as *The Wild Life*, 1957, with a new introduction by the author); *The Optimist*, 1959; *Therefore Be Bold*, 1960; *Salt*, 1963; *Fathers: A Novel in the Form of a Memoir*, 1967 (reprinted as *Fathers*, 1991); *The Great American Jackpot*, 1969; *Biafra Goodbye*, 1970; *My Last Two Thousand Years*, 1972; *Swiftie the Magician*, 1974; *Waiting for Cordelia*, 1977; *Slave Trade*, 1979; *He/She*, 1980; *Family: A Novel in the Form of a Memoir*, 1981 (reprinted as *Family*, 1991); *True Love*, 1982; *Mister White Eyes*, 1984; *A Girl of Forty*, 1986; *She Took My Arm as if She Loved Me*, 1997; *Daughter Mine*, 2000.

NONFICTION: *The Age of Happy Problems*, 1962; *A Walk on the West Side: California on the Brink*, 1981; *Travels in San Francisco*, 1990 (memoirs); *Best Nightmare on Earth: A Life in Haiti*, 1991; *Bohemia: Where Art, Angst, Love and Strong Coffee Meet*, 1993.

CHILDREN'S LITERATURE: *The Young Prince and the Magic Cone*, 1973.

EDITED TEXTS: *Fiction of the Fifties: A Decade of American Writing*, 1959; *Stories of Modern America*, 1961 (with David L. Stevenson); *First Person Singular: Essays for the Sixties*, 1963.

BIBLIOGRAPHY

Hicks, Granville. "Generations of the Fifties: Malamud, Gold and Updike." In *The Creative Present: Notes on Contemporary American Fiction*, edited by Nona Balakian and Charles Simmons. New York: Gordian Press, 1973. A critical essay comparing the work of Bernard Malamud, Herbert Gold, and John Updike.

_____. *Literary Horizons: A Quarter Century of American Fiction*. New York: New York University Press, 1970. A collection of essays and book reviews of various authors, including Gold.

Tooker, Dan, and Roger Hofheins. *Fiction! Interviews with Northern California Novelists*. New York: Harcourt Brace Jovanovich, 1976. Provides a conversational, noncritical look at Gold's writing style, habits, and literary influences.

Waldon, Daniel, ed. *Herbert Gold and Company: American Jewish Writers as Universal Writers*. Studies in American Jewish Literature 10. Kent, Ohio: Kent State University Press, 1991. A collection of critical essays by various authors discussing Gold's fiction in terms of his Jewish American background.

Irene Struthers Rush

OLIVER GOLDSMITH

Born: Pallas, County Longford(?), Ireland; November 10, 1728 or 1730
Died: London, England; April 4, 1774

PRINCIPAL SHORT FICTION

An Enquiry into the Present State of Polite Learning in Europe, 1759
The Citizen of the World, 1762 (collection of essays first published in *The Public Ledger*, 1760-1761)

OTHER LITERARY FORMS

Oliver Goldsmith published a great variety of material including poems, biographies, a novel, essays, and sketches. One of his plays, *She Stoops to Conquer: Or, The Mistakes of a Night* (pr., pb. 1773), is still popular and widely performed.

ACHIEVEMENTS

Oliver Goldsmith was a writer of such range, such enormous output, and such varying quality that he is difficult to categorize easily. Success came slowly for Goldsmith after years of work as a Grub Street hack, but as his style and reputation as a writer developed, he became a member of the eminent London literary circle, which included men of letters such as Samuel Johnson, Edmund Burke, and Sir Joshua Reynolds. Many of his poems and essays attracted favorable notice, and with his novel, *The Vicar of Wakefield* (1766), he achieved a solid reputation as a writer of fiction.

Goldsmith's first play, *A Good-Natured Man* (pr., pb. 1768), failed in its initial production at Covent Garden but went on to become a moderate success. His next play, *She Stoops to Conquer*, earned him greater honor as a playwright. Goldsmith's clear,

Oliver Goldsmith (Library of Congress)

charming style and his gift for humor and characterization have ensured his enduring popularity in the many genres he practiced.

BIOGRAPHY

Oliver Goldsmith received his A.B. from Trinity College in Dublin in 1749. He toyed with the notion of taking holy orders but was refused by a bishop who felt his scarlet breeches reflected a less than serious attitude. In 1752, he left Ireland never to return. His travels to London to study law met with misfortune, but a generous uncle then sent him to study medicine at Edinburgh. Shortly thereafter he traveled by foot through Holland, Switzerland, and France. He settled in England in 1756, supporting himself at various times as a doctor among the poor, an apothecary's assistant, an usher in a school, and finally as a hack writer for Ralph Griffith's *Monthly Review*. His life was marked by continual wandering, and poverty was his constant companion. After establishing himself in the literary world, he was honored by being chosen one of the nine charter members of Samuel Johnson's famous club. He died in 1774, leaving an incredible volume of work and an equal amount of debt.

ANALYSIS

Oliver Goldsmith's essays reflect two significant literary transitions of the late eighteenth century. The larger or more general of these was the beginning of the gradual evolution of Romanticism from the Neoclassicism of the previous one hundred years. Oppressed by the heavy "rule of reason" and ideas of taste and polish, readers of this transitional period gradually began to respond more to the imaginative and the emotional in literature. This transition serves as a backdrop for a related evolution that played an essential role in the development of the modern short story. At this time the well-established periodical essay began a glacially slow movement away from its predominant emphasis on a formal exposition of ideas; contemporary essayists, none more prominent than Goldsmith, began to indulge more their taste for the personal approach and for narrative. The result was increased experimentation with characterization, story line, setting, and imagery; concurrent with these developments, style, theme, tone, and structural patterning received particular attention. Varying degrees and types of emphasis on these elements pushed the essay form in many diverse directions. Of all the contemporary essayists, Oliver Goldsmith best reflects these developments.

THE CITIZEN OF THE WORLD

Goldsmith's *The Citizen of the World* vividly illustrates the variety of experimentation in the contemporary periodical essay and is of great importance in the history of the Asian tale. With its vigorous appeal to the imagination and emotions, the Asian tale marked a major step toward Romanticism. More important, its popularity at a time of significant literary experimentation led to an interesting mixture of two literary traditions, the essay-sketch and the tale, which serves as a bedrock for the development of the modern short story.

Goldsmith incorporated the current enthusiasm for Asian motifs in his collection of essays. He used the device of the frame tale, associated with the recently translated *The Arabian Nights' Entertainments* (1706-1708), to give the collection its unity. The frame is supplied by a traveling Chinese philosopher who observes the customs and society of London and writes his observations to friends in the East. This narrative point of view affords Goldsmith an infinite variety of techniques and subjects. His basic strategy is to start with a discursive essay that leads to one of two general avenues. On the one hand, from this point Goldsmith may proceed to build a soapbox from which the Chinese philosopher expounds on morality and philosophy; in these essays Goldsmith normally maintains the form of the didactic essay. On the other hand, Goldsmith may proceed to an appropriate observation on English culture by the Chinese philosopher; the observation may elucidate a philosophical point or a moral lesson. These essays illustrate the increasing interest in narrative and personality and place a larger than customary emphasis on glimpses of daily life. There are also variations on this idea; for example, the Chinese philosopher's observation may take the form of a tale which completely dominates the essay, or he may focus almost exclusively on descriptive detail of action or people or settings—a strategy which culminates in a sketch rather than an essay.

The latter occurs in Letter 26 where the Chinese philosopher describes for friends in the East his English acquaintance, "the man in black." The Chinese philosopher begins by remarking that his friend's manners "are tinctured with some strange inconsistencies." Curiously, "though he is generous even to profusion, he affects to be thought a prodigy of parsimony and prudence." The Chinese philosopher has known him to "profess himself a man-hater while his cheek was glowing with compassion." By way of example, the Chinese relates the adventures of a walk they shared; they begin by happening "to discourse upon the provision that was made for the poor in England." This discussion fires the indignation of the man in black, who assures the Chinese that the poor "are imposters, every one of them and rather merit a prison than relief." The two suddenly encounter an old man of reduced fortune, whose story has no influence on the Chinese who describes himself as "prepossessed against such falsehoods"; but at the same time he witnesses "it visibly operate" upon the man in black "and effectually interrupt his harangue." His companion clearly burns with compassion yet is

"ashamed to discover his weakness" to the Chinese who turns his head momentarily, affording his friend the opportunity to press coins into the outstretched hand. As they return to their walk, the man in black who "fancied himself quite unperceived" begins again "to rail against beggars with as much animosity as before." His monologue is continually interrupted by more of the poor with the same result until finally he is so distracted he reaches to his pockets in plain view of the Chinese, who vividly portrays his friend's "confusion when he found he had already given all the money he carried about him to former objects." As a last resort the man in black gives this final beggar a "shilling's worth of matches"—and thus the portrayal ends.

This letter brilliantly demonstrates Goldsmith's dominant tendencies in the periodical essay or sketch. The focal character, the man in black, is realistically portrayed and psychologically interesting; Goldsmith subordinates the incidents to his description of the focal character's responses to the beggars; the setting, vaguely in the countryside, is void of descriptive detail and lacks focus; Goldsmith's prose style here is characteristically lucid, natural, and simple, yet capable of genuine subtlety and sensitivity; a characteristic touch of wit occurs when the Chinese turns his head and allows his friend to preserve his pride; Goldsmith structures his piece around his narrative persona, the Chinese philosopher, who describes the subject character, the man in black, in terms of the latter's response to external events. The overall pattern indicates Goldsmith's genius for seizing an idea, purifying and distilling his presentation, and unifying all his narrative elements in a complete development of his central concept.

LETTERS 48 AND 49

In direct opposition to this approach, in Letters 48 and 49 Goldsmith chooses a quite different avenue with an entirely different result. He begins again with the discursive essay but now proceeds to establish a soapbox for the Chinese visitor. What issues from this soapbox is fairly atypical for Goldsmith, yet quite important in terms of the short story's historical development.

At the beginning of Letter 48 the Chinese philosopher strolls into an artist's studio to examine some paintings. He observes a young prince before a canvas surrounded by flatterers "assiduously learning the trade." The scene strikes "very disagreeable sensations" in the visiting philosopher. He disapproves of seeing a youth who "by his station in life, had it within his power to be useful to thousands, thus letting his mind run to waste upon canvas, and at the same time fancying himself improving in taste, and filling his rank with proper decorum." The prince asks for the philosopher's opinion of his art, work filled with Chinese elements crudely used. The rational Chinese, feeling that "seeing an error, and attempting to redress it, are only one and the same," spoke his true but harsh opinion and received a proportion of the same in exchange. Considering, however, that "it was in vain to argue against people who had so much to say without contradicting them," the Chinese begged leave to repeat a fairy tale which would illustrate the "absurdity of placing our affections upon trifles." He adds that he "hoped the moral would compensate for its stupidity." The young artist protests a story with a moral but the Chinese pretends not to hear and proceeds to relate the tale of a young prince in the remote kingdom of Bonbobbin.

The Chinese warms to his tale describing the young prince whose physical beauty inspired the sun to "sometimes stop his course, in order to look down and admire him." "His mind was no less perfect" for "he knew all things without having ever read." His name was "Bonbennin-Bonbobbin-bonbobbinet which signifies Enlightener of the Sun." After vividly detailing the prince's courtship and wedding, the Chinese momentarily digresses to the prince's affection for his collection of mice, with which he would "innocently" spend "four hours a day in contemplating their innocent little pastimes." Returning to the wedding night, the Chinese relates how the joy of the young couple was abruptly interrupted by the appearance of a beautiful white mouse with green eyes, exactly the creature the young prince "had long endeavored to possess." To the utter dismay of the prince, the mouse escapes capture and disappears. After all the efforts of the prince's subjects fail to recover the mouse, the prince sets out to search the world until he finds the mouse, not knowing the mouse was secretly "sent by a discontented Princess and was itself a fairy." In his travels, the prince's only companion was a faithful blue cat with the power of speech. Far from home, the prince relates his story to an ugly old woman who promises him the mouse if he will marry her then and there. After seeking the counsel of the blue cat, the prince marries the old woman and is shocked when she admits to being the mouse. She offers the prince the choice of having her as a woman by day and a mouse by night or vice versa. Taking the advice of the blue cat, the prince decides on the first alternative and the three return to the palace. On the night of their arrival, the prince asks the old woman to resume the appearance of the mouse and to dance on the floor as he sings. As the mouse is gaily dancing, the blue cat rushes forth, gobbles up the mouse thus breaking the charm, and resumes the shape of the young princess. The prince realizes the error of his ways and reconciles himself to his happy marriage. The young couple live long and happily, "perfectly convinced by their former adventures, that they who place their affection on trifles at first for amusement, will find those trifles at last become their most serious concern."

If the sketch of the man in black is contrasted with this pair of letters, it is found that in the latter Goldsmith has moved completely over to the tale tradition generally, to the Asian tale specifically. The focal character, the prince, is not comparatively realistic like the man in black but the epitome of idealized virtues. He has little inner life and is dominated by exotic and magical external actions. The setting, the remote kingdom of Bonbobbin, Goldsmith describes in vivid, exotic detail. The prose style is still lucid and natural but he chooses stronger and more dramatic words. The tone, far less personal than before, now becomes more public and socially directed, as the explicit moral tag demonstrates. The structural pattern is the framed oral retelling of an exotic Asian tale.

LETTER 13

Successes by Goldsmith in the two quite different traditions of sketch and tale have been examined; Letter 13 appears to represent Goldsmith's attempt to balance more perfectly elements of the two. The Chinese philosopher has just returned from a visit to Westminster Abbey where the "monumental inscriptions, and all the venerable remains of the deceased merit" have inspired his feelings of gloom. Upon entering the "temple marked with the hand of antiquity, solemn as religious awe, adorned with all the magnificence of barbarous profusion, dim windows, fretted pillars, long colonnades, and dark ceilings," he stands in oppressed solitude drinking in the atmosphere and wondering at how pride has attended "the puny child of dust even to the grave." He is aware that he possesses "more consequence in the present scene than the greatest hero of them all" who has toiled "for an hour to gain a transient immortality and are at length retired to grave where they have no attendant but the worm, none to flatter but the epitaph." As the Chinese stands alone with his feelings, he is approached by the man in black, who offers to be his guide. While they walk, the Chinese philosopher questions his companion about the man entombed in a particularly magnificent monument, assuming his life to have been one of great merit. The man in black answers with the dead man's biography, concluding that the latter is just one of many "who, hated and shunned by the great when alive, have come here, fully resolved to keep them company now they are dead." When the two men reach the poet's corner, the Chinese asks to be shown the grave of Alexander Pope. The man in black responds that "people have not done hating him yet." The Chinese is amazed that a man who gave the world so much entertainment and instruction should be so hated and is shocked to learn how writers in general suffer at the hands of critics and booksellers and from the ignorance of patrons.

The two men next turn their attention to the tombs of kings. At the entrance gate the Chinese is expected to pay an admission fee which he likens to that required to see a show. Having paid the money, the Chinese expects to see something extraordinary since what he has already seen and heard without charge has genuinely surprised him, but he is disappointed by the "pieces of absurdity" with which the gatekeeper tries to impress him. At the next gate the Chinese is again requested to pay an admission fee. Completely disillusioned, the Chinese refuses, choosing

instead to return to his lodgings "in order to ruminate over what was great, and to despise what was mean in the occurrences of the day."

By combining elements of the essay-sketch and tale traditions in this letter, Goldsmith reached a new plateau in his writing and closely approached the short story. In addition to exterior action and emotional responses, Goldsmith added brilliant dialogue and more completely developed the focal character, the Chinese. While Goldsmith subordinated the narrow action, he also made it intimate and dramatic, thus using it to fulfill a thematic function. The theme, the consideration of fame, is universal and at the same time inherently personal. Goldsmith used the setting in much the same way. The setting is described in exotic detail and possesses a psychological dimension that sets the tone for the theme. Goldsmith's style in this letter combines psychological subtleties with narration and buttresses the nonjudgmental tone essential to the theme. The tone and theme are significant, for Goldsmith now leaves the reader with no flat picture or moral but with the experience of his own feelings. By carefully controlling the exterior elements, Goldsmith holds time still for the reader and draws him in to share the questions and the feelings of the Chinese. With the open lyrical ending, Goldsmith leaves the reader to experience and reflect for himself.

If Goldsmith's genius can be appreciated after a perusal of his essays, the appreciation can only grow when the variety and excellence of Goldsmith's other writings are known. In addition to his essays, Goldsmith also applied his talents to drama and produced the timeless *She Stoops to Conquer*. While sentimental comedy was flourishing, Goldsmith was significant for reviving and purifying the comedy of manners and thus temporarily returning laughter to the stage. His many biographies are enduring and lively, for Goldsmith always maintained his lucid natural style. His poetry was his "solitary pride," for within this form Goldsmith could harmonize both the sad and gay sides of his personality. His novel, *The Vicar of Wakefield*, is one of the best of the sentimental novels and represented an important step toward Romanticism. In addition to his versatility and excellence, Goldsmith is the writer who best exemplified the vast literary transitions of the later eighteenth century.

OTHER MAJOR WORKS

LONG FICTION: *The Vicar of Wakefield*, 1766.

PLAYS: *The Good-Natured Man*, pr., pb. 1768; *She Stoops to Conquer: Or, The Mistakes of a Night*, pr., pb. 1773.

POETRY: "An Elegy on the Glory of Her Sex: Mrs. Mary Blaize," 1759; "The Logicians Refuted," 1759; *The Traveller: Or, A Prospect of Society*, 1764; "Edwin and Angelina," 1765; "An Elegy on the Death of a Mad Dog," 1766; *The Deserted Village*, 1770; "Threnodia Augustalis," 1772; "Retaliation," 1774; *The Haunch of Venison: A Poetical Epistle to Lord Clare*, 1776; "The Captivity: An Oratoria," 1820 (wr. 1764).

NONFICTION: *The Bee*, 1759 (essays); *Memoirs of M. de Voltaire*, 1761; *The Life of Richard Nash of Bath*, 1762; *A History of England in a Series of Letters from a Nobleman to His Son*, 1764 (2 volumes); *Essays: By Mr. Goldsmith*, 1765; *Life of Bolingbroke*, 1770; *Life of Parnell*, 1770; *An History of the Earth, and Animated Nature*, 1774 (8 volumes; unfinished).

MISCELLANEOUS: *The Collected Works of Oliver Goldsmith*, 1966 (5 volumes; Arthur Friedman, editor).

BIBLIOGRAPHY

Brooks, Christopher K. "'Guilty of Being Poor': Goldsmith's 'No-Account' Centinel." *English Language Notes* 36 (September, 1998): 23-38. Argues that Goldsmith's character, the "Private Centinel" in his *Citizen of the World*, is one of the cleverest and most profound uses of a poor, homeless character in eighteenth century literature.

Dixon, Peter. *Oliver Goldsmith Revisited*. Boston: Twayne, 1991. An updated introduction to the life and works of Goldsmith.

Flint, Christopher. "'The Family Piece': Oliver Goldsmith and the Politics of the Everyday in Eighteenth-Century Domestic Portraiture." *Eighteenth-Century Studies* 29 (Winter, 1995/1996): 127-152. Argues that the family portrait in *The Vicar of Wakefield* is typical of family in eighteenth century culture; claims that Goldsmith suggests that both the novel and portraiture are engaged in political acts of domestic regulation free of the corruption often associated with "politics."

Hopkins, Robert H. *The True Genius of Oliver Goldsmith*. Baltimore: The Johns Hopkins University Press, 1969. Hopkins interprets Goldsmith not in the traditional view as the sentimental humanist but as a master of satire and irony. A chapter "Augustanisms and the Moral Basis for Goldsmith's Art" delineates the social, intellectual, and literary context in which Goldsmith wrote. Hopkins devotes a chapter each to Goldsmith's crafts of persuasion, satire, and humor. Includes a detailed examination of *The Vicar of Wakefield*.

Lucy, Séan, ed. *Goldsmith: The Gentle Master*. Cork, Ireland: Cork University Press, 1984. This short but useful collection of essays provides interesting biographical material on Goldsmith, as well as critical comment on his works. An essay on *The Vicar of Wakefield* identifies elements of the Irish narrative tradition in the novel, and other essays examine the themes of exile and prophesy in Goldsmith's poetry and Goldsmith's role as an antisentimental, reforming playwright seeking to revitalize the eighteenth century theater.

Lytton Sells, Arthur. *Oliver Goldsmith: His Life and Works*. New York: Barnes & Nobble Books, 1974. This volume is divided into two sections on Goldsmith's life and works, respectively. Individual chapters focus on particular facets of Goldsmith's work ("The Critic," "The Journalist," "The Biographer") and also feature more detailed studies of major works such as *The Citizen of the World* and *The Vicar of Wakefield*. Contains an extended discussion of Goldsmith as dramatist and poet.

Mikhail, E. H., ed. *Goldsmith: Interviews and Recollections*. New York: St. Martin's Press, 1993. Contains interviews with Goldsmith's friends and associates. Includes bibliographical references and index.

Quintana, Richard. *Oliver Goldsmith: A Georgian Study*. New York: Macmillan, 1967. This work incorporates biography and criticism in a readable account of Goldsmith's colorful life and his development as a writer. Goldsmith's many literary genres are discussed in depth, with chapters on his poetry, drama, essays, and fiction. A lengthy appendix offers notes on Goldsmith's lesser writings, such as his biographical and historical works.

Rousseau, G. S., ed. *Goldsmith: The Critical Heritage*. London: Routledge & Kegan Paul, 1974. A record of critical comment on Goldsmith, this volume is organized by particular works with an additional section on Goldsmith's life and general works. This anthology extends only as far as 1912, but pieces by Goldsmith's contemporaries, such as Sir Joshua Reynolds's sketch of Goldsmith's character, and by later critics such as William Hazlitt and Washington Irving, offer interesting perspectives on Goldsmith's place in literary history.

Swarbrick, Andrew, ed. *The Art of Oliver Goldsmith*. Totowa, N.J.: Barnes & Noble Books, 1984. This excellent collection of ten essays offers a wide-ranging survey of the works of Goldsmith. Essays treat individual works (*The Citizen of the World, The Deserted Village, The Traveller*), as well as more general topics such as the literary context in which Goldsmith wrote, the elements of classicism in his works, and his place in the Anglo-Irish literary tradition.

Kathy Ruth Frazier, updated by
Catherine Swanson

NADINE GORDIMER

Born: Springs, South Africa; November 20, 1923

PRINCIPAL SHORT FICTION

Face to Face: Short Stories, 1949
The Soft Voice of the Serpent and Other Stories, 1952
Six Feet of the Country, 1956
Friday's Footprint and Other Stories, 1960
Not for Publication and Other Stories, 1965
Livingstone's Companions: Stories, 1971
Selected Stories, 1975
A Soldier's Embrace, 1980
Something Out There, 1984
Reflections of South Africa, 1986
Jump and Other Stories, 1991
Crimes of Conscience, 1991
Why Haven't You Written? Selected Stories, 1950-1972, 1992

OTHER LITERARY FORMS

Nadine Gordimer is known for several novels, including *A World of Strangers, Occasion for Loving, The Conservationist* (1974), *Burger's Daughter* (1979), and *The House Gun* (1998), as well as the acclaimed *My Son's Story* (1990). She also contributed to South African scholarship with her books *On the Mines* (1973; with David Goldblatt), *The Black Interpreters* (1973), *Lifetimes Under Apartheid* (1986; with Goldblatt), and *Living in Hope and History: Notes from Our Century* (1999). In 1967, Gordimer edited a study of the literature of her homeland, *South African Writing Today*, with Lionel Abrahams, and in 1988, she published a collection of essays, *The Essential Gesture: Writing, Politics, and Places*, which was edited by Stephen Clingman.

ACHIEVEMENTS

As a courageous chronicler of life in South Africa, Nadine Gordimer is known throughout the world. She received the W. H. Smith and Son Prize in 1971 for *Friday's Footprint and Other Stories*. Two years later she won the James Tait Black Memorial Prize for *A Guest of Honour* (1970). The next year, *The Conservationist* shared with Stanley Middleton's *Holiday* (1974) the prestigious Booker Prize. Gordimer was also a recipient of France's Grand Aigle d'Or, and in 1991 she won the Nobel Prize in Literature.

Gordimer rejected candidacy for the Orange Prize in 1998 because it was restricted to female writers. She is the vice president of PEN International and an executive member of the Congress of South African Writers. Gordimer has been honored with the Modern Literature Association Award and the Bennett Award in the United States and the Chevalier de l'Ordre des Arts et des Lettres in France. Her short fiction has been published in such magazines as *The New Yorker*.

One American reviewer summed up Gordimer's importance in literature, writing: "Gordimer is in the great mainstream of the short story—Maupassant, Chekhov, Turgenev, James, Hemingway, Porter." Most of Gordimer's fiction has been published in paperback form, enabling a greater number of readers and critics to recognize and enjoy her work.

BIOGRAPHY

Nadine Gordimer grew up a rebel. Both parents were immigrants to South Africa; her mother was English, her father an Eastern European Jew. In Springs, the gold-mining town near Johannesburg where she spent her early years, Gordimer frequently played hooky from her convent school. When she did attend, she would sometimes walk out. She found it difficult to tolerate all the pressures for conformity.

In the middle-class environment in which Gordimer grew up, a girl could aspire only to marry and rear a family. After leaving school and then working at a clerical job for a few years, she would be singled out as a prospective wife by a young man who had come from a family very much like her own, and from there, within months she would actualize the greatest dreams of young womanhood: She would have her engagement party, her linen shower, and her wedding ceremony, and she would bear her first child. None of these dreams would be served by a girl's education; books, in perhaps leading her mind astray, would interfere with the years of her preparation for the mold.

At an early age, however, Gordimer did not fit the mold—she was an avid reader. By nine, she was already writing, and at fourteen she won a writing prize. Her favorite authors were Anton Chekhov, W. Somerset Maugham, Guy de Maupassant, D. H. Law-

rence, and the Americans Katherine Anne Porter, O. Henry, and Eudora Welty. As she became a young woman, she became increasingly interested in politics and the plight of black South Africans. She did not, however, launch her writing career as a way to bring change.

A male friend was an important influence on her. He told her that she was ignorant and too accepting of society's values. Gordimer has written, "It was through him, too, that I roused myself sufficiently to insist on going to the university." Since she was twenty-two at the time and still being supported by her father, her family did not appreciate her desire to attend the university.

She commuted to Johannesburg and the University of Witwatersrand. While at the university, she met Uys Krige, an Afrikaans poet who had shunned his Afrikaner heritage, lived in France and Spain, and served with the International Brigade in the Spanish Civil War. He, too, was a profound influence on her. She had been "a bolter," as she put it, at school; she was in the process of bolting from her family and class and the culture of white South Africa, and Krige gave her a final push. She would be committed to honesty alone. She began to send stories to England and the United States. They were well received, and she began to build her reputation as a short-story writer and novelist.

In the 1950's, Gordimer married her first husband, Reinhold Cassirer, a German Jew who had fled Berlin. They had a son, Hugo, with whom she collaborated in the mid-1990's on a documentary about Berlin and Johannesburg. A second marriage produced another child.

In the 1980's Gordimer turned to a new medium. She wrote teleplays of four of her stories—*Praise*, *Oral History*, *Country Lovers*, and *A Chip of Glass Ruby* (all 1985); she also participated in the production of others. Taken together, the films present a compelling vision of Gordimer's South Africa. A filmed interview of Gordimer by Joachim Braun often accompanies the showing of her films. In this interview, Gordimer had many interesting things to say about both her work and the tragic state of her country. Always passionate about politics, Gordimer was a member of the African National Congress during the 1990's.

ANALYSIS

Nadine Gordimer is a distinguished novelist and short-story writer. About *Selected Stories*, drawn from her earlier volumes of stories, a reviewer said, "the stories are marked by the courage of moral vision and the beauty of artistic complexity. Gordimer examines, with passionate precision, the intricacies both of individual lives and of the wide-ranging political and historical forces that contain them." About the stories in *A Soldier's Embrace*, a reviewer wrote, "Their themes are universal: love and change, political transition, family, memory, madness and infidelity, to name a few. . . . What makes Nadine Gordimer such a valuable—and increasingly valued—novelist and short-story writer is her ability to meet the demands of her political conscience without becoming a propagandist and the challenges of her literary commitment without becoming a disengaged esthete." Over the course of her career, three of her books were banned in South Africa.

It would be easy for Gordimer to declare self-exile. Unlike James Joyce, however, she chose not to abandon the inhospitable country of her birth, accepting the obligation of citizenship to help make her country better. She did this by practicing her art, for it is an art that enables her diverse compatriots to understand better themselves and one another.

The settings and characters in Gordimer's stories cut across the whole spectrum of South African life. She writes about black village life and black urban experiences. She writes about the Afrikaans-speaking whites, English-speaking whites, Indians, and others. Her protagonists are as likely to be males as females, and reviewers have commented on her uncanny ability to make her male characters fully realized. In *The House Gun*, Gordimer ponders the deeply personal question of whether parents can even trust their own child not to commit murder. With amazing range and knowledge, she sheds light on the intricacies of individual lives and on the historical and political forces that shape them.

Reading one of Gordimer's stories is always exciting, because one does not know what will have caught her interest—urban or rural blacks, urban or rural Boers, leisured or working or revolutionary whites, an African or a European setting. It is a great surprise, for example, to discover a story in the form of a letter from a dead Prague father to the son who predeceased him. It is a made-up letter in which Hermann Kafka tells off ungrateful, congenitally unhappy Franz.

As she has demonstrated again and again during more than thirty years of writing, Gordimer does not restrict her focus to people and scenes that are the most familiar. One marvels in reading "A City of the Dead, a City of the Living," for example, at what the author, a well-off white woman, knows of black-township life, at the total credibility of characters Samson Moreke and his wife, Nanike. Gordimer's knowledge and credibility are characteristic of all of her short fiction. "A City of the Dead, a City of the Living," "Sins of the Third Age," and "Blinder" could easily be included among the twenty best short stories of the twentieth century.

"IS THERE NOWHERE ELSE WHERE WE CAN MEET?"

Among Gordimer's most gripping stories are those in which blacks and whites are at cross-purposes. "Is There Nowhere Else Where We Can Meet?" from *The Soft Voice of the Serpent and Other Stories*, is one of the simplest and best of this group. On a country road, a young white woman's handbag is torn from her by a passing local, whose bedraggled condition had evoked the woman's pity. The day is very cold, yet he is shoeless and dressed in rags. When she attains safety and has brought her fear under control, she decides not to seek aid or inform the police. "What did I fight for" she thinks. "Why didn't I give him the money and let him go? His red eyes, and the smell and those cracks in his feet, fissures, erosion."

"SIX FEET OF THE COUNTRY"

The title piece of Gordimer's 1956 collection, *Six Feet of the Country*, is another exceptional story. A young black laborer walks from Rhodesia to find work in South Africa, where he has family who are employed on a weekend farm of a white Johannesburg couple. When he arrives at the farm, the illegal immigrant becomes ill and dies. There ensues a prolonged entanglement with the authorities, who insist on having the body so that it can be examined and the bureaucratic requirement for a statement of the cause of death can be fulfilled. With great reluctance, the family surrenders the body. When at last the casket is returned to the farm for burial, they discover that the body in it is that of a stranger. In the course of spinning out a plot about the fate of a corpse, Gordimer provides great insight into the lives of the farm laborers, the proprietors, and the police official, and she also reveals the relative inability of the laborers to deal with illness and the bureaucracy.

"A Chip of Glass Ruby"

"A Chip of Glass Ruby," in *Not for Publication and Other Stories*, is about an Indian family in the Transvaal. The wife and mother is loving and unassuming and a very competent manager of a household that includes nine children. To the chagrin of her husband, Bamjee, she is also a political activist. It makes no sense to him that she takes grave risks for blacks, who are regarded as lower even than Indians. During the course of the story, she is arrested and imprisoned and participates in a prison hunger strike. Bamjee, a poor, small-time fruit and vegetable dealer, cannot understand any of this: He asks, "'What for?' Again and again: 'What for?'" His birthday comes, and he himself does not even remember. The eldest daughter brings word from her mother, in the prison, however, that his birthday must not be forgotten. Bamjee is moved and begins to have a glimmer of understanding of the wonderful woman who is his wife. As the daughter explains: "It's because she always remembers; remembers everything—people without somewhere to live, hungry kids, boys who can't get educated—remembers all the time. That's how Ma is."

"The Intruder"

"The Intruder," which appears in *Livingstone's Companions*, focuses on the decadence of an upper-class man of English descent. After shedding his last wife, hard-drinking, stay-out-late James Seago takes up with the beautiful teenage daughter of Mrs. Clegg, a woman of his age who affects a bohemian morality. Seago refers to the daughter, Marie, whom he uses sexually and enjoys having in his lap as he drinks, as

his teenage doll, his marmoset, his rabbit. Because he has financial problems, Seago is plausibly able to postpone committing himself to her in marriage. Once they are married, Seago's irresponsible life of nightly partying does not change. Having married his pet, however, he must live with her, and so they set up housekeeping in an unpleasant flat. Marie becomes pregnant. The arrival of a child will force changes in Seago's way of life: For one thing, they will have to find living quarters more suitable for a child; for another, his wife-pet will have to give her primary attention to the child, not him. Arriving home early one morning after a night of partying, they fall into bed exhausted. A few hours later, Marie awakens hungry. She wanders out of the bedroom and finds the rest of the flat a wreck. All the kitchen staples have been spilled or thrown about; toothpaste is smeared about the bathroom. In the living room, on one of the sofa cushions, is "a slime of contraceptive jelly with haircombings—hers." Gordimer only hints at the perpetrator. It seems more than likely, though, that it is James Seago, who again is rebelling at the prospect of being forced into a responsible mode of life.

"Abroad"

In "Abroad," the main character is an Afrikaner. Manie Swemmer is a likable, middle-aged widower who has worked hard his entire life at construction and with cars. His grown sons have moved to neighboring black-run Zambia, known as Northern Rhodesia while still a British colony. Manie decides to take the train up to Zambia and visit his sons. Arriving in Lusaka, the capital, Manie is met by his younger son, Willie. Having expected to stay with Willie, Manie is surprised to learn that Willie does not have quarters of his own but is staying at a friend's, where there is no room for his father. To his dismay, Manie learns that all the local hotels are booked. The irrepressible Manie, though, manages to talk the manager of the Regent into placing him in a room that already has been rented as a single. The problem is that it is rented to an Indian, although an educated Indian. Although Manie has been given a key to the room and has placed his belongings inside, when he returns later, the Indian, from the inside, has bolted the door and locked out the Afrikaner. Manie then is offered a bed in a room intended for black guests. The blacks have not yet arrived, and Manie uses the door bolt to lock them out. "Abroad" is a beautiful story about a well-meaning Afrikaner who is excited by the racial mixing of the new nation and who wants to stretch himself to his liberal limit. His feelings toward blacks, though, are still conditioned by his South African base, where all blacks are automatically regarded as inferior. "I've only just got here, give me a bit of time," Manie tells the desk clerk. "You can't expect to put me in with a native, right away, first thing."

"A SOLDIER'S EMBRACE"

Upon gaining its independence from Portugal in 1975, Mozambique became another black-ruled neighbor of South Africa. "A Soldier's Embrace," the title story of Gordimer's 1980 collection, is about the changeover, the exultation, and the disillusionment of a liberal white couple. The story begins with a brilliant scene of the celebration of the victory of the guerrillas who have been fighting the colonial power. Swept up by the street crowd, the woman finds herself embraced by two soldiers, one a white peasant youth, the other a black guerrilla. She puts an arm around each and kisses each on the cheek. Under the new regime, one is certain, a human being will be a human being; all groups will be treated equally. Although many whites take flight to Europe, the woman and her husband, a lawyer, are eager to participate in building the new nation. Weeks and months pass, however, and, despite the friends the lawyer has among highly placed blacks, the government does not ask the lawyer for his services. There is an atmosphere of hostility toward whites. There is looting and violence. When a friend in nearby Rhodesia, soon to be Zimbabwe, offers the lawyer a position in that country, with reluctance and relief he and his wife pack and go. The couple has wanted the country in which they have spent their adult years to be black-run; when that comes about, they find that there is no role for them.

SOMETHING OUT THERE

In the novella that provides the title for Gordimer's volume of short fiction *Something Out There*, a race war looms but has not yet erupted. Acts of violence are taking place; any one of them might well precipitate such a war. In the novella, the "something out there" is a baboon. Gordimer's intention is to suggest that the response of white South Africans to the baboon corresponds to the irrational way they have been responding to the carefully planned symbolic acts of violence by guerrillas. Those acts of violence are handwriting on the wall announcing the coming of race war, which still could be prevented if the writing were read intelligently.

All that the whites want, however, is to be left alone. They want the animal "to be confined in its appropriate place, that's all, zoo or even circus." They want South African blacks to be confined to their appropriate places—locations and townships, black homelands, villages in the bush. As the baboon is "canny about where it was possible somehow to exist off the pickings of plenty," so, too, is the South African black majority, before the cataclysm, somehow able to exist off pickings of white wealth. That wealth will not be shared, only protected, "while charity does not move those who have everything to spare, fear will"—the fear of the baboon, the fear of the guerrilla.

What is the fate of the baboon? It is finally shot and slowly bleeds to death from its wounds. The implication is clear: A similar fate awaits the guerrillas. Gordimer's prime minister speaks: "This government will not stand by and see the peace of mind of its peoples destroyed. . . . We shall not hesitate to strike with all our might at those who harbour terrorists. . . ." The four guerrillas who are the novella's human protagonists, in counterpoint to the movements of the baboon, succeed in blowing up a power station; three escape and it is made clear that they will carry out further attacks. The meaning in this plot—though not in all Gordimer plots on this subject—is that a ruthless government will be a match for those attempting to destroy it.

That the white population is greatly outnumbered makes no difference. They have the honed intelligence, the technology, the will to defend to the death what they have. Racial justice is an idea with which only a few whites—the man and woman on the power-station mission—are concerned. Protecting privilege and property is what most whites care most about. They cannot understand the few who act from disinterested motives. A minor character in "Something Out There" is a decent white police sergeant. He is totally mystified by the white guerrillas whom he interrogates:

> "There's something wrong with all these people who become enemies of their own country. . . . They're enemies because they can't enjoy their lives the way a normal white person in South Africa does."

One of the black guerrillas is dispassionate, determined, fearless Vusi, whose life is dedicated to bringing about black majority rule. Vusi says. "They can't stop us because we can't stop. Never. Every time, when I'm waiting, I know I'm coming nearer." A Vusi, however, is rare. "At the Rendezvous of Victory," another story in this volume, looks ahead to the ultimate black victory. It is about the man who served as commander in chief of the liberation army, known as General Giant. As a warrior, he was invaluable; as a cabinet minister after victory, he is a great burden to his prime minister. He led his people to victory and freedom; in freedom, his chief interest is women.

"A City of the Dead, a City of the Living"

In "A City of the Dead, a City of the Living," a young black man who has committed illegal acts for his people's liberation and who is on the run from the police is given shelter by a township family. With their small house already overcrowded, the family is inconvenienced, but the husband knows his duty. His wife, nursing her fifth child, does not like the idea of taking in a stranger, but the man is pleasant and helpful, and she softens. She softens and begins to feel attracted to him. Frightened, she goes to the police to inform on him, thus betraying the cause of her people's liberation.

"Sins of the Third Age"

"Sins of the Third Age," surprisingly, is not a political story. It is about a couple who survived World War II as displaced persons. Nothing remained of their pasts. They met and in a strange country began to build their lives together. Gordimer is wonderfully evocative as she suggests the passing of years and the

deepening of their love. The wife's job as an interpreter takes her on frequent trips, many times to Rome and Milan. On one of her trips, she gets the idea that they should buy a home in Italy for their retirement, near a Piedmontese village. He retires first and goes to Italy to prepare the house. After several months, he appears suddenly and announces, "I've met somebody." His affair eventually ends, but the betrayal destroys the vitality of the marriage. To have done otherwise than to take her husband for granted would have been betrayal on her part. She trusted, and she loses.

"Blinder"

"Blinder" is still another fine story in the 1984 volume. It is about an aging servant woman's loss of her lover, a man who was the main consolation of her life. Ephraim's first loyalty, however, was to his wife and children in his home village; the wife got his earnings, and after his death, her children get his bicycle. When Ephraim suddenly dies, Rose's white family expected her to increase her drinking, to go on a "blinder." Instead, she plays hostess to Ephraim's wife, who has come to the city to see about a pension.

"The Defeated"

"The Defeated" was originally published in the collection *Why Haven't You Written? Selected Stories, 1950-1972* and was reprinted in 1993. It is a first-person narrative concerning a European Jewish family that runs a concession store for black South Africans in a forbidden, filthy part of town. The narrator, a young girl, befriends Miriam Saiyetovitz, whose immigrant parents work long hours selling goods to indecisive customers. The shop they live above is across from an eating establishment teeming with the smells of slaughtered animals. Mrs. Saiyetovitz, "ugly, with the blunt ugliness of a toad; the ugliness not entirely at home in any element—as if the earth were the wrong place, too heavy and magnetic for a creature already blunt," and her dull husband devote their lives to giving their daughter everything they possibly can. When Miriam describes all the birthday gifts her friend received, her mother assures her they will throw her a huge party. As the two girls grow up together and it comes time for university, Miriam's parents labor to send her to a good college. Miriam grows farther apart from them, moving into the upper classes as she attends pool parties and eventually marries a doctor. Ultimately, she abandons the two people who made her comfortable life possible. When the narrator, now a grown woman, goes to visit Mr. and Mrs. Saiyetovitz, she learns that they hardly see their daughter or her baby son at all.

In "The Defeated," Gordimer conjures up an evocative variety of discordant but powerful moments: the sweaty smell of the black Africans mingling with the odor of bloodied meat, the toadlike mother juxtaposed with her blossoming daughter, the quietly ragefilled father who takes terrible advantage of his status as a white man to humiliate his black customers. Also noticeable is the contrast between the narrator's relatively benign home life and the concession area where black South Africans are forced to shop among the refuse. "The Defeated" deftly envelops in its fold class differences, the burgeoning of female sexuality, and the tragedy of wasted lives, both of immigrants and of dispossessed indigenous peoples. Gordimer does not openly judge Miriam, but it is clear through the telling of her growing alienation that Miriam is only one of the upwardly mobile Afrikaners whose sights are set on material gain and not on remaining true to those who sacrificed happiness for them.

OTHER MAJOR WORKS

LONG FICTION: *The Lying Days*, 1953; *A World of Strangers*, 1958; *Occasion for Loving*, 1963; *The Late Bourgeois World*, 1966; *A Guest of Honour*, 1970; *The Conservationist*, 1974; *Burger's Daughter*, 1979; *July's People*, 1981; *A Sport of Nature*, 1987; *My Son's Story*, 1990; *None to Accompany Me*, 1994; *The House Gun*, 1998.

TELEPLAYS: *A Chip of Glass Ruby*, 1985; *Country Lovers*, 1985; *Oral History*, 1985; *Praise*, 1985.

NONFICTION: *On the Mines*, 1973 (with David Goldblatt); *The Black Interpreters*, 1973; *Lifetimes Under Apartheid*, 1986 (with Goldblatt); *The Essential Gesture: Writing, Politics, and Places*, 1988 (Stephen Clingman, editor); *Conversations with Nadine Gordimer*, 1990 (Nancy Topping Bazin and Marilyn Dallman Seymour, editors); *Three in a Bed: Fiction, Morals, and Politics*, 1991; *Writing and Being*, 1995; *Living in Hope and History: Notes from Our Century*, 1999.

EDITED TEXT: *South African Writing Today*, 1967 (with Lionel Abrahams).

BIBLIOGRAPHY

Bazin, Nancy Topping, and Marilyn Dallman Seymour, eds. *Conversations with Nadine Gordimer*. Jackson: University Press of Mississippi, 1990. The scope of this volume renders it invaluable. It reveals some of Gordimer's insights and attitudes toward her works and their origins, in conversations spanning thirty years. Supplemented by an index and a bibliography.

Cooke, John. *The Novels of Nadine Gordimer: Private Lives, Public Landscapes*. Baton Rouge: Louisiana State University Press, 1985. Cooke discusses Gordimer's development as a writer of fiction. Cooke focuses on the individual, tracing the shift in Gordimer's identity from colonial writer, to South African writer, and, even further, to African writer. Cooke provides valuable interpretation of, and critical insight into, Gordimer's work. Complemented by useful bibliographies and an index.

Ettin, Andre Vogel. *Betrayals of the Body Politic: The Literary Commitments of Nadine Gordimer*. Charlottesville: University Press of Virginia, 1995. Ettin examines all Gordimer's genres of writing and discovers the recurring themes: betrayal, politics of family, concept of homeland, ethnicity, and feminism.

Haugh, Robert F. *Nadine Gordimer*. New York: Twayne, 1974. Haugh provides the first book-length study of Nadine Gordimer's work and places her among the masters of short fiction (he finds her novels less impressive). His analysis stops with *A Guest of Honour* and *Livingstone's Companions*. Includes bibliographical references and an index.

Lazar, Karen. "Feminism as 'Piffling'? Ambiguities in Nadine Gordimer's Short Stories." In *The Later Fiction of Nadine Gordimer*, edited by Bruce

King. New York: St. Martin's Press, 1993. Examines a number of Gordimer's short stories in terms of her changing attitudes toward women's oppression and feminism, ranging from her early view that many women's issues are "piffling" to views that reveal Gordimer's politicization on the question of gender.

Lomberg, Alan R. "Once More into the Burrows: Nadine Gordimer's Later Short Fiction." In *The Later Fiction of Nadine Gordimer*, edited by Bruce King. New York: St. Martin's Press, 1993. An analysis of how Gordimer continues to examine concerns raised in early stories in her later ones. After discussing how two early stories are developed into a later novella, Lomberg analyzes other stories that Gordimer has written again and again, particularly those that treat love affairs.

Smith, Rowland, ed. *Critical Essays on Nadine Gordimer*. Boston: G. K. Hall, 1990. An excellent selection of essays on Gordimer's works. Includes bibliographical references and an index.

Temple-Thurston, Barbara. *Nadine Gordimer Revisited*. New York: Twayne, 1999. Part of Twayne's World Authors series, this is a good updated study of the author and her works. Bibliographical references and an index are provided.

Trump, Martin. "The Short Fiction of Nadine Gordimer." *Research in African Literatures* 17 (Spring, 1986): 341-369. Argues that in her best stories Gordimer describes the hardships of South Africans, particularly women, who suffer social inequality; summarizes a number of stories that illustrate this focus.

Paul Marx, updated by
Carol Bishop

CAROLINE GORDON

Born: Todd County, Kentucky; October 6, 1895
Died: San Cristóbal de las Casas, Mexico; April 11, 1981

PRINCIPAL SHORT FICTION

The Forest of the South, 1945
Old Red and Other Stories, 1963
The Collected Stories of Caroline Gordon, 1981

OTHER LITERARY FORMS

Caroline Gordon was a distinguished novelist, short-story writer, essayist, and literary critic. In the field of literary criticism, she is admired for her contributions to New Criticism and to theories of form and symbolic structure. Her most famous work of literary criticism, written with her husband, Allen Tate, is *The House of Fiction: An Anthology of the Short Story* (1950), an anthology of short stories designed to illustrate methods for reading and interpreting fiction.

ACHIEVEMENTS

Caroline Gordon's novels and short fiction reveal her concerns with a sense of order and tradition in a world where those qualities are increasingly at risk, the world of the rural South. Her interest in those themes and settings reveals her intellectual ties to the New Critics; like them, she rejected popular, sentimental pictures of the region, finding meaning instead in rituals such as hunting and fishing, which gave dignity and moral order to a chaotic world. Her conversion to Roman Catholicism in 1947 gives an extra dimension to her later work. Her careful style and concern with point of view have also caused her to be compared with Henry James. During her lifetime, Gordon received a John Simon Guggenheim Memorial Foundation Fellowship in creative writing, won the O. Henry Short-Story Award for "Old Red," and was given honorary doctorates by Bethany College, Purdue University, and St. Mary's College. In 1966, she received a grant of ten thousand dollars from the National Council of Arts.

BIOGRAPHY

Caroline Gordon was graduated from Bethany College, Bethany, West Virginia, in 1916. From 1920 to 1924, she served as a reporter for the *Chattanooga News*; an article she wrote in 1923 on the Fugitive writers of Nashville brought her to the attention of members of that group, especially Allen Tate, whom she married in 1924 and divorced in 1959. In 1929, she was awarded a John Simon Guggenheim Memorial Foundation Fellowship in creative writing and traveled to England and France; during the year, she also worked, for brief intervals, as a secretary to novelist Ford Madox Ford, who was instrumental in encouraging her to publish several of her short stories and her first novel. Gordon taught at the University of North Carolina, the University of Washington, the University of California, Davis, and Purdue University. In 1947, Gordon became a member of the Catholic Church, a fact which a number of critics have seen as influencing the themes and the highly moral cast of her later writings.

ANALYSIS

A modernist in style and technique, Caroline Gordon is decidedly antimodern in the themes of her writings. Among American authors, she is similar to Willa Cather in decrying the spiritual corruption of the modern industrial age and in lauding as an ideal a return to the humanistic values of an agrarian society. While the frontier serves as the backdrop for Willa Cather's idealizations of pastoralism, the South and its heritage provide the setting for romantic explorations of Nature's influence upon human beings' ethical development in Gordon's fiction.

The thematics of Gordon's fiction and her own avowed interest in the southern gestalt identify her strongly with the literary movement known as the Southern Renaissance. Initiated around 1920 and encompassing the Fugitive writers, the movement worked to revive through art and literature a rebirth of interest in southern ideals and values, particularly those of the agrarian, pre-Civil War South. The renaissance in southern letters strove to eliminate from

Caroline Gordon (Library of Congress)

portrayals of the South the false sentimentality and excessive romanticism characteristic of the writings of the Old South and to uphold, instead, the view of the South as the repository of humanistic values and a viable alternative to the dehumanizing effects of modern materialism and industrialization. The views of the Southern Renaissance can be seen most clearly in Gordon's choice of heroes in her fiction. Her heroes generally are emblematic of the southern agrarian ideal, individualistic, self-reliant characters exemplifying a deep love of Nature and a respect for the values of community and family heritage. A strong sense of place or devotion to the land as symbolic of higher spiritual qualities in human existence is also readily apparent, together with respect for those characters who shape their destinies in accord with ethical values.

A number of Gordon's heroes in her fiction are sportsmen whose dedicated passion for Nature is the focal point of their lives and the source of their awareness of aesthetic and spiritual values. From their relationship with Nature, they learn moral lessons which inspire them to the higher values of courage, compassion, and sacrifice. Often, the sportsman hero is contrasted directly with those characters of lessened moral awareness who see Nature as only a means to an end of self-gratification or materialistic greed.

"THE LAST DAY IN THE FIELD"

Typical of the sportsman hero is Aleck Maury, the protagonist of "The Last Day in the Field" and a character who appears in several of Gordon's short stories in *The Forest of the South* and in the novel *Aleck Maury, Sportsman,* published in London as *Pastimes of Aleck Maury, The Life of a True Sportsman.* In "The Last Day in the Field," Aleck Maury is presented to the reader as a once-vigorous sportsman now grown old and having to confront both his own physical limitations and his own mortality. Aleck is like "the fall when the leaves stayed green so long"; in watching the progress of the frost on the elderberry bushes, he sees symbolized his own existence: "The lower, spreading branches had turned yellow and were already sinking to the ground but the leaves in the top clusters still stood up stiff and straight." Thinking of how the frost creeps higher out of the ground each night, Aleck remarks to himself, "Ah-ha, it'll get you yet!" aware that old age will take its toll upon him soon—but not before he has his "last day in the field."

Aleck's wife, Molly, urges him not to hunt this year, reminding him of the pain in his leg from a previous hunting injury; at first Aleck agrees to her wisdom, but when the killing frost comes, bringing with it the scents and colors of the perfect hunting day, Aleck is off before dawn to awaken Joe Thomas, the young man next door, and go quail hunting. The two men experience the ritualistic pleasure of preparing for the hunt, with Aleck making some sandwiches and coffee to take on the trip while Joe hitches up the buggy and gathers up the hunting gear. When all is ready in preparation, the men get the dogs, Bob and Judy, a matched set of liver-and-white pointers and two of the finest hunting dogs in the country.

The ride from Gloversville to Spring Creek takes more than an hour, and when the men arrive the dogs are eager to track down some quail. Joe sets the dogs free, and they find their first bevy of quail in the bottomlands of a corn field. Joe takes the easiest shot and bags a bird; Aleck, characteristically, takes the shot requiring the most skill and patience and gets the best bird of the lot. After several more shots at singles, the men stop to eat lunch. Aleck notices Bob, the hunting dog, and senses an empathetic comradeship with his spirit. Aleck reflects, "I looked at him and thought how different he was from his mate and like some dogs I had known—and men, too—who lived only for hunting and could never get enough no matter how long the day was." The men walk through several more fields, and Aleck feels the pain building steadily in his leg. He wonders if he will be able to make it through the day, at the same time that he laments deeply that the day is going by so quickly and soon the perfect hunting day of this season will be over. Joe misses an easy shot, and Aleck shares with him some of his accumulated wisdom gathered through many such days in the field. An empathy develops between the two men, and Aleck feels even more keenly his own age and a deep longing to be young again and have so much time ahead.

At twilight, the men begin the walk back to the buggy. Aleck's leg is hurting him badly, and he fears that he cannot make the journey back. At that moment, the men climb a fence and come out at one end of a long field, "as birdy a place as ever I saw," Aleck thinks to himself, and Aleck knows that no matter how much pain he is in he has to hunt that field, "leg or no leg." Aleck and Joe shoot two quail, and, as Aleck is retreating from the field, he spots Bob making a perfect sighting and points on the last quail from the last covey of the day. "Your shot," Aleck tells Joe, but Joe replies, "No, you take it." In the fading light, Aleck gets the bird with the third shot. "I saw it there for a second, its wings black against the gold light, before, wings still spread, it came whirling down, like an autumn leaf, like the leaves that were everywhere about us, all over the ground."

"The Last Day in the Field" is a descriptive story, working to capture a mood and a setting as a man who loves hunting faces the fact that he must soon give it up and seeks to draw all the beauty, feeling, and meaning he can from his last experience. The story's action line is a simple one, and there are no major plot twists or conflicts to be resolved. What gives the story its effect and power is its sustained tonal qualities of mood, imagery, and setting that subtly suggest much about Aleck Maury and the world he faces. Contrasting images—the green of fall and the frost of winter, the sunrise of the perfect hunting day and its peaceful close at sunset, Aleck's age and Joe's youth, Molly's practical wisdom and Aleck's passionate response to the beauty and energy of Nature—combine to create in the reader the mood of "the last day in the field" and to convey the insights acquired in these final moments by a man whose spirit is attuned to the meanings and fulfillment Nature has to impart.

"ONE AGAINST THEBES"

The romanticism that pervades much of Gordon's writing reaches its fullest expression in the story "One Against Thebes," a rewritten version of her first published story, "Summer Dust." The line of thematic development presented is almost Keatsian in asserting the primacy of the imagination over the limitations of the real and clearly defined, and there is, too, in the story a strong romantic emphasis upon the beauty of youth and innocence in contrast to the world of experience in which values and the human spirit become corrupted by expediency and failures of moral courage.

The epigraph of the story, "That you shall forever hold this city safe from the men of Thebes, the dragon's sons," indicates that the story's theme is evil and the necessity to protect the city, or human civilization, from evil's encroachment. The inhabitants of Thebes were said to be descended from dragons and to have borne serpent's tails in earlier times. This motif is presented in the story through a number of images which restate the theme of the serpent and emphasize the omnipresence of evil.

The story's protagonist, a small girl, is walking along a dusty road in midsummer. Ahead of her walks a black girl, a black woman, and a black boy; the boy runs behind the woman and lurches from side to side of the road, stirring up clouds of dust that spiral in a trail at his feet. The child looks at the trail and thinks "how it might have been made by a great snake, a serpent as large as any one of them, hurling itself now to one side of the road, now to the other, and thinks, too, how she and the other girl and the boy and even the old woman seem to move in its coils."

The girl's vision of the serpent trail Son has made in the dust as he plays along the road foreshadows her first encounter with evil—a woman, obsessed with greed, who tries to claim for herself peaches that belong to the girl's grandmother; two young men who run a horse several miles, "in August, too, when you're not supposed to lather horses"; and the poverty and loneliness of an old black woman, Aunt Emily, who lives in one of the cabins "in a row back of the big house." The images of imperfection and suffering in the world leave the girl frightened and filled with revulsion, while her older brother's apparent wisdom about the ways of the world and his discussion of "grownup" matters she does not understand leave her confused and isolated. The girl, however, is the only character in the story capable of an act of kindness and of envisioning a better world than the one she encounters. In a moment of empathy and generosity, she slips the *Green Fairy Book* she has read many times into Son's jacket pocket, knowing all the while she will never see the book again. Son runs off to play in the road again, when he comes to a spot where "the trail his feet had made earlier in the afternoon still showed he would whack the dust—as if he were trying the beat a snake to death." The girl follows slowly behind him, "stepping to one side of the road to avoid the serpentine trail that Son's feet had left in the dust." As she walks along the road and clouds of dust envelop her, she recalls the words from the fairy book about how the Fairy Godmother said to the Little Princess that they would ride a cloud to the crystal palace in the woods and there would be waiting for them a gold crown, silver slippers, and a silver veil embroidered with the sun, the moon, and the stars. The concluding image is of the child lost in dream visions of an ideal world in which an escape from ugliness and evil is possible. In the real world, where no such escape is truly possible, the only avenue of amelioration is compassion and the strength to ward off the serpent.

"THE ICE HOUSE"

One of Gordon's most undervalued stories is "The Ice House," a work which expresses both her interest in southern themes and her allegiance to humanistic values. The story takes place a year after the Civil War and is set in an old ice house in the South where the bodies of Union soldiers were hurriedly buried during a battle in 1862. The story focuses upon two young southern boys, Doug and Raeburn, and a Yankee contractor. The contractor has hired the boys to go into the ice house and dig up the skeletons of the Union soldiers, which he will then place in coffins and deliver to the United States government at so much "a head." After a day of long, hard labor, the contractor pays the boys and tells them he won't be needing them any longer. The boys are surprised, since they were originally told they would be hired for three or four days' work. Doug hangs back in some bushes to see what the contractor will do after they leave and discovers that the man is rearranging the skeletons in the pine coffins. When Raeburn asks Doug what he thinks the contractor is doing, Doug responds, "He dividing up them skeletons so he can get paid double." Later, walking home, Doug stops and tells Raeburn, "There ain't a whole man in any one of them boxes. If that ain't a Yankee fer ye!"

The story would be a slight one in both meaning and impact were it not for the fact that Gordon uses it to contrast, through the characters of Doug and Raeburn, the values of materialism and the values of humanism. Doug shares the values and the worldview of the Yankee contractor; he is a materialist at heart, interested only in opportunity and economic gain. When the boys meet on the road to begin the job, it is Doug who chides Raeburn for being late and for not being excited about all the money they are going to make. When he senses that Raeburn feels uneasy about digging up dead bodies, Doug tells him he can always get somebody else. Digging up the bodies is just a job to Doug, and he is not personally involved with it as Raeburn is. "Handlin' a dead Yankee ain't no more to *me*," Doug says, "than handlin' a dead hawg." As the two boys arrive, the Yankee contractor calls out to them, "Well boys, I see you're like me. Early risers." The emphasis here is upon the work

ethic, and Doug is very much a product of this mind-set, while Raeburn prefers to be a little late and at least get his breakfast. Doug is the first to take a pick and begin the gruesome business of unearthing the bodies after the contractor tells them the faster they get done the sooner they get their money. Raeburn hesitates and moves more slowly, aware of what lies ahead.

As the work progresses, Doug is largely insensitive to the skeletons he unearths and to the lives they once contained. Raeburn, however, pauses to look out over the field where the battle was fought and envisions the suffering that must have occurred. When the boys and the contractor break for lunch, Raeburn cannot eat because of a "sick feeling" that sweeps over him. Doug suffers from no such problem and spends the period discussing with the contractor government jobs and whether the man is paid by the day or by the job. When the boys tell the contractor they plan to do farm work after this job, he tells them that farm work is "all right if you can't get nothing else to do" but that smart young boys like they are should be "looking out for oppertunity." He adds, "The folks at home all thought I was mighty foolish when I come down to this country, but I knew they was oppertunity in the South . . . bound to be."

The contractor, like Doug, sees the South and the skeletons in the ice house as "oppertunity." The reasons the men died and the values they fought to uphold have no meaning. The materialism of the post-Civil War era is rampant; it has invaded the ice house and turned the skeletons of men who died believing in a cause into so many dollars of profit per coffin. The stark contrast in moral values in the story is between the exploiters, who simply profit from other men's battles, and the believers, like the soldiers, who are capable of commitments beyond the self and of sacrifices at great cost. "The Ice House" confirms Gordon's belief, apparent in the entire canon of her writings, that the battle of the modern era is not between sectional rivalries but between those sensitive to man's potential for higher ideals and spiritual purpose in his life and those who wish only to exploit and corrupt for their own self-serving purposes.

OTHER MAJOR WORKS

LONG FICTION: *Penhally*, 1931; *Aleck Maury, Sportsman*, 1934; *None Shall Look Back*, 1937; *The Garden of Adonis*, 1937; *Green Centuries*, 1941; *The Women on the Porch*, 1944; *The Strange Children*, 1951; *The Malefactors*, 1956; *The Glory of Hera*, 1972.

NONFICTION: *How to Read a Novel*, 1957; *A Good Soldier: A Key to the Novels of Ford Madox Ford*, 1963; *The Southern Mandarins: Letters of Caroline Gordon to Sally Wood, 1924-1937*, 1984.

EDITED TEXT: *The House of Fiction: An Anthology of the Short Story*, 1950 (with Allen Tate).

BIBLIOGRAPHY

Arbery, Virginia L. "'Considerable Emphasis on Decorum': Caroline Gordon and the Abyss." *Modern Age* 36 (Winter, 1994): 157-164. Discusses her fiction that makes use of American history and her depiction of the hero and the pattern of sacred marriage. Argues that critics have inadvertently depreciated the centrality of her often stated claim that women are always on the lookout for heroes.

Fritz-Piggott, Jill. "The Dominant Chord and the Different Voice: The Sexes in Gordon's Stories." In *The Female Tradition in Southern Literature*, edited by Carol S. Manning. Urbana: University of Illinois Press, 1993. Argues that the most general fact about gender in Gordon's stories is that they are told by different male and female voices. Analyzes some of Gordon's stories in which an individual confronts a force as the Other against which the self is defined.

Jonza, Nancylee Novell. *The Underground Stream: The Life and Art of Caroline Gordon*. Athens: University of Georgia Press, 1995. A good, updated biography of Gordon. Includes bibliographical references and an index.

Landless, Thomas H., ed. *The Short Fiction of Caroline Gordon: A Critical Symposium*. Irving, Tex.: University of Dallas Press, 1972. Contains one essay on the Aleck Maury stories and another essay that provides an extensive discussion on "The Captive." Nature, sex, and the political implications of the South form subjects for some of the other essays.

Lindberg-Seyersted, Brita, ed. *A Literary Friendship: Correspondence Between Caroline Gordon and Ford Madox Ford*. Knoxville: University of Tennessee Press, 1999. Letters between two acclaimed authors. Provides an index.

Makowsky, Veronica A. *Caroline Gordon: A Biography*. New York: Oxford University Press, 1989. Although this work is primarily a biography, it contains extensive analysis of the fiction, including many of the short stories.

Rocks, James E. "The Short Fiction of Caroline Gordon." *Tulane Studies in English* 18 (1970): 115-135. Discusses the basic theme of natural and supernatural grace in the stories. Analyzes the irony in "Her Quaint Honor," the dichotomy between physical and mental insight in "Last Day in the Field," and the telescoping of time in "Old Red."

Stuckey, W. J. *Caroline Gordon*. New York: Twayne, 1972. A brief biography and a detailed analysis of Gordon's novels and some of the short stories, especially "Old Red," "The Captive," "The Last Day in the Field," "Her Quaint Honor," and "Brilliant Leaves."

Waldron, Ann. *Close Connections: Caroline Gordon and the Southern Renaissance*. New York: Putnam, 1987. A literary biography that concentrates on Gordon's connections with other writers in the "Southern Renaissance" and their mutual influence.

*Christina Murphy, updated by
Ann Davison Garbett*

MARY GORDON

Born: Far Rockaway, New York; December 8, 1949

PRINCIPAL SHORT FICTION
Temporary Shelter, 1987
The Rest of Life: Three Novellas, 1993

OTHER LITERARY FORMS

Mary Gordon has been most recognized for her novels. *Final Payments* (1978), *The Company of Women* (1980), and *Men and Angels* (1985) all received praise for her examination of themes concerning women, Roman Catholicism, and art. Gordon has also published *Good Boys and Dead Girls: And Other Essays* (1991) and a personal memoir of her father, *The Shadow Man: A Daughter's Search for Her Father* (1996).

ACHIEVEMENTS

Mary Gordon received the Janet Heidinger Kafka Prize from the University of Rochester for *Final Payments* in 1979 and for *The Company of Women* in 1981.

BIOGRAPHY

Mary Catherine Gordon was born in 1948 in Far Rockaway, New York, to a working-class, Irish Catholic family. Her father was an important early influence in her life, teaching her to read and encouraging her to write. She was only seven when he died, leaving her devastated. She thus grew up in a female household inhabited by her mother, an aunt, and her grandmother. The latter two were rigid in their piety and unsympathetic toward Gordon's literary interests. Gordon attended parochial school and originally planned to become a nun.

Her rebellious nature began to manifest itself during her high school years, and she chose to attend Barnard College instead of Catholic Fordham University. During her university years in the 1960's, she was exhilarated by the sense of freedom and experimentation on campus. Antiwar demonstrations, the women's movement, and the life of the countercul-

ture caused her to question Catholicism's stance on sex and on the role of women in the church. After college she began graduate work at Syracuse University and participated in a women's writers' group. She began to publish poems and short stories while working on a dissertation on Virginia Woolf. When her third novel was published, she gave up her graduate work.

When Gordon began researching a biography of her father, she was forced to see that most of what he had claimed about himself was untrue. He had come from an immigrant Jewish family and had converted to Roman Catholicism; he had never attended Harvard University or lived in Paris; his writing was labored and pretentious, bigoted and anti-Semitic. These discoveries were painful for Gordon but confronting them marked a new direction in her writing. Gordon married and settled with her husband and children in New York City, teaching creative writing at Barnard College.

ANALYSIS

Mary Gordon's early novels, *Final Payments* and *The Company of Women*, developed religious themes that labeled her a Catholic novelist, a title she rejected. Her later work has moved away from dealing explicitly with religion. In both those early works, a young woman wrestles with conflicts between her repressive Catholic upbringing and her desire for independence. In *Final Payments* the repressive force is a father; in *The Company of Women* it is a priest. Even in *Spending: A Utopian Divertimento* (1998), a novel which seems intent on avoiding expressly religious material, the conflict exists submerged in the novel's narrator.

Parents and children, especially fathers and daughters, play important roles in Gordon's work. The repressive adult, who is unsympathetic to a child's fears, is a common figure and appears repeatedly in the stories of *Temporary Shelter*. Similarly Gordon has been interested in the position of the immigrant Irish person in America, who often faces the same sort of conflict that divides parents and children. How can the children of a New World meet the demands of parents who grew up in the Old? How can immigrants find a place in the New World? These questions form much of the theme of *The Other Side* (1989), a novel about three generations of an Irish American family.

Many critics found Gordon's early work weak in its portrayal of men and ascribed that weakness to Gordon's own conflicts between the official morality of the Church and her understanding of human passions. Her later work, especially *The Rest of Life* and *Spending*, seem determined to correct that weakness by giving close attention to sexual relations between men and women, and in interviews Gordon has wondered how readers of her early work will respond to so much explicit sex.

"Delia"

"Delia" is one of three stories with interrelated characters from Gordon's early collection, *Temporary Shelter*. They focus on four Irish American sisters and their position in America—beautiful Kathleen (whose daughter Nora was born with one leg shorter than the other), sharp-tongued Bridget, tiny Nettie, and Delia, the youngest and best looking of the group, who marries a Protestant and moves away, to the dismay of her sisters. Only Nora's kindly mother defends Delia's husband, John Taylor, because he was kind to Nora. The others assume that he and Delia will have Protestant children and that Delia will be lost to them forever.

After Delia writes that she is pregnant with her first child, no further news is heard. Meanwhile, Kathleen also becomes pregnant. Delia's due date passes without news. At last Kathleen is in labor, and while young Nora is sitting on the porch, listening to her mother's cries, John Taylor appears. He intends to speak to Kathleen, but when he learns that she is in labor, he loses courage and instead gives his message to Nora: Delia died two months earlier while giving birth to a stillborn child. He gives Nora a silver dollar to buy her silence for what he mysteriously says will be their secret. Somehow Delia's exposure to American culture proved toxic, just as her sisters had predicted.

Mary Gordon in 1993 (AP/Wide World Photos)

"Agnes"

"Agnes" is the second of the *Temporary Shelter* stories to deal with Nora's family. Like "Delia," it is told partly from Nora's point of view. Agnes is the common-law wife of Nora's uncle Desmond, a bootlegger. For a decade the family suffered both because of Desmond's periodic skirmishes with the law and because of Agnes's sinful living arrangement with him. Nora once liked Uncle Desmond, but as she has matured she has come to see him as an embarrassment. Agnes also embarrasses her; dowdy and common, she has too little self-respect to leave the affair.

Desmond suddenly leaves Agnes to move to California to marry a girl whom Nora's father labels "a rich girl whose family threw her out for marrying a greenhorn." Nora's contempt for Agnes grows as Agnes continues to write Desmond. When Agnes learns that Desmond's wife is pregnant, she even wonders if she should go to California to help with the new baby. When Desmond's wife learns of their correspondence and forces him to break it off, Agnes hangs herself. For that sin, she must be buried in an unsanctified cemetery by a Presbyterian undertaker. After the death, Nora bitterly concludes that the real lesson is that the world has no place for women like Agnes.

"EILEEN"

"Eileen," the last of the Nora stories, chronicles the fate of Eileen Foley, who left her job in a Limerick orphanage to come to America, where she hoped to make enough money to bring over her youngest brother, Tom. Nora liked Eileen when she lived with Nora's family for a few months, but in the intervening years Nora has learned a cruel lesson. The nuns who had encouraged her to apply to a teachers' college failed to mention her disability in their recommendation. She was thrilled to be accepted to the school, but on her arrival she was quickly dismissed on account of her short leg and crutch. Now she has taken an educational course and become an excellent secretary, but her idealism has been blasted and her new cynicism convinces her that the bright but childish Tom will never be successful in America. When Tom is killed in a freak accident, Eileen decides to return to Ireland. Like Nora, she has lost faith in America as a land of opportunity, the theme suggested by all three stories.

THE REST OF LIFE

In each of the three novellas of *The Rest of Life*, a woman narrates the story of her most important lover. In *Immaculate Man* a social worker describes her long affair with Clement, a priest, and the circumstances that have made an ally of Father Boniface, an older priest who also loves Clement. In *Living at Home*, a psychiatrist, who specializes in work with autistic children, describes her marriage to an Italian journalist, Lauro, a man who seems to be her psychic opposite. In *The Rest of Life*, an old woman (from whose point of view much of the story is told) is taken back to the Italian town of her birth by her eager son and his girlfriend. As she travels, she relives her adolescent romance with Leo, a Marxist and a poet, with whom she made a suicide pact.

Each of the novellas examines the ways in which men and women use each other in love. The narrator of *Immaculate Man* loves Clement but suspects that to him she is a means of leaving the priesthood. The narrator of *Living at Home* feeds on Lauro's vitality but understands that he values her mostly for her body and for the haven their home provides him in his nomadic life. In *The Rest of Life*, the most complex of the narratives, the narrator reveals that Leo used her to massage his own ego. Nevertheless, her guilt at having backed out of the pact while Leo died has tainted her life and added to her guilt at having disappointed her beloved father. Although the three narratives share a focus on character rather than on events, the central character of *The Rest of Life* relives the day of the suicide pact and its humiliating consequences, making this the most conventional of the three works.

OTHER MAJOR WORKS

LONG FICTION: *Final Payments*, 1978; *The Company of Women*, 1980; *Men and Angels*, 1985; *The Other Side*, 1989; *Spending: A Utopian Divertimento*, 1998.

NONFICTION: *Good Boys and Dead Girls: And Other Essays*, 1991; *The Shadow Man: A Daughter's Search for Her Father*, 1996; *Seeing Through Places: Reflections on Geography and Identity*, 2000; *Joan of Arc*, 2000.

BIBLIOGRAPHY

Becker, Brenda L. "Virgin Martyrs." *The American Spectator* 14 (August, 1981): 28-32. This is a stringent but not unfriendly discussion of Gordon's first two novels. Becker praises depictions of female friendships and the workings of the Catholic Church but faults her for her heavy-handed symbolism and her portrayals of men.

Corrigan, Maureen. "*Spending: A Utopian Divertimento*." *The Nation* (March 16, 1998): 29-32. In this review of Gordon's work, Corrigan sees the steamy sexuality of this novel's narrator as a reaction to her earlier models of Catholic guilt. She praises her humor and her sharp portrayal of the artist's vision, but she faults the central theme, which she compares with a Harlequin romance.

Dwyer, June. "Unappealing Ethnicity Meets Unwelcoming America: Immigrant Self-Fashioning in Mary Gordon's *Temporary Shelter*." *Melus* 22 (Fall, 1997): 103-112. Despite the forbidding title and a rather ponderous introduction, this essay is a thoughtful examination of conflicts inherent in the immigrant experience: Immigrants must face the realities of their new country while they must also confront the dominant culture's images of them. Most of the discussion concerns the Nora stories in this collection.

Gordon, Mary. "An Interview with Mary Gordon." Interview by Sandy Asirvatham. *Poets and Writers* (July/August, 1997): 50-61. This meaty interview focuses on Gordon's work methods and influences. It includes some brief analysis of her novels and gives more detailed attention to the significance of her discoveries about her father.

Lee, Don. "About Mary Gordon." *Ploughshares* 23 (Fall, 1997): 218-226. A detailed biography that concentrates on the relationship between Gordon's life and her fiction.

Powers, Elizabeth. "Doing Daddy Down." *Commentary* 103 (June, 1997): 38-42. Powers discusses what she sees as the repudiation of fathers in the work of three recent writers, including Gordon in *The Shadow Man*. In Powers's rather harsh judgment, Gordon's dismay at the truths she discovered about her father stem from her political liberalism and her quarrels with the Catholic Church rather than from any deeper reasons.

Ann Davison Garbett

MAXIM GORKY
Aleksey Maksimovich Peshkov

Born: Nizhniy-Novgorod, Russia; March 28, 1868
Died: Gorki, U.S.S.R.; June 18, 1936

PRINCIPAL SHORT FICTION

"Chelkash," 1895 (English translation, 1901)
Ocherki i rasskazy, 1898-1899 (3 volumes)
Rasskazy i p'esy, 1901-1910 (9 volumes)
Orloff and His Wife: Tales of the Barefoot Brigade, 1901
Skazki ob Italii, 1911-1913 (*Tales of Italy*, 195-?)
Tales of Two Countries, 1914
Po Rusi, 1915 (*Through Russia*, 1921)
Chelkash and Other Stories, 1915
Stories of the Steppe, 1918
Zametki iz dnevnika: Vospominaniia, 1924 (*Fragments from My Diary*, 1924)
Rasskazy 1922-1924 godov, 1925
Selected Short Stories, 1959
A Sky-Blue Life and Selected Stories, 1964
The Collected Short Stories of Maxim Gorky, 1988

OTHER LITERARY FORMS

Maxim Gorky wrote in many genres, including several novels, of which *Foma Gordeyev* (1899; English translation, 1901), *Mat* (1906; *Mother*, 1906), *Delo Artamonovykh* (1925; *Decadence*, 1927; also known as *The Artamonov Business* (1927), and *Zhizn Klima Samgina* (1927-1936; *The Life of Klim Samgin*, 1930-1938) are the best known. He also wrote several plays, among which the most acclaimed is *Na dne* (pr., pb. 1902; *The Lower Depths*, 1912). His three-part autobiography, *Detstvo* (1913; *My Childhood*, 1915), *V lyudyakh* (1916; *In the World*, 1917), and *Moi universitety* (1923; *My Universities*, 1923), is perhaps his most moving work. His reminiscences of literary friends, as well as his letters, are valuable documents for the literary history and atmosphere of his time.

ACHIEVEMENTS

Maxim Gorky appeared at the end of the nineteenth century and of the Golden Age of Russian literature. Thus he spent most of his career writing in the shadow of the giants. Caught in the revolutionary spirit, he spent his entire life fighting for a better lot for his people, mostly through his writings. He was the founder of the new realistic trend best suited for that purpose. To that end he wrote many works, depicting the depth of social injustice and poverty of his people, as best illustrated in his play *The Lower Depths*. During the revolution, he strove to preserve Russian culture threatened by the wanton destruction, and he did his best to help young writers. In the last years of his life, he was revered as the doyen of Soviet literature, even though he distanced himself from the excesses of the revolution. Some of his stories, novels, and plays are considered to belong to the best works in Russian literature of the twentieth century.

BIOGRAPHY

Maxim Gorky was born Aleksey Maksimovich Peshkov on March 28, 1868, in a central Russian town, Nizhniy-Novgorod, into a small-merchant family. The family became impoverished in his child-

Maxim Gorky (Library of Congress)

hood, and when Gorky was three, his father died and his mother remarried. After she died, he went to live with his grandparents but left home at fifteen, looking for work. He wandered through Russia for several years. At one time, he attempted suicide because of his hard life. Then, he met one of the leading Russian writers, Vladimir Korolenko, and his life was changed forever, as he discovered an ability and urge to write. He published his first story, "Makar Chudra," in 1892, under the pseudonym of Maxim Gorky ("Maxim the Bitter"), a name that he kept throughout his career. He continued to write at a steady pace for the rest of his life.

He was arrested as a political activist in 1898, an event that foreshadowed a lifetime of revolutionary activity. The publication in 1899 of his first novel, *Foma Gordeyev*, established him as a leading younger writer and brought him the friendship of Leo Tolstoy, Anton Chekhov, and other well-known writers. He was arrested again but released at Tolstoy's intervention. He fled to Finland, visited the United States in 1906, and settled on the Italian island of Capri, where he met Vladimir Ilich Lenin and other Russian luminaries, who flocked to him as on a pilgrimage. He returned to Russian in 1913, continued the revolutionary struggle, and was arrested several more times before the Revolution of 1917. During the revolution, he lent total support to the Bolshevik cause. At the same time, he was appalled by the excesses and brutality of the civil war, and he tried to save what he could of Russian culture threatened by the revolution. He also helped established writers to survive by organizing, translating, and publishing activities, and he also encouraged the younger ones to write.

By then, he was a world-famous figure, his works having been published in many countries. In 1921, he left Russia for Capri, where he stayed for seven years, ostensibly for his health but more likely because of his disagreement with the developments in postrevolutionary Russia. In 1928, he made peace with the country's leaders and returned to Russia. He spent the rest of his life being revered as the patriarch of Soviet letters, yet, strangely enough, he never wrote anything with the Soviet reality as a subject matter. His health, which was poor throughout his life, deteriorated severely, and he died in 1936 from tuberculosis, although rumors about foul play persist to this day. He was buried in the Kremlin as a national figure, and his hometown was renamed for him.

ANALYSIS

Maxim Gorky's short stories offer a composite portrait of a writer dedicated to his craft but also to the solution of the pressing problems of his society. The main features of this portrait reveal Gorky as an idealist, a humanitarian, a revolutionary, and a realist. Often, several of these traits are combined. There is a distinct constancy in his views and attitudes and in his desire to lend his talent to the service of both his literary vocation and the bettering of the lives of his compatriots.

"THE SONG OF THE FALCON"

Gorky's idealism is best illustrated by the short-short story, actually a poem in prose, "Pesnia o sokole" ("The Song of the Falcon"). In this early story, his belief in human beings' dignity, yearning for freedom, and lofty aspirations is manifested by the glorification of a stately bird, a falcon, which soars majestically through vast blue expanses. At the same time, a snake on the ground is bound to its low-level existence, and when it tries to imitate the falcon, it falls from a cliff from which it attempted to fly. With the help of these symbols, Gorky expresses a notion that human beings' destiny can resemble the soaring flight of a falcon if they strive for it; if not, theirs is the lot of a snake. It is an act of faith on his part, perhaps more of a hope, that humankind can realize its lofty aspirations. This faith or hope reveals Gorky's tendency to romanticize human potential, prompting some critics to call him a romantic idealist.

Further examples of this romantic idealization are found in three other early stories, "Makar Chudra" (English translation), "Starukha Izergil" ("Old Woman Izergil"), and "Chelkash" (English translation). Makar Chudra tells a story of a young Gypsy who kills the girl he loves rather than submit to her demand that he crawl before her if he wants to be her lover. Gorky extols here human beings' determination to preserve freedom and dignity, sacrificing all other considerations. In the second story, "Old

Woman Izergil," based on Russian folklore, Danko is leading his people out of a dark forest by taking his heart out of his chest and using it as a torch. Freedom, Gorky preaches, is not cheap and often requires the ultimate sacrifice, like that of the Gypsy in the preceding story. Gorky's admiration for bravery and boldness is brought to a head in "Chelkash," where the characters of two vagabonds, a thief and a peasant, are contrasted. The thief Chelkash acts like a rapacious beast, whereas the peasant is driven by common greed. Gorky's sympathies are clearly on the side of Chelkash because he follows blindly his instincts, thereby displaying character strength, while the peasant is moved by low, selfish interests.

"TWENTY-SIX MEN AND A GIRL"

Gorky further believes that yearning for freedom and better life, no matter how sincere and justified, is futile if it is not accompanied by resolute action. In perhaps his best story, "Dvadtsat'shest' i odna" ("Twenty-six Men and a Girl"), he confronts twenty-six bakery workers with an opportunity to satisfy their yearning for freedom and beauty in the person of pretty, sixteen-year-old Tanya, who purchases baked goods in their shop every day. To them, Tanya is like a sun, a symbol of life, beauty, and freedom which they crave in their wretched lives but cannot obtain because of their position but also their passivity. When a dashing soldier takes advantage of Tanya's infatuation with him, the workers feel betrayed and leer at her humiliation. Gorky chastises, in symbolic fashion, the passivity of an entire class that, even though it knows what it needs and deserves, will remain frustrated without decisive action.

"A MAN IS BORN"

This story points at other characteristics of Gorky: his humanitarianism, his revolutionary spirit, and his interest in social issues. Love for human beings and belief in their sanctity have always been the cornerstones of his creed. Nowhere is this better depicted than in his short story "Rozhdenie cheloveka" ("A Man Is Born"), in which a traveler, a persona representing Gorky, assists a mother in delivering her baby in the bushes, amid the bleak background of famine and hopelessness. Yet, by ushering a new man-child into the world, Gorky expresses hope that better days are in store if human beings are willing to help one another.

The revolutionary spirit, which informs many of Gorky's stories and novels, is best manifested in his prose poem "Pesnia o Burevestnike" ("The Song of the Stormy Petrel"). He again resorts to nature to symbolize the feelings of human beings, in this case their determination to solve their problems by force, if necessary. While other birds are cowering in the storm, the stormy petrel flies majestically (like the falcon in the earlier prose poem), "laughing at the storm-clouds," which will never obliterate the sun, and crying out, "like a prophecy of triumph": Let the storm break in all its fury. This poem in prose has been adopted by revolutionaries as the hymn of the revolution, prophesying the victory.

"ONE AUTUMN NIGHT"

Preoccupation with social themes pervades many of Gorky's works. Such stories, written in a straight, realistic style, show, more than any others, the quintessential Gorky: his love and respect for humankind and his concern for social injustice but also his realization that poverty and injustice have lowered some human beings to the level of beasts. At times, Gorky is preaching, but most of the time, he depicts settings and simple characters to act out his messages, as in the story "Odnazhdy osen'iu" ("One Autumn Night"), in which two young, hungry, cold, and ill people console each other under an overturned boat; the woman warms the man with her body, a few minutes after she has expressed hatred for another man who has grieved her. Not all stories of this kind are sentimental; sometimes they show callousness and brutality precluding any hope. Such is the story "V stepi" ("In the Steppe"), in which three young tramps (from Gorky's gallery of vagabonds), tortured by hunger, strangle a sick man who has given them food because they want more food and money. As the oldest among them explains, "Nobody is to blame for anything, because we are all beasts." Such pessimistic stories are not common with Gorky; his granite faith in a better life usually prevails.

A good number of Gorky's stories are devoid of moral preaching and ideological colorations. They are concerned mainly with human characters and sit-uations, with an interesting plot for its own sake, and with whatever it is that urges a writer to write a story. Most of such stories are from Gorky's later years. In an early one, "Na plotakh" ("On the Rafts"), a father takes over his son's wife, regretting that he had not met her before. "Suprugi Orlovy" ("Orlov Married Couple") presents a drunken husband who beats his wife until they both go to work in a hospital. There, she finds her vocation, while he is incapable of mending his ways and leaves in rage and defiance. "Varen'ka Olesova" ("Varenka Olesova"), the only story by Gorky that is favorable to the landowning class, presents a landowner who despises Russian novels because of their overly realistic depiction of daily life, exhibiting weak, timid characters, while the woman in the story prefers the adventurous heroes of the French novels, who take her out of the miserable life surrounding her.

In his later stories, Gorky showed that he could rise above mundane topics, as in "Golubaia zhizn'" ("Sky-Blue Life"), whose character copes with approaching insanity but eventually recuperates. "O pervoi liubvi" ("First Love") is an autobiographical story of lovers who part after realizing that they are not meant for each other. Such stories prove that Gorky was a true artist. It is this artistry that built and preserved his reputation as one of the best Russian writers.

OTHER MAJOR WORKS

LONG FICTION: *Goremyka Pavel*, 1894 (novella; *Orphan Paul*, 1946); *Foma Gordeyev*, 1899 (English translation, 1901); *Troye*, 1901 (*Three of Them*, 1902); *Mat*, 1906 (*Mother*, 1906); *Ispoved*, 1908 (*A Confession*, 1909); *Zhizn Matveya Kozhemyakina*, 1910 (*The Life of Matvei Kozhemyakin*, 1959); *Delo Artamonovykh*, 1925 (*Decadence*, 1927; also known as *The Artamonov Business*, 1948); *Zhizn Klima Samgina*, 1927-1936 (*The Life of Klim Samgin*, 1930-1938; includes *The Bystander*, 1930, *The Magnet*, 1931, *Other Fires*, 1933, and *The Specter*, 1938).

PLAYS: *Meshchane*, pr., pb. 1902 (*Smug Citizen*, 1906); *Na dne*, pr., pb. 1902 (*The Lower Depths*, 1912); *Dachniki*, pr., pb. 1904 (*Summer Folk*, 1905); *Deti solntsa*, pr., pb. 1905 (*Children of the Sun*,

1906); *Varvary*, pr., pb. 1906 (*Barbarians*, 1906); *Vragi*, pb. 1906 (*Enemies*, 1945); *Posledniye*, pr., pb. 1908; *Chudake*, pr., pb. 1910 (*Queer People*, 1945); *Vassa Zheleznova* (first version), pb. 1910 (English translation, 1945); *Falshivaya moneta*, wr. 1913, pr., pb. 1927; *Zykovy*, pb. 1914 (*The Zykovs*, 1945); *Starik*, wr. 1915, pr. 1919 (*Old Man*, 1924); *Yegor Bulychov i drugiye*, pr., pb. 1932 (*Yegor Bulychov and Others*, 1937); *Dostigayev i drugiye*, pr., pb. 1933 (*Dostigayev and Others*, 1937); *Vassa Zheleznova* (second version), pr., pb. 1935 (English translation, 1975); *Seven Plays*, 1945; *Five Plays*, 1956; *Plays*, 1975.

NONFICTION: *Detstvo*, 1913 (*My Childhood*, 1915); *V lyudyakh*, 1916 (*In the World*, 1917); *Vozpominaniya o Lev Nikolayeviche Tolstom*, 1919 (*Reminiscences of Leo Nikolaevich Tolstoy*, 1920); *Moi universitety*, 1923 (*My Universities*, 1923); *Vladimir Ilich Lenin*, 1924 (*V. I. Lenin*, 1931); *Reminiscences of Tolstoy, Chekhov and Andreyev*, 1949; *Untimely Thoughts: Essays on Revolution, Culture, and the Bolsheviks*, 1968.

MISCELLANEOUS: *Polnoe sobranie sochinenii*, 1949-1955 (30 volumes); *Polnoe sobranie sochinenii*, 1968-1976 (25 volumes); *Collected Works of Maxim Gorky*, 1979-1981 (8 volumes).

BIBLIOGRAPHY

Barratt, Andrew. *The Early Fiction of Maksim Gorky: Six Essays in Interpretation*. Nottingham, England: Astra Press, 1993. Excellent essays on Gorky's early works. Includes bibliographical references and an index.

Borras, F. M. *Maxim Gorky the Writer: An Interpretation*. Oxford, England: Clarendon Press, 1962. One of the more astute interpretations of Gorky's works, especially his novels and plays. Unlike many other books that concentrate either on biography or political issues, Borras's book emphasizes Gorky's artistic achievements. Chapter 2 analyzes his short stories.

Figes, Orlando. "Maxim Gorky and the Russian Revolution." *History Today* 46 (June, 1996): 16-22. Argues that Gorky's journalism and correspondence revealed in Soviet archives shows Gorky was not a devout Bolshevik and had doubts concerning the revolution and the course it took after 1917, all of which forced him into exile in 1921.

Gorky, Maxim. *Maxim Gorky: Selected Letters*. Edited and translated by Andrew Barratt and Barry P. Scherr. New York: Oxford University Press, 1997. An important collection of letters beginning in 1889 and ending with Gorky's death in 1936. The letters reveal Gorky's life story in his own words, shed light on many writers, including Anton Chekhov and Leo Tolstoy, and are representative of the development of Russian literature.

_____. *Untimely Thoughts: Essays on Revolution, Culture, and the Bolsheviks: 1917-1918*. Translated by Herman Ermolaev. New Haven, Conn.: Yale University Press, 1995. A splendid collection of critical articles that denounce the Bolshevik system of government, depict the Russian national character, and render a vision of the future.

Hare, Richard. *Maxim Gorky: Romantic Realist and Conservative Revolutionary*. London: Oxford University Press, 1962. The first substantial study of Gorky in English since Alexander Kaun's book (listed below). Hare combines the political aspects of Gorky's biography with critical analyses of his works, with the latter receiving the short end. Contains some interesting observations obtained from (anonymous) people who knew Gorky well.

Kaun, Alexander. *Maxim Gorky and His Russia*. New York: Jonathan Cape and Harrison Smith, 1931. The first book on Gorky in English, written while Gorky was still alive and supported by firsthand knowledge about him. It covers literary and nonliterary aspects of Russia's literary life and the atmosphere in Gorky's time. Still one of the best biographies, despite some outdated facts, corrected by history.

O'Toole, L. Michael. "'Twenty-six Men and a Girl.'" In *Structure, Style, and Interpretation in the Russian Short Story*. New Haven, Conn.: Yale University Press, 1982. A structuralist analysis of the story.

Peterson, Dale E. "Richard Wright's Long Journey from Gorky to Dostoevsky." *African American Review* 28 (Fall, 1994): 375-387. Discussion of the influence of Gorky and Dostoevski on Richard Wright. Notes similarities between Gorky's and Wright's writing, but claims that Wright moved away from Gorky's faith in collectivist culture and social engineering.

Terry, Garth M., comp. *Maxim Gorky in English: A Bibliography*. 2d rev. ed. Nottingham, England: Astra Press, 1992. An indispensable aid for any student of Gorky.

Weil, Irwin. *Gorky: His Literary Development and Influence on Soviet Intellectual Life*. New York: Random House, 1966. The most scholarly book on Gorky in English, skillfully combining biography with critical analysis. Valuable especially for the discussion of Soviet literary life and Gorky's connections with, and influence on, younger Soviet writers. Contains select but adequate bibliography.

Vasa D. Mihailovich

WILLIAM GOYEN

Born: Trinity, Texas; April 24, 1915
Died: Los Angeles, California; August 29, 1983

PRINCIPAL SHORT FICTION

Ghost and Flesh: Stories and Tales, 1952
The Faces of Blood Kindred, 1960
Selected Writings of William Goyen, 1974
The Collected Stories of William Goyen, 1975
Had I a Hundred Mouths: New and Selected Stories, 1947-1983, 1985

OTHER LITERARY FORMS

Although William Goyen asserted that "short fiction is what I most care about . . . the short narrative form most challenges and most frees me," he wrote several highly acclaimed novels, including *The House of Breath* (1950, 1975), *Come, the Restorer* (1974), and *Arcadio* (1983). Goyen was also a playwright of some distinction although his plays have never been published. In addition, he wrote two television plays, *A Possibility of Oil* (1958) and *The Mind* (1961). Goyen was the playwright-in-residence at Lincoln Center from 1963 to 1964. He was a brilliant lecturer and critic; his essays appeared in *The New York Times, TriQuarterly, Southwest Review*, and other journals. In 1973, he published a biography of Jesus Christ, *A Book of Jesus*, and at the time of his death, he was at work on studies of Saint Paul and Saint Francis. He was also working on an autobiography/memoir of six influential women in his life. Throughout his life, Goyen was intensely interested in music and was recognized as a composer of considerable ability.

ACHIEVEMENTS

William Goyen won the McMurray Award in 1950 for *The House of Breath*; he was a John Simon Guggenheim Memorial Foundation fellow in creative writing in 1952 and 1954. He received the Texas Institute of Arts and Letters award for the best comic novel of 1962, and he earned a Ford Foundation grant for novelists writing for the theater (Lincoln Center Repertory Company) in 1963 and 1964. In 1965, 1966, 1968, 1969, and 1970, he won the American Society of Composers, Authors, and Publishers award for musical composition. *The Collected Stories of William Goyen* was nominated for a Pulitzer Prize in 1975, and in 1976, Goyen won the O. Henry Award for short stories. The prestigious French journal *Delta* devoted its entire ninth issue to Goyen in 1979. During his distinguished career, Goyen earned what is rarer than any literary award: the unqualified admiration and affection of his peers. He was recognized as being not only a storyteller of originality and consummate skill but also, and more important, an artist and man of genuine integrity, dignity, and spirituality.

BIOGRAPHY

Born in Texas to a lumber salesman, Charles Provine Goyen and his wife, Mary Inez (Trow), on April 24, 1915, William Goyen has said that his first seven years in the small town of Trinity supplied the material for the short stories he wrote. He then moved to Houston. From Rice University he got a B.A. and an M.A. in comparative literature. From 1940 to 1945, he served in the Navy, where he began his first novel. He lived in Taos, New Mexico, where he met Frieda Lawrence, who was to have a profound influence on the young man: "Frieda brought me a sense of the richness of the great world, and that, together with what I had come through—college, Texas, the war—got me ready to move into the real world that I had never been in." After New Mexico, he lived in Europe for some time, staying with Stephen Spender in London in 1949. In 1951 and 1952, he became friendly with Truman Capote and Carson McCullers. After another year in Europe (Italy and Switzerland), he returned to New Mexico. In the 1950's, he began to work in theater, film, and television. On November 10, 1963, he married Doris Roberts, an actress. That same year, he won a Ford Foundation grant. He served as senior editor at McGraw-Hill from 1966 to 1972.

Goyen began a distinguished career as a university professor in 1955 at the New School for Social Research, where he taught until 1960. He was a participant in the Columbia University Writing Program from 1963 until 1965; he also taught at Brown University (1972-1973), Princeton University (1976-1978), Hollins College (1978), Stephens College (1979), the University of Houston (1981), and the University of Southern California (1981-1982). In 1975, an anniversary issue of *The House of Breath* brought considerable critical acclaim and renewed attention to his novels. Goyen was, however, more popular and more highly respected in Europe than in the United States. In 1979, the distinguished French journal *Delta* accorded him an honor theretofore granted to only four other writers (Flannery O'Connor, Eudora Welty, William Faulkner, and Herman Melville) by devoting an entire issue to his work. In spite of his failing health (Goyen died after a protracted

William Goyen, right, in 1954 (AP/Wide World Photos)

struggle with leukemia), he experienced a great surge of creative energy in his last years; his late flowering, like that of William Butler Yeats, yielded works of great power, originality, mystery, and beauty. To the end, Goyen wrote eloquently of the ecstasy and the anguish of human life; he championed the diminished and lost things of this world; he insisted on the holy mystery of each human being; and he proved that, as he said, "Art is an act of hope, and faith. Art is redeeming, and art is an affirmation." In the words of Robert Phillips, "We have been blessed to have had William Goyen among us."

ANALYSIS

"The White Rooster" is the story with which *Ghost and Flesh: Stories and Tales*, William Goyen's first collection, opens. The war between the sexes is being fought out in the hen yard. The story opens and centers upon an unattractive woman who dominates her absent husband, Walter. In his brief appearances, he says little and does not do much, except to obey his domineering wife. According to the code of the Southwest, a woman needs to be mastered in order to be feminine. Marcy Samuels is homicidal. What is ostensibly driving her "insane" is the omnipresence of her scrawny, "white-faced" father-in-law, who scuttles through her house in his wheelchair, hawking and wheezing through his thin white neck. The second thing that aggravates her to dementia is the presence in her backyard of an old, sick white rooster. The scrawny cock is identified with the annoying old man by his movements, his noise, his appearance, and the rage he arouses in her. She determines to kill it while Mr. Samuels, coughing in his wheelchair behind her, recognizes that it is his neck that she would like to be wringing.

Marcy has had many arguments with Walter about putting his father out of the house. The old man has overheard these and is aware of her hatred for him. Marcy bullies Walter into constructing a trap which functions like a guillotine. She sits by the window, the cord pulled taut in her hand, waiting for the rooster to approach so that she can release the rope and decapitate it. At the murdering instant when the white rooster approaches and is about to "get it" in the neck, the old man slits his enemy's throat from behind with a knife. After murdering her, he devastates the house, smashing everything he can reach from his wheelchair: ripping off the wallpaper, slashing up the pillows, tearing and destroying in impotent fury. Walter finds him dead in this chaos.

The violence initiated by Marcy in her hatred of her father-in-law and deflected to the white rooster ricochets back to the old man, is vented by him against her who began it, and then becomes a storm of passion which demolishes the entire house. Goyen shows that hatred vented against one order of being, the bird, infects the human order, and then grows into a storm which destroys the object world, the house. In parentheses beside the title, it is indicated that this is Walter's story. In narrative terms, the perspective would have to be his, since he is the only survivor. In emotional terms this is also his story, because he, alone, is culpable. As "master" of this house, now savaged, he should have assumed the masculine role; then there could have been order and peace in his house instead of this explosion of destructive force unleashed by hate.

"A Shape of Light"

The last story in this collection is called "A Shape of Light." Very different in tone, it is similar rhetorically. The sentences are made of short, repetitive, incantatory phrases. Instead of a linear plot, there are circlings, stalkings, dancings, weavings around an action which the language barely lets the reader glimpse. The author describes the setting of this story in words that might equally apply to his syntax. He says, "you had wandered into a landscape of addict elations, hallucinations and obsessions."

In passages of sharply contrasted dictions, a childhood memory is reclaimed, in the guise of a ghost's being fleshed out. The narrator recalls having triumphantly sent up a homemade kite, constructed by him out of shoe-box tissue paper and kindling wood. He sees it in terms of an artifice sent aloft by the artificer, released into a life of its own. Boney Benson, who flags the trains with a lantern, had asked the boy to let him send up a message, which he scribbles in pencil on the page of a lined tablet. The message flies away and the kite falls. The boy wonders what had been written on it. Now an adult, in a dirty city, he identifies with the impulse to send up a message and allow it to fly high above the sordidness. A piece of paper flies up from the street, and on this transitional symbol the narrator imprints Boney's story.

His wife having died in childbirth, because the baby rose up in her and choked out her breath, Boney lay on her grave to listen for the unborn baby he had so fatally implanted in her. As restitution, he castrates himself and buries his bloody member in Allie's grave. Each night a light seems to arise from the tomb and Boney follows the flickering light. Four strangers had disinterred Mrs. Benson and found a hole where the child had been, and they join in the search for the light which had issued from the grave. Then the story circles back to its beginning in which a man in a city is writing down "the message that was sent and lost" in that long-ago town which is now "reclaimed and fixed forever in the light of so much darkness." The tale is told of a man who saddles his horse to follow a ghostly light. Interspersed with these passages are balladlike stanzas in which Allie speaks: "Oh where you agoing Boney Benson, and it nightfall? Why are you leaving the supper table so suddenly you have galloped your food; your supper will get cold and I will get cold."

This interplay between the real old man and his lantern, the gossip of the town which turns the actuality into a legend through its whispering, and the ballad form which this orally transmitted material assumes resonates against the figure of the author, seated at his writing table in the present inscribing this fiction. Each level of storytelling is indicated in the style appropriate to it. The educated author is presented in poetic prose, the rumors of the townspeople in colloquial speech, the yearnings of Allie in anapestic meter which stomps itself out in primitive rhythms, and the scenes in which the narrator describes his childhood encounter with Boney Benson are in flat, simple sentences. Therefore Goyen can make language, alone, do the work of setting the stage, changing the scenery, identifying the characters, and establishing the mood. He achieves both lighting effects and background music without employing either.

The denouement is implanted in the opening. It is retrospectively illuminated at the end of the story. The reader must return to the beginning to comprehend what he has just experienced. This imposes on the act of reading the same philosophical point made by the story's theme and by the mode of its narration. All three are engaged in parallel processes symbolized by the pursuit of the flickering light. The quest for the truth is like trying to put flesh on a ghost which ever haunts and eludes the reader. When the reader rereads the story, he discovers that this was the lost message which had been inscribed there in the beginning, which was read, but not yet fully understood:

> Walking one day I found a child let down from Heaven on a piece of string, standing in a meadow of bluebonnets and paint-brush, leashed out to me. This was my lost child and I told him what he did not know, left my words with him, our covenant, and laid this charge upon him: "speak of this little species that cannot speak for itself; be gesture; and use the light and follow it wherever it may lead you, and lead others to it."

By recording a local legend that would otherwise have vanished into the darkness and giving the reader simultaneously the popular form and the philosophical implications, Goyen, in the act of writing a story, gave the reader a history of the narrative form, from its inception in inspiration to its embodiment in artifact.

OTHER MAJOR WORKS

LONG FICTION: *The House of Breath*, 1950, 1975; *In a Farther Country: A Romance*, 1955, 1962; *The Fair Sister*, 1963; *Come, the Restorer*, 1974; *Wonderful Plant*, 1979; *Arcadio*, 1983; *Half a Look of Cain: A Fantastical Narrative*, 1994.

PLAYS: *The House of Breath*, pr. 1957; *The Diamond Rattler*, pr. 1960; *Christy*, pr. 1964; *Aimee!*, pr. 1973.

TELEPLAYS: *A Possibility of Oil*, 1958; *The Mind*, 1961.

POETRY: *Nine Poems*, 1976.

NONFICTION: *Ralph Ellison's Invisible Man: A Critical Commentary*, 1966; *My Antonia: A Critical Commentary*, 1966; *A Book of Jesus*, 1973.

TRANSLATION: *The Lazy Ones*, 1952 (by Albert Cossery).

BIBLIOGRAPHY

Bawer, Bruce. "The Lighthouse Keeper's Log." *The New York Times*, July 17, 1994. Bawer reviews Goyen's *Half a Look of Cain: A Fantastic Narrative*; discusses it as a dreamlike, Chinese box of a book with nothing for readers of conventional novels to grasp on to; claims it is the work of a brilliant writer, but is emotionally inert.

Duncan, Erika. "Come a Spiritual Healer: A Profile of William Goyen." *Book Forum* 3 (1979): 296-303. Duncan's sensitive essay is part analysis and part personal reminiscence. She suggests that Goyen's stories and novels involve a search "for the radiance of life and the hidden meaning in the darkness."

Goyen, William. "An Interview with William Goyen." Interview by Reginald Gibbons and Molly McQuade. *TriQuarterly* 56 (1983): 97-125. Goyen gave several illuminating and interesting interviews during the course of his career. This late interview, which is preceded by a brief biography and a critical assessment of Goyen's work, yields a fascinating, in-depth look into Goyen's ideas on life, art, spirituality, and his own works.

Gibbons, Reginald. *William Goyen: A Study of the Short Fiction*. Boston: Twayne, 1991. Part of Twayne's Studies in Short Fiction series, this volume provides an excellent overview of Goyen's short stories. Includes bibliographical references and an index.

Gumm, Clyde. "William Goyen: A Bibliographical Chronicle." *Bulletin of Bibliography* 35 (1978): 123-131. This bibliography is an invaluable resource for anyone working on Goyen's work. Gumm has compiled not only the publication data for all of the author's essays, stories, poems, and novels, but also every essay, review, and interview written about Goyen from 1938 through 1976.

Horvath, Brooke, Irving Malin, and Paul Ruffin, eds. *A Goyen Companion: Appreciations of a Writer's Writer*. Austin: University of Texas Press, 1997. Features essays on Goyen by admiring writers.

Paul, Jay S. "Marvelous Reciprocity: The Fiction of William Goyen." *Critique: Studies in Modern Fiction* 19, no. 2 (1977): 77-92. This study of *The Collected Stories of William Goyen* focuses on Goyen's depiction of love, his use of a storyteller as the central character, and the ways in which the manner of telling shapes a story. Paul's thoughtful analyses of numerous stories from this collection leads him to the conclusion that "the whole of Goyen's work must be thought of as a meditation upon story-telling, which is ideally a means of rescuing one's past, one's self, one's listeners. His concern has been art's power to transform human life."

_____. "'Nests in a Stone Image': Goyen's Surreal Gethsemane." *Studies in Short Fiction* 15 (1978): 415-420. "Nests in a Stone Image," from the collection *Ghost and Flesh: Stories and Tales*, is the story of a writer frustrated by his inability to write and by his more profound inability to love. Paul demonstrates that the writer's vigil "is patterned on Jesus' night of prayer and doubt in Gethsemane." He explains that Goyen's theme is love and argues that Goyen believes that each individual "can be as vital and dynamic as Jesus himself."

Pilkington, Tom. "Goyen's Letters." *The Houston Chronicle Zest*, March 19, 1995, p. 19. A review of Goyen's *Selected Letters from a Writer's Life*, with biographical comments on Goyen's literary career and his affair with Katherine Anne Porter.

Wier, Allen. "William Goyen: Speech for What Is Not Spoken." *Black Warrior Review* 10 (Fall, 1983): 160-164. In his moving meditation on Goyen's life and fiction, written shortly after the writer's death, Wier talks about what knowing Goyen meant to him and what reading Goyen's fiction has meant and will mean to him. He focuses his critical comments on *Arcadio*, and he asserts this final novel, like all Goyen's fiction, "gives the reader a sense of intimacy."

Ruth Rosenberg, updated by
Hal Holladay

SHIRLEY ANN GRAU

Born: New Orleans, Louisiana; July 8, 1929

PRINCIPAL SHORT FICTION

The Black Prince and Other Stories, 1955
The Wind Shifting West, 1973
Nine Women, 1985

OTHER LITERARY FORMS

Other than her collections of short stories, Shirley Ann Grau has written several novels, including *The Hard Blue Sky* (1958), *The House on Coliseum Street* (1961), *The Keepers of the House* (1964), *The Condor Passes* (1971), and *Roadwalkers* (1994). Feature articles have appeared in *Mademoiselle, Holiday*, and *The Reporter*.

ACHIEVEMENTS

Shirley Ann Grau received the 1965 Pulitzer Prize in fiction for *The Keepers of the House*. It was also a selection by both the Literary Guild and the Book-of-the-Month Club and was a condensed selection by *Ladies Home Journal* (January/February, 1964). *The Condor Passes* was also chosen for the Book-of-the-Month Club. Grau received honorary doctorates from Rider College and Spring Hill College.

BIOGRAPHY

Shirley Ann Grau attended Booth School in Montgomery, Alabama, from 1940 to 1945 and graduated in 1946 from Ursuline Academy in New Orleans. She graduated from Newcomb College in 1950 and attended Tulane University for two postgraduate years of study. Grau taught creative writing at the University of New Orleans. In 1955, she married philosopher James K. Feibleman; they had four children.

ANALYSIS

Identified at the beginning of her career as a southern writer following in the path of brilliant storytellers such as Eudora Welty and Katherine Anne Porter, Grau gained quick name recognition based on her remarkable use of local color and sensory details.

Her early settings often reflect both mood and tone and articulate, with symbols, their thematic or atmospheric effect on characters.

Grau, however, is more than a regional author bound to a southern heritage. Indeed, from 1970 on, she began to shift her settings to other locations, most notably to the Massachusetts coast, and she shifted from a strong emphasis on persons living in poverty to a sharp focus on the very wealthy. Whatever the subject matter of Grau's stories, however, most are superbly crafted. Grau writes in the mode of the modern short story, making use of a smooth and usually realistic surface of events with an underlying symbolic structure that carries meaning.

Many of Shirley Ann Grau's early stories are about characters indigenous to the South. They live in bayou villages, in the foothills of the Appalachians, or near the beaches of the Gulf of Mexico. Usually her plots involve a narrator who experiences a difficult or humorous moment in time resolutely with no recourse to emotional abandon. In "Pillow of Stone," from *The Wind Shifting West*, Ann Marie Landry, although she is pregnant and afraid of water, insists that her husband Raoul take her in a shaky little sailboat in a storm to the wake of her father. As she steps from the boat, her unborn child moves. In "The Other Way," a black child is taught by her creole elders that she must return to the all-white school to which she has won a scholarship and not mention quitting. The child finds the isolation unbearable, yet she acquiesces. In "The Thieves," a young woman is able to allow both a real thief and her own young lover to escape without feeling.

"MISS YELLOW-EYES"

"Miss Yellow-Eyes" describes bravery, cowardice, and racial tensions among siblings. Lena, one of three children born to a black couple, is fair-skinned enough to be considered white, while both Celia and Pete have dark complexions. Pete introduces Lena to his white-skinned African American friend, Chris, who becomes Lena's soldier-husband. Both dream of immigrating to Canada and passing as white, while

Pete wants to stay in New Orleans. Chris enlists in the Army and dies fighting in the Korean War; Pete believes Chris's death is a useless waste.

Shortly after Chris dies, Pete loses an arm in a switch-yard mishap. Celia, aware that Pete feared being drafted, questions whether Pete's misfortune was really accidental, for his Army induction notice arrives while he is hospitalized. She also begins noticing contrasts of colors in yellow and blue eyes; white and black taxicabs or beaches; bright moonlight, electric lights, and darkness. She ponders as well the victim-martyr name symbolism of Lena (Mary Magdalene) and Chris (Christ). These environmental elements symbolically project Grau's early ideas and concerns about human subjects and problems.

"JOSHUA"

"Joshua," in *The Black Prince and Other Stories*, concentrates on the universal experience of growing up. The story occurs in the bayou region, Bon Secour, a poor black fishing community. Unpainted houses with tin roofs, a gulf swamp, and constant rain serve as backdrop for Joshua's struggle to become a man. From the beginning, it is clear that eleven-year-old Joshua is the target for many of the tensions between his parents. The immediate difficulty centers on his mother's desire for her husband to return to fishing, so that they will have money to buy Joshua a new coat; he refuses because he has seen his friend blown up in the gulf by a German U-boat.

Joshua leaves his argumentative parents, slips on an oil-dipped canvas to keep warm, and, with his friend Henry Bourgeois, spends the night in their hideaway, an abandoned warehouse. During the night a gigantic explosion awakens them; Joshua lights the lamp and leaves it burning as they return to sleep. The next morning Henry suggests that Joshua had kept the lamp lighted because he was afraid. Joshua denies his fear even though Henry heard him crying during the night.

Returning home, Joshua learns that the noise was the explosion of a U-boat. Joshua's drunken father taunts and physically threatens him if he refuses to take the boat and catch fish for supper. Joshua accepts the dare and, with Henry, sets out in the pirogue. After checking and securing fish from the swamp's edge, Joshua steers the boat into the swamp. Despite

superstitious fears of evil in the icy, water moccasin-filled swamp, he is intent upon seeing where the explosion took place, hoping in this way to prove he is not afraid. When they arrive at the backwater of the river, Joshua spies something blue-colored. He determines to get a closer look, despite Henry's warnings of danger, and wades courageously through waist-deep waters and debris to the lifeless body clothed in bright blue pants and a brown leather jacket. His fingers white with cold, Joshua takes his tangible reward for his courage, the jacket. In his primal world, Joshua has reached his goal and mastered his test; he has accomplished what his father has been too frightened to do. Additionally, he has proven to his friend that a "real" man refuses to let fear prevent him from taking action or responsibility.

THE WIND SHIFTING WEST

Eighteen years later, after publishing three novels and receiving a Pulitzer Prize, Grau released *The Wind Shifting West*. During those years, she replaced the Gulf Coast settings and shifted character emphasis from the poor to the wealthy. Psychological and motivational insights, along with contrast, serve as basic tools to reveal her characters' universal conflicts or experiences. Many tales in this collection showcase the subject of love, especially love unreturned or denied. Others blend this subject, love, with desegregation, tradition, the 1930's Depression, and death.

In most of the stories in *The Wind Shifting West*, Grau carefully describes the colors, clouds, and general plan of the scenery in the first paragraphs. In "The Beach Party," she describes the arrival of a jeep at an isolated area of beach. Three men prepare the beach by choosing a sheltered spot behind a sand dune and by digging a pit. The jeep returns later with girls, including Frieda Matthews, and several sacks. Frieda has been invited to the party to be the date of one of her brother's friends—an arrangement insisted upon by their mother. The story, told from Frieda's point of view, is of a young woman who learns from her isolated position as an outsider about dates and about death.

The tone of isolation is set when Frieda refuses to join the group in the water; she has a terror of the ocean and wanders off down the beach by herself. Unexpectedly, she finds in an adjacent cove several people snorkeling. When she returns to her own group, she again asks if she can do anything. When her brother suggests that she help him with the corn in the water, Frieda chooses to leave with John, her date, and they go off to look at the other beach party. The dialogue between Frieda and John illustrates Frieda's naïveté; she is frightened and yet attracted by John's simple physical affection. Their quiet moment is broken by commotion on the beach.

Everett reports that one of the snorkelers has not come back. John leaves to help, and Frieda is alone once again. She cannot join the group at the water, so she attempts to help the young boy who reported the missing snorkeler, but he requires nothing of her. The young men find the body, and John attempts to revive it with mouth-to-mouth resuscitation. Frieda attempts to help him when he vomits, but he takes care of himself. In the confusion of the police van arriving and the party breaking up, Frieda is left alone on the beach. Finding that she is alone does not terrify her; she decides not to wait for the party; instead she sets out on the four-mile hike home. Grau thus encapsulates in this story the feelings of a young girl not quite ready to participate in adult interaction yet old enough to be aware of the isolation of the environment unpadded by protecting family members.

"THE WAY BACK"

"The Way Back" concerns adultery. A couple has spent two days together, yet the woman, in her internal monologue, reveals no clear memory of any individual moment. Returning to the city, their meaningless conversation underlines the terminal nature of this brief affair. Their formal farewell handshake further emphasizes the absence of love in the relationship. This sterility echoes the closing of the title story, which concerns Carolyn and Giles, a sister-in-law and a brother-in-law. On their way to rescue Carolyn's husband from his damaged boat, they are intimate on the boat deck. After dressing, Caroline notices that all that remains of intimacy is "some weed on the anchor and some salt dried on our skin." Giles replies bluntly, "There isn't ever much left, when it's done."

"THE MAN OUTSIDE"

"The Man Outside" depicts another scenario of love denied. During the 1930's Depression, a husband deserts his wife and eleven children. Several years later she marries Albert Benton, a foreman of a local lumber mill, who has the funds to make needed farm repairs and to support her family. One evening, one of the children notices a man standing outside watching the house. The mother glances out and insists that Benton send the man away. The children never question the man's identity, but the mother's agitation suggests that she denies her first love—the husband watching the house—in favor of the secure life that Benton's money provides.

NINE WOMEN

The stories collected in *Nine Women* reveal Grau's profound understanding of contemporary women's lives, interests, and conflicts. Grau questions what happens to women when they no longer view themselves and their identity solely in relation to a traditional male authority who protects and directs their lives as if they were unthinking, irresponsible children. How do they achieve control of their lives? Do they all even want to find a separate identity? In Grau's portraits, women are separated from their husbands by death, divorce, or choice. Some prefer to remain sheltered in changeless roles that comfort and protect them from doing anything independently. Yet others desire freedom to control and choose their own actions and thoughts.

HUNTER

Nancy Morrison, in "Hunter," is the sole survivor of a plane crash that killed her husband and daughter. Nancy courts death on countless plane flights, hoping that perhaps the next plane will crash and end her misery. Symbolically, if Nancy's family were still alive, her dreams of happiness might be similar to Katy Wagner's in "Summer Shore," who prefers the protection of her sheltering home and the repetitive tasks done regularly for thirty-six years to any changes. Even when her husband knows what she is thinking, it is comfortable and "save[s] talking." One other widow, Mrs. Emmons in "Housekeeper," provides a contrast. She is a very strong-willed, independent woman who builds a separate life for herself, against her children's wishes, not just once but twice. First, she is housekeeper for a widowed doctor. Nine years later, she remarries. After her former employer dies and leaves her an inheritance, Mrs. Emmons and her husband plan a trip to Egypt, something she had wanted to do since childhood.

"WIDOW'S WALK"

In "Widow's Walk," death separates Myra Rowland from her husband, Hugh. Even his name disappears from her beach-club parking space. On opening day of the summer season, Myra struggles to recall the names of people she has known for years; Hugh had always remembered names for her. Unable to cope with a directionless life, she is a ship without a rudder, drifting aimlessly from place to place.

"LETTING GO"

Divorce and choice combine in "Letting Go." Mary Margaret, bored by the monotony of her marriage, chooses both to divorce her husband and to reject the demands of her controlling parents: She wants personal control of her life. As she drives away from her family, her sense of happiness is similar to the relief that Barbara Eagleton in "Ending" feels after taking the last step to dissolve nearly twenty-five years of marriage. With her first taste of freedom, Barbara comfortably watches the television pictures without turning on the sound. A different choice is portrayed in "Home," the story of Angela Taylor, a successful real estate agent and her lesbian lover, Vicky, who decides that she wishes to bear a child and have them raise it together. After angry discussion, Angela agrees to the baby. Ironically, without any men in their lives, Angela assumes the role of protective father figure as she makes arrangements to buy a house that will be safe for a baby.

"FLIGHT"

In "Flight," the ninth tale in *Nine Women*, Willie May, a dying woman, refuses to remain in the hospital or with her son any longer. As she flies home, she recalls her life. As a child, Willie May learned that duty comes first and that she would never be free to have personal choices. Courtship, marriage to her husband John, a war, her son's birth, and the growth of her business happen without any real action on her part. When Willie May discovers that John and his belongings are both gone from their home, his family tells her that John retired after twenty years in the post office. She never searches for his new home, since she accepts his absence as something she cannot control. Willie May exemplifies the hopelessness, passivity, and stoic resignation of the black slaves or women in earlier times who had absolutely no control over the things that happened to them. Willie May's story is a negative touchstone against which women may measure their degree of independence.

"THE BEGINNING"

In "The Beginning," Nanda describes how her mother's imaginary creation of a magical kingdom becomes a life-sustaining myth for her. Her father, the absent Hindu shoe salesman, is given godlike status, while her mother's constant endearments make Nanda believe in her own personal self-worth. Nanda's acceptance that she is the treasured princess in this fantastic realm is so absolute and powerful that she internalizes castle and kingdom; they become the bedrock foundation for her inner world. She carries this sense of self-esteem, along with her wicker basket of toys, to provide continuity and royal identity for her as the family moves from place to place. "The Beginning" serves as a positive example of what a strong, determined woman can achieve by herself when she realizes her own self-worth and instills this sense of value in her own daughter. The tale of Nanda's and her mother's life concludes in Grau's novel *Roadwalkers*.

In this collection, self-confidence, determination, consideration and real love for others provide freedom for both males and females to grow and make choices, to have separate identities, and to still join together as two equals who are able to exercise control over their lives. Grau proves through her penetrating examination of national and universal problems in American society that she is far more than just a southern writer of local color.

OTHER MAJOR WORKS

LONG FICTION: *The Hard Blue Sky*, 1958; *The House on Coliseum Street*, 1961; *The Keepers of the House*, 1964; *The Condor Passes*, 1971; *Evidence of Love*, 1977; *Roadwalkers*, 1994.

BIBLIOGRAPHY

Grau, Shirley Ann. Interview by William Griffin. *Publishers Weekly* 229 (January 10, 1986): 70-71. A brief biographical sketch and conversation, in which Grau talks about her life and her work, including her short-story collection *Nine Women*.

Kissel, Susan S. *Moving On: The Heroines of Shirley Ann Grau, Anne Tyler, and Gail Godwin*. Bowling Green, Ohio: Bowling Green State University Popular Press, 1996. Examines the fictional characters of three contemporary female writers. Includes bibliographical references and an index.

Pearson, Ann. "Shirley Ann Grau: 'Nature Is the Vision.'" *Critique: Studies in Modern Fiction* 17 (1975): 47-58. This article deals with Grau's use of nature, which seems to permeate her novels and stories. Pearson suggests that Grau's vision of the world lies in her perception of the ever-present closeness of nature.

Rohrberger, Mary. "Shirley Ann Grau and the Short Story." In *Women Writers of the Contemporary South*, edited by Peggy Whitman Prenshaw. Jackson: University Press of Mississippi, 1984. Rohrberger argues that Grau's short stories are models of the form, making use of a surface content and substructures pointing to analogues that carry meaning.

Schlueter, Paul. *Shirley Ann Grau*. Boston: Twayne, 1981. The first book-length critical study of Grau's work. Excellent use of details, though somewhat short on interpretation.

Shigley, Sally Bishop. "Refuge or Prison: Images of Enclosure and Freedom in Shirley Ann Grau's *Nine Women*." *Short Story*, n.s. 3 (Fall, 1995): 54-68. Discusses the unifying thematic symbols and images that tie the stories together in Grau's short-story cycle. Argues that the stories express a need for shelter from the sometimes too real aspects of the world and the danger in finding such security.

Wagner-Martin, Linda. "Shirley Ann Grau's Wise Fiction." In *Southern Women Writers: The New Generation*, edited by Tonette Bond Inge. Tuscaloosa: University of Alabama Press, 1990. Argues that Grau's highly stylized manner of narration is in many ways in the style of the folktale. Contends that one of her most distinctive traits is her interest in ceremony and ritual. Makes general comments about Grau's fiction that apply to her stories; for example, that her best fiction deals with the nonwhite culture's impingement on the patriarchal matrix that dominates southern life.

Sylvia Huete, updated by Mary Rohrberger and Betsy Harfst

JOANNE GREENBERG

Born: Brooklyn, New York; September 24, 1932

PRINCIPAL SHORT FICTION

Summering: A Book of Short Stories, 1966
Rites of Passage, 1972
High Crimes and Misdemeanors, 1979
With the Snow Queen, 1991

OTHER LITERARY FORMS

In addition to her collections of short fiction, Joanne Greenberg has written several novels: *The King's Persons* (1963), *I Never Promised You a Rose Garden* (1964), *The Monday Voices* (1965), *In This Sign* (1970), *Founder's Praise* (1976), *A Season of Delight* (1981), *The Far Side of Victory* (1983), *Simple Gifts* (1986), *Age of Consent* (1987), *Of Such Small Differences* (1988), *No Reck'ning Made* (1993), and *Where the Road Goes* (1998). In 1979, her novel *I Never Promised You a Rose Garden* was made into a Hollywood film. Greenberg has also been a regular contributor of articles, reviews, and short stories to many periodicals, including *The Hudson*

Review, The Virginia Quarterly Review, Chatelaine, and *Saturday Review*.

ACHIEVEMENTS

The King's Persons, Joanne Greenberg's novel about the York massacre, won the Jewish Book Council of America Award for Fiction in 1963. *In This Sign* is such a sensitive exploration of the world of the deaf that it is studied by those who deal with the hearing-impaired. *I Never Promised You a Rose Garden* was endorsed by Dr. Karl Menninger as a contribution toward the understanding of schizophrenia; in 1967 she was given the Frieda Fromm-Reichmann Award by the American Academy of Psychoanalysis, an honor seldom accorded to laypersons.

Greenberg also received the Harry and Ethel Daroff Memorial Fiction Award in 1963 and the William and Janice Epstein Fiction Award in 1964, both of them awarded to her by the National Jewish Welfare Board for her book *The King's Persons*. In 1971, she won both the Marcus L. Kenner Award from the New York Association of the Deaf and the Christopher Book Award for *In This Sign*. She received the Frieda Fromm-Reichmann Memorial Award from Western Maryland College in 1977 and from Gallaudet College in 1979. In 1983, she was awarded the Rocky Mountain Women's Institute Award.

BIOGRAPHY

Joanne Greenberg was born in Brooklyn, New York, on September 24, 1932, the daughter of Julius Lester and Rosalie (Bernstein) Goldenberg. She earned a B.A. degree from American University in Washington, D.C., and at the same time she gained an interest in medieval art and music, which led her to write her historical novel *The King's Persons*. On her summer vacations she sang alto at the Tanglewood Music Festival and "was briefly the only white waitress in a Navajo reservation restaurant." This is narrated in "L'Olam and White Shell Woman." Other vacation experiences that contributed to the collection *Summering* were herding horses, tutoring the foreign-born, and being a space-control agent for an airline. Greenberg is also a graduate of the University of London, England. Being a qualified teacher of sign

language afforded her insights into the silent world she depicted in *In This Sign*. On September 4, 1955, she married Albert Greenberg, a vocational rehabilitation counselor; they became the parents of two sons, David and Alan. Her involvement in land reclamation led her to write *Founder's Praise*. Her volunteer work on a fire-fighting and emergency rescue team contributed to "Like a Banner" and "Merging Traffic." Her wide-ranging interests include teaching anthropology and sign language. Greenberg continued to pursue vigorously her writing career and her many and varied interests. She has been a member of the Authors' Guild, the Authors' League of America, the International Association of Poets, Playwrights, Editors, Essayists, and Novelists (PEN), the American Civil Liberties Union, the National Association of the Deaf, and the Colorado Authors' League.

ANALYSIS

A consummate storyteller, Greenberg employs shrewd psychological insights to create characters that draw her readers into the plot, keeping them immersed in her story until the very last page.

"THE SUPREMACY OF THE HUNZA"

Joanne Greenberg's "The Supremacy of the Hunza" is about the responses of two men to ninety-foot towers linked with cables that are erected on their land. Forty-three-year-old Westerbrook is an uncompromising idealist who is looking for a utopia. First he seizes upon the Chontal Indians on the southern Isthmus of Mexico, who are reputed to have a society free of violence and crime. Margolin, an anthropologist, who meets him at a protest organized against the towers, points out that the absence of crime only means the absence of the idea of private ownership. Their peacefulness is due to chronic malnutrition.

Westerbrook tries to enlist Margolin in his causes, conservation groups, fights against pollution, crusades, petitions, and marches. Cynically, Margolin throws away all the pamphlets. Margolin is relieved to be summoned by a therapist at a state institution to interpret the dreams of three Sioux patients so that he can escape from brooding over the towers that are defacing the landscape.

Margolin returns, exhausted by his failures. "The

symbols of The People had become cheapened parodies, like Made in Japan trinkets." The dreams that he had taped had been full of phony images from the movies, fake feather headdresses from cowboy pictures, and carried no cultural weight at all. He is oppressed by the pain of these Indians, "tongue-tied with tranquilizers," and by his inability to help at all. When Margolin discovers a drawer full of leaflets about the air, the water, and the food, he begins, in a rage, to dial Westerbrook's number to tell him that he does not want to be involved in any more of his crusades, but his wife informs him that Westerbrook is sick. Margolin then determines to be kind. He scarcely recognizes the "lowered, pinched quality of the voice; its youthfulness had been conquered, the naïve enthusiasm was gone." There is so much pain in Westerbrook's voice that "suddenly Margolin wanted to beg his forgiveness; for polluting his air and fouling his water and for permitting the hideous towers to stand." When Westerbrook mentions his newest enthusiasm, the Hunza, Muslim herders on the slopes of the Himalayas who live to a vigorous old age because they exist simply on pure food, whose language has no words for greed or envy, Margolin restrains his usual cynical comments. For his restraint he earns a pounding headache and the reward of hearing Westerbrook's voice recover its normal enthusiasm.

The conflict is between two contrasted attitudes toward civilization. The amateur romanticizes the simple life. The professional anthropologist refuses to be enlisted in any campaigns to clean the environment because he recognizes the hopelessness of the struggle, as well as the falsity of all the hyped-up reports from utopia. Margolin's compassionate impulse angers him afterward because his fear of further wounding the idealist has cost him his honesty. His conciliatory remarks about the Hunza restore his friend's dignity, however, and Margolin recognizes in this concession how much envy had been mingled with his previous responses to Westerbrook, and this is a humiliating fact to have to accept.

The imagery in this story is so unobtrusive that one has to search for it. The telephone poles that have upset both of the men remain standing. That is an in-

flexible fact. Neither organized protests nor private broodings have budged them an inch. Yet the ugly poles support cables which permit telephone conversations like the one which closes the story. The skeptic who had maintained his detachment ends by giving emotional support to a man whose naïveté he had scorned, whose social activism has made him feel guilty, whose faith in primitivism he felt was ill-informed, and whose belief that this world could be made better by means of committees he disagreed with. The poles carry the possibility of communication, flawed though it must be by individuals' psychological distances from one another. They bridge the physical distances; one must make the emotional accommodations to bridge the psychic ones. Every technological advance carries its own psychic assault with it. The movie versions of Indian identity have supplanted any authentic feelings about what it means to be a Sioux, just as the tranquilizers have obliterated the dark passions that had placed him in the asylum in the first place. Civilization makes primitive truths difficult to recover.

The story is effective precisely because it permits no easy answers to these hard questions. It raises the possibility that there might be a superior language, like that of the Hunza, which has no words for greed (represented by the individual conglomerates that put up more and more poles) or envy (represented by the academic mentality that feels the need to expose myths). If political activism is futile and dreaming of utopias is childish, what hope is there for this earth? The story provocatively raises profound dilemmas, leaving the reader to search for some solution. This is an example of the polemic genre at its most effective. It derives ultimately from the prophetic books of the Bible, whose rhetorical strategy is always to pose a question that demands to be answered in action: What are *you* going to do about this?

"HUNTING SEASON"
"Hunting Season" tells of a mother's anguished pursuit of her little boy, whom she has allowed to play outside while men are shooting their guns and sometimes killing one another. Fearing that he will have an epileptic attack because he has been on some new medicine only a week, she sets aside the bread

she has been baking to follow him to make sure he does not have another seizure as the guns go off, and the animals burst the thickets in panic. "He could fall, thrashing, unable to breathe, his face growing gray for lack of air, and then down the rocky gully, falling." She begins to run, listening for him, "smelling the air for danger," tracking him warily like a middle-aged huntress. At the sight of his small, thin figure, staring at the creek, she realizes that she is intruding on his privacy and, full of self-reproach, retreats, leaving him to face his dangers alone. He is shouting at the rocks, a big-boy threat that ends with: "Do you hear me?" "It was her intonation exactly, all the querulous anger of her impatience and all the long-suffering in her tone, captured with unconscious, searing honesty."

She whispers back that she has heard him and that she knows he has to make that murdering world his own. The courage involved in the mother's withdrawal of maternal protectiveness shows that she has successfully negotiated her part of this rite of passage. She hears, in his unconscious imitation of her voice, that she has damaged him enough already. He has internalized all the negative aspects when she had so much wanted him to see her as someone spontaneous, who played and laughed and loved the wind. She is ashamed at having lost her youthful joyousness and turned into a scolding woman. In the instant of grace when she decides to leave him his freedom, however, there is the possibility, if not of recovering her own freedom, at least of permitting him to retain his. The suggestion remains poised in the air.

Again, the symbolism is structural, not decorative. The title, "Hunting Season," is explicitly referring to the men who are stalking game. Implicitly, however, it embodies the plot. The mother has become a hunter of her child. She stalks him, holding her breath, keeping her footsteps noiseless, trying not to extrude the scent of her fear, which he might inhale. When she lets him go, she releases a victim. She allows him to fantasize himself as an aggressive male, to enter the murdering world, protected only by his talismanic turquoise jacket on his pathetically thin shoulders. That instant of swerving away from her maternal impulse to enfold him requires enormous control. The

mother's silent surrender of the role of huntress shows she can discipline her feelings. The author's use of a moment of silence to signal emotional growth shows what control she has over her art. The mother's concern builds up, accelerates into anxiety, mounts into panic but, instead of expending itself, is suppressed. The pace of the story augments the jolt of the ending. In that instant she accepts the end of her season as huntress so that he can become the hunter of experience in his own hunting season.

HIGH CRIMES AND MISDEMEANORS

All but three of the stories in *High Crimes and Misdemeanors* are Hasidic tales. These trace the cosmic consequences of human lapses. A lie can extinguish a star; an expression of gratitude can make a tree bloom. The narrator says, "Medieval Jewish mystics held that the acts of men have widespread effects in the heavenly realms." Two old ladies afraid of muggers barricade themselves in their house. Their niece consults a professor of religion, who advises her to fortify them through the mystical word as Rabbi Judah Lowe did his golem, when he fed him the Ineffable Name. So she inscribes Psalm 22 in Hebrew, leaving out all the vowels, so that its "mystical power retained its primal strength," and bakes it into a honey cake so they can ingest its power. At the end, the elderly aunts are no longer afraid to walk in the streets in "The Jaws of the Dog."

"THINGS IN THEIR SEASON"

In "Things in Their Season" intricate calculations are made "from one of the mystical books of the cabala" to discern where time is stockpiled. Four middle-aged Jews succeed in stealing some from the Cosmic Bank for Rabbi Jacob, whose fatal illness had threatened to interrupt their Monday night Talmud discussions. "Certain Distant Suns" takes its title from a Yiddish "commercial" on Aunt Bessie's unplugged television set that reproaches her, through the person of a shabbily dressed Hasid, for having stopped praying. He says,

in every relationship a certain amount of resentment builds up over the years . . . this is especially true in regard to mankind and the Master of the Universe, since the relationship is so—so onesided. I beg all of you, not to stop discussing the Master of the Universe, even if you can no longer praise Him. If it be in anger or despair or even, God forbid, in ridicule, keep His Name aloud in your mouths. It is possible that certain distant suns are powered by the mention of His Name.

WITH THE SNOW QUEEN

In her later collection of short stories, *With the Snow Queen*, Greenberg takes readers on an engaging tour of a fantasyland that only she could have created. People travel backward in time, characters harangue their authors, and an incomplete ritual may have had a disastrous effects on some innocent bystanders. She uses the search for an authentic sense of self that people in their middle years often embark upon as the bridge for this series of short stories. Personal crises help some of her characters change direction, while other characters come to accept a slightly flawed but more authentic self.

Who can resist Sima's freedom—in the title story—to go back to a turning point in her early years and dramatically change her life. In "Persistence of Memory" a prisoner who trades his memories to the inhabitants of Ghenna for oblivion finds that he can change his life by changing his memories. Only at the very end of "Torch Song" can one find out how the Vatican Ski Team fared in the Olympic Games. While older readers may immediately identify with many characters in this collection, *With the Snow Queen* will appeal to readers of all ages.

OTHER MAJOR WORKS

LONG FICTION: *The King's Persons*, 1963; *I Never Promised You a Rose Garden*, 1964 (as Hannah Green); *The Monday Voices*, 1965; *In This Sign*, 1970; *Founder's Praise*, 1976; *A Season of Delight*, 1981; *The Far Side of Victory*, 1983; *Simple Gifts*, 1986; *Age of Consent*, 1987; *Of Such Small Differences*, 1988; *No Reck'ning Made*, 1993; *Where the Road Goes*, 1998.

BIBLIOGRAPHY

Diamond, R. "The Archetype of Death and Renewal in *I Never Promised You a Rose Garden*." *Perspectives in Psychiatric Care* 8 (January-March, 1975): 21-24. Diamond compares the journey and recovery from schizophrenia to the initiation ritual of shamans. A discussion of the myths of death and resurrection is highlighted. The incorporation of Carl Gustav Jung's archetypes of the unconscious in connection with a search for self makes this article distinctive. Includes a bibliography.

Fromm-Reichmann, Frieda. "Frieda Fromm-Reichmann Discusses the 'Rose Garden' Case." *Psychiatry* 45, no. 2 (1982): 128-136. A transcript of a lecture given by Fromm-Reichmann to the Ypsilanti Psychiatric Institute discussing the treatment of a young female adolescent. Greenberg, using the pseudonym of Hannah Green, wrote about a treatment plan she received. Fromm-Reichmann talks about the treatment plan she devised, the outcome, and the book that her patient wrote.

Greenberg, Joanne. "Go Where You're Sent: An Interview with Joanne Greenberg." Interview by K. L. Gibble. *Christian Century* 102 (November 20, 1985): 1063-1067. Greenberg discusses her motivation and writing techniques with Gibble. He induces her to reveal bits and pieces of her personal philosophy. Some valuable clues to her personality can be found in this interview.

_____. Interview by Susan Koppelman. *Belles Lettres* 8, no. 4 (Summer, 1993): 32. Greenberg discusses her work and when she became a writer. She says she began writing to express her unhappiness while living in New York City.

_____. "Joanne Greenberg." Interview by Sybil S. Steinberg. *Publishers Weekly* 234 (September 23, 1988): 50-51. Notes that each of her novels and short-story collections deals with people challenged by a hostile or strange world. Greenberg asserts that she has stood by her publisher, Holt, throughout her writing career because the company gave her a chance when other publishers would not.

Wisse, Ruth. "Rediscovering Judaism." Review of *A Season of Delight*, by Joanne Greenberg. *Commentary* 73 (May, 1982): 84-87. This review is set in the context of Jewish life in the United States. The author compares the heroine's struggle with issues of faith to a reawakening of spiritual values that can be found in modern society as a whole and the Jewish community in particular.

Wolfe, K. K., and G. K. Wolfe. "Metaphors of Madness: Popular Psychological Narratives." *Journal of Popular Culture* 10 (Spring, 1976): 895-907. An eloquent discussion of an emerging genre using *I Never Promised You a Rose Garden* as an ex-ample. This genre, psychological in nature, has a recognizable structure and imagery. The authors turn a spotlight on the implications that many of the protagonists of this type of novel, or autobiography, are women using the metaphor of a journey. Includes notes and a bibliography.

Ruth Rosenberg, updated by
Maxine S. Theodoulou

GRAHAM GREENE

Born: Berkhamsted, England; October 2, 1904
Died: Vevey, Switzerland; April 3, 1991

PRINCIPAL SHORT FICTION

The Basement Room and Other Stories, 1935
The Bear Fell Free, 1935
Twenty-four Stories, 1939 (with James Laver and Sylvia Townsend Warner)
Nineteen Stories, 1947
Twenty-one Stories, 1954
A Visit to Morin, 1959
A Sense of Reality, 1963
May We Borrow Your Husband? and Other Comedies of the Sexual Life, 1967
Collected Stories, 1972
How Father Quixote Became a Monsignor, 1980

OTHER LITERARY FORMS

Graham Greene published twenty-six novels including *The Power and the Glory* (1940; reissued as *The Labyrinthine Ways*), *The Heart of the Matter* (1948), *Brighton Rock* (1938), *The End of the Affair* (1951), and *The Human Factor* (1978). In addition to his many novels and short-story collections, Greene published five plays; three collections of poetry of which the last two, *After Two Years* (1949) and *For Christmas* (1950), were privately printed; travel books, including two centering on Africa; several books of lit-erary essays and film criticism; a biography, *Lord Rochester's Monkey: Being the Life of John Wilmot, Second Earl of Rochester* (1974); and two autobiographical works, *A Sort of Life* (1971) and *Ways of Escape* (1980). In addition, Greene published journals, book reviews, and four children's books.

ACHIEVEMENTS

Although the Nobel Prize eluded Graham Greene, he remains one of the most important novelists of the twentieth century. With more screen adaptations than any other modern author, translations into twenty-seven different languages, and book sales exceeding twenty million dollars, Greene has enjoyed a combination of critical success and popular acclaim not seen since Charles Dickens.

In 1984, Britain made Greene a Companion of Literature, and in 1986, a member of the elite Order of Merit. France bestowed on Greene one of its highest honors, naming him a Commander of Arts and Letters. In addition, Greene's most famous novels—*The Power and the Glory, The End of the Affair*, and *The Heart of the Matter*—have been acknowledged as literary masterpieces. Combining the outer world of political intrigue and the inner world of the human psyche, Greene's world is one of faith and doubt, honor and betrayal, love and hate. Both the depth and breadth of Greene's work make him one of Britain's most prolific and enduring writers.

BIOGRAPHY

Educated at Berkhamsted School and Balliol College, Oxford, Graham Greene served in the Foreign Office, London, from 1941 to 1944. He married Vivien Dayrell-Browning in 1927 and had two children. He was a staff member of the *London Times* from 1926 to 1930, and he served as movie critic (1937-1940) and literary editor (1940-1941) of *The Spectator*. He also served as director for Eyre and Spottiswoode, publishers (1944-1948), and for The Bodley Head, publishers (1958-1968). The recipient of numerous awards, Greene received the Hawthornden Prize for *The Labyrinthine Ways* in 1941; the Black Memorial Prize for *The Heart of the Matter* in 1949; the Shakespeare Prize, Hamburg, 1968; and the Thomas More Medal, 1973. Other awards of distinction include a D.Litt. from the University of Cambridge in 1962, a D.Litt. from Edinburgh University, 1967, Honorary Fellow at Balliol College (Oxford) in 1963, Companion of Honor in 1966, and Chevalier of the French Legion of Honor in 1969. With fifty-four books to his credit, Greene remained a productive writer throughout his life. His last publication was in 1988, but he was said to be working on a new book at the time of his death on April 3, 1991. Greene spent his last years in Antibes, France, and died in Vevey, Switzerland.

ANALYSIS

"Goodness has only once found a perfect incarnation in a human body and never will again, but evil can always find a home there. Human nature is not black and white but black and grey." So said Graham Greene in his essay "The Lost Childhood," and the statement as well as any defines the worldview manifested in his fiction. The "perfect incarnation" is Jesus Christ, and it is against this backdrop of the divine-made-human that Greene draws and measures all the actions of his stories. Whether the stories are explicitly religious in theme, such as "The Hint of an Explanation," or not, or whether Greene chooses to view humanity in a tragic or comic light, the basic vision is the same: human nature steeped in evil and struggling with the fundamental problems of egotism, love and hate, responsibility, innocence and guilt.

As a result of this vision, the central action in Greene's fictional world is invariably betrayal—the Judas complex—betrayal of one's fellow human beings, of one's self, or of one's God. For Greene's heroes and heroines there is no escape; they fall by virtue of their very humanity. Yet their flawed humanity is not presented and then judged from the standpoint of any simplistic orthodoxy. As a thinker and as a fiction writer Greene was a master of paradox, creating a world of moral and theological mystery in which ignobility and failure may often be the road to salvation. Indeed, in Greene's world the worst sin is a presumed innocence which masks a corrosive egotism that effectively cuts human beings off from their fellow creatures and from God.

"THE HINT OF AN EXPLANATION"

Greene's paradoxical treatment of his major themes within a theological perspective is best evident in "The Hint of an Explanation." The story develops in the form of a conversation between the narrator, an agnostic, and another passenger, a Roman Catholic, while the two are riding on a train in England. Although he confesses to have occasionally had intuitions of the existence of God, the agnostic is

Graham Greene (©Amanda Saunders)

intellectually revolted by the whole notion of "such a God who can so abandon his creatures to the enormities of Free Will . . . 'When you think of what God— if there is a God—allows. It's not merely the physical agonies, but think of the corruption, even of children.'" The question posed by the agnostic is the mystery of evil—why an omniscient God permits it. In response, the Catholic reminds him that the limitations of human understanding make a full answer impossible for human beings. Nevertheless, he insists, there are "hints" of an explanation, hints caught by men when they are involved in events that do not turn out as they were intended—"by human actors I mean, or by the thing behind the human actors." The suggested "thing" behind the human actors is Satan, and it is the Catholic traveler's conviction of Satan's ultimate impotence and defeat, derived paradoxically from an experience of evil in his own childhood, that provides the underpinning for his own belief in divine providence.

As a child, the Catholic son of a Midland bank manager was tempted by the town freethinker to steal a consecrated Host while serving Mass and deliver it to him. The tempter, a baker named Blacker, is corruption incarnate; he both entices the boy by letting him play with an electric train and promising to give it to him, and at the same time threatens to bleed him with a razor if the boy will not do his bidding. The boy is conscious of the *eternal* consequences his actions will have: "Murder is sufficiently trivial to have its appropriate punishment, but for this act the mind boggled at the thought of any retribution at all." Still, driven by fear of Blacker, he steals the communion wafer—the Body of Christ—and prepares to deliver it to the baker. Nevertheless, when Blacker appears that evening under the boy's bedroom window to collect the Host, his diabolical purposes are defeated when the boy abruptly swallows the communion wafer rather than deliver it into the hands of the Enemy.

As he now recalls this episode from his childhood for the agnostic stranger, the Catholic sees in it a "hint" of the manner in which the mystery of the divine will operates, for that episode was the "odd beginning" of a life that eventually led him to become a priest. Looking back on it now, he sees in his struggle

with Blacker nothing less than the struggle between God and Satan for the human soul, and the inevitable defeat of "that Thing," doomed to hopelessness and unhappiness.

Although the story is clear in its religious theme, any danger of its being merely a tract disguised as fiction is skillfully circumvented both by the paradoxical quality of Greene's thought and by his technical skill as a writer. For one thing, Greene undercuts the threat of dogmatic rigidity by creating enormous compassion for the malevolent figure of Blacker, imprisoned in his own misery, at the same time leaving the door open for his eventual redemption through defeat. Moreover, much of this compassion derives from the reader's awareness that, as a human being, Blacker is as much the victim of satanic forces working through him as he is agent of his own fate. Greene sustains a delicate dramatic balance between man's free will and responsibility on the one hand, and on the other, the suggestion or "hint" of supernatural forces at work in human affairs. Greene leaves the reader with a sense of the ineffable mystery of reality, and even the rather hackneyed and mechanical surprise ending of the story—the discovery in the last paragraph that the Catholic is indeed a priest—is consistent with the dramatic logic of the story.

"The Hint of an Explanation" bears many of the trademarks that made Greene one of the most important and widely read artists of the twentieth century, earning him both popularity and high critical esteem. His technical skill and sheer virtuosity as a storyteller stemmed equally from his mastery of the high formalist tradition of Henry James and Joseph Conrad and from the conventions of the melodramatic thriller, with its roots in classical, Renaissance, and Jacobean drama. Mastery of the themes and devices of the thriller—love and betrayal, intrigue, unexpected plot turns, the use of the hunt or chase, danger and violence—gave him a firm foundation upon which to base his subtle explorations of the spiritual condition of human beings in the twentieth century. In short, one of his most important contributions to the short story lies in the way in which he took the conventional form of popular fiction and infused it with a dimension of mystery that often penetrates to the deepest theological levels of experience. Although occasionally the action in Greene's stories may seem contrived, it is contrivance brought off with great dynamism—the energy and unpredictability of life's happenstances—and not the sealed, airless contrivance wrought by the aesthetic purists (whom Greene denounced), those modern fiction writers who have elevated artistic form to an absolute.

Although the social milieu of Greene's fiction is most often the commonplace world of modern England and Europe, it is his ability to infuse this landscape with the sense of mystery that gives the stories their imaginative power and depth. Often the most fertile ground for imagination is childhood, and this may well account for the fact that, as in "The Hint of an Explanation," Greene frequently makes childhood the locus of action for his themes of innocence, egotism, and betrayal. Yet his depiction of childhood is not a sentimentalized, romantic portraiture of innocence betrayed by a hostile world. Greene focuses on childhood because he finds in children a sense of reality which is keener and more alive, a sharper moral imagination, and a more vivid awareness of the personal consequences of their choices as they struggle with the demands of love and hate, loyalty and betrayal. In an essay on James, Greene remarked that ". . . to render the highest justice to corruption you must retain your innocence: you have to be conscious all the time within yourself of treachery to something valuable." Greene's fictional children, still unjaded by maturity, *feel* the potential for treachery both within themselves and surrounding them. Greene was able to make this complex childhood world palpable and render it with great psychological fidelity, perhaps seen best in one of his finest stories, "The Basement Room."

"THE BASEMENT ROOM"

Betrayal and the spiritually fatal consequences of choosing a specious innocence over the unalterable fact of the fallen state are the driving forces in "The Basement Room." Phillip Lane, a seven-year-old upper-class boy, develops a strong bond of friendship with Baines, the family butler, while his parents are gone on a fortnight's holiday. With Baines, whom he

sees as a "buccaneer" and man-of-the-world, Philip feels that he has begun "to live," and indeed he *is* initiated into a complex world of love and hate, deceit, the demands of friendship, and eventually betrayal. For Baines and Phillip have a common enemy: Mrs. Baines, a bitter shrew who bullies both her husband and young Phillip. During a day's outing with Baines, Phillip also meets the butler's mistress, Emmy, whom Baines introduces as his "niece." When Mrs. Baines is called away suddenly because of family illness, Baines, in a holiday mood, brings Emmy home for the night, convinced that Phillip will loyally keep his secret.

"Life," however, so complex and confusing in its demands, is too much for young Phillip. The suspicious Mrs. Baines returns unexpectedly during the night and terrifies him, demanding to know where "they" are. Too frightened to answer, Phillip manages to reach the bedroom door in time to see the enraged Mrs. Baines attacking her husband in the upstairs hallway, and in the ensuing struggle she topples over the bannister and is killed. Phillip runs frightened from the house, while the butler quickly removes her body to the foot of the stairs of their basement apartment to make it appear that she has accidentally fallen there. Phillip wanders aimlessly in the streets, waiting for someone to lift the burden of responsibility from him, for "life" has now become intolerable. "He loved Baines, but Baines had involved him in secrets, in fears he didn't understand. That was what happened when you loved—you got involved; and Phillip extricated himself from life, from love, from Baines." So when he is returned home by the police, Phillip betrays Baines, blurting out the facts that condemn the butler.

The effect of Phillip's betrayal—choosing an egotistic "innocence" over the ambiguous responsibilities of love in a fallen world—is disastrous to his own spiritual growth. At the end of the story, Greene skillfully shifts the scene forward to Phillip's own deathbed where, having "never faced it [life] again in sixty years . . . ," he agonizingly relives the moment of his betrayal, murmuring the policeman's question to Baines ("Who is she? Who is she?") as he sinks into death. Greene's point is clear: Phillip's spiritual development stopped at age seven when he refused the consequences of his love for Baines. Instead of the reality of being a fallen, yet free and mature, creature, he chose egotism and the illusion of innocence. The innocence Phillip elects, however, is not a true child-like quality. On the contrary, the childhood Phillip loses is exactly that keen awareness of the potentialities for love and treachery, of the power of evil and the vital sense of mystery inspiring terror and awe which constitutes for Greene the real human condition. We are reminded of Greene's quoting from Æ's poem "Germinal": "In the lost childhood of Judas, Christ was betrayed."

"THE DESTRUCTORS"

Greene's depiction of the lost childhood theme in "The Basement Room" is devastating and terrible, but he can also present the same theme in a manner which is devastatingly funny. Such is the case in "The Destructors," in which the callous youngster Trevor leads a gang of neighborhood boys in the systematic dismantling of the house of Mr. Thomas—"Old Misery" as the children call him—a retired builder and decorator. Because his own father was once an architect, Trevor fully understands the value of Old Misery's house; indeed, it is an elegant, two-hundred-year-old structure built by Sir Christopher Wren, which embodies the refinements of tradition. In fact, Old Misery's house is an emblem of civilization itself, the whole legacy of humane values and order and design passed from generation to generation, still imposing even though it stands amid the ruins of bombed-out postwar London. Fully conscious of its historical and cultural significance, Trevor diabolically mobilizes the gang of youths to bring the house down, working from the inside ". . . like worms, don't you see, in an apple."

Trevor ingratiates himself with Old Misery by asking to tour the inside of the house and then, learning that the owner will be away for a weekend holiday, sets his plan of destruction in motion. Working floor by floor, the gang wrecks everything—furniture, china and ornamental bric-a-brac, doors, personal mementos, porcelain fixtures, the winding staircase, and parquet floors; even Old Misery's hidden cache of pound notes is burned up. The evil inspired by Trevor goes beyond simple thievery; it is destruction for its own sake, a satanic love of chaos. When Trevor's minion Blackie asks him if he hates Old Misery, the leader replies coldly that "There'd be no fun if I hated him. . . . 'All this love and hate,' he said, 'it's soft, it's hooey. There's only things, Blackie. . . .'" In Trevor's remark Greene has touched the nerve of a fundamental side of the modern consciousness, its brutal amorality and contempt for the past.

Still, Greene's inventive genius manages to make "The Destructors" humorous, although terrifyingly so. Trevor's plan to destroy the house is endangered when Old Misery returns prematurely from his holiday, but Trevor is up to the challenge and instantly contrives a plot to trap the aged owner in his own outdoor privy. Locked in by the gang for the night, Old Misery can only sit helplessly and wonder what the faint sounds of hammering and scraping mean. The next morning a driver arrives to remove his lorry from the parking lot next door, and as he pulls away, unaware of the rope tying his truck to the foundation beams, Old Misery's house comes down in a heap of rubble. The driver manages to free Old Misery from the privy, but he cannot restrain himself from laughing at the scene of devastation. "'How dare you laugh,' Mr. Thomas said, 'It was my house. My house.'" The driver can only reply, chuckling, "I'm sorry. I can't help it, Mr. Thomas. There's nothing personal, but you got to admit it's funny."

"The Destructors" represents Greene at his best in presenting his vision of human perversity and folly in a comic vein. The depiction of Trevor's unmitigated evil is frightening, but it is finely balanced by the humor of the final scene; and in the lorry driver's laughter and the absurdly pathetic character of Old Misery the reader finds a basic affirmation of the common values of human existence which, paradoxically, triumph over the cold diabolism of young Trevor. It is he who is the ultimate loser. Knowing the world only as "things," he himself has become a thing—T. the destructor—and he cannot respond either with love or hate to the life around him.

Greene's stories, with their remarkable craftsmanship, exercise a powerful fascination on the reader.

Even at their most melodramatic, his stories unfailingly create a plausible sense of reality because they touch the full range of human experience: petty foibles, corruption, deceit, love, responsibility, hope, and despair. Whether Greene's emphasis is tragic or comic, or a wry mingling of both, the reader is again and again confronted in the stories with the fundamental mystery of existence on earth, making them at once rich, entertaining, and profound.

OTHER MAJOR WORKS

LONG FICTION: *The Man Within*, 1929; *The Name of Action*, 1930; *Rumour at Nightfall*, 1931; *Stamboul Train: An Entertainment*, 1932 (pb. in U.S. as *Orient Express: An Entertainment*, 1933); *It's a Battlefield*, 1934; *England Made Me*, 1935; *A Gun for Sale: An Entertainment*, 1936 (pb. in U.S. as *This Gun for Hire: An Entertainment*); *Brighton Rock*, 1938; *The Confidential Agent*, 1939; *The Power and the Glory*, 1940 (reissued as *The Labyrinthine Ways*); *The Ministry of Fear: An Entertainment*, 1943; *The Heart of the Matter*, 1948; *The Third Man: An Entertainment*, 1950; *The Third Man and The Fallen Idol*, 1950; *The End of the Affair*, 1951; *Loser Takes All: An Entertainment*, 1955; *The Quiet American*, 1955; *Our Man in Havana: An Entertainment*, 1958; *A Burnt-Out Case*, 1961; *The Comedians*, 1966; *Travels with My Aunt*, 1969; *The Honorary Consul*, 1973; *The Human Factor*, 1978; *Dr. Fischer of Geneva: Or, The Bomb Party*, 1980; *Monsignor Quixote*, 1982; *The Tenth Man*, 1985; *The Captain and the Enemy*, 1988.

PLAYS: *The Heart of the Matter*, pr. 1950 (adaptation of his novel; with Basil Dean); *The Living Room*, pr., pb. 1953; *The Potting Shed*, pr., pb. 1957; *The Complaisant Lover*, pr., pb. 1959; *Carving a Statue*, pr., pb. 1964; *The Return of A. J. Raffles: An Edwardian Comedy in Three Acts Based Somewhat Loosely on E. W. Hornung's Characters in "The Amateur Cracksman,"* pr., pb. 1975; *For Whom the Bell Chimes*, pr. 1980; *Yes and No*, pr. 1980; *The Collected Plays of Graham Greene*, pb. 1985.

SCREENPLAYS: *Twenty-one Days*, 1937; *The New Britain*, 1940; *Brighton Rock*, 1947 (adaptation of his novel; with Terence Rattigan); *The Fallen Idol*, 1948 (adaptation of his novel; with Lesley Storm and William Templeton); *The Third Man*, 1949 (adaptation of his novel; with Carol Reed); *The Stranger's Hand*, 1954 (with Guy Elmes and Giorgino Bassani); *Loser Takes All*, 1956 (adaptation of his novel); *Saint Joan*, 1957 (adaptation of George Bernard Shaw's play); *Our Man in Havana*, 1959 (adaptation of his novel); *The Comedians*, 1967 (adaptation of his novel).

TELEPLAY: *Alas, Poor Maling*, 1975.

RADIO PLAY: *The Great Jowett*, 1939.

POETRY: *Babbling April: Poems*, 1925; *After Two Years*, 1949; *For Christmas*, 1950.

NONFICTION: *Journey Without Maps: A Travel Book*, 1936; *The Lawless Roads: A Mexican Journal*, 1939 (reissued as *Another Mexico*); *British Dramatists*, 1942; *Why Do I Write? An Exchange of Views Between Elizabeth Bowen, Graham Greene and V. S. Pritchett*, 1948; *The Lost Childhood and Other Essays*, 1951; *Essais Catholiques*, 1953 (Marcelle Sibon, translator); *In Search of a Character: Two African Journals*, 1961; *The Revenge: An Autobiographical Fragment*, 1963; *Victorian Detective Fiction*, 1966; *Collected Essays*, 1969; *A Sort of Life*, 1971; *The Pleasure Dome: The Collected Film Criticism, 1935-40, of Graham Greene*, 1972 (John Russell-Taylor, editor; published in the U.S. as *The Pleasure-Dome: Graham Greene on Film, Collected Film Criticism, 1935-1940*); *Lord Rochester's Monkey: Being the Life of John Wilmot, Second Earl of Rochester*, 1974; *Ways of Escape*, 1980; *J'Accuse: The Dark Side of Nice*, 1982; *Getting to Know the General: The Story of an Involvement*, 1984.

CHILDREN'S LITERATURE: *The Little Train*, 1946; *The Little Fire Engine*, 1950 (published in the U.S. as *The Little Red Fire Engine*, 1952); *The Little Horse Bus*, 1952; *The Little Steam Roller: A Story of Mystery and Detection*, 1953.

EDITED TEXTS: *The Old School: Essays by Divers Hands*, 1934; *The Best of Saki*, 1950; *The Spy's Bedside Book: An Anthology*, 1957 (with Hugh Greene); *The Bodley Head Ford Madox Ford*, 1962, 1963 (4 volumes); *An Impossible Woman: The Memories of Dottoressa Moor of Capri*, 1975.

MISCELLANEOUS: *The Portable Graham Greene*, 1973 (Philip Stout Ford, editor).

BIBLIOGRAPHY

Bayley, John. "Graham Greene: The Short Stories." In *Graham Greene: A Reevaluation*. New York: St. Martin's Press, 1990. Basing his comments on his analysis of "The Hint of an Explanation," Bayley argues that many Greene stories have a hidden subject in a sense that none of his novels does. Claims that by means of almost invisible contrasts and incongruities, the story leads the reader both away from and toward its central revelation.

Couto, Maria. *Graham Greene: On the Frontier*. New York: St. Martin's Press, 1988. A well-rounded approach to Greene criticism, including a discussion of the final novels and a retrospective on Greene's career. Contains an insightful interview with Greene and a selection of Greene's letters to the international press from 1953 to 1986.

De Vitis, A. A. *Graham Greene*. Rev. ed. Boston: Twayne, 1986. Most interesting in this volume are an overview of critical opinion about Greene, a chronology, and a chapter on the short stories. Supplemented by a thorough primary bibliography and an annotated bibliography of secondary sources.

Evans, Robert O., ed. *Graham Greene: Some Critical Considerations*. Lexington: University Press of Kentucky, 1963. Although published before some of Greene's later works, this collection of critical essays covers the major novels and short stories and contains rare information on Greene's plays and film criticism. Includes an extremely thorough primary and secondary bibliography covering all Greene's literary genres.

Kelly, Richard. *Graham Greene*. New York: Frederick Ungar, 1984. A general introduction to Greene and his work. The chapter on the short stories discusses "The Destructors," "The Hint of an Explanation," and "The Basement Room" as the best of Greene's stories.

_____. *Graham Greene: A Study of the Short Fiction*. New York: Twayne, 1992. Discusses the influence of Henry James, Guy de Maupassant, and W. Somerset Maugham on Greene's stories, but also discusses how the stories reflect Greene's own personal demons. Includes an interview with Greene, his introduction to his *Collected Stories*, and three previously published essays by other critics.

McEwan, Neil. *Graham Greene*. New York: St. Martin's Press, 1988. Combines criticism and autobiography in the opening chapter, "Greene on Greene," and adds chapters on the early novels, Catholic influences, and comedy. Includes a bibliography of major works.

O'Prey, Paul. *A Reader's Guide to Graham Greene*. London: Thames and Hudson, 1988. A critical overview of Greene's fiction, including a chapter on the major short stories. The excellent introduction familiarizes the reader with Greene's major themes. Supplemented by a complete primary bibliography and a brief list of critical works.

Sherry, Norman. *The Life of Graham Greene*. Vol. 2, *1939-1955*. New York: Viking Press, 1995. In the second volume of this three-volume life, Sherry focuses on a narrow span of time during which Greene published most of his best-known fiction. Focuses on Greene as a celebrated public figure as well as a tormented private individual. Charts Greene's growing political activism as he moves more toward the Left.

Smith, Grahame. *The Achievement of Graham Greene*. Sussex, England: Harvester Press, 1986. Includes an excellent introduction, with an overview of themes and biographical data. Contains chapters on "Fiction and Belief" and "Fiction and Politics," as well as sections titled "The Man of Letters" and "Greene and Cinema." Augmented by a select bibliography.

John F. Desmond, updated by Karen Priest

ROBERT GREENE

Born: Norwich, Norfolk, England; c. July, 1558
Died: London, England; September 3, 1592

PRINCIPAL SHORT FICTION

Mamillia, 1583, 1593 (two parts)
The Mirror of Modesty, 1584
Morando: The Tritameron of Love, 1584, 1587
    (two parts)
Planetomachia, 1585
Perimedes the Blacksmith, 1588
Pandosto: The Triumph of Time, 1588
Ciceronis Amor, 1589 (also known as *Tullies Love*)
Menaphon, 1589
Greene's Never Too Late, 1590
Francesco's Fortunes, 1590
Greene's Farewell to Folly, 1591
A Notable Discovery of Cozenage, 1591
The Defense of Conny-Catching, 1592
A Disputation Between a Hee Conny-Catcher and
    a Shee Conny-Catcher, 1592
The Black Book's Messenger, 1592
A Quip for an Upstart Courtier, 1592
Greene's Vision, 1592

OTHER LITERARY FORMS

To please, and to some extent to form the taste of, the London middle class in the 1580's, Robert Greene mixed and invented literary types. *Mamillia*, his first published work, is a two-part romance presented as moral and rhetorical instruction; *Morando: The Tritameron of Love* is romance via *Courtier*-like conversation; *Planetomachia* sets forth tragic tales within a framework of Olympian conversation and adds a philosophical dispute in Latin. The rogue pamphlets of his last two years are collections of tales passed off as actual events.

More conventional forms used by Greene include the dream vision (for example, *A Quip for an Upstart Courtier*), the poetic eulogy (*A Maiden's Dream*, 1591), the political diatribe (*The Spanish Masquerado*, 1589), and the book of proverbs (*The Royal Exchange*, 1590). In drama, Greene's *Friar Bacon and Friar Bongay* (c. 1589) has been called the first English romantic comedy, but Greene composed at least four other plays, including the bitterly satiric *A Looking Glass for London and England* (c. 1588-1589; in collaboration with Thomas Lodge).

ACHIEVEMENTS

Robert Greene was a contemporary of Christopher Marlowe and William Shakespeare. He lived during one of England's most important literary periods—the English Renaissance. Greene was both an academic and a well-traveled student of life. He earned a B.A. from St. John's College at Cambridge. When he was not in school, Greene journeyed to Italy, Spain, France, Germany, Poland, and Denmark. His education served him well, for it was from the early Greek romances and works of other writers that Greene borrowed elements of characterization, form, diction, and plot. Greene, however, achieved more in his works than only an elaboration of previous literary forms; he was innovative and creative. His works appealed to the imaginations of the Elizabethans.

From 1582 to 1592, Greene wrote constantly. His works were well received and widely read in England. His writings included pamphlets exposing London's social ills, prose romances, and plays. His most notable drama, *Friar Bacon and Friar Bongay*, reflects a sixteenth century fascination with magic, along with an optimistic view of English life. Greene's works are also concerned with the question of an individual's role and identity within society and the capacity of human beings to satisfy their desires yet not exceed their human limits.

BIOGRAPHY

Robert Greene keeps the reader so far off-balance about the actual facts of his life that one cannot begin to write a biography of him without putting faith in statements which might otherwise be suspect. Most scholars, for example, accept that Greene was born in Norwich in 1558 and that his father was a saddler; the best evidence for this comes from

Greene's Groatsworth of Wit Bought with a Million of Repentance (1592), which mentions that its main character, Roberto, was born in Norwich. This detail sent scholars to city records, where they discovered a Robert Greene born to a saddler and his wife in 1558, a likely year. The pamphlet, however, is a bad source since it appeared after Greene's death, and scholars label its attribution to Greene himself probably spurious.

It may be said with more certainty that Greene was educated at Cambridge (B.A., St. John's, 1580; M.A., Clare, 1583) because Cambridge records support the "Master of Arts" appended to Greene's name on his title pages. From 1588 onward Greene proclaimed a second master's degree from Oxford, and the records also support this claim. Moreover, no one, including his enemy Gabriel Harvey, has ever denied his academic accomplishments. That Greene was in 1585 a "student of physic," as he claimed in *Planetomachia*, has never been verified. Other speculations—that he was a rural minister and a fencing master, for example—are based solely on the presence of the common name Robert Greene on lists from history turned up by scholars.

History should probably accept Greene's description of himself as a drinking partner of thieves and scoundrels, a denizen of low inns, and a spendthrift. His friend Thomas Nashe corroborates Greene's words: "Hee made no account of winning credite by his workes . . . : his only care was to have a spel in his purse to conjure up a good cuppe of wine with at all times." His self-cultivated reputation as a rakehell aside, there is no foundation for Harvey's assertion that Greene had a whore as mistress (sister of a known killer) and by her a son, Fortunatus, who died in infancy.

That he died in poverty in September, 1592, after a month-long illness is virtually certain. Certain also is the flurry of pamphlets attributed to him, about him, or including him as a character, which appeared in the half dozen years following his death. Of his dealings with patrons it is known that he termed himself the "adopted son" of one Thomas Burnaby, to whom Greene dedicated several works. How much support Burnaby gave is not known, but Greene's

epistles to his middle-class readers show clearly that he knew them to be his main source of income and prestige.

ANALYSIS

Robert Greene's writing should be understood as the work of a man trying always to put forward an image of both himself and his characters to his readers. That image, elucidated in his prefaces, was one of a socially conscious writer using his God-given talents for the good of his countrymen. Specifically, Greene wished his readers to become better citizens and more adept judges of language and personality through exposure to his loyal, learned, patriotic, and humble heroines and penitent heroes.

In the Christian universe of Greene's romances, men and women suffer, and their communities with them, through perversion of virtue into greed, lust, arrogance, and self-pity. All such suffering, however, is seen by Greene as an opportunity for humility and a subsequent return to charity. The Greene romance plot usually moves through fragmentation of both spirit and society to unity and community. The harmonious monarchies which emerge are always based on mutual respect by all social classes; patriotism includes respect and charity toward foreigners, particularly the exiles and prodigals who move through all Greene stories. Rarely does an important character fail to follow the perversion-regeneration path, so that Greene's stories are peopled by the falling and the rising, not by villains and heroes. Ironically, Greene's best-known romance, *Pandosto* (best known because Shakespeare used it for the plot of *The Winter's Tale*, 1610-1611), ends with the suicide of the title character; thus, modern readers who know only this work have misjudged Greene's muse.

MENAPHON

No work better displays the usual Greene pattern than *Menaphon*, his popular attempt to write a brief, uncynical *Arcadia* (1590). In the romance, Arcadia's King Democles, insecure and suspicious because of a Delphic oracle which seems to portend his ruin, discovers that his daughter Sephestia has married a low noble, Maximius, and borne him a son, Pleusidippus. The enraged Democles threatens Maximius's murder and the young man flees at his wife's urging. Soon she, too, escapes, but is shipwrecked with her infant along the Arcadian coast. Fearing discovery, she pretends to be a shepherdess, Samela, and soon is accepted by the pastoral Arcadians as a poor widow. Her new anonymity, however, makes her prey to the arrogant courtship of Menaphon, the king's chief herdsman, who proceeds from love lyrics to bribes to threats of force in order to win her. Meanwhile, Pleusidippus grows up brilliant, but ungoverned. Then, one day, he is carried off by pirates to Thessaly, where he charms the royal court and is further indulged.

Years pass. Menaphon continues to ply his suit, although Samela has fallen in love with another shepherd, Melicertus, who shyly returns her interest. Melicertus, it is learned, is the disguised Maximius; but neither recognizes the other because both are convinced that his/her spouse is long dead—a symbol for Greene of how the fragmented spirit misperceives reality.

The scene shifts to Thessaly. Pleusidippus, now a prince, hears reports of a paragon of shepherdesses in Arcadia, and, inflamed with lust, he sails away to possess her. Back in Arcadia, King Democles, grown even more tyrannical, hears a similar report, and he, too, enters the country to claim the rustic beauty. Thus, father, son, and husband of Sephestia become rivals, and no man recognizes another because time has disguised them all. When they meet, harsh words grow to combat, and combat to warfare, with thousands of Arcadians falling before the army of their own king. Then, just as Democles is about to execute Samela and Melicertus, an old prophetess steps forth proclaiming that the king is about to murder his daughter. Suddenly, truth springs forth out of all the disguises and all realize how close to disaster their perversions and fears had brought them. Democles sees that their adventures have paralleled the oracle, and suddenly humble, he resigns his kingship to his regal grandson. Sephestia and Maximius return to honor. Menaphon, meanwhile, gives up his courtly wooing, returns to his sheep, and marries his rustic sweetheart.

While a plot summary demonstrates the typical movement of the Greene romance from chaos to harmony, distortion to clarity, Greene is more interested in the mental steps by which each character determines and justifies his actions. Greene's characters come to be known through their soliloquies, which always strike one by their logical order, so that the reader often ignores how distorted the character's perspective is until the decisions that arise lead to disaster. Because Greene so fully presents his characters' motives and thought processes, he rarely creates a character with whom the reader cannot to some degree sympathize. In *Menaphon*, for example, the tyrant Democles seems, as a result, more pitiable than odious, even though Greene details his slaughters. It is this sympathy, this feeling which causes the reader to believe that, as fearful and selfish as these figures may be, they are capable of a charity and trust, that keeps the ending's sudden harmony from seeming contrived.

A NOTABLE DISCOVERY OF COZENAGE

Greene set himself a more difficult task when he tried to show that the whores and thieves of his connycatching pamphlets were deserving of the sympathy of his bourgeois, puritanical readers. He increased the potential for his success by putting himself forward in the first pamphlet, *A Notable Discovery of Cozenage*, as an avowed foe of "those pernitious sleights that have brought many ignorant men to confusion." Once having won his readers' confidence that he was on their side, however, he began to discriminate gradually between the lesser evils of nipping purses and prostitution and the greater evils of judicial bribes and merchant fraud. As the connycatching series proceeded, Greene's nips, foists, and whores become more lively personalities, often speaking directly to the reader not so much to defend their trades but to attack what could be called "white-collar" crime. In these monologues, the rogues come across as witty, practical, and satiric while their victims appear to be greedy, fat upstarts trying to pass themselves off as gentlemen. A willing reader might find himself identifying with the thief against the merchant, and that seems to be Greene's purpose, although he continued throughout the six works to call himself the rogues' foe.

A DISPUTATION BETWEEN A HEE CONNY-CATCHER AND A SHEE CONNY-CATCHER

A Disputation Between a Hee Conny-Catcher and a Shee Conny-Catcher, the fifth pamphlet in the series, takes the reader most deeply into the underworld and into the minds of the rogues by making the reader an eavesdropper on an alehouse debate between "Laurence, a foyst, and Nan, a traffique." Authenticity and intimacy are provided by the slangy, joking speech of the pair and by their reference by name to others of their professions. The subject of the dispute—that of which of them more endangers the commonwealth—seems set up by Greene to allow the reader to indulge his self-righteous anger at the evils of the criminal world; but not far into the dialogue Laurence and Nan take aim at their victims. Nan credits her success as a prostitute to the insatiable lust of her clients; this appetite, she continues, also supports the respectable commercial world:

> the Hospitall would want patients, and Surgians much worke, the Apothecaries would haue surphaling water and Potato roots lye deade on theyr handes, the Paynters could not dispatche and make way theyr Vermiglion . . ., why Laurence, [the taverns] would be moord . . . if we of the Trade were not to supply [their] wants. . . .

She spits her choicest venom at the "good auncient Matron" who sets her "faire wench . . . her daughter . . . out to sale in her youth" to draw on "sundrie to bee suters." To Nan and Laurence the underworld has no limits.

This blackening of all humanity by the connycatching pair recalls the similar process in Greene's romances, whereby each character perverts love in some way and thus endangers society. The rising action of the romances, wherein souls and society are reformed, has its parallel in the sequel to Laurence and Nan's dialogue, "The Conversion of an English Courtizan," which makes up the second half of *A Disputation Between a Hee Conny-Catcher and a Shee Conny-Catcher*. Greene presents this as the true story of a country girl, made vain and greedy by her doting, ambitious bourgeois parents, who never learns humility or loyalty and thus takes to crime.

Having gone from bad to worse, she eventually meets a young merchant who differs from all other Londoners she has met by neither buying her nor scorning her; this quiet fellow respects her, wins her confidence, promises his loyalty, and marries her. The community of the story is harmonized, at least for the time being.

"THE CONVERSION OF AN ENGLISH COURTIZAN"

Not until "The Conversion of an English Courtizan" has Greene suggested in the pamphlet series that his rogues have the potential for reform—in fact, he explicity denies it in the first pamphlet. As in the romances, Greene will not allow the rebuilding of his fictional society until all parties have acknowledged their share in the earlier destruction. Since the connycatching series begins as an indictment of one element of the city, Greene will not depict repentance by that element until the entire society has been implicated in the evil, as it is most vehemently in *A Disputation Between a Hee Conny-Catcher and a Shee Conny-Catcher*. In Greene's Christian vision, repentance can be accepted only by a penitent, whose forgiving includes the desire to be forgiven. For Greene, "The Conversion of an English Courtizan" cannot succeed as a story unless the reader understands that the courtesan represents each segment of society, not merely the stereotyped criminal.

OTHER MAJOR WORKS

LONG FICTION: *Arbasto: The Anatomie of Fortune*, 1584; *Penelope's Web*, 1587; *Greene's Mourning Garment*, 1590; *Philomela: The Lady Fitzwater's Nightingale*, 1592.

PLAYS: *Orlando furioso*, pr. c. 1588; *A Looking Glass for London and England*, pr. c. 1588-1589 (with Thomas Lodge); *Friar Bacon and Friar Bongay*, pr. c. 1589; *John of Bordeaux*, pr. c. 1590-1591; *James IV*, pr. c. 1591; *Complete Plays*, pb. 1909.

POETRY: *A Maiden's Dream*, 1591.

NONFICTION: *The Spanish Masquerado*, 1589; *The Royal Exchange*, 1590; *Greene's Groatsworth of Wit Bought with a Million of Repentance*, 1592; *The Repentance of Robert Greene*, 1592.

MISCELLAENOUS: *Life and Complete Works in Prose and Verse,* 1881-1886.

BIBLIOGRAPHY

Carroll, D. Allen. "The Player-Patron in Greene's *Groatsworth of Wit.*" *Studies in Philology* 91 (Summer, 1994): 301-312. Discusses the character and identity of the anonymous actor who recruits Greene's persona to be a playwright; suggests he may be a fictional character rather than based on William Shakespeare or someone else.

Chandler, David. "'Upstart Crow': Provenance and Meaning." *Notes and Queries* 42 (September, 1995): 291-294. Discussion of the "upstart Crow" reference to Shakespeare in Greene's *Groatsworth of Wit*; suggests that the reference may refer to a clash between Shakespeare and Greene in more dramatic terms than was previously suspected.

Crupi, Charles W. *Robert Greene.* Boston: Twayne, 1986. Crupi's publication addresses Greene's life based on relevant biographical and historical research printed since 1960. Crupi includes two comprehensive chapters dealing with Greene's prose works and plays. The work also contains extensive notes and references, a chronology, and a select bibliography of primary and secondary sources.

Davis, Walter R. *Idea and Act in Elizabethan Fiction.* Princeton, N.J.: Princeton University Press, 1969. This work devotes one chapter to Greene's works and the elements of Greek romance inherent in the works. Davis divides Greene's career into four periods—the euphuistic mode, the short tales or novellas, the pastoral romances, and the pamphlets of repentance, roguery, and other nonfiction. The works are discussed in terms of plot and Greene's development among genres.

Jordan, John Clark. *Robert Greene.* New York: Octagon Books, 1965. Jordan's book is considered a main source for critics concerned with Greene's work. He presents Greene as a man of letters, who was an expert at narrative. The text includes a discussion of Greene's poetry, plays, and nondramatic work. A bibliography and appendices are included. The appendices contain a framework for Greene's tales, misconceptions about Greene's life and career, as well as accounts of early allusions to Greene.

Sanders, Norman. "The Comedy of Greene and Shakespeare." In *Early Shakespeare,* edited by John Russell Brown and Bernard Harris. New York: St. Martin's Press, 1961. Sanders traces Greene's development as a writer, particularly his move from imitation to invention and creativity. He discusses the love plots contained in Greene's romantic comedies as compared to those of William Shakespeare. While he mentions the similarities in development of both playwrights, Sanders does not set out to prove that Greene influenced Shakespeare's works.

Simpson, Richard, ed. *The School of Shakespeare.* Vol. 2. New York: J. W. Bouton, 1878. Simpson's work is a nineteenth century account of Greene's life and work. He explores the relationship between William Shakespeare and Greene as contemporaries and rivals. The volume also contains plot information and a discussion of themes in Greene's plays and other fiction.

Christopher J. Thaiss,
updated by Paula M. Miller

THE BROTHERS GRIMM

Jacob Grimm

Born: Hanau, Germany; January 4, 1785
Died: Berlin, Germany; September 20, 1863

Wilhelm Grimm

Born: Hanau, Germany; February 24, 1786
Died: Berlin, Germany; December 16, 1859

PRINCIPAL SHORT FICTION

Kinder- und Hausmärchen, 1812, 1815 (*German Popular Stories*, 1823-1826; 2 volumes; best known as *Grimm's Fairy Tales*.

OTHER LITERARY FORMS

The Brothers Grimm published important studies of German tales and mythology, as well as philological works recognized for their importance to the study of the German language.

ACHIEVEMENTS

The tales collected and edited by the Brothers Grimm are the defining instances of *Märchen*, a term only approximately translated by "fairy tale." At a time when the changes wrought by the Industrial Revolution threatened to make the traditions of oral storytelling disappear, Jacob and Wilhelm Grimm were able to preserve these tales in written form. Now, in the Anglo-Saxon world at least, the tales recounted by the Brothers Grimm are more familiar than any stories except those of the Bible. The literary influence of the collection has been considerable: It has shaped much of subsequent children's literature and has inspired a great many sophisticated fictions, particularly among the German Romantics, the English Victorians, and the so-called Fabulators of the mid-twentieth century. Most important, however, has been the direct human influence of the tales. The collection epitomizes the psychological wisdom of generations of storytellers, and the tales themselves provide for nearly every child in the West a first map of the territory of the imagination.

BIOGRAPHY

Both of the Brothers Grimm devoted their lives to literary and philological scholarship. Following in their father's footsteps, they studied law at Marburg, but, under the influence of Johann Gottfried Herder and Clemens Brentano, they turned from the law, and between 1806 and 1826, first at Marburg and later at the library of the Elector in Kassel, they collaborated in the study of folklore, producing not only the *Märchen* but also *Deutsche Sagen* (1816-1818; *German Legends*, 1981), on local historical legends and other works. In 1830, they left Kassel to become librarians and later professors at Göttingen. After a decade of largely independent work, the two collaborated again on a monumental lexicon of the German language, the *Deutsches Wörterbuch* (1854). The project was begun in 1838, was carried to Berlin when the brothers were appointed professors at the university in 1841, and was completed only in 1961—Wilhelm had died working on the letter *D*, Jacob at *F*).

Wilhelm Carl Grimm was in his own right an editor of medieval texts who did important work on runes and Germanic legend. Jacob Ludwig Carl Grimm was one of the greatest scholars in the history of a nation of scholars. His *Deutsche Mythologie* (1835; *Teutonic Mythology*, 1880-1888), attempted to establish a theoretical base for the *Märchen* collected earlier, viewing them as the detritus of a German mythology suppressed by Christianity. In thus laying the groundwork for all further speculation on the origins of folklore and myth, he has come to be acknowledged as the father of the scientific study of folklore. At the same time, he is the uncontested founder of the systematic study of the German language and indeed of historical linguistics itself; this assessment is based on the strength of his work that begins with the formulation of Grimm's law in *Deutsche Grammatik* (1819-1837) and culminates in the *Deutsches Wörtebuch*.

ANALYSIS

Grimm's Fairy Tales came into being in the context of German Romanticism, particularly with its renewed interest in the medieval past. Just as European society was becoming urban, industrial, and literate, a growing nationalism turned attention to folk culture. The Brothers Grimm first began collecting songs and stories for the poet Clemens Brentano and his brother-in-law Achim von Arnim, who had themselves collaborated on an influential collection of folksongs, *Des Knaben Wunderhorn* (1805, 1808; the boy's wonderhorn), still familiar from Gustav Mahler's many settings of its songs. The Grimms drew on oral as well as printed sources, interviewing both peasant storytellers and middle-class urban informants. The resulting collection of some two hundred stories preserved a substantial body of folklore, fortuitously, at the very moment when its milieu was being irreparably destroyed by the modernization of nineteenth century Europe. Translated into at least seventy languages, *Grimm's Fairy Tales* stands as the model for every subsequent collection of folklore, however much more sophisticated in theory or method. The brothers' own notes and commentaries on the tales, included in the second edition, form the basis of the science of folklore.

One source of the appeal of these tales is their complex chemistry of both art and artlessness. The Grimms did not think of themselves as authors of short fiction but as what would now be considered anthropologists. They set for themselves the task of contriving, from many different versions of any tale, an account that achieved artistic integrity without sacrificing folkloric quality. This meant sometimes restoring details that seemed to have been dropped or distorted in the course of oral tradition, or deleting what seemed purely literary invention. Many decisions were arbitrary since this was, after all, the beginning of a discipline, and the Grimms sometimes changed their minds, as differences between the first and second editions make clear. They were guided on the whole, however, by an aim of reconstructing prototypes which they assumed to be oral. Thus, in each tale they were responding to two different challenges. First, they attempted to preserve and even enhance the atmosphere of performance through traditional rhetorical devices such as repetition of songs and narrative formulas in which the audience would share

Left to right, Jacob and Wilhelm Grimm (Library of Congress)

and through the general circumstantial quality characteristic of every spellbinding teller. At the same time, their versions were meant to be definitive and fixed in print, a medium with aesthetic demands of its own that had to be met.

"SIX SOLDIERS OF FORTUNE" AND "THE FISHERMAN AND HIS WIFE"

As a result, within the Grimm style, which is instantly recognizable as a matter of motif, several substyles of narrative are apparent. There are some tales that strike the reader as archetypal for their transparency of structure. "Six Soldiers of Fortune," for example, assembles a group of soldiers, each with a unique preternatural power, makes use of, and so in a sense exhausts, each power in a deadly contest for the hand of a princess, and then dismisses the group with a treasure to divide. Perhaps most lucid of all is the haunting "The Fisherman and His Wife"; this tale combines heightening ambitions and lowering weather against the measured rhythm of wishes demanded and granted, all strung on the thread of a summoning spell sung six times to the generous fish, an enchanted prince who disturbingly *remains* enchanted throughout the tale, until in the end everything is as it was. In this tale, no wish is offered at first, until the wife, knowing with the logic of fairy tale that enchanted fish grant wishes, sends her husband back. After wishing herself from hovel to cottage to castle, however, her third wish is for a change not of station but of identity. She wishes to be king, and this moves beyond the rule of three to the inordinate and outlandish: emperor, pope, ruler of the sun and moon, things she cannot be.

"THE LADY AND THE LION"

Other tales seem authentic not for their clarity but for a sense of free-ranging invention in loose, barely articulated forms. "The Lady and the Lion" is a prime example of a tale that seems ready to go anywhere a teller is inclined to take it. It relies heavily on familiar but heterogeneous motifs, and so while it fascinates readers from moment to moment (especially if heard rather than read) with an almost Asian opulence of invention, it seems in the end unmotivated.

"GODFATHER DEATH"

The tension between the commitment to transcribe tales as told and the need to devise viable written artifacts can best be exemplified by contrasting two stories. In "Godfather Death," a man seeking a godfather for his thirteenth child rejects God himself and the Devil but accepts Death because he "makes all equal." When the boy is grown, Death gives him an herb that restores life with these instructions: "If I stand by the head of the sick-bed, administer this herb and the man will recover; but if I stand at the foot, the man is mine, and you must say that nothing can save him." The boy becomes a famous healer. Once when the King is sick, with Death at his feet, the boy risks using the herb to save him, but Death pardons him with a warning. Later, however, the King's daughter is in the same situation, and for love of her the doctor again overrules Death. Death seizes him with an icy hand and leads him to a cave where thousands of candles are burning, some very large, some mere stubs. "Show me the light of my life," says the doctor, and he finds it guttering. He begs his godfather to replace it, and the story ends like this:

Death behaved as if he were going to fulfill his wish, and took hold of a tall new candle, but as he desired to

revenge himself, he purposely made a mistake in fixing it, and the little piece fell down and was extinguished. The physician too fell on the ground; now he himself was in the hands of Death.

"THE WONDERFUL GLASS"

Grimm's Fairy Tales preserves another version of this story, "The Wonderful Glass," which is, from the point of view of a written tale, almost incoherent. It is less carefully composed than "Godfather Death": Only one stranger appears, the child is merely "another child," and the gift of healing is given oddly not to the child but to his father; in fact the child plays no role at all. The father never misuses the gift but one day decides to visit the godfather. Five steps lead to the house. On the first a mop and a broom are quarreling, on the next he finds a "number of dead fingers," on the next a heap of human heads give him directions, on the next a fish is frying itself in a pan. At the top the doctor peeks through the keyhole and sees the godfather with a set of horns on his head. When he enters the house, the godfather hides under the bedclothes. When he says, "I saw you through the keyhole with a pair of horns on your head," the godfather shouts, "That is not true," in such a terrible voice that the doctor runs away and is never heard of again. "The Wonderful Glass" is hardly worth preserving except as a transcript of a clumsy horror story. The immense superiority of "Godfather Death" may suggest how the Grimms' decision to proceed by artful selection among versions rather than by wholesale recasting in another mode produced masterpieces. Again and again their editorial tact added formal power to the visual interest and psychological depth of the inherited stories.

"RAPUNZEL"

"Rapunzel," for example, begins like many of the *Märchen* ("Snow White," "Sleeping Beauty," "The Almond Tree"), with a couple who wish for a child. A small window in their house overlooks a witch's garden, and one night the husband climbs over the high wall to steal some "rapunze," a salad green. He is soon caught by the witch, however, and to save his life he promises to amend the theft by giving her his child when it is born. It was pregnancy that made his wife crave rapunze; the unborn child thus causes the theft and by a rough justice replaces the thing stolen. The witch takes her at birth, names her Rapunzel, and walls her up, even more securely than the plant she replaces, in a tower accessible only by a high window. This generates the central image of the tale: the long-haired nubile girl imprisoned in the tower. Like the husband, the Prince (potential husband of the next generation) climbs over the wall to steal the witch's Rapunze(l), and he too is eventually caught by the possessive witch. Learning of the Prince's visits, she banishes Rapunzel to a wasteland, first cutting off her hair which will be used to lure the Prince to a confrontation. He escapes, but in his terror falls on thorns that blind him. After years of wandering, he hears Rapunzel's voice again, they embrace, and her tears restore his sight.

"Rapunzel" is usually read as a story of maturation, with Rapunzel as the central figure, but she is a passive character throughout, an instrument in the relations of others. It is at least equally a tale of possessiveness and longing. The parents desire a child; in the wife's craving for greens the reader sees the child at once gained and lost. Like the parents (although more like Rumpelstiltskin) the witch desires a child, and the Prince's longing is obvious—it is the chief character trait of princes throughout the *Märchen*. The remarkable dearth of magic is related to these themes. In spite of the presence of the witch, the only magic is the healing tears of love. In other versions the witch's magic harms the prince; here it is mysteriously not her doing, but ironic coincidence. The pathos of that reticence is owed to the Brothers Grimm; their instinct for invoking folk style is apparent in the repeated motifs but above all in their inspired invention of the phrase, "Rapunzel, Rapunzel, let down your hair," which sounds, even when the reader knows better, like the archaic root of the whole story.

Thus, the Grimms reconciled the values of folklore with what were recognized as the requirements of short fiction, but they were scrupulously aware that the versions they contrived were only moments seized out of the continuing tradition of telling and retelling. The proper habitation of the *Märchen* is in the mouths of storytellers. Form, the proportion of parts, and even readers' sympathies are always being accommodated to new audiences in new circumstances. As early as 1893, Marian Cox could study 345 variants of "Cinderella" alone. *Grimm's Fairy Tales* then were folktales accommodated to print: more symmetrical, more compressed, as a rule spatially rather than linearly conceived, and with formal rhythms replacing the lost rhythm of speech. The brothers' devotion to their originals or to the sources behind their originals, however, is apparent. As the example of "Rapunzel" suggests, their versions are much less stylized than other literary versions; the reader never feels the presence of an author as in those printed versions that antedate the Grimms, such as Charles Perrault and Giambattista Basile. They would never say, as Perrault does, that Sleeping Beauty was beautiful even though she dressed like someone's grandmother in clothes out of fashion for a century.

Thanks to the Grimms, the *Märchen* have survived in a new kind of world, but the process of accommodation continues. One of the measures of how thoroughly these tales have been internalized in the West is the shock every reader feels on first reading the Grimms' own account of tales so profoundly familiar. This is not how they are remembered, and the difference frankly reveals how tastes have changed in the intervening years. Through several generations of editors, and especially of parents, the *Märchen* have become more magical, much more romantic, and decidedly less violent than the Grimms' own versions.

Magic is a most important variable. Although there is plenty of it in the tales, modern readers will find the Grimms often unexpectedly discreet in the use of magic.

"THE LITTLE FARMER" AND "SLEEPING BEAUTY"

There is even at least one plainly antimagical story, "The Little Farmer," in which the protagonist defeats a whole town because the people are gullible about magic (eventually they are all drowned when, after the farmer tells them he collected a fine flock of sheep under water, they see fleecy clouds reflected on the surface as confirmation of his story and jump in). There is much use of gratuitous magic, not only for ornament but also, in particular, to establish a tone of fantasy at the start of a story. The beginning of "Sleeping Beauty" offers an extreme example: A frog jumps out of the water, prophesies that the queen will soon bear a daughter, and disappears never to be mentioned again. Indeed, supernatural helpers put in abrupt appearances throughout the tales.

"SNOW WHITE"

Often in reading *Grimm's Fairy Tales*, however, the reader finds coincidence or rationalization where memory led him to expect magic. Thus, in "Snow White," although the wicked queen has her magic mirror, much that could be magic is more nearly pharmacology. Even the revival of Snow White is not, as Walt Disney and memory would have it, by the magic of a kiss from Prince Charming, but like this: The dwarfs gave the coffin to the Prince, who had his servants carry it away.

> Now it happened that as they were going along they stumbled over a bush, and with the shaking a bit of the poisoned apple flew out of her throat. It was not long before she opened her eyes, threw open the cover of the coffin, and sat up, alive and well. "Oh dear, where am I?," cried she. The King's son answered, full of joy, "you are near me. . . . Come with me to my father's castle and you shall be my bride." And Snow White was kind, and went with him.

An earlier generation of commentators would have woven from bush and fruit a myth of fall and redemption, but at least as interesting is the calculated avoidance of overt magic even in resurrection. The blinding of the Prince in "Rapunzel" is treated with similar ambiguity.

VIOLENCE

Apart from the treatment of magic, the most unexpected feature of the Grimms' tales is their violence. The stories are full of treachery, mutilation, cannibalism, and over and over again the visual and visceral impact of the sight of red blood against pale skin, white snow, black wood, or stone. This is most shocking in the well-known stories. When Snow White's stepmother cannot resist coming to the wedding to see if the girl really is "a thousand times more fair," she finds that "they had ready red-hot iron shoes, in which she had to dance until she fell down dead."

The ending of "Cinderella" is similar, although it is better integrated with the shape of the story. The two stepsisters cut off parts of their feet to fit into the tiny slipper, but as each in turn passes the grave of Cinderella's true mother, which is marked by a hazel tree grown from a twig she asked as a gift from her father and watered with her tears, two birds perched in the tree, her helpers earlier, make known the mutilations so that at last Cinderella can put on the shoe that was made for her. As a result, she marries the Prince, and the tale ends with the same birds pecking out the eyes of the stepsisters.

Violence in *Grimm's Fairy Tales* nearly always has a human origin. The reader grows accustomed to witches, stepmothers, and evil elder siblings, but the overwhelming sense of the world here is optimistic. The stories regularly assert a harmony between humans and nature, often seen as more reliable than human harmony: The birds will help when other people will not. By their plotting, the stories also project a harmony in time. In the end, the good live happily ever after, while for the evil there are dire and, to most modern readers, disproportionate punishments. The harmonious close of a Grimm tale is grounded on a faith in justice. Indeed, several of the tales have this as their theme: No crime can remain hidden; truth will come to light. Behind this is a sense of divine Providence, for beneath all the magic the milieu of these tales is thoroughly Christian. There is hardly a trace of the tragic weight of Germanic myth in even the most harrowing of the *Märchen*.

"THE SINGING BONE"

Consider "The Singing Bone": Through the clear water of a river, a herdsman sees on the sandy bottom a bone as white as snow. He retrieves it to make a mouthpiece for his horn, and at once it begins to sing its own story, "I killed the wild boar, and my brother slew me,/ Then gained the Princess by pretending it was he." The marvel is brought to the King, the victim's skeleton is found, the wicked brother is ordered drowned, and the bones are "laid to rest in a beautiful grave." This is quite brutal, even in summary, but the formal symmetries of the violence here reinforce the demonstration of justice. If a modern reader tends to worry about the bereft Princess and is less than satisfied with a beautiful grave, it may be that he has lost faith in any ultimate distribution of justice. That may be the chief reason that so much of the violence of the Grimms' tales is now suppressed in the telling.

The Grimms' theory of folklore as the doctrine of a mythology is now discredited, but they were right to sense the tremendous resonance of these tales in the imagination. More recently, psychological approaches from Sigmund Freud and Carl Gustav Jung down to Bruno Bettelheim have pointed to the archetypal force of these stories. This force is not the Grimms' creation; it is a wisdom concentrated through a long process of transmission. What the Grimm brothers contributed was an array of formal devices learned in the context of literate fiction— devices that increased the strength and resilience of the tales in the period when their survival was most threatened.

Along with the form of the stories, what the Grimms' retelling often particularly enhanced were the visual images. The traditional tales were full of images of seminal power from which much of the psychological impact emanated. In stories meant to be heard, however, the visual imagination is free, and images can be invoked by a word or two. Consciously or not, the Brothers Grimm realized that in the act of reading, the visual imagination is engaged, so images must be sharpened and developed in order to act on a preoccupied eye. As a result, *Grimm's Fairy Tales* is crowded with images of emblematic power such as the gingerbread house, the palace of sleepers, Snow White in her glass coffin, and Little Red Riding Hood and the bedded wolf. These images have attracted the finest illustrators (and animators) of every intervening generation to join with storytellers in transmitting a body of tales that speaks to readers, it seems, in the native language of the imagination.

OTHER MAJOR WORKS

NONFICTION: *Deutsche Sagen*, 1816-1818 (*German Legends*, 1981, 2 volumes); *Über deutsche Runen*, 1921 (Wilhelm Grimm only); *Deutsche Grammatik*, 1819-1837 (Jacob Grimm only); *Die deutsche Heldensage*, 1829 (Wilhelm Grimm only); *Deutsche Mythologie*, 1835 (*Teutonic Mythology*, 1880-1888, 4 volumes; Jacob Grimm only); *Geschichte der deutschen Sprache*, 1848 (Jacob Grimm only); *Deutsches Wörterbuch*, 1854.

BIBLIOGRAPHY

Bettelheim, Bruno. *The Uses of Enchantment: The Meaning and Importance of Fairy Tales*. New York: Random House, 1976. Bettelheim's book discusses the major motifs and themes of fairy tales from a Freudian psychological perspective, focusing on their meanings for the growing child. He discusses many of the tales collected by the Brothers Grimm and in part 2 examines in detail eight of the stories still popular today. He includes a useful bibliography, though many of the books listed are in German, and an index.

Dollerup, Cay. "Translation as a Creative Force in Literature: The Birth of the European Bourgeois Fairy-Tale." *The Modern Language Review* 90 (January, 1995): 94-102. Discusses the European bourgeois fairy tale's development as the result of translation of the stories of the Brothers Grimm into Danish and the stories of Hans Christian Andersen into German; claims this is important because children were not familiar with foreign languages. Argues that the Grimms and Andersen were adapted to European middle-class values.

Haase, Donald, ed. *The Reception of Grimms' Fairy Tales: Responses, Reactions, Revisions*. Detroit: Wayne State University Press, 1993. Valuable essays on public and critical opinions of the Grimms' tales.

McGlathery, James M. *Grimm's Fairy Tales: A History of Criticism on a Popular Classic*. Columbia, S.C.: Camden House, 1993. Examines critical response to the works. Includes bibliographical references and an index.

Michaelis-Jena, Ruth. *The Brothers Grimm*. London: Routledge & Kegan Paul, 1970. Michaelis-Jena has written a thorough biography of Jacob and Wilhelm Grimm, and she includes a chapter called "The 'Nursery and Household Tales' and Their Influence," which provides information on early reactions to the collection and its translations, noting that the tales spurred an interest in collection of other national folktales. Contains an index and bibliography.

Tatar, Maria. *The Hard Facts of the Grimms' Fairy Tales*. Princeton, N.J.: Princeton University Press, 1987. Tatar provides close readings of many of the tales, mostly from a psychological perspective, though the book is aimed at a more scholarly audience than Bettelheim's. She examines typical motifs and situations and attempts to bring in the perspectives of folklorists, cultural anthropologists, and literary critics, as well as that of the psychologists. Notes, index.

Ward, Donald. "The German Connection: The Brothers Grimm and the Study of 'Oral' Literature." *Western Folklore* 53 (January, 1994): 1-26. Discusses the influence of the Brothers Grimm on German storytellers; argues that print and oral tales have not joined into a homogeneous mixture.

Zipes, Jack. *The Brothers Grimm: From Enchanted Forests to the Modern World*. New York: Routledge, 1988. Zipes's book arose out of talks he gave at various conferences. The work is quite scholarly, and many of the chapters examine the effects of the tales on modern society and place them in a sociohistorical context. Supplemented by notes, a good bibliography, and an index.

Laurence A. Breiner,
updated by Karen M. Cleveland Marwick

JOÃO GUIMARÃES ROSA

Born: Cordisburgo, Minas Gerais, Brazil; June 3, 1908
Died: Rio de Janeiro, Brazil; November 19, 1967

PRINCIPAL SHORT FICTION

Sagarana, 1946, 1966
Corpo de Baile, 1956 (subsequent editions in three volumes: *Manuelzão e Miguilim*, *No Urubùquaquá, no Pinhém*, and *Noites do Sertão*)
Primeiras Estórias, 1962, 1968 (*The Third Bank of the River and Other Stories*, 1968)
Tutaméia, 1967
Estas Estórias, 1969
Ave, Palavra, 1970

OTHER LITERARY FORMS

João Guimarães Rosa's first work, a collection of poems entitled *Magma*, has never been published, even though it won an important prize in 1937. *Grande Sertão: Veredas* (1956; *The Devil to Pay in the Backlands*, 1963), his masterpiece, is considered the most significant Brazilian novel of the twentieth century.

ACHIEVEMENTS

João Guimarães Rosa's fiction is generally regarded as the watershed work of the twentieth century Brazilian short story and novel, much as the fiction of Joaquim Maria Machado de Assis in the nineteenth century prompted critics to label every work of fiction as either "before" or "after" that writer. Guimarães Rosa was not only a master teller of tales but also a doctor, an amateur naturalist, and a polyglot. All of his stories reflect his fascination with the physical and natural world and the ways language might be bent to describe that world. His fiction always contains an element of moral or spiritual inquiry, and most of it is set in the interior of Brazil. All of his works are characterized by a highly original and perverse diction, which helps account for the paucity of translations. Guimarães Rosa was also a diplomat, having achieved the rank of ambassador in the Brazilian diplomatic service.

BIOGRAPHY

João Guimarães Rosa was a quiet, myopic child with a taste for natural history and a formidable talent for learning languages. After studying medicine, he practiced in a small town in the *sertão*, acquiring there a profound knowledge of the land and people. He divided his subsequent years between various government posts and the diplomatic corps, ending his career with the rank of ambassador. He was elected unanimously to the Brazilian Academy of Letters in 1963, and in 1965, he served as vice president at the first Latin American Writers Conference in Mexico City. He died in November, 1967, of a brain hemorrhage.

ANALYSIS

Latin American literature is filled with narratives that represent the awareness of the physical reality of Latin America and the adoption of an emotional position toward literature. Indeed, the stereotypic caricature of the Latin American narrative, in the eyes of both Latin Americans and their foreign readers, is that of W. H. Hudson (born and reared in Argentina) in *Green Mansions* (1904) or of reductionist readings of classics such as Ricardo Güiraldes's *Don Segundo Sombra* (1926), José Eustasio Rivera's *La vorágine* (1923), or Rómulo Gallegos's *Doña Bárbara* (1929). At its worst this strain of Latin American literature is a blend of romantic ideals (the Pampas and the Andean highlands) and bizarre exotica (the jungles and feudal oppression). At its best, however, as exemplified in the novels of contemporary masters such as Gabriel García Márquez, Juan Rulfo, Mario Vargas Llosa, Augusto Roa Bastos, and Alejo Carpentier, it represents the attempt to come to grips with the paradoxes and the anomalies of a complex sociocultural tradition that seems to defy its Western roots without really opting out of the modern world nourished by those roots. The fiction of João Guimarães Rosa clearly belongs to this view of Latin America as an unstable amalgam of modern Western myths and a sense of experiential reality as something far richer and more profound than nationalism is capable of recognizing or explaining. Hence there appeared terms such as "Magical Realism" or the "marvelous real" that have been applied to writings exemplified by the aforementioned writers. It is a groping for the much-desired terminological exactitude of academic criticism in the attempt to identify a texture of event and experience in modern Latin American fiction that

depends on the reader's recognizing it as *not* consonant with the everyday rational description of reality purveyed by official ideologies.

"THE THIN EDGE OF HAPPINESS"

Guimarães Rosa's "As Margens da Alegria" ("The Thin Edge of Happiness") is deceptively simple, yet its semiological richness is what makes it so indicative of the sort of fiction described above. Five narrative segments that break up the barely five-page story into microtexts seem to describe no more than a young child's sadness over realizing that his initial, spontaneous happiness with a newly beheld nature can be so suddenly shattered by the inexorable needs of human society. Taken by an aunt and uncle to visit a new city being carved out of the wilderness (probably the futuristic capital of Brasília, one of the symbols of the mid-twentieth century economic boom of capitalism in Brazil), "the boy" (he remains nameless throughout the story) is thrilled, amazed, and awestruck by the new reality he discovers at the end of a mere two-hour plane trip from his home. This reality includes the hustle and bustle of a veritable frontier city, a big city being built almost overnight by powerful machines, and the lush and seductive flora and fauna of the wilderness literally at his doorstep. Suddenly, however, one of the wondrous creatures he sees, a prancing turkey, is killed for a birthday party. Just as suddenly, the boy is treated to what the adults intend as a marvelous display of the power of the machines being used to carve the new metropolis out of the jungle: A sort of juggernaut machete slashes down a tree so efficaciously that the boy does not even see it fall. One minute it stood in understated beauty, then the machine leapt, and the tree lay on the ground, reduced to kindling. Rather than amazement at the machine's prowess, the boy feels sick as he contemplates the "astonished and blue" sky, exposed so brutally by the slash of the machine.

Yet it would be an impoverishment of Guimarães Rosa's text to read it as a brief sketch of a child's loss of innocence in the face of the implacable and mindless destruction of what he has held as beautiful and to which he has reacted with spontaneous, childlike joy. To be sure, Guimarães Rosa's text, particularly when one senses the vignette-like effect of the internal divisions, is somewhat of an inverted narrative haiku (Guimarães Rosa was profoundly influenced by Asian culture): A series of spare images describes, rather than the independent glory of nature as perceived by a neutral and respectful observer, the sudden and irrevocable destruction of a sense of the integrity of natural beauty as perceived by an innocent witness. Yet what increases the depth of sociocultural meaning of this story is precisely the nature of the controlling consciousness described by the narrator, the "privileged" status of the consciousness vis-à-vis the situation or reality portrayed and the conjunction of different orders, the mechanical-industrial and the natural-physical, that are arrayed antagonistically.

Guimarães Rosa's narrator tells his story in a tone that is virtually a parody of children's once-upon-a-time tales: "This is the story: A little boy went with his aunt and uncle to spend a few days in a place where the great city was being built." The narrative goes on to describe in a matter-of-fact, short-sentence fashion how the boy leaves behind his parents and the city to fly with his aunt and uncle to the unknown frontier, how the plane trip is a child's delight of new sensations provided by the indulgent and solicitous adults, and how the place where he arrives is a veritable fairyland: "The boy looked around and breathed deeply, wishing with all his heart that he could see even more vividly everything that presented itself in front of his eyes—so many new things!" One of these new things is a spectacular turkey, an animal unknown in the city; but no sooner is the boy's delight with the pompous and loquacious animal described than it "disappears," slaughtered for a birthday meal. The boy's awe turns to terror: The turkey's absence foregrounds the threatening wilderness from which the animal's strutting had distracted him. Just as quickly the narrator moves to the scene of the mechanized machete felling the simple tree.

In rapid succession the narrative juxtaposes implied opposites: known experiences versus unknown delights, childlike and exuberant joy versus unfocused anxiety, wild nature versus "wild" machines, the wilderness versus civilization and progress, childlike wonderment versus adult matter-of-factness, and the comforting versus the terrifying.

More than an anecdote concerning the brutal shattering of youthful and innocent happiness, Guimarães Rosa's text foregrounds, through the boy's mediating consciousness, a paradigmatic Latin American conflict: the natural versus the mechanical, spontaneous sentiment versus artificial power, what is human versus what is artificial and therefore destructive. Whereas United States society might typically see the union of the mechanical and the human as bringing the greater comfort of the latter, a text such as Guimarães Rosa's sees the two as irremediably antagonistic. The boy's loss of innocence is not the product of any routine process of maturation, whereby the child comes to harmonious terms with modern mechanized society. Rather, it is the result of the brutal imposition of the new mechanized society (the adult representatives of progress and their machines, for whom the beauties of nature discovered by the boy are at best food and at worst a nuisance) on an awesome nature. It is only when the boy's perception of his new surroundings has been "conditioned" by the attitudes and action of the adults that he sees the new reality as no longer a fairyland but a threatening and dark void: "The boy could not understand it. The forest, the black trees, were much too much, they were the world."

In the view of one metatheory of contemporary anthropology, acculturation is a process of acquiring a socially conditioned way of seeing unordered events and situations and of giving them structure and meaning. Guimarães Rosa's story proposes the clash of two processes of acculturation, one the unfettered spontaneity of childlike innocence whereby the world is a garden of delightful marvels; and one the harsh dominance of nature by humans' mechanized society, whereby the world is a threatening enemy to be conquered, swept away in the name of civilized progress. While the child cannot adequately assess the clash between these two processes and while the essentially laconic narrator refrains from doing so, the spiritual destruction of the boy evokes much more than a mythic loss of innocence. It bespeaks the semiologically productive clash, between two processes of acculturation, that underlies much of

Guimarães Rosa's writing, making it so characteristic of the literary exploitation of a fundamentally unresolved conflict of Latin American society.

OTHER MAJOR WORKS

LONG FICTION: *Grande Sertão: Veredas*, 1956 (*The Devil to Pay in the Backlands*, 1963).

BIBLIOGRAPHY

Coutinho, Eduardo F. "João Guimarães Rosa." In *Latin American Writers*, edited by Carlos A. Solé and Maria Isabel Abreu. 3 vols. New York: Charles Scribner's Sons, 1989. An excellent introduction to the complete works, including remarks on language, causality, regionalism and universality, the use of myth, the importance of emotion, and the unusual position in Guimarães Rosa's works of madmen, poets, and children.

Daniel, Mary L. "João Guimarães Rosa." *Studies in Short Fiction* 8 (Winter, 1971): 209-216. This essay provides a useful discussion of the oral nature of the narrative and linguistic novelty.

Foster, David William, and Virginia Ramos Foster, eds. *Modern Latin American Literature*. 2 vols. New York: Frederick Ungar, 1975. Contains translations and reproductions of sixteen critical studies, some translated from Portuguese, French, or German, some in the original English, which give a feel for the reception of the works at or near the time of publication.

Hamilton, Russell G., Jr. "The Contemporary Brazilian Short Story." In *To Find Something New: Studies in Contemporary Literature*, edited by Henry Grosshans. Pullman: Washington State University Press, 1969. An overview of the importance of the short-story genre in Brazil, useful for contextualizing Guimarães Rosa's work. The only work studied in detail is *Tutaméia*.

Harss, Luis, and Barbara Dohmann. *Into the Mainstream: Conversations with Latin-American Writers*. New York: Harper & Row, 1967. A fascinating and sometimes illuminating interview with Guimarães Rosa.

Martins, Wilson. "Structural Perspectivism in Guimarães Rosa." In *The Brazilian Novel*, edited by Heitor Martins. Bloomington: Indiana University Press, 1976. Though focusing largely on *The Devil to Pay in the Backlands*, this study is relevant to the short fiction for its discussion of Guimarães Rosa as both a radical innovator of style and a "classic" writer in the traditions of Brazilian regionalism.

Perrone, Charles A. "Guimarães Rosa Through the Prism of Magic Realism." In *Tropical Paths: Essays on Modern Brazilian Literature*. New York: Garland, 1993. Discusses some of Guimarães Rosa's short stories from the perspective of their magical realism; analyzes their relationship to modernity.

Valente, Luiz Fernando. "Against Silence: Fabulation and Mediation in João Guimarães Rosa and Italo Calvino." *Modern Language Studies* 19 (Fall, 1989): 82-92. Compares Guimarães Rosa's treatment of the fable generic form with that of Italo Calvino.

Vessels, Gary M. "The Search for Motives: Carnivalized Heroes and Paternal Abandonment in Some Recent Brazilian Fiction." *Luso-Brazilian Review* 31 (Summer, 1994): 57-65. Discusses the carnivalisque element in the heroes of such Brazilian writers as Jorge Amado and Guimarães Rosa; also discusses the mystery of motivation in Guimarães Rosa's theme of the abandonment by the father.

Vincent, Jon S. *João Guimarães Rosa*. Boston: Twayne, 1978. The first study of the complete works in any language. This critical study contains a brief summary of Guimarães Rosa's life and is divided into seven chapters, one on each of the short fiction books and one on the novel. The bibliography is, however, dated.

David W. Foster, updated by Jon S. Vincent

H

NANCY HALE

Born: Boston, Massachusetts; May 6, 1908
Died: Charlottesville, Virginia; September 24, 1988

OTHER LITERARY FORMS

Nancy Hale's many published books include a biography, an anthology, a series of essays on the writing of fiction, two novels for children, and six novels for adults, as well as collections of short stories and autobiographical fiction. Her novel *The Prodigal Women* (1942) was a great popular as well as critical success; more than two million copies had been sold when it was reissued in paperback in 1980.

ACHIEVEMENTS

The receiver of both the Henry H. Bellamann Award for literature in 1969 and the Sarah Josepha Hale Award in 1974, Nancy Hale is best known for her ability to reveal the depths of the human mind in the style of an acute and objective observer. A common theme in Hale's work is that of maturity attained when one grows out of the dreams and illusions of the past and accepts the present world willingly. This is often manifested through characters moving from one culture to another and facing a new "outer reality" and through her depictions of women in their roles as mothers, friends, and wives.

BIOGRAPHY

The only child of painters Philip L. Hale and Lilian Westcott Hale, Nancy Hale was born in Boston on May 6, 1908. Among her forebears were the patriot Nathan Hale and a number of celebrated writers including Harriet Beecher Stowe, Lucretia Hale (a great aunt), and Edward Everett Hale (her grandfather). Initially she intended to be a painter, like her parents, and, after graduating from the Winsor School in Boston, she studied at the school of the Boston Museum of Fine Arts and in her father's studio. After she married and moved to New York City in 1928, she took a job as an editor first at *Vogue*, then at *Vanity Fair*, then as a news reporter for *The New York Times*. She began writing at night the short stories and novels which immediately established her as a writer of exceptional talent. In 1942 she married Fredson Bowers, professor of English and later chairman of the English Department and Dean of the Faculty at the University of Virginia, and settled in Charlottesville, Virginia. She had two sons, Mark Hardin and William Wertenbaker, by former marriages. She had five grandchildren. In 1933, Hale was awarded the O. Henry Prize for short-short fiction; in 1958, the Benjamin Franklin special citation for the short story. In 1971-1972 she was a Phi Beta Kappa Visiting Scholar, and for eight years, from 1957 to 1965, she gave the lectures on short fiction at the Bread Loaf Writers Conference. These lectures form the nucleus of *The Realities of Fiction* (1962), one of the best books ever written about the process of writing imaginative prose. Hale died on September 24, 1988, in Charlottesville, Virginia.

ANALYSIS

Most writers of fiction who produce what can be classified as literature, sooner or later, consciously or

Nancy Hale in 1958 (Library of Congress)

unconsciously, develop themes which in their various ramifications become identified with their work. With the early Sherwood Anderson of "I Want to Know Why" and the early Ernest Hemingway of the Nick stories the theme of initiation was established and reiterated; with Willa Cather in *O Pioneers!* (1913), *My Ántonia* (1918), and subsequent shorter pieces, the struggle of immigrants and pioneers to adjust to a new life in a new land provided a theme over and over again; and in the stories collected in *A Good Man Is Hard to Find* (1955), Flannery O'Connor makes it clear that her prevailing theme developed from a conviction that before there could be any illumination or epiphany her characters must undergo some devastating experience of a violent nature.

THE EMPRESS'S RING

Like these writers, Nancy Hale also developed a theme or thesis in her work which one recognizes most clearly in its various ramifications through reading her stories not singly as they first appeared in magazines at irregular intervals but as they were collected in book form. When twenty-four stories published originally in *The New Yorker* and elsewhere were brought together in a single volume entitled *The Empress's Ring*, the underlying theme which unified the collection as a whole clearly emerged. In "Miss August," a story about the mentally disturbed and emotionally ill and maladjusted, a psychiatrist tells a patient, "You are regressing. You are looking for something in the past and when you have found it you will come up again. You feel strangely because you are not living in outer reality." Later the psychiatrist amplifies this statement so that both patient and reader may comprehend more clearly its full import. The reader is to understand that there are two realities: the "outer reality," the practical world which one can touch and document, and "the past," which in these and other stories is also the world of the imagination, made up of memories and illusions, which may be considered the reality of fiction.

In one way or another most of Hale's characters in this collection—such as the patient in "Miss August" and the woman in the title story, "The Empress's Ring"—are exploring their past, sometimes trying to resurrect a security they once knew, sometimes trying to free themselves from the world of dreams and illusions in an effort to develop the maturity which will enable them to live in whatever "outer reality" they must without loneliness, hurt, or defeat. This choice of alternatives provides thematic material for much of Hale's work. In such stories as "The Secret Garden" and "Object of Virtue," in which a desperately lonely young woman and an unhappy child seek understanding and companionship, the characters remain bewildered and confused because they cannot adjust to "outer reality." Hale's stories, however, are not always records of frustration and failure. In "The Readville Stars" and in those light-hearted recollections such as "The Copley-Plaza" and "Charlotte Russe," the narrators who are looking back and reminiscing have achieved sufficient maturity through experience in living to view the past with humor, objectivity, and understanding rather than with regret and longing. When Hale's women (the men in these stories are essentially negligible) are not immersed in the past searching for something, they are often acquiring self-knowledge in the present. In a beautifully written story, "On the Beach," a mother during a morning with her young son realizes that an atomic world has not after all destroyed what for her are the deepest values; in such ironic pieces as "Sheltered" and "A Full Life," a girl and a middle-aged woman dramatically discover unsuspected truths about their own lives.

If the stories in this collection represent variations and extensions of a basic theme, they are developed against widely different backgrounds: the North Shore and Litchfield Hills of New England, towns and villages of the South, hospitals and universities, a ballroom, and a highway motel. Whether Hale constructed her stories objectively or as first-person recollections, she quickly established time, place, and situation and created mood and attitude with great economy of language, demonstrating again and again that she was a most accomplished writer.

THE PATTERN OF PERFECTION

In another collection of stories, *The Pattern of Perfection*, Hale presents a similar group of people, this time extroverts instead of introverts but still troubled and bewildered, trying to cope not so much with inner conflicts as with conflicts arising out of unsatisfactory relationships with others. For Hale these conflicts in human relationships—and in these stories the conflicts are usually familial, mostly between parents and children, sometimes between husbands and wives—are partially solved by replacing indifference and malice with the spirit of understanding and love. In the title story, "The Pattern of Perfection" (a wonderfully ironic title not only for this story but also for the collection as a whole), a house-proud southerner dedicated to her tradition becomes capable of understanding her daughter-in-law's loneliness in an alien land; and in "A Slow Boat to China," a mother made momentarily ill through suppressing manifestations of love for her son finally recognizes the need for yielding to natural impulses. When these conflicts remain unresolved (as in "A Long Summer's Dream," the story of a spinster whose life has been blighted if not destroyed by a dominating mother and aunt), the resulting bitter resignation becomes tragic.

In addition to theme, what contributes largely to the underlying unity of this collection as a whole and to the richness of individual pieces is Hale's skill in fusing story and symbol, her awareness of the dis-

crepancy between the apparent and the real, and her ability to achieve in her narrative the irony so characteristic of life. That the frustrated spinster of "A Long Summer's Dream" must refuse an invitation to sail because she "cannot swim" suggests that whatever opportunities her life may have offered have never been realized because she has never learned how to keep herself afloat. In "Entrance into Life," in which a mother and her small son watch the ritual of a college commencement, one senses the approach of death in the very midst of all that is most alive; and in the concluding story "Rich People," in which a woman is meditating on her past, one recognizes that to have lived a life no matter how secure financially without love and understanding is to have experienced the most corrosive form of poverty.

HEAVEN AND HARDPAN FARM

In such books as *Heaven and Hardpan Farm* and *Secrets*, stories which originally appeared in *The New Yorker* or elsewhere are linked together with little or no additional material to form novels constructed around a series of experiences and episodes. Reread in this form, the stories possess a continuity formerly lacking when they first appeared as single pieces. In *Heaven and Hardpan Farm*, Hale writes of a group of women, four extroverts and four introverts of various ages and backgrounds, suffering from a variety of neuroses because they are unable to emerge from their worlds of fantasy and adjust to outer reality, in which they must learn to live if they are to become productive, happy human beings. What makes the stories in *Heaven and Hardpan Farm* such absorbing reading is not only the author's extensive knowledge of Freudian and Jungian psychology and her ability to incorporate it into her narrative, but also her skill in the characterization of each of the highly individualistic patients as well as the wise, lovable, irascible old psychiatrist who is in charge of the sanatorium, of the practical, dependable housekeeper, and of the nurses who come and go. The reader knows them all, their doubts, fears, desires and dreams, as though the reader, too, was in the sanatorium waiting for his hour with the doctor.

Hale's special triumph in these stories of the neurotic, however, is her introduction of a humor and caustic wit which she sustains unfalteringly without a sour note. Much of the humor derives from the character, methods, and personality of the doctor but also from the behavior of the patients in their efforts to find those footholds for what might be "a sort of spiral climbing up" into outer reality. Despite the grim situation, for few patients show improvement, the humor never seems cruel or inappropriate but rather is a contribution toward realism, for, in the life most of us experience, the linking of opposites is the rule rather than the exception.

SECRETS

In the second short novel, *Secrets,* constructed from stories published in *The New Yorker* with some additional material from *A New England Girlhood,* the narrator, who is also the central character, is a woman in middle life, a wife and a mother who tells in a four-part narrative how she grew from a lonely, sensitive, insecure child, the daughter of artists, into a mature adult capable of coping with her past and present and of appraising herself and others objectively. During the early years the narrator experiences childhood and adolescence with the children next door, "the nearest to brother and sister I ever had," and it is they who provide drama and excitement in the various stages of her life. There is far more to *Secrets,* however, than this skeletal narrative. In the stories Hale deals directly or obliquely with many matters: the difference between imagination and fact, social and racial discrimination, the individual and the group.

As her title announces, her stories are concerned with secrets, not only with childhood secrets such as secret drawers and secret passages but also with the more subtle and tragic secrets of later years, and finally with the great secret of all secrets, the riddle of life, which can only be experienced, never solved. Hale excels in her descriptions whether in her account of a day in the life of a thoughtless, immature debutante, in the devastating picture of Huntington Avenue in the dreary dusk of a Boston winter afternoon, or in the characterization of a friend "with round cheeks, pursed lips, and a button nose." *Secrets* may be enjoyed on several levels. It is both funny and serious, joyous and somber, but above all it is the work of a writer who has always been aware of the conflict between the world of imagination and the world of facts, and who has the experience to know that many must learn to live with both worlds if they are to survive.

THE LIFE IN THE STUDIO

Hale's closest approach to the kind of autobiography which more often than not is based on fact and event in contrast to "autobiographical fiction" is her *The Life in the Studio,* a collection of stories for the most part published originally in *The New Yorker* and later skillfully arranged in book form as an informal, vivid narrative of her early life growing up in a family of artists. Her reminiscences, whether in the form of cheerful anecdote or serious comment and discussion, are full of affection for her family. For despite an early rebellion against the unconventional life of her hardworking parents whose daily routine followed the pattern established by her father's reiterated statement, "Art first, life afterwards," Hale became an increasingly devoted, admiring daughter. Through her eyes the reader sees these "singular parents" at work in their studios complementing each other as creator and critic; the reader sees them with other artists, especially at the stone studio on Cape Ann during the summer.

In the final stories, now chapters, entitled "Journeys" and "An Arrangement in Parents," there is the account of the memorable and triumphant trip to Italy, where Hale and her mother, who was in her eighties, viewed the works of the great painters in the churches and galleries of Venice, Florence, and Rome. After her mother's sudden death on their return home one has the impression that the author, now reviewing and analyzing the lives of her parents and her relationship to them, has gained a new perspective and understanding which has produced "a calm of mind, all passion spent." These recollections, *The Life in the Studio,* will remain a touching memorial written by one who grew in the kind of understanding and love which so many of the characters in her fiction try to develop and need to receive.

THE REALITIES OF FICTION

The Realities of Fiction (1962) is based on five years of lecturing on fiction at various academic institutions and on the writing of fiction at the Bread Loaf Writers' Conference at Middlebury College; Hale not only produced one of the most intelligent, lucid, and fascinating books ever written on the role of the imagination in the creative process but also presented criticism, evaluation, and often detailed analyses of the work of writers ranging from Leo Tolstoy, Charles Dickens, and E. M. Forster to Ernest Hemingway, F. Scott Fitzgerald, and William Faulkner, from Jane Austen to Katherine Mansfield and Elinor Wylie, including comments on the genesis and meaning of some of her own stories. In the first chapter, "The Two Way Imagination," and the final chapter, "Through the Dark Glass to Reality," Hale explains her provocative title by showing through ample reference to life and literature that "the realities of fiction" are as real as "outer reality" and closely linked, for without experiencing and understanding the first many cannot successfully make a passage to the second. What is implied in so much of Hale's fiction is made explicit in these chapters.

In this short essay it is impossible to do more than suggest the high quality and variety of Hale's work. Much of her short fiction is not as yet collected in single volumes, but it can be found in various magazines from *The New Yorker* to *The Virginia Quarterly Review*. Such stories as "The Most Elegant Drawing Room in Europe," with its wonderful description of Venice, superb characterizations of the shy, sensitive observer, her dominating mother, and the worldly, ambivalent *contessa*, reaffirm that Hale was an unusually gifted writer with a sure sense of structure and style, a sharp eye for detail, knowledge of many subjects and places, humor and wit, and a profound understanding of human nature.

Although Hale was a highly individualistic writer whose influence cannot yet be measured, she belongs to a great tradition which includes Anton Chekhov, Gustave Flaubert, the Brontë sisters, Katherine Mansfield, J. D. Salinger, and all those whose sympathies are with the alien, the unwanted, the inferior, and the overly sensitive for whom life in outer reality is so difficult and depressing that they must create another more congenial world through their imaginations. For these people Hale had great compassion, but when

they find the strength and courage and understanding needed to "climb the spiral" and take their place in outer reality, which none can reject, she was the first to applaud.

OTHER MAJOR WORKS

LONG FICTION: *The Young Die Good*, 1932; *Never Any More*, 1934; *The Prodigal Women*, 1942; *The Sign of Jonah*, 1950; *Dear Beast*, 1959; *Black Summer*, 1963; *Night of the Hurricane*, 1978.

NONFICTION: *A New England Girlhood*, 1958; *The Realities of Fiction*, 1962; *A New England Discovery*, 1963; *Mary Cassatt*, 1975.

BIBLIOGRAPHY

Barron, James. "Nancy Hale, Fiction Writer." *The New York Times*, September 26, 1988, p. B8. A biographical obituary sketch, with an account of Hale's literary career and comments on her fictional treatment of the follies and foibles of well-bred women.

Callahan, Amy. "Nancy Hale." *The Boston Globe*, September 27, 1988, p. 59. A brief biographical obituary that traces Hale's literary career and comments on her proper Bostonian characters in her humorous novels and short stories.

Gray, James. "Dream of Unfair Women." In *On Second Thought*, edited by James Gray. Minneapolis: University of Minnesota Press, 1946. Gray writes on two of Hale's novels, *The Prodigal Women* and *Between the Dark and the Daylight*, and several of her short stories, drawing the conclusion that Hale "writes her own stuff and writes exceedingly well."

The New Republic. Review of *Between the Dark and the Daylight*. 109 (July 12, 1943): 51. Finds twenty of the twenty-one stories in this collection praiseworthy and admires Hale's neutral treatment of the intense conflict between characters in her stories.

Van Gelder, Robert. "An Analysis of the Feminine." In *Writers and Writing*. New York: Charles Scribner's Sons, 1946. This interview with Hale focuses on her depiction of women and their relationships with men in her novel *The Prodigal*

Women. She reveals that many of her character studies are revelations of herself; much of this work is autobiographical.

Walton, Edith H. Review of *The Earliest Dreams.* *The New York Times,* April 19, 1936, 7. In this review of a collection of stories in *The Earliest Dreams,* the writer does not commit herself to complete admiration of Hale's work. Instead, she points out some of the more "shallow" stories while balancing that with praise for many of her

fine, perceptive works in the collection. The review is favorable overall.

Welty, Eudora. Review of *Between the Dark and the Daylight. The New York Times,* May 2, 1943, 8. In this review, Welty is impressed with the scope of subjects that Hale's twenty-one stories cover as well as with the sustained "good writing" in them.

John C. Coleman,
updated by Laurie Buchanan

LAWRENCE SARGENT HALL

Born: Haverill, Massachusetts; April 23, 1915
Died: Orr's Island, Maine; October 28, 1993

PRINCIPAL SHORT FICTION

"The Ledge," 1959
"Twenty-three, Please," 1982
"The Sequel," 1989

OTHER LITERARY FORMS

Lawrence Sargent Hall received critical acclaim for his novel *Stowaway: A Novel* (1961). He also wrote *Hawthorne: Critic of Society* (1944), *How Thinking Is Written: An Analytic Approach to Writing* (1963), and *A Grammar of Literary Criticism: Essays in Definition of Vocabulary, Concepts, and Aims* (1965), as well as several published essays.

ACHIEVEMENTS

Lawrence Sargent Hall's *Stowaway* was the unanimous winner of the William Faulkner Award in 1961, an award given for the best first novel by an author. "The Ledge" won the O. Henry Award in 1960 for best short story of the year.

BIOGRAPHY

Lawrence Sargent Hall was born in Haverill, Massachusetts, on April 23, 1915, and graduated in 1936

from Bowdoin College, where he won several awards, including the Hawthorne Prize. After graduation he taught at Deerfield Academy in Massachusetts before entering Yale University in 1938. After receiving his doctorate in 1941 (his dissertation was on Nathaniel Hawthorne, also a Bowdoin graduate), he taught at Ohio University and then at the United States Naval Academy until 1942, when he began a four-year tour in the Navy. He served in the South Pacific before being discharged with the rank of lieutenant commander.

After the war Hall returned to Bowdoin as an assistant professor of English and, aside from a year (1955-1956) as a Carnegie Visiting Professor at Columbia University, he spent the remainder of his teaching career at Bowdoin, retiring in 1986. His O. Henry Award-winning short story, "The Ledge," which appeared in 1959, was followed by his Faulkner Award-winning *Stowaway* in 1961, but despite his phenomenal debut in fiction, he published only two additional short stories. His eclectic interests included taking trips down the Mississippi in his dory, *Way Out,* serving on the Ford Foundation committee that created the Advanced Placement Program of the College Entrance Examination Board, teaching at summer institutes under the National Defense Education Act, and serving on the Maine State Commission for the Arts and Humanities. In addition to academic pursuits, Hall was active in environmental matters, cruising the Maine coast in 1970 to prevent the establishment of oil refineries there. He was also given credit for single-handedly preventing the state of Maine from turning Route 24 into a four-lane highway. After a career in teaching and operating a boatyard on the Maine coast, he died October 28, 1993, at his home in Orr's Island, Maine.

ANALYSIS

Lawrence Sargent Hall's literary accolades are remarkable, considering how few fictional works he wrote. His fiction is, for the most part, concerned with life at sea, hardly surprising given his naval career, his cruises off the Maine coast and down the Mississippi River, and his operation of a boatyard. Hall deprecates contemporary, urban life and exalts life at sea, which he describes in technical detail and which provides him with metaphors for relationships. Like Ernest Hemingway, Hall is concerned with behavior under pressure, and he is skeptical of talk. His protagonists are always taciturn, uncommunicative men's men, who are skilled at their professions but unskilled at interpersonal relationships, which tend to be stormy. Hall's concern seems to be the nature of manhood, and his protagonists are alone but not lonely; they test themselves, usually at sea, by pushing limits and by leading "high-risk lives." Hall also resembles Stephen Crane, whose "The Open Boat" focuses on men's behavior at sea and whose *Red Badge of Courage: An Episode of the American Civil War* (1895) concerns the passage from boyhood to manhood. Hall's style is, for the most part, in the realist tradition, except for "Twenty-three, Please," which is experimental in that the story consists of a series of impressions on the mind of a character who does not speak.

"THE LEDGE"

"The Ledge," Hall's award-winning and frequently anthologized short story, concerns the accidental drowning of a Maine fisherman, his son, and his nephew. On a Christmas morning, the three go duck hunting on an offshore ledge, which is submerged at high tide. In the excitement of successful hunting, the skiff they take to reach the ledge somehow gets set adrift and, despite their efforts to attract attention and help, they become marooned and drown when the tide covers the ledge. Hall's plot is as simple as Ernest Hemingway's in *The Old Man and the Sea* (1952); Hall and Hemingway both focus on their protagonists' behavior as they react with "grace under pressure."

Hall's fictional universe tends to be bifurcated, split into opposites. He contrasts the masculine, outside world (the fisherman's wife thinks "anyone going out like that had to be incurably male") with the feminine "close bed" and "woman's fears." Similarly, he pits the sea, represented by the fisherman, against the shore, represented by his farming brother. There are even two kinds of fishermen, those who stay close to the shore and those who venture farther out, pushing against limits. In the story the opposing characters seem unwilling or unable to communicate with one another. The other fishermen consider the protagonist a disdainful braggart; even his wife has, in her loneliness, considered leaving him.

In "The Ledge," Hall also presents an initiation story gone awry. The fisherman mentors his thirteen-year-old son, attempting to make him a man. The son's Christmas gift, an automatic shotgun, represents a change in his status; the son "was fierce to grow up in hunting, to graduate from sheltered waters and the blinds along the shores of the inner bay." When they discover the wayward skiff, the son "cried softly for a moment, like a man," unwilling to show pain. In the final moments of the story the son becomes "old enough to know there were things beyond the power of any man." The fisherman's nephew, also the recipient of an automatic shotgun, receives some tutoring in the art of waiting: "Part of doing a man's hunting was learning how to wait." Later, when the nephew is briefly left by himself on the ledge while the fisherman and his son retrieve the dead ducks, he suffers an anticipatory attack of "ledge fever," which leaves him temporarily paralyzed.

"The Ledge" ultimately concerns the competent, hard, insensitive loner proud of his equipment and abilities and intent on defeating the "element of time" by doing more than his peers. On rare occasions the fisherman even has the "grand illusion" of beating the "game." When he has to confront the reality of their impending deaths, he understands that "their situation was purely mathematical," not subject to his control; and he considers the end "quite scientifically." Even though he knows time and tide will destroy them, he puts his son on his shoulders, wedges one foot between the rocks, and vows to hold him "through a thousand tides." He cannot, but when the fisherman is found the next day, his foot is still wedged in the rocks, and his son's boot is under his right elbow. At this sight his wife absolves him "of his mortality," realizing the enormity of his struggle.

"Twenty-three, Please"

Although "Twenty-three, Please" focuses on a Native American steeplejack, Hall uses sea imagery to portray the city landscape as a "deadly urban reef." The city, with which the steeplejack's wife is associated, is characterized by its "ashen haze" and smog; with their airplanes, people have "lacerated sacred skies." With his telescope, with which he scans the heavens, and his work high above the city, the steeplejack can render the urban landscape "decent by distance." Although in his work he is "selfless as a saint," his wife has forced him to give up the job and become earthbound. Their marriage becomes a battle zone full of military imagery: The telescope is like a machine gun, and her heels "invade the living room."

In the midst of this domestic warfare, a despondent woman in a nearby building strips herself naked and steps out on the ledge of the twenty-third floor. The steeplejack, who is called to rescue her, joins a priest, a psychiatrist, and a police lieutenant. As the scene unfolds, the woman on the ledge becomes dehumanized as she is successively referred to as "it," "thing," "them," "what," "case," and "confrontation," callous responses not lost on the steeplejack, whose silence contrasts with the verbose jargon of the psychiatrist. When he steps out on the ledge and removes his obligatory safety harness, his actions are erroneously interpreted by the three professionals, who see his behavior from their limited perspectives: The lieutenant thinks the steeplejack is excited by the woman's naked body; the psychiatrist sees him as involving the woman in his own problem; and the priest

sees him as offering her "the saving expression of love." The woman on the ledge does not respond to their chatter but instead leans forward in "the supreme airfoil embrace of the ballet partner." She and her steeplejack partner experience "no sense of fall but of ascent, through one clear burst of sheer coital light." Their suicide, sexual and cleansing, is one of triumph, not defeat.

"The Sequel"

In "The Sequel" Hall returned to the sea for his subject matter and for his protagonist, Harry, a crusty old salt with a decided preference for sailboats over "stinkpots," or motorboats. As in Hall's other fiction, there are conflicts: In addition to the sail/motor dichotomy, there are class distinctions (Harry is a sailor, whereas yacht club members are mere "yachtsmen"), geographical differences between the "land he went sailing to get away from" and the open sea, and differences between marriage (a "low-risk life") and bachelorhood and freedom. In fact, the title of the short story refers to the aftermath of a romantic relationship between Harry and a twenty-seven-year-old artist.

When Harry takes Josie, a middle-aged divorcé who is sizing up Harry as a prospective husband, out sailing, all the oppositions surface and are, for the most part, resolved in Harry's favor. Josie, with her "shore-based thoughts," is not the woman for Harry, because they do not speak the same language. Her use of "straighten up," "low side," "up front," and "tippy," in place of nautical terms, makes him realize that she speaks a language "he has to translate." Harry's attitude toward shore women is clearly patriarchal; he compares them to children. However, he is completely entranced by the young artist, who took from him and then mailed him a check with a promise of more money. Although he knows they had "no horizons" together, Harry is still in love with her (the young woman says he is obsessed); when Josie suggests that the young woman might be waiting on the dock for him, he instinctively looks for her, prompting Josie to ask him to take them ashore.

When Harry and Josie sail to secluded Rumrunner Cove, the idyllic mood is shattered by the intrusion of an outboard runabout circling them at full speed.

Harry, who compares sailing to falling in love, feels that his beloved yawl has been "ravished." On the way back to shore, Harry spots the runabout, which has developed engine trouble and is now adrift. He gains his revenge and demonstrates the "superiority of sail over steam" by towing them to the yacht club and setting them adrift again. Things end as they began, except the sequel proves to be a continuation of Harry's obsession with the young artist, an obsession without much risk for him.

OTHER MAJOR WORKS

LONG FICTION: *Stowaway: A Novel*, 1961.

NONFICTION: *Hawthorne: Critic of Society*, 1944; *How Thinking Is Written: An Analytic Approach to Writing*, 1963; *A Grammar of Literary Criticism: Essays in Definition of Vocabulary, Concepts, and Aims*, 1965.

BIBLIOGRAPHY

Hall, Lawrence Sargent. *How Thinking Is Written: An Analytic Approach to Writing*. Boston: Heath, 1963. Discusses Hall's method of achieving good writing. Includes sample readings.

"Lawrence Sargent Hall." In *Contemporary Authors*. Detroit, Mich.: Gale Research, 1967. A good first stop for students. Includes biographical information.

Thomas L. Erskine

DASHIELL HAMMETT

Born: St. Mary's County, Maryland; May 27, 1894
Died: New York, New York; January 10, 1961

PRINCIPAL SHORT FICTION

Secret Agent X-9, 1934 (with Alex Raymond)
The Continental Op, 1945
The Return of the Continental Op, 1945
The Adventures of Sam Spade, and Other Stories, 1945
Hammett Homicides, 1946
Dead Yellow Women, 1947
Nightmare Town, 1948
The Creeping Siamese, 1950
Woman in the Dark, 1951
A Man Named Thin and Other Stories, 1962
The Big Knockover, 1966

OTHER LITERARY FORMS

Dashiell Hammett's published works include five novels and approximately twenty-five short stories, which he refused to republish during his lifetime. During the 1930's, he wrote "continuing story cartoons," creating "Secret Agent X-9" to compete with "Dick Tracy." His five novels have been filmed, and director John Huston's version of *The Maltese Falcon* (1941), starring Humphrey Bogart as Sam Spade, has been called "the best private-eye melodrama ever made." *The Thin Man* (1934) with William Powell and Myrna Loy as Nick and Nora Charles was the first in a series of "comedy-thrillers" which became for a time a minor film industry.

ACHIEVEMENTS

Publishing short stories mainly in *Black Mask* magazine during the 1920's, Dashiell Hammett had become the preeminent writer, perhaps even the originator, of "hard-boiled" or realistic, action-oriented detective fiction even before he produced any of his novels. Though Carroll John Daly introduced two private eyes in *Black Mask* some months earlier, Hammett's Continental Op generally is considered the prototypical one, a credible and unheroic man with whom readers could identify. Drawing from his experiences as a private investigator, Hammett created a thoroughly professional detective: dedicated to his job and usually—though not always—successful at it; more concerned with obtaining facts than with engaging in violent confrontations; and willing to cooperate with the police when necessary. Set in realistic urban America and written in a terse style and often cynical tone, the Continental Op stories to a large extent set the pattern for all subsequent American private eye fiction. Hammett is the first in a continuum that includes Raymond Chandler, Ross Macdonald, Robert B. Parker, and Bill Pronzini.

BIOGRAPHY

Born in Maryland, Samuel Dashiell Hammett spent his early years in Philadelphia and Baltimore. He left school at fourteen and worked at a variety of odd jobs including that of a manual laborer. Between 1915 and 1918, he worked for the Pinkerton's Detective Agency as an operative, finding this work to be interesting, challenging, adventurous, and at times dangerous. While serving as a sergeant in the U.S. Army Ambulance Corps during World War I, he contracted tuberculosis; although it was cured, his health was permanently impaired. Married with two daughters, Hammett returned to the Pinkerton Agency. (In all, he spent eight years in its employ as an investigator.) He then separated from his family and began to write bits of verse and sketches from his experiences as a detective. In October, 1923, the first story in which the Continental Op appeared was published; by the middle of the 1920's, Hammett was known as an original talent, an innovator in a popular form of fiction, and the central figure in a new school of writing about crime. His writings made him the "darling" of the Hollywood and New York sets. He began to drink heavily and continued to do so despite his meeting with Lillian Hellman, who remained his closest friend for the rest of his life. With the onset of World War II, he enlisted in the Army at the age of forty-eight and served in the Aleutians, where he edited a daily newspaper for the troops. He was discharged in 1945 with emphysema and in poorer health than before. He continued drinking until 1948, when an attack of delirium tremens convinced him never to drink again.

During the 1930's, while he had been writing for the film industry, Hammett had become involved with various left-wing and anti-Fascist causes. He had be-

come a Marxist, and, while he never lost his critical sense regarding the absurdities of many of his associates, he remained loyal to communism. During the McCarthy era of the early 1950's, he served six months in prison for refusing to testify in court. Released and blacklisted, he lived a quiet life with the care and companionship of Lillian Hellman. His lung condition was diagnosed as cancerous and he died in 1961.

ANALYSIS

Dashiell Hammett's best-known and most widely read short stories are those in which the Continental Op, a tough, San Francisco-based Continental Detective Agency investigator, serves as the main character and narrator. Unlike the contemporary American private eye, the Continental Op is not a glamorous figure; he is short, somewhat plump, and middle-aged. His name is never revealed in the stories although he uses several false identities for the people he meets during the course of his investigations. He has no home and no personal life apart from his work; his total identity is that of a private detective. Hired by a society which appears on the surface to be real and

Dashiell Hammett (Library of Congress)

respectable, the Continental Op moves through all the social strata from the seediest to the most aristocratic and finds in fulfillment of his cynicism that all segments of the society are equally deceitful, dishonest, and violent.

Hammett's world is one in which society and social relations are permeated by misanthropic suspicion. The criminal world is a mirror image of the respectable side of the society. It is a reflection of the reputable world in that its existence depends on that world, preys on it for its own ends, and, in effect, is really an actual part of it. These worlds—the respectable and the criminal—are intricately connected and interact with each other. The Continental Op, and for that matter all Hammett's detectives, is the guardian of the official society hired to protect it from the criminal world which is continually threatening to take over. He stands aloof from these worlds in which he must function primarily because he lives by a very stringent "code." There are no rewards for concluding an investigation other than drawing his salary and expenses from the Agency, so he cannot succumb to temptations to enrich himself. He expects of himself, and others like him, to accept the failures and disappointments, as well as physical beatings, without complaint. His job is an end in itself, and since his existential identity comes only from his work, he is protected from the temptation to align himself with either sector of the society against the other. Even his conscious refusal to use the speech of the reputable society becomes a form of self-insulation and serves to establish him as an individual apart.

Written in the realistic style, Hammett's works contain a strong strain of Zolaesque naturalism. The Continental Op, as a narrator, makes no moral claims for himself and is dispassionate in his judgment of other people's actions. The characters of the stories are representative types rather than people. Thefts and killings come naturally out of the forces of the environment. The Continental Op survives in a jungle world in which only the "fittest" can survive. In "The House in Turk Street," for example, the reader is made aware from the very beginning that this detective is different from the Sherlock Holmes type of detective. In the conventional detective story, the

sleuth's superior intellect is totally directed toward solving the "challenging puzzle" and discovering the identity of the villain. The actual capture of the criminal does not interest him; this is left to the official police and is usually merely alluded to in passing in the final paragraphs of the stories. In addition, the detective in the conventional story is almost always completely in control of the situation; he makes things happen.

"THE HOUSE IN TURK STREET"

In "The House in Turk Street," the Continental Op, acting on a tip from an informant, is searching for a man by going from house to house ringing doorbells. The flat, deliberate tone of the first few paragraphs conveys the sense that most of the work of this private investigator is pure drudgery, a lot of footwork and trial and error. He definitely is not in charge of the situation, and he has no brilliant scheme for finding his man. He is at Turk Street on the advice of his informant, and the events of the story unfold largely by chance rather than because of anything the detective does or plans. The operative is welcomed into the living room of the Turk Street house and given tea, cookies, and a cigar by a harmless-appearing elderly couple. As the Continental Op relaxes and gets comfortable, he is jarred out of his illusions of security by the pressure of a gun on the back of his neck. Even though he is at this house through sheer happenstance, the criminals assume that he is aware of their dishonest activities and has been tracking them down in order to capture them.

In many ways, Hammett uses the reader's familiarity with the traditional mystery story as a counterbalance for this tale of adventure. What Hammett succeeds in doing in this story and others in the Continental Op series is to introduce a new kind of detective story, one which will replace what the *Black Mask* writer felt was the contrived and unrealistic classical mystery. In "The House in Turk Street," the old and new forms are presented in interaction with each other. When the characters in Hammett's story experience difficulty, it is because they try to apply the rules of the old world of detective fiction in this new world of adventure where the old rules no longer operate.

For example, Hook, one of the thieves, is killed because he still tries to live in a world of sentiment where men are inspired by women to achieve great things in the name of love. Tai, the Chinese mastermind with a British accent, also clings to the illusions of the old mysteries. Defeated at the end of the story, he is convinced that he has been thwarted by superior detective work and refuses to consider the possibility that the Continental Op had merely stumbled upon their criminal lair. As the Continental Op matter-of-factly reports: "He went to the gallows thinking me a liar." For the master criminal, the possibility that it was all an accident is unthinkable; but in this house in Turk Street, it is not only thinkable—it is what happens. In the world in which the Continental Op does his job, detectives happen upon criminals by chance, criminals such as the young woman in the story escape, the Continental Op survives because he kills in self-defense, and bodies are strewn all around.

Although the "hard-boiled detective" form which Hammett's writings made famous has undergone some significant changes over the years, every writer of the American detective story is indebted to the creator of the Continental Op.

OTHER MAJOR WORKS

LONG FICTION: *Red Harvest*, 1927-1928 (serial), 1929; *The Dain Curse*, 1928-1929 (serial), 1929; *The Maltese Falcon*, 1929-1930 (serial), 1930; *The Glass Key*, 1930 (serial), 1931; *The Thin Man*, 1934.

BIBLIOGRAPHY

Johnson, Diane. *Dashiell Hammett: A Life*. New York: Random House, 1983. The most comprehensive biography of Hammett, this book adds considerable information to the public record of Hammett's life but does not provide much critical analysis of the works. More than half the volume deals with the years after Hammett stopped publishing fiction and during which he devoted most of his time to leftist political activism.

Layman, Richard. *Shadow Man: The Life of Dashiell Hammett*. New York: Harcourt Brace Jovanovich/Bruccoli-Clark, 1981. An academic who earlier produced a descriptive bibliography of Hammett,

Layman provides lucid interpretations of the works. While he holds Hammett in high regard as a major figure in twentieth century American fiction, he does not present a totally admiring portrait of the man.

McGurl, Mark. "Making 'Literature' of It: Hammett and High Culture." *American Literary History* 9 (Winter, 1997): 702-717. Discusses Hammett's response to modernism's divide between high and low culture; argues that Hammett's detective fiction is what modernism looks like to mass culture and what mass culture looks like to modernism; discusses Hammett's habitual lack of seriousness in regard to his own representations.

Mellen, Joan. *Hellman and Hammett: The Legendary Passion of Lillian Hellman and Dashiell Hammett*. New York: HarperCollins, 1996. Although primarily a biographical study, this scrupulously researched work provides insight into the backgrounds of Hammett's fiction. Includes very detailed notes and bibliography.

Metress, Christopher, ed. *The Critical Response to Dashiell Hammett*. Westport, Conn.: Greenwood Press, 1994. A generous compilation of reviews and general studies, with a comprehensive introduction, chronology, and bibliography.

Nolan, William F. *Hammett: A Life at the Edge*. New York: Congdon & Weed, 1983. Author of the first full-length study of Hammett in 1969, Nolan here builds upon his earlier work and that of others to present a convincing portrait of a singularly private man with a code of honor that paralleled those of his detectives. The discussions of the works are straightforward and sound.

Skenazy, Paul. "The 'Heart's Field': Dashiell Hammett's Anonymous Territory." In *San Francisco in Fiction: Essays in a Regional Literature*, edited by David Fine and Paul Skenazy. Albuquerque: University of New Mexico Press, 1995. A consideration of the importance of history and place in Hammett's fiction. Argues that it is wrong to associate Hammett's concern with expedience, environment, habit, training, and chance with a specifically Wild West tradition.

Symons, Julian. *Dashiell Hammett*. San Diego: Harcourt Brace Jovanovich, 1985. A brief but substantive book by a leading English writer of crime fiction and criticism. Symons believes that Hammett created "A specifically American brand of crime story . . . that transcends the form and limits of [its] genre and can be compared with the best fiction produced in America between the two world wars." His considerations of the works support this judgment. Contains a useful select bibliography.

Walker, John. "City Jungles and Expressionist Reifications from Brecht to Hammett." *Twentieth Century Literature* 44 (Spring, 1998): 119-133. Discusses how the fiction of Brecht and Hammett presents the urban landscape as technological anti-utopia and primeval jungle. Discusses the urban jungle metaphor as background for both expressionism and noir. Argues that Hammett reproduces the model of human relations in Bertolt Brecht's fiction.

Wheat, Edward M. "The Post-Modern Detective: The Aesthetic Politics of Dashiell Hammett's Continental Op." *The Midwest Quarterly* 36 (Spring, 1995): 237-249. Examines the meaning of the postmodern era through the character and world of the hard-boiled detective. Claims that Hammett's Continental Op is a postmodernist who does not find truth and justice but produces a fictive account.

Wolfe, Peter. *Beams Falling: The Art of Dashiell Hammett*. Bowling Green, Ohio: Bowling Green University Popular Press, 1980. Especially good in his analyses of Hammett's short fiction, Wolfe surpasses other writers in showing the relationship of each work to the total output. The author of books on other crime-fiction writers (Raymond Chandler, John le Carré, and Ross Macdonald), Wolfe has a knowledge and appreciation of the genre that are apparent in this excellent study.

Robert W. Millett, updated by Gerald H. Strauss

BARRY HANNAH

Born: Clinton, Mississippi; April 23, 1942

PRINCIPAL SHORT FICTION
Airships, 1978
Captain Maximus, 1985
Bats Out of Hell, 1993
High Lonesome, 1996

OTHER LITERARY FORMS

Barry Hannah is the author of several novels: *Geronimo Rex* (1972), *Nightwatchmen* (1973), *Ray* (1980), *The Tennis Handsome* (1983), *Hey Jack!* (1987), *Boomerang* (1989), and *Never Die* (1991).

ACHIEVEMENTS

Barry Hannah received the Arnold Gingrich Award for short fiction from *Esquire* (1978), the Henry H. Bellaman Foundation Award in Fiction (1970), the Bread Loaf Fellowship (1971), the William Faulkner Foundation Prize (1972), and an award in literature from American Academy of Arts and Letters (1979). He has also received a John Simon Guggenheim Memorial Foundation Fellowship, a Mississippi Governor's Award in the Arts, and a Mississippi Institute of Arts and Letters Award. His novel *Geronimo Rex* was a finalist for the National Book Award.

BIOGRAPHY

Born and raised in Mississippi, Barry Hannah graduated from Mississippi College in 1964 and later returned to earn an M.A. and an M.F.A. from that college. In 1966, he began teaching creative writing at Clemson University in South Carolina, where he remained until 1973. It was during this period that he also published his first two novels, establishing himself as a writer of note. Although he did not serve in the Vietnam War, Hannah's most formative influence was that conflict, which was brought home to him by the tales of returning veterans and also by its strong impact on American society. His stories bear witness to the fact that he is of the Vietnam generation and also point to his general interest in war and in military history.

In 1980, Hannah moved to Hollywood to write screenplays for director Robert Altman, an interlude which allowed him to overcome a chronic problem with alcohol. After stints at various universities, Hannah settled down as a writer-in-residence at the University of Mississippi at Oxford, where he settled with his wife, Susan. Hannah has been married three times and has three children.

ANALYSIS

Barry Hannah is among the most prominent southern writers of the post World War II period and has been widely praised for producing some of the finest fiction about the South since the work of William Faulkner. Characterized by a surrealistic style and surprising narrative twists, his stories often depict violent and/or sexual situations that oscillate between the bleak and the hilarious.

Hannah is especially interested in depicting a generation of southern men scarred by the Vietnam War, a conflict which repeated the Civil War's pattern of loss and defeat but which was also the harbinger of both a crisis in masculinity and a general social unraveling. His largely male characters consistently suffer from physical or emotional pain and cannot escape the destructive patterns in which they find themselves and for which they are, in part, responsible. These stories of disintegration and fragmentation are seen as representative of the difficulties of life in a post-Vietnam America. However, Hannah's jazzy, meandering style and his absurdist sense of humor add rich dimensions of comedy and tragedy that cannot be communicated by simply delineating his narratives, which often consist of a series of chaotic subplots and digressions.

Hannah's distinctive style, which strikes the reader as both manic and depressive, is perfectly suited to the inner lives of his characters, whose emotional weather ranges from a sense of absurd comedy to feelings of anxiety that leave them on the brink of suicide and de-

Barry Hannah (©Miriam Berkley)

spair. His capacity to write associatively, as if his stories are as much dreams as histories, has also allowed him to develop a unique stream-of-consciousness approach to narrative that is faithful to the strange and intense inner world of his male characters. Notable also are his arresting story titles, which often sum up the themes of his stories.

AIRSHIPS

This first collection by Hannah established both his major themes and his unique style. The theme of war is prominent: "Testimony of Pilot" not only explores the deranging effects of the Vietnam War on a former combatant but also shows the demoralizing impact of the war on those who watched from the sidelines. "Midnight and I'm Not Famous Yet" depicts a civilian who is touched by the troubles of a friend who served in the Vietnam War. In this narrative, Hannah deliberately blurs the distinction between the Civil War and the Vietnam War—in each case life begins to lose its purpose or meaning. This story and "Knowing He Was Not My Kind Yet I Followed" also feature Confederate General Jeb Stuart, who figures centrally in four of the twenty stories in this collection as both hero and fool.

Other stories are set in contemporary times—"Love Too Long" and "Constant Pain in Tuscaloosa" depict deserted husbands who cannot let go of their former wives. "Coming Close to Donna" is about a woman whose obsessional sexuality leads to murderous behavior on the part of the men in her life, and "Our Secret Home" is about a man who is sexually obsessed with his mentally impaired sister. One of his most famous stories, "Water Liars," shows a group of fishermen who enjoy swapping tall tales but who are affronted by a man who makes the mistake of telling the truth about his sexual fears.

The feeling that life is inherently random and disordered is yet another important theme in Hannah's work, which he explores in the domestic vignette "Deaf and Dumb" and in the surreal stories "Green Gets It," "Quo Vadis, Smut?," and "Mother Rooney Unscrolls the Hurt." The latter three stories are vivid stream-of-consciousness stories that attempt to sum up the meaning of lives that seem to be continually in the process of disintegration.

CAPTAIN MAXIMUS

This second collection consists of seven stories, concluding with a long story set in Seattle concerning women employed by an electric power company, a story Hannah originally developed as a film treatment for Robert Altman. The first seven stories draw on material from Hannah's own life, including drunken brawls, plane crashes, and relationships with writer friends. Many of the stories also feature what Hannah calls "interesting monsters," larger-than-life characters such as war heroes, sports figures, musicians, and writers. The most notable of these is Ned Maximus, who gives this collection its name. Maximus, a one-eyed man with second sight, which allows him to see the dark truths those around him deny, gains no consolation from his gift. He sees in America a wasteland society in which he, too, is a lost soul. His story is summed up by its title, "Ride, Fly, Penetrate, Loiter," which describes a life with no overarching point to it.

Other stories, such as "I Am Shaking to Death," "It Spoke Exactly the Things," and "Getting Ready," also use a series of disjunctive images to depict love stories gone mysteriously wrong. The difficulties of

being a man in an unraveling society are also explored in "Even Greenland" and "Jet," which are devoted to masculine role models whose achievements may in fact be dubious. In "Even Greenland," an admired pilot deliberately kills himself in a plane crash, and in "Fans," a masochistic man is tortured by the football star he worships. A more positive story, "Idaho" is a montage of reflections on guns, drinking, suicide, male bonding, and the saving influence of writing.

BATS OUT OF HELL

This collection returns to the theme of war so prominent in *Airships*. In the title story, "Bats Out of Hell Division," the Civil War is the occasion for a meditation on war that moves between reality and the surreal nature of dreams. In "Upstairs, Mona Bayed for Dong," the Persian Gulf War serves as a background for meditations on life and death, while "That Was Close, Ma" is set against the backdrop of Operation Desert Storm. In "Hey, Have You Got a Cig, the Time, the News, My Face?" a veteran of the Vietnam War is overwhelmed by emotional pain.

"High Water Railers" returns the reader to the world of "Water Liars" and to men who are ashamed of their failure to live up to what they understand are infuriating cultural myths about masculinity and whose only recourse is to lie. Other stories deal with bizarre personality changes: "Two Things, Dimly, Were Going at Each Other" is about a disease called "the grofft," which turns men into dogs, and in "Nicodemus Bluff" a boy's father undergoes a strange personality change during a hunting trip.

HIGH LONESOME

This collection is characterized by improbable plots and wildly inventive language. The first story, "Get Some Young," is also typical of Hannah in its gothic approach to sexuality—here a middle-aged couple's refusal to accept growing old ends in their corruption of a beautiful young boy. In the title story, "Uncle High Lonesome," a man reflects on the reasons for his special kinship with his alcoholic uncle, Peter, who suffers lifelong guilt after murdering a man during a poker game. This memory has been passed on to his nephew and to his nephew's nephew, so that each is connected in a dreamlike generational tragedy involving violence and alcohol. His nephew eventually realizes that his uncle was unable to overcome the "high lonesomes," that is, a sense of overwhelming depression. This theme of the "high lonesomes" surfaces in other stories as well. Sometimes, as in "Repulsed," the experience of the "high lonesomes" ends in redemptive acts of generosity, whereas in other stories the outcome is simply diminishment.

Another feature of this collection is the use of biblical language and a strong religious subtext. Christ-like figures or references can be found in "Through Sunset into the Racoon Night," "The Agony of T. Bandini," and "Drummer Down." In "A Creature in the Boy of St. Louis," a young boy is pulled under water, where he has a death-and-resurrection experience.

OTHER MAJOR WORKS

LONG FICTION: *Geronimo Rex*, 1972; *Nightwatchmen*, 1973; *Ray*, 1980; *The Tennis Handsome*, 1983: *Hey Jack!*, 1987; *Boomerang*, 1989; *Never Die*, 1991.

NONFICTION: *Men Without Ties*, 1995.

BIBLIOGRAPHY

Charney, Mark J. *Barry Hannah*. New York: Twayne, 1992. First full-length study of Hannah and an indispensable guide to all his fiction, including the short stories collected in *Airships* and *Captain Maximus*. Makes a case for Hannah as one of the South's freshest and most iconoclastic writers. Features a thorough discussion of *Airships*, which he sees as reflecting a vision of the South as a microcosm of human existence. Also discusses *Captain Maximus* in the light of its preoccupation with violence. Includes an annotated bibliography.

Hannah, Barry. "The Spirits Will Win Through: An Interview with Barry Hannah." Interview by R. Vanarsall. *Southern Review*, Spring, 1983, 314-341. A long, thoughtful interview, which connects Hannah's own biography with the material in his stories. Discusses his alcoholism, his fascination with violence, his work in California as a screenwriter, the influence of other authors, his love of the English language, and his feelings of kinship with rock guitarist Jimi Hendrix.

Shepherd, Allen. "Outrage and Speculation: Barry Hannah's *Airships*." *Notes on Mississippi Writers*, 1982, 63-73. Important analysis of many of the stories and major themes in *Airships*. Notes Hannah's ability to render psychologically impaired narrators convincingly, as well as his gift for dialogue and poetic symbolism.

Weston, Ruth D. *Barry Hannah, Postmodern Romantic*. Baton Rouge: Louisiana State University Press, 1998. Important full-length study discusses Hannah's postmodern style and his ability to express hard truths about the conditions of contemporary life. Provides a serious analysis of all of Hannah's work including his short-story collections. This critique is also notable for its skillful use of current short-story theories to explicate Hannah's work, especially with regard to the idea of "debunking." It is also especially good at discerning the wild, irreverent, "carnivalesque" aspects of Hannah's work and at examining the theme of "the lie" in much of Hannah's work. It correctly identifies a strong religious subtext and sees Hannah as examining the social, cultural, and religious betrayals of the American Dream, especially in terms of defective myths about male prowess. Includes a bibliography.

Wyatt, David. *Out of the Sixties: Storytelling and the Vietnam Generation*. New York: Cambridge University Press, 1993. Analysis of Hannah as a member of a literary generation defined by the Vietnam War, which was experienced as a shared ordeal. Also notes the ways in which Hannah creates parallels between the Vietnam War and the Civil War as unfinished wars in which honor turned to shame, with various issues and emotional wounds remaining unresolved.

Margaret Boe Birns

THOMAS HARDY

Born: Higher Bockhampton, England; June 2, 1840
Died: Dorchester, England; January 11, 1928

PRINCIPAL SHORT FICTION

Wessex Tales, 1888
A Group of Noble Dames, 1891
Life's Little Ironies, 1894
A Changed Man, the Waiting Supper, and Other Tales, 1913
The Complete Short Stories, 1989 (Desmond Hawkins, editor)

OTHER LITERARY FORMS

In addition to his short stories, Thomas Hardy is best known for two distinct literary careers: first as a novelist, author of such classic works as *Far from the Madding Crowd* (1874) and *Tess of the D'Urbervilles* (1891); then, following the hostile reaction to *Jude the Obscure* in 1895, as a poet, especially for his epic verse drama about the Napoleonic Wars, *The Dynasts: A Drama of the Napoleonic Wars* (pb. 1903, 1906, 1908, 1910, verse drama; pr. 1914; abridged by Harley Granville-Barker).

ACHIEVEMENTS

Thomas Hardy is widely regarded as both a major Victorian novelist and a major modern poet. With little formal education, Hardy, who trained and worked as an architect before becoming a professional writer, was largely self-taught and eminently well read, particularly in the philosophical and theological exchange of ideas in the late nineteenth century. In addition to reflecting the intellectual climate stimulated by such thinkers as Charles Darwin, John Stuart Mill, and Herbert Spencer, Hardy's fiction also is recognized for its portrayal of rural southwestern England, vividly and lovingly represented in his fictional region called "Wessex." Many of his tales are based on local folklore, thus preserving this tradition while also recording the historical effects of mid-nineteenth century industrial changes on the agrarian community. Hardy fought critical and popular disapproval

for his frank treatment of then taboo subjects and for what was deemed his inordinately hard pessimism. Hardy was awarded honorary degrees from Oxford, Cambridge, St. Andrews, Bristol, and Aberdeen universities, a medal from the Royal Institute of British Architects, a royal Order of Merit, and a gold medal of the Royal Society of Literature. He was offered, but declined, a knighthood. His burial in Westminster Abbey is a further testament to his status among the great English authors.

BIOGRAPHY

Thomas Hardy was born and reared in the Dorsetshire countryside to which he was to return constantly for the settings of many of his novels, stories, and poems. His family encouraged his reading, and he was educated at local schools. He left formal schooling at sixteen to become an architect's apprentice, although he continued to read and teach himself. In 1862, he went to London to work in an architect's office but returned to Dorsetshire in 1867 to begin a career as a writer. Working part-time with a local architect, he produced his first novels, but he soon took up writing full-time. In 1874, he married Emma Lavinia Gifford. Although their marriage was not entirely happy, it lasted until Emma's death in 1912. He was married again, to Florence Emily Dugdale, in 1914, a time during which Hardy was successful but controversial as a novelist. Following critical outcries over what some considered obscenity of both *Tess of the D'Urbervilles* and especially *Jude the Obscure* in 1895, he turned almost exclusively to poetry, an endeavor in which he was also successful. On his seventieth birthday, he received the Order of Merit. He died in Dorsetshire at the age of eighty-seven.

ANALYSIS

Although the short stories of Thomas Hardy share with his novels the fictional setting of "Wessex," certain character types, and the philosophic concerns of his better-known writing, they necessarily lack the scope and sometimes majestic sweep of his longer

Thomas Hardy (Library of Congress)

works. Nevertheless, many of the short stories stand on their own as effective and moving pieces of literature. Hardy was proud that they were often based on and permeated with local legends and folktales; still, the stories are not merely country fables. Even when they have strong elements of the grotesque or the supernatural, these aspects are not included primarily for the sake of shock or to suggest an allegorical moral. Instead, Hardy builds around these elements to construct telling and convincing psychological portraits of his characters.

"THE WITHERED ARM"

Perhaps the best known of these stories is one with a plot which almost makes it a ghost story, "The Withered Arm." Rhoda Brook, a tenant of Farmer Lodge, has had an illegitimate son by her landlord. When the farmer returns to Wessex with Gertrude, his new wife, Rhoda is intensely jealous. Although she has never seen Gertrude, she is able to imagine

her clearly from her son's descriptions. Finally, one night Rhoda has a dream or vision: "that the young wife, in the pale silk dress and white bonnet, was sitting upon her chest as she lay." The "incubus," as Hardy calls it, taunts Rhoda, nearly suffocating her with its weight. In desperation, Rhoda reaches out and grabs the specter's left arm; she throws the specter to the floor, after which it promptly vanishes. The next day, Rhoda meets Gertrude in person and finds that she actually likes her; in a few days, however, Gertrude complains to Rhoda about a pain in her left arm which had begun at the time of Rhoda's dream. There is a mark on her arm like fingerprints, which shocks Rhoda as much as it dismays Gertrude. The arm begins to waste away and Lodge's love for his wife diminishes in proportion. Gertrude persuades Rhoda to take her to a local medicine man, Conjuror Trendle, in spite of Rhoda's fear that she will be revealed as the source of Gertrude's suffering and lose her new friend. Trendle shows Gertrude the image of the cause of her afflicted arm; although the reader never sees the image directly, Gertrude immediately turns cool toward Rhoda, and soon after Rhoda and her son leave the area.

Some years later, Gertrude has developed into "an irritable, superstitious woman, whose whole time was given to experimenting upon her ailment with every quack remedy she came across," hoping to win back the love of her husband. Finally, she turns again to Conjuror Trendle, who assures her that the one cure for her arm is to touch the neck of a newly hanged man. While Lodge is away on business, Gertrude rides to Casterbridge, where there is to be a hanging. She arranges to be near the body after it is cut down and, in spite of her revulsion, she touches the neck and feels the "turning of the blood" which will cure her arm. She is immediately interrupted, however, by the dead man's parents—Rhoda and Lodge. Gertrude collapses and soon dies from the stress and shock of her experience: "Her blood had been 'turned' indeed—too far." Rhoda Brook finally returns to the area to live out her days in seclusion, refusing the money which Farmer Lodge leaves her when he dies.

Although this tale follows the outlines of the horror story genre, Hardy does not place his emphasis on the horror of the withered arm or the hanged man, as, for example, Edgar Allan Poe would; nor does he seek for a deeper meaning behind the affliction as Nathaniel Hawthorne might. Instead, the supernatural element is almost taken for granted. The tone of the narrator is lightly skeptical, suggesting the possibility of some psychological origin or even physical cause for the disability, but the concentration and the concern of the story are on the characters, first of Rhoda and then of Gertrude. The reader sees a lonely woman who, wronged by a man and deprived of his love, then loses her one friend. The second part of the story concentrates on Gertrude's desperate desire to restore her physical beauty and the love of her husband, even if she must experience horror to accomplish that end.

"The Fiddler of the Reels"

A similar use of the supernatural to build psychological effects is seen in "The Fiddler of the Reels." The Fiddler is Wat or "Mop" Ollamoor, a veterinary surgeon whose pastime is playing the fiddle at inns, parties, and fairs. Although the men of the area do not care much for him, he seems to have an almost magical power over women when he plays. There is, in fact, something slightly satanic in his character; he "had never, in all likelihood, entered a church at all. All were devil's tunes in his repertory." One woman who is particularly affected by his playing is Car'line Aspent, who finds herself forced to dance whenever Mop Ollamoor plays, no matter what she is doing or thinks she desires. She is so caught up by the fiddler that she even detects his footsteps on the road by her house when he is on his way to visit another woman. Her passion is such that she finally rejects the marriage proposal of her former lover, Ned Hipcroft: "He could not play the fiddle so as to draw your soul out of your body like a spider's thread, as Mop did, till you felt as limp as the withywind and yearned for something to cling to."

Ned moves to London where he makes his living as a mechanic for four years; he finally receives a letter from Car'line, telling him that she is now ready to marry him after all. Ned accepts Car'line's reconsideration gratefully, although he is temporarily taken aback when Car'line arrives with the daughter she has had by Mop. The couple marries and the three live happily in London for a few years until they decide to return to their hometown in Wessex. Stopping in an inn on their return, while Ned takes care of some business, Car'line notices Ollamoor sitting in a corner with his fiddle. Her former lover begins to play, and Car'line once again finds herself forced to dance. The fiddler continues, never stopping, until Car'line collapses from exhaustion. When Ned returns to the inn, he finds that his wife has collapsed, and his daughter, whom he has come to love as his own, has disappeared with the fiddler.

The figure of Wat Ollamoor in "The Fiddler of the Reels" is obviously drawn from the legends which associate the devil with music, especially that of the fiddle. (Mop is also compared to Paganini, who was rumored to have drawn his power from the devil.) Once again, however, Hardy does not attempt to concentrate on the unearthly power of the musician; his concern is rather with its effect on his characters, especially Car'line. In this woman's infatuation and helplessness, one can see the obsessiveness and sexual passion which also drive Tess of the D'Urbervilles.

"The Fiddler of the Reels" is set in a time of great change for England in general and Wessex in particular. The events in the story take place during the year of the first world fair, the Great Exposition of 1851. There is a strong contrast between this homage to the industrial revolution and the more mystic and communal affairs of a small, obscure village. The coming of the railroad to that village is just one sign of the disappearance of a way of life which had lasted for centuries. It is because of these changes which were rapidly transforming Hardy's country during his lifetime that many of his short stories and tales are set in the past.

"The Distracted Preacher"

One of Hardy's best re-creations of the past of Wessex is his lengthy story "The Distracted Preacher." The preacher of the title is Mr. Stockdale, a Wesleyan minister living in the 1830's during King William IV's reign. Being new to town, he takes lodgings and discovers his new landlady, Lizzy Newberry, to be a beautiful young widow. The two are almost immediately attracted to each other and soon fall in love. Stockdale soon discovers, however, that Lizzy is not as totally respectable as she appears. First, she obtains some illegal smuggled liquor to cure the preacher's cold; next, Stockdale notices that she seems to sleep late, until he eventually realizes that she is often out of the house all night. Gradually, he realizes and she reveals to him that she is working with a group of smugglers who help to support the town during the winter and that in fact she, with her cousin Jim Owlett, is a leader of the smugglers. Naturally, the minister is shocked and disapproves of such activities, but his concern for Lizzy eventually overcomes his inhibitions. He accompanies her on several of her missions and does not betray her when the king's men search the town for the hidden liquor. In the end, however, Stockdale cannot live with both Lizzy and his conscience, and he leaves the town to take a church elsewhere in England.

Up to this point, Hardy's story is entertaining, humorous, and revealing. The dilemma of the preacher, caught between his strict view of morality and obedience to the state and his love for Lizzy, is presented comically. Stockdale appears naïve and innocent, yet he is tempted to become Lizzy's partner in crime as well as in life. The ending, however, is anticlimactic and disappointing. Two years after Stockdale has left the village, he returns and meets Lizzy again, learning that she has been forced to give up smuggling after a raid in which Owlett has been caught and she has been wounded. This time, the two marry and she writes a religious tract based on her experience:

> Stockdale got it printed, after making some corrections, and putting in a few powerful sentences of his own; and many hundreds of copies were distributed by the couple in the course of their married life.

Although this ending also has humorous overtones, Hardy himself did not care for it. In a later note accompanying the story, he explains that the marriage and "happy ending" "was almost *de rigueur* in an English magazine at the time of writing." The ending which Hardy would have preferred would have corresponded to the end of the "true incidents of which the tale is a vague and flickering shadow." In those true incidents, Lizzy and her cousin Jim marry and eventually go to America while the preacher is left alone. "The Distracted Preacher," then, in addition to being a good example of Hardy's storytelling ability also illustrates the problems which writers can have because of the commercial demands placed on their art.

"A FEW CRUSTED CHARACTERS"

Hardy's affection for Wessex and for the past ways of life of which it still contained traces perhaps comes through most clearly in the collection of character sketches titled "A Few Crusted Characters." These tales are framed by a coach ride during which one of the passengers is revealed to be John Lackland's son, who left Wessex thirty-five years before and has returned with a thought of settling down in his old home area. His presence prompts his fellow travelers to reminisce about people he had known and other local characters, but, at the end of each recollection, it is revealed that the characters are dead or that the places in which they lived and worked have been changed. When the carriage reaches Lackland's hometown of Longpuddle, he walks about the area but finds himself disappointed:

> None of the objects wore the attractiveness in this their real presentation that had ever accompanied their images in the field of his imagination when he was more than two thousand miles removed from them.

Looking at the gravestones of the people he had known in his youth, he realizes, fifty years before Thomas Wolfe, that you can't go home again:

> . . . in returning to this spot it would be incumbent upon him to reestablish himself from the beginning, precisely as though he had never known the place, nor it him. Time had not condescended to wait his pleasure, nor local life his greeting.

Once again, Lackland leaves his village and is never seen again.

"BARBARA OF THE HOUSE OF GREBE"

Hardy's fascination with the past is probably seen most thoroughly in his collection *A Group of Noble Dames*. As in "A Few Crusted Characters," the reader is presented with stories about a number of women of title or property told by a group of men before and after dinner. One of the best of these, "Barbara of the House of Grebe," also demonstrates Hardy's predilection for the grotesque. Lady Barbara is a young woman who spurns the advances of her neighbor, Lord Uplandtowers, and elopes with a commoner, Edmund Willowes. The couple soon discovers that their love cannot overcome their financial needs, and they appeal to Barbara's parents for forgiveness. The parents accept the return of the young people on the condition that Willowes spend a year on the Continent with a tutor to prepare himself for a life in aristocratic society. While traveling, however, Willowes is badly burned while rescuing some people from a burning building. When he returns, he is so disfigured that Barbara cannot bear to look at him, and he leaves again for Europe. Lord Uplandtowers renews his pursuit of Lady Barbara and eventually succeeds in marrying her after she is legally declared a widow.

Uplandtowers is disappointed, however, because he realizes that Barbara does not love him with the same passion she felt for Willowes and because she gives him no male heir. Barbara later receives a statue from Pisa which was commissioned by Willowes while he was traveling in Italy. It is a perfect, full-length replica of her former husband before his disfigurement, and she hides it from her husband. Uplandtowers is annoyed and jealous of the statue's handsome features, but stops thinking of it when it disappears. He soon realizes, however, that Barbara has been leaving her bed at night and wandering off. Following her, he observes her enter a secret room where she has placed the statue and watches as she embraces and kisses the figure, apologizing to her dead husband for not having loved him enough. For revenge, and to turn his wife's thoughts back to him, Uplandtowers has the statue mutilated to resemble Willowes after the fire. The alteration terrifies Barbara, but she still refuses to renounce her love for Willowes. Finally, Uplandtowers locks her in a room with the statue and forces her to gaze on it until her spirit is broken. Uplandtowers's victory, however, becomes a new kind of defeat. His wife becomes obsessively attached to him, "till at length her very fi-

delity became a burden to him, absorbing his time, and curtailing his liberty, and causing him to curse and swear." In addition, although Barbara bears her husband eleven children, only one—a girl—survives to maturity, and the estate passes to a nephew.

Barbara's story illustrates another set of Hardy's concerns: the importance of character rather than mere appearance, the vanity of class prejudice, and the folly of forcing someone to love against his or her will. These themes, expressed in simple, colloquial, and compelling language, make Hardy's tales more than merely an interesting sidelight to the major writings of a great novelist.

OTHER MAJOR WORKS

LONG FICTION: *Desperate Remedies*, 1871; *Under the Greenwood Tree*, 1872; *A Pair of Blue Eyes*, 1872-1873; *Far from the Madding Crowd*, 1874; *The Hand of Ethelberta*, 1875-1876; *The Return of the Native*, 1878; *The Trumpet-Major*, 1880; *A Laodicean*, 1880-1881; *Two on a Tower*, 1882; *The Mayor of Casterbridge*, 1886; *The Woodlanders*, 1886-1887; *Tess of the D'Urbervilles*, 1891; *Jude the Obscure*, 1895; *The Well-Beloved*, 1897; *An Indiscretion in the Life of an Heiress*, 1935.

PLAYS: *The Dynasts: A Drama of the Napoleonic Wars*, pb. 1903, 1906, 1908, 1910 (verse drama), pr. 1914 (abridged by Harley Granville-Barker); *The Famous Tragedy of the Queen of Cornwall*, pr., pb. 1923 (one act).

POETRY: *Wessex Poems and Other Verses*, 1898; *Poems of the Past and the Present*, 1901; *Time's Laughingstocks and Other Verses*, 1909; *Satires of Circumstance*, 1914; *Selected Poems of Thomas Hardy*, 1916; *Moments of Vision and Miscellaneous Verses*, 1917; *Late Lyrics and Earlier*, 1922; *Human Shows, Far Phantasies, Songs, and Trifles*, 1925; *Winter Words in Various Moods and Metres*, 1928; *Collected Poems*, 1931; *The Complete Poetical Works*, 1982-1985 (3 volumes; Samuel Hynes, editor).

NONFICTION: *Life and Art*, 1925 (Ernest Brennecke, editor); *The Early Life of Hardy*, 1928; *The Later Years of Thomas Hardy*, 1930; *Personal Writings*, 1966 (Harold Orel, editor); *The Collected Let-*

ters of Thomas Hardy, 1978, 1980 (Richard Little Purdy and Michael Millgate, editors, 2 volumes).

BIBLIOGRAPHY

Carpenter, Richard C. *Thomas Hardy*. Boston: Twayne, 1964. Carpenter argues that Hardy is a "gloomy philosopher," though he maintains that label is too restricting. In addition to the usual characterization, descriptions, plots, and social themes, Carpenter also looks at elements of symbolism, myth, impressionism, and drama in Hardy's fiction and poetry. Contains a chronology, a bibliography, and an index.

Chew, Samuel C. *Thomas Hardy: Poet and Novelist*. 1928. Reprint. New York: Russell & Russell, 1964. Although it does not lack sentiment, this volume is still one of the most respected of the traditional analyses of Hardy's work. Chew examines Hardy's pessimism, his use of coincidence, his conflict of intellect and intuition, and the structural excellence of his Wessex novels, which Chew considers to be a clarification of Victorian technique. Includes a bibliography and an index.

Daleski, H. M. *Thomas Hardy and Paradoxes of Love*. Columbia: University of Missouri Press, 1997. Argues that Hardy is the premodern precursor of sexual failures and catastrophic ends.

Gatrell, Simon. *Thomas Hardy and the Proper Study of Mankind*. Charlottesville: University Press of Virginia, 1993. A study of Hardy's technique of presenting character in relationship to society. In addition to chapters on individual novels, Gatrell devotes chapters to Hardy's use of the dance as a folk ritual and to the imperial theme in his fiction.

Gibson, James. *Thomas Hardy*. New York: St. Martin's Press, 1996. An introductory guide to Hardy's art, focusing on how Hardy used his own experience in his writing and tracing his development from fiction back to his first love, poetry.

Guerard, Albert J. *Thomas Hardy: The Novels and Stories*. Cambridge, Mass.: Harvard University Press, 1949. One of the classic critical works on Hardy, examining his poetry and fiction in Victorian and modern contexts. In relation to Joseph Conrad and André Gide, Hardy is an old-fashioned storyteller, but he anticipates modern elements of antirealism in his conflicting impulses, his symbolic use of coincidence, and his artful technique.

Howe, Irving. *Thomas Hardy*. New York: Macmillan, 1967. One of the earliest book-length studies of Hardy's short fiction as well as his poetry and novels, tracing the development of Hardy as a writer and the influences of his background and intellectual environment. The chapter "Let the Day Perish" focuses on Hardy's women characters, especially Tess, who illustrates the transformation and ennobling of a cultural stereotype. Complemented by a primary bibliography and an index.

Pinion, F. B. *A Hardy Companion*. New York: St. Martin's Press, 1968. A helpful, comprehensive guide to Hardy's writing, political and philosophical background and biographical influences. Includes maps, illustrations, and a select bibliography. Also contains a handy dictionary of people and places in Hardy's fiction and the locations of Hardy manuscripts.

Plotz, John. "Motion Slickness: Spectacle and Circulation in Thomas Hardy's 'On the Western Circuit.'" *Studies in Short Fiction* 33 (Summer, 1996): 369-386. Claims that Hardy's story reflects his criticism of modernity in relationship to Britain's imperialism; the steam roundabout in the text becomes visible in its full, complicated relationship to other roundabout systems of the modern age.

Seymour-Smith, Martin. *Hardy*. New York: St. Martin's Press, 1994. In this literary biography, Seymour-Smith not only provides a detailed biography of Hardy's life but also summarizes and critiques previous criticism of Hardy and discusses in a straightforward, nontheoretical way, Hardy's most important works; analyzes critical reception to Hardy's work and critiques critical controversies over his fiction and thought.

Webster, Harvey Curtis. *On a Darkling Plain*. Chicago: University of Chicago Press, 1947. An extended, in-depth consideration of Hardy's fiction and poetry in the light of his pessimism, considering how personal experiences and intellectual trends contributed to the development of his melancholy view. Webster discerns a natural "para-disaic tendency" that periodically surfaces in Hardy's work, but he maintains that the world destroyed this "happy outlook."

Donald F. Larsson, updated by Lou Thompson

JOY HARJO

Born: Tulsa, Oklahoma; May 9, 1951

PRINCIPAL SHORT FICTION

"Boston," 1991

"The Flood," 1991

"Northern Lights," 1991

"The Woman Who Fell from the Sky," 1996

"Warrior Road," 1997

A Map to the Next World: Poetry and Tales, 2000

OTHER LITERARY FORMS

Joy Harjo is best known as a poet, but some of her work in this form can best be described as prose poetry, so the difference between the two genres tends to blur in her books. In both the poetry and the prose, Harjo frequently uses Native American spiritual myths and symbols and southwestern settings (Oklahoma and New Mexico). She has also edited (with Gloria Bird) *Reinventing the Enemy's Language: Contemporary Native Women's Writing of North America* (1997).

ACHIEVEMENTS

Joy Harjo's two poetry collections published in the 1990's—*In Mad Love and War* (1990) and *The Woman Who Fell from the Sky* (1994)—won numerous awards. Harjo was a National Endowment for the Arts fellow in 1978, an Arizona Commission on the Arts Creative Writing fellow in 1989, and she won an American Indian Distinguished Achievement Award, in 1990. Through her several volumes of poetry, Harjo has become one of the leading Native American poetic voices.

BIOGRAPHY

Joy Harjo was born and raised in Tulsa, Oklahoma, where she lived until she was sixteen, and has been strongly influenced by her Muskogee Creek heritage. She received her B.A. in 1976 from the University of New Mexico, and an M.F.A. in creative writing from the University of Iowa two years later. She has been an instructor of poetry at several schools, and from 1991 to 1997 she taught at the University of New Mexico, Albuquerque. In addition to her other writing efforts, Harjo is a painter, a musician (she plays the saxophone), who has produced several records with her band, "Joy Harjo and Poetic Justice," and a screenwriter. She has lectured widely on poetry and the arts and has been active in Native American affairs, particularly in cultural organizations. She had two children, Phil and Rainy Dawn.

ANALYSIS

As a writer often working in poetry, Joy Harjo's language tends to be highly charged and full of images (such as "the blue bowl of the sky") and visions. Her writing is also often strongly spiritual, encompassing, as it does, a number of Native American myths and a distinctive Native American viewpoint. Harjo also writes of social issues, particularly the plight of Native Americans in the United States, both historically and in the present, and especially (but not exclusively) the condition of the Native American woman. C. B. Clark has accurately described the scope of Harjo's work, saying that she "recalls the wounds of the past, the agony of the Indian present, and dream visions of a better future for indigenous

Joy Harjo

peoples." Her prose work is generally short (three to five pages), it often mingles realistic and mythic modes, and it is strongly autobiographical.

"THE FLOOD"

"The Flood" is representative of the shape of much of Joy Harjo's prose writing—short and yet deeply visionary. This first-person, three-page narrative alternates between a contemporary, realistic mode (cars, a six-pack, and a convenience store) and deeper elements (a mythical water monster and centuries of legend and history). At the heart of the story is the image of a sixteen-year-old woman walking into a lake to marry a mythic Indian water god. However, the narrative is hardly linear, and the girl is simultaneously a tribal daughter carrying her sister to the lake to draw water in the distant past, a contemporary young woman driving a car into the lake, and a third woman watching the girl walk out of the lake twenty years later. Which is she? All of them, in a

mixture of the poles of the narrative method used here, which employs memory and imagination. The fiction is heavily multilayered: Myth infuses history with meaning, and there is no objective retelling of the story that can adequately capture truth without undue reduction or simplification. The story is less a fiction than a vision—including the rain at the end "that would flood the world." Readers of "The Flood" may be reminded of another native American fictionist, the Chippewa writer Louise Erdrich, whose short story "Fleur," for example, also concerns a young Indian girl meeting a water monster in a lake.

"NORTHERN LIGHTS"

Like "The Flood," "Northern Lights" was first collected in 1991 in *Talking Leaves: Contemporary Native American Stories*, edited by Craig Lesley. While it is also in the first person, "the story doesn't belong to me," the narrator concludes, "but to Whirling Soldier who gifted me with it in the circle of hope." The narrator meets Whirling Soldier at a winter dance. He has returned from duty in Vietnam with many scars, most of them mental. His story is also the history of three generations of an alcoholic family (including his father and his daughter). There is no easy answer here as to how Whirling Soldier is saved, but at the conclusion of the story, there is a kind of redemption for all of the characters:

> After the dance, we all ran out onto the ice to see the northern lights. They were shimmering relatives returned from the war, dancing in the skies all around us. It was an unusual moment of grace for fools.

Like the work of Native American writers Leslie Marmon Silko (*Ceremony*, 1977) and James Welch (*Winter in the Blood*, 1974), this story of a soldier returning from war is an opportunity for the writer to raise a number of other important Native American issues. As in her other stories, Harjo here writes like a poet ("He snuffed his confusion between honor and honor with wine, became an acrobat of pain in the Indian bars of Kansas").

"BOSTON"

This short story varies from the usual Harjo pattern in its taking place outside the southwestern setting of most of her other fiction, and yet even here the view of the world is Native American, for Boston is perceived as sitting at the edge of the Atlantic, where the horizon divides "the Upperworld and the Underworld," and is infused with myth. Once again the story is short (fewer than one thousand words), first person, and strongly autobiographical (the narrator's first name is "Joy"). "Boston" centers on the narrator's father, who once "found himself" in that city, probably because of a woman. Why did he find himself so far away, she wonders, "ten thousand myths away from Oklahoma"? That speculation leads her to the creation story of the "the first Muskogee rising from the mists of the east" and to other myths, like that of the water monster. So, speculation about what might have taken her father from Oklahoma to Boston leads her back to the history and legends of Oklahoma. "At nearly forty," the Harjo persona confesses, "I am thinking of the traps we construct to absent memory." Her father died in 1983 in an aging trailer. The story of her father is thus, like the Muskogee creation story itself, about water, "as if you must wind back through all memory, all history, the water monster the ongoing companion to the left of you." The story of her father has become her own story, the story of her people, and the story of the continuing power of Muskogee myth. Fiction for Harjo cannot leave out history and myth, for all exist on similar planes simultaneously and constantly infuse each other in her writing.

"THE WOMAN WHO FELL FROM THE SKY"

This short work is the title piece from Harjo's 1996 prizewinning poetry collection and may be the best example of the ways in which her poetry bleeds into prose, or vice versa. The central image is taken from an old Iroquois female creation myth, but in the Harjo version "that force operates within the dreadful confines of modern urban life," as Paula Gunn Allen notes in the introduction to the piece collected in her *Song of the Turtle: American Indian Literature, 1974-1994* (1996). "Once a woman fell from the sky," the story begins, and the reader immediately enters a world where myth and reality coincide. On one plane exists much of the ugliness of modern urban life, like poverty and alcoholism, especially as experienced by Native Americans. The Safeway store parking lot,

where Johnny ("Saint Coincidence") witnesses the woman falling from the sky, is also a place of transcendent love and mystery. For Lila, the woman who falls, has also lived in the sky as a star, and her descent into Johnny's arms with her children is the beginning of hope. As the nameless narrator concludes the coda to the story, "*I understood love to be the very gravity holding each leaf, each cell, this earthy star together.*" Native American myth becomes the start of the search for a solution to contemporary Native American problems.

"WARRIOR ROAD"

"Warrior Road" was collected by Harjo in *Reinventing the Enemy's Language: Contemporary Native Woman's Writings of North America*, the volume she edited in 1997 with Gloria Bird. It is longer than her other stories, and less obviously mythic than her earlier work, but it is linked to other prose pieces in being strongly autobiographical and poetic. The story concerns the birth of Harjo's two children, but she uses these events to talk about the treatment of Native Americans in the United States—and particularly by a medical "system in which the wisdom that had carried my people from generation to generation was ignored." Her son was born when Harjo was seventeen, her daughter four years later. When, at age sixteen, Harjo's daughter bore a daughter herself, the narrator realizes "something *had* changed," and Krista Rae is born into a larger and more loving family. Conditions for Native Americans had improved, as Harjo's own life story demonstrates. Four days later, she took her grandchild "to the saguaro forest before dawn and gave her the name I had dreamed for her. . . . A female ancestor approaches on a horse. We are all together."

Toward the end of this account, Harjo writes that her work

> has to do with reclaiming the memory stolen from our peoples when we were dispossessed from our lands east of the Mississippi; it has to do with restoring us.

"Warrior Road," which is less fictional and more autobiographical than many of Harjo's stories, is still doing that work and in a language that has Harjo's distinctive poetic stamp.

OTHER MAJOR WORKS

POETRY: *The Last Song*, 1975; *What Moon Drove Me to This?*, 1980; *She Had Some Horses*, 1983; *Secrets from the Center of the World*, 1989; *In Mad Love and War*, 1990; *The Woman Who Fell from the Sky*, 1994.

TELEPLAY: *Origin of Apache Crown Dance*, 1985.

EDITED TEXT: *Reinventing the Enemy's Language: North American Native Women's Writing*, 1997 (with Gloria Bird).

BIBLIOGRAPHY

Clark, C. B. "Joy Harjo (Creek)." In *The Heath Anthology of American Literature*, edited by Paul Lauter et al. Vol. 2. Boston: Houghton Mifflin, 1998. Clark's brief introduction to selections of Harjo's poetry (including the prose poem "Deer Dancer") in this anthology delineates several of the most important qualities of her writing.

Coltelli, Laura, ed. *The Spiral of Memory: Interviews, Joy Harjo*. Ann Arbor: University of Michigan Press, 1996. These interviews with the poet offer insights into her method of working as well as the continuing concerns of her writing.

Donovan, Kathleen. *Feminist Readings of Native American Literature*. Tucson: The University of Arizona Press, 1998. Donovan's last chapter, "Dark Continent/Dark Woman," is a consideration of Joy Harjo in company with the French literary critic Helene Cixous. Both writers "struggle to reconcile their sense of multiple identities that arise from the displacements of history and family background," Donovan argues, and "by embracing their multiple identities and places of origin, they transform and create, thereby gaining a measured healing that permits them to 'more than survive.'"

Scarry, John. "Joy Harjo." In *Smoke Rising: The Native North American Literary Companion*, edited by Janet Witalec. Detroit, Mich.: Gale Research, 1995. Scarry's brief entry on Harjo recognizes her "need for remembrance and transcendence" and includes several poems demonstrating this duality (including the prose poems "Grace" and "Autobiography," both from *In Mad Love and War*.)

Witalec, Janet, ed. *Native North American Literature: Biographical and Critical Information on Native Writers and Orators from the United States and Canada from Historical Times to the Present*. New York: Gale Research, 1994. The essay on Harjo in this encyclopedia is a very useful survey of the writer's career and includes long excerpts from three essay-reviews of Harjo's work.

David Peck

JOEL CHANDLER HARRIS

Born: Eatonton, Georgia; December 9, 1848
Died: Atlanta, Georgia; July 3, 1908

PRINCIPAL SHORT FICTION

Uncle Remus: His Songs and His Sayings, 1880
Nights with Uncle Remus, 1883
Mingo and Other Sketches in Black and White, 1884
Free Joe and Other Georgian Sketches, 1887
Daddy Jake the Runaway, 1889
Balaam and His Master and Other Stories and Sketches, 1891
Uncle Remus and His Friends, 1892
Tales of Home Folks in Peace and War, 1898
Told by Uncle Remus: New Stories of the Old Plantation, 1905
The Complete Tales of Uncle Remus, 1955 (edited by Richard Chase)

OTHER LITERARY FORMS

Joel Chandler Harris's literary talents were considerably broader than the Uncle Remus tales for which he is so well known. He was an accomplished editor, essayist, folklorist, and biographer, and he wrote several romantic novels.

ACHIEVEMENTS

Joel Chandler Harris was best known in his day for his collections of Uncle Remus tales, particularly *Uncle Remus: His Songs and His Sayings* and *Nights with Uncle Remus*, tales which were not created but recorded by him. When the American Academy of Arts and Letters was founded in 1905, Harris was elected to be one of the inaugural members. The black man/white boy which Harris uses in the Uncle Remus stories was highly influential on Mark Twain's portrayal of the Jim/Huck relationship in *The Adventures of Huckleberry Finn* (1884). With the emergence of the Civil Rights movement, however, and with the portrayal of Uncle Remus as a man among cartoons in Walt Disney's movie *Song of the South*, the figure of Uncle Remus (who was in part based on Harriet Beecher Stowe's character Uncle Tom from *Uncle Tom's Cabin*, 1852) fell into some amount of literary and political disfavor. Twentieth century studies of folklore have, however, established Harris's importance as a folklorist who collected authentic black folk tales.

BIOGRAPHY

Born in Putnam County, Georgia, the illegitimate son of an Irish laborer who deserted the family just after his birth, Joel Chandler Harris spent a rather ordinary boyhood in rural Georgia. He was not very interested in school and seems to have preferred playing pranks to studying. In 1862, at age fourteen, Harris was given a job as a printer's devil by Addison Turner, an eccentric planter who published a rural weekly newspaper, the *Countryman*, on his nearby plantation. It is impossible to overestimate Turner's influence on young Harris, for in addition to allowing him to contribute pieces to the paper, Turner also encouraged him to read extensively in his private library and to roam around his thousand-acre plantation. It was here that Harris first heard the black folk narratives that were later to become the heart of the Uncle Remus stories. After working for Turner for four years, Harris held brief jobs at several newspapers around the South. In 1873 he married Esther LaRose and soon settled in Atlanta, where he lived until his death in 1908.

Joel Chandler Harris (Library of Congress)

In 1876, Harris was hired to do editorial paragraphing for the Atlanta *Constitution*. Soon after his arrival, he was asked to take over a black-dialect column from a retiring writer, and, on October 26, 1876, his first sketch appeared, featuring the witty observations of an older black man. A month later the older black was officially called "Uncle Remus," and a major new voice in American humor was born. Uncle Remus began as a rather thin, almost vaudevillian caricature of a black man, an old urban black who supposedly dropped by the Atlanta *Constitution* office to offer practical comments, and some of Harris's own opinions, on corrupt politicians and lazy blacks. The character grew, however, when Harris transferred the locale of the sketches to a plantation and incorporated tales he had heard in the slave quarters during his early days with Turner. In late 1880, Harris collected twenty-one "urban" and thirty-four "plantation" Uncle Remus sketches along with black songs, maxims, and proverbs in *Uncle Remus: His Songs and His Sayings*. The collection was an immediate success, and, much to Harris's astonishment and embarrassment, he was famous.

ANALYSIS

Most of the Uncle Remus stories follow a similar formula. They begin with a frame narrative, which typically opens in Uncle Remus's cabin behind the "big house" as he discusses daily affairs with the young white son of Mars' John and Miss Sally. Usually something that the boy says reminds Uncle Remus of a story about Brer Rabbit or some other "creeturs." Once the tale is over, Uncle Remus draws a moral lesson for the boy and sends him to bed. The friendship between Uncle Remus and the young boy is worth noting, because in many ways it is Joel Chandler Harris's own idealized version of black/white relations. Both Uncle Remus and the boy have a strong love for each other and represent the best qualities of both races—Uncle Remus considers himself superior to the domestic servants, and he tells the boy not to play with the "riff-raff" Favers children, the poor white trash of the area. Yet Uncle Remus is not afraid to discipline the young boy subtly, and he sometimes pretends to withhold a tale because the boy has misbehaved during the day (chucking rocks at chickens, for example). Sometimes, borrowing a trick from Brer Rabbit, he has the boy bring him food from the kitchen as a means of appeasement. Uncle Remus also functions as the boy's teacher, moving him out of the linear chronology of the present and initiating him into the timeless world of the fables—a lesson the young boy sometimes has trouble understanding.

UNCLE REMUS

In "How Mr. Rabbit Saved His Meat," for example, the boy objects that Uncle Remus is beginning a tale about Brer Wolf, who has already been killed in an earlier story. In mock exasperation, Uncle Remus remarks that the boy "done grow'd up twel he know mo'n I duz." The world of the fables, like the patterns of human nature they depict, is atemporal.

The subtle tensions evident between Uncle Remus and the boy are also reflected in the stories themselves. Most of the Uncle Remus stories center on the best-known trickster in all of folklore, Brer Rabbit, and they present a further allegory of black/white relations in the postwar South. A weaker animal in a world of predatory wolves, foxes, bears, and buzzards, Brer Rabbit is forced to depend on his wits and his creativity for survival. His mischievousness disrupts the traditional roles of success within the established work ethic of the other animals, who raise their own "goobers" and catch their own fish, and his trickery allows him to gain power over, and respect from, a stronger race. Yet Brer Rabbit almost never brings his quarrels to open confrontation, and this reflects Harris's conservatism on racial matters. In "The Wonderful Tar-Baby Story," for example, it is Brer Rabbit's aggressive resistance to the lethargic, silent black tar-baby that gets him trapped by Brer Fox, but his smooth and deceptively conciliatory rhetoric allows him to escape. Brer Rabbit rarely openly accuses the other animals of misdeeds; his struggle for respect in the forest is achieved through the subtleties of role-playing and indirect retribution.

Although the Brer Rabbit tales may represent a projection of the black man's desire for the realignment of the white man's social structure, they have a dark side to them as well. Sometimes Brer Rabbit's overbearing brashness can backfire, as in "Mr. Rabbit Meets His Match at Last." In this tale, Brer Tarrypin and the rabbit agree to a foot race, but the turtle places his wife and children at strategic points around the track and wins the bet, since to Brer Rabbit all turtles look alike. In "Mr. Rabbit Meets His Match Again," Brer Rabbit tries to cheat Brer Buzzard out of some food, but Brer Buzzard flies him high over the river and threatens to drop him until he admits his trickery. On occasion, Brer Rabbit's roguery leads to acts of senseless violence. In "Mr. Rabbit Nibbles Up the Butter," Brer Rabbit steals butter that communally belongs to himself, Brer Fox, and Brer Possum. He then implicates Brer Possum as the thief by smearing some of the butter on him as he sleeps. Declaring his innocence, Brer Possum suggests that all three jump over a brush fire so that the heaviest animal, being full of butter, will be unmasked as the thief. Both the fox and the rabbit make the jump, but Brer Possum dies. In "The Sad Fate of Mr. Fox," the final tale of *Uncle Remus: His Songs and His Sayings*, Brer Fox offers to show Brer Rabbit how to cut meat from inside a cow without killing it. As soon as they are both inside, however, Brer Rabbit purposefully gives the cow a fatal blow.

When the farmer who owns the cow arrives, Brer Rabbit identifies the fox as the thief and the farmer kills him, chopping off his head. Brer Rabbit then takes the head to Mrs. Fox, telling her that it is a fine cut of beef, and Brer Fox's son soon discovers the head of his father floating in the caldron.

The Brer Rabbit tales carry an allegorical message for both blacks and whites. Harris recognizes that white society must learn to make room for a race that it has historically considered to be weak and inferior, yet he advises blacks to be patient and accept a slow rate of change. Too fast a push for power can lead to violence, and killing the fox only angers his son to revenge. Whatever sympathies Harris might have felt for the underdog position of the Reconstruction black were tempered by his political conservatism, which caused him to share some of the racial biases of his time.

NIGHTS WITH UNCLE REMUS

Uncle Remus proved so popular that Harris went on to publish a half-dozen more Uncle Remus volumes in his lifetime. Of these other volumes, his second collection, *Nights with Uncle Remus*, is the most important and the one that most fully shows the fruits of his labor. In it, Uncle Remus is rounded out much more to become a complete character in his own right, and other characters on the plantation are introduced as storytellers, principally Daddy Jack, a character who speaks in a Sea Island dialect called "Gullah," and who Harris used to tell stories he perceived to be of a different cultural origin than the stories that Uncle Remus tells. As popular as these Uncle Remus collections were, Harris never considered that their merit was inherently literary. He always insisted that in them he was the "compiler" of a folklore and dialect that were fast disappearing in the South at the end of the nineteenth century. He was careful to include only the Uncle Remus tales that could be verified as authentic black oral narratives, and, with his usual diffidence, he minimized his own role in elevating them to artistic short fiction.

MINGO AND OTHER SKETCHES IN BLACK AND WHITE

In *Mingo and Other Sketches in Black and White*, Harris surprised his readers by temporarily moving away from the Uncle Remus formula. The collection was favorably reviewed, and Harris showed that his literary talents could be stretched to include what he considered to be more serious forms. The title story, "Mingo: A Sketch of Life in Middle Georgia," is an admirable local-color portrayal of class conflicts. The central conflict is between two white families, the aristocratic Wornums and the poor-white Bivinses. Before the Civil War, the Wornums's daughter, Cordelia, had married the Bivins's son, Henry Clay, much to the displeasure of the Wornum family, who promptly disinherited her. Henry Clay was killed in the war and Cordelia died shortly thereafter, leaving a daughter in the care of Mrs. Feratia Bivins, Henry's mother. Mrs. Wornum is overcome with grief after the death of the children and realizes that she has made a mistake in snubbing the Bivinses, but fiercely proud Feratia cannot forgive her. In a comic yet pathos-filled scene, Mrs. Wornum asks Feratia Bivins to let her see her granddaughter, whom she has never seen. Feratia coolly replies, "if I had as much politeness, ma'am, as I had cheers, I'd ast you to set down," and adamantly refuses to let Mrs. Wornum see the baby. The final wise commentary, however, comes from Mingo, a former Wornum slave who is loyal to his old master and acts as the surrogate father for the surviving child. It is the black man's strength of character and endurance that promises reconciliation and social progress. Harris, a poor white by birth himself, is clearly antiaristocratic and sides with the underdog in times of changing social values, yet by applauding the virtues of loyalty and duty in the black, he comes very close to advocating a servile and passive acceptance, as some of his critics have charged.

FREE JOE AND OTHER GEORGIAN SKETCHES

Harris's *Free Joe and Other Georgian Sketches*, and the frequently anthologized title story, "Free Joe and the Rest of the World," further illustrates his ambivalence on the "Negro question." In 1840, a slave-speculator named Major Frampton lost all his property except one slave, his body-servant Joe, to Judge Alfred Wellington in a famous card game. Frampton adjourned the game, went to the courthouse and gave Joe his freedom, and then blew his brains out. Joe, although freed, remains in town because his wife Lucinda is now the property of the judge. All goes well for Joe until the judge dies and his estate is transferred to the stern Spite Calderwood. Calderwood refuses to let Joe visit Lucinda. Joe's easy life comes to an end: The other slaves will have nothing to do with him, and he is an outcast from the white community, sleeping outside under a poplar tree. When Calderwood learns that in spite of his orders Lucinda has been sneaking out to meet Joe, he takes her to Macon and sells her; he even has his hounds kill Joe's dog. Joe, however, even when told the truth about Lucinda, seems incapable of understanding. Night after night he waits for his wife and his dog to return together in the moonlight, until one night he dies alone under the poplar tree, a smile on his face and humble to the last.

In "Free Joe and the Rest of the World," Harris achieves a balance between sentimentality and realistic portrayal in dramatizing the plight of the freeman in the antebellum South. Even though Joe is the humble, unassuming victim of white cruelty, his freedom also represents the vague, gothic threat of social dissolution to the white community, who come to view him as "forever lurking on the outskirts of slavery, ready to sound a shrill and ghostly signal" of insurrection. Yet unlike Brer Rabbit, Joe is no ingenious trickster, and Harris obliquely hints that, all things considered, Joe may have been better off a slave since his freedom leaves him "shiftless" and incapable of fending for himself.

BALAAM AND HIS MASTER AND OTHER SKETCHES AND STORIES

Of the six stories collected in *Balaam and His Master and Other Sketches and Stories*, three are portraits of loyal blacks and three treat the fate of a white man in a crumbling society. In this collection Harris again illustrates his favorite themes: the changing social values between blacks and whites, and the need for reconciliation through patience and understanding. "Balaam and His Master" is the story of the fiercely loyal manservant of young Berrien Cozart— the sensual, cruel, impetuous, and implacable son of a respected plantation family. As in many of Harris's aristocratic families, the older Cozart practices a benign paternalism toward his slaves, but his young son

Berrien is nothing but a spoiled and dissolute gambler who abuses the privileges of his race. Yet despite his master's excesses, Balaam remains a constant and loyal valet, even to the point of participating in a scam to sell himself to a new master and then returning to Berrien. Berrien is finally arrested for murder, and Balaam breaks into the jail to be with him; but it is too late—Berrien is already dead. The story ends with Balaam loyally crouching over his dead master, who died with a smile as sweet as a "little child that nestles on his mother's breast." Even though Balaam is morally superior to his white master, the message of the story is that loyalty and service are superior to social revolution.

In "Where's Duncan?"—another story in *Balaam and His Master and Other Stories and Sketches*— Harris gives a more apocalyptic version of the changing social values between blacks and whites. The story is narrated by old Isaiah Winchell, who meets a dark stranger named Willis Featherstone as he is hauling his cotton to market. As they camp for the evening, old Isaiah learns that Willis Featherstone is the mulatto son of a plantation owner who had educated him, grown to hate him, and then sold him. The next evening the group camps near the old Featherstone plantation, and a vampirelike mulatto woman comes to invite them to dinner at the "big house." Willis Featherstone, who seems to know the woman, enigmatically asks her "where's Duncan?" and she hysterically replies that old Featherstone has "sold my onliest boy." Later that evening, the camp is awakened by a commotion at the big house. Old Isaiah rushes up to see the house on fire, and through the window he glimpses the mulatto woman stabbing Old Featherstone and screaming "where's Duncan?" Willis Featherstone, say some of the observers, was inside enjoying the spectacle. The story ends with a gothic scene of fiery retribution as the old plantation house burns and collapses, and old Isaiah still dreams of the smell of burning flesh. Violent confrontation is possible, Harris suggests, if white society continues to abuse the black.

As an editorialist, essayist, and humorist, Joel Chandler Harris was instrumental in trying to reconcile the tensions between North and South, black and white, left by the Civil War. Although he shared some of the racial prejudices of his time—one detects a paternalism for the black in much of the short fiction—he was a progressive conservative who, as one critic has said, "affirmed the integrity of all individuals, whether black or white; and he could not countenance unjust or inhumane actions by any member of the human race." In the 1870's and 1880's, his editorials in the Atlanta *Constitution* consistently argue against sectionalism, both literary and political, and in favor of a united country. Any literature, wrote Harris in 1879, takes its materials and flavor from "localism," yet "in literature, art, and society, whatever is truly southern is likewise truly American; and the same may be said of what is truly Northern."

OTHER MAJOR WORKS

LONG FICTION: *Sister Jane*, 1896; *The Chronicles of Aunt Minervy Ann*, 1899; *On the Wing of Occasions*, 1900; *Gabriel Tolliver*, 1902; *A Little Union Scout*, 1904; *The Shadow Between His Shoulder-Blades*, 1909.

CHILDREN'S LITERATURE: *Little Mr. Thimblefinger*, 1894; *Mr. Rabbit at Home*, 1895; *The Story of Aaron*, 1896; *Aaron in the Wildwoods*, 1897; *Plantation Pageants*, 1899; *Wally Wanderoon and His Story-Telling Machine*, 1903.

BIBLIOGRAPHY

Baer, Florence E. *Sources and Analogues of the Uncle Remus Tales*. Helsinki: Academia Scientiarium Fennica, 1980. Essential to anyone trying to study the Brer Rabbit stories. For each tale, Baer gives a summary, the tale type number from *The Types of the Folk-Tale* (1928), motif numbers from Stith Thompson's *Motif-Index of Folk Literature* (1955-1958), and a discussion of possible sources. She also includes an excellent essay discussing Harris's legitimacy as a collector of folktales.

Baker, Margaret P. "The Rabbit as Trickster." *Journal of Popular Culture* 28 (Fall, 1994): 149-158. Discusses the image of the rabbit as trickster in popular culture; concludes that, although some of the traditional folk images of the trickster have changed, twentieth century trickster figures help

people deal with paradox and irony and show their audiences that they are neither totally victims nor victors but can capitalize on their own weaknesses to build strengths for coping with life.

Bickley, R. Bruce, ed. *Critical Essays on Joel Chandler Harris*. Boston: G. K. Hall, 1981. Traces the critical heritage about Harris, including contemporary reviews. Of particular importance is an article by Bernard Wolfe, which was printed in *Commentary* in 1949.

_____. *Joel Chandler Harris*. Boston: Twayne, 1978. A full-length study, including chapters on the major as well as the later Uncle Remus tales, and Harris's other short fiction. Includes a brief, useful annotated bibliography.

_____. *Joel Chandler Harris: An Annotated Bibliography of Criticism, 1977-1996*. Westport, Conn.: Greenwood Press, 1997. A good reference for students of Harris.

Cousins, Paul. *Joel Chandler Harris: A Biography*. Baton Rouge: Louisiana State University Press, 1968. A biography that the author worked on intermittently for more than thirty years and that includes material from interviews with friends of Harris. Not a reliable source for critical evaluations of Harris's work.

Harris, Joel Chandler. *Dearest Chums and Partners: Joel Chandler Harris's Letters to His Children, a Domestic Biography*. Edited by Hugh T. Keenan. Athens: University of Georgia Press, 1993. Reveals aspects of Harris's life through his correspondence with family members.

Hemenway, Robert. Introduction to *Uncle Remus: His Songs and Sayings*, edited by Robert Hemenway. New York: Penguin Books, 1982. Hemenway's introduction is very clear and informative, one of the better all around essays on the Brer Rabbit stories. Contains a brief bibliography.

Keenan, Hugh T. "Twisted Tales: Propaganda in the Tar-Baby Stories." *The Southern Quarterly* 22, no. 2 (Winter, 1984): 54-69. This essay updates some arguments that Bernard Wolfe put forth in his *Commentary* article (included in R. Bruce Bickley's entry above). Better researched than Wolfe's article and more even in tone.

Lester, Julius. "The Storyteller's Voice: Reflections on the Rewriting of Uncle Remus." In *The Voice of the Narrator in Children's Literature*, edited by Charlotte F. Otten and Gary D. Schmidt. New York: Greenwood Press, 1989. Lester discusses the problems he had with his editor when he was

trying to get his retelling of the Uncle Remus stories published; argues that voice is the heart of the story and that he could not be unfaithful to the original folktales.

Robert J. McNutt, updated by Thomas J. Cassidy

JIM HARRISON

Born: Grayling, Michigan; December 11, 1937

PRINCIPAL SHORT FICTION

Legends of the Fall, 1979 (collection of three novellas: *Revenge, The Man Who Gave Up His Name*, and *Legends of the Fall*)

The Woman Lit by Fireflies, 1990 (collection of three novellas: *Brown Dog, Sunset Limited*, and *The Woman Lit by Fireflies*)

Julip, 1994 (collection of three novellas: *Julip, The Seven Ounce Man*, and *The Beige Dolorosa*)

The Beast God Forgot to Invent, 2000 (collection of three novellas: *The Beast God Forgot to Invent, Westward Ho*, and *Forgot to Go to Spain*)

OTHER LITERARY FORMS

Although best known for his prose—novels and novellas—Jim Harrison is an accomplished poet (*After Ikkyu and Other Poems*, 1996; *The Shape of the Journey: New and Collected Poems*, 1998), essayist, and screenwriter. As a man of letters, Harrison made his poetic debut with the publication of *Plain Song* (1965). *The Theory and Practice of Rivers* (1986) represents a continuing pursuit of the poetic muse. Essays concerning food, travel, sports, and critical literary insights appear in *Just Before Dark* (1991). The screenplays *Revenge* (1989), based on the novella in *Legends of the Fall*, and *Wolf* (1994), which he wrote with Wesley Strick and which is based on the novel of the same name, are his most noted works in that genre.

ACHIEVEMENTS

The accumulation of Jim Harrison's writing ensures him a place among important writers of the late twentieth century. The multifarious concerns addressed in his books of fiction, poetry, and numerous nonfiction articles are gleaned from his intense capacity for observation, memory, and experience.

Harrison received a National Endowment for the Arts Award in 1968 and a John Simon Guggenheim Memorial Foundation Fellowship in 1969; he was also awarded twice by the National Literary Anthology.

BIOGRAPHY

James Thomas Harrison was born in Grayling, a small rural community in northern Michigan, in 1937. It was there that he developed his love for the outdoors. At age thirteen, he moved to Lansing, Michigan, when his father took a position at Michigan State University.

Growing up in a family of voracious readers (his father enjoyed William Faulkner, Ernest Hemingway, and Erskine Caldwell) proved beneficial to Harrison's decision at an early age to become a writer. At age nineteen, he left home for New York, where he intended to write poetry and live the life of a bohemian.

Later, he returned to Michigan and received a B.A. from Michigan State University in 1960 and an M.A. in 1964. Shortly thereafter, he took a position as assistant professor of English at the State University of New York at Stony Brook and taught there for one year.

Jim Harrison in 1981 (Library of Congress)

After leaving his position at Stony Brook, Harrison returned to Michigan to take up writing full time. Grants, fellowships, and articles for magazines like *Sports Illustrated* kept Harrison going until the 1979 publication of *Legends of the Fall*, his first commercially successful book. The film rights for the book's three novellas eventually led to Harrison's career as a screenwriter and the popular film adaptation of the *Legends of the Fall* by screenwriters Susan Shilliday and Bill Witliff in 1995. Harrison's film work and the literary strength of books like *The Woman Lit by Fireflies* (1990) and *The Road Home* (1998) have made him a widely read and critically acclaimed author.

ANALYSIS

As a storyteller who experiments with form, Jim Harrison tells stories in a variety of modes. He borrows techniques and literary conventions from romance, adventure, mystery, and comedy. He does not utilize these categories, however, in a formulaic manner, but instead he modifies the conventions of literary genre to dramatize contemporary difficulties.

Harrison is often accused of writing "macho fiction." Some critics agree that, if viewed superficially, the stories appear to be rhetorically macho—rendered from a mythic male viewpoint. In these stories, however, the opposite is true. Although his characters display a penchant for sex, violence, and the sporting life, they do not derive any benefit from their macho behavior. In fact, either they become isolated and lonely, or their dignity and integrity are lost.

REVENGE

In *Revenge*, the first novella in *Legends of the Fall*, the persona weaves a violent tale of vengeance, friendship, and love between three people: Cochran, a former fighter pilot; Tibey, a gangster struggling to legitimize himself; and Miryea, Tibey's beautiful wife. As the tale unfolds, Cochran, the protagonist, develops a friendship with Tibey, a powerful and rich Mexican businessman; the friendship results in a dangerous liaison between Cochran and Miryea. Tibey is obsessed with two things: tennis and his beautiful upper-class wife—not because he loves her but because she provides a degree of status for him in the so-called legitimate world.

The story begins *in medias res* with vultures hovering over the battered naked body of Cochran, who lies dying in the Mexican desert as a coyote nearby watches curiously. The narrative persona informs the reader that "Carrion was shared not by the sharer's design but by a pattern set before anyone knew there were patterns." The natural world is viewed from an objective perspective in Harrison's fiction, and, like the coyote looking on objectively, nature's presence signifies a detached and impersonal environment. Within this environment, Cochran and Tibey find themselves confused and isolated.

A narrative pattern unfolds from Cochran's point of view when a Mexican worker and his daughter find Cochran in the desert. They deliver him to a mission, where he is nursed back to life by Diller, a Mennonite missionary doctor. Cochran's restoration is slow and painful, as are his memories when he begins to recover. Eventually, Cochran and Tibey must have a showdown. Before Cochran's brutal encounter with Tibey, readers see him several evenings earlier in a bar drinking with a friend. Cochran talks too much about his relationship with Miryea. His friend listens patiently, but when he realizes that Miryea is Tibey's wife, he turns pale with fear, and he informs Cochran that Tibey is a Spanish sobriquet for *tiburon*, "the shark."

Tibey learns of the affair at the same time that Cochran wins a tennis tournament. He is delighted with Cochran's win and sends him several thousand dollars and a one-way ticket to Paris. This gift, however, is a veiled warning to leave Miryea alone. Cochran and Miryea, however, have already made arrangement to spend a few days at a mountain cabin in Mexico while Tibey is away on business. Unbeknown to the lovers, Tibey and his henchmen have followed them. Miryea is disfigured by Tibey and forced to watch as Cochran is beaten senseless; she is then drugged and delivered to a brothel, where she is kept against her will. Cochran is pulled from the trunk of a car and left to die in the desert.

As Cochran recovers, he is obsessed with finding Miryea and getting revenge against Tibey. Tibey, unable to assuage his guilt for the brutal treatment that Miryea received, has her placed in a nunnery, where she ultimately dies from sorrow and the abuse she received in the brothel. The tale ends in bitter irony when Cochran finally corners Tibey. Tibey asks for an apology, which Cochran gives him; the two men part in misery, realizing that revenge, as the old Sicilian proverb says, "is a dish better served cold." Engaged in this kind of macho behavior, each man loses his love, integrity, and dignity; each is left in the depths of despair.

THE MAN WHO GAVE UP HIS NAME

The following novella, *The Man Who Gave Up His Name*, focuses on Nordstrom, a man who at forty-three is in a midlife crisis. He is a man whose passions consist of cooking and dancing alone in his apartment to "work up a dense sweat and to feel the reluctant body become fluid and graceful." The dance metaphorically represents Nordstrom's life, for this dance, as readers later learn, is a dance for survival. Nordstrom has all the trappings of success; he has plenty of money, a beautiful wife, and his daughter, a university student, is intelligent and lovely. This ideal existence is set up for the reader through flashback

via Nordstrom's perspective—a literary convention that Harrison uses to establish the central character's point of view.

Ultimately, though, Nordstrom's classic American Dream disintegrates when his wife divorces him, and even though his daughter loves him, she considers him a dolt. He is further distressed by the death of his father, which makes him think of his own mortality. During these events, Nordstrom asks himself the question that modern human beings have been asking since the Industrial Revolution, "What if what I've been doing all my life has been totally wrong," and he begins his quest to discover the answer.

The story takes a violent and surprising turn at the end, when Nordstrom decides to give his money away and take a long trip. He views his achievements and successes with disdain and thinks that giving away his money will help him turn his life around. At a graduation dinner for his daughter, Sonia, he embarrassingly attempts to give her fifteen thousand dollars in one-hundred-dollar bills for a new car, an act for which he is rebuked by his former wife, Laura, whom he has not seen in four years. Inevitably, Sonia refuses the money, making him regret even more what he feels he has become—a kind of middle-aged fop. The violent twist occurs when Sarah, a beautiful waitress and dancer—after whom Nordstrom lusts when he sees her during forays into his New York neighborhood—is invited to the dinner party by one of Sonia's friends.

A ruckus ensues when an Italian, who looks like "a cutout from the movies of a gangster psychopath," enters accompanied by a large black man; together, they bodily remove Sarah, but not before Nordstrom strikes the black man and is threatened with a gun held by the Italian. After the party, Nordstrom realizes that he is being set up when Sarah telephones, asking if they can meet. They have lunch together and return to Nordstrom's room, where they have sex. Afterward, Sarah demands ten thousand dollars from Nordstrom to keep her maniacal boyfriend, Slats, from killing him. Nordstrom refuses to be subjected to extortion by these petty, drug-dealing thugs and relishes the thought that his life has been threatened; he waits in his motel room for retribution, feeling more alive and in tune with himself than he had felt before.

The Italian breaks into his room, unaware that Nordstrom is waiting for him. Nordstrom hears the Italian enter and bursts from the suite. Catching him off guard, Nordstrom manages to throw the man out a seventh-floor window. He feels little remorse, however, explaining his actions away by noting that this man may have threatened his family. He confronts the extortionists at lunch the next day, refusing to knuckle under to their threats, and explains that it was unfortunate that the Italian had to die. Sarah and Slats are bewildered; they give up their ruse, thinking that they have encountered a genuine mad man.

In the epilogue, Nordstrom retreats to a small coastal town in Florida, where he rents a tourist cabin and takes a job cooking seafood in a local restaurant. He buys a boat, fishes in the Gulf, studies marine life, and dances alone at night to music coming from a transistor radio. Nordstrom is an isolated character who resorts to the primitive side of his nature to survive. He searches for self-understanding in a society that constantly negates the natural world. He sheds the burdens of urbanized life—marriage, children, money, and materialism—and for all of his faults, he is an empathetic character, one who is certainly alone and humble in his environment.

BROWN DOG

Harrison's consummate ability to manipulate comedy is exhibited in *Brown Dog*, the first novella in *The Woman Lit by Fireflies*. This humorous tale is about B. D., a footloose scuba diver who shares an illegal salvaging operation with his partner, Bob. The two characters scavenge for artifacts from sunken ships in northern Michigan lakes and sell them to collectors.

The story begins with B. D. writing his memoirs, a mock form that Harrison previously used in *Wolf: A False Memoir* (1971). Having dabbled in psychology, Shelley, B. D.'s girlfriend, convinces B. D. to record, as a form of therapy, the events that led to his eventual arrest for transporting a dead Indian to Chicago in a stolen refrigerator truck. Shelley is an attractive anthropologist twenty years younger than B. D. As B. D.'s version is revealed, readers realize that his re-

liability as a narrator is questionable, which adds to the story's humor.

The plot revolves around two principal events: Shelley's desire to locate an Indian burial mound on which B. D. had previously stumbled, and the dead Indian chief whom B. D. found during one of his dives in Lake Superior. B. D. has a habit of unexpectedly finding things. When he locates the ancient Indian burial ground, his Chippewa friend, Clause, convinces him not to divulge its location. Shelly is very interested in the burial mounds and continually tries to get B. D. to show her where they are so she can study them.

Upon his dive into Lake Superior, B. D. finds a perfectly preserved Indian (except that his eyes are missing) in seventy feet of water. From that moment, the Indian is referred to as Chief. B. D. does not share his find with Bob, however, until he works out a plan, which he admits in retrospect was not a very good one. The problem is that all good plans must begin without a flaw, and this one is unfortunately flawed from the beginning. B. D. is not Native American, but he looks Indian and is often mistaken for one. Like many other roles that he assumes, B. D. plays at being Indian because it is expected of him. He respects and admires Native Americans, having grown up with them, and so he refuses to show Shelley the ancient burial ground but instead hatches a plan to make a little money from the Chief.

The absurd tale gains momentum when B. D. steals a refrigerator truck, and, after salvaging the Chief, includes Bob in a scheme to transport the dead Indian to an artifacts collector in Chicago. The plan goes awry when B. D. and Bob drink too much and are arrested. Bob is given two years in the local penitentiary, but B. D.'s sentence is light—the judge pitying B. D. because, as B. D. explains, he got confused when he heard the Chief ask him to bury him.

B. D. describes events in his "memoirs" with alacrity and comic dismay, but while he admits his ordinariness, he does not think himself stupid. Furthermore, although his attitude is predominately chauvinistic, his commonsense observations provide the reader with viable explanations for his ridiculous behavior.

THE WOMAN LIT BY FIREFLIES

The Woman Lit by Fireflies is the last novella in the collection by the same title. Using a female voice, the narrative represents a sensitive and believable female protagonist. This is not Harrison's first attempt, however, to use a third-person narrative limited to a female viewpoint character. He accomplished this challenge in *Dalva* (1988), a novel that focuses on the personal and historical aspects of a woman's life in a male-dominated society.

For Clare, a wealthy middle-aged woman married to a man whose only concern is the present status of the stock market, the circumstances are similar. Like most of Harrison's central characters, she is desperately alone. After losing her best friend, Zilpha, and her dog, Sammy, to cancer, Clare's migraines intensify, causing her to give in to the whims of those around her, namely her husband, Donald, who exerts his influence over her.

Returning from a visit to her daughter in Colorado, she is plagued by a severe migraine. Donald listens repeatedly to a tape called "Tracking the Blues," which has no connection to music but proves to be an explanation of the current stock market situation. Clare can no longer tolerate Donald and his obsession with money, and when they exit Interstate 80 in Iowa for a rest stop, she leaves a note in the rest room, stating that she has abandoned her husband because he is physically abusive. She escapes into a nearby cornfield, leaving Donald behind.

Once in the cornfield, Clare resorts to basic survival skills to make it through a rainy night without food or water. Meanwhile, the migraine takes control of her, and she drifts in and out of delirium. Intrusive memories invade her consciousness, and detailed events, retrospective insights into past friendships, and various aspects of her marital relationship are revealed to her. These memories form the basis of Clare's enlightenment—the migraine symbolically paralleling life's suffering and pain. At the end of her ordeal, she is able to subdue the migraine and, in effect, subjugate her inability to act for herself. This character's physical pain allows her to get in touch with her subconscious. She does this while the natural world looks on with a placid eye.

JULIP

As in *The Woman Lit by Fireflies*, *Julip*'s female protagonist faces a debilitating masculine world. Unlike Clare, Julip is young, energetic, and capable of correcting the mistakes of male vanity. In *Julip*, Harrison weaves a seamless and comic tale of the protagonist's life. Julip, named for the drink, has a difficult rural Wisconsin childhood. Her father, a trainer of bird dogs, has a weakness for liquor that blunts his success, and his frequent binges often end in physical and mental collapse. Meanwhile, Julip's emotionally cold mother leaves Julip and her brother Billy to their own resources.

Still, Julip loves her father, and, when he dies, she takes over his profession. Unconsciously, Julip also searches for a connection to her father through her affairs with three middle-aged men—Charles, Arthur, and Ted—collectively called "the boys."

Billy learns of "the boys," and, in a demented attempt to revenge what he calls her "defilement," he begins following them. In disguise, he stalks her lovers for two weeks, finally shooting them in their boat as they are passing under a bridge. However, he uses a .22, and none of the men is fatally wounded. Billy receives seven to ten years in prison, but Julip learns that he may be transferred to a mental institution if he admits to being insane. The judge, prosecutor, and victims all agree to the change in sentence.

Feeling responsible for Billy's plight, Julip sets out to release him. Turning to Billy's psychologist for help, she learns that her father had not committed suicide, as her mother claimed. Instead, a group of drunk teenagers had run him over. Released from two years of guilt over the supposed suicide, Julip heals the wound of her father's drinking and death and finally frees herself from her emotional attraction to older men.

When she confronts "the boys" to sign the agreement to place Billy in the mental institution, she can rise above their empty life of drinking, drugs, and sex with younger women. While they display their foolishness—begging her to marry them between bouts of champaign and fishing—she displays cool affection mixed with rationality and self-confidence.

By the novella's end, Julip attains the agreement

and secures a release order from the judge and the prosecuting attorney. Having successfully removed Billy from the horrors of prison, Julip, finished with her empty affairs and her brother's insane version of chivalry, returns to Wisconsin to the peace of a rural life training bird dogs. Thus, with her feminine power, wit, and intelligence, she has triumphed over an absurd society still shaped by decaying, male-generated notions of lust, honor, and power.

In his fiction, Harrison transcends what some critics have unjustly referred to as macho writing. He uses modes of mystery, adventure, romance, and tragic comedy to reflect men and women in conflict with modern society. His characters are on personal quests, searching for enlightenment in a fast-paced techno-industrial society.

OTHER MAJOR WORKS

LONG FICTION: *Wolf: A False Memoir*, 1971; *A Good Day to Die*, 1973; *Farmer*, 1976; *Warlock*, 1981; *Sundog: The Story of an American Foreman*, 1984; *Dalva*, 1988; *The Road Home*, 1998.

SCREENPLAYS: *Cold Feet*, 1988 (with Thomas McGuane); *Revenge*, 1989; *Wolf*, 1994 (with Wesley Strick).

POETRY: *Plain Song*, 1965; *Locations*, 1968; *Outlyer and Ghazals*, 1971; *Letters to Yesenin*, 1973; *Returning to Earth*, 1977; *Selected and New Poems; 1961-1981*, 1982; *The Theory and Practice of Rivers: Poems*, 1986; *The Theory and Practice of Rivers and New Poems*, 1989; *After Ikkyu and Other Poems*, 1996; *The Shape of the Journey: New and Collected Poems*, 1998.

NONFICTION: *Just Before Dark: Collected Nonfiction*, 1991.

BIBLIOGRAPHY

Harrison, Jim. "The Art of Fiction, CIV: Jim Harrison." Interview by Jim Fergus. *The Paris Review* 107 (1988): 53-97. In this interview, Fergus asks the right questions about life, literature, and art. Harrison's responses are personal and enlightening, giving the reader a variety of interesting insights into the craft of fiction and poetry.

_____. Interview by Wendy Smith. *Publishers Weekly* 237 (August 3, 1990): 59-60. A general discussion of some of the basic characteristics of Harrison's writing, followed by comments by Harrison on his work; Harrison notes that, although he still considers fiction and poetry his major work, he is intrigued by the screenplay format.

_____. "Jim Harrison." In *Conversations with American Novelists*, edited by Kay Bonetti, Greg Michaelson, Speer Morgan, Jo Sapp, and Sam Stowers. Columbia: University of Missouri Press, 1997. Harrison discusses how the skills he developed writing poetry were transferred to his fiction; talks about the sometimes negative influence of university writing programs, his reputation as a macho writer, his interest in the novella form, and his work as a screenwriter.

Lorenz, Paul H. "Rethinking Machismo: Jim Harrison's *Legends of the Fall*." *Publication of the Arkansas Philological Association* 15 (1989): 41-52. A concise explanation showing what function macho characters serve in *Legends of the Fall* and *Revenge*. Lorenz explains his interpretation of the cowboy macho mentality, detailing the actions of various characters to prove Harrison's intent, which is to represent the failure of this mentality in civilization. The "mythic cowboy hero" is but a myth and cannot be revived, according to Lorenz's interpretation, and any attempt by these characters to "blaze a solitary path through a senseless world [only] leads to unhappiness, banishment, and death." Bibliography.

Reed, Julia. "After Seven Acclaimed Novels, Jim Harrison Is Finding It Harder to Elude Fame." *Vogue* 179 (September, 1989): 502. A brief biographical sketch, commenting on Harrison's shunning of publishing hype and promotion. Discusses Harrison's screenplays; argues that the strength of his writing lies in his hypnotic use of language, his romantic and compelling characters, and his ability to reveal the human need to be close to nature.

Roberson, William H. "'A Good Day to Live'; The Prose Works of Jim Harrison." *Great Lakes Review: A Journal of Midwest Culture* 8-9 (1983): 29-37. Roberson's reviewlike treatment of selected prose is an overview of basic themes in Harrison's fiction. He disputes the notion that Harrison is writing "macho fiction" by providing a clear analysis to the contrary. Includes notes.

Rohrkemper, John. "'Natty Bumppo Wants Tobacco': Jim Harrison's Wilderness." *Great Lakes Review: A Journal of Midwest Culture* 8 (1983): 20-28. Rohrkemper suggests that Harrison's poetic treatment of nature is closer to a "dark romantic" such as Herman Melville than it is to an Emmersonian transcendentalist outlook. Rohrkemper asserts that Harrison's fiction is based on the tradition of his "literary parents and grandparents," the modernists, but with one significant twist: The modernists show the "pristine beauty of nature first, and then nature spoiled," while Harrison shows how nature exists in spite of human influence. Notes.

Allen Learst, updated by John Nizalowski

BRET HARTE

Born: Albany, New York; August 25, 1836
Died: Camberley, Surrey, England; May 5, 1902

PRINCIPAL SHORT FICTION

The Lost Galleon and Other Tales, 1867
Condensed Novels, 1867
The Luck of Roaring Camp and Other Sketches, 1870
Stories of the Sierras, 1872
Mrs. Skaggs's Husbands, 1873
Tales of the Argonauts, 1875
Thankful Blossom, 1877
The Story of a Mine, 1878
Drift from Two Shores, 1878
The Twins of Table Mountain, 1879
Flip and Found at Blazing Star, 1882
In the Carquinez Woods, 1883
Maruja, 1885
The Crusade of the Excelsior, 1887
A Millionaire of Rough-and-Ready, 1887
A Phyllis of the Sierras, 1888
Cressy, 1889
The Heritage of Dedlow Marsh, 1889
A Waif of the Plains, 1890
A First Family of Tasajara, 1891
Sally Dows, 1893
A Protégée of Jack Hamlin's, 1894
The Bell-Ringer of Angel's, 1894
In a Hollow of the Hills, 1895
Barker's Luck and Other Stories, 1896
Three Partners, 1897
Tales of Trail and Town, 1898
Stories in Light and Shadow, 1898
Mr. Jack Hamlin's Meditation, 1899
Condensed Novels: Second Series, 1902
Trent's Trust, 1903
The Story of Enriquez, 1924

OTHER LITERARY FORMS

Bret Harte attempted practically every form of *belles lettres* common in the nineteenth century. He wrote several collections of poems, almost entirely forgotten in the years since his death. Indeed, his poetic reputation to modern readers depends completely on the success of one poem, his comic verse masterpiece "Plain Language from Truthful James," more commonly known as "The Heathen Chinee," published in 1870. He wrote and edited newspaper material, essays, the novel *Gabriel Conroy* (1876), and some excellent satirical work, notably his *Condensed Novels*; and he collaborated with Mark Twain on a play, *Ah Sin* (1877), based on his poem "The Heathen Chinee."

ACHIEVEMENTS

Bret Harte's influence on "local color" fiction, es-

Bret Harte (Library of Congress)

pecially the literature of the American West, was profound but not totally fortunate. He was one of the earliest writers, and certainly the most influential one, to set stories on the mining frontier that evolved from the California gold rush of 1849. His interest in the Western story and his success in transforming his raw material into popular fiction led many subsequent writers to explore American Western themes that they might otherwise have dismissed as unworthy of serious notice. Harte's stories, however, focusing on colorful characters that he deemed worthy of treatment for their own sake, tend to undervalue plot and setting, and his contrived plots and sentimental treatment of character gave subsequent Western fiction an escapist, juvenile bent, which it took a long time to outgrow.

BIOGRAPHY

Born in Albany, New York, as Francis Brett Harte (he would later drop the "Francis" and change the spelling of his middle name to Bret), Harte went to California in 1854, where for a while he lived many of the lives he was later to re-create imaginatively in the biographies of his fictional characters.

Among other occupations, he worked an unsuccessful mining claim on the Stanislaus River; he may have been a guard for the Wells Fargo stagecoach lines; and he was employed in various capacities at the San Francisco mint before drifting into journalism. He was associated with the founding (1864) of C. H. Webb's journal the *Californian*, in which some of his own early work was published. Subsequently he became editor of the *Overland Monthly* (1868-1870), in which many of his most famous works first saw print. Notable among these are the short story "The Luck of Roaring Camp" and the comic poem "Plain Language from Truthful James," which led to an offer from *The Atlantic Monthly* of a ten-thousand-dollar yearly contract, annually renewable, for exclusive rights to his material. On the strength of this contract Harte moved to Boston, but the contract was never renewed after the first year. Indeed, Harte's later work never came up to the standard of his earlier, and although he was a tireless writer his production rapidly degenerated into hack work. He moved to Europe, serving for a brief time as American consul in Krefeld, Germany, and in Glasgow, Scotland, before finally settling in London, where he lived the rest of his life. He was happy in London, where people viewed his work more charitably than in the United States and where he was respected as an authentic voice of "the '49."

ANALYSIS

In any discussion of Bret Harte, one must begin by making a clear distinction between *importance* and *quality*, that is, between the influence of an author's work and its intrinsic value. That Harte was an extremely important writer, no one will deny. Almost entire credit should be given to him for the refinement of the gold fields of California into rich literary ore. More than a mere poet of "the '49," he firmly established many of the stock character types of later Western fiction: the gentleman gambler, the tarnished lady, the simple though often lovably cantankerous prospector, all invariably possessed of hearts of gold. These prototypes, so beloved of later Western writers both of fiction and film, seemed to spring, like rustic Athenas, full-grown from his fertile brain. Yet with all his admitted importance there have been doubts from the very beginning about the intrinsic quality of his work. After publication of *The Luck of Roaring Camp and Other Sketches* and the overwhelming success of his famous comic poem "Plain Language from Truthful James" in the same year, the set of brilliant tomorrows confidently predicted for him developed instead into rediscovery only of a series of remembered yesterdays. What, the critic should initially ask, is the reason behind Harte's meteoric rise and his equally precipitous fall?

Perhaps a partial answer may be found by examination of a term often applied to Harte's work: It is, critics are fond of saying, "Dickensian." There is much truth to this critical commonplace, for the influence of Dickens is everywhere to be found in Harte's writing, from the often brilliantly visualized characters, through the sentimental description, to the too-commonly contrived plot. Perhaps the first of these influences is the most important, for, like Dickens, when Harte is mentioned one immediately thinks of memorable characters rather than memorable stories. What would Dickens be without his Bob Cratchit, Mister Micawber, and Little Nell? Similarly, what would Harte be without his gambler John Oakhurst or his lovable but eccentric lawyer, Colonel Starbottle? The answer to these rhetorical questions, however, conceals a major limitation in Harte's literary artistry which the often too-facile comparison to Dickens easily overlooks. For in Dickens's case, in addition to the characters mentioned above, equally powerful negative or evil ones may be added who are completely lacking in Harte's own work. Where are the Gradgrinds and Fagins and Uriah Heeps in Harte's writing? The answer, to the detriment of Harte's stories, is that they are nowhere to be found. The result, equally unfortunate, is that Harte's stories lack almost completely any tragic vision of the world or of human beings' place in it. Misfortune in Harte's stories is uniformly pathetic rather than tragic, and the unfortunate result is that too often these stories settle for a "good cry" on the part of the reader rather than attempting any analysis of humanity's destiny or its place in an unknown and often hostile universe.

"THE OUTCASTS OF POKER FLAT"

A brief glance at one of Harte's best-known stories, "The Outcasts of Poker Flat," may serve at once to indicate both the strengths and the limitations of his work. This story tells of the fortunes of four "outcasts" from the California gold camp of Poker Flat, who have been escorted to the city limits by a vigilance committee, operating in the flush of civic pride, and told never to return on peril of their lives. The four outcasts are Mr. John Oakhurst, a professional gambler; "the Duchess" and "Mother Shipton," two prostitutes; and "Uncle Billy," a "confirmed drunkard," suspected as well of the more serious crime of robbing sluices. The four outcasts hope to find shelter in the neighboring settlement of Sandy Bar, a long day's journey away over a steep mountain range; but at noon the saddle-weary Duchess calls a halt to the expedition, saying she will "go no further." Accordingly, the party goes into camp, despite Oakhurst's pointing out that they are only half way to Sandy Bar and that they have neither equipment nor provisions. They do, however, have liquor, and the present joys of alcohol soon replace the will to proceed toward Sandy Bar where, in all fairness to the outcasts, their reception may not be overwhelmingly enthusiastic. Oakhurst does not drink, but out of a feeling of loyalty stays with his companions.

Some time later during the afternoon, the party is joined by two refugees from Sandy Bar, Tom Simson and his betrothed, Piney Woods. They have eloped from Sandy Bar because of the objections of Piney's father to their forthcoming marriage and are planning to be wed in Poker Flat. It transpires that Simson, referred to throughout the story as "the Innocent," had once lost to Oakhurst his "entire fortune—amounting to some forty dollars"—and that after the game was over Oakhurst had taken the young man aside and given his money back, saying simply "you're a good little man, but you can't gamble worth a cent. Don't try it over again." This had made a friend-for-life of the Innocent and also serves to show that Poker Flat's view of Oakhurst as a monster of iniquity is not to be taken totally at face value. Since it is now too late to travel on, both the outcasts and the young lovers decide to encamp in a ruined house near the trial.

During the night Uncle Billy abandons the group, taking all the animals with him. It also begins to snow. The party, predictably, is snowed in, although the situation does not appear too grave since the extra provisions which the Innocent has brought with him and which Uncle Billy did not take in his departure are enough, with careful husbandry, to last the party for ten days. All begin to make the cabin habitable, and they spend the first few days listening to the accordion the Innocent has brought and to a paraphrase of the *Iliad* which the Innocent has recently read and with which, much to Oakhurst's delight, he regales the company.

The situation, however, deteriorates. Another snowstorm totally isolates the camp, although the castaways are able to see, far below them, the smoke of Poker Flat. On the tenth day, Mother Shipton, "once the strongest of the party," who had mysteriously been growing weaker, dies. Her serious decline, it turns out, is a result of the fact that she had not eaten any of her carefully husbanded rations, which she had selflessly saved for her companions. Oakhurst then makes a pair of snowshoes out of a pack saddle and gives them to the Innocent, whom he sends off to Poker Flat in a last attempt to bring aid. If the Innocent reaches Poker Flat within two days, Oakhurst says, all will be well. He follows the Innocent part way on his journey toward Poker Flat, but does not return.

Meanwhile, back at the camp, the situation goes from bad to worse. Only the Duchess and Piney are left, and—although they discover and are properly grateful for the pile of wood which Oakhurst has secretly gathered and left for them—the rigors of a cruel world prove too strong. They die of starvation in the snow, and a rescue party arriving too late is properly edified by their moral courage—and, the reader trusts, properly chastened by recognition of Poker Flat's own despicable conduct. Oakhurst, we discover at the end of the story, in the best tradition of *noblesse oblige*, has committed suicide. The story concludes with a rehearsal of his epitaph, written by himself on a deuce of clubs and pinned to a pine tree with a bowie knife: "Beneath this tree lies the body of John Oakhurst, who struck a streak of bad luck on the

23d of November 1850, and handed in his checks on the 7th of December, 1850."

It is pointless to pretend that "The Outcasts of Poker Flat" does not have a certain power; indeed, the evidence of its continuing popularity, as shown through inclusion in countless anthologies of every persuasion, clearly indicates that the story is not a totally negligible effort. Yet after the thoughtful reader has finished the story, he or she is conscious of a certain dissatisfaction. The question to be asked is, "Why?"

The obvious answer seems to be that the story has little new to say. In European literature, prostitutes with hearts of gold were scarcely novel figures by the 1860's; furthermore, the fact that holier-than-thou individuals are likely not only to cast the first stone but also to be sorry when it hits can scarcely have been moral news to any reasonably perceptive reader. What Harte no doubt intended was to evoke an emotion on the part of the reader, an emotion of sorrow and pity for the poor victims of the social ingratitude (one hates to say *injustice*) of Poker Flat. The argument, from one perspective, is the oldest in the world—the tiresome *tu quoque* statement that the holier-than-thou are little better than the lowlier-than-them. Yet this easy answer will not entirely work. As has been pointed out many times, considered purely from the perspective of "ideas," most literature *is* commonplace.

Perhaps a better question is to ask how Harte approached his parable and whether his fictional method works. To this the answer must be "No," for if the reader considers the story carefully, he or she must agree that it simply is not successful, even in its own terms. We have, as Harte's friend and sometime collaborator Mark Twain would have said, been "sold."

Let us examine the story closely. A group of outcasts is sent up a long day's journey to another place. They stop only halfway—that is, half a day's journey—there. The place they left, in fact, is clearly visible behind them. Four in number, they are joined by two others; when Uncle Billy deserts, their number is five. Harte tells us that with careful management they have ten days' food, even though they have no animals. (What Uncle Billy could possibly have wanted with the seven animals he stole, particularly since he had no provisions to put on them, is never clarified, nor is the bothersome detail of how he could have managed the theft in the first place, considering he had to remove them single-handedly from under the noses of his companions, one of whom, John Oakhurst, is, Harte specifically tells us, "a light sleeper." The animals do not simply wander off; Harte calls our attention to the fact that they had been "tethered." Uncle Billy must therefore have released them on purpose.) In any event, the unfortunate castaways survive on meager rations for a week until Oakhurst suddenly remembers how to make snowshoes. Why he could not remember this skill on the second day or perhaps the third, is never clarified, but no matter. The reason is obvious, at least from Harte's point of view of the logic of the story. It is necessary for Harte to place his characters in a situation of romantic peril in order that their sterling qualities be thrown into high relief; to place his characters *in extremis*, however, Harte totally sacrifices whatever logic the story may have in its own terms.

When Uncle Billy leaves, then, the group discovers that it has sufficient supplies for ten days—that is, fifty man days' worth of food. Mother Shipton eats none of hers, dying of starvation at the end of a week. This means that the party now has some twenty-two man days of food left, with at the most only three people to eat it, since Mother Shipton is already dead and Oakhurst is about to commit suicide. This is, according to the data Harte has previously given, an easy week's rations. Why, then, do the two surviving ladies die of starvation before the rescue party arrives some four days later?

The answer has nothing to do with the story, which is designed, rather, for the moral Harte wishes to impale upon it. For in his single-minded pursuit of the commonplace notion that appearances may be deceiving and that there is a spark of goodness in all of us, Harte has totally sacrificed all fictional probabilities. Any potential tragic effect the story might presumably possess evaporates in the pale warmth of sentimental nostalgia.

This inability to allow his stories to speak for themselves is Harte's besetting fictional weakness.

Rather than allowing his tales to develop their own meaning, he obsessively applies a meaning to them, a meaning which, in far too many cases, cheapens the fictional material at his disposal. Perhaps the fault is that Harte, in his relentless search for this new California literary ore, did not really know where to find it. The mother lode consistently escaped him, and whatever flakes his search discovered were too often small and heavily alloyed.

OTHER MAJOR WORKS

LONG FICTION: *Gabriel Conroy*, 1876.

PLAYS: *Two Men of Sandy Bar*, pr. 1876; *Ah Sin*, pr. 1877 (collaboration with Mark Twain); *Sue*, pr. 1896 (with T. Edgar Pemberton).

POETRY: "Plain Language from Truthful James," 1870 (also known as "The Heathen Chinee"); *Poems*, 1871; *East and West Poems*, 1871; *Poetical Works*, 1880; *Poetical Works of Bret Harte*, 1896; *Some Later Verses*, 1898.

BIBLIOGRAPHY

Barnett, Linda D. *Bret Harte: A Reference Guide*. Boston: G. K. Hall, 1980. With a brief introduction outlining the historical directions of Harte scholarship and criticism, this work provides a good annotated bibliography and checklist through 1977.

Duckett, Margaret. *Mark Twain and Bret Harte*. Norman: University of Oklahoma Press, 1964. Duckett's book is an intriguing and carefully documented history of the friendship and literary association of Twain and Harte and their eventual falling out and feud. Includes illustrations and a bibliography through 1963.

Hall, Roger. "Annie Pixley, Kate Mayhew, and Bret Harte's *M'Liss*." *ATQ*, n.s. 11 (December, 1997): 267-283. Discusses the struggle in 1878 over the rights to *M'Liss*, a play based on a story by Bret Harte; claims that the struggle indicates the chaotic state of copyright laws, contracts, and play "pirates" in the late nineteenth century.

Morrow, Patrick. *Bret Harte*. Boise, Idaho: Boise State College, 1972. This brief but excellent study analyzes Harte's major work in both literature and criticism. Although concise, it is a very helpful introduction. Supplemented by a select bibliography.

_____. *Bret Harte, Literary Critic.* Bowling Green, Ohio: Bowling Green State University Popular Press, 1979. Morrow surveys and analyzes what he considers a very neglected part of Harte's work, his literary criticism. He establishes Harte's significance in the "local color" movement. Contains a useful bibliography of primary sources.

_____. "Bret Harte, Mark Twain, and the San Francisco Circle." In *A Literary History of the American West.* Fort Worth: Texas Christian University, 1987. This important chapter covers the contributors to the Western journals between 1865 and 1875, placing emphasis on Harte.

O'Connor, Richard. *Bret Harte: A Biography.* Boston: Little, Brown, 1966. A lively, anecdotal, and gossipy account limited to Harte's life, this work is not critical in focus. It does list Harte's best-known literary characters.

Scharnhorst, Gary. *Bret Harte.* New York: Twayne, 1992. A critical biography of Harte, providing analyses of stories from four different periods of his life, fully informed by critical reception of Harte's work. An afterword summarizes Harte's critical reputation.

_____. *Bret Harte: A Bibliography.* Lanham, Md.: Scarecrow Press, 1995. An excellent tool for the student of Harte.

_____. "Mark Twain, Bret Harte, and the Literary Construction of San Francisco." In *San Francisco in Fiction: Essays in a Regional Literature*, edited by David Fine and Paul Skenazy. Albuquerque: University of New Mexico Press, 1995. Discusses Harte's acceptance of the Eastern canon's taste in such stories as "The Idyl of Red Gulch" and his romanticized depiction of San Francisco as a rough-and-tumble boomtown in several late stories.

Stevens, J. David. "'She War a Woman': Family Roles, Gender, and Sexuality in Bret Harte's Western Fiction." *American Literature* 69 (September, 1997): 571-593. A discussion of gender in Harte's western fiction; argues that what critics have labeled sentimental excess in Harte's fiction is in fact his method of exploring certain hegemonic cultural paradigms taken for granted in other Western narratives; discusses stories that deal with the structure of the family and how they critique gender roles.

Stewart, George R. *Bret Harte, Argonaut and Exile.* Port Washington, N.Y.: Kennikat Press, 1964. Stewart's is the most scholarly and highly regarded of Harte's biographies. It focuses on Harte's life and defends the writer's achievements against his detractors.

Stoneley, Peter. "Rewriting the Gold Rush: Twain, Harte, and Homosociality." *Journal of American Studies* 30 (August, 1996): 189-209. An examination of authority and gender in gold rush fiction. From the perspective of poststructuralist theories of difference, explores the partnership of Mark Twain and Bret Harte; situates the Harte-Twain relationship within a broader network of late nineteenth century.

James K. Folsom, updated by John W. Fiero

JOHN HAWKESWORTH

Born: London(?), England; 1715(?)
Died: London, England; November 16, 1773

PRINCIPAL SHORT FICTION
Adventurer, 1752-1754

OTHER LITERARY FORMS

John Hawkesworth began his literary career by writing for the *Gentleman's Magazine*; he succeeded Samuel Johnson as the writer of parliamentary debates, and he contributed poems under a pseudonym. After working with Johnson on the periodical the *Adventurer*, Hawkesworth edited the works of Jonathan Swift and adapted several pieces for the stage. In imitation of Johnson's *Rasselas, Prince of Abyssinia* (1759), he wrote a long Oriental tale, *Almoran and Hamet* (1761). Hawkesworth's final publication was a history of British exploratory voyages into the South Seas.

ACHIEVEMENTS

Though not widely read in the twentieth century, John Hawkesworth was an important figure in the eighteenth century world of periodical publishing. Of humble background, Hawkesworth earned his reputation primarily through starting the magazine *Adventurer*, to which he contributed more than seventy essays, and editing the twelve-volume works of Swift. He also took over Johnson's job of recording the parliamentary debates in *Gentleman's Magazine*. To reward Hawkesworth for his literary contributions, the archbishop of Canterbury bestowed on him an honorary Lambeth degree of LL.D., a mere token award that Hawkesworth tried to use to his advantage by embarking on a short-lived career in the ecclesiastical courts. His pretension incurred the derision of such contemporaries as Johnson. Prolific and versatile, Hawkesworth wrote verse as well as prose, essays as well as fiction. His prose reveals a conventional and representative eighteenth century style that is deftly imitative of Johnson.

BIOGRAPHY

Little is known of John Hawkesworth's life until he became associated with the *Gentleman's Magazine* about 1746. Like many men of middle or lower class, he tried to make his reputation and fortune through literature. His *Adventurer* essays and his edition of Swift's works ultimately earned him an honorary degree and a chance to work in the theater; between 1756 and 1761, he composed or adapted several works for the stage. For many years he helped his wife manage a school. He died abused and outcast from society: the man who had sought to promote morality and piety through his essays was accused of indecency and impiety in his *An Account of the Voyages Undertaken in the Southern Hemisphere* (1773).

ANALYSIS

Like all eighteenth century periodical essayists, John Hawkesworth knew the value of fiction to hold an audience from issue to issue and to make moral instruction pleasing. Unlike most essayists, however, he used fictional devices almost exclusively (sixty of seventy *Adventurer* essays employ at least one type) and paid careful attention to the creation of emotional effects: "Those narratives are most pleasing which not only excite and gratify curiosity, but also engage the passions." How to engage the passions and how to discover objects on which to fix their attention became the task of Hawkesworth's *Adventurer* essays.

Periodical writers of the time always professed a moral purpose. It ranged from a commentary on proper notions of dress and behavior to the recommendation of certain virtues to the advocacy of religious doctrines. Hawkesworth gave some attention to popular topics such as the theater and conversation, but he felt a particular duty to advocate two positions. First, he wished to show that morality simply did not mean overt compliance with law; subtle evasions in thought or conduct could have the same dire consequences as outright violations. Second, he judged contemporary society too flippant in its approach to religious questions and too heedless of human dependency on the divine. Although Hawkesworth variously used fable, allegory, or character to discuss either topic, he usually treated the first by a story of contemporary manners and the second by an Oriental tale.

Hawkesworth wrote five narratives of modern manners to illustrate the "excellence and importance" of abstaining from even the appearance of evil. They are the story of Melissa (Nos. 7-8), who is thrice reduced to penury because others believe ill of her; the tale of Eugenio (Nos. 64-66, 70), whose silent devotion to obedience and honor is mistaken for cowardice; the story of Desdamona (Nos. 117-118), whose efforts to reform her philandering husband earn her the imputation of adultery; and the tale of Flavilla (Nos. 123-125), whose careless associations with unprincipled persons alienate her father-in-law and her husband. The best of the five, and the one most revealing about Hawkesworth's efforts to engage the passions, is the story of Captain Freeman and Lady Forrest.

Captain Freeman courts Charlotte and wins her love, but her family rejects his proposal because of his low rank and small fortune. Soon after, Charlotte

John Hawkesworth (Library of Congress)

is wooed by Sir James Forrest, a wealthy baronet whose qualities charm the lady and persuade the family. Captain Freeman then proposes to Charlotte's sister Maria and is accepted. As the two sisters remain close, Charlotte and Captain Freeman often delight in each other's company, much to the suspicion of Maria and Sir James. After staying late one evening with her sister, Charlotte unwillingly accepts the captain's offer to see her home. She knows that his companionship at dawn will seem suspicious, but she does not know how to explain her reservations without implying an affection for him. After a ride home and a morning walk in a nearby park, they separate. Later that morning, Dr. Tattle reports to Maria that he saw Charlotte and the captain near a bagnio that morning. Maria writes to Charlotte urging her to dissemble a little about the adventure lest Sir James be jealous, but Sir James hears a confused version of events from Charlotte, intercepts Maria's note, and concludes the worst. The baronet challenges Captain Freeman, who, thinking to protect Charlotte, accepts the duel without offering an explanation. After the captain is mortally wounded, he confesses the innocent events of that morning. Horrified that he has killed a guiltless man, Sir James takes a boat for France and is lost at sea.

As the plot summary makes clear, the tale hinges on misunderstandings arising out of unspoken feelings and worries. Since the tale takes three *Adventurer* periodicals to tell, Hawkesworth has the space to develop the psychology of his characters and the tensions of each scene. He describes them with what the eighteenth century called "sensibility," that is, with close attention to a range of emotional expression. Blushes, tears, anger, and fears by characters in almost every scene are the essence of sensibility. By detailing each emotion in turn, Hawkesworth sought to drive the moral lesson home by making the reader feel the experience. Characters are described as "horrified," "in agony," or "suffering inexpressibly,"; they "burst into tears," "throw themselves" at someone's feet, or otherwise display the powerful emotions that seethe beneath a calm exterior. Hawkesworth delights in constructing scenes that cause a character to react violently. This heightened vocabulary invites the reader to a heightened awareness; vicariously the reader shares the character's emotion and learns the moral imaginatively rather than logically.

Hawkesworth's Asian tales aim at engaging the passions in a different way; like Addison, he used the Oriental tale to communicate a religious truth or offer a theological statement. Hawkesworth associates the sense of remoteness, the unexpected twists of fate, and the sublime action—on which the Oriental tale builds—with the awe that ought to characterize mediation on divine subjects. Hawkesworth wrote seven such tales on a variety of religious topics: charity in the story of Carazan the wealthy (No. 132), piety in the tale of Almet the dervish (No. 114), and the superiority of the active life to the contemplative life in the account of Mirza (No. 38), among others. The longest, most vivid, and best plotted of the Asian tales is the story of Amurath the Sultan (Nos. 20-22).

AMURATH THE SULTAN

To help Amurath rule wisely, the genius or jinni Syndarac gives him a ring whose ruby grows pale if the wearer contemplates doing evil. After a while, however, Amurath tires of the ring's limitations on his power and desires, especially on his lust for the beautiful Selima, who resists the command to join his seraglio. When Amurath throws off the ring in frustration, he is instantly changed into a monster, half-wolf and half-goat. At once he is captured and thrown into a cage where he is visited only by the slave assigned to feed him. Gradually learning an affection for his keeper, he saves the man from a tiger's attack. Again, Amurath is transformed, this time into a dog. Fleeing the castle, he wanders the streets of the city and witnesses the miseries plaguing humankind; he quickly comes to share them as he eats a piece of poisoned venison that was intended for the master of a house. This death transforms him now into a dove. In search of shelter he flies into a cave where he finds Selima in conversation with a hermit; he overhears her telling the hermit that she loves Amurath, although she resents his attempt to gain her by force. Instantly he feels love for Selima, and love restores him to "the form proper to the nature in which alone it can subsist." Amurath now ascends the throne with the approval of both Selima and Syndarac.

Hawkesworth's Asian tale contains elements that obviously could have been included in the domestic tales: the intervention of Providence (in the guise of a jinni) to correct evil or reward righteousness, the metempsychosis of Amurath into animal forms emblematic of his moral awareness, and the existence of a magical ring to test the hero. Such elements had previously been used in the popular literature of the sixteenth and seventeenth centuries to describe contemporary events, but eighteenth century sentiment preferred a religion universal and rational. Hawkesworth found in the Oriental tale, which emphasized the marvelous, a device which inculcated religious feelings while the reader indulged his fancy by an escape into the exotic.

ALMORAN AND HAMET

Hawkesworth's final fictional work is the long Oriental tale, *Almoran and Hamet*. Although modeled on Johnson's *Rasselas, Prince of Abyssinia* but inferior to it, Hawkesworth's tale is an ambitious attempt to unite the major fictional devices of the *Adventurer* essays. *Almoran and Hamet* combines the attributes of the marvelous with those of sensibility. Its opening paragraph announces the theme, the right of Providence to order the world regardless of humans' wishes: "Who is he among the children of earth, that repines at the power of the wicked? and who is he that would change the lot of the righteous?" The wicked one, in this case, is Almoran, elder son of the sultan, who has been reared to be conscious of his prerogatives and to indulge his whims without limit. The righteous one is Almoran's brother Hamet, reared as a philosopher and an ascetic, who prefers a life of service to one of self-indulgence.

The plot pits the ruthless malignity of Almoran against the indomitable but helpless virtue of Hamet, and until the end, Almoran seems on the verge of triumph. Two things have set Almoran against Hamet: their father's will that his sons should rule jointly and the beautiful foreigner Almeida. In their mutual wooing of Almeida, the brothers reveal most clearly their opposite sensiblities: Almoran tries first to lure and then to kidnap Almeida into his harem; Hamet first wishes to know her mind and converses with her about moral and theological topics. Almeida responds to Hamet, and the lovers are filled with delicate, exquisite, and pure feeling for each other.

Almoran's power, however, allows him to tyrannize each of the lovers. He confines Almeida to a room and forces Hamet to flee into the desert. Alone and seemingly helpless, each lover is prey to "indescribable" doubts, fears, and torments about the other beloved. Almoran has used the power of a jinni to increase his oppression. At one point he employs the jinni's power to change shapes with Hamet, and rushing to Almeida and expecting to be welcomed into her arms, Almoran is instead disappointed that even to her lover she will not yield before the wedding. After Hamet is captured, Almoran risks a second transformation but this one is fatal to him. Disguised as one of his officers, he goes to Hamet's cell to kill him; but one of the officer's rivals stabs Almoran. Hamet succeeds to the throne, wins Almeida, and commences a prosperous and just rule which seeks to imitate that of Providence; "Let us govern as we are governed; let us seek our happiness in the happiness we bestow, and our honour in emulating the benevolence of heaven."

Ultimately Hawkesworth's mixture of sensibility and orientalism is unsatisfactory; the emotional extravagance cheapens the religious theme. If not profound, however, *Almoran and Hamet* is readable, and although its particular mixture was not influential, its general recipe was copied later. At the end of the century the gothic novelists such as Ann Radcliffe and Matthew Gregory Lewis proved how readable was the combination of the exotic and the emotional.

OTHER MAJOR WORKS

LONG FICTION: *Almoran and Hamet: An Oriental Tale*, 1761.

PLAYS: *Amphitryon*, pr. 1756; *Oroonoko*, pr. 1759; *Edgar and Emmeline*, pr. 1761.

NONFICTION: *An Account of the Voyages Undertaken in the Southern Hemisphere*, 1773.

BIBLIOGRAPHY

Burney, Fanny. *Memoirs of Dr. Burney*. London: Edward Moxon, 1832. The author's father, Dr. Burney, had supported Hawkesworth's nomination to edit the accounts of the voyages of Captain James Cook and John Byron. Fanny Burney recalls a social meeting between Hawkesworth and Dr. Burney a month before the former died, presumably as a result of the ensuing controversy and criticism over Hawkesworth's theological speculations.

Clifford, James L. *Pope and His Contemporaries*. Oxford, England: Clarendon Press, 1949. Clifford deals briefly but informatively with Hawkesworth as Swift's editor and biographer. Although as an editor Hawkesworth apparently made many inaccuracies, as a biographer he was discerning and judicious.

Drake, Nathaniel. *Essays: Biographical, Critical, and Historical*. London: Suttaby, Evance, and Fox, 1814. Includes discussions of Joseph Addison and Richard Steele. Treats *The Tatler, The Spectator, The Guardian*; the style and content of these periodicals; and the ethical character of their writers, including Hawkesworth.

Eddy, Donald D. "John Hawkesworth: Book Reviewer in the *Gentleman's Magazine*." *Philological Quarterly* 43 (1964): 223-238. Eddy suggests that, in addition to the reviews Hawkesworth contributed to the *Monthly Review* in his own name, he also wrote reviews anonymously in *Gentleman's Magazine* from 1767 to 1773. Contains a table of books reviewed in both magazines.

Sambrook, James. *The Eighteenth Century: The Intellectual and Cultural Context of English Literature, 1700-1789*. London: Longman, 1986. Discusses Hawkesworth's idealized and sentimental treatment of the Noble Savage in describing the Tahitians in his collation of the more sober accounts of Captain James Cook and other explorers. Hawkesworth noted the natives' easy subsistence, and their guilelessness and bravery. Chronology, bibliography, index.

Williams, Harold. "Dean Swift, Hawkesworth, and *The Journal to Stella*." In *Essays on the Eighteenth Century*. New York: Russell & Russell, 1963. Hawkesworth edited the *Journal to Stella* (1766, 1768), a collection of Jonathan Swift's letters to a woman in Ireland. Williams evaluates the accuracy of Hawkesworth's transcription and studies earlier speculation that his edition in fact more closely resembles the originals than Swift's own later publication. Williams concludes that in fact Hawkesworth resorted to considerable polishing of passages. Very detailed.

Robert M. Otten, updated by Lou Thompson

NATHANIEL HAWTHORNE

Born: Salem, Massachusetts; July 4, 1804
Died: Plymouth, New Hampshire; May 19, 1864

PRINCIPAL SHORT FICTION

Twice-Told Tales, 1837, expanded 1842
Mosses from an Old Manse, 1846
The Snow-Image and Other Twice-Told Tales,
   1851

OTHER LITERARY FORMS

Nathaniel Hawthorne is a major American novelist whose early *Fanshawe: A Tale* (1828) did not lead immediately to further long fiction. After a period largely given to tales and sketches, he published his classic study of moral prejudice in colonial New England, *The Scarlet Letter* (1850). In the next decade, three more novels—he preferred to call them romances—followed: *The House of the Seven Gables* (1851), *The Blithedale Romance* (1852), and *The Marble Faun* (1860). He wrote books for children, including *A Wonder-Book for Boys and Girls* (1852), and travel sketches of England, *Our Old Home* (1863). His posthumously published notebooks and letters are also important.

ACHIEVEMENTS

This seminal figure in American fiction combined narrative skill and artistic integrity as no previous American writer had done. A dozen of Nathaniel Hawthorne's short stories remain anthology favorites, and few modern American students fail to become familiar with *The Scarlet Letter*.

His influence on subsequent American writers, especially on his younger American friend Herman Melville, and on Henry James, William Faulkner, and Robert Lowell, has been enormous. Although he wrote comparatively little literary theory, his prefaces to his novels, preeminently the one to *The House of the Seven Gables*, and scattered observations within his fiction reflect a pioneering concern with his craft.

BIOGRAPHY

It is fitting that Nathaniel Hawthorne's birth in 1804 came on the Fourth of July, for, if American writers of his youth were attempting a literary declaration of independence to complement the successful political one of 1776, Hawthorne's fiction of the 1830's, along with Edgar Allan Poe's poetry and fiction and Ralph Waldo Emerson's essays and lectures of the same decade, rank as the fruition of that ambition.

Undoubtedly his hometown of Salem, Massachusetts, exerted a powerful shaping influence on his work, even though his sea-captain father died when Nathaniel, the second of three children, was only four and even though Nathaniel did not evince much interest in the sea. No one could grow up in Salem without a strong sense of the past, especially a boy one of whose ancestors, John Hathorne (as the family name was then spelled), had served as a judge in the infamous witchcraft trials of 1695.

In 1813, confined to home by a foot injury for two years, young Nathaniel formed the habit of reading for hours at a stretch. On graduating from Bowdoin College in 1825, where he was a classmate of Franklin Pierce, the future president, and Henry Wadsworth Longfellow, the future poet, the bookish Hawthorne returned to Salem and began a decade of intensive reading and writing. He published a novel,

Nathaniel Hawthorne (Library of Congress)

Fanshawe: A Tale (later repudiated), in 1828 and began to compose the short stories that eventually brought him into prominence. The first collection of these, *Twice-Told Tales*, appeared in 1837.

In 1838, he became engaged to Sophia Peabody, of Salem, and the following year was appointed to a position in the Boston Custom House, but he left in 1841 to join the infant Brook Farm community in West Roxbury, Massachusetts. As a rather solitary man with no prior practical experience of farming, he did not thrive there and left before the end of the year. Marrying in 1842, the couple settled at the Old Manse in Concord. Although he befriended Henry David Thoreau, Hawthorne found the Concord Transcendentalists generally pretentious and boring. During the administration of James K. Polk, he left Concord for another customhouse appointment, this time back in Salem. From this period comes his second short-story collection, *Mosses from an Old Manse*.

Moving thereafter to Lenox in the Berkshires, Hawthorne met the younger writer Herman Melville and produced, in a few weeks in 1850, *The Scarlet Letter*, which was the first of his successful novels;

The House of the Seven Gables and another collection of short fiction, *The Snow-Image and Other Twice-Told Tales*, followed the next year. Back in Concord at "The Wayside" in 1852, he wrote a campaign biography for his friend Pierce, which resulted in Hawthorne's appointment as United States Consul in Liverpool, England. That same year he also wrote the novel *The Blithedale Romance*, based loosely on his Brook Farm experience.

In England, Hawthorne kept an extensive journal from which he later fashioned *Our Old Home*. Resigning his office in 1857, Hawthorne traveled with his family on the Continent; in Florence, he began his last novel, published in 1860 as *The Marble Faun*. By the time he returned to Concord, his health was failing, and although he worked at several more novels, he did not get far into any of them. In 1864, he set forth on a trip with Pierce but died in Plymouth, New Hampshire, on May 19.

ANALYSIS

Nathaniel Hawthorne's reading in American colonial history confirmed his basically ambivalent attitude toward the American past, particularly the form that Puritanism took in the New England colonies. Especially interested in the intensity of the Puritan-Cavalier rivalry, the Puritan inclination to credit manifestations of the supernatural such as witchcraft, and the psychology of the struggle for liberation from English rule, Hawthorne explored these themes in some of his earliest stories. As they did for his Puritan ancestors, sin and guilt preoccupied Hawthorne, who, in his move from Salem to Concord, encountered what he considered the facile dismissal of the problem of evil by the Concord intellectuals. He developed a deeply ambivalent moral attitude that colored the situations and characters of his fiction.

In the early masterpiece "My Kinsman, Major Molineux," his concern with the United States' coming of age blends with the maturation of a lad on the verge of manhood. Introduced to the complexities of evil, characters such as Robin of this story and the title character of "Young Goodman Brown" have great difficulty summoning the spiritual strength to resist dark temptations.

Often, Hawthorne's characters cannot throw off the burden of a vague and irrational but weighty burden of guilt. Frequently, his young protagonists exhibit a cold, unresponsive attitude toward a loving fiancé or wife and can find no spiritual sustenance to redeem the situation. Brown, Parson Hooper of "The Minister's Black Veil," and Reuben Bourne of "Roger Malvin's Burial" are examples of such guilt-ridden and essentially faithless men.

Another prevalent type of protagonist rejects love to become a detached observer, such as the husband of "Wakefield," who for no apparent reason deserts his wife and spends years living nearby in disguise. In the stories of his middle and later periods, these detached characters are usually scientists or artists. The former include misguided idealists such as Aylmer of "The Birthmark" and the scientist Rappaccini in "Rappaccini's Daughter," who experiments remorselessly on female family members in search of some elusive abstract perfection. Hawthorne's artists, while less dangerous, tend also to exclude themselves from warm and loving relationships.

At their most deplorable, Hawthorne's isolated, detached characters become, like Ethan Brand in the story of the same name and Roger Chillingworth of *The Scarlet Letter*, violators of the human heart, unreclaimable souls whose estrangement from normal human relationships yields them little in compensation, either material or spiritual.

Characteristically Hawthorne builds his stories on a quest or journey, often into the woods or wilderness but always into an unknown region, the protagonist emerging enlightened or merely chastened but invariably sadder, with any success a bitterly ironical one, such as Aylmer's removal of his wife's birthmark, which kills his patient. The stories are pervasively and often brilliantly symbolic, and Hawthorne's symbolic imagination encompasses varieties ranging from more or less clear-cut allegory to elusive multiple symbolic patterns whose significance critics debate endlessly.

A century and a half after their composition, Hawthorne's artistry and moral imagination, even in some of his seriously flawed stories, continue to engage readers and critics. Two of Hawthorne's most enduringly popular stories—"Roger Malvin's Burial" and "My Kinsman, Major Molineux"—appeared initially in the 1831 edition of a literary annual called *The Token* but remained uncollected until long afterward. Both seem to have been intended for a book, *Provincial Tales*, that never materialized, and both begin with paragraphs explicitly linking the narratives to historical events.

"ROGER MALVIN'S BURIAL"

"Roger Malvin's Burial" is set in the aftermath of a 1725 confrontation with Native Americans called Lovell's Fight. Roger is a mortally wounded soldier; Reuben Bourne, his less seriously injured companion, must decide whether to stay with his older friend on the desolate frontier or make his way back to his company before he becomes too weak to travel. Urged to the latter course by Roger, his prospective father-in-law, Reuben makes the older man as comfortable as he can at the base of a huge rock near an oak sapling, promises to return as soon as he can, and staggers away. Eventually, he is discovered by a search party and taken home to be ministered to by Dorcas, his fiancé. After several days of semiconsciousness, Reuben recovers sufficiently to answer questions. Although he believes he has done the right thing, he cannot bring himself to contradict Dorcas's assumption that he had buried her father, and he is undeservedly lionized for his heroic fidelity.

Eighteen years later, this unhappy and uncommunicative husband takes Dorcas and their fifteen-year-old son Cyrus to the frontier, presumably to resettle but really to "bury" Roger and expiate his own guilt. On the anniversary of the day Reuben had left Roger, Dorcas and Cyrus are led to the rock and the now blasted oak tree, a fatal gunshot is fired, and in a chillingly ambiguous way Reuben relieves himself of his "curse." This pattern of irrational guilt and ambivalent quest would be repeated in other stories, using New England historical incidents and pervasive symbols such as the rock and oak of "Roger Malvin's Burial."

"MY KINSMAN, MAJOR MOLINEUX"

"My Kinsman, Major Molineux" is justly considered one of Hawthorne's greatest stories. The historical introduction here serves to establish the setting as a time of bitter resentment toward Massachusetts colonial governors. The location is left deliberately vague, except that Robin, the young protagonist, must arrive by ferry in a town where he hopes to meet his kinsman, a colonial official. Robin has come from the country with an idea of getting a boost toward a career from Major Molineux. The town is tense and lurid when he enters at nightfall, and the people act strangely. In particular, whenever Robin mentions the name of his kinsman, he is rebuffed. While frequently described as "shrewd," Robin seems naïve and baffled by the events of this disquieting evening.

Eventually, he is treated to the nightmarish spectacle of the public humiliation of his kinsman, though it appears that Major Molineux is the more or less innocent victim of colonial vindictiveness toward the authority of the Crown. At the climax, Robin finds himself unaccountably laughing with the townspeople at Molineux's disgrace. By the end of the evening, Robin, convinced that nothing remains for him to do but to return home, is counseled by the only civil person he meets to wait a few days before leaving, "as you are a shrewd youth, you may rise in the world without the help of your kinsman, Major Molineux."

At one level, this is clearly a rites-of-passage story. Robin has reached the point of initiation into an adult world whose deviousness and obliquity he has hardly begun to suspect, but one in which he can hope to prosper only through his own efforts. The conclusion strongly implies that he cannot go home again, or that if he does, life will never be the same. As the stranger suggests, he may well be obliged to stay and adjust to the new world that he has discovered. The historical setting proclaims "My Kinsman, Major Molineux" an imaginative account of the colonial struggle toward the challenges and perils of an independence for which the people are largely unprepared. The ferry ride, reminiscent of the underworld adventures of epic heroes such as Odysseus and Aeneas—and perhaps more pointedly yet, the Dante of the *Inferno*—leads to a hellish region from which newcomers cannot normally expect to return. The multiplicity of interpretations that this story has provoked attests to its richness and complexity.

Several of Hawthorne's best stories first appeared in 1835. One of these, "Wakefield," has been criticized as slight and undeveloped, but it remains intriguing. It poses in its final paragraph an exacting problem: "Amid the seeming confusion of our mysterious world, individuals are so nicely adjusted to a system, and systems to one another and to a whole, that, by stepping aside for a moment, a man exposes himself to a fearful risk of losing his place forever." Wakefield "steps aside" by leaving his wife for no apparent reason and secretly taking up residence in the next street. The setting of this story, unusual for Hawthorne, is London, and the couple have been married for ten years. Wakefield seems to be an embryonic version of the ruthless experimenter of several later stories, but here his action is more of a joke than an experiment. He is "intellectual, but not actively so"; he lacks imagination; and he has "a cold but not depraved nor wandering heart." When he leaves, he promises to be back in three or four days, but he stays away for twenty years. He adopts a disguise, regularly walks by his old home and peers in, and even passes his wife in the street. Wakefield has a purpose that he cannot define, but the author describes his motive merely as "morbid vanity." He will frighten his wife and will find out how much he really matters. He does not matter that much, however, for his wife settles to the routine of her "widowhood." Finally, passing his old home in a rain shower, he suddenly decides to enter, and at this point the story ends, leaving unanswered the question of whether he has lost his place forever.

"THE MINISTER'S BLACK VEIL"

Of the many Hawthorne stories that point toward his masterpiece in the novel *The Scarlet Letter*, "The Minister's Black Veil" boasts the character most akin to Arthur Dimmesdale of the novel. Like Dimmesdale, Parson Hooper has a secret. He appears one morning at a Milford meeting house (a reference to "Governor Belcher" appears to place the story in Massachusetts in the 1730's or early 1740's) with his face shrouded by a black veil, which he never thereafter removes. Unlike Dimmesdale, he thus flaunts his secret while concealing it. The whole story revolves around the veil and its meaning. His sermon, unusually energetic for this mild minister, is "secret sin." That afternoon, Hooper conducts a funeral service for a young woman, and Hawthorne hints darkly that Hooper's sin may have involved her. In the evening, at a third service, Hooper's veil casts gloom over a wedding ceremony. The congregation speculates endlessly but inclines to avoid the minister.

One person who does not avoid him is a young woman named Elizabeth, who is engaged to Hooper. Elizabeth unavailingly begs him to explain or remove the veil and then breaks their engagement. In the years that follow, the lonely minister exerts a strange power over his flock. Dying sinners always insist on his visiting them and never expire before he reaches them, although his presence makes them shudder. Finally, Hooper himself sickens, and Elizabeth reappears to nurse him. On his death bed, he questions the aversion of his onlookers and insists that he sees a similar veil over each of their faces. He then expires and is buried with the veil still over his face. A question more important than the nature of Hooper's transgression concerns his increase in ministerial efficacy. Is Hooper's veiled state a kind of extended stage trick? (In death a smile lingers on his face.) Is it advantageous to be ministered to by a "mind diseased?" Is Hooper's effectiveness an implicit condemnation of his and his congregation's religion? Such questions Hawthorne's story inevitably raises and just as inevitably does not presume to answer directly.

"The May-Pole of Merrymount"

"The May-Pole of Merrymount" is simple in plot but complex in theme. One midsummer's eve, very early in the colonial life of the Massachusetts settlement at Mount Wollaston, or Merry Mount, a reenactment of ancient Maypole rites accompanies the wedding of an attractive young couple, Edith and Edgar. Into the scene storms a belligerent group of Puritans under John Endicott, who hacks down the Maypole, arrests the principals, including the flower-decked priest and the bridal couple, and threatens punishment to all, though Edith's and Edgar's will be light if they can accommodate themselves to the severe Puritan life hereafter.

Hawthorne uses history but does not follow it strictly. The historical Endicott's main motive in at-

tacking Merry Mount was to stop its denizens from furnishing firepower and firewater—that is, guns and liquor—to Native Americans. The real Merry Mounters were not so frivolous, nor the Puritans necessarily so austere as Hawthorne depicts them. His artistic purpose required the sharp contrast of two ways of life among early Massachusetts settlers, neither of which he is willing to endorse. The young couple are caught between the self-indulgence of their own community and the "dismal wretches" who invade their ceremony. Like many of Hawthorne's characters, Edith and Edgar emerge into adulthood in an environment replete with bewildering moral conflicts. It is possible to see the conflict here as one between "English" and "American" values, the Americans being the sober seekers of a new, more disciplined, presumably more godly order than the one they chose to leave behind; the conflict can also be seen as one between a form of religion receptive to "pagan" excesses and a strict, fiercely intolerant one; yet another way of seeing it is as one between hedonists and sadists—for the pleasure principle completely dominates Hawthorne's Merry Mount, while the Puritans promise branding, chopping of ears, and, instead of a Maypole, a whipping post for the miscreants.

The resolution of the story echoes John Milton's description of Adam and Eve leaving Eden at the end of *Paradise Lost* (1667), but Hawthorne has Endicott throw a wreath of roses from the Maypole over the heads of the departing newlyweds, "a deed of prophecy," which signifies the end of the "systematic gayety" of Merry Mount, which also symbolizes the "purest and best of their early joys" that must sustain them in the strict Puritan regimen that lies ahead.

"Young Goodman Brown"

"Young Goodman Brown," first appearing in print in 1835, is set in Salem at the end of the seventeenth century—the era of the witchcraft trials. Again, the names of some minor characters are historical, but Brown and his wife, Faith, whom the young protagonist leaves one night to go into the woods, are among his most allegorical. In its outline the allegory is transparent: When a "good man" abandons his faith, he can expect to go to the devil. Hawthorne complicates his story by weaving into it all sorts of subtleties and ambiguities. Brown's guide in the woods is simultaneously fatherlike and devilish. He encounters a series of presumably upright townspeople, including eventually Faith herself, gathering for a ceremony of devil-worship. At the climactic moment, Brown urges Faith to "look up to heaven, and resist the wicked one." The next thing he knows, he is alone in the forest, all his companions having fled—or all having been part of a dream. Brown returns home in the morning, his life radically altered. He can no longer trust his neighbors, he shrinks from his wife, and he lives out his years a scowling, muttering misanthrope.

As in "The May-Pole of Merrymount," Hawthorne's motive in evoking an episode of New England history is not primarily historical: No one proceeds against witches; there is no allusion to Judge John Hathorne. Rather, the setting creates an atmosphere of guilt, suspicion, and unstable moral imagination. Breathing this atmosphere, Brown falls victim not to injustice or religious intolerance but to himself. In a sense it does not matter whether Brown fell asleep in the woods and dreamed the Black Sabbath. Regardless of whether he has lost faith, he has manifestly lost hope. His apparent capacity to resist evil in the midst of a particularly unholy temptation dispels his own guilt no more than the guilt he, and seemingly only he, detects in others. "Young Goodman Brown" is a masterful fictive presentation of the despairing soul.

All the preceding stories had been published by the time Hawthorne turned thirty-one. For about three more years, stories continued to flow, although most of those from the late 1830's are not among his best. He broke a subsequent dry spell with a series of stories first published in 1843 and 1844, many of which were later collected in *Mosses from an Old Manse* in 1846. Most notable of these later stories are "The Birthmark," "The Artist of the Beautiful," and "Rappaccini's Daughter."

"THE BIRTHMARK"

In these later efforts, the artist-scientist appears frequently. Aylmer of "The Birthmark" becomes obsessed by the one flaw in his beautiful wife, Georgiana, a birthmark on her left cheek that had not

previously bothered her or her prior lovers. To Aylmer, however, it is a "symbol of imperfection," and he undertakes its removal. Hawthorne foreshadows the result in many ways, not the least by Georgiana's observation that her brilliant husband's "most splendid successes were almost invariably failures." She submits to the operation nevertheless, and he succeeds at removing the mark but fails to preserve her life, intertwined somehow with it.

Aylmer equates science with religion; words such as "miracle," "votaries," "mysteries," and "holy" abound. He is also an artist who, far from subjecting Georgiana to a smoky laboratory, fashions an apartment with beautiful curtains and perfumed lamps of his creation for her to inhabit during the experiment. Neither hero nor villain, Aylmer is a gifted man incapable of accepting moral limitations and therefore unable to accept his wife as the best that life could offer him.

The artist appears in various guises in Hawthorne's later stories and novels. He may be a woodcarver as in "Drowne's Wooden Image," a poet like Coverdale of *The Blithedale Romance*, a painter like Kenyon of *The Marble Faun*, or, as in "The Artist of the Beautiful," a watchmaker with the ambition "to put the very spirit of beauty into form." Owen Warland is also a peripheral figure, not yet alienated from society like many twentieth century artists real and fictional but regarded as quaint and ineffectual by his companions. Like Aylmer, he attempts to improve on nature, his creation being a mechanical butterfly of rare and fragile beauty. Owen appears fragile himself, but it is part of Hawthorne's strategy to reveal his inner toughness. He can contemplate the destruction of his butterfly by a child with equanimity, for the artifact itself is only the "symbol" of the reality of art. Owen suffers in living among less sensitive and spiritual beings and in patiently enduring their unenlightened patronization, but he finds security in his capacity for beauty.

"RAPPACCINI'S DAUGHTER"

"Rappaccini's Daughter" has three familiar Hawthorne characters. His young initiate this time is an Italian university student named Giovanni Guasconti, whose lodgings in Padua overlook a spectacular garden, the pride and joy of a scientific experimenter, Dr. Rappaccini, whose human subject is his daughter Beatrice. A scientific rival, professor Baglioni, warns Giovanni that Rappaccini much prefers science to humankind, but the young man falls in love with Beatrice and thus comes within Rappaccini's orbit. This scientist is more sinister than Aylmer and exerts his power over Beatrice more pervasively than does Aylmer over Georgiana. Beatrice's very life is bound up with the powerful poison with which he grows the exotic flowers in his garden. Giovanni, who has himself imbibed the poison, tries to counter its effect on Beatrice by offering her a medicine obtained from Baglioni, but its effect on her, whose whole life has depended on the poison, is fatal.

This story and its four main characters have generated a bewildering variety of interpretations. One reason for the critical quarrels is a subtle shift in point of view late in the story. For most of the way, the reader is with Giovanni and knows what Giovanni knows, but about four-fifths of the way, an omniscient narrator begins to comment on the limitations of his perceptions, the truth being deeper than he can plumb. This double perspective creates difficulties in gauging his character and that of the other three principals.

Hawthorne's allegorical propensities also complicate one's understanding of the story. For example, Beatrice can be seen as an Eve, an already corrupted temptress in the garden; as a Dantean, who guides her lover through what is for him, initially at least, Paradise; and as the Pomona of Ovid's tale of Vertumnus, the vegetarian god who wins her love and takes her away. (There is a statue of Vertumnus in Rappaccini's garden.) Obviously, Beatrice is not consistently any of these figures, but each of them leads to further allegorizing.

Perhaps the ultimate explanation of the interpretative difficulties arising from "Rappaccini's Daughter" is the author's profound ambivalence. In this fictional world, good and evil, beauty and deformity, are inextricably intermingled. Is Baglioni, for example, wise counselor or jealous rival, the protector of Giovanni or the vindictive agent of Beatrice's destruction? He fulfills these roles and others. In this story he conjoins with three other familiar Hawthorne

types, the young initiate into life's malignities, the trusting victim of a detached manipulator, and the insensitive violator of his victim's integrity. Nearly every conceivable critical method has been applied to "Rappaccini's Daughter"; ultimately each reader must make up his or her own mind about its primary significance.

After these three stories of the mid-1840's, all viewed incidentally as landmarks of science fiction by historians of that genre, Hawthorne, back in Salem and busy with his customhouse duties, wrote little for several years. Before turning his attention to long fiction in 1850, however, he completed a few more short stories in the late 1840's, the most important of which is "Ethan Brand."

"ETHAN BRAND"

Like several of his best stories, this one occupies the time from nightfall to the following dawn, but unlike "Young Goodman Brown" and "My Kinsman, Major Molineux" it has a contemporary setting. Bartram is a lime burner attending his fire on Mount Greylock in northwestern Massachusetts with his son Joe, when a man appears, a former lime burner who long ago decided to devote his life to searching for the Unpardonable Sin, which, by cultivating his intellect at the expense of his moral sense, he found in his own heart. All this he explains to the unimaginative and uncomprehending Bartram. The sensitive son fears the glint in the stranger's eye, and even Bartram cringes at Ethan Brand's sinister laugh. Since Brand has passed into local folklore, Bartram dispatches Joe to inform the villagers that he is back, and soon a contingent of neighbors comes on the scene. When Brand demonstrates his abrogation of human brotherhood, they retire, and Brand offers to watch Bartram's fire so that the latter and his son can retire for the night to their nearby hut. When Bartram and Joe awake in the morning, they find Brand gone, but a look into the fire reveals his skeleton burned to lime, his hardened heart also burnt but distinctly outlined.

What was the sin? Hawthorne subtitled this story "A Chapter from an Abortive Romance." No fragments of such a romance have ever turned up, although the story alludes briefly to past relationships between Brand and some of the villagers, including an "Esther" on whom Brand had performed a "psychological experiment, and wasted, absorbed, and perhaps annihilated her soul, in the process." Hawthorne seems to have intended no specifying of this or any other of Brand's activities but succeeded in delineating a character who represents the ultimate development—at least in his short fiction—of the coldly intellectual seeker who has denied his heart, exploited others in relentless quasi-scientific experimentation, and isolated himself from humanity. Hawthorne would depict such characters in more detail in his novels but never one who acknowledged his sin so completely and regarded suicide as the only act remaining to him.

At one time, Hawthorne's short stories were viewed mainly as preliminaries to the novels to which he turned shortly after publishing "Ethan Brand" in January of 1850, but he is now recognized as a master of the short story. Unlike all other major American writers of his time, he devoted his creative energies almost exclusively to fiction. Only Edgar Allan Poe, who began to publish his fiction shortly after Hawthorne's early stories appeared, approaches his position as the United States' first artist of short fiction. If Poe excelled at the psychology of terror, Hawthorne prevailed at the psychology of guilt. Both brilliantly characterized the isolated or alienated individual, but only Hawthorne regularly enriched the cultural significance of his stories by locating these characters within the context of an American past and thus contributing imaginatively to his readers' sense of that past.

OTHER MAJOR WORKS

LONG FICTION: *Fanshawe: A Tale*, 1828; *The Scarlet Letter*, 1850; *The House of the Seven Gables*, 1851; *The Blithedale Romance*, 1852; *The Marble Faun*, 1860; *Septimius Felton*, 1872 (fragment); *The Dolliver Romance*, 1876 (fragment); *The Ancestral Footstep*, 1883 (fragment); *Doctor Grimshawe's Secret*, 1883 (fragment).

NONFICTION: *Life of Franklin Pierce*, 1852; *Our Old Home*, 1863; *The American Notebooks*, 1941; *The French and Italian Notebooks*, 1980; *Letters of Nathaniel Hawthorne*, 1984-1987 (4 volumes).

CHILDREN'S LITERATURE: *Grandfather's Chair*,

1841; *Biographical Stories for Children*, 1842; *True Stories from History and Biography*, 1851; *A Wonder-Book for Boys and Girls*, 1852; *Tanglewood Tales for Boys and Girls*, 1853.

EDITED TEXT: *Peter Parley's Universal History*, 1837.

MISCELLANEOUS: *Complete Works*, 1850-1882 (13 volumes); *The Complete Writings of Nathaniel Hawthorne*, 1900 (22 volumes).

BIBLIOGRAPHY

Bunge, Nancy. *Nathaniel Hawthorne: A Study of the Short Fiction*. New York: Twayne, 1993. Discusses Hawthorne's major short stories in three categories: isolation and community, artists and scientists, and perspective, humility, and joy. Includes excerpts from Hawthorne's journals, letters, and prefaces; also includes excerpts on Hawthorne from Herman Melville, Edgar Allan Poe, Henry James, and several contemporary critics.

Charvat, William, et al., eds. *The Centenary Edition of the Works of Nathaniel Hawthorne*. Columbus: Ohio State University Press, 1963-   . This continuing multivolume edition of Hawthorne's works will, when complete, contain the entire canon. Somewhat unevenly accomplished by a variety of editors, the volumes contain a considerable amount of textual apparatus as well as biographical and critical information. Volumes 9, 10, and 11 give the texts of all known Hawthorne short stories and sketches.

Doubleday, Neal Frank. *Hawthorne's Early Tales: A Critical Study*. Durham, N.C.: Duke University Press, 1972. Doubleday focuses on what he calls "the development of Hawthorne's literary habit," including Hawthorne's literary theory and the materials from which he fashioned the stories of his twenties and early thirties. The index, while consisting chiefly of proper names and titles, includes some features of Hawthorne's work ("ambiguity," "irony," and the like).

Fogle, Richard Harter. *Hawthorne's Fiction: The Light and the Dark*. Rev. ed. Norman: University of Oklahoma Press, 1964. One of the first critics to write full analytical essays about the short stories, Fogle examines eight stories in detail as well as the four mature novels. He sees Hawthorne's fiction as both clear ("light") and complex ("dark"). He is particularly adept, although perhaps overly ingenious, in explicating Hawthorne's symbolism.

Keil, James C. "Hawthorne's 'Young Goodman Brown': Early Nineteenth-Century and Puritan Constructions of Gender." *The New England Quarterly* 69 (March, 1996): 33-55. Argues that Hawthorne places his story in the seventeenth century to explore the nexus of past and present in the attitudes of New Englanders toward theology, morality, and sexuality. Points out that clear boundaries between male and female, public and private, and work and home were thresholds across which nineteenth century Americans often passed.

Kelsey, Angela M. "Mrs. Wakefield's Gaze: Femininity and Dominance in Nathaniel Hawthorne's 'Wakefield.'" *ATQ*, n.s. 8 (March, 1994): 17-31. In this feminist reading of Hawthorne's story, Kelsey argues that Mrs. Wakefield finds ways to escape and exceed the economy of the male gaze, first by appropriating the look for herself, then by refusing to die, and finally by denying her husband her gaze.

Mackenzie, Manfred. "Hawthorne's 'Roger Malvin's Burial': A Postcolonial Reading." *New Literary History* 27 (Summer, 1996): 459-472. Argues that the story is postcolonial fiction in which Hawthorne writes the emerging American nation and recalls European colonial culture; claims that Hawthorne rehearses the colonialist past in order to concentrate and effectively "expel" its inherent violence.

McKee, Kathryn B. "'A Small Heap of Glittering Fragments': Hawthorne's Discontent with the Short Story Form." *ATQ*, n.s. 8 (June, 1994): 137-147. Claims that Hawthorne's "Artist of the Beautiful" and "Downe's Wooden Image" are examples of his dissatisfaction with the short story as a form; argues that the fragile articles at the center of the tales mirror the limitations Hawthorne saw in the short-story genre.

Mellow, James R. *Nathaniel Hawthorne and His Times*. Boston: Houghton Mifflin, 1980. In this substantial, readable, and illustrated biography, Mellow provides a number of insights into Hawthorne's fiction. Refreshingly, the author presents Sophia Hawthorne not only as the prudish, protective wife of the Hawthorne legend but also as a woman with an artistic sensibility and talent of her own. Mellow's book is a good introduction to a very interesting man. Suitable for the student and the general reader.

Miller, Edward Havilland. *Salem Is My Dwelling Place: A Life of Nathaniel Hawthorne*. Iowa City: University of Iowa Press, 1991. A large biography of more than six hundred pages, illustrated with more than fifty photographs and drawings. Miller has been able to draw on more manuscripts of family members and Hawthorne associates than did his predecessors and also developed his subject's family life in more detail. He offers interpretations of many of the short stories.

Newberry, Frederick. "'The Artist of the Beautiful': Crossing the Transcendent Divide in Hawthorne's Fiction." *Nineteenth-Century Literature* 50 (June, 1995): 78-96. Argues that the butterfly's appearance is Hawthorne's endorsement of the transcendent power of imagination over nineteenth century empiricism.

Newman, Lea Bertani Vozar. *A Reader's Guide to the Short Stories of Nathaniel Hawthorne*. Boston: G. K. Hall, 1979. For each of fifty-four stories, this valuable guide furnishes a chapter with four sections: publication history; circumstances of composition, sources, and influences; relationship with other Hawthorne works; and interpretations and criticism. The discussions are arranged alphabetically by title and keyed to a bibliography of more than five hundred secondary sources.

Swope, Richard. "Approaching the Threshold(s) in Postmodern Detective Fiction: Hawthorne's 'Wakefield' and Other Missing Persons." *Critique* 39 (Spring, 1998): 207-227. Discusses "Wakefield" as a literary ancestor of "metaphysical" detective fiction, a postmodern genre that combines fiction with literary theory. "Wakefield" raises many of the questions about language, subjectivity, and urban spaces that surround postmodernism.

Thompson, G. R. *The Art of Authorial Presence: Hawthorne's Provincial Tales*. Durham, N.C.: Duke University Press, 1993. Argues that for Hawthorne the art of telling a story depends on a carefully created fiction of an authorial presence. Examines Hawthorne's narrative strategies for creating this presence by using contemporary narrative theory. Analyzes a small number of early Hawthorne stories and the criticism that has amassed about Hawthorne's fiction.

Waggoner, Hyatt. *Hawthorne: A Critical Study*. Rev. ed. Cambridge, Mass.: Harvard University Press, 1963. Waggoner is acute in his tracing of patterns of imagery in Hawthorne's fiction. This book is both a clear exposition and an incentive to plumb Hawthorne more deeply—virtues that have impelled some readers to challenge Waggoner's interpretations. For Waggoner, intuition, rather than biographical data, is the better tool to bring to the study of fiction.

Robert P. Ellis

BESSIE HEAD

Bessie Amelia Emery
Born: Pietermaritzburg, South Africa; July 6, 1937
Died: Serowe, Botswana; April 17, 1986

PRINCIPAL SHORT FICTION

The Collector of Treasures and Other Botswana Village Tales, 1977
Tales of Tenderness and Power, 1989
The Cardinals, with Meditations and Short Stories, 1993

OTHER LITERARY FORMS

Bessie Head's reputation was established by her novels *When Rain Clouds Gather* (1969), *Maru* (1971), and *A Question of Power* (1973). After that, she shifted her attention to historical chronicles of her adopted country, Botswana, producing *Serowe: Village of the Rain Wind* (1981) and *A Bewitched Crossroad: An African Saga* (1984). In 1991 Head published *A Gesture of Belonging: Letters from Bessie Head, 1965-1979*.

ACHIEVEMENTS

Bessie Head's *A Question of Power* was a finalist for the Booker McConnell Prize in 1973. Her short-story collection *The Collector of Treasures and Other*

Botswana Village Tales was nominated for the Jock Campbell Award for literature by new or disregarded talent from Africa or the Caribbean in 1978.

BIOGRAPHY

The career of Bessie Amelia Head (née Emery) falls naturally into three parts: first, her childhood and youth in South Africa; second, her exile in the neighboring country of Botswana; and third, her life there as a citizen of that country, tragically cut short at the age of forty-eight by hepatitis. Head's mother was a rich white woman, who was committed to a mental hospital at the time of her birth. The insanity was real but also covered the fact that Head's father was a black stableman. Head was thus "colored"— the South African term for being of mixed race. She was fostered with a white couple, then passed on to a colored couple, whom she thought of as her natural parents. Her foster father died when she was six, and their situation deteriorated to the extent that, at thirteen, she was sent away to a mission school. There, the principal told her the truth of her birth at the traumatic end of her first term.

She was a good scholar and finally graduated in 1955 with a Natal Teachers' Senior Certificate. She taught briefly in Durban, then entered journalism, writing for the *Post*. In 1960, she left for Cape Town and then Johannesburg, writing for *The New African* and *Drum*, radical literary and political journals. This brought her to the notice of the apartheid authorities. In 1961 she was briefly married to a fellow journalist, Harold Head, by whom she had one child, a son, Harold.

In 1964 she left for Botswana on an exit visa to become an exile. She taught for two years and then devoted herself again to writing, living very simply, recovering from a mental breakdown, and adjusting gradually to the rural life of Serowe, the largest village in South Africa. Gradually her novels won her recognition, and after one refusal she gained citizenship in 1979.

She turned her attention to the history of her new country, which had never been fully colonialized, and produced several remarkably conceived books. She began to travel to writers' conferences and had just embarked on her autobiography when she died.

ANALYSIS

Although Bessie Head's reputation was based initially on her long fiction, her short fiction has confirmed it. Although some of the short stories date back to her days as a journalist in South Africa, most derive from her period in Botswana, when she interviewed people to compile her two chronicle histories. This activity generated so much material from the personal testimonies of her subjects and their own stories that she had plenty left over to fashion into short stories. In fact, much of the material is not fiction at all but oral history written down. Head dissolves genre boundaries between documentary, traditional tale, folklore, memories, and fiction in a unique style.

Journalism had taught her to write economically. Her style and subject matter are deceptively simple. Her themes are universal, although the setting is emphatically local, rural, and everyday. They deal with the harshness of nature, especially ever threatening drought, the tension between newer ways and tribal traditions (a universal African theme), the position of women, and the abuse of power. Ordinary people are dealt with sympathetically; but in celebrating their or-

dinariness, she avoids the simplicities of good (peasant, rural, traditional, black) against bad (white, modern, urban).

Although Head apparently avoids political statement or stance, her short stories can be fully analyzed in terms of a liberal and humane politics, unlike many of her black South African contemporaries. Similarly, while avoiding religious belief statements, her beliefs in the power of love to overcome are tautly idealistic in the way religious fiction at its best demonstrates.

As a writer of short stories, it is her own humility and self-effacement that come through, even while she is working out her own life traumas in her fictions of powerless women. Such tensions between objective and subjective stance produce a delicate counterpointing that eschews the big rhetoric in which other contemporaries engage. It would not be too much to suggest parallels with the short fiction of her white South African contemporary, Nadine Gordimer.

THE COLLECTOR OF TREASURES AND OTHER BOTSWANA VILLAGE TALES

This volume consists of thirteen short stories of village life, specifically of the village life Head observed during thirteen years of exile in Serowe. They partly chronicle the social history of the village, although that is much more systematically done in *Serowe: Village of the Rain Wind* (1981); more particularly, they explore the conflicts around the changing status and identity of women in rural African society. They are thus susceptible to a thoroughgoing feminist analysis, even though Bessie Head denied she was a feminist. The resulting sophisticated analyses often seem at odds with the studied simplicity of Head's technique, which is closely modeled on traditional oral storytelling.

The title story is perhaps the best known of this carefully arranged collection. Dikeledi is a model wife married to a ne'er-do-well. Even while unhappily married, she manages to collect "treasures" of love, friendship, community, and good deeds from the women of the neighborhood. The real shock of the story is her desperate act of killing her husband by castrating him. The judicial system shows little mercy for her, and she is given life in prison. While in prison she meets other women who have also killed their husbands, and a new community of suffering is set up.

The story is crisscrossed with all sorts of issues with wider ramifications than the purely domestic. Head presents the ideal marriage of Paul Thebolo and his wife as a paradigm for the future. Paul becomes the ideal husband—clearly Head is trying to point the way ahead for men also. Dikeledi's husband has lost his own identity in his oppression by both tribal custom and colonial exploitation. His abuse of Dikeledi is the one act of power he can make.

Another story, "Life," contrasts interestingly with this one. The heroine, Life, is a "good-time girl" returning from the bright lights of South African city life to set herself up as a prostitute. She is quite open about the economic power and independence this brings her. The husband she takes, a simple shepherd, kills her. This time, the courts are merciful—it is a crime of passion. This slanting of the justice system is a token of the whole male-dominated society, whether tribal or colonial.

Other stories in the collection deal with religion, especially the clash of tribal religion and Christianity, as in "Heaven Is Not Closed" and "Witchcraft." Head's anti-Christian bias is muted here as she does not wish to appear supportive of tribal religion either. Both are part of a wider conflict between tradition and modernity, yet other stories deal with love and marriage and the conflict between traditional arranged marriage and romantic marriage.

"THE LOVERS"

This story appears in her second collection, *Tales of Tenderness and Power*. It has parallels with "The Deep River: A Story of Ancient Tribal Migration" of the first collection. Both are mythic, placed in a legendary past; both portray the conflict between romantic love and arranged marriage. In "The Lovers," the young man, Keaja, is already an independent thinker, willing to step out of the collective mentality of the tribe. The girl, Tselane, is mesmerized by such free-thinking and by Keaja's proposal of marriage, whether her parents approve of it or not. They do not, and neither do his; eventually the lovers are forced to flee. The legend has it that the earth was so offended by their behavior that the hill where they had their

meetings opened up and swallowed them. Head delicately describes passion and desire in Tselane, despite the fact that there is no language, let alone any model, for such emotions.

"THE PRISONER WHO WORE GLASSES"

The story represents a move away from the village tales. It is set in a prison camp, presumably in South Africa, and involves a group of political prisoners apparently powerless against the oppression of the white prison guard yet managing to control him and break his dominance. The hero, Brille, is so called because he wears glasses. He is an older man, whose spirit has not been broken mainly because the prisoners of "Span One" work as a team. This theme of solidarity and community is an important one for Head. It is not the same as the tribal collective, however, which she questions. It is much more a willed community of support and respect working in a highly democratic way, not easily subverted. This is what the warder, Hannetjie, discovers. He is brought into line by the determination of the prisoners and his own need to survive in an oppressive regime. At the end, roles are reversed in a "live and let live" cooperation.

"THE COMING OF THE CHRIST-CHILD"

This, again, is an exceptional story for Head. It is again set in South Africa but this time makes very explicit political and religious comments. The hero, known only as "the young man" comes from a long line of black African pastors, but the social injustices of apartheid and the inability of his father to withstand them make him feel that God is dead.

His academic education resembles the political education of many young black Africans of the 1960's and 1970's—the young man could be a young Nelson Mandela in his struggles, as he absorbs socialism and a hatred of racial oppression. He sees the limits of the peaceful protest of the African National Congress. His protests lead to imprisonment, exile, and eventually death.

However, in this apparently bleak ending, Head sounds a note of optimism: The "winds of change" blowing over the rest of Africa will eventually reach South Africa, and the Christ-Child, the Messiah, will eventually come to deliver his people.

OTHER MAJOR WORKS

LONG FICTION: *When Rain Clouds Gather*, 1969; *Maru*, 1971; *A Question of Power*, 1973.

NONFICTION: *Serowe: Village of the Rain Wind*, 1981; *A Bewitched Crossroad: An African Saga*, 1984; *A Woman Alone: Autobiographical Writings*, 1990 (Craig Mackenzie, editor); *A Gesture of Belonging: Letters from Bessie Head, 1965-1979*, 1991 (Randolf Vigne, editor).

BIBLIOGRAPHY

Abrahams, C., ed. *The Tragic Life: Bessie Head and Literature in Southern Africa*. Trenton, N.J.: Africa World Press, 1990. This collection of essays on Head is one of the best full studies available. Chapters deal with the short stories. Includes bibliography and index.

Chapman, Michael. *Southern African Literatures*. New York: Longman, 1996. One of the Longman "Literature in English" series, this is one of the fullest overviews of South African literature. Sets Bessie Head well into context in the section "Writing in the Interregnum." An excellent chronology and a full bibliography of individual authors.

Eilersen, Gillian Stead. *Bessie Head: Thunder Behind Her Ears, Her Life and Writing*. Portsmouth, N.H.: Heinemann, 1995. Discusses the relationship between Head's life and her writing.

Ibrahim, Huma. *Bessie Head: Subversive Identities in Exile*. Charlottesville: University Press of Virginia, 1996. A feminist account of Head, dealing with powerlessness and marginality in terms of actual exile. *The Collector of Treasures* forms the subject of her chapter "Women Talk: A Dialogue on Oppression."

Lionnet, Francoise. "Geographies of Pain: Captive Bodies and Violent Acts in the Fictions of Gayl Jones, Bessie Head, and Myriam Warner-Viegra." In *The Politics of (M)Othering: Womanhood, Identity, and Resistance*, edited by Obioma Nnaemeka. New York: Routledge, 1997. This deals specifically with *The Collector of Treasures and Other Botswana Village Tales* from a generally feminist point of view.

Mackenzie, C. "Short Fiction in the Making: The Case of Bessie Head." *English in Africa* 16, no. 1 (May, 1989). Mackenzie is one of the leading South African exponents of Bessie Head, having edited her *A Woman Alone*. He traces the interweaving of the making of *Serowe* and *The Collector of Treasures and Other Botswana Village Tales*.

Ola, Virginia Uzoma. *The Life and Works of Bessie Head*. Lewiston, N.Y.: The Edwin Mellen Press, 1994. One of the most useful introductions to Head's work. In seven chapters, Ola deals with the topics of good and evil, women's roles, nature, and her ability to tell stories. She concludes by comparing Head to other African women writers.

Olaussen, Maria. *Forceful Creation in Harsh Terrain: Place and Identity in Three Novels by Bessie Head*. New York: Peter Lang, 1997. An overview of three Head novels.

David Barratt

LAFCADIO HEARN

Born: Levkás, Ionian Islands, Greece; June 27, 1850
Died: Tokyo, Japan; September 26, 1904

PRINCIPAL SHORT FICTION

Stray Leaves from Strange Literature, 1884
Some Chinese Ghosts, 1887
Kotto: Being Japanese Curios, with Sundry Cobwebs, 1902
Kwaidan: Stories and Studies of Strange Things, 1904
The Romance of the Milky Way, 1905
Fantastics and Other Fancies, 1914

OTHER LITERARY FORMS

Lafcadio Hearn's travel sketches include *Two Years in the French West Indies*, *Glimpses of Unfamiliar Japan*, and *In Ghostly Japan* (1899). He is also remembered for his more comprehensive assessments of Japan, *Kokoro: Hints and Echoes of Japanese Inner Life* (1896), *Gleanings in Buddha-Fields* (1897), *Exotics and Retrospectives* (1898), and *Japan: An Attempt at Interpretation* (1904). His numerous other nonfiction works and his long fictions, *Chita: A Memory of Last Island* (1889) and *Youma: The Story of a West-Indian Slave* (1890), have been less influential.

ACHIEVEMENTS

The author of more than sixty books (if one includes posthumous collections and translations), Lafcadio Hearn was one of the most successful travel writers in history, known during his lifetime as Japan's principal interpreter to the Occident.

BIOGRAPHY

The child of Charles Hearn, a British surgeon-major, and Rosa Tessima, a Greek, Patricio Lafcadio Tessima Carlos Hearn spent his first two years on the island of Santa Maura and the remainder of his childhood in Ireland. In 1884, alienated and mentally ill, his mother abandoned him with a pious great-aunt, who fostered his fears of the supernatural. He was first educated by tutors, then at a church school in Normandy, and finally at Saint Cuthbert's College in England, which he left without receiving a degree, primarily for financial reasons but also because of the accidental loss of an eye.

In 1868, he went to America, where, after an impoverished stay in New York, he made a name for himself in Cincinnati as a reporter (1869-1877). During ten years in New Orleans, he rose to the position of literary editor of *The Times-Democrat*. The fruits of two trips to the West Indies, his travel sketches received a sufficient audience, so that his departure to Japan in 1890 was under the auspices of Harper and Brothers.

Entranced by Japan, Hearn married a Japanese woman (Setsu Koizumi), became a Japanese citizen, and accepted a professorship at the Imperial University of Tokyo. According to a 1903 letter first published in 1998, in his final years Hearn was lonely, alienated from most Westerners in Japan, who saw him as a religious heretic, and embittered by salary negotiations that caused him to leave his university position.

ANALYSIS

Lafcadio Hearn's apprenticeship was in the translation of French works. In translating these works, he learned how to make the exotic and the bizarre evocative in a Latinate style redolent of *fin-de-siècle* decadence. To achieve this mannered effect, he would often make extensive use of thesauri and etymological dictionaries, but he would also go to the opposite extreme of relying on his own unconscious. By the time *Some Chinese Ghosts* was written, his style was artificial enough that he was criticized for it and thereafter learned to moderate it somewhat, but his model was never Hemingwayesque simplicity. Rather, he admired the way William Butler Yeats retold Irish folklore in a dreamlike manner, echoing French symbolism. The brevity of Hearn's and Yeats's tales keeps their mannerisms from being as distracting as they would be at novel length.

Lafcadio Hearn (Library of Congress)

Hearn's Irish and French models did not mean that he had nothing in common with American short narratives. His morbidity earned for him the nickname "The Raven," because it was reminiscent of Edgar Allan Poe; Hearn's fascination with retelling old narratives was shared by other nineteenth century Americans, such as Nathaniel Hawthorne in his *Twice-Told Tales* (1837, expanded 1842). More clearly than Hawthorne, however, Hearn adopted the traditional role of the storyteller, perpetuating what might otherwise be lost. A lifelong outsider, Hearn accepted his role as spokesman for the ghostly and exotic—what modernism excluded from the Occident. His success depended on his representing alien cultures in a form that the skeptical West could accept; thus, as mediator, he placed himself in a position in which he risked suspicion from both hemispheres.

FANTASTICS AND OTHER FANCIES

Although this collection was not published until after Hearn's death, it contains his earliest, extant short fictions, most of which are in a genre he developed—brief, impressionistic sketches. Each presents a *Liebestod* (love/death) theme, softened as in a dream or in a story for children. A whimsically de-

scribed, brave, female cat in "The Little Red Kitten" adopts a kitten; they die looking for each other and are thrown by chance on the same ashes. In "The Ghostly Kiss," the narrator wishes to embrace the woman in front of him in a theater, even if he should die for it. When he succumbs to this temptation, she announces that the kiss has forged an eternal compact, and he finds himself alone in a graveyard. In "The Vision of the Dead Creole," despite serpents, bats, and vampires, a lover opens the grave of his beloved and in his dying vision, the two of them become strangely mingled with the Virgin Mary. Designed for newspaper consumption, these stories are obviously popular literature, some owing much to Poe. However, Hearn's stories are forged to create reverie, whereas Poe's comparable ones elicit terror. Hearn himself deprecated these apprenticeship pieces, yet his fusing of journalistic conciseness with what he had learned from translating French literature produced a unique style.

SOME CHINESE GHOSTS

In his preface, Hearn explains the shortness of the volume and, by implication, the brevity of the tales by quoting Sir Walter Scott's observation that, despite the inherent appeal of the supernatural, reading about it requires a stretching of credulity that soon becomes exhausting. Subsequent to J. R. R. Tolkien's *The Lord of the Rings* (1955), epic fantasies became common. Scott and Hearn, however, are speaking for a period when the fantastic was palatable only if presented as a refined version of the inherently short folktale; Jacob and Wilhelm Grimm's collection, for example, was simultaneously esteemed for its powerful portrayal of emotion and deprecated for its outgrown superstitions. The tone of Hearn's volume is set by the first story, "The Soul of the Great Bell." Because an astrologer forecasts that the bell's forging will require a human sacrifice, the daughter of a master craftsman throws herself into the molten metal, and the completed bell's sound is exceptional because of the influence of her ghost. Hearn expands and embellishes a French translation so that the details become vivid. He ends with the story being mentioned to toddlers, as if he were asking his readers themselves to return to childhood and suspend adult disbelief. The book ends with notes and a glossary of Chinese (particularly Buddhist) terms.

STRAY LEAVES FROM STRANGE LITERATURE

Similar to the previous volume but larger in scope, this is a retelling of traditional narratives from Egyptian, Polynesian, Finnish, Hindu, Buddhist, Islamic, and Jewish sources. That Buddhism is particularly noted may owe something to Hearn's having researched the subject for his previous book and to the popularity that Sir Edwin Arnold's 1879 life of the Buddha, *The Light of Asia*, enjoyed in America. He adapts the tales freely, sometimes condensing, sometimes combining elements from several stories into one. For instance, by using indexes to the Talmud, he builds a character sketch of a rabbi, amalgamating anecdotes scattered throughout that tome. What holds Hearn's book together is, paradoxically, its very diversity, its exoticism—a melange of bizarre behavior, quaint turns of phrase, ghosts, demons, and miracles. On a popular level, he is continuing the work of the American Transcendentalists, showing that neglected traditions, particularly those of Asia, still have cultural value. Even while treasuring the unfamiliar, he must excise whatever seems to him too strange, too divergent from Christian morals and sentiments. Certainly, like most of Hearn's Eastern fictions, these stories may be accused of what Edward Said calls "Orientalism": the imperialistic appropriation of the Orient to satisfy Occidental desires (thus betraying its reality). Such a charge suits these first two volumes better than the ones written after Hearn committed himself to the East.

KOTTO

Dedicated to Sir Edwin Arnold, this collection actually diverges significantly from the Orientalism of Arnold's *The Light of Asia* and Hearn's two previous collections of (mostly) Asian tales. In all three, the narrators are primarily modern believers in magic—a device with prejudicial implications that Easterners are perennially childlike and credulous. In contrast, the tone of *Kotto* is set by two stories in which Hearn speaks in his own voice and emphasizes that the narrative's origins are very old. "In a Cup of Tea" makes particularly significant use of this distancing frame. He begins by comparing the reading of interrupted

narratives to the act of stepping into an abyss and then gives as an example an old tale about someone who swallowed a soul (at which point, the original narrative breaks off). He adds that he could provide various endings but nothing that would please "an Occidental"; thus, he admits his difference from both the Occidental reader and Oriental author. Hearn is left in the vertiginous gulf between them, not a comfortable position but an honest one, which does not try to appropriate East or West.

KWAIDAN

Adapted by Masaki Kobayashi into the classic film *Kwaidan* (1964) and used as a source for new No plays, Hearn's book has continued to appeal to the Japanese. Perhaps one reason for this is that after much modernization, they are themselves distanced from their own heritage, making them comparable to the Western readers Hearn addressed. He comments on this situation at the book's close, where he imagines westernization as a wind stripping fairylike beauty from Japan. In the next to last story, a Japanese word reminds him of a Welsh one, and he recalls a time in his childhood when he sought fairy rings in the grass. Just as English modernism and imperialism pushed aside Celtic culture in Britain, the Occident had begun a cultural deracination in Japan. One of the most frequent themes in the stories of *Kwaidan* is making love to ghosts, for it represents the necessary and nourishing traditions of Japan, which have been reduced to that spectral condition.

OTHER MAJOR WORKS

LONG FICTION: *Chita: A Memory of Last Island*, 1889; *Youma: The Story of a West-Indian Slave*, 1890.

NONFICTION: *Historical Sketch Book and Guide to New Orleans and Environs*, 1885; *Two Years in the French West Indies*, 1890; *Glimpses of Unfamiliar Japan*, 1894; *Kokoro: Hints and Echoes of Japanese Inner Life*, 1896; *Gleanings in Buddha-Fields*, 1897; *Exotics and Retrospectives*, 1898; *In Ghostly Japan*, 1899; *Some Strange English Literary Figures of the Eighteenth and Nineteenth Centuries*, 1899; *Shadowings*, 1900; *Japan: An Attempt at Interpretation*, 1904.

BIBLIOGRAPHY

Bisland, Elizabeth. *The Life and Letters of Lafcadio Hearn.* 2 vols. Boston: Houghton Mifflin, 1906. An authorized biography.

Cott, Jonathan. *Wandering Ghost: The Odyssey of Lafcadio Hearn.* New York: Knopf, 1991. Particularly valuable for literary analysis.

Dawson, Carl. *Lafcadio Hearn and the Vision of Japan.* Baltimore: Johns Hopkins University Press, 1992. This book's strength is in its examination of Hearn's European background.

Hasegawa, Yoji. *A Walk in Kumamoto: The Life and Times of Setsu Koizumi, Lafcadio Hearn's Japanese Wife: Including a New Translation of Her Memoir "Reminiscences."* Folkestone, Kent: Global Oriental, 1997. As informant and translator, Setsu provided Hearn with many of sources for his tale adaptations. Her reminiscences of her husband thus contain valuable accounts of his short-story production.

Hirakawa, Sukehiro, ed. *Rediscovering Lafcadio Hearn: Japanese Legends Life and Culture.* Folkestone, Kent: Global Oriental, 1997. Although quite miscellaneous, this important collection includes treatment of Hearn's short fictions, such as the influence on one of them by Charles Baudelaire.

Murray, Paul. *A Fantastic Journey: The Life and Literature of Lafcadio Hearn.* Folkestone, Kent: Japan Library, 1993. Like a number of the new works on Hearn, this one emphasizes the Irish influences on Hearn.

Ronan, Sean G., ed. *Irish Writing on Lafcadio Hearn and Japan: Writer Journalist and Teacher.* Folkestone, Kent: Global Oriental, 1997. A former Irish ambassador to Japan, Ronan assembles tributes.

Yu, Beongcheon. *An Ape of Gods: The Art and Thought of Lafcadio Hearn.* Detroit: Wayne State University Press, 1964. It assesses the degree to which Hearn managed to intuit a universal "philosophy" based on a combination of European and Japanese attitudes.

James Whitlark

ROBERT A. HEINLEIN

Born: Butler, Missouri: July 7, 1907
Died: Carmel, California; May 8, 1988

PRINCIPAL SHORT FICTION

The Man Who Sold the Moon, 1950
Waldo and Magic, Inc., 1950
The Green Hills of Earth, 1951
Universe, 1951 (as *Orphans of the Sky*, 1963)
Revolt in 2100, 1953
Assignment in Eternity, 1953
The Menace from Earth, 1959
The Unpleasant Profession of Jonathan Hoag, 1959 (as *6 × H*, 1962)
The Worlds of Robert A. Heinlein, 1966
The Past Through Tomorrow, 1967
Destination Moon, 1979
Expanded Universe: The New Worlds of Robert A. Heinlein, 1980

OTHER LITERARY FORMS

Robert A. Heinlein was prolific in the science-fiction genre, producing many novels as well as several volumes of short stories. He also wrote a number of science-fiction novels for young adults and a handful of nonfiction pieces about science fiction or the future. In the 1950's he worked as an adviser and occasional script writer for the television program *Tom Corbett: Space Cadet,* and he also worked on the screenplays for two films, *Destination Moon* (pr. 1950) and *Project Moonbase* (pr. 1953).

ACHIEVEMENTS

With his first published story, "Lifeline," Robert A. Heinlein became a major influence on other science-fiction writers who have emulated his crisp "insider" style, his matter-of-fact acceptance of projected innovations, and his Social Darwinist expansionist philosophy. His name is synonymous with the "realist" school of science fiction in the public mind, and his work is reprinted repeatedly in science-fiction anthologies. Heinlein's stories are generally fast-moving and full of realistic detail, anticipating scientific and technological advances. He has been praised for his ability to create future societies in convincing detail and is considered one of the masters of the science-fiction genre. Heinlein received four Hugo Awards: in 1956 for *Double Star* (1956), in 1959 for *Starship Troopers* (1959), in 1961 for *Stranger in a Strange Land* (1961), and in 1966 for *The Moon Is a Harsh Mistress* (1966). In 1975 he was awarded the Grand Master Nebula Award for his contributions to science-fiction literature.

BIOGRAPHY

Robert Anson Heinlein was born and reared in Missouri and attended the University of Missouri before going to the United States Naval Academy at Annapolis. He served in the navy for five years until he contracted pulmonary tuberculosis and was forced to retire in 1934. After graduate school at the University of California at Los Angeles, he worked at a variety of jobs, including stints as an architect, a real estate agent, an owner of a silver mine in Colorado, and a civil engineer in a navy yard in Philadelphia during World War II. After the war, he devoted himself to writing full-time. He sold his first story in 1939 to *Astounding Science Fiction* and contributed other stories to various magazines over the years. In the 1960's, he became well known for the Hugo Award-winning novel *Stranger in a Strange Land* (1961), which became a kind of a religious guide for some hippies.

In 1966, he moved to California, where he lived for the rest of his life. In 1969, he was asked to be a guest commentator alongside Walter Cronkite on the Apollo 11 mission that put the first man on the Moon.

Heinlein was active at times in Democratic and Libertarian politics, and many of his books reflect his libertarian philosophy that the government should avoid meddling in people's lives. He was married twice, first to Leslyn McDonald and in 1948 to Virginia Doris Gerstenfeld, but had no children. He died in 1988 in Carmel, California, at the age of eighty.

ANALYSIS

With few exceptions, Robert A. Heinlein's best-known stories are from his "Future History" series, conceived in 1939-1941 as taking place in a consistent fictional universe over the next two to seven centuries. Ordered by fictional chronology in one 1967 volume, that series is less consistent in detail than in general outlines, leading up to and taking place in "The First Human Civilization," an ideal social arrangement allowing maximum liberty for the responsible individual. This ideal of human progress, not without setbacks, is also evident in tales and novels not explicitly set against the "Future History" setting, variations of which have formed the backgrounds of many subsequent writers' works as well.

As a storyteller, Heinlein seems less concerned with perfect craftsmanship than with what the story can point to; overt didacticism was a feature in his fiction long before the novels of his later career, in which it became a problem. What is the use, Heinlein seems to ask, of thinking about the future except as an arena for testing various strategies for living? Heinlein characters learn mostly from themselves, however, or older versions of themselves, in a deterministic cycle that leads to social progress and individual solipsism, or to the belief that nothing outside oneself really exists. Heinlein was a craftsman, however, whose plots are generally adequate and sometimes brilliant, whose style is authoritative and concise at best, whose concern with process did not blind him to human goals, and whose command of futuristic details was often overpowering.

"—WE ALSO WALK DOGS"

The best-crafted story from Heinlein's early, most influential period, "—We Also Walk Dogs," does not strictly fit the parameters of the "Future History." It does, however, illustrate the underlying theme of progress, by means of roughly equal parts of scientific and social innovation, fueled by the desire for personal gain, enabled by the freedom to pursue it. Begun for the purpose of walking dogs for a fee, General Services, Inc., the story's "corporate hero," has grown into a multimillion-dollar "credit" business with tens of thousands of employees near the turn of the twenty-first century. A "typical" job is shown at the start, when a wealthy dowager asks the company to help her greet her party guests by "stereo vision," while they speed her by interurban rocket to the side of her injured son. Doing this relatively simple service for her, they revel in their organizational abilities and overcharge her for her spoiled incompetence.

The sideshow she causes is only a prologue to the story's central action, which requires the company to do what is practically impossible. For an interplanetary conclave on Earth, the government wants all the aliens to be provided with approximations of their homeworld environments. The major problem is nullifying gravitation, which requires a new field theory and the practical harnessing of it within ninety days. Locating the one man, O'Neil, who could possibly do it is simple; convincing him to do so is not. Independent and reclusive, he can be bought only by an exquisite china bowl, the "Flower of Forgetfulness," the priceless property of the British Museum.

The ease with which the General Services team manipulates people to buy O'Neil off is mirrored by the ease with which he devises an antigravity effect, both accomplishments resulting from proper organization and application of resources. The story does not stop there, however; with an eye on the profitability of the "O'Neil effect" in "space navigation, colonization, recreation," General Services maneuvers both the naïve inventor and the slow-acting government into an "independent" corporation with Earth as its sole customer and O'Neil as figurehead. The physicist's reluctance finally is overcome when the General Services team request "visiting rights" to the bowl now in his possession.

The pieces dovetail perfectly; the craftsmanship is fine; and the manner of telling and the social attitudes conveyed are vintage Heinlein. The future setting is indicated not only by the existence of planetary governments, intelligent aliens, and powerful "service" occupations but also by abbreviated references to futuristic technology. Some of it is today outmoded ("voders," or wire-spooled vocal recorders), routine (punch-carded data banks), or environmentally unsound (interurban rocket transport). Still exotic are "sky cars," stereo-vision telephones, "pneumatic" lifts in place of elevators, monetary "credits," and "gravity shields." Introduced unobtrusively in action rather than digressive exposition, these developments, taken for granted, underline the alien feel of this future world, even as the story line turns on its essential similarity to our own. Fast action, crisp dialogue, and technical ingenuity save the day and serve humankind, thanks to the profit motive. The potential of General Services and new technology for harm is ignored, since these are all good people, competent in science and business and appreciative of good art.

"THE GREEN HILLS OF EARTH"

"The Green Hills of Earth," an often reprinted story, is one of Heinlein's most romantic. Its appeal lies presumably in the figure of its protagonist, Rhysling, "the Blind Singer of the Spaceways," whom it claims to portray, warts and all. Directly addressing his audience, the unnamed narrator alludes to our common knowledge of a history yet to come, sketching out an insider's view of Solar System colonization and changes in space brought about by progress.

Punctuating the tale with quotations from and allusions to his hero's published and unpublished repertoire, the narrator takes us from world to world with Rhysling in his dual career as jet-man and minstrel. Part 1 discusses how, as a scapegrace spaceman, he rescues a ship and loses his sight to runaway radioactivity. Part 2 is more complicated, explaining how his doggerel grows to poetry as ribaldry gives way to remembered beauty, the effect of which is poignant on those who can see the despoliation of that which he celebrates in song. Part 2 also ends with heroics, however, as the long-blind former jetman calls upon memory to save the ship taking him home to Earth at last. Rhysling does not live out the trip, but he does manage to record for posterity the definitive version of the title song.

The story is a model of artistic economy, sketching the outlines of technological and social development as well as of one man's lifetime as a crewman, bum, and artist, in a framework pretending to give an objective account when in fact it sentimentalizes its hero and romanticizes the course of history. Ever cognizant of the frontier motif in American consciousness, Heinlein extends the casual recklessness of the Old West and traditional life at sea into a sphere where it may not belong, given the physical and economic restraints of space travel.

"THE MENACE FROM EARTH"

The Moon is a favorite setting for Heinlein, never more tellingly than in "The Menace from Earth." Like his contemporary "juvenile" novels, it has a teenage protagonist, a girl more believable than her counterpart in *Podkayne of Mars* (1963). Contrary to the lurid connotations of the title, the "menace" is a platinum blonde entertainer, Ariel Brentwood, whose Luna City vacation precipitates an emotional crisis in the life of the narrator, Holly Jones.

Practical and scientifically educated at fifteen, Holly has no qualms about opting for a career as a spaceship designer in partnership with eighteen-year-old Jeff Hardesty. When Ariel monopolizes the time of Jeff as her guide, Holly does not recognize the emotional cause of her depression. Her neglected emotional education sneaks up on her, causing her first to endanger, then to save Ariel's life. Although she is wary about Ariel's advice on manipulating men, Holly does find there is more to Jeff and to herself than engineering specifications.

Although the plot is trite, Holly's style, replete with unexpected applications of engineering terms, keeps the clichés at a distance. Her lunar provincialism, even as she is exposing Ariel's terrestrial naïveté, lends charm and verisimilitude to the story. Since Holly finds it difficult to talk about her own emotions, her descriptions are mainly of the artifacts and processes which are the tale's real focal point.

Taking Ariel from the spaceport to her hotel, Holly also gives the reader a guided tour of the multileveled honeycomb of corridors and apartments, shops and labs, patterns and people that make up Luna City. Extended description does not slow the action, however, even when it shifts midway to the "Bat's Cave," where residents take advantage of low gravity and convection currents to experience arm-powered winged flight. Heinlein's feeling for process is exhibited in Holly's account, emotionally freighted with mythic references (from Icarus and Lucifer to Circe), of the practice, preparation, and instruction leading to the crucial rescue that gives Ariel a sprained ankle, Holly two broken arms, and the story a happy ending.

"'ALL YOU ZOMBIES'"

Alongside his social commentary and technological extrapolation, Heinlein also incorporated softer speculation, less anchored to the real world. Depending more on the artist's ability to make the impossible come true by means of words, many of these stories flirt with solipsism, the belief, perhaps endemic among writers, that nothing and no one outside oneself is real. This is particularly well illustrated in "'All You Zombies,'" a story of sex change and time travel. As with God and godlike aliens, introducing time travel into a story makes it impossible to say just *what* is "impossible"; what *will* happen is as real as what *has* happened, and either is subject to change at the traveler's option.

To make sure the right choices are made, Heinlein makes his narrator's existence depend on his manipulating events in the past so that boy meets girl, girl has baby, baby is displaced backward in time, and boy joins the Temporal Bureau. All four main characters are versions of the narrator, whose whole existence is a closed loop, himself or herself both creature and creator. Directing our attention away from the impossibility of creation out of nothing and the arbitrariness of revising the past, Heinlein focuses on the inevitability of these events and their effect on the narrator. Mixing dialogue with monologue, he preserves the simplest possible narrative sequence to make the story lucid and convincing. For all its machinelike precision, however, the story ends with a hint of terror, since the narrator, aware of his/her own origins, cannot quite believe that anyone else exists.

An ingenious puzzle whose internal consistency defies logical disproof, "'All You Zombies'" calls attention to its elaborate stage management and suggests the perpetual dilemma of Heinlein's protagonists. Supremely competent at what they do, they count others only as aids or obstacles. Subject to such authorial determinism, disguised as historical inevitability in the "Future History" stories, his heroes are projections of the author's will to master the world, which makes them enormously appealing to many readers.

Heinlein's methods for getting the future under control in a fictional setting were highly influential in science fiction. Almost always entertaining and thought provoking, he often told a superior story in the process.

OTHER MAJOR WORKS

LONG FICTION: *Rocket Ship Galileo*, 1947; *Beyond This Horizon*, 1948; *Space Cadet*, 1948; *Red Planet*, 1949; *Sixth Column*, 1949 (as *The Day After Tomorrow*, 1951); *Farmer in the Sky*, 1950; *Between Planets*, 1951; *The Puppet Masters*, 1951; *The Rolling Stones*, 1952; *Starman Jones*, 1953; *The Star Beast*, 1954; *Tunnel in the Sky*, 1955; *Double Star*, 1956; *Time for the Stars*, 1956; *Citizen of the Galaxy*, 1957; *The Door into Summer*, 1957; *Have Space Suit—Will Travel*, 1958; *Methuselah's Children*, 1958; *Starship Troopers*, 1959; *Stranger in a Strange Land*, 1961; *Glory Road*, 1963; *Podkayne of Mars: Her Life and Times*, 1963; *Farnham's Freehold*, 1964; *The Moon Is a Harsh Mistress*, 1966; *I Will Fear No Evil*, 1970; *Time Enough for Love*, 1973; *The Notebooks of Lazarus Long*, 1978; *The Number of the Beast*, 1980; *Friday*, 1982; *Job: A Comedy of Justice*, 1984; *The Cat Who Walks Through Walls*, 1985; *To Sail Beyond the Sunset*, 1987.

SCREENPLAYS: *Destination Moon*, 1950; *Project Moonbase*, 1953.

NONFICTION: *Of Worlds Beyond: The Science of Science-Fiction Writing*, 1947 (with others); *The Science Fiction Novel*, 1959 (with others).

MISCELLANEOUS: *The Best of Robert A. Heinlein, 1939-1959*, 1973.

BIBLIOGRAPHY

Aldiss, Brian, and David Wingrove. *Trillion Year Spree: The History of Science Fiction*. London: Victor Gollancz, 1986. Aldiss's general survey of the history of science fiction includes a discussion of several of Heinlein's works. His focus is on Heinlein's novels, but Aldiss's comments also provide useful insights into the short stories and place them in a historical perspective. Includes an index.

Franklin, H. Bruce. *Robert A. Heinlein: America as Science Fiction*. New York: Oxford University Press, 1980. Franklin has written an excellent, scholarly full-length study of Heinlein's work. He assesses Heinlein's important themes and discusses his libertarian politics. Franklin is an academic Marxist.

Hantke, Steffen. "Surgical Strikes and Prosthetic Warriors: The Soldier's Body in Contemporary Science Fiction." *Science-Fiction Studies* 25 (November, 1998): 495-509. Discusses how the technologically augmented body in the science fiction of Heinlein and others raises issues of what it means to be male or female, or even human, since the use of prosthetics to heal or strengthen the body is accompanied by the dissolution of the body.

Hull, Elizabeth Anne. "Heinlein, Robert A(nson)." In *Twentieth Century Science Fiction Writers*, edited by Curtis C. Smith. Chicago: St. James Press, 1986. Hull's entry on Heinlein's work provides an overview that focuses on his novels. Supplemented by a bibliography of Heinlein's works and a critical bibliography.

McGiveron, Rafeeq O. "Heinlein's Inhabited Solar System, 1940-1952." *Science-Fiction Studies* 23 (July, 1996): 245-252. Discusses Heinlein's population of a solar system in his early work by four different extraterrestrial civilizations, which serve the purpose of humbling the brash young human species.

Nicholls, Peter. "Robert A. Heinlein." In *Science Fiction Writers: Critical Studies of the Major Authors from the Early Nineteenth Century to the Present Day*, edited by E. F. Bleiler. New York: Charles Scribner's Sons, 1982. Nicholl's essay on Heinlein is quite long and an excellent introductory overview of Heinlein's work. His focus is on the novels, but his comments are useful in looking at the short stories as well. He too discusses Heinlein's politics. Contains a Heinlein bibliography and a critical bibliography.

Olander, Joseph D., and Martin Harry Greenberg, eds. *Robert A. Heinlein*. Edinburgh: Paul Harris, 1978. This work collects a number of essays on Heinlein by various writers. Includes discussions of sexuality, politics, and Social Darwinism in Heinlein's work, as well as an essay on Heinlein's "Future History" series. Complemented by a critical bibliography.

Slusser, George Edgar, and Daniele Chatelain. "Spacetime Geometries: Time Travel and the Modern Geometrical Narrative." *Science-Fiction Studies* 22 (July, 1995): 161-186. Compares time travel narratives with modernist geometrical narratives; claims that in both, plot is reduced to a game of logic and traditional story space/time is transposed into the realm of temporal paradox. Compares Jorge Luis Borges's "Death and the Compass" with Heinlein's "By His Bootstraps."

Williams, Donna Glee. "The Moons of Le Guin and Heinlein." *Science-Fiction Studies* 21 (July, 1994): 164-172. Compares Heinlein's *The Moon Is a Harsh Mistress* with Ursula K. Le Guin's *The Dispossessed*; in both cases, selective immigration, harsh new environment, and enforced isolation from the decaying parent culture dictate new social patterns.

David N. Samuelson,
updated by Karen M. Cleveland Marwick

MARK HELPRIN

Born: New York, New York; June 28, 1947

PRINCIPAL SHORT FICTION

A Dove of the East and Other Stories, 1975
Ellis Island and Other Stories, 1981
"Last Tea with the Armorers," 1995

OTHER LITERARY FORMS

Though Mark Helprin is best known as a writer of short fiction, the genre in which he has excelled, he is also the author of several substantial novels: *Refiner's Fire: The Life and Adventures of Marshall Pearl, a Foundling* (1977), *Winter's Tale* (1983), *A Soldier of the Great War* (1991), and *Memoir from Antproof Case* (1995). In 1989, Helprin switched genres to children's literature for the writing of *Swan Lake* (1989), with the story taken from the ballet of the same name. It was the first of a trilogy that later would include *A City in Winter: The Queen's Tale* (1996) and *The Veil of Snows* (1997). Two-time Caldecott winner Chris Van Allsburg provided the illustrations.

Helprin's stories and essays on politics and aesthetics have appeared in *The New Yorker, Atlantic Monthly, New Criterion, The New York Times*, and *The Wall Street Journal*. He also served as a speech writer for 1996 presidential candidate Bob Dole, authoring his Senate resignation speech in preparation for his candidacy.

ACHIEVEMENTS

Hailed as a gifted voice when his first book of short stories appeared, Mark Helprin confirmed such judgments with *Ellis Island and Other Stories*, a volume that won the National Jewish Book Award in 1982. That same year, the American Academy of Arts and Letters awarded Helprin its Prix de Rome. Among his other honors are a John Simon Guggenheim Memorial Foundation Fellowship and nominations for both the PEN/Faulkner Award and the American Book Award for Fiction. Helprin is one of the most accomplished of the younger generation of Jewish American writers, and his fiction self-consciously attempts to extend and deepen the significant contribution those writers have made to American literature since World War II.

BIOGRAPHY

Born in New York City, Mark Helprin grew up an only child in Ossining, New York. His mother, Eleanor Lynn, was a Broadway leading lady in the late 1930's; his father Morris Helprin was a graduate of Columbia University and worked as a reporter, a film reviewer, and an editor for *The New York Times* before entering the film industry. Eventually, the elder Helprin became president of Alexander Korda's London Films.

After graduating from high school in 1965, Helprin attended Harvard University, receiving a B.A. in English in 1969. He then entered the English doctoral program at Stanford University but left after one term and moved to Israel. He returned to Harvard University in 1970, and after finishing an M.A. in Middle Eastern studies in 1972, Helprin went back to Israel, where he was drafted into the Israeli army (he had become a dual citizen). He served from 1972 to 1973 in the army and in the air force. He has also served in the British Merchant Navy.

Helprin's main hobby is mountain-climbing, and he has climbed Mount Rainier, which is local to his home in Seattle, as well as Mount Etna. Aside from a short stint at Princeton University and a year of postgraduate work at Magdalen College, University of Oxford, in 1976-1977, Helprin concentrated mainly on the writing of fiction after his return to the United States. In 1986 Helprin moved from New York to Seattle, Washington. A reclusive man, Helprin seldom grants interviews or appears in public forums.

ANALYSIS

Mark Helprin is an author whose imaginative resources seem inexhaustible. His prose has economy, grace, and a rich yet accessible metaphorical texture, qualities that combine to make his stories eminently readable. Helprin writes of an astonishing range of times, places, and characters in stories that often move from realistic narrative to fable. Yet his fiction is unified by what William J. Scheick has called Helprin's "fascination with the human spirit's impulse for transcendence." Helprin himself once remarked, "I write only for one reason—and that's a religious one. Everything I write is keyed and can be

Mark Helprin (©Jerry Bauer)

understood as . . . devotional literature." At their best, his stories disclose a world of values that does not simply reflect a personal metaphysics but also links Helprin's work to both the Jewish religious tradition and to the Transcendentalist heritage of Ralph Waldo Emerson, Walt Whitman, and Henry David Thoreau.

Not surprisingly, those stories often turn on moments of revelation, on various epiphanies. The beauty of nature and the beauty of human action combine to awaken many of his characters to a world that transcends human making. Helprin has noted that "vision and redemption" are two of the principal elements in his writing. Throughout that fiction, he moves his readers toward an enlarged conception of both their own capacities and the wondrous transformations of the world they inhabit.

While Helprin's voice is essentially an affirmative one, his affirmations are usually earned—the product not simply of visionary moments but also of experiences of suffering, anguish, and loss. His characters are frequently presented as survivors, sustained by their memories of an earlier love or by their commitments to art. War is one of the most common events in these characters' lives. Like Stephen Crane and Ernest Hemingway, whose influence is often apparent in Helprin's style and subject matter, Helprin makes the experience of war one of his central metaphors.

The most important lessons his characters learn through their varied experiences are spiritual, moral, and emotional. One of the major attractions of Helprin's writing, in fact, is its moral energy and its author's willingness to make assertions of value. "Without sacrifice the world would be nothing," one story begins. In his visionary novel *Winter's Tale*, which projects a transfigured urban world, Helprin describes the four gates that lead to the just city: acceptance of responsibility, the desire to explore, devotion to beauty, and selfless love. These qualities might be said to define the central themes of Helprin's stories as well.

A DOVE OF THE EAST AND OTHER STORIES

Helprin's first book, *A Dove of the East and Other Stories*, contains twenty stories, many of them so brief that they depend almost entirely on the creation of a mood rather than on the development of plot, character, or theme. For the book's epigraph Helprin uses a line from Canto 2 of the *Inferno* from Dante's *La divina commedia* (c. 1320; *The Divine Comedy*, 1802; 3 vols.): *Amor mi mosse, che mi fa parlare* (love that has moved me causes me to speak), words that anticipate the book's concern with the redemptive power of love. Helprin has called Dante his single greatest influence, and many of Helprin's portraits of female characters suggest that they function—much as Beatrice did for Dante—to mediate the spiritual vision his male characters strive to attain.

In "Katrina, Katrin'," for example, two young clerks returning home from work are discussing women and marriage, when one of them suddenly launches into an account of his loss of Katrina, to whom he had been engaged some two or three years earlier. Biferman's tale of Katrina's illness and death

links this story with the Romantic tradition and its fascination with doomed love and with the strength of human fidelity despite the power of death. Moreover, through allusions to the biblical Song of Solomon, Helprin recalls an even more ancient tradition that conceived of love in terms of both profound passion and passionate commitment, a conception of love all too rare in an age of casual sexual liaisons and disposable spouses. "Katrina, Katrin'" leaves the reader not only with a sense of Biferman's tragic loss but also with a sense of love's shimmering possibilities.

An even greater emphasis on life's possibilities infuses "Katherine Comes to Yellow Sky," which Helprin plays off against a similarly titled story by Stephen Crane. In contrast to Crane's "The Bride Comes to Yellow Sky," in which the bride remains nameless and the story is told from the perspective of its male characters, Helprin focuses on Katherine, who arrives in Yellow Sky alone. Here Helprin employs two of his most recurrent symbols—light and a mountain landscape—to emphasize Katherine's potential for personal growth and transcendence. Katherine is a dreamer, in fact something of a visionary, who has come west after her parents' death to begin a new life. In Yellow Sky, with its "lantern mountains glowing gold in all directions, catching the future sun" and its peaks still gleaming after the sun has set, Katherine finds herself in the presence of "the source." Her journey's end is essentially a beginning. What Helprin says about Katherine's dreams might be said about his own approach to fiction. Katherine, he writes, "believed incessantly in what she imagined. . . . And strangely enough these substanceless dreams . . . gave her a strength, practicality, and understanding which many a substantial man would never have." For Helprin, the imagination projects and confirms life's promise.

Among the best of the briefer stories in *A Dove of the East and Other Stories* are "Ruin," "The Home Front," and "First Russian Summer." In both "Ruin" and "The Home Front," violence is a central, though understated, element. The latter story, set during the Civil War, is again reminiscent of Crane, as Helprin depicts a group of soldiers assigned to burial detail, awaiting a June battle. During an idyllic interlude, the men fraternize with a unit of nurses and luxuriate in the beauty of nature. The air of unreality the war has assumed is soon shattered, however, when the men are commanded to dig five enormous pits. In these mass graves, they later bury more than a thousand dead. The story concludes with a reference to "the high indifferent stars" that oversee the bloodshed below, an image that parallels the "high cold star on a winter's night" in Crane's "The Open Boat."

"The Home Front" is informed by Helprin's awareness of the potential for violence in human nature and the indifference with which the physical world often greets human need. Both humanity and nature have other dimensions, however, as additional stories in *A Dove of the East and Other Stories* suggest. In "First Russian Summer," for example, an eighty-year-old man named Levi recalls the words of his grandfather some seventy years earlier. Gazing upon forest and mountain, his grandfather had urged the boy to note "the shape of things and how astonishing they are" and had commended the trees, "not any painting or books or music," as "the finest thing on earth." The aged Levi has retained his grandfather's conviction that nature is a miracle which attests God's creative power. Yet he knows that he lives in "a world blind to the fact of its own creation." Levi's desire, like Helprin's, is to awaken humanity to the mystery that attends its being.

The most accomplished stories in this first collection are "A Jew of Persia" and the title story, which open and close the book. "A Jew of Persia" combines the fable with elements of literary realism, for it makes use of the supernatural as Nathaniel Hawthorne does in his tales and romances, and as Isaac Bashevis Singer does in his stories. Here, Helprin presents the reader with a protagonist who struggles with the Devil himself, a conflict that begins in the mountains of Persia and ends in a barbershop in Tel Aviv, where Najime slays his adversary.

Helprin endows Najime with qualities that are central to his own artistic vision. The Jew not only possesses courage and ingenuity but also demonstrates vital piety. Before his final confrontation with the Devil, Najime prays for the strength both to rec-

ognize evil and to resist it, and he finds himself endangered in Tel Aviv precisely because he had earlier thwarted an attempt to rob him of the wealth of his village—gold and silver which he had been conveying to the Persian capital to help other Jews emigrate to Israel. Najime resists the robbers not to preserve his own life or his own property but to fulfill his communal responsibilities. Similarly, in Tel Aviv he acts to free the residents of the Ha Tikva Quarter from the misfortunes that have overtaken them on his account. As Helprin presents him, Najime is a heroic figure: not only a survivor but also a savior. In addition to his courage and piety, his greatest weapons are "the strength of the past" and "the power of memory," qualities that Helprin stresses in story after story. "A Jew of Persia" establishes Helprin's relationship to traditional Jewish characters and concerns, including the dramatic conflict between good and evil. Najime's triumphant encounter with the Devil also sounds the note of optimism that predominates in this collection.

In "A Dove of the East," that optimism is again present, though somewhat muted. Like "A Jew of Persia," this story is set in Israel, where its protagonist, Leon Orlovsky, herds cattle on the Golan Heights. Originally from Paris, Leon has become a skilled horseman and an excellent scout. On the day the story opens, he discovers an injured dove that his horse accidentally trampled during a frenzied ride prompted by Leon's desire to exorcize his memories. In a long flashback, Helprin reveals Leon's history: his training as a chemist, his love for Ann in Paris, their courtship and marriage, and her disappearance during World War II. Though Leon is endangering the cattle by remaining with the dove, he refuses to abandon it, seeing in the dove an emblem of suffering humanity. Like the bird he nurses, Leon himself "is moved by quiet love," and his fidelity to the dove's need reflects his continuing commitment to Ann, with whom he still hopes to be reunited. Like the wartorn Nick Adams of "Big Two-Hearted River," Leon carefully ritualizes his daily activities, for such self-discipline helps to insulate him from the ravages of modern history. Though bereft of Ann and unable to save the injured dove, Leon nevertheless affirms love and compassion while awaiting "a day when his un-raveled life would again be whole."

ELLIS ISLAND AND OTHER STORIES

Ellis Island and Other Stories, published some six years after Helprin's first collection, shows a marked increase in artistic achievement. The book contains the title novella, in addition to ten other stories. Four of those ten deal with war or the threat of war, while two others present characters who must cope with the accidental deaths of their loved ones. In almost all these stories ("White Gardens" is a notable exception) both plot and characterization are much more fully developed than in many of the briefer mood pieces in *A Dove of the East and Other Stories*.

This second volume opens with one of Helprin's most visionary tales, "The Schreuderspitze," whose central character, a photographer named Wallich, has recently lost his wife and son in an automobile accident. To escape his grief, Wallich moves to a tiny Alpine village, where he takes up mountain climbing. "He was pulled so far over on one side by the death of his family," Helprin writes, "he was so bent and crippled by the pain of it, that he was going to Garmisch Partenkirchen to suffer a parallel ordeal through which he would balance what had befallen him."

To prepare for his ascent of the Schreuderspitze, Wallich begins a rigorous period of physical training and ascetic self-discipline that lasts nearly two years. The story culminates, however, not in Wallich's actual ascent of the mountain but in a climb undertaken in a series of dreams that extends over three nights. In this dream vision, Wallich mounts into the *Eiswelt*, the ice world, with an ever-increasing sense of mastery and control. There he achieves a state of mystical insight in which he recognizes "that there was life after death, that the dead rose into a mischievous world of pure light, that something most mysterious lay beyond the enfolding darkness, something wonderful." These discoveries Wallich associates with the quality of light in the *Eiswelt*, but he also links them to the artistry of Ludwig van Beethoven's symphonies, which he compares to "a ladder of mountains" leading into "a heaven of light and the dead." In its use of this imagery of mountains and light, "The

Schreuderspitze" resembles "Katherine Comes to Yellow Sky." Like Katherine, Wallich is nourished by his dreams, for they enable him to rise "above time, above the world" to a Blakean vision of eternity ("Starry wheels sat in fiery white coronas"). Restored by this experience, Wallich returns to Munich to re-enter an everyday world now imbued with the extraordinary.

"The Schreuderspitze," perhaps more than any other story in *Ellis Island and Other Stories*, bears the imprint of Helprin's religious concerns. Moreover, by grounding Wallich's vision in his encounter with the sublime in nature, Helprin places the story squarely in the Romantic tradition. Like his Transcendentalist predecessors, Helprin seeks to promote the reign of wonder as one means of recovering a sense of the sacred, an awareness of mystery.

"Letters from the *Samantha*," one of the most intriguing stories in *Ellis Island and Other Stories*, records this eruption of the mysterious in a minor rather than a major key. Influenced by Edgar Allan Poe, this story is told through a series of letters that recount events on board the *Samantha* after it rescues a large monkey adrift at sea. From the first, the creature undermines the ship's morale, and its presence sets many of the sailors against the vessel's master, one Samson Low, the author of the letters. Deciding that the ape must again be set adrift, Low finds himself strangling the creature when it resists him. Although Low informs his crew that the monkey is not a symbol and that no significance invests its coming and going, the power of Helprin's tale lies in just such suggestiveness. As the master's name indicates, Samson Low is himself a fallen creature who destroys what he cannot understand. Locked in battle, Low and the monkey mirror each other: "I gripped so hard that my own teeth were bared and I made sounds similar to his. He put his hands around my neck as if to strangle me back." This tale, which immediately follows "The Schreuderspitze," counterpoints the initial story. Low's movement, in contrast to Wallich's, is downward.

Several of the stories in *Ellis Island and Other Stories*—"Martin Bayer," "A Vermont Tale," "Tamar"—create or build upon a sense of nostalgia.

They are tales that record the loss of innocence, the vanishing of an ideal, while at the same time they affirm the value of that ideal. "A Vermont Tale," for example, recalls the month-long visit the narrator and his younger sister make to his grandparents' farm while his parents contemplate divorce. Though the month is January, with its "murderous ice," the narrator's prose celebrates nature's grandeur. The highlight of this visit is the grandfather's lengthy tale of a pair of Arctic loons. As the old man describes the birds, he humanizes them, so that the marital difficulties he identifies in their relationship seem to parallel those of the narrator's parents. In the grandfather's dramatic and moving story, the unfaithful male loon is ultimately reunited with its mate. Helprin's tale ends, however, not on this optimistic note but rather with the boy's recognition that his parents' marriage will not follow his grandfather's plot. Yet the ideal of fidelity remains an ideal that this story discovers, significantly, in nature itself.

Several of the other stories in Helprin's second collection of short fiction return to the concern for war and its effects that is so evident in his first collection. Two of those stories, moreover, appear to draw upon Helprin's own experiences in the Israeli army. The first of these, "North Light," although nominally a first-person narrative, is dominated by the "we" of the soldiers' shared perspective. In only five pages, the story explores the psychology of warfare as an army unit is held back from the battlefield. Helprin's analysis of the anger that this delay generates—an anger that will be the men's salvation in combat—is thoroughly convincing.

The other war story set in Israel, "A Room of Frail Dancers," focuses on a soldier named Rieser, whose brigade has just been demobilized. The title of this story becomes a metaphor for human existence itself, especially when Rieser images the dancers as "figures of imperfection in constant striving." The frailty of the dancers suggests the fragility of the order they establish, though Helprin's title also hints at humanity's perennial desire to achieve the grace and harmony associated with dance. Rieser's own frailty is evinced when he pronounces the dancers' movements "purposeless" and commits suicide.

Another story whose title functions metaphorically is "Palais de Justice." Whereas Rieser's struggle is largely internal, the conflict in this story involves a sculling contest between an attorney in his early sixties and a scornful young man. Using the wisdom of experience, the aging attorney unexpectedly triumphs over his adversary, whom he identifies with the barbarism and violence of the twentieth century, a century contemptuous of tradition and of the older generation that transmits its values, a theme Helprin also addresses in "First Russian Summer." The Palais de Justice is also "the place of the world," Helprin suggests, and he implies as well that every individual has a responsibility to affirm the humane values embodied in this story's protagonist.

The novella that gives Helprin's second collection its title is a comic mixture of realism and fantasy. Divided into four sections, *Ellis Island* recounts the first-person narrator's arrival in the United States and his initial experiences there. The plot is complicated and its events often implausible, but the novella's central thematic concern is the narrator's discovery of selfless love. As is often the case in Helprin's fiction, this discovery is made possible by the protagonist's encounter with a woman, in this case with two women: Elise, a striking Danish immigrant with whom he falls in love on Ellis Island, and Hava, who attempts to teach him the tailor's trade once he reaches New York City. When Elise, his "pillar of fire" (the title of the novella's first section), is refused entry into the United States because she has no one to support her, the narrator agrees to find a job as a tailor to secure her freedom.

After having undergone several amazing changes of identity on Ellis Island, the narrator continues his extraordinary adventures in New York City, adventures that display Helprin's imagination at its most whimsical. Once the narrator obtains a position as a tailor (a trade about which he knows nothing), he meets Hava. It is from Hava, whose name is the Hebrew word for Eve, that he learns the lesson of selflessness, for she works twice as hard as usual to complete his tailoring along with her own. The narrator moves in with Hava, is ironically given the certificate of employment he needs not for winning a job but for quitting it, and begins a career as a journalist. His very success, however, causes him to forget Elise. Only after he and Hava are married does he recall his pledge "to redeem Elise." Returning to Ellis Island he learns that she has died while aiding those aboard a typhus-ridden ship. Her death, he recognizes, demands of him "a life of careful amends."

In this novella, as elsewhere in his fiction, Helprin does not shy away from the didactic. Even in so whimsical a tale, he manifests his pervasive concern for health of heart and soul. "Hardened hearts and dead souls" are the price that people pay for ignoring the demands of justice, compassion, and self-sacrifice. "To give to another without reward," writes Helprin's narrator, "is the only way to compensate for our mortality, and perhaps the binding principle of this world."

"LAST TEA WITH THE ARMORERS"

In portraying his characters as survivors, Helprin views them as individuals capable of either being sustained or restrained by remembrances of their difficult past. In one of his later works, "Last Tea with the Armorers," he once again juxtaposes the beauty of nature and human action to construct an old-fashioned romance with modern-day overtones in which the reality of love is shown to overcome suffocating social influences and human self-perceptions. It is a simple story of a father, a night watchman in a language school, and his thirty-four-year-old daughter Annalise, a hospital microscopist, both of whom are holocaust survivors who settled into a small Israeli border community in 1947 following the war in Europe. For the next twenty-five years they spend their lives in a small set of rooms "now impossible to leave because of its perfect familiarity." Their highly structured lives take a turn when the father takes a liking to an Australian immigrant attending the language school where he works. Immediately, the father begins to sing the praises of the student to his daughter in the hope she might take a romantic interest in the fellow. The father's role of matchmaker is both simple and complicated—to create a bond between a man whose reason for not being married is simply that he never believed anyone would want to marry him and a woman who "already dismissed him, because she herself had been dismissed so many

times before." Helprin reinforces the powerful pull of self-perception by placing Annalise within the ranks of an Israeli army reserve unit and next to a clerical coworker Shoshanna who was "so beautiful that half of her life was closed to her, as she was always the object, and never the observer." The constant presence of Shoshanna and the attraction she represents to the soldiers serves to underscore Annalise's view of herself as a woman almost "invisible to men." It is a classic Helprin theme, that of individuals locked in self-perceptions that limit their capability to experience life's higher emotional callings. Only through her loving father's nudging is Annalise able to take the first step toward her own personal epiphany by initiating a simple dialogue with the Australian, setting in motion a series of events that best can be described as a reaffirmation of the traditional view that beauty is indeed in the eye of the beholder. Helprin's gift of imagery and his ability to identify the walls that separate individuals, families, and societies, while at the same time making them appear impenetrable, provides a basic framework for his stories. Within the walls reigns a conflux of chaotic experiences fully capable of debasing the human spirit yet never quite able to extinguish it. Invariably, one of those virtuous absolutes, most notably love, comes along at a critical juncture to rescue and preserve it. In Helprin's world the absolutes represent eternal truths which can be applied to any age or situation that threatens the human condition.

It is the pursuit of such binding principles that energizes Helprin's fiction. His stories record his character's encounters with or longing for those perennial absolutes: love, goodness, beauty, justice, God. They also celebrate what "Palais de Justice" calls "this intricate and marvelously fashioned world." Though at times too rarefied in plot and character, at their best these stories become windows on the infinite, while grounded in the particular. They thus confirm the claim Helprin makes on his readers in the epigraph to *Winter's Tale:* "I have been to another world, and come back. Listen to me."

OTHER MAJOR WORKS

LONG FICTION: *Refiner's Fire: The Life and Adven-*

tures of Marshall Pearl, a Foundling*, 1977; *Winter's Tale*, 1983; *A Soldier of the Great War*, 1991; *Memoir from Antproof Case*, 1995.

CHILDREN'S LITERATURE: *Swan Lake*, 1989; *A City in Winter: The Queen's Tale*, 1996; *The Veil of Snows*, 1997.

BIBLIOGRAPHY

Alexander, Paul. "Big Books, Tall Tales: His Novels Win Critical Acclaim and Hefty Advances, So Why Does Mark Helprin Make Up Stories About Himself?" *The New York Times Magazine*, April 28, 1991, 32-33, 65, 67, 69. This article probably comes closest to penetrating the mystique with which Helprin has surrounded himself. From stories that his mother was once a slave to others that stretch credulity even further, Helprin has fictionalized his life much as he has his books. Alexander calls Helprin a compulsive storyteller, although Helprin himself claims that he has now learned "to deal in facts—not dreams," especially when talking to journalists. Alexander provides biographical details and discussion of much of Helprin's work (including critical reaction to it) in addition to interview excerpts with Helprin.

Butterfield, Isabel. "On Mark Helprin." *Encounter* 72 (January, 1989): 48-52. Butterfield views Helprin's writing as following in the footsteps of American literary giants such as Mark Twain, William Faulkner, Nathanael West, William Gaddis, and Thomas Pynchon. The article focuses specifically on two stories from *Ellis Island and Other Stories:* "Letters from the *Samantha*" and "The Schreuderspitze." Useful for the interpretative information, although no references are included.

Feldman, Gayle. "Mark Helprin's Next Ten Years (and Next Six Books) with HBJ." *Publishers Weekly* 235 (June 9, 1989): 33-34. This piece, found in the "Trade News" section of *Publishers Weekly*, is illuminating for its insight on what Helprin wants out of his writing career. In negotiating a multimillion-dollar, long-term deal with Harcourt Brace Jovanovich, Helprin's real goal was stability—in fact, he could have actually received more money per book if he had negotiated each work individually, a fact that he readily acknowledges. Helprin likens this contract to the arrangement between the publisher Alfred A. Knopf and the writer Thomas Mann; in essence, Knopf said to Mann, "You write for me and I'll take care of you—that's all you have to do." Includes much firsthand (interview) information from Helprin but no outside references.

Green, Michelle. "Literary Acrobat." *People Weekly* 35 (June 24, 1991): 105-106. A brief biographical sketch that discusses Helprin's childhood, education, and service in the Israeli military.

Goodman, Matthew. "Who Says Which Are Our Greatest Books? The Politics of the Literary Canon." *Utne Reader* (May/June, 1991): 129-130. Discusses Helprin's introduction to *The Best American Short Stories*, in which he attacks revisionists for desecrating the cause of American literature; notes that, although Helprin's argument implies that only revisionists have a political agenda, traditionalists such as former Education Secretary William Bennett use political arguments to advance the cause of Western literature.

Shulevitz, Judith. "Research Kills a Book." *The New York Times Book Review*, May 5, 1991, 26. This brief article provides insight into Helprin's writing priorities. For example, Helprin believes that impersonal facts, or "research," kills the spirit of his writing, and therefore he does not like to place too much importance on historical accuracy. Helprin also states his belief in the idea that "politics should be the realm of reason and art should be the realm of passion."

John Lang, updated by Jo-Ellen Lipman Boon

ERNEST HEMINGWAY

Born: Oak Park, Illinois; July 21, 1899
Died: Ketchum, Idaho; July 2, 1961

PRINCIPAL SHORT FICTION

Three Stories and Ten Poems, 1923
In Our Time, 1924, 1925
Men Without Women, 1927
Winner Take Nothing, 1933
The Fifth Column and the First Forty-nine Stories, 1938
The Snows of Kilimanjaro and Other Stories, 1961
The Nick Adams Stories, 1972
The Complete Stories of Ernest Hemingway, 1987

OTHER LITERARY FORMS

During the four decades in which Ernest Hemingway worked at his craft, he published seven novels, a collection of fictional sketches, and two nonfiction accounts of his experiences in Spain and in Africa; he also edited a collection of war stories and produced a considerable number of magazine and newspaper articles. The latter have been collected in posthumous editions. Manuscripts of two unfinished novels, a series of personal reminiscences, and a longer version of a bullfighting chronicle have been edited and published posthumously as well. In 1981, Hemingway's first biographer, Carlos Baker, brought out an edition of the writer's correspondence.

ACHIEVEMENTS

After spending a decade in relative obscurity, Ernest Hemingway finally became a best-selling author with the appearance of *A Farewell to Arms* in 1929. His long association with the publishing firm Charles Scribner's Sons, where the legendary Max Perkins was his editor for more than two decades, assured him wide publicity and a large audience. His passion for high adventure and his escapades as a womanizer made him as famous for his lifestyle as for his literary accomplishments.

For Whom the Bell Tolls (1940) was selected to receive the Pulitzer Prize in 1940, but the award was vetoed. In 1952, the Pulitzer committee did give its annual prize to *The Old Man and the Sea* (1952). Two years later, Hemingway was awarded the Nobel Prize in Literature.

Even more significant than these personal awards has been the influence that Hemingway has exerted on American letters. His spare style has become a model for authors, especially short-story writers. Further, Hemingway has received significant critical attention, though not all of it laudatory. His tough, macho attitude toward life and his treatment of women have been the subjects of hostile reviews by feminist critics during the 1970's and 1980's.

BIOGRAPHY

Ernest Hemingway was born in Oak Park, Illinois, a Chicago suburb, in 1899, the second child of Clarence (Ed) and Grace Hemingway's six children. Growing up in a doctor's house, under the domination of a forceful mother, would provide Ernest grist for his literary mill in years to come. The family's frequent trips to northern Michigan would also figure in his development as a writer, providing him a locale for numerous stories and an appreciation for wild terrain.

After graduating from high school, Hemingway left Chicago to take a job on the Kansas City *Star*. Shortly after the United States entered World War I, he quit his job and went to Italy as a Red Cross volunteer. There, he was wounded while assisting Italian soldiers. He spent several weeks in a Milan hospital, where he met Agnes von Kurowsky, who would serve as a model for Catherine Barkeley in *A Farewell to Arms*.

Hemingway returned to the United States in 1919 and began writing stories—none of which sold. In 1920, he met Hadley Richardson, whom he married the following year. They returned to Europe late in 1921, and for the next decade, Hemingway spent his time in Paris or in other locales on the Continent, sharpening his skills as a short-story writer. Two collections of his work were published by literary

Ernest Hemingway, Nobel Laureate for Literature in 1954 (©The Nobel Foundation)

While in Spain, he spent most of his time with Martha Gellhorn, a young writer whom he had met the previous year in Florida. They were married in 1939 after Hemingway divorced Pauline. The Spanish Civil War furnished him materials for a major novel, *For Whom the Bell Tolls*, and a play, *The Fifth Column* (1938), which had a brief run on Broadway.

After the outbreak of World War II, Hemingway found a way to be with the American troops, joining his third wife as a war correspondent in Europe. His relationship with Martha deteriorated as the war progressed, and by 1945, they had agreed to divorce. Hemingway made Mary Welsh his fourth wife in 1946, after courting her for two years. The two spent Hemingway's remaining years together in Cuba or in various retreats in the United States and in Europe. During the years following World War II, Hemingway started several major projects, but few came to fruition. A notable exception was *The Old Man and the Sea*, which ran in *Life* magazine, sold millions in hardback, and became a motion picture. Growing bouts of depression became harder and harder to fight off, however, and in 1961, Hemingway finally committed suicide while staying at his second home, in Ketchum, Idaho.

presses. The many expatriates whom he met in Paris served as models for his first full-length novel, *The Sun Also Rises*, which appeared to favorable reviews in 1926. In the same year, he and Hadley separated, and Hemingway pursued his relationship with Pauline Pfeiffer, whom he married in 1927.

In 1928, Hemingway began the novel that would establish his reputation, *A Farewell to Arms*. Published in 1929, it sold quite well and freed the novelist to pursue other interests for several years. Though he had his residence in Key West, Florida, during the 1930's, he spent considerable time in Spain studying the art of bullfighting and took Pauline on a big-game safari in Africa. Out of these experiences came *Death in the Afternoon* (1932) and *The Green Hills of Africa* (1935); neither received the acclaim that the earlier novels had enjoyed.

In 1937, Hemingway managed to secure a position as a reporter to cover the Spanish Civil War.

ANALYSIS

Any study of Ernest Hemingway's short stories must begin with a discussion of style. Reacting against the overblown, rhetorical, and often bombastic narrative techniques of his predecessors, Hemingway spent considerable time as a young man working to perfect the spare form of narration, dialogue, and description that became the hallmark of his fiction. Nowhere does he achieve greater mastery of his medium than in his short stories. He expressed his belief and described his own method in a passage in *Death in the Afternoon:* "If a writer of prose knows enough about what he is writing about he may omit things that he knows and the reader, if the writer is writing truly enough, will have a feeling of those things as strongly as though the writer has stated them." Following this dictum, Hemingway constructed stories that sometimes make readers feel as if they are unseen auditors at some closet drama, or silent observers at intimate moments in the lives of characters struggling with important, although often private, issues.

"HILLS LIKE WHITE ELEPHANTS"

The technique is readily apparent in "Hills Like White Elephants." Set in Spain during the hot summer, the story contains little overt action. Hemingway sketches the background deftly in a single opening paragraph of half a dozen sentences, each of which provides vital information that establishes a physical setting and a symbolic backdrop for the tale. On one side of the little junction station, there are fertile fields; on the other, a barren landscape. Only three characters appear: a man identified as an American, a girl, and a woman who serves them in the little café at which they have stopped to wait for the train that passes through the unnamed town on the route from Barcelona to Madrid. The entire story consists of a single scene in which the man and the girl sit in the café, drink various alcoholic beverages, and converse.

Much of the dialogue seems little more than small talk, but there is an underlying sense of tension from the very first exchange between the man and the girl after they order their beer. The girl mentions that the hills in the distance "look like white elephants," to which her companion replies, "I've never seen one." She immediately responds, "No, you wouldn't have," and he fires back, "I might have. . . . Just because you say I wouldn't have doesn't prove anything." The harshness of their responses contrasts with the inconsequential nature of the subject of their discussion, suggesting that the relationship between them is somehow strained but that neither wishes to discuss openly the real issue over which they are at odds.

For nearly half the story, the two try to make conversation that will ease the tension, but their remarks serve only to heighten it. The man finally mentions, in an almost offhand way, the subject that is really on his mind: He wants the woman to have an abortion. "It's really an awfully simple operation," he tells her. "It's just to let the air in. . . . it's all perfectly natural." The woman, who sits silent through his pleading, finally replies, "Then what will we do afterward?" The man repeatedly assures her that things will be fine if she agrees only to terminate her pregnancy, since in

his view the baby will destroy the lifestyle to which they have become accustomed. The woman is wiser; she knows that their relationship has already been poisoned forever and that her pregnancy is not the sole cause. Theirs has been a peripatetic, rootless life, as barren in some ways as the countryside in which they now find themselves.

This summary of the story, like summaries of so many of Hemingway's stories, is inevitably an artificial construct that does not convey the sense of significance that readers get from discovering the larger issues lurking beneath the surface of the dialogue and description. This story is about choice, a vital choice for the woman, who must face the dilemma of either acquiescing to the man's wishes and undergoing what is for her more than a routine operation or risking the loss of a man for whom she has had some genuine feelings of love. Ultimately, either through his insistence or through her own realization that she must try to salvage their relationship even though she senses it will be futile to do so, she agrees to his demands. Her closing remark, on which the story ends, carries with it the strong note of cynicism that pervades the entire story: "I feel fine," she tells the man as they wait for the train's imminent arrival.

In addition to his distinctive style, Hemingway has made his mark in the literary world through the creation of a special kind of hero. The "Hemingway hero," as this figure has come to be known, is usually a man scarred by some traumatic experience—war, violence, a love affair gone bad. Often a physical maiming serves as a symbolic reminder of the psychological dysfunction that characterizes these figures. Despite having received a bad deal from the world, the Hemingway hero perseveres in his search for a good life, creating his own meaning out of the chaos of existence—the hallmark of existential heroes in both American and continental literature. These heroes do what is right without expecting reward, either in this life or in the next.

"IN ANOTHER COUNTRY"

Two fine examples of Hemingway heroes appear in the story "In Another Country." The tale is set in Italy during World War I. A young American officer is recuperating at an Italian hospital, where he mingles with Italian soldiers who have seen considerably more action than he has seen. The extent of their physical injuries mirrors the psychological scars that the war has inflicted on them. One of them, a major who had been a champion fencer before the war, diligently undergoes therapy on a machine designed to restore his withered hand. He is hard on the young American for entertaining thoughts that full recovery for any of them is possible, yet he insists that they all go through the motions—not only with their therapy but also with other activities as well. He demands that the young man learn Italian correctly, for example, arguing that one must follow the rules in life, even when they seem meaningless. Clearly bitter over his fate, he nevertheless keeps up his treatment, until an even more ironic blow strikes him: His young wife contracts pneumonia, and while he is going through the motions to recover the use of a hand damaged beyond restoration, she lies dying. His anger at the cruelty of her impending senseless death drives him to lash out at the institution of marriage; when she dies, however, he breaks down in tears and abandons his therapy. The young American, witness to the Italian's great love, comes to understand how nothing of value can last in this world. The lesson is bitter, but it is one that Hemingway heroes must learn if they are to go on living in a world where the only certainties are chance and chaos.

The young American in "In Another Country" is similar to the main figure in Hemingway's stories, Nick Adams. Seen often as an alter ego for the writer himself, Nick appears in almost twenty stories, and from them readers can piece together his history. A youth who spends time in Michigan and who has many of his ideals shattered by his participation in World War I, Nick develops the characteristics of the Hemingway hero: He becomes convinced of the world's essential callousness, yet he steels himself against its cruelties by observing the rituals that give his own life meaning. Hence, in "Big Two-Hearted River," Nick uses the activities associated with fishing as a kind of therapy to recover from the trauma of war.

"THE KILLERS"

One of the most anthologized of the Nick Adams stories is "The Killers." In this tale, Nick is a young man, still quite naïve and still given to romanticizing events in his life. Two Chicago gunmen arrive at the small diner where Nick is eating. They bully the waiter, bind and gag Nick and the cook, and wait impatiently for a boxer named Ole Andresen, a frequent patron of the diner, so that they can kill him. When Andresen fails to come to dinner, the gangsters finally leave. Knowing that they will seek out Andresen, Nick runs to the boxer's boarding house to warn him. Surprisingly, Andresen refuses to run away; he is content to wait for whatever fate brings him. Nick cannot understand how anyone can accept his lot with such resignation. The lesson for him— and for Hemingway's readers—is that there comes a point when it is impossible to keep moving on, to keep effecting changes by running away. All people must stand and meet the destiny allotted to them, no matter how bitter and unfair that may seem.

"SOLDIER'S HOME"

Like Nick Adams and the young American in "In Another Country," the hero of "Soldier's Home" has been scarred by his experience in World War I and has discovered upon his return to his hometown that he cannot find a sympathetic audience for his complaints. The people who did not go to war have already formed their opinions of what happened "over there" and have spent their patriotic energies feting the first groups of returning servicemen. Krebs, the protagonist of the tale, had remained in Germany with the occupation forces for a year beyond the declaration of the armistice. He is greeted with suspicion by his fellow townspeople; they cannot understand why he has waited so long to come home. When he tries to tell people what the war was actually like for him, he is rebuffed. He finds that only when he invents tales of heroism do people pay attention to him. Krebs has slipped into a continual state of ennui; no suggestion for action, either from family or friends, strikes him as worthwhile. In this sense, he fails to fulfill the role of typical Hemingway heroes, most of whom go on doggedly with their lives, all the while knowing that their efforts are doomed to failure. The overriding atmosphere of this story is one of pessimism, almost defeatism without hint of defiance—a rather unusual stance for Hemingway.

Two of Hemingway's greatest short stories are set in Africa, a land to which the author traveled on safari in 1933-1934. Often anthologized and frequently the subject of critical discussion, both "The Snows of Kilimanjaro" and "The Short Happy Life of Francis Macomber" detail relationships between weak men and strong women, displaying Hemingway's hostility toward females who seem to prey upon men, sapping their creativity and in some cases emasculating them.

"THE SNOWS OF KILIMANJARO"

"The Snows of Kilimanjaro" tells the story of a writer who is no longer able to practice his craft. Harry, the protagonist, has lost his ability to write well, having chosen to live a life of adventure and luxury. When the story opens, Harry is lying on a cot in the African plains, dying of the gangrene that he contracted by failing to take routine care of a scratch. Much of the story is given over to dialogue between Harry and his wife (presumably his second or third wife), a rich woman on whom he depends now for his livelihood; the tension in their marriage is seen by Harry at times as the cause of his inability to produce the kind of work that had once made him the darling of critics and the public. As Harry sees it, "He had destroyed his talent by not using it, by betrayals of himself and what he believed in." In his imagination, he writes fragments of the wonderful tales that he wishes to tell; these are presented in italic passages interspersed throughout the story.

Though the wife holds out hope that she will be able to get Harry back to a hospital, the writer knows that he is condemned to die of his wound—itself a trivial cut, but in this case fatal because of the circumstances in which Harry finds himself. The physical landscape mirrors Harry's failed aspirations. He is dying on the plains in sight of Africa's highest mountain; he can see the summit, but he knows he will never reach it. Similarly, the gangrenous wound and the resultant decay parallels the decay of the writer who fails to use his talents. Both the striving for some imaginary heights and the senseless destruction of the hero are highlighted in the short epigraph that begins the story. In it, Hemingway notes the presence of a leopard carcass, frozen near the summit of Kilimanjaro. "No one has explained," Hemingway writes,

"what the leopard was seeking at that altitude." No one can really explain, either, why men such as Harry strive to be good writers, nor can anyone explain why some succeed while others are blocked from achieving their goals.

Hemingway portrays the wife in this story with only a modicum of sympathy. She seems concerned about her husband, but only because she entertains some romantic notion that believing strongly in something will make it so; she is convinced that she can save her husband despite clear evidence that he is beyond hope. Harry calls her names and blames her for his failure, and though he realizes in the moments before he dies that she is not actually the cause of his failure—"when he went to her [to marry her] he was already over"—she never achieves a level of dignity that merits the reader's sympathy.

"THE SHORT HAPPY LIFE OF FRANCIS MACOMBER"

The story that critics often cite as Hemingway's finest is also set in Africa. "The Short Happy Life of Francis Macomber" details the relationship of Francis and Margot Macomber, wealthy Americans on an extended hunt with their professional guide, Robert Wilson. Told nonchronologically, the story reveals Francis's initial cowardice in the face of danger, his eventual triumph over his fear, and his untimely death at the moment when he is able to display his courage.

It would be hard to characterize Francis Macomber as a Hemingway hero. In fact, he is quite the opposite. He has money, but he possesses none of the qualities that Hemingway considers admirable in a man. Francis is dominated psychologically by his wife, and much of what he does is aimed at proving his manhood to her. Their African safari is but another effort on his part to display his worthiness for her continued affection. Unfortunately, Francis is a coward. The story opens with a scene that displays the strain that he is under, having just displayed his inability to stand up to danger. Through conversation among the three principal characters, the reader is able to infer that Francis had failed to complete a kill on a lion he had wounded. When he had gone into the bush to finish off the animal, the lion had charged, and Francis had run away; Wilson had been forced to kill the animal. Margot had observed his behavior, and she is now openly disdainful of her husband. She even plays up to Wilson right in front of Francis. As a final insult, after the Macombers retire to their tent for the evening, Margot slips out and goes to Wilson's tent to spend the night with him.

The following day, Francis has a chance to redeem himself. He and Wilson go out to hunt again; this time the quarry is buffalo. Margot remains in the vehicle once more, and the incident with the lion is repeated: Macomber wounds a bull, which slumps off deep into the brush, and he must go in after the beast to finish the job that he started. This time, when the bull charges, Francis holds his ground and fires at the animal, but the beast keeps on coming at him. Almost immediately, Margot fires from the car, but she hits her husband rather than the buffalo. Francis is killed instantly.

Margot Macomber is a classic Hemingway woman—the kind for which Hemingway has been criticized severely in the years since feminist critics have gained influence in American literary studies. She is physically attractive, though she is reaching the age at which her beauty is starting to fade. She is portrayed as being almost desperate to find some kind of security and is willing to use her sexual wiles to obtain it. She is cruel toward Francis when he shows himself a coward: She rejects physical contact with him and openly fawns over Wilson, though she taunts him too about his rather callous attitude toward killing. When Wilson mentions that hunting from a car (which he had done with the Macombers earlier) is a violation of the sport hunting laws and doing so could cost him his license, Margot leaps on the opportunity to suggest that she will use this information to blackmail him at some later time.

Unlike the Macombers, Wilson, Hemingway's white hunter, possesses several of the qualities that the author admires. He is good at his job. He understands people like Francis and Margot, and he has little respect for either of them because they are essentially fakes. He makes his living by taking advantage of the desires of people like them to dabble in life's more dangerous experiences. Having confronted dan-

ger almost every day, Wilson has become accustomed to living with his fears. He has even developed a certain callousness toward hunting and especially toward people who go on safaris. The behavior of the Macombers does not shock him. On the contrary, he is prepared for Margot's gesture of infidelity; he carries a double cot with him so he can accommodate wives like her who find their husbands despicable and the white hunter irresistible. Though Wilson is not admirable, in his self-awareness he achieves a certain esteem that is clearly missing in either of the Macombers.

The major critical question that dominates discussion of this story is: Did Margot kill her husband intentionally, or is Francis's death an accident? This is not idle speculation, for the answer at which one arrives determines the interpretation of the story's central theme. If Francis's death is indeed accidental, one can argue that Hemingway is making an ironic statement about the nature of self-fulfillment. At the moment that Francis achieves his greatest personal triumph, his life is ended. The fates simply destroy the possibility of his taking control of his life now that he has displayed himself capable of facing danger. Few details in the story, however, suggest that Francis should be considered a real hero. He may appear heroic at the instant of his death, but nothing he does before he faces the buffalo makes him worthy of emulation, and little that follows his death indicates that he has won new respect or lasting remembrance. Wilson does remind Margot that, had he lived, Francis would have had the courage to leave his wife. One must remember, though, that Wilson is the person who accuses Margot of murdering her husband, and he is searching to attach a motive to Margot's actions.

If one assumes that Margot shoots her husband intentionally, the ending of the story prompts a different interpretation. Francis is a type of the man struggling to break free of the bond that strong women have placed on weak men—and, by extension perhaps, on all men. This harsh antifeminist viewpoint is supported by Hemingway's portrayal of Margot as a classic femme fatale, valued for her beauty and grasping for security in a world where men ostensibly are dominant but where in reality women use their sexuality to gain and maintain control. Francis's killing of the buffalo is symbolic of his ability to destroy the barriers that are keeping him from breaking free of his wife; when she realizes what the event means, Margot takes immediate action to prevent her husband from carrying through on his triumph. Unfortunately, Hemingway never lets the reader see into the mind of Margot Macomber (though he does share the inner thoughts of Francis, Wilson, and even the lion), so it is impossible to settle on a definitive reading of the wife's motivation and hence of the story itself. As so often happens in real life, readers are left to draw conclusions for themselves from the events which they witness.

A key scene in "The Short Happy Life of Francis Macomber" may serve as a key to understanding Hemingway's philosophy of life. After Macomber has wounded the lion, he and Wilson have a lengthy discussion about the necessity of going after the animal to kill it. "Why not leave him there?" Macomber asks. "It isn't done," Wilson replies; "But," the professional hunter continues, "you don't have to have anything to do with it [the final kill]." Wilson seems to be speaking for Hemingway here. Once something is started, it must be completed. Society depends on that dictum. This is more profound than it may seem at first. As anyone who has read Hemingway's *The Green Hills of Africa* knows, the author sees the safari as a metaphor for life itself. The activities on the safari are self-generated: No one is forced to undertake anything on the hunt, but once one agrees to participate, one has an obligation to carry through according to the rules of the game. Wilson, who sees himself in terms of his profession, must finish the kill even if his dilettante employer refuses to do so. One's duty, Hemingway says in *Death in the Afternoon*, is what one decides to do. Men and women are free to choose their destiny, knowing their struggle will always end in death; doing well that which they choose to do is what makes people heroic.

OTHER MAJOR WORKS

LONG FICTION: *The Sun Also Rises*, 1926; *The Torrents of Spring*, 1926; *A Farewell to Arms*, 1929; *To Have and Have Not*, 1937; *For Whom the Bell Tolls*, 1940; *Across the River and into the Trees*, 1950; *The Old Man and the Sea*, 1952; *Islands in the Stream*, 1970; *The Garden of Eden*, 1986; *True at First Light*, 1999.

PLAYS: *Today Is Friday*, pb. 1926; *The Fifth Column*, pb. 1938.

POETRY: *Three Stories and Ten Poems*, 1923.

NONFICTION: *Death in the Afternoon*, 1932; *The Green Hills of Africa*, 1935; *A Moveable Feast*, 1964; *By-Line: Ernest Hemingway, Selected Articles and Dispatches of Four Decades*, 1967; *Ernest Hemingway: Selected Letters, 1917-1961*, 1981; *The Dangerous Summer*, 1985; *Dateline, Toronto: The Complete "Toronto Star" Dispatches, 1920-1924*, 1985.

BIBLIOGRAPHY

Benson, Jackson J., ed. *New Critical Approaches to the Short Stories of Ernest Hemingway*. Durham, N.C.: Duke University Press, 1990. Section 1 covers critical approaches to Hemingway's most important long fiction; section 2 concentrates on story techniques and themes; section 3 focuses on critical interpretations of the most important stories; section 4 provides an overview of Hemingway criticism; section 5 contains a comprehensive checklist of Hemingway short fiction criticism from 1975 to 1989.

Berman, Ron. "Vaudeville Philosophers: 'The Killers.'" *Twentieth Century Literature* 45 (Spring, 1999): 79-93. Discusses the influence of the modernist reevaluation of vaudeville on Ernest Hemingway's short story; notes that Hemingway's interest in vaudeville resulted from its pervasive presence in society and its acceptance in the intellectual world; argues that vaudeville scripts inspired Hemingway's interest in the juxtaposition of urban sophistication and rural idiocy.

Dubus, Andre. "A Hemingway Story." *The Kenyon Review*, n.s. 19 (Spring, 1997): 141-147. Dubus, a respected short-story writer himself, discusses Hemingway's "In Another Country." States that, whereas he once thought the story was about the futility of cures, since becoming disabled he has come to understand that it is about healing.

Flora, Joseph M. *Ernest Hemingway: A Study of the Short Fiction*. Boston: Twayne, 1989. An introduction to Hemingway's short fiction that focuses on the importance of reading the stories within the literary context Hemingway creates for them in the collections *In Our Time, Winner Take Nothing*, and *Men Without Women*. Argues that Hemingway devises an echo effect in which one story reflects another.

Hays, Peter L. *Ernest Hemingway*. New York: Continuum, 1990. A brief but instructive overview of Hemingway's life and his achievement as a writer. Offers brief critical summaries of the novels and many short stories. Contains a useful chronology.

Lamb, Robert Paul. "The Love Song of Harold Krebs: Form, Argument, and Meaning in Hemingway's 'Soldier's Home.'" *The Hemingway Review* 14 (Spring, 1995): 18-36. Claims that the story concerns both war trauma and a conflict between mother and son. Discusses the structure of the story; argues that by ignoring the story's form, one misses the manner of Hemingway's narrative argument and the considerable art that underlies it.

Leonard, John. "'A Man of the World' and 'A Clean, Well-Lighted Place': Hemingway's Unified View of Old Age." *The Hemingway Review* 13 (Spring, 1994): 62-73. Compares the two Hemingway stories in terms of the theme of age. Notes also the themes of aloneness, consolation of light, loss of sexuality and physical prowess, depression, violence, and the need for dignity.

Mellow, James R. *Hemingway: A Life Without Con-sequences*. Boston: Houghton Mifflin, 1992. A well-informed, sensitive handling of the life and work by a seasoned biographer.

Nolan, Charles J., Jr. "Hemingway's Complicated Enquiry in *Men Without Women*." *Studies in Short Fiction* 32 (Spring, 1995): 217-222. Examines the theme of homosexuality in "A Simple Enquiry" from Hemingway's *Men Without Women*. Argues that the characters in the story are enigmatic, revealing their complexity only after one has looked carefully at what they do and say.

Tetlow, Wendolyn E. *Hemingway's "In Our Time": Lyrical Dimensions*. Lewisburg, Pa.: Bucknell University Press, 1992. Argues that the collection is a "coherent, integral work" unified by such elements as the character Nick Adams, image patterns, symbols, and recurrent themes. Claims the book is analogous to a poetic sequence, a group of works that tend to interact as an organic whole. Discusses the lyrical elements in Hemingway's self-conscious juxtaposition of stories and interchapters.

Wagner-Martin, Linda, ed. *Hemingway: Seven Decades of Criticism*. East Lansing: Michigan State University Press, 1998. A collection of essays ranging from Gertrude Stein's 1923 review of Hemingway's stories to recent responses to *The Garden of Eden*. Includes essays on "Indian Camp," "Hills Like White Elephants," and *In Our Time* as self-begetting fiction.

Laurence W. Mazzeno

AMY HEMPEL

Born: Chicago, Illinois; December 14, 1951

PRINCIPAL SHORT FICTION

Reasons to Live, 1985
At the Gates of the Animal Kingdom, 1990
Tumble Home: A Novella and Short Stories, 1997

OTHER LITERARY FORMS

Amy Hempel was a contributing editor to *Vanity Fair* in 1985-1986 and was the editor of *Unleashed: Poems by Writers' Dogs* in 1995.

ACHIEVEMENTS

Amy Hempel's stories have appeared in leading American journals and have been widely anthologized in publications such as *The Best American Short Stories* and *The Best of the Missouri Review, 1978-1990* ("Today Will Be a Quiet Day" appeared in both), *The Pushcart Prize*, *The Norton Anthology of Short Fiction* (1978), and *New American Short Stories: The Writers Select Their Own Favorites* (1987).

BIOGRAPHY

Amy Hempel was born in Chicago, the eldest of three children (she has two younger brothers). Her family moved to Denver when she was in the third grade, and when she was in high school they moved to San Francisco. Her mother committed suicide when Hempel was eighteen, and at about the same time, Hempel was involved in two serious auto accidents. She spent a number of years in California and studied at both Whittier College and San Francisco State University, and she held a variety of jobs in her twenties. She attended the Bread Loaf Writers' Conference in Vermont for a while but started writing in earnest when she studied with author Gordon Lish in a fiction workshop at Columbia University in 1982. (Lish arranged for her first collection of stories to be published in 1985.) After settling in New York City with her husband, Hempel worked as an editor and contributor to several periodicals and taught and lec-

tured at a number of writing programs and workshops.

ANALYSIS

Amy Hempel is one of the original short-story writers upon whom the term "minimalist" was conferred but, as several critics have noted, "miniaturist" may be a more accurate term. Some of her stories are very short (including the one-sentence "Housewife," which appears in *Tumble Home*). Even in her longer stories the style is compressed and economical in the extreme, the action limited, and the characters constantly making cryptic, ironic comments to one another. In an interview, Hempel said:

> A lot of times what's not reported in your work is more important than what actually appears on the page. Frequently the emotional focus of the story is some underlying event that may not be described or even referred to in the story.

Her stories demonstrate this minimalist philosophy again and again. Hempel's stories often revolve around sadness, loss, and survival: Characters are in hospitals or in recovery or in trouble. However, even in these stories of crisis, Hempel is distinguished by her humor; characters, even children, always have clever things to say to one another, and their conversations are full of metaphors, parables, and symbolic lessons. Hempel's stories often feature dogs, other animals, and best girlfriends, thus often bordering on sentimentality. What saves the stories from falling into that easier literary condition, if anything, is their sardonic wit.

"IN THE CEMETERY WHERE AL JOLSON IS BURIED"

"In the Cemetery Where Al Jolson Is Buried" is probably Hempel's best-known work. Originally published in *Tri-Quarterly*, it has been reprinted in *The Editors' Choice: New American Stories* (1985) as well as in the popular *Norton Anthology of Short Fiction*, and it is quintessentially Hempel. The situation is dire: The narrator is visiting a friend in the hospital whom she has avoided visiting for two months; the friend is dying, and both women are in denial. Their conversation is filled with popular trivia, jokes, and funny stories—but many of these hint at the situation (like the narrator's fear of flying). After an earthquake, the narrator relates, a teacher got her sixth-grade students to shout, "*Bad* earth!" at the broken playground. She asks her friend, "Did you know when they taught the first chimp to talk, it lied?" In the end, the friend dies, although the narrator cannot express the thought and says euphemistically, "On the morning she was moved to the cemetery, the one where Al Jolson is buried." In the last image of the story, the narrator describes what happened when the signing chimp had a baby and it died: "her wrinkled hands moving with animal grace, forming again and again the words: Baby, come hug, Baby, come hug, fluent now in the language of grief." Only the narrator is inarticulate in that language, but the sublimation of her feelings makes the story a powerful emotional experience for readers. As is often the case in reading Amy Hempel, less is surely more.

"TODAY WILL BE A QUIET DAY"

This short story was also published in Hempel's first collection, *Reasons to Live*, and was later included in *The Best American Short Stories*, *The Pushcart Prize XI*, and *The Best of the Missouri Review: Fiction, 1978-1990*, the journal where it first appeared.

The story describes a father in San Francisco taking his son and daughter out for the day. The father drives north across the Golden Gate Bridge; the three eat lunch in Petaluma, and then the daughter drives them home by a different route. Little happens, in other words, and the story is filled with their conversation, joke-telling, and jousting—like the title, an inscription the son once imagined on his tombstone. The father has taken them out for the day because

> He wanted to know how they were, is all. Just—how were they. . . . You think you're safe, the father thought, but it's thinking you're invisible because you closed your eyes.

A friend of the boy has recently killed himself, readers learn, and the father wants to make sure his own

Amy Hempel (©Miriam Berkley)

kids are okay. The imagery of the story underlines the question of the difference between appearance and reality: The restaurant where they have lunch still looks like the gas station it originally was; the daughter discovers that the dog she thought was taken to live on a ranch has been put to sleep. At the end of the story, all three are in sleeping bags in the master bedroom of their house. Has the mother died recently? Are the parents divorced? Something hidden has given a tension to the simple events of the story. As they fall asleep, the father asks if they want the good news or bad news first and then says he lied, that there is no bad news. For a little while longer, perhaps, he is going to be able to protect his two teenagers from the dangers of the world, but this protective posture, as Hempel intimates to readers, is precarious.

"THE HARVEST"

"The Harvest" was originally published in *The Quarterly* and collected in *At the Gates of the Animal Kingdom*, Hempel's second collection of stories, and it is the best example of her metafictional style, a style which has occasionally appeared in her fiction.

The story is narrated by a young woman who has been in an auto accident: She and her date were headed for dinner in his car when they were hit, and in the accident the narrator almost lost her leg—or did she? In the second half of the story, she starts to unravel her narrative, and to describe the things she left out of the story, made up, or exaggerated—the marital status of the man, the seriousness of her injuries—and by the end, readers question what, if anything, took place. A psychiatrist tells the girl that victims of trauma often have difficulties distinguishing fiction from reality, and the insight underlines what Hempel is doing in "The Harvest": telling a story that becomes a narrative about making up a story—or about storytelling itself.

"THE MOST GIRL PART OF YOU"

This story was first published in *Vanity Fair* and was subsequently reprinted in *New American Short Stories* and in *At the Gates of the Animal Kingdom*, and it displays the basic Hempel style. A teenage narrator tells of her relationship with her friend, "Big Guy," whose mother hung herself eight days earlier. While the surface conversation is, as usual, full of jokes, clearly there is something deeper going on. Big Guy sews the girl's name into the skin of his hand, sucks ice to try to crack his teeth, and cuts the insect bites on her body with a razor. When Big Guy starts to make love to her after a dance, the girl claims she is "ready to start to truly be alive," but readers sense something else—his instability, her insecurity, and her obvious pity for his tragedy. The title of the story comes from a film she was forced to watch at school years earlier, *The Most Girl Part of You*, and her own mother has apparently encouraged her sexual initiation. To readers, that introduction to adult sexuality seems wrong. Like the iceberg Ernest Hemingway used to describe a story's hidden content, a large part of this story's cryptic meaning may lie beneath the tense fictional surface.

TUMBLE HOME: A NOVELLA AND SHORT STORIES

This collection contains seven stories and the title novella, an eighty-page letter the narrator is writing to an artist she may or may not have met, describing her life inside a mental hospital. Little happens, and readers learn more about the narrator's friends in the institution—Karen, Warren, and Chatty—than about the narrator's own life. There is hardly anything remarkable in their conversations except the wit and sardonic humor of Hempel's elliptical, first-person style. The other stories in the collection—several of them just a few pages long—reflect typical Hempel concerns. "Sportsman," probably the strongest story here, for example, describes the breakup of Jack and Alex. Jack drives east from California to stay with his friends Vicki and her husband, "the doctor," who live on Long Island. Vicki arranges for Jack to see Trina, a psychic, but then Alex calls from California to say that her mother has suffered a stroke. The story ends with Jack and Trina headed into New York City on a date, but the resolution of the relationships here is far from certain. As usual, appearances can be deceiving. The city looks pretty good, Jack comments; "Give it a minute," the psychic responds. Like Raymond Carver, Hempel often tells deceptively simple stories about contemporary characters in deeper trouble than they realize.

BIBLIOGRAPHY

Aldridge, John W. *Talents and Technicians: Literary Chic and the New Assembly-Line Fiction.* New York: Charles Scribner's Sons, 1992. In a chapter that considers Carver, Ann Beattie, and Frederick Barthelme, Aldridge accuses Hempel of "chronic minimalist constipation" and claims that behind her stories, several of which he analyzes, "there seems to be nothing but a chilly emotional void generated by either an incapacity to feel or a determination to express no feeling if one is there."

Blythe, Will, ed. *Why I Write: Thoughts on the Craft of Fiction.* Boston: Little, Brown, 1998. As one of twenty-six contributors to this collection, Hempel suggests some of the reasons that she creates her short fiction.

Hallett, Cynthia J. "Minimalism and the Short Story." *Studies in Short Fiction* 33 (1996): 487-495. In an essay that uses Hempel, Raymond Carver, and Ernest Hemingway as primary examples, Hallett attempts to lay down a theoretical foundation for minimalist fiction.

Hemple, Amy. Interview by Suzan Sherman. *BOMB*, Spring, 1997, 67-70. In this wide-ranging interview, Hempel talks about her background as a

writer, the origins of many of her stories, and her theories about reading and writing short fiction.

David Peck

O. HENRY
William Sydney Porter

Born: Greensboro, North Carolina; September 11, 1862
Died: New York, New York; June 5, 1910

OTHER LITERARY FORMS

While almost all of O. Henry's literary output is in the short-story form, he contributed verse and anecdotes to *Rolling Stone*, the humorous weekly magazine which he founded and edited in 1894. He also experimented with play writing, collaborating on a musical comedy based on "He Also Serves," with two other gentlemen; the play was staged once, in mid-1909. He also prepared a play based on "The World and the Door."

ACHIEVEMENTS

A widely read and published writer, O. Henry's short stories influenced not only the development of magazine fiction as a popular form but also the evolution of modern narrative. Indeed, even very diverse European and South American writers adopt the devices O. Henry perfected. This phenomenon is no accident: His short stories have been widely reprinted and translated, especially in Russia and France, and have been adapted for radio, stage, and television performances.

O. Henry was, however, especially popular in the United States. Extremely humorous, clever, and entertaining, he also managed to capture all that was recognizably and uniquely American—the variegated language, attitudes, spirit, geographical locations, social environments, and, most important, the inclination to identify with the downtrodden, the underdog. O. Henry's contribution to American letters was so obvious that a long-lived literary prize—the annual O. Henry Memorial Award for Prize Stories—was established in 1918 by the New York Society of Arts and Sciences.

BIOGRAPHY

Receiving little formal education, O. Henry, pseudonym of William Sydney Porter, found themes and plots for his short stories in his early jobs as pharmacist, ranch hand, draftsman, and bank teller. After being arrested for embezzlement in 1894, he fled to Honduras, where much of the material for *Cabbages and Kings* was acquired. He returned to Texas in 1897 to be with his dying wife and was convicted and sent to prison one year later. During his imprisonment he began to achieve national prominence for his stories and subsequently continued his writing career in New York. He signed contracts with the *Sunday World* and *Munsey's* for weekly stories drawn from his own experiences in the city. In 1907, he married his childhood sweetheart; three years later he died, fi-

O. Henry (Library of Congress)

nally succumbing to alcohol-induced cirrhosis of the liver and diabetes.

ANALYSIS

O. Henry's widely varied background provided not only plots for his tales but also characters drawn from all walks of life. Ham in "The Hiding of Black Chief," Caesar in "A Municipal Report," and Lizzie in "The Guilty Party" are only isolated examples of O. Henry's proficiency in creating a vivid sense of the texture of language for the reader by reproducing native dialect, be it Western, southern, or even "New Yorkese." This linguistic sensitivity contributes to O. Henry's versatility as a local colorist, as does his literary self-education. Echoes of Charles Dickens appear in "Elsie in New York," allusions to Greek and Roman mythology in "Hygeia at the Solito" and "The Reformation of Calliope," and parodic references to Arthur Conan Doyle in "The Adventure of Shamrock Jolnes."

O. Henry's popularity stems not only from his depiction of commonplace events and human responses but also from the surprise endings of his "well-made" plots. Talented as an ironist, he both comments upon

and sympathizes with the ranch hands, bank clerks, and shop girls whose sorrows and foibles he recreates. While much of his humor redounds from his likely use of puns and literary allusions, much might be called the humor of recognition—the rueful grin that occurs when a reader sees his or her own petty flaws mirrored in a character and predicts the inevitable downfall. The downfall, however, is often given the comic turn which made O. Henry famous. Kid Brady in "Vanity and Some Sables," for example, would rather go to jail for the theft of furs than tell his girlfriend that her "Russian sables" cost $21.50 in a bargain basement; Maida, the shop girl in "The Purple Dress" who "starves eight months to bring a purple dress and a holiday together," gives up her carefully garnered money to save a spendthrift friend from eviction. Molly sacrifices her furs—and her vanity—to prove Kid's honesty, and Maida is outdone by her tailor in generosity so that she gets both her dress and the marriageable head clerk: These are the twist endings that turn minor personal tragedies into comic triumphs.

"THE GIFT OF THE MAGI"

Possibly one of the most anthologized of O. Henry's stories is "The Gift of the Magi," a tale about the redeeming power of love. The protagonists, a couple named James and Della Young, struggle to live on a small salary. By Christmas Eve, Della's thrift has gained her only $1.87 for her husband's gift, which she had hoped would be "something fine and rare and sterling." She decides to sell one of the family "treasures"—her long, beautiful chestnut hair—to buy a platinum chain for her husband's prized possession, his watch. The first reversal is that he has bought her a set of pure tortoiseshell combs with which to adorn her long hair; the second, that he has sold his watch to do so.

In this story about the true spirit of gift-giving, both the family treasures and the protagonists take on Old Testamentary significance. Della's hair, the reader is told, puts the Queen of Sheba's wealth to shame; Jim's watch rivals all of Solomon's gold. Both unselfishly sacrifice their most precious possession for the other, thereby ushering in a new dispensation on Christmas Eve. Even more, these "two foolish children" acquire allegorical value in their act of giving insofar as they replicate the giving of the three wise men: "Of all who give and receive gifts, such as they are the wisest," O. Henry tells us: "They are the magi." In O. Henry's version, then, the "Gift of the Magi" turns out not to be gold, frankincense, or myrrh, not even hair-combs or a watch chain, but rather selfless love.

"PAST ONE AT ROONEY'S"

This love is what O. Henry posits as a cure for such social ills as the inevitable gang fights and prostitution he portrays in his New York stories. In "Past One at Rooney's," a tale introduced as a modern retelling of William Shakespeare's *Romeo and Juliet* (c. 1595-1596), a gangster, hiding from the police, falls in love with a prostitute. They lie about their occupations for the sake of the other: Eddie MacManus pretends to be the son of a Wall Street broker, while Fanny claims to be a factory girl. When a policeman recognizes MacManus, however, she gives up her new identity to prevent the arrest. Pulling her night's money out of her garter, she throws it at the policeman and announces that MacManus is her procurer. Once they are allowed to leave, MacManus confesses that he really is wanted by the police but intends to reform; and seeing that she still loves him, saves her (as she had "saved" him by sacrificing her hoped-for respectability) through marriage. Such stories of the "golden-hearted prostitute" are plentiful in the O. Henry canon and in themselves provide another clue to O. Henry's popularity—his emphasis on the remnant of human compassion in the most cynical of characters.

ROADS OF DESTINY

O. Henry is interested as well in what might be called the moment of choice: the decision to act, speak, or dress in a way which seems to determine the whole course of a life. The title story of the volume *Roads of Destiny*, a story allegorical in nature, suggests that the choice is not so much among different fates as among different versions of the same fate. Environment, in short, determines character, unless some modicum of self-sacrificing love as in "The Gift of the Magi" intervenes. More concretely, O. Henry saw poverty and exploitation as the twin evils

of urban life. Often cited for his sympathetic portrayal of the underpaid store clerk who struggles to survive, he is, as well, a biting critic of those who perpetuate an inhumane system to satisfy personal greed or lust. "An Unfinished Story," for example, castigates an aging lady-killer who is "a connoisseur in starvation. He could look at a shop-girl and tell you to an hour how long it had been since she had eaten anything more nourishing than marshmallows and tea." Piggy, with whom O. Henry himself ruefully identified, preyed on shop girls by offering them invitations to dinner. The working girl might thus keep her conscience and starve, or sell herself and eat: This was her condition as well as her choice.

"THE TRIMMED LAMP"

Where a choice need not be made through hunger alone is the middle moral ground on which many of O. Henry's stories take place. "The Trimmed Lamp," the titular story of another volume, suggests two opposing ways to deal with an exploitative economic system. Nancy, a country girl content to work for small wages in a department store, mimics not only the quietly elegant dress but also the manners of her wealthy customers, while her friend Lou, a highly paid laundry presser, spends most of her money on expensive, conspicuous clothing. Nancy exploits the system by educating herself in the best it has to offer; Lou works for the system and profits monetarily. In the long run Nancy's education teaches her the difference between purchased quality, such as the clothes Lou wears, and intrinsic quality, which cannot be bought. She refuses an offer of marriage from a millionaire because he is a liar: As O. Henry writes, "the dollar-mark grew blurred in her mind's eye, and shaped itself into . . . such words as 'truth' and 'honor' and now and then just 'kindness.'" Lou, in contrast, becomes the mistress of a wealthy man, leaving her quiet, serious fiancée to Nancy. The final vignette, a plainly clothed but vibrantly happy Nancy trying to comfort her sobbing, fashionably dressed friend, illustrates the divergence between their two philosophies. While neither can escape completely from the economic system, Nancy refuses to measure human worth in monetary terms; instead, she adopts the same set of values posited in "The Gift of the Magi."

"THE RANSOM OF RED CHIEF"

Many of the stories O. Henry writes are quite outside the moral framework that is suggested in "The Trimmed Lamp." Like others written about the "gentle grafters" which populated the nether side of his world, the story of "The Ransom of Red Chief" is of the "biter bit" variety. O. Henry's humorous focus on the problems that two kidnappers have with their charge—a redhaired version of Tom Sawyer with the same unflagging energy for mischief—deflects the moral question about the criminal action. Johnny enjoys his adventure; he styles himself Red Chief and tries to scalp one of his captors at daybreak, then rides him to the stockade to "rescue" settlers, feeds him oats, and worries him with questions about why holes are empty. His father's reply to a demand for ransom shows that he understands *who* is in captivity; he offers to take his son back for a sum of $250.

THE GENTLE GRAFTER

Similarly, the exploits recounted in *The Gentle Grafter* are modern tall tales, the heroes at times acquiring a mythological aura, at times appearing to be no different from the average man on the street. Grafting, in short, is an occupation which carries the same code of responsibilities as any legitimate business, as is made clear in "Shearing the Wolf." When two con men, Jeff Peters and Andy Tucker, discover that the leading hardware merchant in town intends to frustrate someone else's scheme to sell forged money, they agree that they cannot "stand still and see a man who has built up a business by his own efforts and brains and risk be robbed by an unscrupulous trickster." The twist is that the "trickster" is the merchant and the "businessman" is the forger.

In a number of respects, then, O. Henry contributed immeasurably to the development of the American short story. To be sure, many of his works are considered ephemeral today, primarily because they first appeared as magazine fiction; but a careful perusal reveals that behind the humor lies the mirror of the social reformer. In the characters and situations one notices common human problems of the beginning of the twentieth century; in the humor one notices the attempt to deal with apparently insurmount- able social problems. With his clever plot reversals, O. Henry does more than create a new story form; he keeps the reader alive to the connotations of language and aware that in a world dominated by an unfair economic system, human kindness may be the answer.

BIBLIOGRAPHY

Arnett, Ethel Stephens. *O. Henry from Polecat Creek.* Greensboro, N.C.: Piedmont Press, 1963. Described by Porter's cousin as a delightful and authentic story of O. Henry's boyhood and youth, this entertaining biography of the early years goes far in illuminating the character-shaping environment and experiences of both Porter and his fiction. Supplemented by illustrations, notes, a bibliography, and an index.

Current-Garcia, Eugene. *O. Henry: A Study of the Short Fiction.* New York: Twayne, 1993. An introduction to O. Henry's stories, largely drawn from Current-Garcia's earlier Twayne volume. Focuses on O. Henry's frequent themes, his romanticism, and his narrative techniques, such as his use of the tall-tale conventions. Includes critical excerpts from discussions of O. Henry by other critics.

Eichenbaum, Boris. *O. Henry and the Theory of the Short Story.* Translated by I. R. Titunik. Ann Arbor: University of Michigan, 1968. Originally published in Russia in 1925, this study reflects both the Russian interest in O. Henry as a serious writer and the brand of criticism known as Russian Formalism. Because Formalism was more concerned with technical achievement than thematic profundity, O. Henry, who was a technical master, is a perfect candidate for the exercise of this kind of analysis.

Evans, Walter. "'A Municipal Report': O. Henry and Postmodernism." *Tennessee Studies in Literature* 26 (1981): 101-116. Recognizing modern criticism's either trite interpretation or complete indifference to O. Henry's work, through the fiction of postmodernists like Vladimir Nabokov, John Barth, Robert Coover, and William Gass, Evans embarks on a radical revisioning of Porter's literary contributions.

Gallegly, Joseph. *From Alamo Plaza to Jack Harris's Saloon: O. Henry and the Southwest He Knew.* The Hague: Mouton, 1970. By investigating contemporary photographs, literature, popular pursuits, news items, and personalities—both real and fictional—from the contemporary scene of the author, Gallegly provides significant insight into the Southwestern stories.

Langford, Gerald. *Alias O. Henry: A Biography of William Sidney Porter.* New York: Macmillan, 1957. A well-documented biography that considers in detail Porter's marriages and the evidence used in his embezzlement trial. The foreword provides a brief but penetrating overview of O. Henry's critical reputation (including overseas) and his place within the context of American literature. Supplemented by illustrations, an appendix about *Rolling Stone*, notes, and an index.

Monteiro, George. "Hemingway, O. Henry, and the Surprise Ending." *Prairie Schooner* 47, no. 4 (1973-1974): 296-302. In rehabilitating O. Henry and his most famous technique, Monteiro makes comparisons with Hemingway's own—but very different—use of the same device. This significant difference Monteiro ascribes to Hemingway's essentially uneasy reception of Porter's work and to the two authors' divergent outlooks on life.

Pattee, Frederick Lewis. *The Development of the American Short Story.* New York: Harper and Brothers, 1923. Although this is an old study of the short story, the O. Henry chapter represents an influential negative criticism of his fiction.

Stuart, David. *O. Henry: A Biography of William Sydney Porter.* Chelsea, Mich.: Scarborough House, 1990. A good, updated volume on O. Henry. Includes bibliographical references and an index.

Patricia Marks,
updated by Terri Frongia

HERMANN HESSE

Born: Calw, Germany; July 2, 1877
Died: Montagnola, Switzerland; August 9, 1962

PRINCIPAL SHORT FICTION

Eine Stunde hinter Mitternacht, 1889
Hinterlassene Schriften und Gedichte von Hermann Lauscher, 1901
Diesseits: Erzählungen, 1907
Nachbarn: Erzählungen, 1908
Umwege: Erzählungen, 1912
Aus Indien, 1913
Am Weg, 1915
Schön ist die Jugend, 1916
Märchen, 1919 (*Strange News from Another Star and Other Tales,* 1972)
Piktors Verwandlungen: Ein Märchen, 1925
Die Nürnberger Reise, 1927
Kleine Welt: Erzählungen, 1933

Stunden im Garten: Eine Idylle, 1936
Traumfährte: Neue Erzählungen und Märchen, 1945 (*The War Goes On,* 1971)
Späte Prosa, 1951
Beschwörungen, 1955
Gesammelte Schriften, 1957
Stories of Five Decades, 1972

OTHER LITERARY FORMS

Although Hermann Hesse is known primarily for his novels, he also wrote poems and essays on art, literature, and society as well as short stories. In addition, he wrote reviews and articles for numerous journals and newspapers and compiled critical editions of a wide variety of literary works.

ACHIEVEMENTS

Hermann Hesse's maiden novel *Peter Camenzind*

(1904; English translation, 1961) won the Bauernfeld Prize of Vienna in 1904, the first of myriad awards bestowed on the author in his lifetime. Interestingly, most of Germany's prestigious awards were not accorded to Hesse until after World War II, when he was near seventy. Other significant awards include the Goethe Prize and the Nobel Prize in Literature, both awarded in 1946. Hesse also contributed the so-called cult book *Demian* (1919; English translation, 1923), which took the German literary scene by storm when it was published, providing, as Hesse's biographer Joseph Mileck purports, "a veritable bible for German youth." This same novel produced a huge following in American colleges in the 1960's and 1970's, with its focus on the unintegrated hero as outsider and his accompanying quest for a self-identity, a matrix of personal values, and a means of facilitating moral and philosophic commitment.

Hermann Hesse, Nobel Laureate for Literature in 1946
(©The Nobel Foundation)

BIOGRAPHY

After attending various schools, including the Protestant church school at Maulbronn from which he fled, Hermann Hesse became an apprentice in a tower-clock factory in 1894; later he became an apprentice in the book trade. In 1904, he became a freelance writer and contributed to a number of journals and newspapers. From 1907 to 1912, he was coeditor of the journal *März* (March). In 1911, he traveled to Ceylon, Sumatra, and Malaya, although because of illness he did not actually visit India itself. In 1912, he moved to Switzerland. A nervous breakdown in 1916 led to psychotherapy sessions in 1916-1917 with Dr. J. B. Lang, a student of Carl Jung. In 1919, he moved to Montagnola in Swiss Ticino, where he lived for the rest of his life, and in the same year he began painting seriously. He was analyzed by Jung in 1921. Hesse's pacifism during World Wars I and II led to sharp criticism from his fellow compatriots. Hesse died in 1962.

ANALYSIS

Although they are not as well known as the novels, Hermann Hesse wrote many short stories; in fact, the short story was one of the two genres (the other was poetry) which preoccupied him all of his life. The stories show a variety of themes; the early ones tend to aestheticism and decadence. Those written in Hesse's middle years are realistic with touches of humor or irony, and the later ones are frequently magical or surreal. The themes of Hesse's short stories parallel those in his novels. As in other works by Hesse, the short stories emphasize inwardness and subjectivity and are often autobiographical. Many of the protagonists are outsiders who are alienated from the bleak reality of civilization and who try to find self-fulfillment. This inner quest for self-awareness and fulfillment, frequently unsuccessful, is a central theme in Hesse's stories.

"A MAN BY THE NAME OF ZIEGLER"

"A Man by the Name of Ziegler" foreshadows the surrealistic style of Hesse's later works and shows his predilection toward Eastern pantheism, even before his trip to the East. In this story, Hesse depicts modern civilization as empty. Ziegler, the protagonist, is representative of modern human beings: He is smug and self-satisfied; he exists rather than really lives. Ziegler is unaware of the emptiness of his own life. At the beginning of the story, Hesse describes Ziegler as one of those people whom one sees everyday yet never remembers because he has a "collective" face. Ziegler is neither stupid nor gifted; he likes money, pleasures, and dressing well and is always concerned about what other people think of him. He judges people only from the outside, by how they are dressed, and treats them accordingly. Ziegler respects money and science; he has no appreciation for beauty but values practical results alone. Because his father has died of cancer, he admires cancer research, hoping that a cure can be found so that he will not suffer the same fate. Hesse shows readers a mediocre, superficial person who is full of his own importance. Ziegler's life is not ruled by the promptings of his inner nature but rather by prohibitions and fear of punishment. He believes that he is an individual; in reality, Hesse explains, he is merely a specimen. Hesse describes him ironically as a "charming young fellow."

After arriving in a new town, Ziegler decides to go sightseeing. His choice of where to go is determined by money: The museum is free on a Sunday, and the zoo can be visited for a moderate fee on the same day. The museum bores him. While killing time there until lunch, he notices a display of medieval witchcraft which he dismisses contemptuously as childish nonsense. He nevertheless takes a pellet from the display, and when another visitor enters the room, he hurriedly hides it in his pocket. While waiting for lunch in a restaurant, he smells the pellet and then swallows it. After lunch he goes to the zoo.

To his surprise, the pellet has given him the power to understand what animals say. To his horror, he hears the contempt and disdain that the animals have for humans; to them Ziegler is no better than vermin, "an absurd and repulsive bug." The animals themselves are more noble than human beings. Ziegler is dejected and wrenched from his usual habits of thought in which he thinks of human beings (and himself in particular) as the pinnacle of creation. Ziegler now also looks at people through the eyes of animals and finds no dignity in them at all; he sees only a "degenerate, dissembling mob of bestial fops."

In despair, he throws away his formerly treasured fashionable gloves, shoes, and walking cane and sobs against the bars of the elk's cage. He is taken away to an insane asylum. The sudden realization that he is nothing drives him mad.

"WALTER KÖMPFF"

"Walter Kömpff," set in Gerbersau, a thinly disguised Calw, is a good example of Hesse's Swabian tales. In these stories, Hesse emphasizes realistic portrayals of people. The humor and irony with which he describes people's failings is reminiscent of the nineteenth century Swiss writer Gottfried Keller, particularly *The People of Seldwyla* (1856, 1874) tales. The story opens with the death of Walter's father, Hugo, whose dying wish is that Walter should carry on the family business. Against the wishes of his mother, Cornelia, Walter accedes to this request. In so doing he makes a fatal mistake, choosing a false way of life at odds with his real nature. Although Walter has certain traits of his father, he also has his mother's more sensitive soul. In him, maternal and paternal traits are unable to blend and remain in conflict with each other.

Walter's first position as an apprentice shows him the essential dishonesty of the merchants; he is taught how to shortchange the customer, and his conscience rebels, forcing him to leave the job. His second position with the pietist Leckle is more successful. Later, however, his guardian forces him to leave Leckle in order to travel and see something of the world. For Walter the struggle for money seems crude and cruel; it cannot satisfy the demands of his imagination, and he has to struggle constantly with himself not to run away. Unable to find meaning in life, he becomes melancholy and resigns. He does not remain true to his inner nature, which wants a life of freedom and fulfillment.

Eventually against his will he has to return home to take over the business, and he performs his duties diligently and efficiently. It becomes increasingly clear to his mother, however, that Walter is merely playing a role that has been forced upon him: His heart is not in the work, and he is unhappy, although lulled by routine. After his mother's death, Walter feels as if he were in a void. His soul longs for freedom and a balanced existence, but his mind is that of a merchant, and these aspects of his personality are at war. In his search for meaning, he turns to God, but the pietist meetings he attends disappoint him since the people he meets there lack spiritual integrity.

Eventually, completely alienated from society and from himself, he closes up his shop. By now his eccentricity, which his fellow merchants do not understand, has made him the laughingstock of the town. Walter realizes that he has misspent his life, but he lacks the energy to begin anew. Instead, he becomes increasingly introverted, helpless, and dispirited; he sinks deeper and deeper into a "morass of self-tormenting speculations." Even his belief in God has vanished. Walter feels that he has tested God, only to find that He is a myth. In a desperate attempt to force God to give proof of his existence, he blasphemes against him. Finally he hangs himself, unable to live life any longer as a lonely misfit, unable to live a life that has no meaning. At the end of the story, few of the townspeople understand Walter's fate, but, as Hesse says, few people understand how close they all are to the darkness that Walter experiences.

"THE POET"

"The Poet" deals with the theme of the artist and the divorce between art and life—a frequent theme in Hesse's works. The story also shows Hesse's interest in China. At the outset, Han Fook longs to be a great poet. He comes from comfortable circumstances and is engaged to be married. Han Fook attends a lantern festival and watches the festivities from the opposite bank, a lonely observer in the midst of merriment. Although he longs to participate in the festival, his much deeper longing is to observe and then to reproduce the experience in a perfect poem. Alone, he ponders the meaning of art and decides that it is to mirror the world in such a way that "in these mirror images he would possess the essence of the world, purified and made eternal." Art for him, as for Hesse, is thus a way of transcending the ephemerality of the world. In his musings on the nature of art, he is suddenly interrupted by the Master of the Perfect Word who invites him to join him at the source of the great river to perfect his art. After receiving his father's permission, Han leaves to join the Master.

After two years with the Master, Han returns home to see his family, but he watches from outside the house, suddenly aware of how incompatible life and art are. He sees that in the poet's dreams reside "a beauty and enchantment that one seeks in vain in the things of the real world." Time passes, and again Han yearns for his hometown; he feels a murderous hatred of the Master whom he blames for having, as he believes, destroyed his life. In his hatred, he attempts to murder him, but the Master reminds Han that he is there of his own free will. Many years pass and Hans's artistic talents grow until, one day, the Master disappears; Han is now Master in his own right. Han returns to his hometown but discovers that all the members of his family have died. A lantern festival is again taking place. Han plays the lute and finds that there is now no difference between the reflections and reality; art and life have merged into one. Despite the lonely years of renunciation for his art and despite the need as an artist always to be an observer rather than participant, Han Fook has followed his inner voice and is at peace with himself.

"AN EVENING WITH DR. FAUST"

"An Evening with Dr. Faust," one of Hesse's later stories, is a satirical treatment of modern culture. After a sumptuous dinner, Dr. Faust and his friend Dr. Eisenbart are sitting comfortably replete. Faust tells his friend that his famulus (servant) has invented a machine with which they can hear what is taking place in the same room in the future. The machine is brought in and turned on. At first they hear a wild, evil, diabolical howling which makes Dr. Eisenbart turn pale. Then come snatches of a speech in which there is talk of industrial progress and modern techniques, then a banal poem full of clichés. An eruption of strongly rhythmical music, jangling and languid by turns, follows, and then a mysterious couplet (an advertisement). When the demonstration is over, Faust and Eisenbart are perplexed. Dr. Eisenbart believes that future humanity has gone mad, while Faust believes that it is not all humanity but that perhaps there is an insane asylum on this spot in the future or else the people are drunk.

Clearly, Hesse is satirizing the radio here as a representative of mass culture. Unlike the music which Han Fook plays in "The Poet," which expresses happiness and wholeness, this music is discordant and chaotic. Hesse admired the music of the sixteenth, seventeenth, and eighteenth centuries, which he thought of as music of light and enlightenment. Music for Hesse was a means by which the individual could see into his soul and develop himself. The music in this story, however, is not symbolic of development but rather of anarchy and chaos, typical of the state of society, in Hesse's view. Not only music has declined but also poetry, as demonstrated by the jangling rhythm and nonsense character of the poem they hear. Although the depiction of Dr. Faust here is ironical—he is not a great, tragic figure searching for self-knowledge but rather a comfortable bon vivant—nevertheless Johann Wolfgang von Goethe's *Faust* (1808, 1832) and the whole Classical tradition of German literature which Hesse so admired is brought to mind. In comparison with this tradition, modern culture is found wanting.

As these stories show, Hesse's concern is with the inner life of his protagonists. Only Han Fook in these stories attains self-knowledge and is at peace with himself. Walter Kömpff struggles unsuccessfully to find his identity. In Hesse's view, it is better, however, to struggle and suffer unsuccessfully than to be complacent like Ziegler. Hesse emphasizes the need for people to grow constantly and develop; otherwise they stagnate and grow self-satisfied. Hesse's stories are essentially optimistic. Although he is pessimistic about the directions that modern society and culture are taking, he nevertheless believes in human's ability to transcend themselves and to overcome their limitations—a very Nietzschean view of human beings. Growth and becoming are important concepts for Hesse and the measure of success lies not only in reaching the goal but also in the intensity of the struggle, even if it fails.

OTHER MAJOR WORKS

LONG FICTION: *Peter Camenzind*, 1904 (English translation, 1961); *Unterm Rad*, 1906 (*The Prodigy*, 1957; also known as *Beneath the Wheel*, 1968); *Gertrud*, 1910 (*Gertrude and I*, 1915; also known as

Gertrude, 1955); *Rosshalde*, 1914 (English translation, 1970); *Knulp: Drei Geschichten aus dem Leben Knulps*, 1915 (*Knulp: Three Tales from the Life of Knulp*, 1971); *Demian*, 1919 (English translation, 1923); *Klingsors letzter Sommer*, 1920 (*Klingsor's Last Summer*, 1970; includes the three novellas *Klein und Wagner*, *Kinderseele*, and *Klingsors letzter Sommer*); *Siddhartha*, 1922 (English translation, 1951); *Der Steppenwolf*, 1927 (*Steppenwolf*, 1929); *Narziss und Goldmund*, 1930 (*Death and the Lover*, 1932; also known as *Narcissus and Goldmund*, 1968); *Die Morgenlandfahrt*, 1932 (*The Journey to the East*, 1956); *Das Glasperlenspiel: Versuch einer Lebensbeschreibung des Magister Ludi Josef Knecht samt Knechts hinterlassenen Schriften*, 1943 (*Magister Ludi*, 1949; also known as *The Glass Bead Game*, 1969).

POETRY: *Romantische Lieder*, 1899; *Unterwegs: Gedichte*, 1911; *Musik des Einsamen: Neue Gedichte*, 1915; *Gedichte des Malers*, 1920; *Ausgewählte Gedichte*, 1921; *Krisis*, 1928; *Trost der Nacht: Neue Gedichte*, 1929; *Vom Baum des Lebens*, 1934; *Neue Gedichte*, 1937; *Die Gedichte*, 1942; *Späte Gedichte*, 1946; *Poems*, 1970.

NONFICTION: *Boccaccio*, 1904; *Franz von Assisi*, 1904; *Zarathustras Wiederkehr: Ein Wort an die deutsche Jugend von einem Deutschen*, 1919; *Blick ins Chaos*, 1920 (*In Sight of Chaos*, 1923); *Betrachtungen*, 1928; *Kleine Betrachtungen*, 1941; *Krieg und Frieden: Betrachtungen zu Krieg und Politik seit dem Jahr 1914*, 1946, rev. ed. 1949 (*If the War Goes On . . . Reflections on War and Politics*, 1971); *Hermann Hesse: Essays*, 1970; *Autobiographical Writings*, 1972; *My Belief: Essays on Life and Art*, 1974; *Reflections*, 1974.

BIBLIOGRAPHY

Boulby, Mark. *Hermann Hesse: His Mind and Art*. Ithaca, N.Y.: Cornell University Press, 1967. An extensive examination of Hesse's novels from the perspective that there are definable, basic, and yet complex structural patterns revealed in a survey of all the longer works. Underlying the examination is the assertion that the pivotal point of Hesse's work is his universalization of a personal conflict in artistic from. Provides an in-depth analysis of each of the major novels, including the earlier *Peter Camenzind* and *Beneath the Wheel*.

Brink, Andrew. *Obsession and Culture: A Study of Sexual Obsession in Modern Fiction*. Madison, N.J.: Fairleigh Dickinson University Press, 1996. Examines sexual behavior in Hesse's works and others of the twentieth century.

Donovan, Josephine. *Gnosticism in Modern Literature: A Study of the Selected Works of Camus, Sartre, Hesse, and Kafka*. New York: Garland, 1990. A good study of Hesse's fiction that reveals gnosticism.

Field, George Wallis. *Hermann Hesse*. New York: Twayne, 1970. This work concentrates on the novels, integrating Hesse's themes with biographical concerns and outlining some of the historical and literary influences on the author, such as the tradition of the *Bildungsroman* (the novel of personal evolution).

Howard, Patricia J. "Hermann Hesse's 'Der Dichter': The Artist/Sage as Vessel Dissolving Paradox." *Comparative Literature Studies* 22 (1985): 110-119. Argues that "The Poet" foreshadows many of Hesse's later works, especially the idea of the artist performing a special and magical role in apprehending the unity of nature and spirit, art and science.

Lapham, Lewis H. "Magic Lanterns." *Harper's* 294 (May, 1997): 11-13. Argues that Hesse's novel *The Glass Bead Game*, published in 1943, anticipated the compression of the narrative voice into pithy poetic statement best rendered as metaphor. Hesse proposed a vast inventory of recombinant algorithms, each reduced to the form of a symbolic glass bead, as a means of expressing every noble or worthy thought produced in Western civilization.

Mileck, Joseph. *Hermann Hesse: Life and Art*. Berkeley: University of California Press, 1978. A comprehensive biography of Hesse. Traces and emphasizes the reflective aspects of Hesse's life and art while delineating the nature of his creative impetus and process. Mileck includes extensive data and background for Hesse's many *Novellen*, tales, fantasies, essays, and other genres. Includes a German/English index of Hesse's works.

Richards, David G. *Exploring the Divided Self: Hermann Hesse's "Steppenwolf" and Its Critics*. Columbia, S.C.: Camden House, 1996. An excellent study of the seminal novel. Includes bibliographical references and an index.

_____. *The Hero's Quest for the Self: An Archetypal Approach to Hesse's "Demian" and Other Novels*. Lanham, Md.: University Press of America, 1987. This modern analysis applies the theories of Carl Jung to Hesse's novels. Asserts that Hesse anticipated Jung and that his works serve as "poeticized" models of Jungian concepts. Explores issues central to the author, whose conflicts primarily deal with German dualism and the need for self-integration.

Rose, Ernst. *Faith from the Abyss: Hermann Hesse's Way from Romanticism to Modernity*. New York: New York University Press, 1965. Takes a biographical approach to Hesse's works, contending that many of them "read almost like a spiritual autobiography" and that they illustrate "the reality of an existential problem" raised by Hesse in his artistic response to Romanticism. This problem—the nature of reality—emphasizes Hesse's concern with a means by which to resolve polarities into a coherent worldview.

Tusken, Lewis W. *Understanding Hermann Hesse: The Man, His Myth, His Metaphor*. Columbia: University of South Carolina Press, 1998. Tusken examines Hesse's major novels.

Ziolkowski, Theodore. *Hermann Hesse*. New York: Columbia University Press, 1966. A forty-eight page pamphlet-sized volume that provides a lucid and general overview of the author, his works, and his basic themes. Examines Hesse's split heroes tormented by chronic dualism, the dialectical rhythm of their internal action, and the nature of Hesse's prose that depicts people's basic dilemma.

Ziolkowski, Theodore, ed. *Hesse: A Collection of Critical Essays*. Englewood Cliffs, N.J.: Prentice-Hall, 1973. The introduction to this volume discusses the phenomenon of "Hessomania," the cultlike response to Hesse's works, and the crossing-over of Hesse's icons to the popular culture.

Provides an overview of the critical reactions to Hesse's works while outlining major reasons for their popularity. Includes ten essays by renowned writers such as Martin Buber and Thomas Mann.

Jennifer Michaels
updated by Sherry Morton-Mollo

PATRICIA HIGHSMITH

Born: Fort Worth, Texas; January 19, 1921
Died: Locarno, Switzerland; February 4, 1995

PRINCIPAL SHORT FICTION

The Snail-Watcher and Other Stories, 1970 (also known as *Eleven*)
Kleine Geschichten für Weiberfeinde, 1974 (*Little Tales of Misogyny*, 1977)
The Animal-Lover's Book of Beastly Murder, 1975
Slowly Slowly in the Wind, 1979
The Black House, 1981
Mermaids on the Golf Course and Other Stories, 1985
Tales of Natural and Unnatural Catastrophes, 1987

OTHER LITERARY FORMS

Patricia Highsmith is best known for her highly original psychological studies of the criminal mind, particularly in the Ripley mystery series. She coauthored a children's book and wrote material for television programs, including *Alfred Hitchcock Presents*. A number of her novels were made into films, including the 1951 Alfred Hitchcock production of *Strangers on a Train* (1950) and another version, produced in 1969, entitled *Once You Kiss a Stranger* (1969); *The Talented Mr. Ripley* (1955), produced by Times Film in 1961 as *Purple Noon* and also filmed by Anthony Minghella in 1999; *The Blunderer* (1954) as *Le Meurtrier* (1963) and *Enough Rope* (1966); *This Sweet Sickness* (1960) as the French film *Tell Her That I Love Her* (1977); and *Ripley's Game* (1974) as *The American Friend* (1978). In the 1990's she published the novels *Ripley Under Water* (1991) and *Small g: A Summer Idyll* (1995).

ACHIEVEMENTS

Patricia Highsmith won high critical and commercial acclaim in England, France, Germany, and eventually her native country. A member of the Detection Club, she received both the Edgar Allan Poe Scroll of the Mystery Writers of America and the Grand Prix de Littérature Policière award in 1957, for *The Talented Mr. Ripley*. In 1964, she received the Crime Writers Association of England Silver Dagger Award for the best foreign crime novel of the year, *The Two Faces of January* (1964). She was made an Officier de l'Ordre des Arts et des Lettres in 1990.

BIOGRAPHY

Born on January 19, 1921, the daughter of Jay Bernard Plangman and Mary (Coates) Plangman Highsmith, Mary Patricia Highsmith was reared by her grandmother for the first six years of her life. Her parents (both commercial artists) had separated over her mother's relationship with Stanley Highsmith. When her mother remarried, Highsmith rejoined her in New York City, a time she recalled as "hell" because of constant conflicts and arguments.

Highsmith began writing at the age of seventeen. She was the editor of the Julia Richman High School newspaper and received a B.A. from Barnard College in 1942. For a brief interval after graduation she made her living writing scenarios for comic books. Her first story, "The Heroine," was published in *Harper's Bazaar* in 1945 and selected for inclusion in the collection *O. Henry Prize Stories of 1946*. With the help of writer Truman Capote, she was admitted into the Yaddo artists' colony in 1948, where she completed *Strangers on a Train*. The novel, her third written but first published, did not see print until two years later, but the 1951 film adaptation by Alfred Hitchcock and

Patricia Highsmith (Archive Photos)

the subsequent sale of its stage rights helped launch her career.

Highsmith traveled extensively in the United States, Mexico, and Europe in 1940's and 1950's, before moving to England in 1963. She lived a solitary life in France from 1967 to 1982, then in Switzerland, where she died in 1995 from a combination of lung cancer and aplastic anemia. She never married, and she left a bequest valued at $3 million to Yaddo.

ANALYSIS

Patricia Highsmith is certainly better known for her novels, especially the Ripley series, than for her short stories. Nevertheless, her work in the demanding shorter medium was diverse and of very high literary quality. She was praised by no less a master of the well-told tale than Graham Greene, who in his foreword to *The Snail-Watcher and Other Stories* calls her "a writer who has created a world of her own—a world claustrophobic and irrational which we enter each time with a sense of personal danger." Highsmith is not simply a teller of interesting stories

but also a master of the intellectually unsettling, a goad and a gadfly who clearly means to upset readers' smug comfort with the everyday world that they take for granted. Greene's word "danger" is precise: Highsmith in a sense threatens the reader with a world in which everything seems normal until a sudden off-kilter event puts all in doubt. Her stories focus on the abnormal psychology of seemingly conventional people, on bizarre natural and supranatural events, and on the animal world upsetting the "natural" superiority of humans.

Highsmith's contribution to the short-story genre has been in a number of very different areas. Her control of the very short, very mordant, and very elegant tale is complete and puts her in the ranks of the French masters of such forms. Not a word is wasted; not a sentence departs from the general train of thought. Her pieces about animals open readers' anthropocentric minds to other possibilities, just as the first-person (using "person" loosely) narration by animals allows readers to see their world afresh. Animal matters aside, Highsmith's territory is also human psychology, particularly the aberrant and the marginal. She is very skilled at tying the particular psychological quirk to what might be called the psychosocial, the point at which individuals affect the group around them and begin to suffer repercussions because of the complex of reactions of others.

THE SNAIL-WATCHER AND OTHER STORIES

The Snail-Watcher and Other Stories features some of Highsmith's sharpest psychological studies. The oft-reprinted title tale is one of several in which a character's neuroses and repressed emotions are reflected grotesquely in the behavior of animals. Peter Knoppert, a proper middle-aged broker with a secure if sexless marriage, develops a passion for keeping snails. The energy he devotes to breeding them as pets provides him with relaxation that has a beneficial effect on his performance at work. As his work becomes more challenging Knoppert neglects to keep an eye on the snails' reproduction, and they quickly overrun the study where he keeps them, setting up a spectacularly loathsome finale in which he is literally consumed by his hobby.

A similar fate befalls the protagonist of "The

Quest for *Blank Claveringi*." Egotistical biologist Avery Clavering is so zealous in his determination to discover and name for himself an appropriately gigantic species of snail reputed to inhabit a remote Pacific island that he fatally miscalculates their predatory behavior. Whereas both these stories reveal Highsmith's underappreciated talent for black comedy, others are deadly earnest in their use of human-animal relationships to explore aspects of failed human intimacy. In "The Terrapin," a young, friendless boy briefly makes a pet from a live turtle his mother has brought home for a stew. The mother's casual indifference toward the animal's fate—she throws it live into a pot of boiling water, then chops it apart—mirrors her domination and emotional brutalizing of her son. In "The Empty Birdhouse," a childless couple approaching middle age (common character types in Highsmith's work) go to increasingly greater extremes to exterminate an unidentifiable animal that has taken up residence in their house, which proves by its indestructibility to be a symbol for the couple's unhappiness and lack of fulfillment.

The Snail-Watcher and Other Stories also includes some of Highsmith's finest tales about obsessed, perhaps mentally disturbed individuals, conditions she describes with great precision. "When the Fleet Was in at Mobile" tells the story of Geraldine, a country girl from Alabama who is rescued from a Mobile brothel by a Louisiana farmer. When the farmer becomes abusive because of jealousy about her past, she sees no solution except murder, and the description of Geraldine's actions and attempted escape has a dreamlike quality suggestive of a tenuous grasp on reality. Only at the end of the story, however, do readers appreciate how unreliable a source of information Geraldine has been. Highsmith gives an unsentimental picture of the making of a prostitute out of a simple young woman and of her subsequent mental disarray, but in such a way that readers can feel only empathy, in spite of her murderous intentions.

Another fine portrait of a marginally competent young woman pushed over the edge is in "The Heroine." Lucille goes to work for the wealthy and happy Christiansen family as a nurse to the two children. Her pyromaniacal background—she likes to start fires with pieces of paper in ashtrays—is never revealed to the family, and Lucille's subsequent fanatical devotion to the Christiansen children requires, in her own simplistic terms, a heroic act of unselfish devotion. She therefore torches the house with gasoline, before charging in with the intention of saving the children. The story taps the very human fantasy of acting heroically before admiring loved ones but shows a diseased mind blurring the fantasy into reality in a way that can only make readers nervous about the quiet intense strangers who surround them.

"Another Bridge to Cross" focuses on Merrick, a successful businessman who has lost his wife and son in a car accident. Merrick travels to Italy to try to regain some purpose to his life but witnesses the suicide of a poverty-stricken Italian worker. He befriends a street urchin (a theme in Highsmith short stories) who then robs a woman in Merrick's hotel. Merrick next learns that the suicide's wife has killed their children and herself in grief. Like Herman Melville's "Bartleby the Scrivener" (1856) in a parallel that must be intentional, Merrick remains in a garden at his hotel paraphrasing one of Bartleby's lines ("I prefer not to"): "I prefer the garden." Highsmith's story, however, ends more naturalistically than Melville's, for when the hotel staff calls a doctor to examine Merrick, clearly meaning to have him removed and institutionalized, Merrick continues his journey, but no more relieved of his despair than when he arrived. Highsmith's version of "Bartleby" is "modern" in that it does not resolve in a neat literary fashion; Merrick must simply carry on, as usually happens in real life.

LITTLE TALES OF MISOGYNY

Little Tales of Misogyny is accurately named: The longest is nine pages, most are three or four pages, and all are about the downfall of women and girls. Highsmith does not see women as victims of men or even of other women but rather as—mostly—subject to willful obsessions and compulsions. Flirtatious sexuality ("The Coquette," "The Dancer," "The Victim"), an inexorable drive to procreate ("The Breeder"), a lazy desire to be taken care of by men ("The Invalid: Or, The Bed-Ridden," "The Mobile Bed-Object," "The Fully-Licensed Whore: Or, The Wife")—all familiar but potentially destructive responses by women to the roles they play in society—overcome the individual characters, dominating, controlling, and ultimately destroying the role-players themselves. These reactions include jealousy over imagined betrayal by lovers ("The Female Novelist"); over being the perfect little girl ("The Perfect Little Lady"), the perfect mother-in-law ("The Silent Mother-in-Law"), the perfect mother ("The Prude"), the perfect religionist ("The Evangelist"); or over simply being perfect. A few women in the stories are victims of their own beauty or of their own circumstances or of the equally driven men around them ("The Hand," "Oona, the Jolly Cave Woman"), but most choose their fate, if choice is even possible for people who are virtually humorous characters. The relationship of these women to men, their "meal-tickets," often arises as a theme, yet Highsmith clearly means only to observe, not to analyze causes. All the tales read like sardonic, modern allegories yet with no moral lesson intended beyond the mordant observation of the stubborn foolishness of (female) human nature. The effect has the oddness of medieval misogynist tracts told by a modernist sensibility: There is no comfort here for anyone.

THE ANIMAL-LOVER'S BOOK OF BEASTLY MURDER

The title of *The Animal-Lover's Book of Beastly Murder* puns on British tabloid headlines: Here the murder is *by* (and occasionally *of*) beasts. Each story covers the experience of a different animal, some in first-person narration. Highsmith's daring in attempting to show the world from inside the brain of elephant and cockroach, cat and camel is admirable for its high credibility and lack of sentimentality. While not all the stories are equally successful, some are among Highsmith's best.

"Chorus Girl's Absolutely Final Performance" contrasts the title's elephant character as a cheerful youngster working for a kind trainer and, thirty years later, as a grumpy oldster under a cruel elephant wrangler. The first-person narration captures a ponderous heaviness to Chorus Girl's thought and "language" that is highly persuasive. "Djemal's Revenge" follows a working camel in an Arab country as he is abused by his master and then as he gets even

with a violence most satisfying and quite in accord with his environment. "There I Was, Stuck with Busby" is about The Baron, a large old dog whose master dies, leaving him with an uncaring and nasty new owner. The Baron finally gets to live with Marion, his old master's adored girlfriend, but not until he takes things into his own hands, so to speak.

"In the Dead of Truffle Season" stars Samson the pig, whose greed for truffles overcomes the tenuous control that his master Emile has over him. Pigs are as unsentimental about farmers, readers learn, as farmers are about pigs, and Samson is quite happy to change his loyalties. "The Bravest Rat in Venice," one of the best stories in the book, manages to create sympathy even for a rat that gnaws off a baby's nose—no mean feat. The rat's-eye view of Venice is as precise and as visual as a motion-picture camera. "Engine Horse" traces the revenge of a horse whose pet kitten is carelessly killed by a loutish young man and whose act saves a decent old woman in the bargain. In the other stories, which feature chickens, monkeys, hamsters, and ferrets as their protagonists, Highsmith draws similarly perceptive and provocative parallels between animal and human experience.

SLOWLY SLOWLY IN THE WIND

Slowly Slowly in the Wind is hard to categorize. Some stories, notably the title story, continue Highsmith's examination of disturbed characters. Edward "Skip" Skipperton is a highly successful businessman who can barely keep his anger and aggression under control. When poor health puts him into semiretirement as a gentleman farmer, he turns his energy and his fury on a neighbor, losing his daughter, and ultimately his freedom, in the process. While Skipperton's revenge on his neighbor is spectacularly horrible, his motives and uncontrolled emotions are immediately recognizable as very human and thus distressingly familiar: Unable to tolerate the frustration of his wishes, Skipperton responds childishly with simple and overwhelming force. A less common phenomenon, though by no means rare in modern society, is handled in "Woodrow Wilson's Neck-Tie." Serial murderer Clive Wilkes kills to become known, to lift himself out of his banal and mediocre life. He has no emotion, handling his victims like effigies to be posed for comic effect. The result is chilling, evoking newspaper stories of real-life killers of similar coldness. The murderer in "The Baby Spoon" at least has an understandable, if twisted, motive: revenge on a manipulative former professor who has used him and embarrassed him.

Highsmith often writes about New York City, having grown up there, and two works in this collection are in what might be called her New York story mode. "The Network" traces a group of friends who help one another survive the competition and depredations of violence in the city. A young newcomer at first rejects the group's smothering attentions in order to assert his independence but soon changes his mind after a mugging and a robbery. In "Broken Glass," an octogenarian widower is mugged by a teenage thug but responds with unexpected violence that at least gives him the satisfaction of striking back. In the typical Highsmith New York story, there is an "us against them" theme in which a civilized protagonist attempts to ward off the barbarians who run unchecked in the city. Two anomalous stories in this collection are "One for the Islands," an allegory about death and the hereafter expressed in terms of a cruise ship and island destinations, and "Please Don't Shoot the Trees," a futuristic fantasy in which pollution-beset trees grow breastlike protuberances that shoot burning poison at passersby. Highsmith's territory includes the bizarre, the inexplicable, and the satiric, but the usual setting for the aberration is a highly realistic and normal world, not a milieu already topsy-turvy as in these two stories.

THE BLACK HOUSE

Highsmith's juxtapositions of human and animal behavior, most notable in the collections *The Snail-Watcher and Other Stories* and *The Animal-Lover's Book of Beastly Murder*, are a subtle means of addressing the bestial side of human nature. Animals are less in evidence in *The Black House*, but the book's eleven stories can be read as interpretations of a theme first articulated by Peter Knoppert, the ill-fated pet owner in "The Snail Watcher," who proclaims, "'You can't stop nature.'" Repeatedly in these tales, intelligent and respectable people find themselves in unusual situations that provoke them to

irrational, beastly behavior. "The Dream of the *Emma C*" tells of a fishing smack that rescues an exhausted young woman swimming in the waters two miles off the coast of Cape Cod. Immediately, the crew of six men, who hitherto have gotten along on the ship, begin squabbling among themselves. The men are attracted almost instinctively to the woman, and as each tries to ingratiate himself with her fights break out, leading to the accidental bludgeoning death of one by the story's end.

Sexuality and violence are similarly conjoined in the title story, about an abandoned house in a small working-class town in upstate New York. The house is reputedly haunted, and many of the older men in town boast of enjoying their first sexual conquests there. Timothy Porter, a young educated man, decides to explore the house and finds it completely empty, making it unlikely to have played a role in any of the tales told about it in the local bar. When Tim mentions this at the bar, the previously friendly patrons take it as a challenge to the personal and social mythology they have constructed about the house. Tim is called outside to fight and is beaten to death.

There is no brutality in "The Terrors of Basket-Weaving," only the disturbing expression of an inexplicable, seemingly innate talent. While scavenging on the beach one day, a sophisticated modern woman finds an old wicker basket with a hole in it and repairs it without thinking. She is so unnerved by her near-instinctive grasp of the primitive craft of basket-weaving that she can only reclaim peace of mind by destroying the basket.

Responsibility and guilt—feelings that separate the civilized from the savage—are constantly complicated and compromised in Highsmith's stories. In "Something the Cat Dragged In," a perfectly ordinary afternoon tea is interrupted when the house cat pulls a severed human hand through the cat door. The guests' immediate feelings of shock and disgust are mitigated when it is discovered the hand belonged to an unscrupulous man who was murdered and dismembered with just cause by a local farmer. The guests decide not to report the murder, concluding that any guilt over its concealment is the farmer's to feel.

In "Under a Dark Angel's Eye," a man discovers

that his family's insurance agent has swindled him out of money under the pretense that it went to the care of his mother in a nursing home. His mother actually died five years earlier, and the money was diverted to the care of the agent's dissolute son. Shortly afterward, the agent's son dies in a car wreck, and the agent and nursing-home manager who conspired with him commit suicide. The man interprets events as a working out of the biblical axiom "an eye for an eye" and assuages feelings of guilt he felt for his own vengeful thoughts by burning his copy of the Old Testament. In "Not One of Us," a clique of successful and fashionable people ostracize one of their own and, through devious acts of seeming friendship, drive him to suicide. At his funeral, when it is discovered that each member of the group did something secretly to ruin the man, the ringleader thinks, "Anyone might have said 'We killed him, you know' but no one did." Typical of Highsmith's characters, women express mild surprise but virtually no remorse at their personal capacity for evil.

MERMAIDS ON THE GOLF COURSE AND OTHER STORIES

Mermaids on the Golf Course and Other Stories, like *Slowly Slowly in the Wind*, is a set of disparate tales rather than a medley with coherent themes. "The Romantic" is a New York story about a young secretary who discovers that she would rather live a safe fantasy life of romance fiction and imaginary dates than take her chances on the singles scene. Another such tale depicts the private emotions of the father of a child with Down syndrome. Tortured by the unfairness of the child's suffering from Down syndrome and driven to fury by the effects the condition has had on the street for no visible reason. The murder is cathartic, somehow balancing with his son's bad luck and giving Roland a sense of control that he lacked before. "Where the Action Is" is an ironic look at fate and fame. A young, barely professional news photographer in a small Wyoming town misses the climax of a bus hijacking because he has to visit the restroom but casually takes a grab shot of one of the victims, a young woman who may or may not have been raped. His chance photograph captures the poignancy of the victim and also fits in with various "crime in the streets" themes being exploited in the press, and his photograph wins the notice of *The New York Times*, then a Pulitzer Prize. Craig, the photographer, finds his career is made, as he parlays his lucky break into a lecture series and then an apologetic book about the invasion of his subject's privacy, though she too seems to have a private agenda. The story neatly depicts how fame can feed on itself, "creating facts" out of chance events.

"Not in This Life, Maybe the Next" presents another situation in which a woman suffering psychic pain begins to notice a small creature around the house, in this case a very stocky, two-foot-tall "man" of enormous strength. As in the other stories of this type, no rational explanation is offered for this manifestation of emotional states. "The Stuff of Madness" is wonderfully mordant, as Christopher and Penny clash over publicity about her hobby of stuffing her dead pets and installing them in the garden, where they rot and mold. Before the news photographers come, Christopher rigs a department store mannequin in the garden to look like one of his past mistresses, triggering a heart attack in Penny and a fitting end for himself. Perhaps the most haunting story is "A Shot from Nowhere," a situation like that of Julio Cortázar's "Blow-Up," in which Andrew, a young painter, witnesses a murder in a small Mexican town. No one is willing to pursue the crime or the criminals, and Andrew himself is blamed. The story ends with Andrew free but the situation unresolved.

TALES OF NATURAL AND UNNATURAL CATASTROPHE

Highsmith's collection *Tales of Natural and Unnatural Catastrophe* is among her best, with lively stories mostly taking a definite turn toward political and social satire. "Operation Balsam: Or, Touch-Me-Not" is a scathing indictment of the morality of nuclear regulators, in this case of a bureaucrat who finds a suitably secret storage place for deadly waste under a football stadium on a university campus and who sacrifices a friend and colleague to a horrible end in order to maintain this secrecy. "Nabuti: Warm Welcome to a UN Committee" is a devastating send-up of a newly independent African country, corrupt and incompetent, attempting to cover up its malfeasance with United Nations money and instead covering up the investigating committee itself. "Sweet Freedom! And a Picnic on the White House Lawn" addresses the policies that have spilled the lunatic, but supposedly benign, out onto the streets of the United States; in this version, the homeless wreak their revenge in a variety of fashions.

"Rent-a-Womb vs. the Mighty Right" satirizes conservative attacks on the surrogate mother phenomenon, while "Sixtus VI, Pope of the Red Slipper" postulates a pope who publicly reverses all significant Vatican policies toward women and procreation. "President Buck Jones Rallies and Waves the Flag" is a heavy-handed satire in the tradition of Stanley Kubrick's film *Dr. Strangelove* (1964), amusing for its outrageousness. Four stories return to traditional Highsmith concerns. "Moby Dick II: Or, The Missile Whale" is told from the whale's point of view, as in the stories in *The Animal-Lover's Book of Beastly Murder*; like the great white whale, this cetacean does not take kindly to being hunted but has a modern weapon. "Trouble at the Jade Towers" is not an animal revenge story in the earlier pattern but does feature a cockroach occupation of a prestigious Manhattan address. "No End in Sight" and "The Mysterious Cemetery" invoke again the mood and tone of earlier Highsmith, the first about an old lady in a nursing home who refuses to die decently and save everyone a lot of trouble, the second a spooky tale of human cancer experiments which, when buried in the graveyard, grow enormous, mushroomlike simulacrums of human bodies. Thus, Highsmith, late in her career, moved into more political and satiric writing but also kept her touch for her traditional approaches.

OTHER MAJOR WORKS

LONG FICTION: *Strangers on a Train*, 1950; *The Price of Salt*, 1952 (initially under pseudonym Claire Morgan; also pb. as *Carol*); *The Blunderer*, 1954 (also as *Lament for a Lover*, 1956); *The Talented Mr. Ripley*, 1955; *Deep Water*, 1957 (also as *Deep Water: A Novel of Suspense*, 1957); *A Game for the Living*, 1958; *This Sweet Sickness*, 1960; *The Cry of the Owl*, 1962; *The Two Faces of January*, 1964; *The Glass Cell*, 1964; *The Story-Teller*, 1965 (also as *A Suspension of Mercy*, 1965); *Those Who Walk Away*, 1967; *The Tremor of Forgery*, 1969; *Ripley Under Ground*, 1970; *A Dog's Ransom*, 1972; *Ripley's Game*, 1974; *Edith's Diary*, 1977; *The Boy Who Followed Ripley*, 1980; *People Who Knock on the Door*, 1983; *The Mysterious Mr. Ripley*, 1985 (contains *The Talented Mr. Ripley*, *Ripley Under Ground*, and *Ripley's Game*); *Found in the Street*, 1986; *Ripley Under Water*, 1991; *Small g: A Summer Idyll*, 1995.

NONFICTION: *Plotting and Writing Suspense Finction*, 1966

CHILDREN'S LITERATURE: *Miranda the Panda Is on the Veranda*, 1958 (with Doris Sanders).

BIBLIOGRAPHY

Brophy, Brigid. "Highsmith." In *Don't Never Forget: Collected Views and Reviews*. New York: Henry Holt, 1966. Brophy compares Highsmith's artistic achievements to those of Georges Simenon to argue that Highsmith's crime novels, with their moral ambiguity, "transcend the limits of the genre while staying strictly inside its rules." She claims that "what Sophocles did for the tragedy of fate Miss Highsmith does for the melodrama of coincidence."

Chin, Paula. "Through a Mind, Darkly." *People Weekly* 39 (January 11, 1993): 93-94. A biographical sketch of Highsmith's eccentric, reclusive, and forbiddingly private life. Discusses her popularity in Europe and her cult status in America; lists her many honors.

Coburn, Marcia Froelke. "And the Enemy Is Us: Patricia Highsmith." *Film Comment* 20 (September/October, 1984): 44-45. Argues that Highsmith is something of an anomaly among writers of hardboiled mystery, since she concentrates on the criminals' point of view and often allows them to avoid being caught. Notes Highsmith's focus on the inescapable effects of thought in which consideration of sin is as bad as sinning and often leads inextricably to a forbidden act.

Dupont, Joan. "Criminal Pursuits." *The New York Times Magazine*, June 12, 1988, p. 60. Notes that although Highsmith is a celebrity in the rest of the world, she is relatively unknown in her native United States; suggests that because Highsmith has lived abroad and has never been in the United States to promote her books, she has never developed a strong link with publishers or readers. Others believe it is because her books are not clearly classifiable as thrillers, mysteries, or literature.

Harrison, Russell. *Patricia Highsmith*. New York: Twayne, 1997. This first book-length study of Highsmith in English explores the aesthetic, philosophical, and sociopolitical dimensions of her writing. Study of her short fiction is limited to discussion of *Slowly Slowly in the Wind* and *The Black House*, which represent, in Harrison's opinion, the strongest collections.

Highsmith, Patricia. Interview by Craig Little. *Publishers Weekly* 239 (November 2, 1992): 46-47. A brief biographical and critical discussion of Highsmith, commenting on the Hitchcock film version of her first novel, *Strangers on a Train*, and her popularity in Europe over the last forty years.

_____. "Not Thinking with the Dishes." *Writer's Digest* 62 (October, 1983): 26. Highsmith says she follows no set rules for story writing; she begins with a theme, an unusual circumstance or a situation of surprise or coincidence, and creates the narrative around it. Her focus is on subjective attitudes, what is happening in the minds of her protagonists. Her settings are always ones she knows personally.

Hilfer, Anthony Channell. "Not Really Such a Monster: Highsmith's Ripley as Thriller Protagonist and Protean Man." *Midwest Quarterly: A Journal of Contemporary Thought* 25 (Summer, 1984): 361-374. Hilfer studies Highsmith's Ripley as a "subversive variation" of a suspense thriller protagonist, one through which Highsmith flouts moral and literary expectations. He argues that Ripley's lack of a determinate identity makes his role-playing credible.

Summers, Claude J., ed. *Gay and Lesbian Literary Heritage*. New York: H. Holt, 1995. Includes an excellent essay by Gina Macdonald on Highsmith's life work to the time of her death in 1995.

Sutcliffe, Thomas. "Graphs of Innocence and Guilt." *The Times Literary Supplement*, no. 4696 (October 2, 1981): 1118. Sutcliffe argues that the uneasy, disquieting force of Highsmith's works comes from her depiction of reason persisting in inappropriate conditions. Her focus on "what it is like to remain sane" while committing horrendous deeds blurs complacent distinctions. At their best, her short stories are brilliant studies of "fear and loathing, moral absolution and culpability"—"the fragility of . . . untested moral structures."

Symons, Julian. *Mortal Consequences: A History from the Detective Story to the Crime Novel*. New York: Harper & Row, 1972. Symons calls Highsmith "the most important crime novelist at present," more appreciated in Europe than in the United States, but a fine writer, whose tricky plot devices are merely starting points "for profound and subtle character studies," particularly of likable figures attracted by crime and violence. It is her imaginative power that gives her criminal heroes a "terrifying reality" amid carefully chosen settings. She is at her best describing subtle, deadly games of pursuit.

Andrew F. Macdonald

WOLFGANG HILDESHEIMER

Born: Hamburg, Germany; December 9, 1916
Died: Poschiavo, Switzerland; August 21, 1991

PRINCIPAL SHORT FICTION

Lieblose Legenden, 1952 (revised 1962)
Ich trage eine Eule nach Athen, 1956
The Collected Stories of Wolfgang Hildesheimer,
  1987

OTHER LITERARY FORMS

Wolfgang Hildesheimer wrote one novel and two prose monologues. His book *Mozart* (1977) is a well-researched essay on the composer. It was followed by *Marbot: Eine Biographie* (1981; *Marbot: A Biography*, 1983), the biography of a fictional artist. Hildesheimer also wrote numerous radio plays and stage dramas and was a literary translator and reviewer. In 1996, a posthumous collection of Hildesheimer's collages, *Schönheit als Therapie: Bilder gegen die Verzweiflung*, was published.

ACHIEVEMENTS

Wolfgang Hildesheimer received the Blind Veterans' Prize for Radio Plays in 1954, the City of Bremen Prize for Literature and the prestigious Georg Büchner Prize in 1966, and the Premio Verinna-Lorenzon for *Mozart* in 1977. He was awarded the Bavarian Academy of Fine Arts Prize for Literature, an honorary doctorate from the University of Gießen in 1982, and the City of Weilheim Prize for Literature in 1991.

BIOGRAPHY

Wolfgang Hildesheimer was born in Hamburg, Germany, on December 9, 1916. The Hildesheimers were Jewish and emigrated to England after Adolf Hitler came to power in 1933. Wolfgang learned fluent English, trained as an artist in Jerusalem and London, then worked as an English teacher and British information officer in Palestine. From 1946 to 1949 he was a simultaneous translator at the Nuremberg Trials.

Writing was Hildesheimer's second profession. He began writing fiction in 1950 and stopped in 1983. As he explained in his lecture "The End of Fiction," he had become increasingly concerned about the world population explosion, the threat of ecological disaster, and technological developments "outside the scale of moral values." Before, during, and after his literary career, Hildesheimer worked as a graphic artist. His work in the studio gave him a sense of peace he could not find elsewhere. His book of collages, *Schönheit als Therapie: Bilder gegen die Verzweiflung* (beauty as therapy: images of despair), was published in 1996.

Hildesheimer married the artist Silvia Dillman in 1953. They chose to live in the Italian-speaking part of Switzerland, in picturesque Poschiavo. He died there of a heart attack on August 21, 1991. In the year of his death, the German publisher Suhrkamp put out a seven-volume edition of Hildesheimer's complete works, including his illustrations.

ANALYSIS

Hildesheimer's literary biographer, Henry A. Lea, was a translator with him at the Nuremberg Trials. In 1997's *Wolfgang Hildesheimers Weg als Jude und Deutscher* (Wolfgang Hildesheimer's path as Jew and German), Lea shows that it was not until several years after the Trials that the reports of Nazi atrocities had their full impact on Hildesheimer. In 1957 he emigrated from Germany a second time. From then on, he saw the world in terms of victims and oppressors. The main characters in Hildesheimer's works are victims, alone in an absurd world.

Hildesheimer's short stories, collected in *Lieblose Legenden* (loveless legends), were written over a period of twelve years, from 1950 to 1962. During those years, the first-person narrator experienced changes in the world and in his perception of the world. Hildesheimer suggested in 1983 that tracing those changes is the key to understanding the book.

The stories are loveless only insofar as they do not include a love story; Hildesheimer later stated that he regarded the world quite lovingly at the time. They are also not legends. The alliterating title is appropriate in tone: It sounds ludicrous. Most of these early works are relatively carefree and are often humorous.

Hildesheimer's approach to language is analytical. He enjoys plays on words and literal interpretations of figurative expressions. For example, one of the *Lieblose Legenden* has the main character carry an owl to Athens, a mockery of the German saying whose English equivalent is to carry coals to Newcastle.

The Scottish critic Roderick Watt has shown that Hildesheimer's humor often alienates the reader. Unlike his contemporary and fellow German, Nobel Prize laureate Heinrich Böll, Hildesheimer presupposes considerable erudition, then satirizes the very group that possesses the cultural knowledge to understand his references. His irony is born of pessimism.

"THE LIGHT GRAY SPRING COAT"

"Der hellgraue frühjahrsmantel" ("The Light Gray Spring Coat") is the first story in *Lieblose Legenden* and a fine illustration of Hildesheimer's complexity of composition. A letter arrives from a cousin, Edward, who disappeared twelve years ago. At the same time, the piano tuner arrives. The main character, Mr. Holle, mistakenly sends the piano tuner's coat to the cousin in Australia but makes amends by giving the piano tuner the cousin's coat. The humor of the story derives not only from the confusion but also from the trivialization of potentially extreme events: the disappearance of the cousin, the reaction of the piano tuner to losing his coat, and the behavior of the main character. All require background knowledge.

The story was written in 1950. If the cousin disappeared twelve years earlier, that means he disappeared in 1938, a year before the Germans initiated World War II but already five years into the Nazi persecution of Jews and intellectuals. One can realistically fear the worst for Cousin Edward. Against this background, his simple request for his light gray spring coat brings comic relief.

The identity of the piano tuner is also cause for alarm, because his name, A. M. Kolhaas, is clearly a play on the main character in Heinrich von Kleist's novella *Michael Kohlhaas* (1810). After Kleist's

Kohlhaas has his horses confiscated, his quest for justice leads him to take extreme measures. He exhausts the corrupt legal system, wages war, and is finally executed. By comparison, Kolhaas the piano tuner is a mild-mannered man, who does not seem likely to take retaliatory action.

Likewise, Mr. Holle is a reference to Mother Holle of *Grimm's Fairy Tales* (1812), the old woman who rewards two girls with different attire: The industrious daughter is showered with gold coins, the lazy one with tar. Hildesheimer's Mr. Holle has two light gray spring coats to dispense, but in this case both recipients seem satisfied. The reader feels relief that disruptive, potentially disastrous events subside with barely a ripple. Nevertheless, there is knowledge of danger lurking below the surface, danger that may erupt at any time. Hildesheimer was only too aware of the fragility of civilized life.

"I AM NOT WRITING A BOOK ON KAFKA"

"Ich schreibe kein Buch über Kafka" ("I Am Not Writing a Book on Kafka") is a hilarious satire of shallow academic pretentiousness, of self-important, second-rate people, who write more and more about less and less. Hildesheimer uses the jargon well. His first-person narrator is working on a nine-volume biography that "fills a gap" but whose explication "would go beyond the parameters of this brief apologia." He is writing a biography of Ekkehard Golch, who wrote a biography of James Boswell, who actually did write a biography of Samuel Johnson.

The point of the satire is that, by the time one is three times removed from the main subject, all relevance is lost. Golch's life sounds very monotonous, not to mention the narrator's. Hildesheimer makes the project utterly ridiculous by having the narrator claim to have written reverse biographies as well—Johnson's experience of Boswell, Boswell's of Golch, and Golch's of the narrator himself—a self-serving exercise.

Despite this satire, Hildesheimer went on to write an acclaimed biography of the composer Wolfgang Amadeus Mozart and realized the potential of a fictional biography for self-expression in his book *Marbot*.

"THE END OF A WORLD"

Hildesheimer wrote "Das Ende einer Welt" ("The End of a World") in 1951 and adapted it for a radio opera in 1953, with music by Hans Werner Henze. An artificial island sinks, drowning a high society hostess and all her guests but one, who is smart enough, like the rats he sees, to desert the proverbial sinking ship.

The story is often interpreted as yet another of Hildesheimer's witty attacks on pretentious people of "culture," but the opera invites a political interpretation as well. In it, Hildesheimer calls the main character and sole survivor Fallersleben, a clear reference to Hoffmann von Fallersleben, who wrote the words to the German national anthem. Implicit in Hildesheimer's story/opera is the observation that Fallersleben himself would feel alienated in modern Germany. He would jump ship, as does his fictional namesake, as did Hildesheimer's family when Adolph Hitler came to power in 1933, and as would Hildesheimer himself in 1957. Hildesheimer was intimately acquainted with the horrible revelations of the Nuremberg Trials and viewed German culture with scepticism and irony.

"SLEEP"

"Schläferung" ("Sleep") is the last and longest of the *Lieblose Legenden*. Hildesheimer's point of departure is a 1983 poem by Hans Magnus Enzensberger, "Meine Gedichte," a poem Hildesheimer later described as "seductively beautiful." There is humor in his interpretation and expansion of the poem, for Hildesheimer typically takes literally that which Enzensberger meant metaphorically and describes why it is preferable to sleep in a guitar as opposed to a cello.

Hildesheimer's significant addition is the presence of three women to watch over the first-person narrator's final rest. His choice of the Mona Lisa, a Catholic nun, and the beheaded Mary Stuart may seem bizarre but is indicative of the extent to which he is anchored in human history and culture. While entering the guitar to escape the "murderers and idiots," he remains very much immersed in their world.

Hildesheimer's fanciful variation on the poem is a vehicle for his comments on civilization. He conveys a strong sense that most human endeavor is meaningless and should be taken lightly. While searching the attic, the narrator comes across clothing and objects that evoke the people of past generations. A suit of armor that fascinated him in childhood is now nothing more than a reminder of someone who was "a servant of many servants of many systems."

OTHER MAJOR WORKS

LONG FICTION: *Paradies der falschen Vögel*, 1953; *Tynset*, 1965; *Masante*, 1973; *Marbot: Eine Biographie*, 1981 (*Marbot: A Biography*, 1983).

PLAYS: *Die Eroberung der Prinzessin Turandot*, pb. 1955; *Pastorale*, pr. 1958; *Spiele, in denen es dunkel wird*, pb. 1958; *Das Opfer Helena*, pr. 1959 (*The Sacrifice of Helen*, 1968); *Die Verspätung*, pr., pb. 1961; *Nachtstück*, pr., pb. 1963 (*Nightpiece*, 1967); *Mary Stuart*, pr. 1970 (English translation, 1972).

NONFICTION: *Mozart*, 1977 (English translation, 1980).

MISCELLANEOUS: *Schönheit als Therapie: Bilder gegen die Verzweiflung*, 1996 (collages).

BIBLIOGRAPHY

Hildesheimer, Wolfgang. "The End of Fiction." In *Wolfgang Hildesheimer: Gesammelte Werke*, edited by Christiaan Nibbrig and Volker Jehle. Vol. 7. Frankfurt am Main: Suhrkamp, 1991. A lecture given at University College, Dublin, in 1975. The same detached, analytical outlook as in the early stories but without the humor. Hildesheimer questions the validity of culture in a time of impending ecological disaster. Ends with an imaginary dialogue between a novelist and a scientist, which foreshadows Hildesheimer's decision to cease creative writing. States his belief that the writer should support a good cause.

Lea, Henry A. "Wolfgang Hildesheimer and the German-Jewish Experience: Reflections on *Tynset* and *Masante*." *Monatshefte* 71 (Spring, 1979): 19-28. Places Hildesheimer in historical context and explains his distrust of all things German. Helps the reader recognize references used in the short stories as well. Identifies the basic tone as fear and compares Hildesheimer's precise prose to Franz Kafka's. This article is an English precursor of Lea's excellent book on Hildesheimer that appeared in German in 1997.

_____. *Wolfgang Hildesheimers Weg als Jude und Deutscher*. Stuttgart: Hans-Dieter Heinz, 1997. Includes bibliographical references and an index.

Sacker, H. D. "Hildesheimer's Vision of Literature." *Hermathena* 121 (Winter, 1976): 198-213. An appreciation of Hildesheimer written after his lecture, seminar, and readings in Dublin, Ireland, in 1975. Focuses on Hildesheimer's criterium that literature must make the reader see something not actually in the outer world.

Stanley, Patricia H. *Wolfgang Hildesheimer and His Critics*. Columbia, S.C.: Camden House, 1993. A thorough, systematic overview of the critical reception of Hildesheimer's works. The first ten pages deal with the *Lieblose Legenden*. English translations for all German titles and quotations. Includes mention of Hildesheimer's graphic art and suggests topics for further investigation.

Watt, Roderick H. "Self-Defeating Satire? On the Function of the Implied Reader in Wolfgang Hildesheimer's *Lieblose Legenden*." *Forum for Modern Language Studies* 19 (January, 1983): 58-74. Explains many of the references in the stories and shows how Hildesheimer both aligns himself with and satirizes the culturally educated upper middle class. Casual asides and name-dropping presuppose common knowledge, but some of Hildesheimer's cultural allusions are fictional, and he parodies critical and scholarly jargon. Contains German quotations but is quite understandable and worthwhile.

Jean M. Snook

CHESTER HIMES

Born: Jefferson City, Missouri; July 29, 1909
Died: Moraira, Spain; November 12, 1984

PRINCIPAL SHORT FICTION
The Collected Stories of Chester Himes, 1990

OTHER LITERARY FORMS

Chester Himes wrote many novels, including *If He Hollers Let Him Go* (1945), newspaper articles, and two autobiographies. His crime novels set in Harlem were the first to bring him international fame.

ACHIEVEMENTS

Best known for the series of detective stories called the Harlem Domestic, Chester Himes wrote in many genres and with an impressive variety of techniques and themes. Because throughout his career, even after he had emigrated abroad, he confronted without flinching the wrenching effects of racism in the United States, he is sometimes categorized into the group of protest writers. What distinguishes him is his humor, often necessarily grotesque in the grimmest of circumstances.

Upon the publication of *The Collected Stories of Chester Himes*, a brief review in the magazine *Essence* recommended his stories, written over a forty-year span, because he showed African Americans to themselves as they really are, in all facets of their lives. Such relevance suggests that he captured an essence of African American life, one that is often tragic and violent, and also passionate, tender, sensual. He was awarded the Rosenwald Fellowship in 1944 and the Grand Prix de Littérature Policière in 1958.

BIOGRAPHY

Born on July 29, 1909, in Jefferson City, Missouri, to middle-class black parents, Chester Himes had an emotionally traumatic home life. Estelle Boman, his light-skinned mother, and Joseph Sandy Himes, his much darker-skinned father, lived perpetually at war with each other. The racial tension within the family affected the three brown-skinned sons and led to the decline of the family's lifestyle. His father, a professor of metal trades and African American history at southern black colleges, had to keep taking more and more menial jobs because his wife's contempt for his colleagues forced the family to keep moving.

After living in several places in the South, the Himeses finally settled in Ohio. Himes entered Ohio State University at seventeen. Crippled by a fall into an open elevator shaft and then angered by the racial segregation on campus, Himes did not adapt well to the academic life. He failed all his courses the first semester and had to withdraw the next. His subsequent life as a juvenile delinquent came to an abrupt end when, in 1928, he was arrested, badly beaten at the police station, tried and convicted of armed robbery, and sentenced to twenty years.

Oddly enough, the incarceration may have given Himes the time and the calm away from his tense family life to discover his talent. His first stories were published by the vitally important black magazine *The Crisis*. By the time he was released in 1936, he was twenty-six and a writer. A year later, he married Jean Johnson, a woman he had known before his imprisonment.

Himes continued to write as he explored the United States for work. During World War II, he was a shipfitter and riveter in California. The bitter racial experiences in Los Angeles led to the novel *If He Hollers Let Him Go*. In 1954, as so many American writers, including frustrated black writers, have done before him, Himes left the United States and traveled through Europe. The French admired his life, particularly appreciating the satire of *Pinktoes* (1961), a ribald novel proposing the solution to racial tensions through indiscriminate sexual relationships. It was his French editor who encouraged Himes to write the

Chester Himes (Library of Congress)

detective novels set in Harlem, featuring Grave Digger Jones and Coffin Ed Johnson. Himes wrote these in a hurry, desperate for the money, but they turned out to be the perfect match of form and content. Increasingly pessimistic about the violence of his native country, Himes wrote more and more about the radical solution to the racial problem—violence. The Harlem of his detectives, the detectives the detectives themselves, the people among whom they move are all caught up, trapped in a cycle of violent behavior from which they cannot escape.

With so much pain, personal and cultural, from the beginning of his life, Himes did what talented artists do: He confronted it, fashioned it into a personal vision, and, living fully, even found the love and humor in it. He died in Spain, in 1984, of Parkinson's disease, without returning to the homeland that he had described so vividly.

ANALYSIS

Chester Himes's short stories, he believed, served as his apprenticeship as a writer. They were the first of his writings to be published, and he continued in the genre intermittently for more than forty years. When an anthology of his short fiction was proposed in 1954, he revealed in his autobiography that he could not feel proud of it. The anthology finally published in 1973, *Black on Black: Baby Sister and Selected Writings*, was highly selective, concentrating on the stories of the first two decades of his career. A 1990 edition, *The Collected Stories of Chester Himes*, contains sixty-one pieces, ranging from 1933 to 1978, with nine updated. Many are prison stories, and not all are of even quality, but as a whole, they demonstrate Himes's remarkably versatile range of techniques and the ongoing themes and preoccupations of his longer pieces.

"HIS LAST DAY"

Prison life, horrible as it was, gave Himes the subject of several short stories. "His Last Day," about a condemned man's last few hours before the electric chair, already shows some of Himes's trademarks. Spats, a hardened, ruthless criminal who is condemned to death for killing a police officer, reflects wryly that he would not have been identified if the one person left alive during his robbery of a club had not recognized his fawn-colored spats. Even when he manages to hide out for a few days, he is finally trapped—by his past and by a woman. An old sweet heart whom he had abandoned in her pregnancy shoots the man who had provided Spats with refuge, thus attracting the police. Rivetingly grim, this early effort is marred by the dated slang, but even so, Himes's characteristic grisly humor comes through.

"HER WHOLE EXISTENCE"

James Baldwin wrote of Himes that he was the only black writer to describe male-female relationships in terms other than violence. One of Himes's earliest love stories, "Her Whole Existence: A Story of True Love," verges on parody in its clichéd language but also shows Himes's imaginative skill. Written from the point of view of Mabel Miles, the beautiful daughter of a successful African American politician, the story leaps suddenly from the romanticism of Mabel's attraction for Richard Riley, an ambitious, successful, and handsome criminal, to an analysis of class conflict. Trapped between the respect for law instilled by her family and her own passion, Mabel first betrays Richard and then helps him to escape. It is the first of Himes's portrayals of unpredictable but strong women.

"A NIGGER"

"A Nigger" suggests, with its shockingly simple denouement, Himes's bitter observations about the sexual relationship between blacks and whites. Mr. Shelton, a rich old white man, drops in unexpectedly on Fay, a black prostitute who lives with a light-skinned common-law husband and who is currently involved with another black man, Joe Wolf. Taken by surprise, Fay shoves Joe into the closet to receive her white lover. Joe hears her cajole and flatter Mr. Shelton out of two hundred dollars and, crouched in the dark, recalls other tired, unattractive white men he has known who have turned to black women not in appreciation but in exhaustion. Such men have convinced themselves, he thinks, that it is only black flesh they touch, animal flesh that has no mind or power to judge. When he is ready to leave, Mr. Shelton opens the door of the closet by mistake, looks in, turns away, and leaves. While Fay is jubilant that Joe was not detected, Joe is so furious that he tries to strangle her. He knows that the white man saw him and simply refused to recognize his existence. Back in his own tiny room, he reflects bitterly that he must count himself a "nigger" for allowing his poverty and dependence on a prostitute to rob him of his manhood.

"HEADWAITER"

Though many of Himes's stories—and novels—ram home the pain of being black in the United States, there are other works that portray individuals who can carve a dignified niche in the limited ways available to them. "Headwaiter" presents Dick Small, an African American man in charge of an old-fashioned dining room patronized by a regular white clientele. Imperturbable in this familiar atmosphere, Dick watches over everyone in his care, remembering the personal details of individual customers, waiters, busboys. In his small way, he does what he can for the less fortunate. When the diners are horrified to learn that one of the best waiters is an former convict, Dick stands firmly by his decision to give the man a second chance, and his polite firmness quells the furor. He is unable, however, to save another waiter who acts drunk; when he has to dismiss him, he does so with sympathy and compassion.

"LUNCHING AT THE RITZMORE"

The complementary story "Lunching at the Ritzmore" differs in tone. A satiric view of the laws that required separate public establishments for blacks and whites, this story suggests, lightheartedly, what Himes was seriously to advocate later: the power that lies in a large crowd to hurl down racist barriers. In "the mecca of the motley" in Pershing Square, Los Angeles, a young college student from Vermont argues that there is no discrimination against Negroes. A drifter in the crowd bets him the price of dinner that a young brown-skinned Negro, an unemployed mechanic, will be refused service if the three eat at a restaurant. As the three set off in search of a suitably challenging place to eat, the crowd around them grows and grows because people think that a free giveaway must be the goal of such a gathering. A policeman follows them, wanting to arrest them but not being able to think of a good reason to do so. Finally, an enormous crowd halts outside the very fancy Ritzmore Hotel; there, the debate shifts slightly from race to class, as none of the three is dressed well enough. The diners, the waiters, and the cooks, however, are so stunned by the crowd that the three men are immediately served the only item that they can read on the French menu— ironically enough, it is apple pie. The student wins his bet but has to pay because the drifter is broke.

"ALL HE NEEDS IS FEET"

Few other stories exhibit such lighthearted irony in the face of racial discrimination. "All He Needs Is Feet" is ironic, in the horrifying, brutal way that shocks the reader into realizing why Himes later saw violence as the only solution for African Americans, because they are mistreated so violently by a violent society. Ward, a black man, walking down the sidewalk in Rome, Georgia, steps off to let a white woman and two white men pass. One white man bumps into Ward anyway and provokes him to fight. A crowd that gathers, thinking a lynching is too severe, pours gasoline on Ward's feet and sets him on fire. In jail for assault with a deadly weapon, Ward has his feet amputated. He goes to Chicago with money sent by his family and learns to use crutches and knee pads to work at shining shoes, saving enough money to buy war bonds. In a theater, his crutches tucked out of everyone's way under the seats, Ward cannot stand up for the national anthem at the end of the film. A big, burly man from Arkansas hits him for disrespect to the flag. The ultimate cruelty of the story come as a punch line, when a policeman arrests the white man: The man from Arkansas blubbers that he could not stand a "nigger" sitting through the national anthem, even if he did not have feet.

The issue of patriotism became very complex for African Americans during World War II, especially for those who fought for democracy against Adolf Hitler and his blatantly racist and fascist goals of a super race and then had to reflect on the racism in their own democracy. Several of Himes's war stories, such as "Two Soldiers," reveal a man struggling to remain patriotic and optimistic. The most effective of these, "So Softly Smiling," springs from the war atmosphere but is really a beautiful love story. Roy Jonny Squires, a lieutenant in the U.S. Army, returns to Harlem for thirty days. Exhausted by the warfare in North Africa, he heads for a bar late at night and meets Mona Morrison, a successful poet. Her "tawny skin like an African veld at sunset" exactly fulfills the ache for love that fiery raids at dawn have brought upon him. This delicate love story is punctuated throughout with dramatic reminders that the lovers' time together is very short, and their courtship and married life proceed at breakneck speed. It is in this story that Himes touches on the race issue during war, lightly, positively; Roy says that he finally enlisted because he heard someone say that the United States belonged to the Negro as much as it did to anyone.

"TANG"

More than two decades later, Himes seemed to have lost such patriotic optimism. In "Tang," a tired, hungry couple sit watching television in their cold-water slum flat in Harlem, when a long cardboard box with a florist's label is delivered to them. They discover inside it an M-14 army gun and a typewritten sheet warning them to learn how to use their weapon and wait for instructions, for freedom is near. The man, T-bone Smith, who had used such a weapon in the Korean War, is absolutely terrified and wants to report the gun to the police. The woman, Tang, once a beautiful, softly rounded woman who has become hard and angular from her life as a poor prostitute, is ecstatic. She hugs the gun as if it were a lover and cherishes the thought that the gun could chop up a white policeman. She is ready to fight for freedom, even pointing the gun at T-bone to stop him from calling the police. Her defiance enrages him; he whips out a spring-blade knife and slashes her to death, crying that he might not be free of whitey, but he is now free of her.

Writing twenty years before Himes's death, the critic Edward Margolies noted that Himes's characters tend to be reflective, interested in ideas and in intellectualizing the predicaments in which they find themselves. As such, they are quite different from such characters as Bigger Thomas, with whom Richard Wright shocked the United States in his *Native Son* (1940). Wright's success trapped other African American writers whom the literary establishment then automatically described as, or expected to be, "protest" writers. Certainly, the range of Himes's short fiction is so vast that it includes stories of strong protest. He wrote, however, stories of individuals caught up in a web of many circumstances. Race is clearly an issue in his fiction, but so are love, sex, poverty, class, war, prison, violence, success, failure, and humor. His short fiction is not only a prelude to his better known novels but also a rewarding world in itself.

OTHER MAJOR WORKS

LONG FICTION: *If He Hollers Let Him Go*, 1945; *Lonely Crusade*, 1947; *Cast the First Stone*, 1952 (unexpurgated edition pb. as *Yesterday Will Make You Cry*, 1998); *The Third Generation*, 1954; *The Primitive*, 1955 (unexpurgated edition pb. as *The End of a Primitive*, 1997); *For Love of Imabelle*, 1957 (revised as *A Rage in Harlem*, 1965); *Il pleut des coups durs*, 1958 (*The Real Cool Killers*, 1959); *Couché dans le pain*, 1959 (*The Crazy Kill*, 1959); *Dare-dare*, 1959 (*Run Man, Run*, 1966); *Tout pour plaire*, 1959 (*The Big Gold Dream*, 1960); *Imbroglio negro*, 1960 (*All Shot Up*, 1960); *Ne nous énervons pas!*, 1961 (*The Heat's On*, 1966; also pb. as *Come Back Charleston Blue*, 1974); *Pinktoes*, 1961; *Une Affaire de viol*, 1963 (*A Case of Rape*, 1980); *Retour en Afrique*, 1964 (*Cotton Comes to Harlem*, 1965); *Blind Man with a Pistol*, 1969 (also pb. as *Hot Day, Hot Night*, 1970); *Plan B*, 1983.

NONFICTION: *The Autobiography of Chester Himes: The Quality of Hurt, Volume I*, 1972; *The Autobiography of Chester Himes: My Life of Absurdity, Volume II*, 1976.

MISCELLANEOUS: *Black on Black: Baby Sister and Selected Writings* (1973).

BIBLIOGRAPHY

Cochran, David. "So Much Nonsense Must Make Sense: The Black Vision of Chester Himes." *The Midwest Quarterly* 38 (Autumn, 1996): 1-30. Examines Himes's creation of the hard-boiled cop figure as a reflection of his own experience in Harlem. Argues that he presents Harlem as the underside of American capitalism.

Crooks, Robert. "From the Far Side of the Urban Frontier: The Detective Fiction of Chester Himes and Walter Mosley." *College Literature* 22 (October, 1995): 68-90. Analyzes the emergence of African-American detective fiction in the works of Walter Mosley and Chester Himes. Shows how Himes develops a strategy for disrupting the frontier narrative in a way that lays it bare.

Fabre, Michel, Robert E. Skinner, and Lester Sullivan, comps. *Chester Himes: An Annotated Primary and Secondary Bibliography*. Westport, Conn.: Greenwood Press, 1992. This is a comprehensive annotated bibliography of writings by and about Himes.

Himes, Chester. *Conversations with Chester Himes*. Edited by Michel Fabre and Robert Skinner. Jackson: University Press of Mississippi, 1995. This collection of interviews with Himes provides information about his life and work.

Lundquist, James. *Chester Himes*. New York: Frederick Ungar, 1976. An introductory volume to Himes's life and works, with chapters on the war novels, confessional novels, and detective novels. The first chapter, "November, 1928," describes the armed robbery for which Himes was arrested and subsequent arrest and trial, in detail. Chronology, notes, bibliography of primary and secondary sources, index.

Margolies, Edward. "Race and Sex : The Novels of Chester Himes." In *Native Sons: A Critical Study of Twentieth-Century Negro American Authors*. Philadelphia: J. B. Lippincott, 1968. A discussion of the major novels. The author sees Himes as considerably different from the group of protest writers following Richard Wright and believes that his European sojourn weakened his writings about the United States. Bibliography and index.

Margolies, Edward, and Michel Fabre. *The Several Lives of Chester Himes*. Jackson: University Press of Mississippi, 1997. This full-length biography of Himes is indispensable for information about his life.

Milliken, Stephen F. *Chester Himes: A Critical Appraisal*. Columbia: University of Missouri Press, 1976. Contains an excellent chapter, "Take a Giant Step," on Himes's short stories. This study includes sections on the protest, autobiographical and detective novels. Chronology, bibliography of primary sources, and annotated bibliography of secondary sources.

Muller, Gilbert. *Chester Himes*. Boston: Twayne, 1989. An excellent introduction to Himes's life and works. Traces the evolution of Himes's grotesque, revolutionary view of life in the United States for African Americans, in several literary modes, culminating in his detective fiction. Chronology, appendix, index, and annotated bibliographies of primary and secondary works.

Rosen, Steven J. "African American Anti-Semitism and Himes's Lonely Crusade." *MELUS* 20 (Summer, 1995): 47-68. Discusses an anti-Semitic streak that runs through Himes's work alongside an anxiety to assert masculinity. Shows how Himes used Jewish characters or formulated Jewish traits as a foil to black American masculinity.

Rosenblatt, Roger. "The Hero Vanishes." In *Black Fiction*. Cambridge, Mass.: Harvard University Press, 1974. Briefly compares Himes's hero to Richard Wright's *Native Son* (1940). Particularly interesting is the introduction, which provides a broad-ranging discussion of the relationship of black literature to American literature as a whole. Index, bibliography.

Shakuntala Jayaswal

EDWARD D. HOCH

Born: Rochester, New York; February 22, 1930

PRINCIPAL SHORT FICTION

City of Brass and Other Simon Ark Stories, 1971

The Judges of Hades and Other Simon Ark Stories, 1971

The Spy and the Thief, 1971

The Thefts of Nick Velvet, 1978

The Quests of Simon Ark, 1984

Leopold's Way, 1985

The Spy Who Read Latin and Other Stories, 1990

The People of the Peacock, 1991

The Night, My Friend: Stories of Crime and Suspense, 1992

Diagnosis: Impossible—The Problems of Dr. Sam Hawthorne, 1996

The Kipper of Storyville and Other Ben Snow Tales, 1997

OTHER LITERARY FORMS

Edward D. Hoch, in addition to his own short-story collections, has published hundreds of uncollected stories, which have appeared in periodicals and books. (He has written these under his own name and the pseudonyms Anthony Circus, Stephen Dentinger, R. L. Stevens, Pat McMahon, Ellery Queen, and Irwin Booth.) Hoch is a well-known editor of short-story anthologies and, in 1976, began editing the annual collection of the year's best mysteries. He has also written several novels. From August, 1980, through March, 1985, under the pseudonym R. E. Porter, he wrote "Crime Beat," a column of mystery news, for *Ellery Queen's Mystery Magazine (EQMM)*. Hoch has also been a frequent contributor of mystery articles to magazines and reference books in the genre. Many of his stories have been dramatized on television for *The Alfred Hitchcock Hour, Night Gallery, McMillan and Wife, Tales of the Unexpected*, and other series.

ACHIEVEMENTS

By the mid-1980's, it was generally accepted that Edward D. Hoch, almost single-handedly, was keeping alive the tradition of the classic detective puzzle invented by Edgar Allan Poe in his Dupin stories. With great success, at least once each month since 1973, he has presented intricate mysteries and seemingly impossible crimes solved through the mental prowess of his detective. Clues are invariably fairly presented, so that the reader may match intelligence with the story's protagonist.

In addition to being the most prolific short-story writer in the mystery field (having written nearly a thousand stories by century's end), Hoch has been highly regarded by fans and his peers for the quality of his work. His story "The Oblong Room" (in *The Saint Magazine*, June, 1967) won the Mystery Writers of America annual Edgar Allan Poe Award, being selected in a year in which a story by John le Carré was also nominated. A later story, "The Most Dangerous Man Alive," was nominated for an Edgar Allan Poe Award. Hoch was elected president of the Mystery Writers of America in 1982. At the twenty-second annual Anthony Boucher Memorial Mystery Convention (Bouchercon), in 1991, Hoch was the guest of honor, in recognition of his long and distinguished writing career.

BIOGRAPHY

As a nine-year-old in Rochester, New York, Edward Dentinger Hoch began a lifelong love affair with the mystery story, starting with the works written under the omnibus pseudonym Ellery Queen, generally considered classic detective puzzles. He continued to read widely in the field and eventually, as a teenager, began writing mystery fiction himself. In 1949, though still unpublished, he was given affiliate membership in the Mystery Writers of America.

For eight years, he wrote whenever he could—while attending school, serving in the U.S. Army (1950 to 1952), and working at various jobs—but all the stories that he submitted were rejected. Finally, a story, "Village of the Dead," was published in the December, 1955, issue of *Famous Detective Stories*, one of the last of the "pulp" magazines. Hoch began to be published with increasing frequency, though at first most of his sales were to ephemeral pulp and digest-sized magazines with such titles as *Keyhole Detective Stories* and *Two-Fisted Detective Stories*. From 1954 until 1968, he worked full time as a public relations writer for a Rochester advertising agency, writing fiction in his spare time. Gradually, he broke into the more prestigious, better-paying mystery periodicals such as *EQMM* and *Alfred Hitchcock's Mystery Magazine*. In 1965, he sold one of his stories to television, for *The Alfred Hitchcock Hour*. With a contract for his first novel in 1968, he was able to leave his job and become a full-time writer.

Despite several novels, Hoch has become known for his short stories. Starting in May, 1973, and for many years thereafter at least one of his stories appeared in every issue of *EQMM*, the leading magazine in the genre. Realizing that the short story was his métier, he abandoned novels after 1975. Hoch remained active in the Mystery Writers of America and became a trustee of the Rochester Public Library, where, as a student, he once worked as a research assistant. He settled in Rochester, with his wife, the former Patricia McMahon, whom he married in 1957.

ANALYSIS

From the outset, Edward D. Hoch's writing has followed two tracks, though they frequently merge. In his debut story, he created the first of his more than twenty series detectives, Simon Ark, and provided him with a bizarre, seemingly impossible crime to solve. It is the first of literally hundreds of stories by Hoch in which he shows his endless inventiveness in presenting perplexing problems and their resolutions, without repeating himself. Yet, in the same story, there is a plot that reflects Hoch's Catholic roots and the influence, which he has acknowledged, of G. K. Chesterton and Graham Greene. As a writer who finds his audience in magazines of mystery fiction, Hoch realizes that his primary "product" is providing escape, through brain-teasing mysteries, and he knows that in mystery short stories, there is insufficient length for deep characterization. One need not

read too far between Hoch's lines, however, to see important issues also being treated.

THE QUESTS OF SIMON ARK

Simon Ark, the series detective introduced in "Village of the Dead," owes much to the pulp tradition of the infallible superhero, though he resolves his cases by ratiocination, not physical strength or firepower. He claims to have been a Coptic priest in Egypt, two thousand years earlier, and he presently investigates strange happenings, while he searches for and tries to eradicate evil. Ark is introduced as he arrives in the remote western United States village of Gidaz (a deliberate reversal of Voltaire's Zadig) after hearing of the mass suicide of the entire population. Seventy-three people leaped to their deaths from a hundred-foot cliff. A strong religious leader, calling himself Axidus, had come to town and had great influence on its inhabitants. He is Ark's leading suspect, though he denies responsibility for the deaths. The story's basis is a North African cult, the Circumcellions, part of the Donatist schism from the Catholic Church.

Despite the religious trappings and potential for supernaturalism, Hoch established here his practice of resolving all cases rationally and through evidence that he makes as available to the reader as to his detective. The Ark stories—the early ones, in particular—are enlivened by mystical elements that add the suggestion of the supernatural to their characteristically complex puzzles. Just as Ark himself purports to be immortal, so does he consider the criminals whom he brings to justice avatars or incarnations of the "Ultimate Evil" he seeks. "The Man from Nowhere" is based on the true mystery of Kaspar Hauser, a nineteenth century celebrity whose bizarre murder was never solved. In this story, Ark must discover how a pair of false mystics have staged a stabbing death by an apparently invisible entity, patterned on Hauser's own death. "Sword for a Sinner" concerns a murder among a radical set of Catholic penitents who endure mock crucifixions as part of their purification ritual. Hoch occasionally adds a believable element of pathos to the stories by way of Ark's "Watson," the nameless New York publisher who narrates all the stories and whose fallible character represents the human weakness that gives evil its foothold in the world.

In "The Vicar of Hell," Ark fights a historical order of Satanists as his sidekick fights to resist temptations of the flesh offered by the cult's nubile quarry. "The Judges of Hades" involves the murder of the narrator's father and sister and an inquiry into his family's background complicated by his estrangement from them.

"I'D KNOW YOU ANYWHERE"

Though best known for series detectives, in his early years Hoch wrote many stories without continuing characters. Some of the best of these deal with good and evil on a global level, using the Cold War as metaphor. "I'd Know You Anywhere" starts during World War II with the first encounter between the protagonist, Contrell, and Willoughby Grove, a soldier with no qualms about killing enemy soldiers after they have surrendered. They meet again in the Korean War, and again Grove has disdain for any rules, preferring to kill the people he calls "gooks." At a third meeting in Berlin, shortly after the East Germans erected the Wall in 1961, Grove would shoot communist border guards, even if that might start World War III. Finally, the story flashes to the future, 1969, with Grove an army general. To the concern of Contrell, the president of the United States promises free rein to this man who loves to kill.

THE SPY AND THE THIEF

Though the titles of Hoch's spy stories about Jeffrey Rand, head of Britain's Department of Concealed Communications, are reminiscent of le Carré's first best-seller, the stories are far different. Though Rand is fully aware that spying is a dirty business, much of the cynicism and angst of le Carré's characters is missing, replaced by taut action and neat, often ironic, resolutions of cases.

In early stories such as "The Spy Who Came to the End of the Road" and "The Spy Who Came Out of the Night," Rand is pitted against Russian agents, such as his counterpart in Russian Intelligence, Taz. Though Rand accepts counterintelligence activities, such as reading Russian or Chinese messages and capturing their spies, he is troubled when he must share the responsibility for assassinating enemy agents. He refuses to accept all the conventional wisdom about espionage and believes that there are decent men. He even comes to share a close kinship with Taz, an implicit recognition that even spying can be a profession that goes beyond boundaries and ideologies.

"SACAJAWEA'S GOLD"

Hoch has created two amateur detectives whose cases reflect the United States' past. One of them, Ben Snow, roams the frontier in the late nineteenth and early twentieth centuries, and though he seems law-abiding, a legend has grown that he is actually Billy the Kid. Snow is the character through whom Hoch introduces historical events into his stories, and often it is Native Americans and their mistreatment that come under scrutiny. In "Sacajawea's Gold," Ben is traveling through Yellowstone Park during the 1890's, shortly after the battle at Wounded Knee, when he helps Floating Cloud, a lovely Shoshone, by capturing her runaway pinto. She is seeking her missing father and also a leather pouch of gold coins reputedly given to Sacajawea, guide to Lewis and Clark, by the explorers. Ben decides to help her but finds that there is a third aspect to the investigation, the murder of a half-breed. As often happens, his reputation has preceded him, and an army officer, Captain Grant, assumes that Ben is a gunfighter. Ben finds that his interest in Floating Cloud and in solving the mystery causes conflict with her proud brother, Swift Eagle.

DIAGNOSIS: IMPOSSIBLE

Hoch's tales of Dr. Sam Hawthorne, a small-town New England doctor, are concerned with more recent history. Though the first story appeared in 1974, the series tells of events beginning in the 1920's and moves gradually through the Depression. (In one story, Ben Snow, then a very old man, combines with Hawthorne to solve a mystery involving an Indian tepee.) Changes in American lifestyle and medicine are subtly used as background. Hoch has made Northmont the impossible crime capital of the world, and his Hawthorne series is probably his most ingenious. The stories are classic locked-room mysteries, which call for the solution of seemingly impossible crimes committed under circumstances where it would be impossible for anyone to have been at the scene of the crime or to have left it unnoticed. Among dozens of cases, Hawthorne has solved the mystery of a horse and carriage that disappeared after entering a covered New England bridge, the murder of a victim who was alone in a voting booth, and the murder of an escape artist locked by himself in a shack in front of witnesses. The Hawthorne stories are frequently complicated by clues that implicate an "innocent" bystander as the perpetrator.

In "The Problem of the General Store," Madge Murphy, a former suffragist and now an early advocate of job opportunities for women, has settled in Northmont in 1928. Many men appear alienated by her equal rights advocacy. Madge is suspected of the shotgun slaying of Max Harkner, proprietor of the general store, because she was found near his body. Hawthorne wonders why, if she committed the murder, she was unconscious at the scene of the crime. He also explores whether her outspokenness brought her an enemy willing to frame her. Hoch gives the mysteries added credibility through references to period history and plot twists that hinge on an appreciation of small-town life and prejudices in times past. "The Problem of the Little Red Schoolhouse," in which Hawthorne must solve the kidnapping of a young boy, deliberately evokes the Leopold and Loeb and Lindbergh kidnapping cases. In "The Problem of the Haunted Bandstand," the criminal exploits the town's memory of a racially motivated lynching decades earlier. In "The Problem of the Old Gristmill," a key clue to an otherwise insoluble murder is an understanding of how icehouses work. In "The Problem of the Lobster Shack," the motive for murder proves to be the then-unspeakable shame of a homosexual relationship.

"THE THEFT OF THE GENERAL'S TRASH"

A long-standing tradition in mystery fiction is the rogue, such as Arsène Lupin or the saint, who, like Robin Hood, robs those who "deserve" it but helps those in need. Hoch's Nick Velvet provides an interesting variation on that theme. He makes a surprisingly good living by stealing only objects of little value yet charging a minimum of twenty thousand dollars per theft when the series began in 1966.

Though suspension of disbelief helps, Hoch has made it plausible that Velvet would be hired to steal, variously, the water from a swimming pool, the remaining tickets for a Broadway show that has closed, a last-place baseball team, a toy mouse, some exposed film, a used tea bag, and an overdue library book.

Velvet is being paid by newspaper columnist Sam Simon to steal that epitome of worthless items, a bag of garbage, in "The Theft of the General's Trash." The General, however, is Norman Spangler, the president's adviser on foreign affairs. Velvet is reluctant at first (it is shortly after the Watergate political scandal), and he agrees only after he ascertains that no military secrets will be involved. Velvet learns that Simon is really trying to track down the missing Carter Malone, a Watergate figure who jumped bail and disappeared rather than go to prison. As happens throughout the Velvet series, a more serious crime (usually murder) occurs while Velvet is stealing the insignificant object. Typically, he must find the killer, sometimes to help an innocent person but often to keep from being arrested himself.

LEOPOLD'S WAY

Captain Jules Leopold of the police department in a large northeastern city is arguably the most famous soldier in Hoch's small army of detectives. He also has been the subject of more stories than any of Hoch's other sleuths. Hoch's "The Oblong Room" features Leopold and is typical of the early stories in the series in that the policeman's compassion and insight into character are as important as his deductive abilities. In "The Oblong Room," which evokes the 1960's, a college student is suspected of killing his roommate. He is found standing over the victim, with whom he has been alone for the twenty hours after death. In the room are found six sugar cubes saturated with LSD. Leopold enters a world alien to him, one in which college students experiment freely with drugs and sex, looking for what they claim are religious experiences. The murder room is analogized to a Poe story, "The Oblong Box." Though Leopold never loses his humanity, in later stories, especially beginning in the 1980's, Hoch has him solve very complex, impossible crimes. In one story, a bride disappears just as she is about to walk down the aisle to be married.

"THE SWEATING STATUE"

Hoch has made no secret of his Catholicism and interest in the church; he even edited, with Martin H. Greenberg, a collection of mystery stories in which that religion is important to each story. One of his lesser known detectives is Father David Noone, who has appeared a few times. By far the most interesting Noone story is "The Sweating Statue," a story suggested by an incident in Central America related by Graham Greene in *Getting to Know the General* (1984). Noone is parish priest at Holy Trinity, a poor inner-city church. After the report that a statue of the Blessed Virgin has repeatedly been seen sweating, people descend on the church and its contributions soar. The Cardinal sends Monsignor Thomas Xavier to help Noone investigate, though the woman who discovered this phenomenon asks why the church is reluctant to accept a miracle when the world needs one so badly. With the murder of a church employee, Noone and Xavier have two mysteries to solve.

"THE GYPSY DELEGATE"

One of Hoch's later series, begun in 1985, has had to keep up with changing conditions in Eastern Europe. The series character is Michael Vlado, a Romanian Gypsy, created for an anthology about ethnic detectives. In the early stories in the series, Vlado helps Captain Segar, an honest police officer, solve crimes. Events occur in the context of a dictatorship, one supported in Moscow, in which the Gypsy people, as a minority group, are subjected to discrimination, as they were in the Nazi era.

"The Gypsy Delegate" takes place after the December, 1989, uprising. Segar is now part of the new government, though, when Michael congratulates him, he confesses that his goal is getting through the first month without being shot. Vlado, as king of a tribe of Gypsies, is one of five Romanian delegates sent on the Orient Express to Switzerland to meet with King Michael, Romania's exiled ruler. One of the delegates, a famous educator, is murdered on the train, and the weapon, a dagger, is termed "a gypsy weapon," so Vlado, a suspect, is determined to solve the case.

"THE CHRISTMAS CLIENT"

Hoch's mastery of the puzzle story has led inevitably to contributions to anthologies of new stories featuring Sherlock Holmes. His various pastiches of Arthur Conan Doyle have all been respectful and informed extensions of the Holmes canon and come near to making Holmes a minor series character of Hoch's own. "The Return of the Speckled Band," written for *The New Adventures of Sherlock Holmes: Original Stories* (1987), gives a new twist to events modeled on one of the original Holmes stories. Both "The Manor House Case," in *Resurrected Holmes: New Cases from the Notes of John H. Watson, M.D.* (1996), and "The Adventure of Vittoria the Circus Belle," in *The Mammoth Book of New Sherlock Holmes Adventures* (1997), challenge the master sleuth to unravel mysteries involving concealed identities and wild animal killings. "The Adventure of the Dying Ship," from *The Confidential Casebook of Sherlock Holmes* (1998), pits the aging Holmes against a sham spiritualist aboard the Titanic.

One of Edward Hoch's more intriguing Sherlock Holmes tales is "The Christmas Client," written for *Holmes for the Holidays* (1996). Holmes is sought out by Charles Dodgson, best known for his Alice books written under the pseudonym Lewis Carroll. Dodgson is being blackmailed by Holmes's nemesis Professor Moriarity with some amateur photographs he has taken and fears will be considered scandalous. Holmes rightly intuits that the extortion is a subterfuge to distract authorities from an even graver crime Moriarity plans to commit. Clues vital to stopping Moriarity must be deduced from a bit of nonsense verse the criminal has composed in Carrollian style and passed to Dodgson. The story is a showcase for Hoch's research of history and period detail and also an ingenious mystery that has Victorian England's master of logical detection grappling with intrigue grounded in Carroll's special brand of literary illogic.

"THE DETECTIVE'S WIFE"

In a nonseries 1990 story, "The Detective's Wife," Roger and Jenny seem to be an ideally suited couple. Roger works as a police detective and Jenny for an advertising agency. Early in their marriage, they often discuss his cases, and Jenny tries to help solve them through use of deduction. His reference to her as "Watson" is an affectionate inside joke between them. Long hours and his frustration at the volume of drug-related crime cause Roger to become depressed and then paranoically jealous of Jenny. In hopes of saving their marriage, she tries to help him with a current criminal who has eluded him, a serial killer. Detection is important to this story, yet it also explores the effect of urban crime on those who must try to cope with it.

When his "streak" in *EQMM* began in 1973, Hoch started to concentrate mainly on stories of puzzle and detection involving his many series detectives. This was especially true in the 1980's. "The Detective's Wife" appeared in a nongenre magazine, the California literary quarterly *Crosscurrents*. It, along with other evidence, is an indication of Hoch returning to more varied mysteries and, without abandoning his famous puzzle stories, exploring larger issues in society.

OTHER MAJOR WORKS

LONG FICTION: *The Shattered Raven*, 1969; *The Transvection Machine*, 1971; *The Blue Movie Murders*, 1972 (as Ellery Queen); *The Fellowship of the Hand*, 1973; *The Frankenstein Factory*, 1975.

EDITED TEXTS: *Dear Dead Days*, 1972; *Best Detective Stories of the Year*, 1976-1981; *All But Impossible!*, 1981; *The Year's Best Mystery and Suspense Stories*, 1982-1995; *Great British Detectives*, 1987 (with Martin H. Greenberg); *Women Write Murder*, 1987 (with Martin H. Greenberg); *Murder Most Sacred: Great Catholic Tales of Mystery and Suspense*, 1989 (with Martin H. Greenberg).

CHILDREN'S LITERATURE: *The Monkey's Clue, and the Stolen Sapphire*, 1978.

BIBLIOGRAPHY

Adey, Robert. *Locked Room Murders*. 2d ed. Minneapolis: Crossover Press, 1991. Adey analyzes eighty-one of Hoch's impossible crime stories. Each entry has a brief description of the impossible problem (usually, but not limited to, a locked-room murder) presented and, in an appendix at the end of the book, how the crime was solved.

Barzun, Jacques, Taylor Hertig, and Wendell Hertig. *A Catalogue of Crime*. 2d ed. New York: Harper & Row, 1989. The authors single out eleven short stories and one anthology for discussion. They emphasize the consistency of his work and praise the complexity and lifelike quality of his plots.

Hoch, Edward D. "Shortcut to Murder: An Interview with Edward D. Hoch." Interview by John Kovaleski. *The Armchair Detective* 23 (Spring, 1990): 152-169. Considered the definitive interview with the author, it contains detailed descriptions of many aspects of his career, including his early writing, his writing habits and methods, and the origin of his major series characters. Hoch frankly discusses the reasons for his preference for the short story over the novel. He admits that characterization is often the weak point in his work, a function of the limitations imposed by short-story length.

Kovaleski, John. "Shortcut to Murder." *Armchair Detective* 23 (Spring, 1990): 152-169. An interview with Hoch, who talks about his detective fiction and its relationship to the rest of his work.

Moffatt, June M., and Francis M. Nevins, Jr. *Edward Hoch Bibliography, 1955-1991*. Van Nuys, Calif.: Southern California Institute for Fan Interests, 1991. A complete listing of the writings of Hoch through the end of 1991, with complete publishing information, including reprints, identification of those stories about continuing characters, and adaptations to other media.

Nevins, Francis M., Jr. Introduction to *Leopold's Way*, by Edward D. Hoch. Carbondale: Southern Illinois University Press, 1985. Nevins discusses the series character Captain Leopold in the context of Hoch's many other series characters. He considers the stories among Hoch's best because they are classic detective tales but, in the tradition of crime fiction by Georges Simenon and Graham Greene, they reveal "unexpected nuances of character and emotion and meaning beneath the surface of his deceptively simple style."

_____. *Twentieth-Century Crime and Mystery Writers*, edited by Lesley Henderson. 4th ed. London: St. James Press, 1998. In addition to brief biographical information and an extensive bibliography of Hoch's work, this volume contains an analysis of Hoch's work and place in the genre. Nevins finds the Roman Catholic viewpoint of the early Hoch obtrusive but notes the writer's growth and the stimulating concepts behind many of his plots. Hoch's stories are described as perfect miniatures of the novels of such detective-story giants as Ellery Queen and John Dickson Carr.

Skillman, Brad. "Edward Hoch: Master in His Own Write." *The Drood Review of Mystery* 11 (October, 1991): 4-5. Largely based on an interview with Hoch, this article elicited his opinion on the reasons for the relative decline of the mystery short story, including the shrinkage of magazine markets for new writers. Hoch also discusses the continuing trend, begun at the end of World War II, toward the psychological crime story and away from the detective tale.

Spoto, Mary Theresa. "Needing Burial: Horror and Reconciliation in Edward D. Hoch's 'The Faceless Thing.'" *Studies in Weird Fiction* 20 (Winter, 1997): 13-17. A close reading of Hoch's short horror story "The Faceless Thing," which Spoto praises for an ending different from traditional horror story endings that re-establish the natural order. Instead, Hoch offers an alternative type of reconciliation that is consistent with the psychology of its characters and provides a closure "that is in harmony with the disharmony of a universe of horror."

Steinbrunner, Chris, and Otto Penzler, eds. *Encyclopedia of Mystery and Detection*, New York: McGraw-Hill, 1976. This early, unsigned article gives a general overview of Hoch's work and refers to his short stories as highly regarded, though his novels had been greeted indifferently.

Marvin Lachman, updated by Stefan Dziemianowicz

E. T. A. HOFFMANN

Born: Königsberg, East Prussia; January 24, 1776
Died: Berlin, Germany; June 25, 1822

PRINCIPAL SHORT FICTION

Fantasiestücke in Callots Manier, 1814-1815
Nachtstücke, 1817
Klein Zaches, Genannt Zinnober, 1819 (*Little Zaches, Surnamed Zinnober*, 1971)
Die Serapionsbrüder, 1819-1821 (4 volumes; *The Serapion Brethren*, 1886-1892)
Prinzessin Brambilla: Ein Capriccio nach Jakob Callot, 1821 (*Princess Brambilla: A "Capriccio" in the Style of Jacques Callot*, 1971)
Meister Floh: Ein Märchen in sieben Abenteuern zweier Freunde, 1822 (*Master Flea: A Fairy Tale in Seven Adventures of Two Friends*, 1826)
Four Tales, 1962

The Best Tales of Hoffmann, 1967
Selected Writings of E. T. A. Hoffmann, 1969

OTHER LITERARY FORMS

A genius with versatile talents in graphics, music, and theater, E. T. A. Hoffmann first achieved artistic distinction as a musician. He composed symphonies, operettas, sonatas, and the first romantic opera *Undine* (1816), based on a *Nouvelle* by Friedrich Heinrich Karl de la Motte Fouqué, and he wrote perceptive, progressive music criticism on Ludwig van Beethoven's Fifth Symphony, Wolfgang Amadeus Mozart's *Don Juan* and *The Magic Flute*, and other musical topics. He also wrote two major novels: *Die Elixiere des Teufels: Nachgelassene Papiere des Bruders Medardus, eines Kapuziners* (1815-1816; *The Devil's Elixirs: From the Posthumous Papers of*

E. T. A. Hoffmann (Library of Congress)

though it would be difficult to trace completely his worldwide influence, his work certainly inspired writers such as Washington Irving, Nathaniel Hawthorne, and Edgar Allan Poe in the United States, Alexandre Dumas, Honoré de Balzac, and Victor Hugo in France, and Alexander Pushkin, Nikolai Gogol, and Fyodor Dostoevski in Russia. His tales have also inspired many composers, perhaps most notably Jacques Offenbach (*The Tales of Hoffmann*) and Peter Ilych Tchaikovsky (*The Nutcracker* and *The Queen of Spades*). His short fiction introduced many modern themes, including parapsychology and abnormal psychology, alienation of humans from life and society, the subconscious, the use of robots and automatons, and the fantastic and the grotesque. Hoffmann has also been credited with writing the first detective story in 1820, "Das Fräulein von Scudéri" ("Mademoiselle de Scudéry").

Brother Medardus, a Capuchin Friar, 1824), a Jekyll-Hyde psychological novel exploring the darker side of human nature, and *Lebensansichten des Katers Murr, nebst fragmentarischer Biographie des Kapellmeisters Johannes Kreisler in zufälligen Makulaturblättern* (1819-1821; *The Life and Opinions of Kater Murr, with the Fragmentary Biography of Kapellmeister Johannes Kreisler on Random Sheets of Scrap Paper*, 1969), a structurally innovative novel which contains interspersed pages from the life of a fictitious musician, used as blotting paper and underlay by the main narrator, the cat.

ACHIEVEMENTS

E. T. A. Hoffmann is a major figure of the romantic period and among the best-known writers of the German Romantic movement outside Germany. Al-

BIOGRAPHY

Ernst Theodor Amadeus Hoffmann's parents, of Polish-Hungarian background, were divorced when he was only two. As a child he received private tutoring in painting and piano. He studied law at the University of Königsberg and passed a government examination in 1795, but he gave private music lessons until his second exam in 1798, when he was assigned to courts in Berlin, then in Posen. In 1802, he was given a punitive transfer to a small town, Plock, for having drawn caricatures of Prussian officers, and there he married a Polish girl, Michelina Rohrer-Trzcinka, who remained his wife to the end. In 1806, Napoleon's army occupied Warsaw, and Hoffmann, like other Prussian officials who refused to sign an oath of allegiance to the French, lost his position and returned to Berlin, where he endured a year of hunger and hardship. From 1808 to 1812, Hoffmann worked with the Bamberg Theatre, first as orchestra-director, then as composer, stage-designer, and general assistant, during which time he had a serious platonic love affair with his teenage music student Julia Marc, who appears frequently in his fiction. In 1813, Hoffmann worked for the theater in Dresden and witnessed the siege of the city by the French forces. Reemployed by the Prussian bureaucracy from 1815 until his death, Hoffmann displayed great civil courage in opposing the "persecutions of demagogues," notably "Father" Jahn, a pioneer in athletics. For satirical passages against the chief prosecutor in his work *Master Flea*, Hoffmann was subjected to an investigation which lasted until his death from a paralytic disease on June 25, 1822. Contrary to the traditional image of him as a shiftless alcoholic, Hoffmann was a highly capable, conscientious, and just court official.

ANALYSIS

E. T. A. Hoffmann's fiction moves on two levels: a fantastic, imaginary level and an everyday, realistic one. The basic worldview underlying Hoffmann's "higher realm," the "marvellous magical world" beyond ordinary earthly reality, is German Classical Idealism in its late Romantic form as developed by thinkers such as Georg Hegel, Friedrich Schelling, and Johann Fichte, who saw external nature as a complex, contingent manifestation of the absolute spirit world. Literarily, this idea took the form of interpreting nature, especially its strangest or most symbolic phenomena (hypnosis, the occult, somnambulism, mental telepathy, insanity, dreams, mythology, music, religion) as hieroglyphics and evidences of the deeper strata of being, which could be "higher," as in the aesthetic and religious sublimity intimated in the great music of Johann Sebastian Bach, Ludwig van Beethoven, or Wolfgang Amadeus Mozart, or could open mysterious abysses of darkness as in Gotthilf Heinrich von Schubert's book on the "dark side of nature." In the words of critic Kenneth Negus, Hoffmann's myths "pictorialize invisible truths of nature."

The principle governing the depiction of this mythical, transcendental level in Hoffmann's stories is described in the framework story of *The Serapion Brethren*.

"THE STORY OF SERAPION"

In "The Story of Serapion," an insane man living in the woods in southern Germany in modern times believes himself to be the hermit Serapion who suffered martyrdom in Alexandria under the Emperor Decius. He is perfectly rational apart from this "idée fixe" with its aftermath that, having passed through martyrdom, by God's omnipotence he now lives on for centuries in great serenity "in the Theban desert" and receives visits from great men of history: Ariosto, Dante, Petrarch. When the realistic narrator challenges him that these interesting events really happen only in his mind, he answers, in accord with the subjectivistic philosophy of the time, that "if it is the mind only which takes cognizance of events around us, it follows that what it has taken cognizance of has actually occurred." The Serapion Brothers, a group of writers, including the narrator—who meet regularly to read to one another the stories that constitute the book—adopt Serapion's name and creative fantasy as their ideal, stressing both concrete vividness and Romantic sovereignty over the artistic material. A counterpointed realistic principle stated more than once later in the framework is that "the foot of the heavenly ladder, which we have got to mount in order to reach the higher regions, has got to be fixed firmly in every-day life," for "it is the outer world which causes the spirit to exercise those functions which take cognizance." The charm of "The Story of Serapion" consists in the interplay of attitudes between the totally subjective title figure and the realistic narrator. The very first story Hoffmann wrote, "Ritter Gluck," is much like "The Story of Serapion" in describing a genial delusionary who masterfully plays the famous composer's music from blank pages and at the end identifies himself with the words, "I am Ritter Gluck."

Far from being all of one type, the greatness of Hoffmann's works resides precisely in his awareness of point of view, in his expert modulation of perspective and narrative texture, thus creating a great number of styles and genres, depending on the narrator stance within the realism-Romanticism spectrum. In some stories, such as the famous *The Golden Flower Pot* (1814) and "The Mines of Falun," the balance shifts away from normal reality to the fantastic and mythical, while in others, such as "Councillor Krespel," "A Fragment of the Lives of Three Friends," and "Automatons," the marvelous and imaginary does not shatter the stance of an urbane, rational narrator.

THE GOLDEN FLOWER POT

The Golden Flower Pot, a fantastic *Märchen*, sharply contrasts the two conflicting strata and focuses mainly on the spirit realm. The student Anselmus struggles between the two perspectives represented by his love for Serpentina, a blue-eyed little green snake, daughter of Archivist Lindhorst, a powerful age-old Salamander (spiritprince) of the paradisaic Atlantis Kingdom, and his love for Veronica, whose aspirations are purely prosaic and conventional. In the end, the imaginary realm wins out; Anselmus marries Serpentina and vanishes from the earth, and the beautiful Xanadu-like dream realm is given an allegorical explanation as "life in poetry," which reveals "the sacred harmony of all begins, . . . the deepest secret of nature." The story's fame stems from the scintillating descriptions of the Romantic realm, such as the Fairyland Atlantis and the Archivist's fabled chambers with their strange unearthly trees and flowers, birds and insects, as well as from the ironic effects produced by the clash of perspectives.

"THE MINES OF FALUN"

"The Mines of Falun" strikes a more somber tone. Based on a true incident depicted in Schubert's book, the basic plot was already narrated with beautiful simplicity by J. P. Hebel in his anecdote "Unexpected Return": A young miner dies when a mine shaft caves in; fifty years later his body is discovered perfectly conserved by the metallic water of the mine; and his bride, now a wrinkled old woman, embraces her youthful fiancé and (in Hoffmann's version) dies as the corpse begins to disintegrate from contact with the air. In elaborate arabesques of Romantic imagination, Hoffmann relegates this core plot to the end and places the focus mainly on symbolic forces of the underworld (the Queen of Metals, a ghostly miner, metallic hieroglyphics, and the visionary mother lode) which lure the main character to his doom. The trau-

matic impact of his mother's death at the very beginning suggests a possible psychological interpretation of the beautiful, eerie sequences. The vast dark mine shaft of Falun, with its lifeless, weird-shaped rock masses "like gigantic petrified animals," sulfurous vapors, and dark-burned miners crawling out like insects, is heightened to a visible symbol of the gaping abyss of hell itself.

"MADEMOISELLE DE SCUDÉRY"

Written in a similar somber tone is "Mademoiselle de Scudéry," the first detective story (1820, thus antedating Edgar Allan Poe's Auguste Dupin stories). Many of its scenes take place at night, and it depicts the "night side" of the human psyche. The master goldsmith Cardillac cannot bear to part with his creations, so in the night he murders his customers to steal back their jewelry; he is so thorough in his crimes that the baffled Paris police think an entire gang of hoodlums is at work. Contrasting with this mad Jekyll-Hyde figure, the refined, humane author Mademoiselle de Scudéry clears an innocent suspect and solves the case. At the end, in the manner of late-Romantic and Biedermeier stories about weird events as well as of the modern detective story, all mysterious occurrences are given a natural explanation.

"COUNCILLOR KRESPEL"

"Councillor Krespel," one of the stories that uses an urbane modern narrator to observe strange persons or events, tells of an eccentric who buys expensive old violins, plays them once, then dismantles them to find the secret hidden in their inner structure. The tragic ending, anticipating Thomas Mann's *Tristan* (1903), is the death of his daughter Antonie, whose great singing talent is inseparable from a fatal illness. The story is narrated as a true experience by Theodor, one of the Serapion Brothers, rather than read as a piece of creative fiction, and it is meant as a transition "from pure insanity (Serapion), *via* eccentricity (Krespel), to the realms of everyday rationality" ("A Fragment of the Lives of Three Friends," "Automatons"). It is perhaps Hoffmann's most tragic tale.

THEMES AND STYLE

"A Fragment of the Lives of Three Friends," combining a ghost story with that of three young men's love for the same girl, has bidirectional irony between the rational perspective and the preternatural phenomena. "Automatons" explores the eeriness of various mechanical oddities, especially "The Talking Turk," from an inquisitive but cool and empirical standpoint. "The Sandman," in which a traumatic childhood "experience" leads to madness, attempted murder, and suicide, features Olimpia, the scientist's automaton "daughter," who is familiar from Offenbach's opera. In "A New Year's Eve Adventure," which recounts Hoffmann's frustrated love for Julia Marc, who is depicted as a sirenlike enhantress luring the protagonist to his doom, Chamisso's shadowless Peter Schlemihl and Erasmus Spickher, who lost his mirror reflection to the seductive Giulietta, are mythical figures. Other characters seem to have been suggested by a New Year's candy display—for example, the chancellor "was a splendid gumdrop with a coat made of pleated notepaper. . . ." All these stories maintain the tone of a suave and cultivated narrator.

Artists play a considerable role in Hoffmann's tales; indeed, some stories were suggested by paintings. "Doge and Dogaressa" is based on a painting by Wilhelm Kolbe exhibited in Berlin in 1814, depicting an eighty-year-old Doge marrying a beautiful eighteen-year-old girl before a background of Venice. Hoffmann develops this into a love-triangle story. The tragicomic "An Interrupted Cadence" begins with the description of a painting by J. F. Hummel from the same Berlin exhibition: two young women singing under the direction of a man in a cassock. In the story, the narrator Theodore falls in love with two Italian singers and goes with them as their composer and accompanist. Once, on a capricious impulse, Theodore strikes the final chord too early and interrupts the older sister's artificial coloratura. Hearing the two women discuss him pejoratively, he breaks up the friendship. Years later, himself an accomplished musician, he meets them again in scene exactly like the painting. Time has not been very kind to his former friends; he has a sense of relief that he has not remained associated with them—for that would have meant artistic stagnation—mingled with a reminiscent sadness at the "interrupted cadence" not only of Lauretta's coloratura but also of their friendship itself.

The collection *Princess Brambilla* is based on eight fantastic caricatures by Jacob Callot. One artist-story not based on a painting but in which paintings play a prominent part, the hilariously comical novella *Signor Formica* (1819), in which the famous Italian artist Salvator Rosa through clever machinations removes the obstacles to the marriage of two young friends, abounds with side-splitting humor about the medical profession, miserliness, and artistic jealousy.

In conclusion, a few peculiarities of Hoffmann's style are as follows. First, in dialogues, he often repeats a phrase before and after the identification of the speaker: "'I still,' cried the prince in supreme annoyance, 'I still don't understand you, incomprehensible man.'" Second, E. T. A. Hoffmann appears in his works in many ways as a narrator (indeed, in the Serapion framework, three of the narrators are alter egos of Hoffmann) or as a character (for example, the frustrated lover in "A New Year's Eve Adventure"), but one oft-repeated striking self-caricature is a physical trait of his various magicians, master artists, or scientists (such as Coppelius, Dr. Dapertutto, Professor X., Archivist Lindhorst, Godpapa Drosselmeier, and Cardillac): They have a hooked Roman nose and a contorted sarcastic sneer, interpreted by Hoffmann as resulting from the perception of the dichotomy that exists between the "other realm" and the outer world of reality. Third, as shown above, amid the many genres and styles one certain mythical structure animates all his works and is well summed up in a quotation from the Serapion framework about the gothic cathedral of Strasburg:

> . . . the beholder gazes with a strange inward disquiet upon the Strasburg Minster, as it soars aloft in the most daring curves, and the most wondrous interlacings of varied, fantastic forms and ornamentation. And this very unrest awakens a sense of the Unknown, the Marvellous; and the spirit readily yields itself to this dream, in which it seems to recognize the Superearthly, the Unending. Now this is exactly the effect of that purely romantic element which pervades Mozart and Haydn's compositions.

This also is the quintessence of Hoffmann's aesthetic endeavor.

Finally, however arabesque the "interlacings" and "fantastic forms" of Hoffmann's works may be, they are not the result of purely subjective arbitrariness; whatever subject he wrote about was well researched. The works and frameworks themselves often cite historical sources or books on psychology, parapsychology, and occult and preternatural phenomena which he had consulted. Although he wrote so long before the greatest advances in psychology, psychologists who have studied his works confirm the accuracy of his treatment, and a Prussian general praised Nutcracker's deployment of troops in his war against the mice. Hoffmann's castle in the clouds has a foundation built on the solid rock of reality.

OTHER MAJOR WORKS

LONG FICTION: *Die Elixiere des Teufels: Nachgelassene Papiere des Bruders Medardus, eines Kapuziners*, 1815-1816 (*The Devil's Elixirs: From the Posthumous Papers of Brother Medardus, a Capuchin Friar*, 1824); *Lebensansichten des Katers Murr, nebst fragmentarischer Biographie des Kapellmeisters Johannes Kreisler in zufälligen Makulaturblättern*, 1819-1821 (*The Life and Opinions of Kater Murr, with the Fragmentary Biography of Kapellmeister Johannes Kreisler on Random Sheets of Scrap Paper*, 1969; also as *The Educated Cat*).

NONFICTION: *Briefwechsel*, 1967-1969 (3 volumes; correspondence); *Tagebücher*, 1971 (4 volumes; diaries); *Selected Letters*, 1977.

MUSICAL COMPOSITIONS: *Liebe und Eifersucht: Oper*, 1807; *Trois Canzonettes*, 1808; *Arlequinn: Ballett*, 1811; *Undine*, 1816; *Musikalische Werke*, 1922-1927.

BIBLIOGRAPHY

Allen, Richard. "Reading Kleist and Hoffmann." In *Romantic Writing*, edited by Stephen Bygrave. London: Routledge, 1996. Discusses alienation, the Freudian notion of the uncanny, the relationship between love and death, and the sense of strangeness in Hoffmann's "The Sandman."

Daemmrich, Horst S. *The Shattered Self: E. T. A. Hoffmann's Tragic Vision*. Detroit: Wayne State University Press, 1973. An important study of the literary work of Hoffmann. After his introduction, which places Hoffmann in historical context and outlines critical appraisals of his work, Daemmrich analyzes Hoffmann's major themes and motifs. He sees a "dynamic structural pattern" as a basis for humans' search for identity and finds in Hoffmann's work a portrayal of "the disintegration of the individual in a world uncontrolled forces." Contains extensive notes to individual chapters, a bibliography, and an index.

Hewett-Thayer, Harvey W. *Hoffmann: Author of the Tales*. Princeton, N. J.: Princeton University Press, 1938. A comprehensive biography of Hoffmann and a discussion of his works. The footnotes are very informative, containing comments and suggestions for further reading, as well as the original German for many passages when these appear in English translation in the main text. Includes very readable story analyses, often with a summary of the story line. Supplemented by a listing of Hoffmann's literary works with dates of publication, a bibliography, and an index of names and works. Intended as an introduction for both the student and the general reader.

Kohlenbach, Margarete. "Women and Artists: E. T. A. Hoffmann's Implicit Critique of Early Romanticism." *The Modern Language Review* 89 (July, 1994): 659-673. Notes the psychic limitation and misogynistic implications in several of Hoffmann's narratives; examines "Der Sandmann" to determine the importance of the text's ambiguity with respect to the Romantic discourse on femininity.

Kropf, David Gleen. *Authorship as Alchemy: Subversive Writing in Pushkin, Scott, Hoffmann*. Stanford, Calif.: Stanford University Press, 1994. Discusses the story "Das Fräulein von Schdern" in terms of how it reveals different ways in which authorship puts pressure on the creative process and undermines the workings of authorship.

Lazare, Christopher, ed. Introduction and biographic note to *Tales of Hoffmann*. New York: Grove Press, 1946. The introduction contains helpful comments on Hoffmann's importance in nineteenth century European literature, and the biographical note is an informative essay, giving the general reader details of Hoffmann's biography along with some insights into his attitudes and way of viewing life. The main body of the book contains modern English translations of ten of his most important stories.

McGlathery, James M. *E. T. A. Hoffmann.* New York: Twayne, 1997. A critical introduction to Hoffmann's life and work, focusing on critical reception to his work, his own critical writings, and analysis of his major works of fiction. Includes discussions of "The Sandman" and "Ritter Gluck," as well as several lesser-known stories and Hoffmann's fairy tales.

Negus, Kenneth. *E. T. A. Hoffmann's Other World: The Romantic Author and His "New Mythology."* Philadelphia: University of Pennsylvania Press, 1965. A very readable and useful monography, focusing on Hoffmann's development of a coherent body of myth in his fantasy world—a "new mythology" founded on an inner spiritual (or psychological) world but extending to form a "cosmic myth." In the process, Negus examines all Hoffmann's major, and many of the minor, literary works, with a view to laying a critical foundation for his narrative art. The book includes a select bibliography and an index.

Passage, Charles E. *The Russian Hoffmannists.* The Hague: Mouton, 1963. Intended for readers interested in comparative literature, this study focuses on the significance of Hoffmann's work for Russian literature. Among the authors examined at length are Nikolai Gogol and Fyodor Dostoevski. Passage attempts to show real areas of influence and correct claims of influence where none exists. The appendices include a helpful listing of Hoffman's works with the original publication dates (even of individual stories when published elsewhere before appearing in a collection), a chronology, and a parallel listing of Hoffmann's work in relation to works of Russian Hoffmannists.

David J. Parent, updated by Susan L. Piepke

HOMER

Born: Ionia(?), Greece; c. ninth century B.C.E.
Died: Greece; c. eighth century B.C.E.

PRINCIPAL SHORT FICTION

Iliad, c. 800 B.C.E.
Odyssey, c. 800 B.C.E.

OTHER LITERARY FORMS

Homer is noted as the author of two magnificent works: the *Iliad* and the *Odyssey.*

ACHIEVEMENTS

Homer's position at the headwaters of Western literature has assured him an unparalleled influence. Writers from antiquity through the twentieth century are in his debt, and, as the principal repository of Greek legend, his work is an important source of knowledge about the classical world. Homeric epic in particular presents a complete world of remote time and space, offering the full range of human experiences, integrated into one complex social and ideological nexus.

While modern readers have nothing at stake in this remote past in and of itself, those who became the "things of song" as well as those who were "the singers of tales" are their ancestors, culturally if not biologically. One of the functions of Homeric epic was to set in motion "for the future" the singing itself. The dimensions of the *Iliad* and the *Odyssey* are respectively 15,693 and 12,110 metrical lines; Greek text consists of 115,477 and 87,765 words. It was the genius of Homer to create such an ancestral literary heritage.

BIOGRAPHY

A careful study of the Homeric Greek language, and of references to social customs that do not belong to that heroic age, or late Bronze Age, toward which the story line and some material objects point back, permits one to fix the time of Homer within that era of commercial redevelopment that occurred in the Aegean Basin during the Early Iron Age. Geometric art documents both the transitional era and the emergence of epic themes and characters. The earliest direct quote from the *Iliad*, by Semonides (c. 630 B.C.E.), calls its author "man of Chios." Homer was identified and censured by Xenophanes (c. 550 B.C.E.); the poems were named specifically and Homer dated by Herodotus (c. 450 B.C.E.) as having lived "four hundred years earlier." Some ancient commentators accepted the existence of an old, blind, wandering bard who composed first the *Iliad* and then the *Odyssey*. Nineteenth century scholarship was inclined to doubt that both works are by one man, and some doubted that either poem is the work of a single author. Nevertheless, as scholarly debate sharpens and arguments become more sophisticated, scholars continue to use the name "Homer" when speaking of the poems, and almost all readers of whatever maturity think of a man, Homer, who created two epic masterpieces.

ANALYSIS

Homer was the beneficiary of earlier, disparate stories, some mythical, some legendary, and some doubtless historical. Like William Shakespeare so many centuries later, although in an oral medium rather than a written one, Homer combined, rearranged, and shaped with artistic purpose these earlier narrative materials. The writing down of Homeric epic must be nearly contemporary with the advent of the Greek alphabetic script within the eighth century B.C.E., for the vocabulary retains hints of letters subsequently discarded, and the earliest inscriptions on pottery include fragments of catalectic dactylic hexameter—the heroic scansion.

ILIAD

The *Iliad* remains the first of Western war stories and the *Odyssey*, the greatest of adventures. Each, for all its episodic variety, is a unity. The *Iliad* begins with the indignant wrath of Achilles which affects the last events before the walls of Troy and ends with the replacement of wrath by a personal humanity shown

Homer (Library of Congress)

to the grieving Priam, King of Troy. The *Odyssey* develops the adventures of Odysseus (already praised for his ingenuity in the *Iliad*), who left his wife and home in Ithaca twenty years before to bring Helen back from Troy, until he triumphantly returns to Ithaca and his wife, the faithful Penelope—the moral obverse of Helen. In the creation of these unities, Homer utilized a number of techniques which later poets (and prose writers) would adopt. Among these are: the announcement of an anticipated action which is then suspensefully delayed; the invocation to the muse (with which each poem begins); the beginning of the action *in medias res*; the consequent use of flashbacks; and telling repetition by epithet and formulas, catalogue, and the epic simile.

The simplicity and directness of Homer's vignettes have produced some immortal images for subsequent Western artists—literary, pictorial, and plastic. Among these are the parting of Hector and Andromache with the child Astynax frightened by the horse-haired helmet of his father, the death of Hector at the hands of Achilles, Priam's visit to Achilles, the Greek leaders going to the tent of the sullen Achilles (used by Shakespeare in *Troilus and Cressida*, 1601-1602, and through Shakespeare by Alfred, Lord Tennyson in "Ulysses"), and even the Telemachia, the sequence of episodes which makes up the first four books of the *Odyssey*. These episodes and characters remind the reader that they and the rest of the poem are both poetry and educational lesson. For the Greeks and Westerners who succeeded them, Homer is both "poet" and "educator"; some have gone so far as to seek lessons in every aspect of the poems, and they piously created them when they were not to be found. This moralizing bent has often led to rampant allegorizing. It is one thing to claim, in however a reductionist spirit, the *Iliad* as a textbook for governors and the *Odyssey* as a guide to household economy, but quite another to find anagogical and tropological meaning in verses singularly free from such designed levels of significance. Such, however, has been part of the interpretive history of these epics.

Those not understanding the wholeness of each poem have found inconsistencies and contradictions; book 10 of the *Iliad* (the Doloneia) and book 11 of the

Odyssey (the summoning of the disembodied personalities in Hades) looked like interpolations. Yet in large the poems are most carefully structured, for the oral nature of their composition obviously did not preclude subtle balancing and contrasting.

The *Iliad* begins with the wrath of Achilles at the injustice done to him by Agamemnon and ends with the clemency of Achilles, who returns to Priam the body of Trojan Hector slain and dishonored by Achillean wrath. In between, the reader is shown the effects of Achilles' withdrawal from the fight before the walls of Troy. Books 2 to 9 present the preparation for battle, the triumph of Diomedes, an only slightly less powerful Achilles, and the setback of the Greeks, whose leaders in book 9 come in an embassy to Achilles, who still refuses to fight, although in his refusal there are signs of hope.

Book 10, sometimes viewed as an interlude, involves the slaying of the Trojan spy, Dolon, and the capture by Diomedes and Odysseus of Trojan horses. Books 11 to 22 show more fighting, which brings about the wounding of the leading Greeks, Agamemnon, Diomedes, and Odysseus; the breaching of the Greek wall by Hector, a temporary Greek rally; a return to Trojan advantage; the pivotal decision by Achilles (book 16) to allow Patroclus to wear Achilles' own armor in order to save the Greek cause; the subsequent triumph of Patroclus over Zeus's own son, Sarpedon; Patroclus's death at the hands of Hector; the fight for the body of Patroclus; the grief of Achilles for the death of his friend; the creation of new arms for Achilles, including the richly designed shield; the reconciliation of Achilles with Agamemnon and the public presentation of the compensatory gifts to Achilles by Agamemnon; the arming of Achilles; his destruction of many Trojans, but not Aeneas, who is rescued that he may live and eventually rule over the surviving Trojans; and Achilles' great fight with the River Scamander, the battle amongst the gods, somewhat of a comic relief before the climactic fight between Achilles and Hector and the dishonoring of Hector's body.

Book 23 provides the funeral of Patroclus and the funeral games, which offer a lessening of tension and further revelation of the characters of the Greek heroes. Achilles is still the dominant figure, but one almost purged of his wrath. In book 24 Achilles suppresses his need of vengeance and grants Priam the body of Hector, well aware of the imminence of his own death. The poem ends with the Trojans mourning the death of their bulwark and champion. The *Iliad* is the first of Western books, and its characters, themes, and structure have provided more than two millennia of subsequent narrative artists with materials for their own poetry and prose. None of them, however, with good reason, has matched the *Iliad*'s presentation of the glory and limitations of perfected martial honor.

ODYSSEY

The *Odyssey* is a more varied work than the *Iliad*, even as its eponymous protagonist, the man of many wiles, is a far more multifaceted character than Achilles. Not only is Odysseus (Ulysses) more complex but also his enemies are of different kinds, not only men and gods but also sorceresses and giants. The fact that Odysseus overcomes monsters and women alters the tone of this poem, but as in the *Iliad*, the author can rely on his audience's knowing most of the background of the events in his work, a knowledge that increases the pleasure derived from the heightened expectation. The suspense begins with books 1-4, which are devoted to the difficulties of Penelope, Telemachus, and Ithaca in general as they suffer the degradations and plots of the suitors. Only the return of Odysseus himself can save matters. Telemachus goes in search of information regarding his father's whereabouts. The largely domestic considerations of the opening lay the groundwork of the plot and promise the return of the hero. In addition, there is an element of the fantastic, an important aspect of the entire poem, in the story of Proteus, the old man of the sea who is tricked by Menelaus into telling of Odysseus. Books 5-12 are framed by two magical women, the nymph Calypso, who, after saving Odysseus from shipwreck and loving him for eight years on her hidden island, only reluctantly and at the command of the gods releases him; and Circe, initially a powerful but evil witch who is overcome by Odysseus and, after loving the hero for a year, releases him with a helpful warning of future dangers.

In between, the plot includes the contrast of life among the aesthetically attractive Phaeacians and the adventure with the monster cannibal Polyphemus who, blinded, is tricked by Odysseus at nearly the cost of his own life. In addition there is the haunting episode (book 11) of the descent into Hades. The fantastic adventures, dangers, and magical devices (the plant *moly* given to Odysseus by Hermes to protect him against the charm of Circe) are perhaps the best-known aspects of the *Odyssey* (well-known also in their domesticated modernizations to readers of James Joyce's *Ulysses*, 1922). These adventures are told by Odysseus himself (to the King and Queen of the Phaeacians) while functioning as narrative retrospect, and they remind the audience also of the important role of the "singer of tales" within the dramatic nature of narrative poetry.

Book 13 brings Odysseus back to Ithaca (by magic ship) and again within the protective care of Athena. In this and the following books, he learns of events in his beleaguered home, is disguised (as a beggar), and begins a series of discrete revelations and recognition scenes. These occur first with his son (book 16); then most touchingly with his old dog Argos (book 17); then with his ancient nurse Euryclea, who recognizes his boar-scar (book 19); then with his swineherd Eumaeus (book 21); after the slaying of the suitors, with his wife Penelope, who recognizes his unique knowledge of the structure of their marriage bed (book 23); and finally by means of his scar, with his father Laertes. Book 24 brings "this Odyssey" to its rightful conclusion with harmony reestablished by Athena.

The ferocity of Odysseus's revenge upon the suitors serves to remind the audience of the ethics of a far earlier culture, even as modern readers marvel at the skillful narrative devices and the remarkable aesthetic compression of long-term physical action. No summary or analysis of this most intricately woven of ancient poems—woven of the threads of myth, fairy tale, legend, and geographical fact—can convey its delight or indicate the fascination of its protagonist, a hero who is a complete man, son, husband, and father.

How an epic poet is of influence upon other narrative writers using shorter forms and sometimes, indeed in the twentieth century, almost always, prose, remains an open question. The days of verse narrative seem to have ended with the death of John Masefield. Yet all narrators who have read Homer are themselves open to the force of the dramatic nature of the narrative; the diversity of his episodes; the unity of total design; the consistency and contrasting nature of his characters; the relative simplicity of his syntax and the clarity of his similes (even the celebrated extended or "Homeric" similes, which, if not equal to the Miltonic simile in homologation, are easily as memorable); the concentration of action into a few days out of very many; the devices of flashback and foreshadowing; the effect of augmentation and iteration by catalog and epithet; and, finally, the choice of themes of love, war, and personal integrity, however these terms are defined today. Homer is, after all, the first—perhaps the greatest—of Western storytellers.

BIBLIOGRAPHY

Carlisle, Miriam, and Olga Levaniouk, eds. *Nine Essays on Homer.* Lanham, Md.: Rowman & Littlefield, 1999. This collection of essays offers insight into Homer's themes and style.

Clarke, Howard W. *Homer's Readers: A Historical Introduction to the "Iliad" and the "Odyssey."* Newark: University of Delaware Press, 1981. Within a format of five chapters, the reading of Homer, over the long period since the inception of the epics, is sequentially viewed as "romanticized, allegorized, criticized, analyzed, and anatomized." Under the final and contemporary category, one sees successively the historical, anthropological, geographical, oral, and literary Homer. Detailed notes, extensive bibliography, and index.

Clay, Jenny Strauss. *The Wrath of Athena: Gods and Men in the "Odyssey."* Princeton, N.J: Princeton University Press, 1983. By asking and then answering the question of Athena's withdrawal from Odyseus, which takes one through a closely considered, carefully argued, and elaborately documented discussion of gods and humans within Homeric poetry, one discerns how the entirety of the *Odyssey* has coherence. This reading, with full use of ancient and scholarly commentaries, of Homer from within Homer, illustrates how the *Odyssey* and the *Iliad* are interrelated. Extensive bibliography and detailed indices.

Dalby, Andrew. "The *Iliad*, the *Odyssey*, and Their Audiences." *The Classical Quarterly*, n.s. 45, no. 2 (1995): 269-279. Contends the society that appears in Homer's epics is built on the perceptions of the poorest and least powerful Greeks of that time. The power, actions, and possessions of the heroes are enlarged because this is the most satisfactory means by which to depict the life of the rich in a literature that is in essence a popular discourse.

De Jong, Irene J. F., ed. *Homer: Critical Assessments.* New York: Routledge, 1999. Thoughtful critical interpretations of Homer's works.

Foley, John Miles. "Signs, Texts, and Oral Tradition." *Journal of Folklore Research* 33 (January-April, 1996): 21-29. Discusses an episode in the *Odyssey* as a species of oral traditional communication; argues that only when we put aside our culturally constructed, unexamined notions of "signs" and "reading" can we grasp the richness of Homer's poems, which effectively lie between performance and text.

Friis Johansen, K. *The "Iliad" in Early Greek Art.* Copenhagen: Munksgaard, 1967. While discussing and detailing a complete representation of epic themes in archaic art (before 475 B.C.E.), Friis Johansen provides a comprehensive catalog (pp. 244-280) of all that pertains to the *Iliad*, in a work unmatched for comparable materials in English.

Parry, Milman. *The Making of Homeric Verse: The Collected Papers of Milman Parry.* Oxford England: Clarendon Press, 1971. By focusing on the formulaic nature of repeated passages and units within the traditional meter, Parry radically altered the way in which heroic and oral poetry was to be studied and what constituted its style. Well indexed, but requires a capacity to work with the Greek text.

Redfield, James M. *Nature and Culture in the "Il-*

iad": The Tragedy of Hector. Chicago: University of Chicago Press, 1975. Depends on a careful reading of Aristotle's *The Poetics* relative to the *Iliad*, which allowed access to the central themes of the comparisons and contrasts between Achilles and Hector. Five chapters, enriched by extensive notes, references, and indices, provide a view of the poem under the categories of imitation, tragedy, the hero, error, and purification.

Richardson, Scott. "Truth in the Tales of the *Odyssey*." *Mnemosyne* 49 (September, 1996): 393-402. Discusses the difficulties involved in determining the truth value of long narratives told by characters in the *Odyssey*; a number of tales told by characters cannot be authenticated because the main narrator does not include these episodes in his own narrative; explains how the idea of an "ideal narrative audience," one that believes all the incidents related as factual, can be helpful in dealing with falsehoods in the *Odyssey*.

Scodel, Ruth. "Bardic Performance and Oral Tradition in Homer." *American Journal of Philology* 119 (Summer, 1998): 171-194. Claims that the care with which Homer presents bardic performance as uncontaminated and free, even while he reveals the forces that would realistically limit its freedom.

Wace, Alan J. B., and Frank H. Stubbings, eds. *A Companion to Homer.* London: Macmillan, 1962. A collection of twenty-three major essays contributed by sixteen of the more important British and American scholars. The issues involved in the discussion of Homer, the poetry, its study, its world, and its material culture are adumbrated within three historical frameworks: that to which Homer points, that of which "he" was a member, and that from which "he" has been successively read ever since. A thorough index complements the select bibliographies and notes found within each essay.

Wood, Michael. *In Search of the Trojan War.* New York: Facts on File, 1985. This volume is the published version of a popular and eminent British Broadcasting Corporation's television series. It reviews the history of the archaeological investigation into the Homeric sites throughout their Late Bronze Age, beginning with the discoveries of German archaeologist Heinrich Schliemann; also reviews the historical impact of those discoveries on the way in which the historical question can be put concerning the Trojan War, the cast of Homeric characters in that war, the story of the *Iliad*, and Homer himself. This beautifully and extensively illustrated volume is a splendid accompaniment to the reading of the *Iliad*.

Rosemary Barton Tobin,
updated by Clyde Curry Smith

JANETTE TURNER HOSPITAL

Born: Melbourne, Australia; November 12, 1942

PRINCIPAL SHORT FICTION

Dislocations, 1986
Isobars, 1990
Collected Stories: 1970-1995, 1995

OTHER LITERARY FORMS

Although Janette Turner Hospital's short stories have been widely praised, she is probably best known for her novels *The Ivory Swing* (1982), *The Tiger in the Tiger Pit* (1983), *Borderline* (1985), *Charades* (1988), *The Last Magician* (1992), and *Oyster* (1996). Hospital has also written a crime thriller, *A Very Proper Death* (1990), under the pseudonym Alex Juniper.

ACHIEVEMENTS

Janette Turner Hospital's short story "Waiting" won a first short-story award, presented by *Atlantic Monthly*; her first novel, *The Ivory Swing*, won Canada's Seal First Novel Award, presented by Seal Books. She has also received a gold medal from the Canadian National Magazine Awards; a Torgi Award, presented by the Canadian Association for the Blind; and an Australian National Book Council Award. Her collection of short stories *Dislocations* won the Fellowship of Australian Writers Award, and her novel *Charades* was a finalist for the Booker McConnell Prize. Many of her short stories have appeared in England's *Annual Best Short Stories*, and her novel *Oyster* was a finalist for awards in both Australia and Canada. Griffith University awarded her an honorary doctorate in 1995 for her contributions to Australian literature.

BIOGRAPHY

Janette Turner Hospital was born in Melbourne, Australia, on November 12, 1942, but her family soon moved to Brisbane, Queensland, where she received her B.A. from the University of Queensland in 1966. After teaching school in Queensland for a short time, Hospital moved to the United States, where she worked as a librarian at Harvard University. She and her husband moved to Kingston, Ontario, in 1971, where she received an academic appointment in religious studies. In 1977 she lived in India, where she developed material for her novel *The Ivory Swing*. She has been a writer-in-residence and a lecturer at the Massachusetts Institute of Technology, the University of East Anglia, Colgate University, and other schools in the United States, Canada, and Australia. Thereafter, she became a professor of English at the University of South Carolina.

ANALYSIS

The most common critical remarks made about the fiction of Janette Turner Hospital focus on her geographical and cultural dislocation. Although she has encouraged such a multicultural approach in an era fascinated by marginality by titling her first short-story collection *Dislocations* and her second *Isobars* (imaginary lines on a map connecting points of equal pressure), Hospital's focus on political and cultural issues has tended to neglect the universal psychological and philosophical implications of her short fiction.

While Hospital's stories are often more conventionally structured than her frequently experimental novels, they are also more personal, arising from what author Elizabeth Bowen once called "necessariness"; Hospital's stories, as Bowen says about the short story, seem to spring from an "impression or perception pressing enough, acute enough to make the writer write."

Although many of Hospital's stories focus on cultural differences, the emphasis is not on their social or political implications but rather on the more profoundly philosophical implications of the tensions between the concrete and the abstract, the poetic and the physical, between primeval spirituality and culturally constructed religion, between restraint and release, and, ultimately, between civilization and its discontents.

"LITANY FOR THE HOMELAND"

This story is important for understanding the uniquely personal and psychological way Hospital treats the theme of the relationship between two cultures. "Litany for the Homeland," written in response to an Australian multicultural festival's request that writers compose a piece on the subject of homelands, is the most explicit treatment of the theme. In this lyrical meditation, the female narrator recalls a time in Queensland when she was looking at the stars through a telescope and noticed a wild boy with a glittering eye beckoning to her from behind a rotten fence. She describes different embodiments of the boy with the glittering eye, all of whom have since seduced her away from abstraction and idealization. One of them, Paddy McGee, a young Irish Catholic boy, who rebels against schoolteachers, takes his beating and leaves, never to return.

"AFTER LONG ABSENCE"

Another incarnation of the Paddy McGee character, Patrick Murphy, appears in "After Long Absence," the story of a woman who visits her home in Queensland. She recalls that, when she was in the fifth grade, she was stigmatized by teachers and students for her parents' fundamentalist religious beliefs. In the central event of the story, she remembers one Friday night in Brisbane, when she was with her father and others preaching against sin outside a theater. Patrick Murphy came out of the theater accompanied by a brassy platinum blond with big breasts and spiked heels. When the blond laughed at the "Holy Rollers," Patrick said that such people have guts and that he "always did go for guts"; significantly, he gave the young protagonist a wink and a thumbs-up. The adult narrator, who has long since rebelled against her parents' religious fundamentalism, thinks she has always been a pagan at heart.

"YOU GAVE ME HYACINTHS"

The allure of the pagan is also at the heart of "You Gave Me Hyacinths," in which the female protagonist remembers her first teaching job in Cairns, Australia, and the young working-class girl who was her student. The girl hates poetry and scolds the teacher for spoiling things by always asking why. The protagonist urges her to escape the small, tropical town, but

Janette Turner Hospital (AP/Wide World Photos)

when the two of them go for a swim, the teacher realizes that the girl belongs in Cairns, and she envies her comfortable sense of being at home. The story ends with the girl giving the teacher a stolen orchid and the teacher reading her the passage from T. S. Eliot's *The Waste Land* (1922) that is the source of the story's title. The gap between the stolen orchid and the Eliot poem is similar to the gap between the telescope and the wild boy's glittering eye in "Litany for the Homeland"—a tension between the ideal and the real, which occurs often in Hospital's stories.

"GOLDEN GIRL"

The tension between body and mind in "Golden Girl" takes place within a single character, Cilla, a beautiful young woman disfigured in an accidental fire. The poetic allusion that serves as a metaphor for this story—for poetry is never very far from Hospital's language-conscious vision—is Alfred, Lord Tennyson's "The Lady of Shalott." Cilla, while still swathed in bandages, decides, like the Lady of Shalott, to be "mysterious and desirable and infinitely remote." Brilliant as well as beautiful, Cilla controls her story and her situation through her literate and ironic point of view, deciding she will exist as her own literary commentary—beautiful, though tragic.

Describing herself as looking like the bride of Tutankhamen, driving dead lovers crazy, Cilla says her headgear is as white as a virgin's underwear and jokes about her thighs, "gallantly doffing their cloak of flesh to cover her cheeks." With the protection of this comic deprecation, she endures being locked inside her mask. At the end of the story, she transcends the revelation of the stranger who stares back at her in the mirror and affirms her love for her friend, who feels responsible for the accident. Ultimately, the girl is golden, not because of her physical appearance but because of the glow of her mind.

"UNPERFORMED EXPERIMENTS HAVE NO RESULTS"

This late Hospital story, included in *The Best of Best Short Stories, 1986-1995*, but appearing for the first time in book form in her *Collected Stories*, opens with Phillipa, the female narrator, feeling uncertain about the temporal and causal relationships between certain events and about whether the events are dreams or reality. Thematically, this uncertainty is combined with the narrator's consideration of chance and coincidence; she says she has become "obsessed with patterns of chance, the neatness of them, the provocation such neatness gives"; however, she also says the more she tries to focus on the neatness of chance the hazier things become.

The central problematical event in the story occurs while she is sitting at the end of her dock reading a book and watching the "theatre of wind and water." She sees a man in a canoe and, astonished, thinks she is imagining things. She considers that it is odd how certain body shapes and gestures remain like templates in the memory; she believes the figure of the man looks much like her friend Brian, and she remembers her senior year in Queensland, when she and Brian climbed a waterfall and floated into a "long sensuous silence . . . sweeter than sleep." The story then shifts to a dream in which she sees Brian's drowned body under water. She assumes there is a simple logic to this sequence of events (seeing the man in the canoe and then having the dream), but she cannot be sure. The relationship between past and

present is emphasized when she receives an e-mail message from Brian, saying he wishes they could go backward, "unclimb the waterfall."

Brian, a scientist, understands the artistic nature of the narrator—that she lives inside the vague world of her mind, making things up and believing they are real. When she accuses him of dong the same, he says that as a scientist, his fictions are verifiable but admits that "half the battle is how you frame the question. Unperformed experiments have no results." In this story, Hospital explores key issues about the relationships and differences between science and art, sympathetic magic and synchronicity. The experiments the artist performs do not seek results, for the artist wishes to remain in a realm without verification, a realm of synchronicity, magic, mythical thinking, and negative capability. In the realm of art, one never wants to get where one is going; one does not really want the answers to questions; one wants the mystery of imminence.

OTHER MAJOR WORKS

LONG FICTION: *The Ivory Swing*, 1982; *The Tiger in the Tiger Pit*, 1983; *Borderline*, 1985; *Charades*, 1988; *A Very Proper Death*, 1990 (as Alex Juniper); *The Last Magician*, 1992; *Oyster*, 1996.

BIBLIOGRAPHY

Callahan, David. "Acting in the Public Sphere and the Politics of Memory in Janette Turner Hospital." *Tulsa Studies in Women's Literature* 15 (Spring, 1996): 73-81. Discusses Hospital's "feminist postmodernism," how conflict between moral concerns and memory creates displacements in her work; argues that her fiction reflects a tension between reality as a construct and the demand for moral responsibility.

_____. "Janette Turner Hospital and the Discourse of Displacement." In *Nationalism vs. Internationalism: (Inter)national Dimensions of Literatures in English*, edited by Wolfgang Zach and Ken L. Goodwin. Tübingen: Stauffenburg, 1966. Argues that whereas in her earlier stories, Hospital presents cultural conflict arising from differences in individuals, in later stories she explores the more complex issue of accommodating otherness within ourselves.

Cowley, Julian. "'Violent Times': Janette Turner Hospital's Art of Memory and the History of the Present." In *Image and Power: Women in Fiction in the Twentieth Century*, edited by Sarah Sceats and Gail Cunningham. New York: Longmans, 1996. Discusses the relationship between history and storytelling in two of Hospital's novels; points out a common theme in her work relating to storytelling as a way to find meaning and as a strategy for survival.

Hamelin, Christine. "'Novelist as Urgent Quester.'" *Australian and New Zealand Studies in Canada* 9 (June, 1993): 106-111. Hospital insists that she is not writing propaganda or didactic art; says that her fiction does not begin with ideology, but with a sense of irresistiblility and inevitability; says that she is not in the business of telling readers what political stance they should take.

Hospital, Janette Turner. Interview by Missy Daniel. *Publishers Weekly* 239 (September 14, 1992): 80-81. Hospital discusses the methods by which her fiction is generated, the effect of dislocation on her writing, her academic background in medi-eval literature, and the issue of nationality among writers.

McGregor, Cynthia. "Voyages Between Two Worlds." *Books in Canada* 21 (November 1, 1992): 11-16. Hospital talks about her relationship to Canadian critics, her experience with intolerance toward her fundamentalist upbringing, and the difference between the way she approaches writing short stories and writing novels.

Schramm, Margaret K. "Identity and the Family in the Novels of Janette Turner Hospital." In *Canadian Women: Writing Fiction*, edited by Mickey Pearlman. Jackson: University Press of Mississippi, 1993. Discusses Hospital's focus on the conflict between sensuality and moral responsibility, her use of doubles or mirror characters, and her experiments with narrative structure.

Stoneham, Geraldine. "Dislocations: Postcolonialism in a Postmodernist Space." In *Postmodern Subjects/Postmodern Texts*, edited by Jane Dowson and Steven Earnshaw. Atlanta, Ga.: Rodopi, 1995. Discusses Hospital's use of tactics of deconstruction while engaging in a dialogue between postcolonialism and feminism.

Charles E. May

PAM HOUSTON

Born: New Jersey; 1962

PRINCIPAL SHORT FICTION

Cowboys Are My Weakness: Stories, 1992
Waltzing the Cat, 1998

OTHER LITERARY FORMS

Pam Houston began her writing career contributing nonfiction and short stories to numerous popular and literary periodicals such as *Vogue*, *The New York Times*, *Quarterly West*, and *The Gettysburg Review*. Some of these stories later appeared in her 1992 *Cowboys Are My Weakness* and her 1998 *Waltzing the Cat*. She is also the editor of *Women on Hunting: Es-says, Fiction, and Poetry* (1995) and has had her stories selected for many works such as *The Best American Short Stories 1990* and *Prize Stories: The O. Henry Awards* in 1999. Her autobiography, *A Little More About Me*, was published in 1999.

ACHIEVEMENTS

Pam Houston's collection of short stories, *Cowboys Are My Weakness: Stories*, was a New York Times Notable Book in 1992 and won the 1993 Western States Book Award. In 1999, *Waltzing the Cat* won the first Willa Literary Awards (named after Pulitzer Prize-winning author Willa Cather) for best contemporary fiction.

BIOGRAPHY

Described by many critics as "a modern Annie Oakley," Pam Houston was born in New Jersey but spent much of her childhood in Bethlehem, Pennsylvania. The only child of an actress and unsuccessful businessman, her childhood was filled with parental alcoholism and physical abuse and unmet expectations. Her father wanted her to become a tennis star; her mother wanted her to be thin and perfectly made-up. Houston wanted to be neither.

When Houston was two and a half years old, her baby-sitter encouraged her to learn to read and write. This became a means of escape from a childhood often fraught with great danger, including sixteen car accidents (once with each of her parents) in as many years of age. Houston graduated second in her class with a degree in English from Denison University in Granville, Ohio. In 1992 she married (and later divorced) a South African safari guide, Mike Elkington. Later, she received a Ph.D. from the University of Utah.

Because she spent much of her childhood afraid for her personal safety, Houston claims her attraction to dangerous white-water rafting and emotionally withdrawn cowboy types was a response to feelings of fear and lack of control as a child and a way of returning to an unfortunate but familiar lifestyle. Her work as a hunting and rafting guide in the American West and Alaska forms the basis for most of her literary work.

ANALYSIS

Relying on her outdoor adventures, Pam Houston has carved out her unique niche as a female author writing about topics normally associated with male writers like Ernest Hemingway or Edward Abbey: exotic landscapes, wanderlust, and struggles against unpredictable natural elements, such as mother grizzlies and deep river currents.

Influenced by D. H. Lawrence and other modernists, Houston's short stories have an autobiographical flavor to them. They are infused with what the *East Bay Express* describes as "an embedded irony in . . . that the tough, outdoorsy heroines could navigate dangerous rapids with expertise, but couldn't quite get a handle on their love lives—especially in relationships with terse men of the west." Yet, Houston's female characters know that they are responsible for their own lives, truths, and desires for love.

Houston explores these themes of self-reliance and love by mixing personal experience with metaphor in an attempt to discover the real truth behind not only her wilderness experiences but also her relationships with parents, friends, and lovers. Instead of planning out her narrative before she sits down to write, Houston first tries to write out as much as she can remember about a place first to keep herself from consciously controlling the meaning of the story because, she claims, "When I'm looking the other direction, that's when the truth emerges."

WALTZING THE CAT

Houston's second book of short stories, *Waltzing the Cat*, is a collection of eleven linked stories about the life of Lucy, a photographer, whose adventures with nature and relationships seem to be metaphors for much of Houston's own life. Leaving the Rockies for Oakland, California, Lucy experiences all kinds of emotional and physical turmoil—hurricanes, rafting accidents, and parents and lovers who are distant and self-obsessed—in what has been described as "a vigorous, often lyrical rendition of a young woman's quiet but intense search for herself."

For example, in "The Best Girlfriend You Never Had," Lucy and her friend Leo recount stories about people they have known, including themselves, who "have their hearts all wrapped around someone who won't ever love them back." In this story, Leo and Lucy, whose relationship parallels that of the story's title, are reading poetry about love aloud while watching various weddings take place in the gardens of the Palace of the Fine Arts in San Francisco. As Lucy takes photos of the couples, we learn how Leo, an architect, is in love with Guinevere, a Buddhist weaver, who "seems not to know Leo is alive." From Lucy we learn of her involvement with Gordon, a college professor with an angry, possessive streak who, after dragging Lucy's self-confidence down to his own level, begins stalking her. It is in this story that the reader is introduced to Lucy's parents. Their biting comments about her in front of a traffic cop cause the officer to decide not to give her a ticket for her numerous violations because, as he puts it, "there's nothing I could do to you that's going to feel like punishment."

In the title chapter "Waltzing the Cat," Lucy must face her mother's death and her father's retreat from reality. The narrator tells the story of the family cat that has become a waddling, overstuffed storehouse for her parent's unexpressed emotions and expectations for each other and their daughter. As Lucy tells the reader, "For as long as I can remember, my parents have eaten vicariously through the cat. Roast chicken, amaretto cheese spread, rum raisin ice cream" was fed to the cat while she was offered "carrots and celery, cauliflower and radishes." At the end of the story, Lucy's hopes for becoming the focus of her father's affections are quickly dashed when, upon hearing her father say "I love you so much," she turns around to find him talking to the cat.

In subsequent stories, Lucy plunges into adventure after adventure as a means of finding some kind of emotional fulfillment. Then in "Moving from One Body of Water to Another," the narrator has a chance encounter with Carlos Castanada which leads her to finally understand that the spiritual reality and emotional balance that she has been seeking is much closer to home than she realizes. In later stories, Lucy returns to the Rockies and her grandmother's old ranch house to live, concluding a collection of stories that one critic has described as a "consistent pattern of seeking, discovery, loss and compromise." It is in the epilogue that the narrator understands that to find her emotional balance she does not need to try to fulfill parental expectations or find a man. Instead of mastering dangerous rivers and currents, she needs only be brave enough to seek out her true self.

OTHER MAJOR WORKS

NONFICTION: *Men Before Ten A.M.*, 1996 (photographs by Veronique Vial); *A Little More About Me*, 1999.

EDITED TEXT: *Women on Hunting: Essays, Fiction, and Poetry*, 1995.

BIBLIOGRAPHY

Fanselow, Julie. "The Emotional Truth: Writings of Author Pam Houston." *Writer's Digest* 76, no. 10 (October, 1996): 6. Houston's first collection of stories "Cowboys Are My Weakness" continues to sell well since its publication in 1992. She feels that stories always change in the retelling.

Gilbert, Elizabeth. "Risky Business." Review of *A Little More About Me*, by Pam Houston. *The New York Times Book Review*, September 12, 1999, p. 25. Review of the author's autobiography which also discusses Houston's numerous adventures and the path that her autobiographical stories take.

Houlihan, Mary. "Wild World of Words; Her Tales Mix Love, Adventure." *Chicago Sun-Times*, October 10, 1999, p. G17. Interview with the author in which she discusses her early family history, mentors, teaching, and future adventures.

Houston, Pam. "On the River with Pam Houston: Adventure, a Cure for Bad-Love Blues." Interview by Molly O'Neill. *The New York Times*, July 15, 1992, p. C1. Interviewer goes on a three-day river trip with the author while they discuss Houston's childhood, men and first book, *Cowboys Are My Weakness: Stories*.

_____. "Truth and Dare: Pam Houston's Greatest Adventure Is Within Herself." Interview by Lori Tobias. *Denver Rocky Mountain News*, September 12, 1999, p. 1E. Houston discusses her early childhood and autobiography. Her use of personal experiences in her short stories is also addressed.

Reynolds, Susan Salter. "I Love Lucy: *Waltzing the Cat*, by Pam Houston." *The Los Angeles Times Book Review*, November 15, 1998, 12. Reviews her second book with a special emphasis on the author's use of personal experience and metaphor as writing strategies.

See, Carolyn. "Running Life's Rapids." *The Washington Post*, October 30, 1998, p. D02. Discusses the issues of concern to Lucy, the main character in *Waltzing the Cat*, such as men, her parents, and risking her life.

Lisa-Anne Culp

WILLIAM DEAN HOWELLS

Born: Martin's Ferry, Ohio; March 1, 1837
Died: New York, New York; May 11, 1920

PRINCIPAL SHORT FICTION

A Fearful Responsibility and Other Stories, 1881
Selected Short Stories of William Dean Howells, 1997

OTHER LITERARY FORMS

William Dean Howells is known primarily as a novelist, especially for his two acknowledged master-pieces, *The Rise of Silas Lapham* (1885) and *A Hazard of New Fortunes* (1889). He was also a distinguished journalist and editor, who presided for years over the "Editor's Easy Chair" column for *Harper's Monthly*. In *Criticism and Fiction* (1891) and *My Literary Passions* (1895) Howells expounded the principles that made him known as a champion of literary realism.

ACHIEVEMENTS

Besides his enormous output in several literary genres, from 1866 until 1881 William Dean Howells was an editor for the *Atlantic*. Beginning in 1886, he was for many years an editorial columnist for *Harper's Monthly*. Howells received an honorary degree from Oxford University in 1904 and was elected first president of the American Academy of Arts and Letters in 1908.

BIOGRAPHY

William Dean Howells was born in Martin's Ferry, Ohio, on March 1, 1837, and he received much of his early education in the Hamilton printing office of his father's *Intelligencer* before working on the *Ohio State Journal* from 1858 to 1861. His campaign biography of President Abraham Lincoln earned him an appointment as United States consul in Venice (1861-1865). In 1861 he married Elinor Mead, and they had three children, Winifred (born 1863), John (1868), and Mildred (1872). After his return from Venice, Howells moved to Boston, where he lived until 1888, when he moved to New York City.

Howells was one of the most distinguished men of letters in his day and a close friend of other notables, such as Henry James and Mark Twain, many of whom he wrote about in *Literary Friends and Acquaintances* (1900) and *My Mark Twain* (1910). In his criticism, he championed a realistic approach to fiction but a realism too genteel for some critics, like the naturalistic novelist Frank Norris. The high esteem of the world of letters was reflected in a seventy-fifth birthday gala held for him, with President William Howard Taft attending.

Howells consistently displayed a social conscience. He angered a great many influential people by his vigorous defense of the Haymarket anarchists in 1887, and he helped found the National Association for the Advancement of Colored People (NAACP) in 1909.

ANALYSIS

William Dean Howells is best remembered in literary history for two things: He wrote more than twenty novels, and he tirelessly defended realism over Romanticism. Howells's earliest short stories are weak and imitative, often more sketch than story, and not until 1868 in "Tonelli's Marriage" does he achieve a convincing story by focusing on European social customs as he observed them as consul in Venice.

The death of Howells's daughter Winifred in 1889 may have prompted him to write several stories treating the subject of immortality, including the so-called Turkish Room tales, a series of "psychic romances" named for a small group who gather at a private club in New York City to explore supernatural themes. The narrator of the stories is a novelist, Acton, who, amid the club's exotic Indian and Middle Eastern furnishings, reports the conversations that loosely shape the narratives. As a champion of literary realism, Howells justifies these tales by a distinction between romance and Romanticism:

Romance [good], as in Hawthorne, seeks the effect of reality in visionary conditions; romanticism [bad], as in Dickens, tries for a visionary effect in actual conditions.

This scheme suggests the famous complementary intentions of Samuel Taylor Coleridge, by Howells's definition a romancer, and William Wordsworth (a Romanticist) in their *Lyrical Ballads* (1798).

Other groupings of Howells's stories include the Dulldale tales, inspired by small towns like Jefferson, Ohio; several children's stories; and the pair of stories about Basil and Isabel March, "A Circle in the Water" and "A Pair of Patient Lovers." Only the March narratives have prompted much significant critical attention.

"THE MAGIC OF A VOICE"

"The Magic of a Voice" is a love story. Stephen Langbourne is awakened one night in his New Hampshire hotel by the voices of two young women in the room next to him, and when he falls in love at first sound with one of the girls, Barbara Simpson, he contrives to get her name and address and even to initiate

William Dean Howells (Library of Congress)

a winter-long correspondence with her from New York City. Barbara even sends him a photograph of herself. Come spring, Langbourne journeys to New Hampshire and boldly arrives at the home of the two girls, Barbara and her friend from the hotel, Juliet Bingham. Langbourne is dismayed to find Barbara not as attractive as he had imagined, for, as a joke, she had sent Juliet's photograph instead. Eventually, once Langbourne gets to know both girls, he discovers, after all the misunderstandings are played out, that it is really plain Barbara whom he loves, and they brace themselves to live happily ever after. Although critics have sneered at this story—when condescending to notice it—it has elements that deserve attention, such as the implications of Langbourne's aural voyeurism. More interesting, however, for gender critics are Howells's remarks about Barbara—that "there was something almost mannish in her essential honesty," that "her companionship would be as easy and reasonable as a man's, while it had the charm of a woman's," and that "the [hotel register] entry was in a good, simple hand, which was like a man's in its firmness and clarity."

"A DIFFICULT CASE"

"A Difficult Case" is one of Howells's finest stories, a probing of the questions about immortality that had troubled Howells since his daughter's death. A middle-aged minister, Clarence Ewbert, takes a position in a church in a small university community, but his wife's hopes for social success are frustrated when the university members fail to join the small congregation. One faithful parishioner, the aging Ransom Hilbrook, lives alone on a crumbling farm and becomes Ewbert's "difficult case." When Hilbrook makes frequent, long evening visits to the Ewberts' to pursue tortuous arguments about immortality, the Reverend Ewbert reveals a kind interest in the lonely eccentric, but Mrs. Ewbert judges him a socially inconsequential nuisance who is exhausting her husband. Hilbrook's war experiences and the deaths of his wife and child have soured him on life, and he prays not for immortality but for an annihilation that will guarantee he never wakes up in his "old identity, with the potentiality of new experiences in new conditions." Ewbert's task becomes, then, to argue for a satisfying immortality, but the process of winning over Hilbrook saps both his health and his own faith. Mrs. Ewbert then turns Hilbrook away one evening and takes Ewbert for a seaside holiday, from which he returns refreshed and gratified by a university congregation. Hilbrook, though, apparently crushed by Mrs. Ewbert, retires to his bed and dies of loss of interest in life. The appeal of this story lies not in the observations on immortality, which are trivial, but in the contrast between Ewbert, a caring man, and his hard wife, and in this respect it reveals the influence on Howells of a writer he greatly admired, Nathaniel Hawthorne, who regarded a lack of charity as an unpardonable sin.

"THE ANGEL OF THE LORD"

The first of Howells's nine Turkish Room stories is "The Angel of the Lord." The rambling narrative of a psychologist, Wanhope, is reported by the first-person narrator, Acton, a novelist. Minver, an artist, and Rulledge, an idler of no apparent occupation, listen and contribute *ad libitum*. The subjects of Wanhope's tale are a now-dead couple, the Ormonds, and the history of the husband's debilitating obsession with death. When the Ormonds bought an old home in the Connecticut countryside, Ormond (the husband) had found in its library the works of the eighteenth century English poets known as the Graveyard School,

> like Gray and Collins and Young . . . who personified nearly everything from Contemplation to Indigestion, through the whole range of the Vices, Virtues, Passions, Propensities, Attributes, and Qualities, and gave them each a dignified capital letter to wear.

Ormond somehow finds in personification "the reason of things," and the revelation transforms his life as he enjoys perfect tranquillity in his new freedom from his old obsession. In his Bible reading, he fixes on the epithet "The Angel of the Lord," which so consumes his imagination that a passing tramp assumes a holy mission in Ormond's mind, and he bounds joyfully into the woods after the vagrant and falls to his death. This odd story should be seen in the context of its time, when psychologists like Wanhope were investigating psychic phenomena and the Soci-

ety for Psychical Research flourished. Howells himself pronounced that visions, whether natural or supernatural, were "precious."

"EDITHA"

When Editha Balcom becomes excited by the prospect of an impending war—presumably the Spanish-American War—she urges her fiancé, George Gearson, to enlist. However, George, much more sensible and realistic than the romantic Editha, reveals a coolness to the idea, which briefly lowers their mutual ardor. Editha magnifies this rift to dramatic proportions: "It all interested her intensely; she was undergoing a tremendous experience, and she was being equal to it." She then composes a naïve letter to George expressing a shallow patriotism, which makes it clear that he must enlist if he wishes to marry her. Before she can send her ultimatum, George appears with the news that he has been commissioned a captain and will lead his own company into battle, and with that news Editha gives him the letter to read "sometime" and experiences a near swoon of desire. Editha prays for George's safety, speaking to God with "the implication of a mutual understanding," but the inevitable happens, and George dies in his first skirmish. Editha and her father then travel from upstate New York to visit George's mother in Iowa. The old lady has received Editha's letter among George's things, and she reproves Editha bitterly:

> You thought it would be all right for my George, *your* George, to kill the sons of those miserable mothers and the husbands of those girls that you would never see the faces of.

With that, Mrs. Gearson orders Editha to remove her mourning black: "Take it off, take it off, before I tear it from your back." Edith is left to revel in her tragedy, consoled by her judgment of Mrs. Gearson as vulgar. "Editha" has been much anthologized and is usually praised for its dramatic clash between the realistic and the romantic temperaments.

OTHER MAJOR WORKS

LONG FICTION: *Their Wedding Journey*, 1872; *A Chance Acquaintance*, 1873; *A Foregone Conclusion*, 1875; *The Lady of Aroostook*, 1879; *The Undiscov-*

ered *Country*, 1880; *Dr. Breen's Practice*, 1881; *A Modern Instance*, 1882; *A Woman's Reason*, 1883; *The Rise of Silas Lapham*, 1885; *Indian Summer*, 1886; *A Minister's Charge: Or, The Apprenticeship of Lemuel Barker*, 1887; *April Hopes*, 1887; *Annie Kilburn*, 1888; *A Hazard of New Fortunes*, 1889; *The Shadow of a Dream*, 1890; *An Imperative Duty*, 1891; *The Quality of Mercy*, 1892; *The Coast of Bohemia*, 1893; *The World of Chance*, 1893; *A Traveler from Altruria*, 1894; *The Day of Their Wedding*, 1896; *A Parting and a Meeting*, 1896; *The Landlord at Lion's Head*, 1897; *An Open-Eyed Conspiracy: An Idyl of Saratoga*, 1897; *The Story of a Play*, 1898; *Ragged Lady*, 1899; *Their Silver Wedding Journey*, 1899; *The Kentons*, 1902; *The Son of Royal Langbirth*, 1904; *Miss Bellard's Inspiration*, 1905; *Through the Eye of the Needle*, 1907; *Fennel and Rue*, 1908; *New Leaf Mills*, 1913; *The Leatherwood God*, 1916; *The Vacation of the Kelwyns*, 1920; *Mrs. Farrell*, 1921.

PLAYS: *The Parlor Car*, pb. 1876; *A Counterfeit Presentment*, pb. 1877; *Out of the Question*, pb. 1877; *The Register*, pb. 1884; *A Sea-Change*, pb. 1887; *The Albany Depot*, pb. 1892; *A Letter of Introduction*, pb. 1892; *The Unexpected Guests*, pb. 1893; *A Previous Engagement*, pb. 1897; *An Indian Giver*, pb. 1900; *Room Forty-five*, pb. 1900; *The Smoking Car*, pb. 1900; *Parting Friends*, pb. 1911; *The Complete Plays of W. D. Howells*, pb. 1960 (Walter J. Meserve, editor).

POETRY: *Poems of Two Friends*, 1860 (with John J. Piatt); *Poems*, 1873; *Samson*, 1874; *Priscilla: A Comedy*, 1882; *A Sea Change: Or, Love's Stowaway*, 1884; *Poems*, 1886; *Stops of Various Quills*, 1895; *The Mother and the Father*, 1909.

NONFICTION: *Lives and Speeches of Abraham Lincoln and Hannibal Hamlin*, 1860; *Venetian Life*, 1866; *Italian Journeys*, 1867; *Tuscan Cities*, 1885; *Modern Italian Poets*, 1887; *A Boy's Town*, 1890; *Criticism and Fiction*, 1891; *My Literary Passions*, 1895; *Impressions and Experiences*, 1896; *Stories of Ohio*, 1897; *Literary Friends and Acquaintances*, 1900; *Heroines of Fiction*, 1901; *Literature and Life*, 1902; *Letters Home*, 1903; *London Films*, 1905; *Certain Delightful English Towns*, 1906; *Roman Holidays*, 1908; *Seven English Cities*, 1909; *Imaginary Interviews*, 1910; *My Mark Twain*, 1910; *Familiar Spanish Travels*, 1913; *New Leaf Mills*, 1913; *Years of My Youth*, 1916; *Eighty Years and After*, 1921; *The Life in Letters of William Dean Howells*, 1928 (M. Howells, editor).

CHILDREN'S LITERATURE: *"Christmas Every Day" and Other Stories Told for Children*, 1893.

BIBLIOGRAPHY

Bardon, Ruth, ed. *Selected Short Stories of William Dean Howells*. Athens: Ohio University Press, 1997. Indispensable. A meticulously edited collection of thirteen stories plus generous annotations of thirty-three more. The introduction, the notes, and the works cited list make this a valuable work for Howells scholars.

Cady, Edwin H. *The Road to Realism: The Early Years, 1837-1885, of William Dean Howells*. Syracuse, N.Y.: Syracuse University Press, 1956.

_____. *The Realist at War: The Mature Years, 1885-1920, of William Dean Howells*. Syracuse, N.Y.: Syracuse University Press, 1958. These two volumes by Cady are standbys for Howells's life and the shaping of his theories of literature.

Carter, Everett. *Howells and the Age of Realism*. Philadelphia: J. B. Lippincott, 1954. Howells has always been identified with the critical dicta of realism, and this book establishes the historical context well.

Eble, Kenneth E. *William Dean Howells*. 2d ed. Boston: Twayne, 1982. An excellent introduction to Howells in the Twayne series, if devoted almost entirely to the major novels.

Klinkowitz, Jerome. "Ethic and Aesthetic: The Basil and Isabel March Stories of William Dean Howells." *Modern Fiction Studies* 16 (Autumn, 1970): 303-322. A good analysis, and one of the few periodical essays devoted to Howells's short fiction.

Lynn, Kenneth S. *William Dean Howells: An American Life*. New York: Harcourt Brace Jovanovich, 1970. Excellent critical and biographical study.

Frank Day

LANGSTON HUGHES

Born: Joplin, Missouri; February 1, 1902
Died: New York, New York; May 22, 1967

PRINCIPAL SHORT FICTION

The Ways of White Folks, 1934
Simple Speaks His Mind, 1950
Laughing to Keep from Crying, 1952
Simple Takes a Wife, 1953
Simple Stakes a Claim, 1957
The Langston Hughes Reader, 1958
The Best of Simple, 1961
Something in Common and Other Stories, 1963
Simple's Uncle Sam, 1965

OTHER LITERARY FORMS

Although perhaps best known for his poetry, Langston Hughes explored almost every literary genre. His prose fiction includes novels, humorous books, historical, biographical, autobiographical, and cultural works, translations, lyrics, librettos, plays, and scripts. His total output includes more than seventy volumes, as well as numerous articles, poems, and stories that have not yet been collected.

ACHIEVEMENTS

Langston Hughes has been acknowledged both before and after his death as the most influential African American writer in the English-speaking world. As a leader of the Harlem Renaissance, he not only wrote in a variety of genres but also edited and encouraged the literary, dramatic, and musical productions of other people of color. Recognition came during his lifetime as early as 1925, when he won the Poetry Prize given by *Opportunity* magazine and the Spingarn prizes of *Crisis* magazine for both poetry and essay writing. His novel *Not Without Laughter* (1930) won the Harmon Gold Medal in 1931. That year he received his first Rosenwald Fellowship, an award repeated in 1941. The John Simon Guggenheim Memorial Foundation Fellowship in 1935, the National Academy of Arts and Letters Award for Literature in 1946, and the Ainsfield-Wolf

Award in 1953 continued to keep him in the forefront of the literary community, particularly in New York, throughout his life. His alma mater, Lincoln University, awarded him an honorary doctorate in 1943, and he received others from Howard University and Case Western Reserve University in 1963 and 1964, respectively.

BIOGRAPHY

James Mercer Langston Hughes came from an educated family whose energies were spent primarily in entrepreneurial efforts to combat poverty and institutionalized racism in order to survive. His life repeats a well-known pattern of early twentieth century African American families: a resourceful mother who rented out their home to boarders, a father who had to leave home to find work, a grandmother who cared for him during his early years, and a stepfather. He grew up in the Midwest—Kansas, Illinois, and Ohio—and participated in athletics as well as in literary activities in high school.

Graduating from Central High School in Lincoln, Illinois, in 1920, Hughes attended Columbia University before shipping out on liners bound for Africa and Holland. He also traveled extensively in Europe before returning to the United States in 1925. Then, in 1929, he received a B.A. from Lincoln University, Pennsylvania. Hughes at first subsisted with the help of patrons, but gradually began to earn a living on the proceeds from his writings and his poetry readings. Although mainly basing himself in Harlem, New York City, Hughes continued to travel extensively. He won numerous prizes, grants, and fellowships for his literary achievements before his death in 1967.

ANALYSIS

Langston Hughes records in *The Big Sea: An Autobiography* (1940) his feelings upon first seeing Africa: ". . . when I saw the dust-green hills in the sunlight, something took hold of me inside. My Africa, Motherland of the Negro peoples! And me a Negro! The real thing!" The trip to Africa confirmed what he

Langston Hughes (Library of Congress)

already knew—that the subject matter of his writings would reflect his desire "to write seriously and as well as I knew how about the Negro people." Most of Hughes's short stories concern themselves with black people presented from many different perspectives and in both tragic and comic dimensions. Even when a white is the protagonist of a story, as in "Little Dog," the gentle black man to whom Miss Briggs is attracted is given special focus. Hughes, however, is not racist in his presentation. People, regardless of their racial background, are people first participating in a common humanity before they are individuals distorted by prejudice based on ignorance, by fear, or by social conditions which create a spiritual and psychological malaise, sometimes crippling in its effect.

"LITTLE DOG"

"Little Dog" tells the story of a white and gaunt middle-aged woman, head bookkeeper of a coal and coke firm for twenty-one years, who, because of her own sense of prudence, responsibility, and concern, sublimates her own desires to care for her mother, and then, after her mother's death, is left alone and lonely. Although she keeps busy, is comfortably situated, and does not think too much of what she may be

missing, she occasionally wonders why she knows no one whom she can appreciate as a friend. One day she inexplicably stops the taxicab in which she is riding in front of a pet shop featuring in its window "fuzzy little white dogs," and she purchases for herself a puppy at a very steep price. She arranges with the janitor of her apartment building, "a tow-headed young Swede," to provide food for her dog, which she names Flips, and soon her life revolves around activities centering on Flips.

One day the janitor does not show up to feed the dog; several days pass until Miss Briggs decides she needs to go down to the basement to search out the janitor. With her dog by her side, she knocks at a door behind which she hears sounds of "happy laughter, and kids squalling, and people moving." The door is opened by a small black boy and soon Miss Briggs discovers that the "tall broad-shouldered Negro" standing amidst the children is the new janitor.

The image patterns and juxtapositions in the story now begin to form meaningful patterns. The white woman, living "upstairs" with the "fuzzy white dog," is contrasted with the black man and his "pretty little brown-black" children who live "downstairs." The gentle and kind black man begins to service Miss Briggs's needs, bringing more food than is good for the dog because he believes the woman desires it and because he is being paid for it; Miss Briggs, however, never tells him that meat every few days is sufficient. Soon Miss Briggs finds herself hurrying home, never realizing that it is no longer the dog but rather the nightly visits of the janitor that compel her to hurry. One evening her words inadvertently reveal her subconscious needs. The black janitor has just left after delivering Flips's food and she can hear him humming as he returns to his family. Suddenly Miss Briggs says to Flips: "Oh, Flips . . . I'm so hungry."

Now, although she never consciously knows why, Miss Briggs decides she needs to move; ". . . she could not bear to have this janitor come upstairs with a package of bones for Flips again. . . . Let him stay in the basement, where he belonged." The accumulation of references to bones, meat, and services provides for the reader, if not for Miss Briggs, a moment of epiphany: "He almost keeps me broke buying bones,"

Miss Briggs says to the tall and broad-shouldered black janitor. "True," the janitor answers her. The sustenance the black man provides for the dog is no sustenance for the gaunt and bony woman, nor is the dog, like children, sufficient to keep memory of the departed alive. Miss Briggs moves and shortly is completely forgotten by the people in the neighborhood in which she had lived.

"Thank You Ma'am"

If Miss Briggs seems a portrait of a woman dead before she is buried, Mrs. Luella Bates Washington Jones of "Thank You Ma'am" is a picture of middle-aged woman still vital and vigorous, although she, too, lives alone; and although it appears she has no children of her own, she is still potent, giving new life to a young black boy who attempts to mug her. The child is no match for the woman, who is identified with her purse so large "that it had everything in it but a hammer and nails." She drags him home with her, sees that he washes, and shares with him her frugal meal. Her presence is so overpowering that the boy is more fearful of trying to get away than of staying, but she breaks down his resistance when she speaks to him of common problems. "I was young once and I wanted things I could not get." The boy waits expecting the "but" to follow. The woman anticipates: "You thought I was going to say, *but I didn't snatch people's pocketbooks*. Well, I wasn't going to say that. . . . I have done things, too, which I would not tell you, son. . . . Everybody's got something in common." The woman's actions, however, tell the boy more than her words do, and at the end of the story the boy is unable to use words, although his lips try to phrase more than "Thank you Ma'am."

"Professor"

One of Hughes's most frequently praised stories is "Professor." Focused through the point of view of its protagonist Dr. T. Walton Brown (*T* for Tom, Uncle Tom?), the story examines how a black professor of sociology "bows" and "bobs" like a puppet on a string to members of the wealthy white establishment, doing only those things of which they approve, saying what they want to hear, and, although at times he knows the lies diminish him, still allowing his own needs to determine his behavior patterns.

Bitterly ironic in tone, the story begins with the juxtaposition of Brown in dinner dress against the lobby of a run-down segregated hotel and Brown cared for by a white chauffeur who tucks the professor carefully into the luxury of a limousine to carry him through the black ghetto to a private house as large as a hotel. Brown's posture and attire are carefully contrasted with the "two or three ash-colored children" who run across the street in front of the limousine, "their skinny legs and poor clothes plain in the glare of the headlights." So also are the streets and buildings contrasted—"the Negro streets": "pig's knuckle joints, pawnshops, beer parlors—and houses of vice, no doubt—save that these latter, at least, did not hang out their signs" with the "wide lawns and fine homes that lined the beautiful well-lighted boulevard where white people lived."

Brown has bought entry into the white establishment by prostituting himself, by accepting the degradation of the constant diminishing of his selfhood and his negritude. He listens to his white counterpart say: "Why, at our city college here we've been conducting some fine interracial experiments. I have had some colored ministers and high school teachers visit my classes. We found them most intelligent." Although at times Brown is moved to make slight and subtle protest, in the end he agrees with the biased white people, saying "You are right."

Brown's behavior is dictated by his desire for the money the white people offer him as long as he conforms to their expectation. Money will buy Brown prestige, will enable his college to survive, and will further his career. Money will also "take his family to South America in the summer where for three months they wouldn't feel like Negroes." Thus, he dances to the "tune of Jim Crow education," diminishing both himself and his race. Although carefully constructed, the story offers no subtleties beyond the ironies present; image patterns are at a minimum, complex symbolism nonexistent. Characterization, too, is sparse. The reader learns only enough about the professor to make his behavior immediately credible, but a traditional plot line moves with careful pacing to climax and pointed resolution, and the theme overshadows technique.

"FINE ACCOMMODATIONS"

Similar in theme and technique to "Professor" is "Fine Accommodations." In this story, a young black porter learns that the Dr. Jenkins, booked into sleeping car accommodations, is not the leader of his race and "fine man" the naïve porter expects but rather another Uncle Tom who keeps on "being a big man" by "bowing to Southern white customs," by helping to keep poor black people just where they have always been "all the time—poor and black." At the end of the story, the porter makes the point of the story: "The last Negro passenger I had in that drawing room was a pimp from Birmingham. Now I got a professor. I guess both of them have to have ways of paying for such fine accommodations."

"BIG MEETING"

From the perspective of complexity, subtlety, and power, "Big Meeting" is a considerably better story. Told in the first person by a young black boy who with a companion is observing a church revival meeting held in the woods, the story recounts the boy's moment of epiphany when he realizes, if only subconsciously, that as a cynical observer rather than a participant in the ritual he is more akin to the white folks gathered to watch than to his own people. Making use of dialect and gospel songs, Hughes builds the story to a powerful sermon where the preacher recounts the betrayal of Christ to the accompaniment of echoing refrains and then moves the sermon to the cadences of poetry:

They brought four long nails
And put one in the palm of His left hand.
The hammer said . . . Bam!
They put one in the palm of His right hand.
The hammer said . . . Bam!
They put one through His left foot . . . Bam!
And one through His right foot . . . Bam!
. . . "Don't drive it!" a woman screamed. "Don't drive
them nails! For Christ's sake! Oh! Don't drive 'em!"

In the woods observing the action, the narrator and his companion are near enough to a car full of white people to overhear what they are saying as they comment in ways showing their biases, limitations, and prejudices. As the narrator hears these comments, he begins to respond, but not enough to cause him to identify with the participants in the service. Rather, both he and his companion seem more concerned with the behavior of their mothers who are taking part in the church rituals.

At the climax of the story, the narrator hears his mother's voice: "Were you there when they crucified my Lord?/ Were you there when they nailed Him to the tree?" At the same time as the mother cries out the questions, the preacher opens his arms wide against the white canvas tent, and his body reflects a crosslike shadow. As the mother asks the question again, the white people in the car suddenly drive away creating a swirl of dust, and the narrator cries after them, "Don't go. . . . They're about to call for sinners. . . . Don't go!"

The boy's cry to the white people reflects his understanding of the parallel setup between the white people and the betrayers of Christ. Hughes goes further than this, however, and provides in the last sentence of the story an epiphanic moment: "I didn't realize I was crying until I tasted my tears in my mouth." The epiphany projects a revelation dimly understood by the narrator but clearly present—that as bad as the white people's behavior seemed, his own rejection of his people and heritage was worse.

OTHER MAJOR WORKS

LONG FICTION: *Not Without Laughter*, 1930; *Tambourines to Glory*, 1958.

PLAYS: *Mulatto*, pb. 1935; *Little Ham*, pr. 1935; *Don't You Want to Be Free*, pb. 1938; *Freedom's Plow*, pb. 1943; *Simply Heavenly*, pr. 1957; *Black Nativity*, pr. 1961; *Tambourines to Glory*, pr., pb. 1963; *Five Plays*, pb. 1963; *Jerico-Jim Crow*, pr. 1963; *The Prodigal Son*, pr. 1965.

POETRY: *The Weary Blues*, 1926; *Fine Clothes to the Jew*, 1927; *Dear Lovely Death*, 1931; *The Negro Mother*, 1931; *The Dream Keeper and Other Poems*, 1932; *Scottsboro Limited*, 1932; *A New Song*, 1938; *Shakespeare in Harlem*, 1942; *Jim Crow's Last Stand*, 1943; *Lament for Dark Peoples*, 1944; *Fields of Wonder*, 1947; *One Way Ticket*, 1949; *Montage of a Dream Deferred*, 1951; *Selected Poems of Langston Hughes*, 1959; *Ask Your Mama: Or,*

Twelve *Moods for Jazz*, 1961; *The Panther and the Lash: Or, Poems of Our Times*, 1967.

NONFICTION: *The Big Sea: An Autobiography*, 1940; *The First Book of Negroes*, 1952; *The First Book of Rhythms*, 1954; *Famous American Negroes*, 1954; *Famous Negro Music Makers*, 1955; *The First Book of Jazz*, 1955; *The First Book of the West Indies*, 1955; *A Pictorial History of the Negro in America*, 1956; *I Wonder as I Wander: An Autobiographical Journey*, 1956; *Famous Negro Heroes of America*, 1958; *First Book of Africa*, 1960; *Fight for Freedom: The Story of the NAACP*, 1962; *Black Magic: A Pictorial History of the Negro in American Entertainment*, 1967; *Arna Bontemps-Langston Hughes Letters*, 1980.

TRANSLATIONS: *Masters of the Dew*, 1947; *Cuba Libre*, 1948; *Gypsy Ballads*, 1951; *Selected Poems of Gabriela Mistral*, 1957.

MISCELLANEOUS: *Troubled Island*, c. 1930 (opera libretto); *Popo and Fifina: Children of Haiti*, 1932 (with Arna Bontemps); *Street Scene*, 1947 (lyrics); *The Poetry of the Negro, 1746-1949*, 1949 (with Arna Bontemps); *Simply Heavenly*, c. 1959 (opera libretto); *New Negro Poets: U.S.A.*, 1964; *The Book of Negro Humor*, 1966; *The Best Short Stories by Negro Writers: An Anthology from 1899 to the Present*, 1967.

BIBLIOGRAPHY

Borden, Anne. "Heroic 'Hussies' and 'Brilliant Queers' Genderracial Resistance in the Works of Langston Hughes." *African American Review* 28 (Fall, 1994): 333-345. Discusses Hughes's focus on the interrelationship between gender and racial issues, as well as his treatment of gender issues within the black community—particularly the ways in which gender affects the struggle to maintain community in racist society.

Chinitz, David. "Rejuvenation Through Joy: Langston Hughes, Primitivism, and Jazz." *American Literary History* 9 (Spring, 1997): 60-78. Argues that in freeing himself from the primitivist movement, Hughes struggled to undo ideas long fused in primitivist discourse and attempted to rescue elements of primitivism that he continued to find meaningful, especially those pertaining to African American jazz.

Cooper, Floyd. *Coming Home: From the Life of Langston Hughes*. New York: Philomel Books, 1994. A thoughtful look at Hughes's life and works.

Dickinson, Donald C. *A Bio-Bibliography of Langston Hughes, 1902-1967*. 2d ed. Hamden, Conn.: Archon Books, 1972. With its preface by Arna Bontemps, a major scholar and critic of the Harlem Renaissance and a contemporary of Hughes, the reader has both older and updated assessments of Hughes's achievement. Part 1 is the biography, which incorporates information throughout Hughes's life; part 2 includes all of his work through 1965, except short newspaper articles, song lyrics, and phonographic records. Even a glance at the bibliography gives an indication of the range of Hughes's imaginative achievement.

Emanuel, James A. *Langston Hughes*. New York: Twayne, 1967. This survey of Hughes's work as a poet and fiction writer emphasizes the reflection of African American speech patterns, rhythms, and idiomatic expressions in Hughes's work, as well as the folk culture behind these, which he turned into literary devices. The book also points out pan-African themes and the peculiar struggle of a writer with Hughes's background in both the sociological and literary contexts.

Harper, Donna Sullivan. *Not So Simple: The "Simple" Stories by Langston Hughes*. Columbia: University of Missouri Press, 1995. A good analysis of Hughes's tales. Includes bibliographical references and an index.

Haskins, James. *Always Movin' On: The Life of Langston Hughes*. Trenton, N.J.: Africa World Press, 1993. A good, updated biography of Hughes.

Hokanson, Robert O'Brien. "Jazzing It Up: The Bebop Modernism of Langston Hughes." *Mosaic* 31 (December, 1998): 61-82. Examines how Hughes uses be-bop jazz to challenge both the boundaries between music and poetry and the distinctions between popular and high culture; argues that Hughes's work constitutes a distinctively "popular" modernism that uses jazz to ground its poetic experimentation in the vernacular tradition of African American culture.

Jemie, Onwuchekwa. *Langston Hughes: An Introduction to the Poetry*. New York: Columbia University Press, 1976. This study of the collected poems omits a number of later works but provides an important focus on the poetic techniques and themes of Hughes. Jemie defends Hughes against charges of being merely popular and emotional, pointing out the African oral tradition as well as African American music as influences on Hughes's poetry and Hughes's role in the development of a black consciousness in American poetry.

Rampersad, Arnold. *The Life of Langston Hughes*. 2 vols. New York: Oxford University Press, 1986-1988. This major critical biography illustrates not only the triumphs but also the struggles of the man and the writer. The importance of Hughes in the Harlem Renaissance and his symbolic significance in the developing artistic and imaginative consciousness of African American writers come alive in concrete examples in volume 1, *I, Too, Sing America*, and volume 2, *I Dream a World*. These titles, drawn from Hughes's poetry, reveal the themes illustrating the writer's life and the points in his own characterization of his struggle.

Tracy, Steven C. *Langston Hughes and the Blues*. Urbana: University of Illinois Press, 1988. This book uses the folk traditions of African and African American culture as background but concentrates primarily on the blues tradition within that culture as a way of interpreting Hughes's work. The intellectualizing of this tradition and the deliberate incorporation of the blues dimension in imaginative literature is a major emphasis, along with the oral tradition in African culture. This historical survey of the blues as an art form and its application in criticism seeks to counteract the dismissal of some of Hughes's more popular works by critics such as Donald C. Dickinson (see above).

Mary Rohrberger,
updated by Emma Coburn Norris

WILLIAM HUMPHREY

Born: Clarksville, Texas; June 18, 1924
Died: Hudson, New York; August 20, 1997

PRINCIPAL SHORT FICTION

The Last Husband and Other Stories, 1953
A Time and a Place, 1968
The Collected Stories of William Humphrey, 1985
September Song, 1992

OTHER LITERARY FORMS

Novelist William Humphrey began his literary career in the late 1940's as a short-story writer, contributing to a number of the United States' better magazines—*The New Yorker, Accent, Esquire*, and *The Atlantic*—and publishing a collection of stories before his first novel appeared. His stories have attracted favorable critical comment, but most commentators rate his novels above his stories. Of his novels, the best known are *Home from the Hill* (1958) and *The Ordways* (1965); he also wrote *Hostages to Fortune* (1984) and *No Resting Place* (1989). Many critics think Humphrey's best piece of writing is *Farther Off from Heaven* (1977), a memoir of the first thirteen years of his life. In addition to his fiction, Humphrey authored several hunting and fishing stories first published in magazines and later reprinted as small books: *The Spawning Run* (1970), *My Moby Dick* (1978), and *Open Season: Sporting Adventures* (1986).

ACHIEVEMENTS

The publisher Alfred A. Knopf called William

Humphrey's *Home from the Hill* the best novel to come out of Texas. The book earned for Humphrey the Carr P. Collins Award of the Texas Institute of Letters for best book of fiction by a Texas author in 1958, and it was a finalist for the National Book Award. The success of Humphrey's first novel, which was made into a popular motion picture in 1960, led to his winning a grant from the National Institute of Arts and Letters, which aided him in the writing of his second novel, *The Ordways*, which was selected by the Literary Guild, enjoyed six printings in its first year, and won for Humphrey a second Texas Institute of Letters prize. In 1995 Humphrey also received the Lon Tinkle Award from the Texas Institute of Letters for excellence sustained throughout a career.

Biography

William Humphrey was very secretive about his life, saying once that he considered it bragging to fill out forms sent by *Who's Who* and other dictionaries of biography. Therefore, the entries about Humphrey in such publications are limited to the kind of material found on dust jackets. In later years, he was slightly more forthcoming in interviews and published a memoir which covers the first thirteen years of his life, the years he spent in his native Clarksville, Texas. From notes, hints, and "slips" by the author, it is possible to reconstruct some parts of his life. He was the son of working-class parents (his father was an auto mechanic), and he suffered an affliction as a child that required braces for his legs. He and his mother left Clarksville never to return after his father was killed in a car wreck in 1937. Humphrey and his mother moved to Dallas, Texas. He attended Southern Methodist University and the University of Texas at Austin, apparently never taking a degree. He mentioned in an interview published in 1988 that he left Texas in 1943 during his last semester of college. He decided to leave while sitting in the middle of a German class, so he stood up and walked out, telling the professor that he was headed for Chicago. Where he went is not clear, but for most of the rest of his life he lived in the state of New York, residing in the city of Hudson beginning in the early 1960's. Humphrey,

William Humphrey in 1958 (Library of Congress)

apparently without benefit of a degree, lectured at several colleges, but for most of his life he supported himself, his wife Dorothy, and his daughter Antonia by his writing.

Humphrey told interviewer Ashby Bland Crowder that he studied art between the ages of thirteen and eighteen. Then he found, when he tried to join the navy during World War II, that he was color-blind. He gave up art and turned to writing, going to New York with a five-act play about Benjamin Franklin. The play was never produced, and Humphrey turned to the writing of fiction. The short-story writer he most admired was fellow Texan Katherine Anne Porter. She wrote her nephew, after reading two of Humphrey's stories in *Accent*, that the young writer had taken two of her stories, "The Cracked Looking-Glass" and "A Day's Work," and turned them into his own. The Humphrey stories, "In Sickness and in Health" and "Man with a Family," do indeed bear remarkable resemblances to Porter's stories. Later, in a letter cited in Joan Givner's *Katherine Ann Porter: A Life* (1982), Humphrey admitted to Porter that he had stolen his first published story from "A Day's Work" and that he always wrote with her stories open to the paragraphs that he most admired. There is no question that Humphrey's stories owe a great debt to Porter's works, especially in their irony and emphasis on place.

Humphrey, whose interest in hunting and fishing can be traced to his father, devoted much of his writing in later years to nonfiction stories about outdoor sports, though his interest in the out-of-doors has not produced a large body of work. The same can be said of his fictional output. In more than forty years, he produced five novels and more than twenty stories.

Humphrey's best work is about Red River County, Texas, but after 1977, the year he published his memoir *Farther Off from Heaven*, about his childhood there, he wrote a number of novels about life in other places. *Hostages to Fortune* is set in Hudson, New York, and describes the effects of a young person's suicide on his parents; *No Resting Place* is about the Cherokees' being uprooted from the South and marched to Texas along the "Trail of Tears" in the 1830's.

In April, 1997, Humphrey was diagnosed with cancer of the larynx. Despite his illness, Humphrey continued to write almost until the end. He died on August 20, 1997, at the age of seventy-three.

ANALYSIS

Most of William Humphrey's stories are set in and around his native Red River County, Texas, which is located in the far northeastern corner of the state. The county borders the state of Oklahoma, and many of the stories take place across the Red River in "the Little Dixie" section of Oklahoma. Northeastern Texas and southeastern Oklahoma were settled by southerners who came West before and after the Civil War, Indians driven West when the South was being cleared of Native Americans during the rapid expansion of the 1820's and 1830's, and slaves—later freed—brought in by both whites and Indians.

THE LAST HUSBAND AND OTHER STORIES

Humphrey's ancestors came into his part of Texas following the Civil War, and it is this part of the world that Humphrey always understood best, even though he left Clarksville for good in 1937. His best stories and novels are about the people and places he knew when he was a boy growing up in Clarksville. His first book of stories *The Last Husband and Other Stories* shows clearly how much Humphrey is dependent on his homeland for the success of his work. The six best stories in the volume are Texas-based. Five take place in and around Clarksville, and one is about a transplanted Texan isolated in a northern city and longing for home. The four stories set in the East, where Humphrey lived during his writing apprenticeship, lack the life found in his Clarksville stories. It is not that the themes are deficient or that the style suffers in his eastern stories. There are excellent scenes and some of the characters are as well developed as those in his regional works. Something is missing, however, and it is very clear that it is a sense of time and place that Humphrey must have in order to tell his stories and develop his points. He understands the people of Red River County and can make them speak a language that is real. When he shifts to New York, his "other" setting, place becomes unreal for him. The sense of kinship with the people who speak his language and share his customs disappears. The stories and novels suffer. Even his later works—produced after a lifetime as a fiction writer—lack the immediacy of his earlier works, his works about Clarksville.

The non-Texas stories, written while he was still in his Katherine Anne Porter phase, are technically correct and usually well written. They are typical of the pieces published in highbrow magazines in the years immediately following World War II. The people are modern and sophisticated, and their lives in the suburbs are as hollow as up-to-date social critics and old-fashioned moralists would like one to believe they are. Furthermore, following the modern mode of fiction, the stories are ironic and ultimately depressing.

The book's title story is about a man named Edward Gavin who has a series of mistresses in a desperate attempt to get his wife, an unsuccessful artist with a successful sister, to pay attention to him and live the kind of life that married people are traditionally supposed to live. Edward, whom the reader knows only through a narrator, loses his battle with his wife of two decades, proving that his infidelities netted him nothing. His wife's winning gets her nothing either. They are as dead as people in a wasteland always are.

"The Last Husband" is not a bad story until one begins to compare it to Humphrey's best regional work. His early story "The Hardys" makes a nice contrast to "The Last Husband." The Hardys are an old couple closing their home to move in with their children. Mr. Hardy was widowed before he met his present wife, and Mrs. Hardy has spent years being jealous. The reader learns, in this story, told first from one point of view, then from another, that Mr. Hardy has long since forgotten his first wife and that Mrs. Hardy has no need to be jealous. (Interestingly, Edward Gavin summarizes "The Hardys" for the narrator when the two are riding the train home from Grand Central Station one night.) "The Hardys" is filled with the homey regional details and carefully rendered speech that make for excellent fiction.

"Quail for Mr. Forester" is a typical Humphrey story in that the reader sees the changing ways of the South through the eyes of a young boy—a method Humphrey uses again and again. Mr. Forester's family once made up the local aristocracy, but in recent years the Foresters have come down in the world. The narrator's father, a top-notch hunter, kills some excellent quail and invites Mr. Forester to dine. The dinner conversation is all about the decline of the Old South, which, ironically, is felt much more keenly by the narrator's family of working-class people than by Mr. Forester. At the end of an evening talking about the glory days before the Civil War, the boy, still awed, muses, "I felt that there was no hope for me in these mean times I had been born into." The mean times of the North also trouble the southern woman in "A Fresh Snow." She married a man from outside her region and is now sitting sadly in her room watching the flakes fall and thinking how far she is from home and how different the customs are. When her young son comes home and speaks in the harsh dialect of the industrial East, "she sat him on her lap and rocked him softly, his head against her breast, while she told him all about the South, where he was born."

A TIME AND A PLACE

The stories in William Humphrey's second vol-

ume *A Time and a Place* are all set in Depression-era Texas and Oklahoma. Heavily ironic, as most of his stories are, these narratives depict the harshness of life during the years of the Dust Bowl, the oil strikes, and the closing years of the Old South in Texas and Oklahoma, a world eradicated by World War II. There are a number of good stories among the ten in this volume. One of the best and most often discussed is "A Voice from the Woods," which flashes back from the undefined present to the time when the outlaws Bonnie and Clyde and Pretty Boy Floyd were heroes to the poor people of Texas and Oklahoma. The narrator, who grew up in Clarksville, lives in the East. His mother is visiting him and his eastern wife, and as they sit drinking beer, they hear the cooing of a mourning dove. The sound recalls to the mother the time that a man she once loved and considered marrying robbed the bank in Clarksville and was killed in a gunfight on the street. She and the son, a very small boy at the time, witnessed the death of the robber. She sits thinking how different her life might have been had she married Travis Winfield, who died in the arms of his latest love, a redheaded woman. The mother recalls how she had a good life with a good husband, but she says, "And yet, thinking of that redheaded woman . . . I felt, well, I don't know what else to call it if not jealousy."

There is a certain sentimentality to the story, but Humphrey evokes the time and the place and the attitude of the people as well as anyone writing about Texas in the 1930's ever has. An equally effective story at evoking the era is "Mouth of Brass," about a brief friendship between a small boy and a black tamale vendor. The vendor travels all over town during the week, but on Saturdays he sets up his tamale boxes in the town square, where "the population doubled—in ginning season tripled—as country folks poured in. . . ." One Saturday, Finus—the vendor—sells a dozen tamales to a little boy who is buying them for his family waiting just off the square. When the boy wolfs down five of the tamales on the way back to the family, the father thinks Finus took advantage of the child's age to cheat him, becomes enraged, and confronts the vendor. One thing leads to another, and the man knifes Finus. Naturally, in the Deep South of the 1930's, it is determined that the white man was provoked, and he is let off on self-defense. The little boy, who was once allowed to make his rounds with Finus, experiences an epiphany about race relations and will never be the same.

These stories and many others in Humphrey's collections paint vivid pictures of the South as it was when Humphrey was a boy and was learning about the injustices of life. His works are filled with the ironies to be encountered in a merciless universe devoid of justice and quick to plunge human beings into misery. His stories are often bleak and hopeless: Men are forced into crime by circumstances and then are punished unmercifully; the underclass are beaten down by the rich; children are jerked suddenly into adulthood by death and destruction. Bad as it is, however, there is a richness to the life found in northeast Texas. There were traditions and stories and customs that were passed down from generation to generation by word of mouth. There were moments of unsurpassed joy to balance—at least partially—the violence and cruelty found there and so well described in the writings of William Humphrey.

SEPTEMBER SONG

This collection of twenty stories was also Humphrey's final published book, appearing five years before he died. These stories revolve around themes of aging, from the frustrations of dealing with one's declining physical capacities to the need to attach meaning and purpose to one's life. Their quality is uneven, but included here is some of Humphrey's best writing.

Not surprisingly, the stories assume a somber, sad tone, yet they are also full of humor. In "The Dead Languages," for example, hearing loss is both amusing—as the protagonist, a retired reporter, confuses words, such as "cows" with "clouds"—and poignantly tragic in the accuracy and detail with which both the physical loss and others' reactions to the reporter are described. In the opening story, "Portrait of the Artist as an Old Man" (a reference to the novel by James Joyce, who enjoys other allusions in Humphrey's work), an aging Texas-born writer fabricates wild stories about his life during an interview with the young journalist who has been asked to prepare the writer's obituary.

Human beings' ultimate lack of control over the outcome of life, despite best-laid plans, is a recurring theme, perhaps best developed in the longest story of the collection, "The Apple of Discord." Here, an apple farmer hopes to be able to pass his land to one of three daughters but instead is compelled to sell the land to a developer. The farmer then attempts to give the money to his daughters and follows that with a suicide attempt to spite his girls. One daughter, however, upsets his plan.

The collection's title story is one of Humphrey's best, featuring a seventy-six-year-old protagonist who decides to divorce her husband and reunite with a former lover. The very decline in her husband that has partially prompted the decision is what forces her, in the end, to stay, as she realizes that "he could not look after himself."

Molly Giles, reviewing the book in *The Los Angeles Times* and observing that some of the male characters could easily be "the same boys in Mr. Humphrey's Texas novels, grown up," noted that their older counterparts serve to remind readers that "there isn't such a long long time between May and September." Jonathan Yardley, in a review of the collection appearing in *The Washington Post*, summed up not only *September Song* but also Humphrey's work in general when he described the stories as "interesting and admirable" achievements in serious fiction rather than commercial success and "fashionable glitz."

OTHER MAJOR WORKS

LONG FICTION: *Home from the Hill*, 1958; *The Ordways*, 1965; *Proud Flesh*, 1973; *Hostages to Fortune*, 1984; *No Resting Place*, 1989.

NONFICTION: *The Spawning Run*, 1970; *Ah, Wilderness: The Frontier in American Literature*, 1977; *Farther Off from Heaven*, 1977; *My Moby Dick*, 1978; *Open Season: Sporting Adventures*, 1986.

BIBLIOGRAPHY

Almon, Bert. *William Humphrey: Destroyer of Myths*. Denton: University of North Texas Press,

1998. A comprehensive critical study of Humphrey's fiction, including a discussion of the role of Texas as a setting in his work. Includes a bibliography and an index.

Givner, Joan. "Katherine Anne Porter: The Old Order and the New." In *The Texas Literary Tradition*, edited by Don Graham et al. Austin: University of Texas Press, 1983. Though Humphrey's name does not appear in the title, Givner argues that Humphrey and fellow Texan William Goyen were greatly under the influence of Porter. Here and in the biography that she wrote on Porter, Givner traces Porter's influence on the two younger writers and says that they were eager to imitate Porter and win her favor with letters and flowery dedications. The essay is interesting also in showing the treatment Porter received in the male-dominated Texas literary establishment of the 1930's and 1940's.

Graham, Don. "Regionalism on the Ramparts: The Texas Literary Tradition." *USA Today* 115 (July, 1986): 74-76. Discusses five distinct literary regions in Texas: East Texas, West Texas, the Gulf Coast, the Border Valley, and Urban Texas. Notes how the southern culture of Texas was depicted by George Sessions Perry during the 1940's and by three East Texans—William Goyen, William Humphrey, and William A. Owens—during the 1950's and 1960's.

Grider, Sylvia, and Elizabeth Tebeaux. "Blessings into Curses: Sardonic Humor and Irony in 'A Job of the Plains.'" *Studies in Short Fiction* 23 (1986): 297-306. The authors of this essay focus on Humphrey's short story "A Job of the Plains," an ironic retelling of the Book of Job as it might have happened in the Dust Bowl of Oklahoma during the Great Depression of the 1930's. Humphrey's story, the authors say, delves into the meaninglessness of life, the cruelty of God's universe, and the pointlessness of human suffering. The theme becomes "the controlling theme for the remaining stories in the collection. In every story, Humphrey weaves a similar naturalism into the Dust Bowl/Depression worldview." Grider and Tebeaux compare *A Time and a Place* to Sherwood Anderson's *Winesburg, Ohio* (1919).

Humphrey, William. Interview by Jose Yglesias. *Publishers Weekly* 235 (June 2, 1989): 64-65. A brief discussion of Humphrey's life and career, noting the regional background of some of his best-known fiction; in the interview section of this piece, Humphrey discusses his writing habits, his disdain for the literary establishment, and his relationships with editors, publishers, and other literary figures.

_____. "William Humphrey: Defining Southern Literature." Interview by Ashby Bland Crowder. *Mississippi Quarterly* 41 (1988): 529-540. Humphrey reveals some hitherto unknown facts about his life and gives a hint about his method of working. The interviewer is at great pains to fix Humphrey in the canon of southern literature and to question the author closely on his relationship to William Faulkner and others. The persistent attempts to direct the flow of the interview to "southernness" often interrupts Humphrey's commentary on his general attitudes and his view of his place in American literature.

Lee, James Ward. *William Humphrey*. Austin, Tex.: Steck-Vaughn, 1967. One of the volumes in the Southwest Writers series, this pamphlet of sixty pages is the longest work on Humphrey, but it was written when Humphrey had only two novels, a volume of stories, and four uncollected stories in print. The first twenty pages discuss Humphrey's fourteen stories, while the rest of the study analyzes *Home from the Hill* and *The Ordways*. One of the major emphases in the pamphlet is on Humphrey's use of regional materials—the folklore, the naturalistic descriptions, and the customs of northeast Texas.

_____. "William Humphrey." In *American Novelists Since World War II*, 2d ser., edited by James E. Kilber, Jr. Detroit, Mich.: Gale Research, 1980. In this six-page essay, Lee updates the pamphlet he wrote in 1967, placing more emphasis on the novels, the sporting stories, and the memoir *Farther Off from Heaven*. Lee predicts that *Farther Off from Heaven* may be Humphrey's farewell to Red River County and the Clarksville of his boyhood.

Tebeaux, Elizabeth. "Irony as Art: The Short Fiction of William Humphrey." *Studies in Short Fiction* 26 (Summer, 1989): 323-334. Asserts Humphrey's complex irony is the defining characteristic of his art. His nonheroic, dirt-farmer protagonists often make errors of judgment that lead to an ironic reversal that deepens their dilemma. Analyzes a number of stories to illustrate Humphrey's irony and parody of the tragic.

Winchell, Mark Royden. *William Humphrey.* Boise, Idaho: Boise State University, 1992. A brief pamphlet that provides a short biographical sketch and introduction to Humphrey's fiction. Suggests that the stories are best when describing a place or exploring the psychological subtleties of human relations. Discusses "The Hardys," "Quail for Mr. Forester," and "The Ballad of Jesse Neighbours" as representative of Humphrey's thematic concerns and technical skill. Discusses "Mouth of Brass" and "The Human Fly" as two of his best stories.

James Ward Lee

ZORA NEALE HURSTON

Born: E0atonville, Florida; January 7, 1891
Died: Fort Pierce, Florida; January 28, 1960

PRINCIPAL SHORT FICTION

Spunk: The Selected Short Stories of Zora Neale Hurston, 1985

OTHER LITERARY FORMS

Though best known for her novels, especially *Their Eyes Were Watching God* (1937), Zora Neale Hurston wrote in most major genres during her forty-year career. In addition to the posthumously published collection of short stories, she wrote a few early poems, several short plays, folklore collections, essays, reportage, and an autobiography.

ACHIEVEMENTS

Zora Neale Hurston is best known as a major contributor to the Harlem Renaissance literature of the 1920's. Not only was she a major contributor, but also she did much to characterize the style and temperament of the period; indeed, she is often referred to as the most colorful figure of the Harlem Renaissance. Though the short stories and short plays that she generated during the 1920's are fine works in their own right, they are nevertheless apprentice works when compared to her most productive period, the 1930's. During the 1930's, Hurston produced three novels, all telling examples of her creative genius, as well as two collections of folklore, the fruits of her training in anthropology and her many years of fieldwork. It is Hurston's interest in preserving the culture of the black South that remains among her most valuable contributions. Not only did she collect and preserve folklore outright, but also she used folklore, native drama, and the black idiom and dialect in most of her fiction.

Although Hurston's popularity declined during the 1940's and 1950's, and although she died in relative obscurity in 1960, scholars and critics sparked a Hurston revival during the mid-1970's. Hurston's popularity has never been greater, as her works are considered mainstays in any number of canons, among them African American literature, folklore, southern literature, feminist studies, and anthropology.

BIOGRAPHY

Zora Neale Hurston was born in 1891 in the all-black town of Eatonville, Florida, near Orlando. She was the youngest daughter and the seventh of eight children born to John and Lucy Hurston. Her father was a minister and local government official who

Zora Neale Hurston (Library of Congress)

wrote many of Eatonville's laws upon its incorporation and served several terms as mayor. Her mother was a homemaker who cared not only for her children but also for an extended family that included, at various times, her own mother and her brother Jim. By all accounts, Hurston's childhood was happy, almost idyllic, free from the poverty and racism that characterized much of the black experience in the South. Indeed, this wholesome upbringing informed much of Hurston's later work and earned for her the designation as an early black cultural nationalist.

Whatever idyllic aspects Hurston's childhood possessed were shattered when Hurston was about nine. The death of Hurston's beloved mother, who encouraged the young Zora to "jump at the sun," precipitated a change. This was followed by her father's remarriage to a woman who had no interest in the children and the subsequent dismantling of the relative happiness of the Hurston household. The next several years of Hurston's life found her much displaced, living variously with older siblings and receiving only sporadic schooling.

Although exact dates are difficult to place in Hurston's early chronology because she frequently

lied about her age, various sources reveal that Hurston joined a Gilbert and Sullivan traveling show when she was about fourteen as a wardrobe maid to one of the show's stars. Hurston worked for this show for several years, traveling throughout the South, sometimes without pay. It was with this show, however, that Hurston's talents as raconteur were first noticed, as she often entertained the company with stories, anecdotes, and tales from the black South, told with their own humor, mimicry, and dialect.

Hurston left her job with the Gilbert and Sullivan show in Baltimore, and, out of an intense desire to complete her education, she enrolled in the high school department of the Morgan Academy (now Morgan State University) in that city, completing the high school program in 1919. From Morgan, Hurston entered Howard University, at that time known as "the Negro Harvard," in Washington, D.C. At Howard, Hurston soon came to the attention of Alain Locke, adviser to the Howard Literary Society and later a principal critic of the New Negro movement. Locke invited Hurston to join the literary society, and she soon began publishing in *Stylus*, the Howard University literary magazine. Her first published short story, "John Redding Goes to Sea," appeared in *Stylus* in 1921.

Hurston's talent soon came to the attention of Charles S. Johnson, founder and editor of the National Urban League's magazine *Opportunity*, which held annual contests for young writers. Johnson encouraged Hurston to submit her works to *Opportunity*, which she did; "Drenched in Light" appeared in December, 1924, and "Spunk" in June, 1925. Both "Spunk" and a short play, "Color Struck," were second-place prizewinners in their respective divisions in *Opportunity*'s 1925 contest, and another short story, "Black Death," won honorable mention.

Hurston traveled to New York to attend the 1925 contest awards banquet and found herself in the midst of the Harlem Renaissance, the great outpouring of artistic expression revolving around Harlem. She became an active member of the Harlem literati and soon became the Harlem Renaissance's most colorful figure. In the fall of 1925, Hurston entered Barnard, the women's college of Columbia University, on a scholarship arranged by Annie Nathan Meyer. There, she studied anthropology under Franz Boas and received her degree in 1928.

Beginning in 1927, Hurston traveled throughout the South, collecting folklore, first under the sponsorship of the Association for the Study of Negro Life and History, and later through various fellowships, including a Guggenheim, and the private sponsorship of Charlotte Osgood Mason, a wealthy white patron of Harlem Renaissance writers including Langston Hughes and Alain Locke.

In 1930, Hurston and Hughes collaborated on a black folk play, *Mule Bone*, an undertaking that severed the personal and professional relationship between Hurston and Hughes; the break was never mended and kept the play from being published in its entirety until 1991, long after the deaths of both authors. The dispute, precipitated by the question of principal authorship, while certainly unfortunate, nevertheless illustrates the fiercely independent temperament that Hurston maintained throughout her lifetime.

Though the 1930's got off to a rough start with the controversy with Hughes, the decade proved to be Hurston's most productive. Hurston published her first novel, *Jonah's Gourd Vine*, in 1934, followed in rapid succession by the folklore collection *Mules and Men* in 1935; another novel, the now classic *Their Eyes Were Watching God* in 1937; another folklore collection, *Tell My Horse*, in 1938; and another novel, *Moses, Man of the Mountain*, in 1939. In addition, Hurston wrote several short stories and several essays, notably those on black culture, published in Nancy Cunard's massive collection, *Negro*, in 1934.

In 1942, Hurston published her autobiography, *Dust Tracks on a Road*. While the book won the *Saturday Review*'s Ainsfield-Wolf Award for race relations, it proved to be the last significant work of Hurston's career, although she did publish another novel, *Seraph on the Suwanee*, in 1948. There are several reasons for the decline in Hurston's popularity, the most important among them being that her folk-based literature did not fit into protest literature, the dominant literary trend of the 1940's, coupled

with Hurston's growing conservatism. Further, in September, 1948, shortly before the publication of *Seraph on the Suwanee*, Hurston was falsely charged with seducing a minor, but before the charges could be dismissed as unfounded, the black press, in particular the *Baltimore Afro-American*, had spread the story to its readers and had severely, almost irreparably, damaged Hurston's reputation. Disillusioned and outraged at her treatment by the court and the black press, Hurston moved back to the South, where she lived for the remainder of her life.

The 1950's was a tragic decade for Hurston. Her career was stagnant, and although she kept writing, she received rejection after rejection. She did, however, do some reporting for the *Pittsburgh Courier*, a black paper with a national circulation; published several essays; and accepted several speaking engagements. She supported herself with occasional work, including substitute teaching and writing freelance articles for various papers.

Toward the end of the 1950's, Hurston's health became increasingly fragile. She suffered from overweight, hypertension, poor diet, gallbladder trouble, ulcers, and various stomach ailments. In 1959, she suffered a stroke, and in October of that year was placed in the Saint Lucie County welfare home, where, alone and penniless, she died on January 28, 1960. She was buried by subscription a week later in Fort Pierce's segregated cemetery, the Garden of the Heavenly Rest.

ANALYSIS

The bulk of Zora Neale Hurston's short fiction is set in her native Florida, as are most of her novels. Even when the setting is not Florida, however, the stories are informed by the life, habits, beliefs, and idioms of the people whom Hurston knew so well, the inhabitants of Eatonville primarily. One criticism often leveled at Hurston was that she frequently masqueraded folklore as fiction, or, in other cases, imposed folklore on the fictive narrative. Whatever the merits of such criticism may be, Hurston's short stories abound with an energy and zest for life that Hurston considered instructive for her readers.

"JOHN REDDING GOES TO SEA"

Hurston's first published short story is entitled "John Redding Goes to Sea." It was published in the May, 1921, issue of the *Stylus*, the literary magazine of Howard University, and was reprinted in the January, 1926, issue of *Opportunity*. While the story is obviously the work of a novice writer, with its highly contrived plot, excessive sentimentality, and shallow characterizations, its strengths are many, strengths upon which Hurston would continue to draw and develop throughout her career.

The plot is a simple one: Young John Redding, the titular character, wants to leave his hometown to see and explore parts and things unknown. Several circumstances conspire, however, to keep him from realizing his dream. First, John's mother, the pitifully possessive, obsessive, and superstitious Matty Redding, is determined not to let John pursue his ambitions; in fact, she pleads illness and threatens to disown him if he leaves. Second, John's marriage to Stella Kanty seems to tie him permanently to his surroundings, as his new wife joins forces with his mother to discourage John's desire to travel. Further, his mother's tantrums keep John from even joining the Navy when that opportunity comes his way. Later, when John is killed in a tempest while working with a crew to build a bridge on the St. John's River, his father forbids his body to be retrieved from the river as it floats toward the ocean. At last, John will get his wish to travel and see the world, although in death.

If the plot seems overdone and the sentimentality overwhelming, "John Redding Goes to Sea" does provide the reader with the first of many glimpses of life among black Floridians—their habits, superstitions, strengths, and shortcomings. For example, one of the more telling aspects of the story is that Matty believes that her son was cursed with "travel dust" at his birth; thus, John's desire to travel is Matty's punishment for having married his father away from a rival suitor. Hurston suspends judgment on Matty's beliefs; rather, she shows that these and other beliefs are integral parts of the life of the folk.

Another strength that is easily discernible in Hurston's first short story is her detailed rendering of setting. Hurston has a keen eye for detail, and nowhere is this more evident than in her descriptions of the lushness of Florida. This adeptness is especially present in "John Redding Goes to Sea" and in most of Hurston's other work as well.

By far the most important aspect of "John Redding Goes to Sea" is its theme that people must be free to develop and pursue their own dreams, a recurring theme in the Hurston canon. John Redding is deprived of self-expression and self-determination because the wishes and interpretations of others are imposed upon him. Hurston clearly has no sympathy with those who would deprive another of freedom and independence; indeed, she would adamantly oppose all such restrictive efforts throughout her career as a writer and folklorist.

"SPUNK"

Another early short story that treats a variation of this theme is "Spunk," published in the June, 1925, issue of *Opportunity*. The central character, Spunk Banks, has the spunk to live his life as he chooses, which includes taking another man's wife and parading openly around town with her. While Hurston passes no moral judgment on Banks, she makes it clear that she appreciates and admires his brassiness and his will to live his life according to his own terms.

When the story opens, Spunk Banks and Lena Kanty are openly flaunting their affair in front of the Eatonville townspeople, including Lena's husband, Joe Kanty. The other town residents make fun of Joe's weakness, his refusal to confront Spunk Banks. Later, when Joe desperately attacks Spunk with a razor, Spunk shoots and kills him. Spunk is tried and acquitted but is killed in a work-related accident, cut to death by a circle saw.

Again, superstition plays an important role here, for Spunk claims that he has been haunted by Joe Kanty's ghost. In fact, Spunk is convinced that Joe's ghost pushed him into the circle saw, and at least one other townsman agrees. As is customary in Hurston's stories, however, she makes no judgment of the rightness or wrongness of such beliefs but points out that these beliefs are very much a part of the cultural milieu of Eatonville.

"SWEAT"

Another early Eatonville story is "Sweat," published in 1926 in the only issue of the ill-fated literary magazine *Fire!*, founded by Hurston, Hughes, and Wallace Thurman. "Sweat" shows Hurston's power as a fiction writer and as a master of the short-story form. Again, the story line is a simple one. Delia Jones is a hardworking, temperate Christian woman being tormented by her arrogant, mean-spirited, and cruel husband of fifteen years, Sykes Jones, who has become tired of her and desires a new wife. Rather than simply leaving her, though, he wants to drive her away by making her life miserable. At stake is the house for which Delia's "sweat" has paid: Sykes wants it for his new mistress, but Delia refuses to leave the fruit of her labor.

Sykes uses both physical and mental cruelty to antagonize Delia, the most far-reaching of which is Delia's intense fear of snakes. When Delia's fear of the caged rattlesnake that Sykes places outside her back door subsides, Sykes places the rattlesnake in the dirty clothes hamper, hoping that it will bite and kill Delia. In an ironic twist, however, Delia escapes, and the rattlesnake bites Sykes as he fumbles for a match in the dark house. Delia listens and watches as Sykes dies a painful, agonizing death.

While "Sweat" makes use of the same superstitious beliefs as Hurston's other stories, a more complex characterization and an elaborate system of symbols are central to the story's development. In Delia, for example, readers are presented with an essentially good Christian woman who is capable of great compassion and long suffering and who discovers the capacity to hate as intensely as she loves; in Sykes, readers are shown unadulterated evil reduced to one at once pitiful and horrible in his suffering. In addition, the Christian symbolism, including the snake and the beast of burden, adds considerable interest and texture to the story. It is this texture that makes "Sweat" Hurston's most rewarding work of short fiction, for it shows her at her best as literary artist and cultural articulator.

"THE GILDED SIX-BITS"

Although Hurston turned to the longer narrative as the preferred genre during the 1930's, she continued writing short stories throughout the remainder of her career. One such story is "The Gilded Six-Bits," published in 1933, which also examines relationships between men and women. In this story, the marriage bed of a happy couple, Joe and Missie May Banks, is defiled by a city slicker, Otis D. Slemmons. Missie May has been attracted by Slemmons's gold money, which she desires to get for her husband. The gold pieces, however, turn out to be gold-plated. Hurston's message is nearly cliché—"all that glitters is not gold"—but she goes a step further to establish the idea that true love transcends all things. Joe and Missie May are reconciled at the end of the story.

"COCK ROBIN, BEALE STREET"

Hurston's last stories are fables that seem to have only comic value but do, however, advance serious thoughts, such as the ridiculousness of the idea of race purity in "Cock Robin, Beale Street" or the equal ridiculousness of the idea that the North was better for blacks, in "Story in Harlem Slang." While these stories are not artistic achievements, they do provide interesting aspects of the Hurston canon.

In many ways, Hurston's short stories are apprentice works to her novels. In these stories, she introduced most of the themes, character types, settings, techniques, and concerns upon which she later elaborated during her most productive and artistic period, the 1930's. This observation, however, does not suggest that her short stories are inferior works. On the contrary, much of the best of Hurston can be found in these early stories.

OTHER MAJOR WORKS

LONG FICTION: *Jonah's Gourd Vine*, 1934; *Their Eyes Were Watching God*, 1937; *Moses, Man of the Mountain*, 1939; *Seraph on the Suwanee*, 1948.

PLAYS: *Color Struck*, pb. 1926; *The First One*, pb. 1927; *Mule Bone*, pb. 1931 (with Langston Hughes).

NONFICTION: *Mules and Men*, 1935; *Tell My Horse*, 1938; *Dust Tracks on a Road*, 1942; *The Sanctified Church*, 1981.

MISCELLANEOUS: *I Love Myself When I Am Laughing . . . and Then Again When I Am Looking Mean and Impressive: A Zora Neale Hurston Reader*, 1979.

BIBLIOGRAPHY

Chinn, Nancy, and Elizabeth E. Dunn. "'The Ring of Singing Metal on Wood': Zora Neale Hurston's Artistry in 'The Gilded Six-Bits.'" *The Mississippi Quarterly* 49 (Fall, 1996): 775-790. Discusses how Hurston uses setting, ritual, dialect, and the nature of human relationships in the story; argues that the story provides a solution to the problem of reconciling her rural Florida childhood with her liberal arts education and training.

Cobb-Moore, Geneva. "Zora Neale Hurston as Local Colorist." *The Southern Literary Journal* 26 (Spring, 1994): 25-34. Discusses how Hurston's creation of folk characters enlarges the meaning of local color; shows how Hurston proves that while physical bodies can be restricted, the imagination is always free.

Cooper, Jan. "Zora Neale Hurston Was Always a Southerner Too." In *The Female Tradition in Southern Literature*, edited by Carol S. Manning. Urbana: University of Illinois Press, 1993. Examines the hitherto neglected role that Hurston played in the Southern Renaissance between 1920 and 1950. Argues that Hurston's fiction is informed by a modern southern agrarian sense of community. Suggests that the Southern Renaissance was a transracial, cross-cultural product of the South.

Donlon, Jocelyn Hazelwood. "Porches: Stories: Power: Spatial and Racial Intersections in Faulkner and Hurston." *Journal of American Culture* 19 (Winter, 1996): 95-110. Comments on the role of the porch in Faulkner and Hurston's fiction as a transitional space between the public and the private where the individual can negotiate an identity through telling stories.

Glassman, Steve, and Kathryn Lee Siedel, eds. *Zora in Florida*. Orlando: University of Central Florida Press, 1991. This collection of essays by seventeen Hurston scholars explores the overall presence and influence of Florida in and on the works of Hurston. This collection grew out of a Hurston symposium held in Daytona Beach, Florida, in November, 1989, and includes an excellent introduction to the importance of Florida in the study of Hurston.

Hemenway, Robert E. *Zora Neale Hurston: A Literary Biography*. Urbana: University of Illinois Press, 1977. Perhaps the best extant work on Hurston. Hemenway's painstakingly researched study of Hurston's life and literary career was crucial in rescuing Hurston from neglect and establishing her as a major American writer. Although some of the facts of Hurston's chronology have been corrected by later scholarship, Hemenway's study is the most valuable introduction to Hurston's work available. Includes a bibliography of published and unpublished works by Hurston.

Hill, Lynda Marion. *Social Rituals and the Verbal Art of Zora Neale Hurston*. Washington, D.C.: Howard University Press, 1996. Chapters on Hurston's treatment of everyday life, science and humanism, folklore, and color, race, and class. Hill also considers dramatic reenactments of Hurston's writing. Includes notes, bibliography, and an appendix on "characteristics of Negro expression."

Howard, Lillie P. *Zora Neale Hurston*. Boston: Twayne, 1980. A good general introduction to the life and works of Hurston. Contains valuable plot summaries and commentaries on Hurston's works. Supplemented by a chronology and a bibliography.

Lyons, Mary E. *Sorrow's Kitchen: The Life and Folklore of Zora Neale Hurston*. New York: Charles Scribner's Sons, 1990. Perhaps the only straightforward biography of Hurston, written with the younger reader in mind. Especially useful for those who need a primer in Hurston's background in all-black Eatonville.

Newsom, Adele S. *Zora Neale Hurston: A Reference Guide*. Boston: G. K. Hall, 1987. A catalog of Hurston criticism spanning the years 1931-1986, arranged chronologically with annotations. This source is an invaluable aid to serious scholars of Hurston. Also contains an introduction to the criticism on Hurston. An especially useful resource for all inquiries.

Walker, Pierre A. "Zora Neale Hurston and the Post-Modern Self in *Dust Tracks on a Road*." *African American Review* 32 (Fall, 1998): 387-399. Uses poststructuralist theory to discuss Hurston's autobiography, showing how she avoids certain autobiographical conventions; argues that Hurston focuses on the life of her imagination, on the psychological dynamics of her family, on retelling

community stories, on portraying the character of certain friends, and on her ambiguous pronouncements about race.

Warren J. Carson

ALDOUS HUXLEY

Born: Laleham, near Godalming, Surrey, England; July 26, 1894

Died: Los Angeles, California; November 22, 1963

PRINCIPAL SHORT FICTION

Limbo, 1920

Mortal Coils, 1922

Little Mexican, and Other Stories, 1924 (pb. in U.S. as *Young Archimedes, and Other Stories*, 1924)

Two or Three Graces, and Other Stories, 1926

Brief Candles: Stories, 1930

The Gioconda Smile, 1938 (first pb. in *Mortal Coils*)

Twice Seven: Fourteen Selected Stories, 1944

Collected Short Stories, 1957

OTHER LITERARY FORMS

The diversity of Aldous Huxley's more than sixty books encompasses nine collections of poetry (the largest selection being in *Verses and a Comedy*); several plays (*The Gioconda Smile*, pb. 1948, based on his short story of this title, also was the basis of Huxley's screenplay for the 1948 feature film *A Woman's Vengeance*); numerous essays, gathered in several collections (the most convenient being the *Collected Essays* of 1959); and monographs on biography (for example, the 1941 study of Cardinal Richelieu, *Grey Eminence*), travel (for example, *Beyond the Mexique Bay*, 1934), politics and science (for example, *Brave New World Revisited*, 1958), philosophy (for example, *The Perennial Philosophy*, 1945), art and literature (for example, *Vulgarity in*

Literature, 1930), and psychology and religion (for example, *The Doors of Perception*, 1954). He also wrote eleven novels, from *Crome Yellow*, in 1921, to *Island*, in 1962. He is perhaps most famous for his dystopian novel *Brave New World* (1932), which in many ways eerily prefigured modern society.

ACHIEVEMENTS

The recipient of awards from the American Academy of Arts and Letters (1959) and the British Royal Society of Literature (1962), Aldous Huxley has been most praised and studied for his novels, in which—as with his short fiction—he distinctively blends witty prose style, allusion, irony and satire, and symbolism. His targets have ranged from modern British society (as in *Point Counter Point*, 1928), to modern American society (particularly Los Angeles and Hollywood, as in *After Many a Summer Dies the Swan*, 1939, and *Ape and Essence*, 1948), to the bleak view of a future totalitarian world, dominated by sex and drugs, in his science-fiction work *Brave New World*. Huxley's essays have been widely commended, though not much written about, while his short fiction has not received the attention that it merits.

BIOGRAPHY

Aldous Leonard Huxley was born on July 26, 1894, in Godalming, Surrey, to a family with eminent intellectual credentials in both the arts and the sciences. Often cited by critics are elements in Huxley's work related to Huxley's genealogical connections with science on one hand and the liberal arts on the other. His scientific connections came through his pa-

Aldous Huxley (CORBIS/Bettmann)

ternal grandfather, T. H. Huxley, an eminent biologist, and his elder brother, Julian Huxley, also an eminent biologist, while his liberal arts connections came through his mother's relation to the important literary critic, poet, essayist, and moralist, Matthew Arnold.

Huxley was educated at Hillside School, Eton, and Balliol College, Oxford University; Oxford University serves as the background of some of Huxley's short stories, such as "Happily Ever After" and "Cynthia." Huxley's early serious eye ailment, which abated after almost resulting in blindness and an end to his education, is partly reflected in his treasuring of the visual arts and classical music, which are constantly referred to in both his nonfiction and fiction. During World War I, which is referred to in many of his short stories, Huxley was exempted from military service but did agricultural work (like the protagonist of "Farcial History of Richard Greenow") in aid of the war effort.

After graduation with an honors degree in English literature from Oxford, Huxley briefly taught school and then became a full-time writer, supporting himself and his Belgian wife, Maria Nys (and after her death, his second wife, longtime friend and Italian concert violinist Laura Archera), with his esteemed and widely read novels and journalistic nonfiction, plus some screenplays when he changed his home base from England to Southern California in 1937. His wide and long-term travels in Latin America and continental Europe throughout his life are reflected not only in his nonfiction travel writings but also in several short stories. Huxley's continued friendship with and then literary executorship of British fiction writer D. H. Lawrence parallel Huxley's own enduring interests in the instinctive and sexual bases of human behavior, which are recurrent subjects of both his fiction and nonfiction. Acquaintances in Southern California led to Huxley's interest in and writing about Eastern religion and the achievement of transcendental perception and religious consciousness through the use of certain hallucinogenic drugs. In his later years, Huxley became a highly regarded cultural elder statesman and continued public statements, in his writings and interviews, aimed at attaining a just, sensitive, and culturally aware society that would allow, along with transcendental religion, the full and undeceived self-realization of every individual.

ANALYSIS

All twenty-one of Aldous Huxley's short stories, ranging from the five pages of "The Bookshop" and the six pages of "Fard" to the thirty-eight pages of "Happily Ever After" and "Chawdron," are gathered in *Collected Short Stories*, which remains one of Huxley's books readily available to readers. Omitted from *Collected Short Stories* are three novelettes scattered in Huxley's five principal early story collections: "Farcical History of Richard Greenow" (in *Limbo*), "Uncle Spencer" (in *Little Mexican*), and "After the Fireworks" (*Brief Candles*). In nearly all these works, as in his longer fiction, Huxley's witty prose style is used to expose, with irony and satire, the gap between the ideal and the real in various societies, individual human personalities, and human behavior. An example of how Huxley's prose style skewers the greed, indolence, and parasitism of the British aristocracy can be found in the following sentence describing the forebears of Baron Badgery—

Huxley frequently uses comic names for satire—in the opening of "The Tillotson Banquet":

> They had been content to live and quietly to propagate their species in a huge machiolated Norman castle, surrounded by a triple moat, only sallying forth to cultivate their property and to collect their rents.

With adroit irony, Huxley counterbalances his hallmark polysyllabism in "propagate" and "machiolated" with the plainer, parallel, and alliterating "cultivate" and "collect"; he counterbalances the lazy pacifism behind the moated castle with the warlike "sallying forth" not for glory but for money. The pervasive reversal structure or ironic surprise ending of the stories, like Huxley's prose style, helps convey the discrepancy between what people say or think and what they do, between plans or intentions and results, or between appearances and realities.

Frequently in the stories a main character attempts to impose on the world an oversimplified idealistic mental construct that must and does fail. Indeed, a recurrent theme is the duality in life between mind and body, idealism and pragmatism, or spirituality and high culture versus the physical world or materialism. Such duality is ingrained in the title character of "Farcical History of Richard Greenow," who suffers a dissociative personality split between a male, antiwar, hard-edged, intellectual essayist of moderate means and a female, jingoistic, sentimental, middlebrow, monetarily successful novelist. In "The Death of Lully," based on real persons and events, the spirituality of the title character, which drives him to Christian martyrdom in Muslim North Africa, contrasts with the carnality of a young couple on his sea-going transport, as well as with the commercialism of the captain, who wonders how to profit financially from his famous dying passenger. In "Sir Hercules," the title character, a British baron, whose dwarf stature contradicts his given forename, attempts to build a miniaturized utopia on the family estate, with his equally diminutive, attractive, and aesthetically oriented wife; ironically, their son grows up large, loutish, cruel, and insensitive, spurring his parents' suicide. In "The Monocle," the title helps symbolize the story's theme of defective or partial vision, which almost all the characters have, derived from their single, usually egocentric, focus on something, including young Gregory, the main character, who wears the monocle to appear to be more detached and upperclass than he really is, as well as the intellectual Spiller, who actualizes his name by his continual talk, often oblivious to his immediate surroundings. In "Fairy Godmother," the rich Mrs. Escobar attempts to create the fairytale role of the story's title for herself, heedless of the rarity of her good deeds toward the family she is giving charity to, as well as of the reality of what a young child might really want as a gift. Finally, in "The Claxtons," the parent Claxtons, especially the wife, endeavor to create an idealized spiritual, vegetarian, economical household, despite Mrs. Claxton's real envy of her rich relations and eventually her clandestine dietary cheating.

"HAPPILY EVER AFTER"

Interconnected with the conflict between ideal and real, mental and physical, is the persistent focus in the stories on romantic love—its sources, development, illusions, delusions, endurance, or transitoriness. In "Happily Ever After," Huxley uses the fairytale overtones of the title as part of his satire on the real lives of characters, which contradict their romantic illusions; thus Guy Lambourne has the deluded naïveté, suggested by his surname, to believe that he is above the physical side of romantic love, realizing his mistake too late, since he is killed in World War I; also, at the story's end his sweetheart and his good friend, in sentimentalizing over Guy's death, unwittingly push themselves toward an affair that will betray him. In "The Gioconda Smile" and "After the Fireworks," the main male character in each story—Henry Hutton and Miles Fanning, respectively—is an intellectual, art lover, and writer who is flirtatious despite struggling, unsuccessfully, against yielding to a string of sexual liaisons; each pays a drastic price: Hutton is tried and executed for the death of his wife, who was actually murdered by Janet Spence, with whom Hutton flirted and whose Gioconda smile belied such violence, and Fanning wanes in health and in the affection of his young mistress, the course of their affair running as he had understood and predicted. The duality between mind and body in romantic love is also evident in "Cynthia" and "The Rest Cure."

"CYNTHIA" AND "THE REST CURE"

In "Cynthia," consistently threaded with classical allusions, the skeptical narrator's university friend, Lykeham (who has actualized his surname—"like 'em"—by a series of love affairs), claims, with apparent romantic hyperbole, to have met an actual goddess at a playhouse; at story's end, Lykeham, with the narrator in tow, seems, to the narrator's surprise, drawn into a genuinely supernatural outdoors nocturnal pursuit that leads to union with the goddess; however, the skeptical narrator wonders whether the female, identified as the chaste Cynthia, or moon goddess, would not descend to the physical side of the mythological tale of Cynthia's presumably very physical union with the carnal god Pan. In "The Rest Cure," Mrs. Moira Tarwin is transformed by her husband's jealousy of her young Italian factotum, Tonino, from a neurasthenic repulsed by the sexual component of romantic love to a passionate lover; ironically, Tonino is transformed by Mrs. Tarwin's passion from an idealistically chaste admiration, to physical rapture, to bored apathy—the last to Mrs. Tarwin's great distress.

"UNCLE SPENCER" AND "CHAWDRON"

How lovers may superimpose imagination on their partner or some other aspect of the relationship is shown in "Uncle Spencer," "Chawdron," "Green Tunnels," "Hubert and Minnie," "Fard," and "Half-Holiday." In "Uncle Spencer" and "Chawdron," the both gentle Uncle Spencer and the ruthless Chawdron recreate a clearly flawed, self-centered female companion, of opposite temperament to the title character, into an idealized image of a romantic partner; neither achieves a true romantic union, Uncle Spencer's beloved disappearing as soon as their World War I internment ends, and Chawdron's beloved actualizing her childishly attention-getting hypochondria into a fatal illness.

"GREEN TUNNELS" AND "HUBERT AND MINNIE"

In "Green Tunnels" and "Hubert and Minnie," the main female character—Barbara and Minnie, re-spectively—through imagination transforms a male acquaintance into lover and is disappointed when reality contradicts the illusion; Barbara's illusion corresponds to the symbolism of the mazy green tunnels growing where she is staying in Italy, and Minnie's illusion corresponds to the symbolism of the passionate thunder of mill water at the inn where she is to meet her prospective lover, which gives way to the silence of the mill being stopped and his reneging on the assignation.

"FARD" AND "HALF-HOLIDAY"

Finally, in "Fard" and "Half-Holiday," the interrelation of Huxley's concerns—in these instances, delusions in love and societal inequities—emerges from a household marital contretemps in France and a spat between two dogs being walked at a London park, respectively. In "Fard," the title derives from the French word referring to facial cosmetics and thus points to the superficiality of Madame, proud of her good looks and sex appeal, who imaginatively overdramatizes a quarrel over acceding to her husband's will, while ignoring the real health and socioeconomic plight of her maid, Sophie. In "Half-Holiday," impoverished Peter Brett, on a "half-holiday" walk in the park from his low-paying job, imagines himself a fairytale romantic prince and then attempts to implement his daydream by rescuing a dog belonging to two attractive upperclass young women from a dogfight; but instead of winning a princess, he is offered money, dismissed, and quickly forgotten, being of little notice to the young women's social class.

"THE PORTRAIT"

The topic of the fine arts is pervasive in the stories, related to Huxley's preoccupation with the collision between mind and matter, imagination and reality, as well as Huxley's personal interest in painting, music, and literature. As usual in Huxley's short fiction, as well as in his longer fiction, this recurrent theme is often intertwined with Huxley's other recurrent themes. For example, in "The Portrait," the intrinsically interesting and ironic story of a love triangle associated with a painting turns out to be wholly invented by art dealer Mr. Bigger to sell the painting to a prospective parvenu buyer; further expressing the theme of the conflict between art and money in a materialistic society is the climactic revelation that the art dealer has all this time kept the painting's actual artist disconsolately waiting around the gallery, paying him only a fraction of what will be realized from the sale. The relation between literary art and romantic love may be seen in "After the Fireworks" in how an artist succumbs to the pursuit of a beautiful young female reader, more in love with his art than with him, and in "Nuns at Luncheon," in which two writers at luncheon in a fashionable restaurant dispassionately discuss as a potential work of art the tragic love affair of a nun seduced by a confidence man who is a prisoner-patient at a hospital where she is a nurse.

ART AND CULTURE

As in "The Portrait," art or culture versus society's materialistic concern with money and commerce is also evident in "The Bookshop," in which the narrator notices that the title's small repository of culture is squeezed symbolically between a furniture store and cheap diner; in "The Tillotson Banquet," in which a famous artist is fleetingly retrieved from extreme poverty only because a British aristocrat initially but incorrectly thinks the artist can decorate a room in the aristocrat's manor; and in "Little Mexican," in which the narrator, on an extended visit to Italy, is mistaken for a painter because of his hat, a "little Mexican" (that is, sombrero), by an Italian aristocrat, who is interested in business and manufacturing rather than art, and who tries to secure the narrator's help in peddling priceless frescoes that are degenerating on the degenerating family estate.

"YOUNG ARCHIMEDES"

Harking back to the two strains in Huxley's lineage—art and science—are "Eupompus Gave Splendour to Art by Numbers" and "Young Archimedes," which deal with the interrelation of these two fields. In the first of these stories, the narrator's friend Emberlin, having read ancient references to the use of mathematics in art, becomes intrigued and then obsessed by arithmetic; he endangers the ideal of the sane and cultured human being, whose interests ought to be diverse. In "Young Archimedes," set in Italy, a dominating and controlling woman, Signora Bondi, reminiscent of Mrs. Escobar in "Fairy God-

mother," descends on a young impoverished prodigy, Guido, who has talents in both music and mathematics; despite the boy's greater inclination to pursue science, however, Signora Bondi tries to impose her will and cultural hierarchy on the boy, isolate him from his family, and rigidly steer him into music, resulting in the boy's tragic suicide. In this story, as well as Huxley's collected works and life, the implied ideal is a balanced and humane combination of the dualities that pervade existence.

OTHER MAJOR WORKS

LONG FICTION: *Crome Yellow*, 1921; *Antic Hay*, 1923; *Those Barren Leaves*, 1925; *Point Counter Point*, 1928; *Eyeless in Gaza*, 1936; *After Many a Summer Dies the Swan*, 1939; *Time Must Have a Stop*, 1944; *Ape and Essence*, 1948; *The Genius and the Goddess*, 1955; *Island*, 1962.

PLAYS: *Happy Families*, pb. 1919; *Permutations Among the Nightingales*, pb. 1920; *Albert, Prince Consort*, pb. 1923; *The Ambassador of Capripedia*, pb. 1923; *The Discovery*, pb. 1924; *The World of Light*, pb. 1931; *The Gioconda Smile*, pr., pb. 1948.

POETRY: *The Burning Wheel*, 1916; *Jonah*, 1917; *The Defeat of Youth*, 1918; *Leda*, 1920; *Selected Poems*, 1925; *Arabia Infelix*, 1929; *The Cicadas and Other Poems*, 1931.

NONFICTION: *On the Margin: Notes and Essays*, 1923; *Along the Road: Notes and Essays of a Tourist*, 1925; *Jesting Pilate*, 1926; *Essays New and Old*, 1926; *Proper Studies*, 1927; *Do What You Will*, 1929; *Holy Face and Other Essays*, 1929; *Vulgarity in Literature*, 1930; *Music at Night*, 1931; *Texts and Pretexts*, 1932; *Beyond the Mexique Bay*, 1934; *The Olive Tree*, 1936; *Ends and Means*, 1937; *Grey Eminence*, 1941; *The Art of Seeing*, 1942; *The Perennial Philosophy*, 1945; *Themes and Variations*, 1950; *The Devils of Loudun*, 1952; *The Doors of Perception*, 1954; *Adonis and the Alphabet*, 1956 (pb. in U.S. as *Tomorrow and Tomorrow and Tomorrow*, 1956); *Heaven and Hell*, 1956; *Brave New World Revisited*, 1958; *Collected Essays*, 1959; *Literature and Science*, 1963.

MISCELLANEOUS: *Rotunda: A Selection from the Works of Aldous Huxley*, 1932; *Retrospect: An*

Omnibus of Aldous Huxley's Books, 1933; *Stories, Essays and Poems*, 1937; *The World of Aldous Huxley: An Omnibus of His Fiction and Non-Fiction over Three Decades*, 1947.

BIBLIOGRAPHY

Baker, Robert S. *The Dark Historic Page: Social Satire and Historicism in the Novels of Aldous Huxley, 1921-1939*. Madison: University of Wisconsin Press, 1982. An interesting study of history and satire in Huxley's work. Includes a bibliography and an index.

Brander, Laurence. *Aldous Huxley: A Critical Study*. Lewisburg, Pa.: Bucknell University Press, 1970. One of the few general studies of all Huxley's major work, going beyond most other book-length Huxley studies, which focus on the novels. Includes a short, nineteen-page chapter on all the short stories, arranged chronologically by separate sections on each of Huxley's five collections from 1920 to 1930; consequently, "Sir Hercules," one of Huxley's more important stories, lifted by Huxley directly from his novel *Crome Yellow* and only included for the first time in *Twice Seven*, and then the *Collected Short Stories*, is omitted.

Deery, June. *Aldous Huxley and the Mysticism of Science*. New York: St. Martin's Press, 1996. Examines Huxley's knowledge of science and the place of mysticism and science in history. Includes and bibliography and an index.

Holmes, Charles M. *Aldous Huxley and the Way to Reality*. Bloomington: Indiana University Press, 1970. A survey of autobiographical meanings and development in Huxley's works, with brief treatment of "After the Fireworks," "Cynthia," "Eupompus Gave Splendour to Art by Numbers," "Farcical History of Richard Greenow," "The Gioconda Smile," "Green Tunnels," "The Monocle," "Nuns at Luncheon," "The Rest Cure," "The Tillotson Banquet," and "Young Archimedes."

Schubert, Maria. "The Use of Irony in Aldous Huxley's Short Fiction." In *A Salzburg Miscellany: English and American Studies, 1964-1984*. Vol. 2. Edited by James Hogg. Atlantic Highlands, N.J.: Humanities Press, 1984. 181-214. Interesting discussion of the contrast between Huxley's life and the irony and satire of his short fiction, along with patterns and groupings among the stories.

Woodcock, George. *Dawn and the Darkest Hour: A Study of Aldous Huxley*. New York: Viking Press, 1972. Stresses the novels and nonfiction, but has brief comments on all the short stories in separate brief sections on each of Huxley's five story collections from 1920 to 1930 scattered throughout the book, which is chronologically arranged. "Sir Hercules" is treated in a section dealing with Huxley's *Crome Yellow*.

Norman Prinsky

I

IHARA SAIKAKU

Born: Osaka, Japan; 1642
Died: Osaka, Japan; September 9, 1693

OTHER LITERARY FORMS

Ihara Saikaku's best-known work is the picaresque novel *Kōshoku ichidai otoko* (1683; *The Life of an Amorous Man*, 1964). He first won fame as a poet, however, with *Ikudama manku* (1673; ten thousand verses at Ikudama), a compilation that includes *haikai* (comic linked verse) of Saikaku and more than two hundred of his associates. His solo *haikai* performances are recorded in *Dokugin ichinichi senku* (1675; solo verses, one thousand in one day), *Saikaku haikai ōkuzaku* (1677; Saikaku's haikai, a great many verses), and *Saikaku ōyakazu* (1681; Saikaku's a great many arrows). Saikaku also wrote two puppet plays, *Koyomi* (calendar) and *Gaijin Yashima* (triumphant return from Yashima), both of which were staged in 1685.

ACHIEVEMENTS

Ihara Saikaku first gained literary repute as a leading member of Osaka's innovative *Danrin* school of *haikai*. Like others in this group, he wrote with verve and abandon. In 1673, he was a central participant in a twelve-day poetry party that produced ten thousand verses; later, prodigious solo poetizing marathons solidified his fame as a poet. Saikaku's lasting reputation, however, would come from prose fiction. In 1682, he created a new genre, *Ukiyo-zōshi* (books of the floating world) with the publication of his novel *Kōshoku ichidai otoko*, the first of two dozen books written during his last decade. They made him—with *haiku* poet Matsuo Bashō and dramatist Chikamatsu Monzaemon—one of the three dominant figures of Tokugawa literature and earned him a place second only to Murasaki Shikibu, author of *Genji monogatari* (c. 1004; *The Tale of Genji*, 1925-1933, 1935) as a premodern Japanese writer of narrative fiction. He gave the *chonin* (townsmen) heroes and heroines from their own class and made colloquial Japanese a literary language. While his stories sometimes treated the mores of the samurai or Confucian ethics, his most enduring works chronicled with stylistic originality, detached wit, and sharp insight the chief preoccupations of Japan's new urban class: love and money.

BIOGRAPHY

Little is known of Ihara Saikaku's personal life.

He was most certainly born in Osaka in 1642, there being sufficient indication that he considered this city to be his hometown. His real name was, according to one source, Hirayama Tōgo; Ihara was, most likely, his mother's maiden name, which he later adopted for his professional name. "Saikaku" is the last of a series of noms de plume that he used. According to the same source, he was a merchant in an unspecified trade who could afford to leave the management of the business to trusted clerks and devote his life to literary pursuits and to travel.

He took an early interest in *haikai* and is believed to have qualified in his twenty-first year to become a *haikai* teacher (*tenja*). In the early 1670's, he became a disciple of Nishiyama Sōin (1605-1682), the head of the Danrin school of *haikai* and a major challenger to the traditional Teimon school. By 1673, when *Ikudama manku* was performed, Saikaku had established himself as a leading force under Sōin.

Traditionally, *haikai* poetry is composed in linked sequences by several poets as a ritualized social and literary activity. Saikaku was by no means the first to break from this tradition—there had been others before him, most notably Arakida Moritake (1473-1549), who is credited with *Dokugin senku* (compiled 1536-1540; a thousand verses composed by one man). Nevertheless, he was the first to compose one thousand verses in a single day in 1675. The occasion was an emotional one: a memorial tribute to his young wife, who had died after a brief illness. Saikaku titled the compilation *Dokugin ichinichi senku*. This effort was followed in 1677 by *Saikaku haikai ōkuzaku*, another solo performance in which sixteen hundred verses were composed in a single day and night. When rivals bested him, first with eighteen hundred verses, then with twenty-eight hundred, Saikaku returned in 1680 with a public performance of four thousand verses in a single day and night. The record of this feat was published the following year as *Saikaku ōyakazu*. When rivals reported besting him again, Saikaku was determined to put an end to all such rivalry. In 1684, he assembled an audience, and in the presence of referees and scribes he composed 23,500 verses in a twenty-four-hour period. Unfortunately, he delivered the verses so fast that the scribes could only draw hash marks for each verse.

Saikaku proved his point, and as a result the Danrin school embarked on a path of self-destruction. It was not, however, the end of Saikaku. As long as linked verse remained a group activity, fettered by the constraints of traditional versification, it allowed little room for the genius of any single individual to bloom. It is not surprising that Matsuo Bashō (1644-1694) and Saikaku, the two leading men of the Danrin school, discovered a way to free themselves from these limitations and so unleash their talents. Bashō's concentration on the opening verse (*hokku*) of the *haikai* sequence allowed him to reach unsurpassed heights in his endeavor. As for Saikaku the raconteur, performing rapid-fire solo *haikai* gave him experience in weaving together *haikai* sequences with something approaching narrative content and led the way to the development of an idiosyncratic narrative that displayed *haikai* techniques.

With the death of his teacher Sōin, in 1682, Saikaku was emboldened to proceed with the publication of his first attempt at fiction, *The Life of an Amorous Man*. The work was so well received that publishers encouraged him to continue; he was thus embarked on a brief but prolific career as a writer of fiction, producing more than two dozen novels and collections of short stories in the last decade of his life. When he died in 1693, one of his disciples moved into his residence as a caretaker; he edited and possibly made additions to the unfinished manuscripts he found before he had them published. Saikaku's enormous popularity can be seen in that a succession of works purporting to be sequels or written in a style and vein emulating Saikaku's began to appear almost immediately and continued to be published for decades after his death.

Saikaku's last words summarize his attitude toward life. Noting that he had exceeded man's allotted span of fifty years, he gave thanks in this deathbed poem:

> The moon of this Floating World
> I have enjoyed a surplus
> These last two years

ANALYSIS

Ihara Saikaku was a poet who turned to writing prose fiction late in his life. As a *haikai* poet he had distinguished himself as a daredevil maverick with his rapid-fire performances. Yet his focus in *haikai* was the real world of the commoner's life. Unlike the poems of his contemporary Bashō, which tended to be sublimated, Saikaku's poems deal squarely with the diurnal activities of the men and women of the cities. When he turned to fiction, he continued to draw his materials directly from the commercial, urban society of his day.

Saikaku was a consummate storyteller who told his stories with relish. He was also a supreme stylist who wrote in a terse, innovative style that was emulated by his contemporaries and followers. To a large extent, Saikaku's style derived from his training as a *haikai* poet whose medium required communication by splashes of imagery rather than articulated narrative. (Unfortunately, such matters of style are usually lost in translation and can be seen only in the original text.) Saikaku's genius lay in the brilliant insight with which he wrote about sex and money in the life of the townsmen. His earliest work was imbued with optimism and an exuberant air, while his later works turned increasingly pessimistic. Yet throughout his writing career, Saikaku displayed a rare talent of intermingling the comic with the tragic.

FIVE WOMEN WHO LOVED LOVE

Five Women Who Loved Love is generally considered to be Saikaku's masterpiece. It is a rather carefully crafted collection of five scandalous love stories. In contrast to Saikaku's other works on "love," which were in reality about mere sexual encounters, these are stories that dwell more extensively on the portrayals of men and women in love and the often tragic consequences which follow. All but the last of these love stories end tragically; the protagonists pay for their indiscretions with their lives. Punishments for crimes considered subversive to the hierarchical order were harsh in the Tokugawa period. A hired hand who had illicit intercourse with his master's daughter, for example, could have been sentenced to death. Adultery by a married woman was also punishable by death, and a husband who caught his wife in the act could kill her and her lover on the spot. Death was also often the penalty for kidnapping, or even for the embezzlement of ten *ryō* or more. These stories acquired additional poignancy as each of them was based on actual scandals, some still very fresh in the minds of Saikaku's readers. Saikaku freely altered and embellished the incidents and, in typical Saikaku style, added comical touches.

The first story is that of Onatsu, the younger sister of a shopkeeper in the regional town of Himeji, who falls in love with Seijūrō, a clerk in her brother's employ. At an outing carefully staged by Seijūrō, they fulfill their desire. The liaison cannot go unnoticed, however, and fully aware of the penalty for Seijūrō, they flee by boat to reach Osaka but are tracked down and brought back to face the consequences. When Seijūrō is executed, Onatsu loses her mind; at one point she tries to kill herself but is restrained. She then becomes a nun in order to care for Seijūrō's grave, and she prays for his soul day and night. Saikaku comments, "This then is my creation, a new river and a boat for the lovers to float their love downstream, like bubbles in this sad fleeting world." He makes no comment on the harshness of the punishment or the injustice of the law. Yet this final line makes it clear where his sympathy lay: They had violated no moral law; they were simply two hapless lovers caught in an unreasonable legal system.

The second story is about adultery between a barrelmaker's wife, Osen, and her neighbor Chōzaemon. Osen is falsely accused of adultery by Chōzaemon's wife. Incensed, she vows to give the accuser real cause to worry. Her desire for revenge, however, soon turns to lust. One evening after a party, when Chōzaemon follows her home, she invites him in. They are no sooner in bed when the barrelmaker appears and discovers them in the act. Chōzaemon flees the scene, only to be caught and later executed. Osen chooses a more heroic path to death, plunging a carpenter's chisel-like plane into her heart. Osen had acted out of vengeance, rather than love. Chōzaemon's conduct, too, was deficient. Saikaku comments, "The scoundrel's and her corpse too were put on public display at Togano to expose their shame. Their names, through countless ballads, spread to far-away provinces; there's no escaping from one's own misdeeds. Frightful, this world of ours!" Although Osen is spared the indignity of public execution, Saikaku leaves no doubt as to his disapproval of the conduct of Osen and Chōzaemon: unmitigated adultery stemming from revenge or lust.

The third and perhaps most effective of the five stories is about Osan, the beautiful wife of an almanac-maker, and Moemon, a clerk in her husband's Kyoto shop. The almanac-maker has hired Moemon specifically to look after the shop and Osan while he takes an extended business trip to Edo. During her husband's absence, Osan and her maid Rin, who is attracted to Moemon, play a trick on him. The prank backfires, however, and Osan ends up in bed with Moemon. Moemon has come to Rin's bed in response to a note from her; meanwhile Osan has taken Rin's place in her bed to surprise him. Osan, however, falls asleep and is taken unaware. In the morning, when Osan realizes what has happened, she is mortified about the "shame" as well as the nature of her transgression. The only honorable way to salvage the situation, she believes, is to "sacrifice her life in order to save her honor," and she asks Moemon to "join her in her journey to death." They elope, stage a mock suicide to fool pursuers and flee to a mountain hamlet where they find momentary bliss. One day, unable to suppress an urge to reconnoiter the situation back in the capital, Moemon slips back into the city and is spotted; the misadventure leads to their demise: They are paraded through the streets and executed.

In spite of the essentially tragic nature of the incident, the story is told with humorous turns of phrases and is sprinkled with comic interludes. In less skilled hands, it could easily have become a farce; in Saikaku's, it has been crafted into a thoroughly enjoyable tragicomedy. The adultery is unintended, but Osan has made an irrevocable mistake. To validate her good-faith effort to maintain her honor, Saikaku portrays her as an admirable woman, truly in love with Moemon. She is further portrayed as a spirited woman, full of life, who makes the most of the last days of her life and does not regret her action. Saikaku's final comment: "At dawn of the twenty-second of the

Ninth Month they met their end as in a fleeting dream, an end far from dishonorable. Their story is widely known and even in the twentieth century the name of Osan is remembered as vividly as her lovely figure in the pale-blue robe she wore to her death."

The fourth story unfolds with a greengrocer's family taking temporary refuge in a temple when their shop is destroyed by fire. As they await the rebuilding of the shop, an adolescent love affair develops between Oshichi, the fifteen-year-old daughter, and Kichisaburō, a temple page from a samurai family. When the shop is rebuilt and the family returns to their new quarters, Oshichi yearns to see Kichisaburō again. Blinded by love, she sets fire to the new building, believing that the family will then return to the temple again. The fire is stopped at an early stage, but Oshichi is paraded about the city and eventually burned at the stake. Saikaku comments, "No one should ever commit such an evil act. Heaven does not tolerate it." He continues,

> Since it was something Oshichi had done with conviction, knowing full well its consequences, she did not allow herself to waste away. Instead, each remaining day, she had her black hair done up and looked as beautiful as ever. Early in the Fourth Month, alas at sixteen she was in the spring of her youth, as the cherry blossoms were falling to the ground and even the cuckoos cried out in unison their songs of lament, she was finally told that her time had come. She remained as calm and collected as ever, ready to accept life as an illusory dream of an existence and earnestly awaited rebirth in the Land of the Buddha. How very sad!

Saikaku is emphatic in his condemnation of the grave crime of arson and does not question the harshness of the punishment. Yet he allows an outpouring of sympathy for Oshichi. Although she has been illogical and foolish, she has acted out of pure love, Saikaku seems to suggest, when the more common cause of criminal transgressions are greed, jealousy, and spite. Her motive is honorable. Furthermore, faced with death, Oshichi conducts herself with dignity. Saikaku portrays her as showing no remorse but as being sincere in her acceptance of death as the consequence of her act.

Saikaku continues the story beyond the death of the heroine, relating an aspect of the young man's life that had only been hinted at earlier: his homosexual relationship with another youth. Kichisaburō had been so weakened with lovesickness that he had not been told of Oshichi's fate. When he learns of it, he quickly reaches for his sword, but the monks restrain him from killing himself, reminding him of the pledge of homosexual love that he has made to his "sworn brother." He is torn between his obligation to his lover and what he believes is his duty to the girl he once loved. He is relieved, however, when his sworn brother releases him from the obligation, counseling him to join the priesthood to look after Oshichi.

Saikaku's aim was to cover the spectrum of love "in all its varied forms" and particularly to show how duty, honor, and dignity play key roles in the relationships among men. The homosexual segment here anticipates the fifth story, in which a handsome young man who has suffered the loss of two male lovers is relentlessly pursued by a young woman. Madly in love with him, she visits him dressed as a young boy to attract his attention. In the end, they marry, inherit a fortune, and, presumably, live happily ever after.

The success of *Five Women Who Loved Love* and Saikaku's stories in general derives from the wry humor and detachment with which he tells his stories. He maintains a distance from his characters yet manages to portray them sympathetically. The women in these stories are portrayed as independent and strong-willed, undaunted by the harsh laws of society and able to risk their lives for love.

SAIKAKU SHOKOKU-BANASHI

Saikaku traveled extensively around the country and wrote hundreds of short stories which were published over the years as collections, usually with specific themes. Legends and tales with strong local flavor, for example, were brought together in *Saikaku shokoku-banashi* (Saikaku's tales of the provinces), a collection of thirty-five stories told with typical Saikakuesque humor. This short-story form, rooted in the oral tradition and no more than several pages long, was to become with appropriate refinement Saikaku's favorite and most effective form in the

years to come. With Saikaku's background and genius in *haikai* versification and with his talent as a raconteur, it was inevitable that he would abandon the novel in favor of the short story. In time, he began to produce collections of short stories with more distinct themes.

HONCHŌ NIJŪ FUKŌ

As the Bakufu mounted a renewed campaign to encourage filial piety in the early 1680's, Saikaku responded characteristically with the publication in 1686 of his *Honchō nijū fukō* (twenty cases of unfilial conduct in Japan), a gleeful collection of stories about the most reprehensible sort of children, sons and daughters who plot against one another and who would even murder their parents for money. Though doomed by the very odious nature of the stories, the work opened the way for Saikaku to explore the use of themes as a unifying device for other collections of stories.

NANSHOKU ŌKAGAMI

Saikaku returned to the theme of male homosexuality in earnest with the publication of *Nanshoku ōkagami* (*The Great Mirror of Male Love*, 1990) in 1687. In this collection of forty stories, he focused on two groups: samurai and their "sworn brothers" and Kabuki actors and their townsmen patrons. In these stories, particularly in the former group, conflicts arise from triangular relationships, with honor and dignity playing key roles in their resolution. Samurai morality, especially as it pertained to the codified vendetta of the Tokugawa period, is the theme for the thirty-two stories in *Budō denraiki* (the transmission of martial arts), while it is the gnarled notion of samurai honor that serves as the thematic unifier for the twenty-six stories in *Tales of Samurai Honor*. These works of the samurai world are usually criticized as being inaccurate depictions of the samurai mind-set. Yet viewed as humorous portrayals of the strange world of the samurai, they are as entertaining as the bulk of Saikaku's writing.

THE JAPANESE FAMILY STOREHOUSE

While Saikaku had begun his career as a novelist with an unmistakable optimism, he entered a new phase in 1688 with the publication of *The Japanese Family Storehouse*. Perhaps he had become disillusioned with life under the Tokugawa regime; certainly, the seemingly unlimited economic opportunities that were in evidence earlier were rapidly disappearing. His focus took a pragmatic turn, and he began to write stories that revolved almost exclusively around the economic life of the townsmen. The theme to which he turned for *The Japanese Family Storehouse* was the economic life of the wealthy merchants. Of its thirty stories, seventeen are lively, humorous stories on how to become a millionaire, while the remaining thirteen serve as warnings to the merchants on how easy it is to lose their fortunes. Interestingly, many of the stories were based on true stories. Here, Saikaku unabashedly exhorts his fellow merchants not to neglect their family trade, to pay close attention to their business on a daily basis, advising them on how to manage their household finances. The didactic tone, however, is held in check by Saikaku's skill as an effective storyteller.

WORLDLY MENTAL CALCULATIONS

While there are positive aspects of *The Japanese Family Storehouse*, the success stories are by and large based on events that had taken place decades earlier. In the late 1680's, the economic outlook was bleak; it was no longer easy to amass a fortune. Saikaku's next important work, the last to be published during his lifetime, was *Worldly Mental Calculations*, whose theme concerns the merchants' year-end struggle to settle their accounts. Here, Saikaku turns his attention to the poor merchants, portraying their struggles to escape the harangues of the bill collectors. With irony, detachment, and humor, Saikaku tells tales of the poor, who will manage, by hook or by crook, to see the New Year in even when they have no resources except their wits. To Saikaku's credit, even the bleakest story somehow ends on a light note.

SAIKAKU OKIMIYAGE

In both his earliest works, which dealt with the themes of pleasure and sensuality, and his latest, which dealt with economic realism, Saikaku had turned from the optimistic to the pessimistic. In his last memorable work, *Saikaku okimiyage* (Saikaku's parting present), published in 1693, a few months after his death, Saikaku returned to the men who squandered their fortunes on the denizens of the pleasure quarters. They are portrayed as living in poverty, typically with the courtesans on whom they spent a fortune to ransom them from their indentured service. They show no remorse, and, significantly, although they are penniless in the slums, they have not lost their self-respect: They are managing their lives with dignity.

Saikaku was, above all, a raconteur who wrote to entertain. He was a highly original writer, and he wrote in a distinct individual style, a combination of the oral tradition and the ornate literary style. His use of subject matter drawn from contemporary society as well as his use of seventeenth century colloquialism for dialogue contributes to a sense of realism. Saikaku's stories, especially the novels, are weak in plot development; it must be remembered, however, that the concept of plot construction is largely alien to traditional Japanese literature. Saikaku's stories, and much of traditional Japanese literature, must be appreciated more as segments in sequence than in consequence.

OTHER MAJOR WORKS

LONG FICTION: *Kōshoku ichidai otoko*, 1683 (*The Life of an Amorous Man*, 1964); *Shoen ōkagami*, 1684; *Wankyū isse no monogatari*, 1685; *Kōshoku ichidai onna*, 1696 (*The Life of an Amorous Woman*, 1963).

PLAYS: *Koyomi*, pr. 1685; *Gaijin Yashima*, pr. 1685.

POETRY: *Ikudama manku*, 1673; *Dokugin ichinichi senku*, 1675; *Saikaku haikai ōkukazu*, 1677; *Saikaku ōyakazu*, 1681.

NONFICTION: *Yakusha hyōbanki*, 1683?

BIBLIOGRAPHY

Danly, Robert Lyons. "Ihara Saikaku and 'Opening Night in the Capital.'" *The Literary Review* 39 (Winter, 1996): 214-215. A translation of the story, accompanied by comments on the problems of translating Saikaku; discusses the difficulty of explaining a temporally distant culture and capturing a fugitive linguistic charm.

De Bary, Wm. Theodore. Introduction to *Five*

Women Who Loved Love. Rutland, Vt.: Charles E. Tuttle, 1956. An excellent introduction to both Saikaku and the urban environment of large Tokugawa cities such as Osaka, against which most of Saikaku's fiction is set.

Hibbett, Howard. *The Floating World in Japanese Fiction*. New York: Oxford University Press, 1959. This volume is an excellent introduction to late seventeenth century society, including the licensed pleasure quarters, and it thus provides the social background of much of Saikaku's fiction. A chapter is devoted to Saikaku (pp. 36-49), and a sizable portion of his *The Life of an Amorous Woman* is translated. Illustrations include block prints by artists such as Hishikawa Moronobu and also by Saikaku himself.

_____. "Saikaku and Burlesque Fiction." *The Harvard Journal of Asiatic Studies* 20 (June, 1957): 53-73. This essay illuminates a central quality in the culture of Tokugawa Japan's new urban class: mocking irreverence toward established social and cultural norms. Contains examples from Saikaku and other writers of *Ukiyo-zōshi* and compares their use of burlesque with English authors such as Henry Fielding and Daniel Defoe.

Keene, Donald. *World Within Walls: Japanese Literature of the Pre-Modern Era, 1600-1867*. New York: Holt, Rinehart and Winston, 1976. Part of a multivolume history of Japanese literature, this volume devotes a chapter to Saikaku's fic-tion as well as one to Saikaku and others in the Danrin school of *haikai*. Beyond making perceptive critical comments, Keene summarizes many of Saikaku's stories and sets them in historical context.

Lane, Richard. "Saikaku's 'Five Women.'" In *Five Women Who Loved Love*. Rutland, Vt.: Charles E. Tuttle, 1956. An interesting interpretation of what is perhaps Saikaku's finest work. Lane reviews other accounts of the historical incidents on which the stories are based and notes what is distinctive about Saikaku's treatment of them.

Miner, Earl, Hiroko Odagiri, and Robert E. Morrell. *The Princeton Companion to Classical Japanese Literature*. Princeton, N.J.: Princeton University Press, 1985. A brief but judicious characterization of Saikaku's contribution to Tokugawa literature.

Rimer, J. Thomas. *A Reader's Guide to Japanese Literature*. New York: Kodansha International, 1988. A brief review of Saikaku's place in Japanese fiction. Focuses on what is probably his finest work, *Five Women Who Loved Love*.

"Saikaku." In *Kodansha Encyclopedia of Japan*. 9 vols. New York: Kodansha International, 1983. A succinct summary of Saikaku's career. Includes perceptive critical comments on his major works of fiction.

Ben Befu, updated by R. Craig Philips

WASHINGTON IRVING

Born: New York, New York; April 3, 1783
Died: Tarrytown, New York; November 28, 1859

PRINCIPAL SHORT FICTION

The Sketch Book of Geoffrey Crayon, Gent., 1819-
    1820
Bracebridge Hall, 1822
Tales of a Traveller, 1824
The Alhambra, 1832
Legends of the Conquest of Spain, 1835

OTHER LITERARY FORMS

Washington Irving distinguished himself in a variety of genres. His finest and most typical book, *The Sketch Book of Geoffrey Crayon, Gent.*, blends essay, sketch, history, travel, humor, and short story; his first best-seller was a satire, *A History of New York* (1809); he coauthored a successful play, *Charles the Second: Or, The Merry Monarch* (1824); but he devoted the latter and most prolific part of his career to books of travel and especially of history.

ACHIEVEMENTS

Washington Irving was America's first internationally recognized author. While he achieved national notoriety with his satiric *A History of New York*, his fame abroad was made with *The Sketch Book of Geoffrey Crayon, Gent.* Irving was a prolific writer throughout his life, from his first collaborations with his brother William and friend James Kirke Paulding, to his many biographies of well-known historical figures, including George Washington. Among his most successful works were his collections of sketches and tales, a distinction then made between realistic and imaginative types of fiction. His sketches often make use of historical sources, while the tales usually derive from traditional folktales. His best-known stories, "Rip Van Winkle" and "The Legend of Sleepy Hollow," although largely copied from German folktales, still maintain an originality through their American settings and Irving's own gently humorous style.

BIOGRAPHY

The eleventh and last child of a successful merchant, Washington Irving, somewhat frail and indulged as he was growing up, was the favorite child of his Anglican mother and Presbyterian minister father. As a young man, Irving studied law in the office of Josiah Ogden Hoffman, to whose daughter he was attracted, and enjoyed the social and cultural advantages of New York City as something of a gentleman-playboy. At this time, he dabbled in satirical writing in serial publications. He gained a certain amount of cosmopolitan sophistication with a tour of Europe in 1804-1806, during which time he kept a journal.

Irving was admitted to the New York bar at the age of twenty-three and nominally began to work as a lawyer on Wall Street, although he practiced little. Instead, he wrote serial essays with his brother and James Kirke Paulding for a periodical they called *Salmagundi*, modeled on Joseph Addison's *Spectator*, "to instruct the young, reform the old, correct the town, and castigate the age." This amounted to making light fun of fashion and social mores in high society, although occasionally they made jabs at Thomas Jefferson's "logocratic" democracy.

"Diedrich Knickerbocker's" *A History of New York* followed in 1809; originally intended as a parody of a pretentious New York guidebook, it had become instead a comic history of the Dutch in New York. When Matilda Hoffman died in the same year, Irving, distraught, stopped writing for a time. He moved in 1811 to Washington, D.C., to lobby for the Irving brothers' importing firm. Still affected by Matilda's death, he drifted into several different occupations, lost the brothers' firm to bankruptcy, yet benefitted from his literary contacts to the point where he began to pursue writing with renewed effort. By the time he published *The Sketch Book of Geoffrey Crayon, Gent.* in 1819, he was on his way to supporting himself through his writing. In order to find original materials for his sketches, he made various trips through Europe and America, including a ministry to Spain; he returned to New York finally in 1832. His long ab-

Washington Irving (Library of Congress)

sence, reminiscent of Rip Van Winkle's, provided him with a new perspective on the United States, whose western frontier was beginning to open; he packed again, this time for the West, and wrote many of his books out of the experi ence. He finally returned home to the Hudson, ensconced in family and friends, where he died in 1859.

ANALYSIS

Washington Irving's masterpiece, *The Sketch Book of Geoffrey Crayon, Gent.*, has a historical importance few American books can match. No previous American book achieved a really significant popular and critical success in England, the only arena of opinion which then mattered; but Irving demonstrated that an American could write not only well but also brilliantly even by British standards. In fact, throughout the century English as well as American schoolboys studied Irving's book as a model of graceful prose.

Irving had achieved some popularity in his own country well before the British triumphs. In 1807-1808, Irving, his brother William, and James Kirke Paulding collaborated on the independently published periodical series, *Salmagundi*. Since the project was a true collaboration, scholars are in doubt as to precisely who deserves credit for precisely what, but two pieces deserve particular notice. "Sketches from Nature" sentimentally sketches two old bachelors, one of whom restores the spirits of the other by leading him through scenes reminiscent of their youth. "The Little Man in Black" is supposedly a traditional story passed through generations of a single family. Irving here introduces another old bachelor, who wanders into the village a stranger to all and sets up housekeeping in a decrepit house rumored to be haunted. First ostracized by the adults, then tormented by the local children, ultimately he dies by starvation, in his last moments forgiving all, a true but misunderstood Christian.

Both pieces display Irving's graceful style, his prevalent sentimentality, and his wholehearted commitment to charming, pleasing, and entertaining his audience. Both feature an old bachelor stereotype which he inherited from the Addisonian tradition and continued to exploit in later works. The pieces differ in their formal focus, however, and aptly illustrate the two poles of Irving's fictional nature. The second shows his fondness for the tale tradition: He cites a source in family folklore; the narrative hangs on striking incident; and he flavors the atmosphere with a suggestion of the supernatural. The first features virtues of the periodical essay: evocation of character divorced from dramatic incident; a style dominated by smoothness (Edgar Allan Poe's term was "repose") and by descriptions strong on concrete detail; and an essentially realistic atmosphere. Irving's unique genius led him to combine the best of both traditions in his finest fiction and thereby to create the modern short story in America.

Irving's early career coincided with the rise of Romanticism, and the movement strongly influenced his greatest book, *The Sketch Book of Geoffrey Crayon, Gent.* Here he capitalized on the element which strongly marks his most successful stories: imagination. Consistently, Irving's most successful characters, and stories, are those which most successfully exploit the imagination.

"THE SPECTRE BRIDEGROOM"

In "The Spectre Bridegroom," the title character triumphs not through strength, physical skills, or intelligence, but rather through manipulating the imaginations of those who would oppose his aims. The story's first section humorously describes a bellicose old widower, the Baron Von Landshort, who has gathered a vast audience, consisting mostly of poor relatives properly cognizant of his high status, to celebrate his only daughter's marriage to a young count whom none of them has ever seen. In the story's second part, the reader learns that as the count and his friend Herman Von Starkenfaust journey to the castle, they are beset by bandits; the outlaws mortally wound the count who, with his last breath, begs Von Starkenfaust to relay his excuses to the wedding party. The story's third part returns to the castle where the long-delayed wedding party finally welcomes a pale, melancholy young man. The silent stranger hears the garrulous Baron speak on, among other matters, his family's longstanding feud with the Von Starkenfaust family; meanwhile the young man wins the daughter's heart. He shortly leaves, declaring he must be buried at the cathedral. The next night the daughter's two guardian aunts tell ghost stories until they are terrified by spying the Spectre Bridegroom outside the window; the daughter sleeps apart from her aunts for three nights, encouraging their fears the while, and finally absconds. When she returns with her husband, Von Starkenfaust, who had pretended to be the Spectre, they both are reconciled with the Baron and live happily ever after.

By becoming in one sense artists themselves, Herman and his bride both manipulate the imaginations of the Baron, the aunts, and the entire wedding party to make their courtship and elopement possible; here, happily, the dupees lose nothing and share the ultimate happiness of the dupers. There are at least three dimensions to "The Spectre Bridegroom": As it is read, one can imaginatively identify with the duped family and believe the Spectre genuine, or alternately identify with the young couple innocently manipulat-

ing their elders. A third dimension enters when the reader recalls the personality of the frame's Swiss tale-teller, occasionally interrupting himself with "a roguish leer and a sly joke for the buxom kitchen maid" and himself responsible (it is surely not the modest and proper Geoffrey Crayon or Washington Irving) for the suggestive antlers above the prospective bridegroom's head at the feast.

"RIP VAN WINKLE"

The narrative perspectives informing Irving's single greatest achievement, "Rip Van Winkle," radiate even greater complexities. At the simplest level the core experience is that of Rip himself, a good-natured idler married to a termagant who drives him from the house with her temper. While hunting in the woods, Rip pauses to assist a curious little man hefting a keg; in a natural amphitheater he discovers dwarfish sailors in archaic dress playing at ninepins. Rip drinks, falls asleep, and awakens the next morning alone on the mountainside. In a subtle, profound, and eerily effective sequence, Irving details Rip's progressive disorientation and complete loss of identity. The disintegration begins mildly enough—Rip notices the decayed gun (a thief's substitute he thinks), his dog's absence, some stiffness in his own body—each clue is emotionally more significant than the last, but each may be easily explained. Rip next notices changes in nature—a dry gully has become a raging stream, a ravine has been closed by a rockslide; these are more dramatic alterations, but still explainable after a long night's sleep.

Upon entering the village, he discovers no one but strangers and all in strange dress; he finds his house has decayed, his wife and children have disappeared; buildings have changed as well as the political situation and even the very manner and behavior of the people. In a terrible climax, when Irving for once declines to mute the genuine horror, Rip profoundly questions his own identity. When he desperately asks if anyone knows poor Rip Van Winkle, fingers point to another ragged idler at the fringe, the very image of Rip himself as he had ascended the mountain. Even Poe or Franz Kafka never painted a loss of identity more absolute, more profound, more credible, more terrible. After a moment of horror, Irving's sentimental good humor immediately reasserts itself. Rip's now-adult daughter appears and recognizes him; the ragged idler turns out to be his son, Rip, Jr. Rip himself hesitates for a moment, but, upon learning that his wife has died "but a short time since," declares his identity and commences reintegrating himself in the community, eventually to become an honored patriarch, renowned for recounting his marvelous experience.

Thus is the nature of the core narrative, which is almost all most people ever read. The reader values the story for its profound mythic reverberations; after all, throughout Western civilization Irving's Rip has become an archetype of time lost. The reader may also appreciate Irving's amoral toying with lifestyles, although the Yankee/Benjamin Franklin lifestyle Rip's wife advocates and which leads to her death (she bursts a blood vessel while haggling) fails to trap Rip, he triumphs by championing the relatively unambitious, self-indulgent lifestyle Irving identifies with the Dutch. Still, many people feel tempted to reject the piece as a simplistic fairy tale dependent on supernatural machinery for its appeal and effect. This is a mistake.

Those who read the full story as Irving wrote it will discover, in the headnote, that Irving chose to relate the story not from the point of view of an omniscient narrator but from that of Diedrich Knickerbocker, the dunderheaded comic persona to whom years earlier he had ascribed the burlesque *A History of New York*. The presence of such a narrator—and Irving went to some trouble to introduce him—authorizes the reader to reject the supernatural elements and believe, as Irving tells us many of Rip's auditors believed, that in actuality Rip simply tired of his wife, ran away for twenty years, and concocted a cock-and-bull story to justify his absence. Looking closer, the reader discovers copious hints that this is precisely what happened: Rip's reluctance to become Rip again until he is sure his wife is dead; the fact that when his neighbors hear the story they "wink at each other and put their tongues in their cheeks"; the fact that, until he finally established a satisfactory version of the events, he was observed "to vary on some points every time he told it." In the concluding footnote, even

dim Diedrich Knickerbocker acknowledges the story's doubtfulness but provides as evidence of its truth the fact that he has heard even stranger supernatural stories of the Catskills, and that to authenticate his story Rip signed a certificate in the presence of a justice of the peace. "The story, therefore, is beyond the possibility of doubt." Irving clearly intends to convince his closest readers that Rip, like the couple in "The Spectre Bridegroom," triumphed over circumstances by a creative manipulation of imagination.

"THE LEGEND OF SLEEPY HOLLOW"

In "The Legend of Sleepy Hollow" our source is again Diedrich Knickerbocker, and again, creatively manipulating the imaginations of others proves the key to success. The pleasant little Dutch community of Sleepy Hollow has imported a tall, grotesquely lanky Yankee as schoolmaster, Ichabod Crane. Although he is prey to the schoolboys' endless pranks, he himself ravenously and endlessly preys on the foodstuffs of the boys' parents. Ichabod finally determines to set his cap for the pretty daughter of a wealthy farmer, but Brom Bones, the handsome, Herculean local hero, has likewise determined to court the girl. The climax comes when the principals gather with the entire community at a dance, feast, and "quilting frolic" held at Katrina Van Tassel's home. Brom fills the timorous and credulous Ichabod full of tales of a horrible specter, ghost of a Hessian soldier beheaded by a cannonball, who inhabits the region through which Ichabod must ride that night to return home. As he makes his lonely journey back, Ichabod encounters the dark figure who carries his head under his arm rather than on his neck and who runs him a frightful race to a bridge. At the climax the figure hurls his head and strikes Ichabod, who disappears, never to be seen in the village again. Brom marries Katrina, and years later the locals discover that Ichabod turned lawyer, politician, newspaperman, and finally became a "justice of the Ten Pound Court."

Again it is the character who creatively manipulates the imagination who carries the day; the manipulatee wins only the consolation prize. Again the Dutch spirit triumphs over the Yankee. In this story there is something quite new, however; for the first time in American literature there is, in the characterization of Brom Bones, the figure of the frontiersman so important to American literature and American popular culture: physically imposing, self-confident, rough and ready, untutored but endowed with great natural virtues, gifted with a rude sense of chivalry, at home on the fringes of civilization, and incorporating in his own being the finer virtues of both the wilderness and the settlements. Irving here brilliantly anticipated both the essence of Southwestern humor and of James Fenimore Cooper's seminal Westerns.

Irving wrote a great many other stories, including several romantic tales set in Spain, most of them flawed by superficiality and sentimentality; he also produced a number of gothic stories, some of which are still read with pleasure, among them "The Adventure of the German Student" and "The Devil and Tom Walker." Irving, however, reached his highest point in his first published short story, "Rip Van Winkle." He never equaled it in any subsequent story—but then, only a tiny handful of writers ever have.

OTHER MAJOR WORKS

PLAY: *Charles the Second: Or, The Merry Monarch*, pb. 1824.

NONFICTION: *A History of New York*, 1809; *Biography of James Lawrence*, 1813; *A History of the Life and Voyages of Christopher Columbus*, 1828; *A Chronicle of the Conquest of Granada*, 1829; *Voyages and Discoveries of the Companions of Columbus*, 1831; *A Tour of the Prairies*, 1835; *Astoria*, 1836; *The Adventures of Captain Bonneville*, 1837; *The Life of Oliver Goldsmith*, 1849; *The Life of George Washington*, 1855-1859 (5 volumes).

BIBLIOGRAPHY

Aderman, Ralph M., ed. *Critical Essays on Washington Irving*. Boston: G. K. Hall, 1990. A collection of essays on Irving, from both the nineteenth and twentieth centuries. Includes discussions of Irving's art and literary debts, the relationship of his stories to his culture, and his generic heritage.

Antelyes, Peter. *Tales of Adventurous Enterprise: Washington Irving and the Poetics of Western Ex-*

pansion. New York: Columbia University Press, 1990. Explores the theme of the western frontier in Irving.

Bowden, Mary Weatherspoon. *Washington Irving*. Boston: Twayne, 1981. Bowden's general study of Irving discusses the major works in chronological order of composition. While her focus is literary, Bowden begins each chapter with useful biographical information about Irving at the time. The section dealing with *The Sketch Book of Geoffrey Crayon, Gent.* is particularly successful in describing Irving's attitudes toward England and how these are revealed in the sketches.

Hiller, Alice. "'An Avenue to Some Degree of Profit and Reputation': *The Sketch Book* as Washington Irving's Entree and Undoing." *Journal of American Studies* 31 (August, 1997): 275-293. Claims that some of Irving's personal correspondence reveals that *The Sketch Book* may have been pitched deliberately at the British market, resulting in a paralysis of Irving's powers of writing.

McFarland, Philip. *Sojourners*. New York: Atheneum, 1979. While not a conventional biography, this study of Washington Irving's life situates the writer in his various geographic, historic, and literary contexts. McFarland explores in detail the life of Irving, interweaving his biography with those of other important Americans of the time, among them Aaron Burr, the abolitionist John Brown, and John J. Astor.

Murray, Laura J. "The Aesthetic of Dispossession: Washington Irving and Ideologies of (De)colonization in the Early Republic." *American Literary History* 8 (Summer, 1996): 205-231. Argues that Euro-Americans cultivated their sense of vulnerability with respect to Britain and in so doing rhetorically excused themselves from their colonizing role with regard to Native Americans.

Myers, Andrew B., ed. *A Century of Commentary on the Works of Washington Irving*. Tarrytown, N.Y.: Sleepy Hollow Restorations, 1976. This collection, divided into four chronologically ordered sections, offers writings on Washington Irving. Part 1 includes essays by contemporaries of Irving, such as William Cullen Bryant and Henry

Wadsworth Longfellow; part 2 covers evaluations from the beginning of the nineteenth century. Early twentieth century scholars of American literature, such as Fred Lewis Pattee, Vernon Louis Parrington, and Van Wyck Brooks, are represented in part 3, and part 4 covers the period 1945 to 1975. The collection gives an excellent overview of the development of Irving criticism and provides a point of departure for further investigations.

Piacentino, Ed. "'Sleepy Hollow' Comes South: Washington Irving's Influence on Old Southwestern Humor." *The Southern Literary Journal* 30 (Fall, 1997): 27-42. Examines how nineteenth century southern backwoods humorists adapted Washington Irving's "The Legend of Sleepy Hollow" to a southern setting; discusses a number of works with clear parallels to Irving's story.

Plummer, Laura, and Michael Nelson. "'Girls Can Take Care of Themselves': Gender and Storytelling in Washington Irving's 'The Legend of Sleepy Hollow.'" *Studies in Short Fiction* 30 (Spring, 1993): 175-184. Argues that Sleepy Hollow is female-centered; the tales that circulate in the region focus on emasculated, headless spirits and serve to drive out masculine interlopers like Ichabod and thus preserve the old Dutch domesticity based on wives' tales.

Rubin-Dorsky, Jeffrey. *Adrift in the Old World: The Psychological Pilgrimage of Washington Irving.* Chicago: University of Chicago Press, 1988. In this study of Irving's short fiction, Rubin-Dorsky sets out to establish Irving's Americanness, thus reversing a critical tradition that marked him as primarily imitative of British prose style. By placing Irving within his historical context, Rubin-Dorsky underscores Irving's central position in early American letters.

Tuttleton, James W., ed. *Washington Irving: The Critical Reaction.* New York: AMS Press, 1993. Essays of critical interpretation of Irving's works.

Wagenknecht, Edward. *Washington Irving: Moderation Displayed.* New York: Oxford University Press, 1962. Wagenknecht has divided his study of Irving into three parts: The Life, the Man, and the Work. "The Man" is by far the largest section and provides an engaging portrait of Irving's personal life and development as a writer. Wagenknecht's biography offers a more streamlined alternative to Stanley T. Williams's two-volume work (see below).

Williams, Stanley T. *The Life of Washington Irving.* 2 vols. New York: Oxford University Press, 1935. This very thorough biography of "the first American man of letters" provides a wealth of biographical and literary detail about Washington Irving. Volume 1 is most useful for those interested in Irving's short fiction, as it covers his life and his work up to *The Alhambra*. The chapters are organized according to Irving's places of travel or the titles of his works, an arrangement which highlights the various contexts in which Irving wrote.

Walter Evans, updated by Ann A. Merrill

J

SHIRLEY JACKSON

Born: San Francisco, California; December 14, 1919
Died: North Bennington, Vermont; August 8, 1965

PRINCIPAL SHORT FICTION

The Lottery: Or, The Adventures of James Harris,
    1949
Come Along with Me, 1968 (Stanley Edgar Hyman,
    editor)

OTHER LITERARY FORMS

Shirley Jackson's dozen published books include
novels, humorous fictionalized autobiographies, and
children's books. Many of her stories, essays, and
public speeches remain uncollected. Several works
have been adapted to other media: "The Lottery" for
television, *We Have Always Lived in the Castle*
(1962) for stage, and *The Bird's Nest* (1954) and *The
Haunting of Hill House* (1959) for the cinema.

ACHIEVEMENTS

Shirley Jackson is probably best known for her
short story "The Lottery," which was first published
in the June 26, 1948, edition of *The New Yorker*. As
with the majority of her works, both short stories and
novels, "The Lottery" explores the darker side of the
human psyche, often in a manner disturbing to the
reader. In addition to using ordinary settings for extraordinary occurrences, Jackson often injects an element of the supernatural. This is seen, for example, in
the story "The Visit" and in the novel *The Haunting
of Hill House*. In addition, Jackson has published *Life
Among the Savages* (1953), a highly humorous account of her home life. In 1961, Jackson received the
Edgar Allan Poe Award for her story "Louisa,
Please." She was awarded the Syracuse University
Arents Pioneer Medal for Outstanding Achievement
in 1965.

BIOGRAPHY

Shirley Jackson was born in California on December 14, 1919, and moved with her family to New
York when she was sixteen. After an unsuccessful
year at the University of Rochester, Jackson enrolled,
at age twenty, in the University of Syracuse. This was
to be the beginning of an independent life for the author, as she would finally be away from the dominating presence of her mother. At Syracuse, Jackson met
Stanley Edgar Hyman, the man she would marry in
1940. Hyman achieved notoriety in his own right as a
teacher, writer, and critic. The marriage between
Jackson and Hyman was tumultuous in many ways
but provided a stabilizing factor for Jackson. Her literary production increased markedly after the marriage and the birth of their four children. Jackson's
own phobias, however, kept creeping into this successful, if odd, relationship. She was an agoraphobic
and a depressive. Part of the latter affliction was contributed to by her asthma and arthritis, as well as
Hyman's extramarital affair in the early 1960's. In
addition, Jackson had never really been a social person—she was much too individualistic to fit into any
of the polite social molds. In 1963, Jackson began to
turn around psychologically. Her husband made a
new commitment to the marriage, and an enlightened
psychiatrist began to help her work with the agora-
phobia. Her writing continued to be an outlet for her.
Although Jackson recovered emotionally, she never
recovered physically. She was obese and a chain
smoker. She died on August 8, 1965, at the age of
forty-five.

ANALYSIS

Shirley Jackson's stories seem to center on a single concern: Almost every story is about a protagonist's discovering or failing to discover or success-

fully ignoring an alternate way of perceiving a set of circumstances or the world. Jackson seems especially interested in how characters order their worlds and how they perceive themselves in the world. Often, a change in a character's perspective leads to anxiety, terror, neurosis, or even a loss of identity. While it is tempting to say that her main theme is the difference between appearance and reality, such a statement is misleading, for she seems to see reality as Herman Melville's Ishmael comes to see it, as a mirror of the perceiving soul. It is rarely clear that her characters discover or lose their grasp of reality; rather, they form ideas of reality that are more or less moral and more or less functional. For Jackson, reality is so complex and mysterious that one inevitably only orders part of it. A character may then discover parts that contradict a chosen order or that attract one away from the apparent order, but one can never affirm the absolute superiority of one ordering to another. In this respect, Jackson's fictional world resembles those of Stephen Crane and Ernest Hemingway. Perhaps the major differences between her fiction and theirs is that her protagonists are predominantly women; she explores some peculiarly feminine aspects of the problem of ideas of order.

Jackson's middle-class American women seem especially vulnerable to losing the security of a settled worldview. Their culture provides them with idealistic dream visions of what their lives should be, and they have a peculiar leisure for contemplation and conversation imposed upon them by their dependent roles. Men in her stories seem so busy providing that they rarely look at and think about the order of things. Her career women are more like these men. In "Elizabeth" and "The Villager," the protagonists succeed, albeit precariously, in preserving ideas of themselves and their worlds despite the contradictory facts that seem increasingly to intrude. In these two stories, one sees a sort of emotional cannibalism in the protagonists as they attempt to preserve belief in an order that reality seems no longer disposed to sustain. Several stories show a woman's loss of an ordering dream. These divide into stories about women who experience the terror of loss of identity and those who may find a liberating and superior order in what

would ordinarily be called infantile fantasy.

Among those who lose a dream are the protagonists of "The Little House" and "The Renegade." In "The Little House," a woman's first possession of her own small country house is ruined by the terrifying insinuations of her new neighbors; they leave her alone on her first night after relating to her their fears that the previous owner was murdered and that the murderer will return. In "The Renegade," a mother discovers an unsuspected cruelty in her neighbors and even in her children when her dog is accused of killing chickens. Although Jackson's humorous autobiographical stories are of a different order, the often anthologized "Charles" tells of a mother's discovery that the nemesis of the kindergarten whose antics her son reports each day is not the mythical Charles, but her own son, Laurie.

Perhaps the most successful escape into fantasy is Mrs. Montague's in "The Island." All her physical needs are provided by a wealthy but absent son and the constant attendance of Miss Oakes. Mrs. Montague lives in her dream of a tropical paradise, virtually untouched by her actual world. This escape is judged by the ironic frame of Miss Oakes's relative poverty and her inevitable envy, suffering, spite, and ugliness; she has no chance of such an escape herself. Some movements into fantasy are terrifying or at least ambiguous. In "The Beautiful Stranger," Margaret resolves a tension in her marriage by perceiving the man who returns from a business trip as a stranger, not her husband. By the end of the story, this fantasy has led to her losing herself, unable to find her home when she returns from a shopping trip. A similar but more ambiguous situation develops in "The Tooth," in which a woman escapes into a vision of an island to evade the pain of an aching tooth. Many of Jackson's protagonists conceive of an island paradise as an ideal order when their control of the immediate is threatened.

Some ideas of order remain impenetrable. In "Louisa, Please," a variation on Hawthorne's "Wakefield," a runaway daughter returns home after a long absence to discover that her family has built a life around her loss and will not be convinced of her return. In "Flower Garden" and "After You, My Dear

Alphonse," protagonists find themselves unable to change or to abandon racist ideas because the ideas are too strong or because of community pressure.

"THE VISIT"

A closer look at three especially interesting stories reveals more about Jackson's themes and give some indication of her technical proficiency. In "The Visit," Margaret comes to visit a school friend, Carla Rhodes, for the summer. The beautiful Rhodes estate includes a dream house with numerous fantastic rooms. The house seems not quite real; nearly every room is covered with tapestries depicting the house in different hours and seasons, and there is a mysterious tower of which no one speaks. For Margaret, the house and the family are ideal, especially when Carla's brother, Paul, arrives with his friend, the Captain. This idyll lasts until the evening of Paul's departure, when Margaret discovers that Paul has been a hallucination or a ghost, for the Captain is Carla's brother and no one else has seen Paul. This revelation clarifies several mysteries that have developed, especially that of Margaret's strange visit to the tower. Paul has told Margaret that an old aunt often secludes herself in the tower. When Margaret pays her a visit, she undergoes a not really frightening but certainly haunting experience with old Aunt Margaret. At the end of the story, the reader must conclude Aunt Margaret to be an apparition, that she is probably the Margaret who died for love and whose picture in mosaic appears on the floor of one room. Young Margaret has lost a phantom lover as old Margaret lost her Paul. Young Margaret realizes this at the same time that she is made aware of time's effect on the house: the age and weakness of the Rhodeses, the bitter darkness of their true son, and the physical decay of the buildings. Furthermore, she begins to doubt her own place and identity as she wonders if her visit to the house will ever end. The home of her dreaming now threatens to become an imprisoning nightmare.

In retrospect, the device by which Jackson encourages the reader to share Margaret's hallucination or haunting may seem contrived. This choice, however, seems effective because the more fully the reader shares Margaret's perceptions and the more subdued (without being absent) are the disturbing elements,

the more fully will the reader share the shock of her awakening into nightmare. Also technically effective are the apparent connections with Poe's "The Fall of the House of Usher." Most important among these is the succession of mirror images: multiple pictures of the house, between the house and Mrs. Rhodes, among members of the family, between the two Margarets, and between the decline of the family and of the house. These connections seem deliberately chosen in part to emphasize the contrasts between Margaret and Poe's narrator. Because Margaret's response to the house is so positive, the shock of her discovery is greater by contrast. Furthermore, when she discovers this house to be like what one knows the House of Usher to be, one sees the analogy between her terror at imprisonment and that of Poe's narrator when he sees a universe unnaturally lit by a blood red moon, yet another image of the coffin lit from within. Margaret actually enters one of the dream worlds promised American girls. Under its spell, she overlooks its flaws and forgets about time, but when the Captain breaks the spell, pointing out signs of decay, Paul departs and Margaret becomes acutely aware of time as her nightmare begins.

"PILLAR OF SALT"

Time is often the destroyer of feminine ideals in Jackson's stories because they seem to depend on a suspension of time. In "Pillar of Salt," another Margaret loses her secure world. A trip to New York City with her husband forces a new perspective on her which produces her anxiety and, finally, paranoia. It remains unclear, however, whether her paranoia is illness or a healthy reaction to an inimical environment.

The couple's first week in the city is idyllic, and the fast pace is a pleasant change from New Hampshire. At a party at the end of the first week, however, Margaret begins to feel isolated, unnoticed among strangers who behave in strange ways. She learns there is a fire in the building but is unable to convince anyone else to leave. The fire turns out to be two buildings away, but she is the only one to heed the warning and flee the building. She comes to see this nightmarish experience as symbolic of her experience in New York and perhaps of her life as a whole. She begins to notice new details about the city: dirt, decay, speed, stifling crowds. She feels increasingly isolated and insignificant. Of this life she thinks, "She knew she was afraid to say it truly, afraid to face the knowledge that it was a voluntary neck-breaking speed, a deliberate whirling faster and faster to end in destruction." Even her friends' Long Island beach cottage shows the spreading blight; there they find a severed human leg on the sand. Margaret comes to believe that her former order was illusory. Upon returning to the city, she begins to hallucinate, to see the destruction of the city in fast motion. Windows crumble. Her bed shakes. Driven from her apartment, she finds herself unable to return, paralyzed in a fast-moving, anonymous crowd on the wrong side of a mechanical and murderous river of traffic.

Margaret comes to see herself in a modern Sodom, paralyzed not because she has disobeyed God, but because she has seen in prophetic vision the truth about the city: It is no home for human beings but rather is impersonally intent upon destruction. The allusion of the title and her critique of city life verify her perception; however, those who do not share her vision remain capable of functioning. As in "The Visit," the internal view of Margaret encourages a close identification between reader and character which makes judgment difficult until the reader can step back; but stepping back from "Pillar of Salt" plunges the reader deeper into mystery. In both stories, the protagonist moves from dream to nightmare, but in "Pillar of Salt," the reader is much less certain that the move is to a better or more accurate view of reality.

"THE LOTTERY"

Shirley Jackson's reputation rests primarily upon her most anthologized story, "The Lottery." Her lecture on this story (printed in *Come Along with Me*) suggests that her creation of a normal setting convinced many readers that the story was largely factual. In fact, the central problem of the story seems to be to reconcile the portrait of typical small-town life in which the characters seem just like the reader with the horrifying ritualistic killing these people carry out. Here, apparently incompatible ideas of order are thrust upon the reader for resolution, perhaps in order to complicate the reader's conceptions.

"The Lottery" develops by slowly raising the level of tension in the semipastoral setting until a series of carefully arranged revelations brings about a dramatic and shocking reversal. The villagers gather at mid-morning on a late June day for an annual event, the lottery, around which a great deal of excitement centers. Jackson supplies details which arouse reader curiosity: Nearly all towns have a similar lottery; it is as old as the town; it has an elaborate ritual form which has decayed over time; every adult male *must* participate; some believe the orders of nature and of civilization depend on carrying it out correctly. The family of the man who draws the marked lot must draw again to determine the final winner. The tension built out of reader curiosity and the town's moods reverses toward the sinister when the "winner's" wife reveals that she does not want to win. Once this reversal is complete, the story moves rapidly to reveal the true nature of the lottery, to choose a victim for annual sacrifice by stoning. Jackson heightens the horror of this apparently unaccountable act with carefully chosen and placed details.

Several commentators have attempted to explain the story through reconstructing the meaning of the ritual and through carefully examining the symbols. Helen Nebeker sees the story as an allegory of "man trapped in a web spun from his own need to explain and control the incomprehensible universe around him, a need no longer answered by the web of old traditions." These attempts to move beyond the simple thriller seem justified by the details Jackson provides about the lottery. This ritual seems clearly to be a tradition of prehistoric origin, once believed essential for the welfare of the community. Even though its purpose has become obscure and its practice muddled, it continues to unify and sustain the community. Critics tend to underemphasize the apparent health and vitality of the community, perhaps feeling that this ritual essentially undercuts that impression. It is important to notice that one function of the lottery is to change the relationship between community and victim. The victim is chosen at random, killed without malice or significant protest, and lost without apparent grief. This story may be what Richard Eastman has called an open parable, a fable which applies at several levels or in several contexts. "The Lottery" creates an emotional effect of horror at the idea that perhaps in human civilization, the welfare of the many depends often on the suffering of the few: the victim race, the exploited nation, the scapegoat, the poor, the stereotyped sex, the drafted soldier. In these cases, instead of a ritual, other aspects of the social order separate oppressor and victim, yet the genuine order and happiness of the majority seems to depend on the destruction of others. In this respect, "The Lottery" resembles many stories of oppression, such as Franz Kafka's "The Bucket Rider" and some stories by Richard Wright; its purpose may be to jar readers into thinking about ways in which their lives victimize others.

Jackson places the reader of "The Lottery," which lacks a protagonist, in a position similar to that of the protagonists of "The Visit" and "Pillar of Salt." The story moves from a relatively secure agrarian worldview to an event which fantastically complicates that view. Here, as in most of her stories, Jackson emphasizes the complexity of reality. Nature and human nature seem unaccountable mixtures of the creative and destructive. Her best people are in search of ways to live in this reality without fear and cruelty.

OTHER MAJOR WORKS

LONG FICTION: *The Road Through the Wall*, 1948 (also published as *The Other Side of the Street*); *Hangsaman*, 1951; *The Bird's Nest*, 1954 (also published as *Lizzie*); *The Sundial*, 1958; *The Haunting of Hill House*, 1959; *We Have Always Lived in the Castle*, 1962.

PLAY: *The Bad Children*, pb. 1958.

NONFICTION: *Life Among the Savages*, 1953; *The Witchcraft of Salem Village*, 1956; *Raising Demons*, 1957.

CHILDREN'S LITERATURE: *Nine Magic Wishes*, 1963; *Famous Sally*, 1966.

BIBLIOGRAPHY

Cleveland, Carol. "Shirley Jackson." In *And Then There Were Nine . . . More Women of Mystery*, edited by Jane S. Bakerman. Bowling Green, Ky.: Bowling Green State University Popular Press, 1985. This chapter provides the reader with an overview of Jackson's major works. In addition, Cleveland provides some useful critical insights.

Friedman, Lenemaja. *Shirley Jackson*. Boston: G. K. Hall, 1975. Friedman provides the reader with both a biographical and critical study of Jackson and offers information on both her short stories and novels. The volume includes an extensive secondary bibliography.

Hall, Wylie. *Shirley Jackson: A Study of the Short Fiction*. New York: Twayne, 1993. An introduction to Jackson's stories, with comments by Jackson herself, and a few short, previously published, critical articles by others. Discusses Jackson's interest in the occult, her fascination with dream situations, her focus on children, and her most famous story, "The Lottery."

Kittredge, Mary. "The Other Side of Magic: A Few Remarks About Shirley Jackson." In *Discovering Modern Horror Fiction*, edited by Darrell Schweitzer. Mercer Island, Wash.: Starmont House, 1985. A useful study of the use of magic and the supernatural in Jackson's works. The author draws interesting comparisons between Jackson's fiction and nonfiction works.

Oppenheimer, Judy. *Private Demons: The Life of Shirley Jackson*. New York: G. P. Putnam's Sons, 1988. This volume is the first extensive biography of Jackson. It is finely detailed and provides the reader an excellent view of this author. Oppenheimer interviewed close to seventy persons for this book, including Jackson's family members, friends, and neighbors. Contains numerous photographs.

Parks, John G. "'The Possibility of Evil': A Key to Shirley Jackson's Fiction." *Studies in Short Fiction* 15, no. 3 (Summer, 1978): 320-323. This useful article concentrates on Jackson's short stories. Parks draws useful comparisons with authors such as Flannery O'Connor and Nathaniel Hawthorne.

Rubinsein, Roberta. "House Mothers and Haunted Daughters: Shirley Jackson and Female Gothic." *Tulsa Studies in Women's Literature* 15 (Fall, 1996): 309-331. Explains how Jackson's fiction demonstrates her increasingly gothic representation of the bonds between mothers and daughters; discusses this theme in a number of Jackson's stories.

Schaub, Danielle. "Shirley Jackson's Use of Symbols in 'The Lottery.'" *Journal of the Short Story in English* 14 (Spring, 1990): 79-86. Discusses how Jackson distracts the reader's attention into thinking the story is a fable or fairy tale; discusses the symbolic use of setting, atmosphere, numbers, names, and objects in the story.

Stark, Jack. "Shirley Jackson's 'The Lottery.'" In *Censored Books*, edited by Nicholas Karolider, Lee Burgess, and John M. Kean. New York: Scarecrow Press, 1993. Discusses some of the rea-

sons for the story's being censored in schools and some of the values of teaching the story to teenagers; argues that it encourages reflection on some of the issues teens need to understand to become good citizens.

Yarmove, Jay A. "Shirley Jackson's 'The Lottery.'" *The Explicator* 52 (Summer, 1994): 242-245. Discusses the importance of setting, historical time, and irony of character names in the allegorical meaning of the story. Compares the ending of the story to the ending of Hardy's *Tess of the D'Urbervilles*.

Terry Heller, updated by Victoria E. McLure

W. W. JACOBS

Born: Wapping, England; September 8, 1863
Died: London, England; September 1, 1943

PRINCIPAL SHORT FICTION
Many Cargoes, 1896
The Brown Man's Servant, 1897
The Skipper's Wooing, 1897
Sea Urchins, 1898 (published in the United States as *More Cargoes*)
Light Freights, 1901
The Lady of the Barge, 1902
Odd Craft, 1903
Captains All, 1905
Short Cruises, 1907
Sailor's Knots, 1909
Ship's Company, 1911
Night Watches, 1914
Deep Waters, 1919
Sea Whispers, 1926
Snug Harbor, 1931, 1942
The Nightwatchman and Other Longshoremen, 1932
Cargoes, 1965

Selected Short Stories of W. W. Jacobs, 1975
"The Monkey's Paw" and "Jerry Bundler," 1997

OTHER LITERARY FORMS
W. W. Jacobs's novels include *A Master of Craft* (1900), *At Sunwich Port* (1902), *Dialstone Lane* (1904), *Salthaven* (1908), and *The Castaways* (1916). Seventeen of his stories have been dramatized, and "The Monkey's Paw" has been adapted for opera, radio, film (1937), and audiocassette (1998).

ACHIEVEMENTS
W. W. Jacobs's storytelling skill was admired by his contemporaries J. B. Priestley, Evelyn Waugh, G. K. Chesterton, V. S. Pritchett, Jerome K. Jerome, and P. G. Wodehouse. If his byline appeared on a story in *Strand* magazine, sales of the magazine increased to 500,000 copies. Jacobs's humor has been compared to that of Aristophanes and Charles Dickens, his realistic use of language and river settings to those of Mark Twain, his "pastoral" tone to that of Jane Austen, and his supernatural horror stories to those of Edgar Allan Poe.

BIOGRAPHY

William Wymark Jacobs spent his childhood in Wapping, on the Thames estuary, where his father worked as a wharf manager. After graduation from school at sixteen, he worked for the civil service. For amusement and extra money, Jacobs wrote humorous stories about the activities of people in villages along the Thames. In 1885 Jacobs was first published in *Idler* and *To-Day* magazines. Later, his works were published exclusively in the *Strand*. His stories were illustrated by his friend, Will Owen. In 1898, when Jacobs's writing produced enough income to support him, he quit his civil service job to write full time.

In 1900, he married Agnes Eleanor Williams, a feminist and socialist. Jacobs's philosophy was conservative. Even though the marriage suffered from irreconcilable political and social differences, they had two sons and two daughters.

Jacobs wrote more than 158 short stories under his byline and anonymously. By 1916, his prolific writing had slowed, and he began converting his stories into plays. He died in 1943.

ANALYSIS

Humor is the single effect W. W. Jacobs creates in his dockside stories, based on the lives of working-class people before socialism and war changed the British social structure. He uses exaggeration and overstatement to create laughter-provoking farce. However, his stories cannot be classified as satire as he makes no attempt to reform society or his characters' ridiculous and entertaining behavior.

Jacobs uses a third-person observer as narrator. For a mug of beer, the Nightwatchman, a retired seaman, or the Old Timer at the Cauliflower Inn will entertain travelers with their tales. Dialogue includes just enough Cockney dialect to add authentic speech patterns without confusing the reader. Nearly half of Jacobs's stories feature the escapades of sailors on schooners going up or down the Thames estuary or in places like Wapping. The rest feature villagers in towns like Claybury. He is especially adept at describing funny looking or eccentric characters. Female characters are either pretty, deceitful flirts or bossy old women. Fans easily recognize stock char-

acters similar to those in British music hall farces.

Plots revolve around devious and complicated schemes to make money without doing any work, to "get even" with rivals, or to play practical jokes. Jacobs skillfully weaves in complications and polishes off each story with a surprise ending. His stories contain no moral dilemmas, no social problems, and no sex. They are simply good, clean fun, written for middle class readers of *Strand* magazine. Each story is approximately five thousand words long. Jacobs skillfully creates scenes that move slowly and allow readers a chuckle before each new complication begins.

In addition to humorous stories, Jacobs wrote a few suspenseful mysteries: "His Brother's Keeper," "The Well," "The Interruption," "Jerry Bundler," and a novella, *The Brown Man's Servant*. Only "The Monkey's Paw," a horror-fantasy story, remains well known. As in Jacobs's humorous stories, a familiar theme in his horror-mysteries is the futility of trying to "get something for nothing."

"CONTRABAND"

Seaman Dan enters the fo'c'sle of the schooner *Greyhound* and persuades the crew to help him smuggle a runaway soldier to London without the skipper finding out. Private Smith is "six foot four of underdone lobster" and difficult to hide in his red uniform. After the boat gets under way, Smith confesses that he deserted the army because his fickle girlfriend wants him back. He has no clothes except for his uniform, and he will surely be arrested when he steps on shore. Dan expects to get twenty-five shillings from the stowaway, but after he comes aboard, Smith reveals he has only "fi'pence ha' penny."

Complications arise. Two days into the voyage down the Thames, Billy reports the captain is coming to inspect the fo'c'sle prior to having it painted. The crew must decide what to do with the stowaway. Suggestions include "chuck him overboard" with a life preserver and hope another ship picks him up or paint stripes on his body and say he is an insane runaway. Adventurous young Billy comes up with the solution: Toss "Her Majesty's uniform" overboard; then Smith can jump over the side and pretend he has fallen from another boat.

Joe "rescues" him with a line and pulls him aboard. The skipper interrogates Smith, who claims he has been afloat for six hours. He has stripped off his clothes to keep from sinking and has lost a gold watch, his wallet, and three friends, all of whom drowned. After Smith recovers with brandy and warm blankets, the skipper provides him with some too-short castoff clothing.

The crew is anxious to find suitable clothes for Smith and get rid of him. Dan will be arrested for aiding a deserter if Smith is captured, so he goes ashore at Limehouse and buys Smith a tweed suit, a pair of boots, and a bowler hat. Dan's "a regular fairy godmother, ain't he?" says Joe. The other men chip in enough money for Smith's carfare and wave goodbye, but Dan is below "with a stump of lead-pencil and a piece of paper doing sums."

"Blundell's Improvement"

Farmer Turnbull is aggravated and inconvenienced because two men are courting his fickle daughter Venia: stolid John Blundell and handsome and charming army sergeant Daly. Unknown to Venia, the wily old widower Turnbull wants to marry Miss Sippet, but as long as Venia lives at home he cannot do so. He knows that Sergeant Daly will soon be going overseas, so he is not a good marriage prospect. Turnbull advises the lovesick Blundell to use his imagination and become more aggressive in his courtship. He suggests that while the four of them are walking along the quay, Blundell stumble and "accidentally" shove Daly into the water. Then Blundell can "save" Daly and become a hero in Venia's eyes. "Improve upon the plan," says Turnbull.

On a hot Sunday afternoon, Turnbull insists that he and Venia and the two suitors take a stroll on the quay. When Blundell makes no move to shove Daly into the water, Turnbull scolds him and accuses him of cowardice. Blundell says, "You told me to improve on your plan, you know, and I've been thinking out improvements." Then he shoves Turnbull into the water and dives in to save him.

After a sailor drags them both out with a rope, an angry Turnbull tries to convince bystanders that Blundell shoved him into the water. They shame the old man for being ungrateful to his rescuer and say he

must have had a sunstroke to make such a false accusation. "He nearly lost 'is life over you." Blundell pretends unconsciousness. He sputters and "comes to" before fishermen can resuscitate him by rolling him on a barrel. Venia kneels at Blundell's side and holds his hand. Turnbull recovers from the "sunstroke" and sees that Blundell's improved plan is best. Venia marries Blundell, and Turnbull proposes to Miss Sippet.

"The Monkey's Paw"

The single effect that Jacobs creates in this story is horror. The theme involves an evil attempt to gain money by supernatural means. He uses the same method of plot development that is successful in his humorous stories. Each suspenseful scene moves slowly toward a miniature climax. The final black moment and denouement are emotional shockers.

The first scene is a cottage on a rainy night. Mr. White and his son are playing chess, a game of chance. The game foreshadows conflict when White inadvertently places his king in jeopardy. In the second scene, their guest, a British soldier, entertains them with stories about India. He exhibits a mummified monkey's paw, which can grant its owner three wishes. White snatches the paw from the fire and buys it. The solder warns White against using the paw to interfere with fate, an underlying theme of the story. White uses the first wish for money to pay off the home mortgage. In the third scene, a stranger arrives and informs the Whites that their son has been killed in an industrial accident. The company offers a compensatory payment in the exact amount of the outstanding mortgage. In the fourth scene, Mrs. White grieves over her son's death and begs her husband to wish on the monkey's paw for his return from the grave. Reluctantly, he uses his second wish. Not until he hears his son's mutilated corpse banging on the front door does White fully realize the consequences of his meddling with fate. He uses his last wish to return his son's mangled corpse to its grave.

Jacobs uses action and dialogue to develop his characters. For example, the sergeant warns White about the evil nature of the monkey's paw but sells it to him anyway without any sense of moral responsibility. White's actions reveal his attempt to break the narrow circle of his middle-class life. He entertains a stranger who has been to India; he dares to use supernatural means to pay off his mortgage and later to restore life to his dead son's body. The wife behaves in a passive way about the evil monkey's paw until her son dies, and she loses emotional control.

White gives in to his wife's hysteria but finally realizes the evil consequences of trying to change fate. Then he uses the last wish to restore order.

OTHER MAJOR WORKS

LONG FICTION: *A Master of Craft*, 1900; *At Sunwich Port*, 1902; *Dialstone Lane*, 1904; *Salthaven*, 1908; *The Castaways*, 1916.

PLAYS: *Beauty and the Barge*, pr. 1904 (with Louis Napoleon Parker); *The Ghost of Jerry Bundler*, pb. 1908 (with Charles Rock); *In the Library*, pr. 1913 (with Herbert C. Sergent); *A Love Passage*, pr., pb. 1913 (with Philip E. Hubbard); *Keeping Up with Appearances*, pb. 1919; *Establishing Relations*, pb. 1925; *Master Mariners*, pb. 1930; *Matrimonial Openings*, pb. 1931; *Dixon's Return*, pb. 1932; *Double Dealing*, pb. 1935.

BIBLIOGRAPHY

Adcock, Arthur St. John. *The Glory That Was Grub Street: Impressions of Contemporary Authors*. London: S. Low, Marston, 1928. Discussions of various writers, including Jacobs.

Adrian, Jack, ed. *Strange Tales from the Strand*. New York: Oxford University Press, 1991. Analyses of Jacobs's horror-fantasy "The Monkey's Paw" and a novella of psychological realism, *The Brown Man's Servant*.

Chesterton, G. K. "W. W. Jacobs." In *A Handful of Authors: Essays on Books and Writers*, edited by Dorothy Collins. New York: Sheed and Ward, 1953. Compares Jacobs's humor to Dickens's and his farce to Aristophanes'. Other contemporary humorists are found to be witty but without mirth. Jacobs finds jokes in "funny looking people" and their eccentricities. His stories mimic sailors' insults and the real speech of the British working class.

Cloy, John D. *Pensive Jester: The Literary Career of W. W. Jacobs*. Lanham, Md.: University Press of America, 1996. Includes bibliographical references and index.

James, A. R. *The W. W. Jacobs Companion*. Southwick, W. Sussex, England: A. R. James, 1990. An overview of Jacobs's work.

Priestley, J. B. "Mr. W. W. Jacobs." In *Figures in Modern Literature*. London: John Lane, The Bodley Head, 1924. Critics do not classify Jacobs as a literary artist because his popular farces have no depressing messages for the age, no new religion, and no solution for social problems. Fans simply enjoy his stories about characters, like Bob Pretty, "saucy girls, love-lorn third mates, henpecked sea-captains, and observant night-watchmen." He creates a safe "little world," leaving out crime, passion, and tragedy. Jacobs's careful plotting, comic dialogue, and memorable characterizations serve as models for short-story writers.

Pritchett, V. S. "W. W. Jacobs." In *Books in General*. New York: Harcourt, Brace, 1953. Jacobs depicts a "world at its moment of ripeness and decline." Working- and middle-class characters are concerned with the "eternal human problem of how to get the better of one another." His ribald and witty writing develops the traditional characters of English music hall farce. Like Mark Twain's realistic use of dialect, "the langwidge 'e see fit to use was a'most as much as I could answer." A "supreme craftsman of the short story."

Martha E. Rhynes

CRITICAL SURVEY
OF
SHORT FICTION

GEOGRAPHICAL INDEX

GEOGRAPHICAL INDEX

GEOGRAPHICAL INDEX

CATEGORY INDEX

CATEGORY INDEX

SOCIAL SATIRE. *See also* MANNERS, FICTION OF, SOCIAL REALISM

SOUTH AFRICAN CULTURE

SOUTHERN UNITED STATES

SOUTHWESTERN UNITED STATES

SPANISH CULTURE

SUPERNATURAL STORIES. *See also* GHOST, GOTHIC, GROTESQUE STORIES, HORROR, MAGICAL REALISM, OCCULT, SUSPENSE